Mystery & History In Georgia

(Volume II)

By R. Olin Jackson III
B.A., M.Ed.

Published by Whippoorwill Publications, LLC
Roswell, GA 30075

Publisher's Cataloging-in-Publication Data
provided by Five Rainbows Cataloging Services
Names: Jackson III, Ralph Olin, 1951- author.
Title: Mystery & history in Georgia (volume 2) / R. Olin Jackson III.
Description: Roswell, GA : Whippoorwill Publications, 2023. | Includes bibliographical
    references and index.
Identifiers: LCCN 2023904167 (print) | ISBN 979-8-9872286-2-3 (hardcover) |
    ISBN 979-8-9872286-3-0 (paperback) | ISBN 979-8-9872286-4-7 (ebook)
Subjects: LCSH: Georgia—History. | Georgia—History—Anecdotes. | Georgia—History,
    Local—Anecdotes. | Legends—Georgia. | Curiosities and wonders—Georgia. | BISAC:
    HISTORY / United States / State & Local / South (AL, AR, FL, GA, KY, LA, MS,
    NC,SC, TN, VA, WV)
Classification: LCC F286.6 .J33 2023 (print) | LCC F286.6 (ebook) | DDC 398.209758—dc23.

Also By R. Olin Jackson:

A North Georgia Journal of History, Volume I (1989)
A North Georgia Journal of History, Volume II (1991)
A North Georgia Journal of History, Volume III (1996)
A North Georgia Journal of History, Volume IV (1999)
Moonshine, Murder & Mayhem in Georgia (2003)
Tales of the Rails in Georgia (2004)
Georgia Backroads Traveler (2005)
Georgia's Doc Holliday (2006)
We Shall Die Together (co-authored with Daniel Roper) (2008)
Traced with Fire, Written in Blood (co-authored with Daniel Roper) (2009)
Mystery & History in Georgia (Volume I) (2022)
Some Genealogy Keys to Some Georgia Family Trees (2023)
Whippoorwill Hill (2023)

*Grateful appreciation is expressed herewith to Daniel M. Roper and Legacy Communications, Inc. (2005 to present), Rome, Georgia, and **A North Georgia Journal of History, Volumes 1-4** by R. Olin Jackson (Legacy Communications, Inc., 1987-2005) for reprint rights to selected articles within this publication.*

Contents

Wilkes County

The Amazing Story of Evangelist Sam Jones

*He has been gone for more than 117 years as of this writing (2023),
but his storied accomplishments and electrifying religious crusades
across the United States remain the stuff of legends, and just as impressive
today as they were over a century ago, while many modern-day
evangelical counterparts are being held up to ridicule for their misdeeds,
greedy excessive lifestyles – and yes, just plain deceitfulness.*

Samuel Porter Jones was born on October 16, 1847 in Oak Bowery, Alabama, the son of Nancy "Queenie" and John Jones. Throughout his lifetime, he "owned" several different identities: those of "lawyer," "drunkard," "gambler," and "evangelist," to name the most prominent. It was nevertheless his "resurrection" as a devout Christian and one of the most dynamic and influential evangelists of all time which ultimately gained him national renown. He is credited, at a minimum, of more than 500,000 conversions to Christianity (out of an estimated audience of approximately 25,000,000) during his short lifetime.

While on her death-bed in 1856, Sam's mother, Nancy, tried to comfort her then-nine-year-old son with the words, "Sam, I will never be able to return to you, but you can come to me," referring to her unalterable belief in God and Heaven. Sam reportedly was greatly touched by his mother's words, and never forgot her.

When Sam's father, John, remarried and settled in Cartersville, Georgia, a few years later, the children relocated there with him in 1858. John set up law practice in Cartersville, and was a man of outstanding reputation as a Christian. After the terrible U.S. Civil War broke out shortly thereafter, John, as did many leaders in communities all across the South, raised a company of soldiers to which he was named captain in the Confederate Army.

In early 1864, with the Union Army of Gen. W.T. Sherman bearing down upon Georgia, young Sam was relocated to Kentucky for safety. Whether he was taken there by family members is unknown today, but the devastation and accompanying lawlessness caused many families to flee Georgia, and young Sam was among them.

Still in the throes of alcoholism in the 1870s, a young Sam Jones – prior to the days of his ministry when he still frequented the saloons of Cartersville – holds his child, Mary, in his right arm and his cousin, Minnie Edwards in his left.

While in Kentucky, Sam met his future wife, Laura McElwain. Returning to Cartersville at the war's conclusion, the lawlessness and unmitigated dangerous circumstances continued to pervade north Georgia, just as was the case all across the South. All former law enforcement had disappeared. Most able-bodied men – and even young boys – had all been killed or maimed, and there was no manner in which to re-establish order in a lawful society.

Addicted to Liquor

Young Sam attended and was graduated from nearby Euharlee High School, and his father wished to send him for further education to a college or university in the North, but the young man was plagued by what was known as "nervous dyspepsia" (essentially constant upset of the stomach and bowels). With the assumption that a minor alcoholic beverage of some form might aid in quieting his nervous stomach, Sam partook of the drink, and his nervousness did subside, but he inevitably was also ensnared by the addictive quality of the remedy.

It wasn't long before Sam's "remedy" had advanced into full-fledged alcoholism. Despite his addiction, the young man was nevertheless able to set up a successful law practice which flourished for a short time, but his poor judgment in the face of his alcoholism lured him to further drink and substantial habits of gambling. He soon had lost his law practice and was reduced to working as a common laborer just to make ends meet.

Despite the constant pleas of his wife and the responsibilities of his growing family, nothing could sway Sam Jones from drinking and gambling and living, in general, the life of a degenerate. A daughter, Beulah was born October 31, 1869, but died in August of 1871. Mary was born in September of 1871. Other children born to the Jones's were Annie (May 11, 1873), Sam Paul (May 31, 1875), Robert (Dec. 24, 1876), Laura (October of 1881), and finally Julia (April of 1885).

Sam eventually was reduced to shoveling coal into a furnace hours on end to obtain the necessary funds to feed his family, and still he drank and gambled away his meager earnings. Finally, in August of 1872, Sam received the jolting news that his father was seriously ill.

On his deathbed – just as had his mother's – his father's final words broke his son's heart. In an autobiographical sketch in *Thunderbolts* – a recently re-printed volume of his sermons – Sam Jones wrote, *"As I stood by the bedside of my dying father, I grasped his hand to bid him farewell. He looked up into my eyes and asked me to make him a promise to meet him in Heaven. Sinful, wretched and ruined as I was, I made the promise, and every willful step of my life from that bedside to this hour has been an honest effort to redeem that promise."*

Overcome with guilt and emotion, Sam reportedly fell to his knees as he grasped his dying father's hand, and plaintively responded, "I promise, I'll quit drinking and set things straight. I'll meet you and mother in heaven." It, nevertheless, was still a harrowing task to conquer the demons which possessed him. He reportedly described to later congregations his epic battle with his addictions:

"The final time I walked into a public bar, I begged for a glass of liquor," he stated. "When presented with the whisky-filled tumbler, I started to drink and happened to look up into the mirror behind the bar. The man looking back at me was filthy with matted hair and vomit upon his clothes, and one of his eyes was totally closed and lips swollen from some previous conflict.

"I remember thinking, 'Is that all that is left of me?' Without hesitating, I smashed the glass of liquor upon the floor and fell to my knees and cried out publicly 'Oh God! Oh God, have mercy!'

"The bartender, thinking I was dying – and I actually was – ran to my side. Wallowing in my despair and self-pity, I said, 'Just let me alone.' I picked myself up and staggered away.

Jones reportedly then began a series of horror-filled days and nights as he struggled to purge the demons of alcohol from his addiction-riddled body. Many days later, though recovering slowly, he became aware that something had dramatically changed within him, and he no longer was helpless against a craving for

Old Van Wert Methodist Church, constructed in 1846, was one of the few structures in the town which was not burned in 1864 by troops commanded by Gen. William T. Sherman in the U.S. Civil War. It was in this worship facility only ten years later in 1874 that famed evangelist Samuel Jones of Cartersville, Georgia, began his ministry. This photo (circa 1920) shows the church, and possibly its congregation of that day. The poverty-stricken community at that time no doubt had no funds for painting or maintaining the somewhat derelict-appearing facility. (Photo courtesy of GA Dept. of Archives & History, Atlanta, GA)

Present-day view of old Van Wert Methodist Church. Van Wert, Georgia, was the county seat of government for Paulding County from 1838-1852. When a section of Paulding was reconfigured by the State Legislature to create adjoining Polk County, Van Wert lost its status as the seat of government, and shriveled and died. The once-vibrant main street of this community originally included a county courthouse, hotels, saloons, shops and businesses, but has been reduced to little more than a few homes - and the historic church - today. (Photo by Olin Jackson)

a modern Ezekiel, entreating his listeners to give up their sinful ways to make the world a better place.

Sam Jones spoke out not only against the evils of alcohol and gambling, but also against the encroachment of external influences on the spiritual and moral lives of his congregational followers. "The roar of commerce, the click of the telegraph, and the whistle of the engine have well-nigh drowned the voice of God," he told them. "The tune of America is pitched to the dollar."

Called To Ministry

It was only a few weeks after his father's death that the young Jones decided he had been called by God to the ministry. His initial sermon was entirely unplanned, and, in fact, completely unexpected. Accompanying his grandfather to one of the elder Jones's churches in the Bartow Circuit near Cartersville, Sam learned that the speaker for the evening was unable to be present. The elder Jones reportedly laid a hand upon Sam's shoulder and said, "You must preach for us tonight."

Young Sam, as might be expected, protested. He felt he was sorely ill-equipped to pursue any type of ministry. His grandfather, however, reportedly persisted. "My grandson," he said, "if God has called you to preach, you can preach."

Fearfully, Sam stood behind the pulpit to read the text, *"I am not ashamed of the Gospel of Christ, for it is the power of God unto salvation to everyone that believeth."*

"I looked out over a congregation every member of which knew me," he later wrote. *"They knew what my past had been. They knew me only as a wild, reckless boy. I began to talk with fear and trembling. I do not remember my exegesis or analysis of the text. . . Before I had*

alcohol. From that point forward, Sam Jones was indeed a different person.

His alcoholism, however, had made fierce in-roads into his life, and years later, in pleading with others to give up the liquor habit, he proclaimed, "Those years of dissipation formed habits of thirst that have followed me on." Through his own struggle and defeat of alcoholism, he was able to counsel other young men and persuade them to give up a habit that could spell disaster for them.

Known for his eventual outspoken denouncement of the evils of his day, Sam Jones rose from the depths of his own experiences in those evils to become

The home pictured here in Van Wert was rented by Evangelist Sam Jones circa 1874 for his family for $10.00 per month for one year, which he paid in advance. At the time that he rented this property, the main street of Van Wert had numerous saloons and enjoyed an exceedingly unsavory reputation. (Photo courtesy of GA Dept. of Archives & History, Atlanta, GA)

proceeded far into the text I adopted the plan of a good old Methodist preacher 'in the bush' who shuts up his Bible and says 'Brethren, I can't preach the text, but I can tell my experience in spite of the devil.' Out of a heart gushing full of love to God and to man, I told them of God's gracious dealings with me."

Most of his audience was reduced to tears. Many found their way to the altar afterward, eager to change their lives as this "wild, reckless boy" had been willing to change his. In this, his first sermon, Sam Jones had found one secret to becoming a successful evangelist: touch the emotions of the listeners and bring them to decisions for their lives.

After the sermon, his grandfather again laid a hand upon young Sam's shoulder, saying, "Go ahead, my boy. God has called you to the work." Thus began the auspicious career spanning

more than thirty years that would make Sam Jones one of the greatest ministers of God of all time.

His ministry began with his appointment to the Van Wert Circuit centered in present-day Polk County near the tiny rough-and-tumble mill-town of Rockmart. Through this ministry, he served the churches in that area of the North Georgia (Methodist) Conference. The tiny church in which he began his ministry – though unmarked historically – still stands today in Van Wert.

When told that his predecessor had been paid a grand total of $65.00 for a year's work, Sam reportedly replied that salary was of little importance. "I had a field to work in," he said, "and I was going to it gladly."

Acting entirely upon faith, young Sam – with wife and family, a bob-tail pony and only eight dollars remaining

The impressive final home of Rev. Sam Jones still stands in a shady residential area in Cartersville, Georgia. It was to this home that he was returning by train in 1907, when he died of heart failure at the relatively youthful age of 54. The heavy alcoholism of his earlier life quite possibly played a role in his early demise. (Photo by Olin Jackson)

in his pocket – had rented a house, paying one year's rent in advance at $10.00 per month. He found favor in the churches in the circuit, and at the end of three years, "the salary and perquisites totaled $2,100.00, or over $700.00 a year," he said.

During those first years, Sam Jones formed his own philosophy of preaching. "I saw," he said, "that there either were two distinct kinds of Christianity, or else a majority of my people had Christianity and I did not have it, or vice versa. They had indifference and carelessness and prayerlessness, and I found no room for any of them in my religious life."

Rev. Jones said he spent many hours as a youthful pastor trying to solve the problem and to know his duty toward his people. "It was more than three years," he said, "before my courage was screwed up to the sticking point where I could preach the truth in such a pointed way as to leave no one in doubt that I meant him."

Thus began his preaching not of the gospel alone, but of the application of the gospel to the conscience of the listener. "The intellects of men," he said, "when taken in the whole, vary in altitude like mountains and valleys, but the consciences of men form a vast plain without an undulation from shore to shore, and he who stands on a level like this will move not only the peasant and laborer, but the intellectual giants of the earth alike, for the conscience of a Webster is on the same plane and level with the conscience of a brakeman or any other laborer. . . When you arouse the conscience, amid its ferocious lashings, the only alternative . . . is a better life or complete abandonment."

For the next three decades, the philosophy of Sam Jones was to challenge the consciences of his listeners throughout the United States and much of Canada. In the first eight years of his ministry to the Methodist churches in the four circuits to which he was assigned, it was estimated that he preached no less than 400 sermons a year, and no less than 2,000 members were taken into those churches.

A decade after Sam had begun his ministry, the Reverend Joseph Key, a bishop of the Methodist Episcopal Church South wrote:

"For twelve years or more, this unique man has been conspicuously before the people as pastor, evangelist, reformer, benefactor, leader of men and private citizen. Never has the searchlight of scrutiny been more severely used. Friends have watched his upward course with an interest born of love and fear, while enemies have exhausted all agencies to find his weak points, that they might overthrow him.

"At first, he startled and confused his hearers. His abrupt and intense manner divided every congregation. Some praised and some blamed. Both, perhaps were, and still are, extreme. But, applauded, hated, ridiculed, or feared, he still holds his place, and multitudes flock to hear him."

Sam, to his credit, never made theology a study. He declared, "I have never tried to prove there was a God, or that Christ was divine, or that there was a Heaven or Hell. I have made those things not an objective point, but a starting point. . . My idea has always been

Friends have watched his upward course with an interest born of love and fear

that Christ meant what he said when he said 'Preach the gospel,' not defend it; 'Preach the Word,' not try to prove that the Word is true."

The great evangelist was said to have preached to the heart and conscience of the listener, never preaching above the reach of the uneducated, and never down to the intellectual in his audience. Even children understood his homiletics. He loved to tell of the little boy who asked his father, "Will Mr. Jones be returned to the circuit this year?"

"I hope so," answered the father. "Why do you ask?" "Well," replied the child, "he's the only preacher I ever listened to that I can understand what he said."

The story was told of Sam Jones stopping to watch a group of boys playing marbles. "Will you be at my meeting tonight?" he asked them. One of the youngsters teased, saying "If you'll come play marbles with us, we'll come to your meeting."

Sam reportedly never missed a beat. Tying his horse to a nearby fence, he knelt, flexed his hands then gripped a marble between his thumb and forefinger. To the surprise of the boys around him, he not only could play marbles, he "plumbed out the middle man" the first shot, and in a few minutes more, he had won all the marbles, concluding by marching the whole crowd off to his meeting. Within a month, every lad in the area reportedly had become a church-goer.

Full-Time Evangelist

Sam Jones's gift of oratory and his determination to speak the truth as he saw it soon became known throughout Georgia, and after a few years as a circuit rider and pastor of local churches, he was challenged to carry his message to greener pastures.

In 1885, the Methodist churches in Nashville invited him to conduct a revival meeting in that Tennessee city. This meeting was so successful that Sam Jones gave up his pastoral work to become a full-time evangelist. He accepted invitations to hold evangelistic services in widely separated sections of the country.

Rev. Jones's revivals, at first, were attended by hundreds, and later, amazingly, by thousands. At many of his meetings there was standing room only, and more than one great tabernacle was built to shelter the crowds that came to hear him.

A handsome tabernacle eventually was built on a hillside in Cartersville and named in Jones's honor. The local Methodist Episcopal Church named for him is still in use today, and is a handsome structure built in the early part of the 20th century. Likewise, the Sam Jones Female Seminary built in Cartersville was also named in his honor.

Following the conversion of a Captain Tom Ryman, owner and operator of a fleet of pleasure boats plying the Cumberland River in Tennessee in the late 1800s, the Union Gospel Tabernacle in Nashville was completed in 1892. Ryman had vowed to build a tabernacle "so that Sam Jones will never have to preach in a tent again."

In a story, *"The Captain and the Preacher,"* published in **Echoes of the Grand Old Opry** on the 60th anniversary of the building (which later became Ryman Auditorium, home of the Nashville country music organization), Ryman's conversion was described:

"(Ryman). . . the operator of a fleet of pleasure boats . . . dedicated to dancing, gambling and drinking. . . a rough fellow was Captain Ryman, a man of the world.

"It is part of the legend that Tom and members of his rowdy crew went to a tent revival service in Nashville intent upon disrupting it. They meant to make sport of the evangelist Sam Jones.

"Reverend Jones, however, was a preacher of considerable power. In the course of the evening's revival service, and during a Jones peroration on the subject of Motherhood, the rough Tom Ryman was brought to his knees, converted to the ways of Christ. It is said that Captain Ryman led his crewmen back to the boat to throw gaming tables and teakwood bars overboard."

The Grand Old Opry publication described Sam Jones as a man with *"a square, handsome face, with dark, deep-set eyes that one historian has said 'flashed with indignation at one moment and twinkled with merriment the next.'*

"Sam Jones," the story went on, *"had the common touch. 'God projected this world on a root-hog-or-die principle,' he would tell his audience. 'If the hog, or man either, don't root, let him die. . .'"*

Jones was an innovator. He was probably the first evangelist to turn revival meetings into civic reform crusades in the cities in which he preached. He was also the first evangelist, to quote one of his contemporaries, "to make revival meetings as entertaining and applause-conscious as the theater."

After Nashville, Rev. Jones went on to preach in St. Louis, Boston, Cleveland, and many other cities, where he lashed out at the evils of the day. Both men and women by the scores responded to his message by going forward to embrace a new-found faith. A number of times Jones was invited to hold meetings abroad, but he always chose not to leave the country, except for his meetings in Canada.

Sparing No Sinner

No matter where he preached, or to whom, the famed evangelist never pulled his punches. In a revival meeting in California, he lashed out at the state legislature. "The only reason," he shouted from a Los Angeles pulpit, "I can find 50 rascals in town to one in the Legislature, is because there are more people in town. I can take the records of some of you legislators and, with the laws of California, consign you to the penitentiary before tomorrow night... You are the most corrupted people by liquor I have ever seen."

Along with the liquor traffic, gambling came in for its share of his wrath too. To him, gambling was one of the most demoralizing vices, destructive alike to character, home and business.

The media in Sam Jones's day consisted primarily of the newspaper, with its hirelings as bent upon getting a scoop

Rev. Jones and his family were photographed on the front porch of his spacious home in Cartersville shortly before his death. The diminutive evangelist and his wife sit in the chairs to the rear.

or a different slant on a story as their modern counterparts. While the successes of his evangelistic meetings were heralded across the country, he was at times the target of criticism and ridicule. He had a few words too, for some of those who set out to influence their readers in such a way:

"You little sap-headed reporters, with eyes so close together that you can see through a keyhole with both of them, are sent here at night to take down my sermons. You seem to think your mission is to make my sermons funnier and more sensational. Now, bud, if you are doing the best that you can, your paper had better put you on a job that is small enough for your caliber, and let them send a man here who is big enough for the occasion."

Commenting in his later years about his incisive criticism, the by-then-famous evangelist said, "When I first started out, I was afraid I would hurt somebody's feelings. Now, I'm afraid I won't."

Lest it appear that Sam Jones did nothing but criticize his listeners (who seemed always willing to come back for more), it should be remembered that he preached a fundamental gospel based, as he said, on the **Bible** as a starting point, and he had an answer from the "Good Book" for every question.

Reforms in many cities following month-long revivals were credited to his influence; church rolls grew after his visits across the land. He was invited year after year to return to hold services in cities where as many as 20,000 persons would turn out for a single evening's revival meeting.

One of Rev. Jones's most publicized meetings was held in the Cincinnati Music Hall in 1886, at which time the **Cincinnati Times-Star** estimated that 50,000 persons were *"left outside to hear the man that fought the devil and his crowd."*

Sam Jones was richly rewarded for his evangelistic crusades. The **Atlanta Constitution**, on November 21, 1961, in a story on the celebrated evangelist, said, *"At 59, Sam Jones was famous, wealthy, and tired. He had made an estimated $750,000 from his lectures and writings, and he had given a substantial amount of it away."*

One of famous evangelist Sam Jones's most cherished positions was that of agent in 1890 for the Decatur, Georgia Orphan's Home, for which he raised over $60,000 in contributions, freeing the home from debt. He supported the home thereafter from his own funds.

Sudden Death

Sam Jones's career ended abruptly, when he died on a train enroute to Georgia on October 15, 1906, following a successful evangelistic meeting in Oklahoma City, Oklahoma. A funeral train bearing his body bore him back home to Cartersville for the final time. Long lines of mourners awaited him on each side of the track. The remains had lain in state for two days in the state capital building in Atlanta.

The body of the famous evangelist was then returned to be laid to rest on a hillside in his beloved home town. His family had seen to it that his monument would be seen from all three railroads converging on the town, because "all railroad men loved their great friend."

Prior to his burial, when his body had lain in state in the capitol rotunda building in Atlanta, it was never alone, being guarded there around the clock by 16 girls from the Decatur Orphan's Home as thousands honored the fallen evangelical leader for the last time.

Indians and Pioneers
In Old Pine Log, GA

*It began as an aboriginal Indian village in its earliest inhabited days,
and there are sites there where primitive arrow tips and other relics can
still be found today. Later, a pioneer community sprang up there, since
one of the routes westward across Georgia passed through the town.
Though it remains a sleepy community even today, "progress"
and development are fast approaching historic Pine Log.*

Travelers, some daily commuters, and area residents alike travel through the tiny community each day, most of them unaware of just how historic this little crossroads town actually is. Some people stop to peer into the smattering of aged shops, the antique brush arbor, and other sites, but most people don't tarry if they stop at all.

In its earliest days – before Georgia was even a colony – the site became active due to the fact that two primitive Indian trails intersected at the site. One pathway led from Coosa *(Fort Strother, Alabama)* to Tugaloo *(present-day Toccoa)*. The other led from Suwanee Old Town *(near present-day Suwanee, Georgia)* to the Cherokee capitol of New Echota *(near present-day Calhoun, Georgia)* and continued northward into Tennessee *(following much of the route of present-day U.S. Highway 411)*.

Original Owners

Many present-day area residents presume – incorrectly – that the town of Pine Log was named in memory of an Indian head-man who once lived in the area. Others think the name originated from nearby Pine Log Creek, a moniker from the days when a popular pine log once allowed easy fording of the creek. Some people offer other explanations, but according to long-time resident Elizabeth Garrison – a local historian, educator and descendant of the area's earliest pioneers – none of these explanations are quite true.

Garrison, co-author of the ***History of the Pine Log Methodist Church***, and a school teacher for 32 years in Bartow County explains that if one actually researches the history of the site, he or she will discover that in 1738, a tribe of Indians called the *Natchez* were driven out of the lower Mississippi valley. The aboriginals to whom today's residents refer to as "Cherokees," allowed the displaced Natchez natives to settle on one bank of the creek and start a new community there.

"According to tradition, the word 'Natchez' sounded like the Cherokees'

11

word for a pine tree or pine log *(after translation into English of course)*," Garrison said. "It was the custom of the Indians at that time to name the mountains and creeks after *the occupants living on the site*, so the area came to be known as 'Pine Log.'"

Sadly, in the 1830s, the peace-loving Cherokees – who had accepted the ways of white civilization and begun assimilating into the white culture – were nevertheless removed to reservations out west by greedy officials with the state of Georgia who coveted the gold which was newly-discovered on the Indian lands in present-day north Georgia. As a child, Mrs. Garrison says she frequently stumbled upon arrowheads and other Indian artifacts in the Pine Log area which positively identify the site as an active village in pre-history.

Once the Indians had been removed, their land was distributed to white settlers through a land lottery. Just as with many of the original Pine Log community settlers, however, Mrs. Garrison maintains that her ancestor at the site – Charles Baker – didn't obtain his land in the lottery, but purchased it from an individual who did.

"The land in Pine Log valley was fertile and thus very valuable as farm land, not gold-mining property," Garrison said. "The persons drawing such land were sought out by prospective buyers and the property was often sold by the lucky drawers without their ever having even seen it."

Early Religion

Most of the settlers moving across America in the late 1700s and early 1800s were God-fearing Anglo-Saxon protestants, and one of the first structures often built in the pioneer communities was what was known as a "brush arbor" as an early place of worship.

Historic Pine Log Methodist Church, which still stands today, was built by the early settlers in 1842.

Since the Western & Atlantic Railroad at nearby Cass Station was still several years in the future, and the L&N Railway which eventually passed through Pine Log was still some 60 years in the future, the materials for the church had to be laboriously hauled to the site by mule-pulled wagons. Some of the materials, however, were fabricated in Pine Log from the tremendous stands of nearby timber and other area raw materials.

"I remember hearing stories as a child about several men from the community journeying from Pine Log on the Tennessee Road all the way to the port city of Augusta by wagon train to bring back hardware, windows and other building materials for the church," Mrs. Garrison added.

The church and grounds, both of which are now included on the *National Register of Historic Places*, are still in use today. Notable among the original features are the marks of the hand-planed wall boards and the wavy irregularities in the hand-poured glass of the windowpanes, many of which are still in place in the original sashes.

"It is believed that some of the craftsmen who built the church were slaves," Mrs. Garrison notes. "According to the church's early records, many of these same slaves also attended the Methodist Church regularly; were accepted as full members, and were eventually buried in the church's cemetery."

Ancient Burial Site

Interestingly, the church's cemetery also includes an Indian burial ground. A knoll in the southeast portion has been left undisturbed for more than 175 years because the Indians – some in

Known as the Horace Howard home, this structure, which still stood in Pine Log as of 2023, was constructed in the 1830s by a resident and his bride who was part Cherokee. Because of her heritage, she reportedly was forced to depart the community on the "Trail of Tears" in 1838. Her husband, rather than remain behind with this fine home, chose to abandon it and depart with her. Whether they successfully completed the bitter-cold journey to the Indian reservation in the West is unknown today. True love knows no bounds.

pre-history – were buried there before the church was built.

"The earliest dated tombstones are from the 1850s, because prior to that time, white settlers customarily buried their dead in private family cemeteries near their homes," the long-time teacher explained. "Slaves were generally buried near family members."

Church records indicate that 26 of Mrs. Garrison's ancestors are buried in the cemetery – five generations on her father's side and eight generations on her mother's side. Charles Barker, the first of Mrs. Garrison's Pine Log ancestors, is buried nearby in a private plot on land he once farmed.

According to a census published in the *Cassville Standard* newspaper, by 1852, the population of Pine Log had climbed to 944, with 120 families and 278 slaves. The town, by this time, was a thriving agrarian community, but its productive tranquility was about to be seriously tested.

The U.S. Civil War

The advent of the war which ultimately resulted in the devastation of the South, also ended a 25-year period of prosperity and development in Pine Log. The construction of the Western & Atlantic Railroad (W&A) from Atlanta to Chattanooga; the abundance of fertile land, rich iron ore and limestone deposits; and the completion of the Tennessee Road through north Georgia to Augusta; had all nurtured the economic and cultural development of Pine Log, as well as Cass *(present-day Bartow)* County. Ironically, some of these same factors contributed to the area's decline during the war.

"Pine Log was especially susceptible to bushwhackers, thieves, and raiders because of its location on Beasley's Gap Road which provided the easiest crossing of the Pine Log Mountain range," Mrs. Garrison explained. "This road intersected the Tennessee Road in Pine Log."

It was during the many raids and general lawlessness that the outlaws – often disguised as "Home Guard" units – "requisitioned" food, horses and whatever else appealed to them from the unfortunate residents of Pine Log in the name of war-time requirements. In actuality, it represented little more than "theft by taking." Repeated losses of food supplies and other possessions in this manner led to abject poverty and despair in the once-thriving community.

Although Pine Log was spared a direct blow by General Sherman's troops on his infamous 1864 *"March To The Sea"* in which he burned most of the major towns and cities in Georgia, nearly every building in neighboring Cassville – the county seat of Cass County – was destroyed by fire, plunging both Cassville and Pine Log into an impoverished state.

One time-honored Pine Log tradition that did survive the chaos of the Civil War (and which continues today) is the annual camp meeting at the Methodist Church. For more than 100 years, church members have gathered in this quiet rural community in late August for a week-long series of church services in an open-air arena.

In its earliest days, this meeting was comprised of area Methodists who congregated in tents near what was known as a "brush arbor," camping and living at the site for the week services were held. Before the advent of the train and the automobile, participants came by horse and buggy and mule-drawn wagons from places like White, Rydal and even

as far away as Waleska, Georgia, where a Methodist School (present-day Reinhart College) had been established.

Earthquake!

During the hard times following the Civil War, the camp meetings in Pine Log were abandoned, and the religious and social life was neglected as the area's remaining residents struggled to survive. This trend, however, was reversed in dramatic fashion by a single event in August of 1886.

Mrs. Garrison says her Aunt Lula, who was present on that day, passed down a description of the event. According to her memories of that day, the last service in a week-long series of meetings was in progress. The minister – Rev. J.N. Sullivan – had preached fervently, but the congregation wasn't responding like he had hoped.

"On his knees, the reverend prayed for divine intervention, reportedly stating 'Lord, if it takes it to move the hearts of these people, shake the ground on which this old building stands.' According to tradition, these words were scarcely out of the minister's mouth, when the building commenced shaking perceptibly," Mrs. Garrison laughed. "My Aunt Lula remembered opening her eyes and seeing the preacher's water glass and pitcher on the pulpit shaking."

The reaction among the congregation reportedly was both immediate and profound. They rushed down the isles to pray, and people in the village came immediately from their homes to the church that very night. It was several days later before word arrived of the devastating earthquake which had struck Charleston, South Carolina, and Pine Log residents realized what they had experienced were shock waves from the quake.

Regardless of the circumstances, the Sullivan prayer brought a renewed religious zeal, particularly since some people still weren't convinced that it was just an earthquake, and not the hand of God. *(What this circumstance doesn't take into consideration, however, is that earthquakes are from the hand of God too!)* Records indicate that contributions and attendance increased dramatically. The camp meetings were resumed, and within a couple of years, the congregation had built a new outdoor tabernacle where the annual meetings are still held today.

More recently, concrete has replaced the sawdust on the tabernacle floor. The old kerosene lamps were eventually retired too in favor of electricity and electric lights. The religious fervor, nonetheless, persists.

All things eventually change, and the same must be said for Pine Log. The cotton gin the Maxwell family once owned and operated for 100 years is now gone – shut down in 1974 from lack of business. "Soybeans don't need ginning," Ben Maxwell once lamented with a flourish, "and that's about all folks around here grow now."

Gas heaters replaced the pot-bellied stove as the primary source of heat in Bradford's General Store. Serving as the area's official U.S. Post Office until 1979, the old mercantile center eventually closed down after being operated for a number of years by Willis Bradford, whose father, Sam, opened the store in 1904.

Shortly before it closed permanently, Bradford explained in a 1990s interview that *"We don't sell farming supplies anymore, but we still sell quite a few groceries. I also used to get a good many tourists who stopped by on their way to the Smokies (Great Smoky Mountains National Park in Tennessee). Most were in a hurry, but a few remained a bit and visited, interested in our history."*

Hollywood In Pine Log?

Hollywood filmmakers, impressed with the unspoiled scenery of the historic community, eventually began using it as a film site. Several scenes for a *CBS* Made-For-TV movie entitled **Shenandoah** were filmed in the community. The location manager for the movie contacted Mrs. Garrison after seeing photos of her family's 150-year-old home-place – the Mahan homestead – in a Bartow County historical book.

"I told them it didn't look as good now, because we hadn't kept it up," she smiled. "We'd mostly used it just for storage, but they came and looked at it and said it would be perfect."

As a result, *Lauren Film Productions* filmed segments for a couple of days at the old homestead. "There were lots of people, big lighting and equipment trucks and trailers parked everywhere," Garrison related. "Folks said it looked like a little town had grown up overnight.

"The oldest portion of the house was built by an Indian family prior to the Cherokee land lottery," she added. Her grandfather – Joseph Mahan – bought the house in 1866. Mrs. Garrison was born in the house, as was her father before her.

And just as her ancestors before her, Mrs. Garrison said at that time that she planned to live out her days in scenic little Pine Log. By the time you read this article, she very well may have done just that.

Pioneer Relics
At Mosteller Spring

On a quiet wooded roadside along scenic GA 140 highway, an unmarked historic site with deep roots in the antebellum plantation days in Georgia, has somehow survived for over 180 years.

At a site in northern Bartow County just a short distance from the tiny historic community of Folsom and just prior to intersecting Interstate Highway 75, travelers over the years have occasionally noticed the rustic remains of an old gristmill and other aged historic structures on the left side of the road as one travels west. Those individuals with a studied eye for historic remains are suddenly jarred to attention upon seeing this site known by locals as "the old Mosteller Mills property."

In the decades immediately following the close of the War of 1812, a number of events in the southern United States – not the least of which was the Georgia Gold Rush of 1829 – became the catalyst for westward expansion across the state and expulsion of the native Indians of the area. One aspect of this expansion involved the development of farming enterprises for the production of what at that time was the world's most sought-after fiber – cotton.

As the Cherokee and Creek Indians were forcibly removed to reservations farther out west, public lotteries were conducted to encourage settlement of the state's new land acquisitions and to expand the state's boundaries. The South – and especially Georgia – was rich in natural resources, and its rivers and streams offered abundant sources of water power to facilitate the new development.

The Travel Route

Men of all rank and stripe ultimately flooded into the region to seek the gold of north Georgia and to acquire the land with its valuable mineral, timber, and farming resources. Most of these new settlers came down the eastern seaboard of the newly-developing United States, skirting the great Appalachian Mountain Range before turning westward into north Georgia.

One extended family that traveled to what then was old Cass County (present-day Bartow Co.) in north Georgia was the Mosteller clan from South Carolina. Daniel (1800-1855) and Jacob Mosteller joined the Floyds, Bartons, Ellises, Hayes, Murphys, Pinsons, and others in the Salacoa (present-day Folsom) community of Cass.

The Mosteller family was German in origin and Baptist in religion.

Pennsylvania had been their original American home after these immigrants made landfall in the new world and then migrated inland. They eventually moved on to new opportunity in North Carolina and South Carolina, before finding the opportunity they sought in Georgia.

Today, tradition maintains the Mostellers and their families traveled from South Carolina to Georgia in what was known as "prairie schooners" or "Conestoga wagons" such as later became so associated with early travel in the old West. If this is accurate, then it, at best, was a harrowing and slow journey for the Mostellers and their fellow migrants, since the only "roads" across north Georgia at that time were the crude trails which had originated centuries earlier with the migratory movements of large herds of wild buffalo, antelope, deer and other cloven-hooved denizens. The trails cut by these animals had been semi-improved by the native Indians for trading and warring purposes by the time the early settlers such as the Mostellers began arriving, but remained exceptionally crude and few in number.

The Mostellers and their fellow travelers almost certainly reached their new home in north Georgia's Cass County by traveling what then (and still today) was/is known as *"the Old Alabama Road,"* one connection of which followed almost exactly the same route as exists today via Georgia Highway 140 from Roswell, Georgia, to its intersection with Interstate 75 *(Readers please see "Retracing the Old Alabama Roads, Part II, Lower Route" in Mystery & History in Georgia, Volume I)*.

Both the Mostellers and the Pinsons apparently enjoyed a strong affinity for the development of water power to assist them in their endeavors wherever they lived. Their efforts in this regard eventually proved very fruitful, and their new home in north Georgia offered considerable opportunities for this commercial tool. Since they lived within a very close proximity to each other – the Pinsons on Pine Log Creek and the Mostellers on Cedar Creek – they no doubt assisted each other considerably in harnessing the power from these streams.

Source of Water Power

Other early settlers who eventually traveled the same route into Georgia – particularly the wealthier landed class – ultimately required (or desired) necessities such as material to make clothing; milled wood for homes and structures; window sashes for their plantation homes; ground grain for foodstuffs; repaired buggies for travel accommodations; and even distilled liquor. The industrious Mostellers had learned to manufacture and/or provide all these things and more if they had water power.

According to records, the Mostellers arrived in Cass County in 1838, not coincidentally the same year the native Cherokees were permanently and finally removed from the same land – land which the Indians previously had claimed as their own. William C. Blalock owned a sizeable tract of property in the 6th District of the 3rd Section of the Cherokee cession, land which Daniel Mosteller apparently immediately desired to own after chancing upon it.

The specific reason for Daniel's interest in this property is unknown today. No record for this desire exists. However, this property included a very substantial natural spring with cool water which literally boiled and churned up from the ground (and still does today). Even the Native Americans knew the

The Daniel Mosteller (1800-1855) home still stands as of this writing at Mosteller Spring near the community of Folsom in Bartow County. Daniel arrived in Cass (present-day Bartow) County in 1838, the same year the Cherokees were removed from what today is the state of Georgia. (Photo by Olin Jackson)

value of such a source of water. Not only did they understand the purity of the water it provided, they attached super-natural significance to it, since they had no understanding of the reason that it just suddenly appeared on the surface of the earth in an endless quantity.

It is unknown by this writer whether this large spring produces water with limestone, sulfur, iron, or other mineral content. Regardless, Daniel himself, no doubt was also awed and enamored with this unusual natural resource, knowing that it not only would provide a healthful source of water for his family, but also an abundant source of "water power" for the operation of the numerous commercial enterprises he knew could be erected and developed at this site.

Ownership of Slaves

Once established in this new homeland, the Daniel Mosteller family erected mills – with overshot water-wheels – on a substantial stream which did indeed originate from the large natural spring surging up from the ground on their property. The **1840 Cass County Census** records for posterity the residence of Daniel and Jacob in the county that year. Daniel is shown with a wife and five slaves. His brother, Jacob, is listed as the head of a family of six, counting himself, and four slaves.

They were a hard-working family, and their efforts eventually began bearing fruit. They would not have been considered members of the planter elite, since as mill operators, they basically were industrial in classification. They nevertheless were solidly steeped in small-scale mill operations.

The water-powered gristmills, sawmills, and wool carding mills, etc. which they built and operated, no doubt required more skill than that possessed by the average slave of that day. It is proba-bly for that reason the later census years indicate the Mostellers, in fact, owned very few slaves.

This, however, is not to imply that skilled slaves were not necessarily avail-able. It merely indicates the obvious: skilled slaves were very expensive, espe-cially as late as the decade prior to the U.S. Civil War after the importation of slaves had been outlawed, so this no doubt would have discouraged their pur-chase by the Mostellers. The few slaves they did purchase no doubt were used es-sentially for subsistence farming, domes-tic labor, and general maintenance.

As a result of their industrial, rath-er than agricultural focus, the farming endeavors on Mosteller land primarily involved the production of corn, hogs, wheat, and cotton. Any surpluses of hogs and corn quite likely were sold to the plantation region in south Georgia to sustain the "pork and pone" diet of hordes of field slaves.

The cotton produced on the Mo-steller operation was used either for homespun cloth or as a commodity from which to earn additional cash. Late in the eighteenth and into the twenti-eth century – following recovery of the economy from the disastrous effects of the U.S. Civil War – timber and lumber processing played an ever-increasing role in their agricultural pursuits.

Though the former Mosteller prop-erty remains in private ownership as of this writing, a number of the old mill structures, along with their associated aged equipment are still visible on the grounds, as is the huge natural spring which once was such a strategic aspect of the milling operations.

Interestingly, the *1850 Cass Coun-ty Census* labeled Daniel Mosteller as a "farmer," with an estate valued at $4,000.

In 1850, $4,000.00 was the equivalent of just over $140,000.00 today. This in-vestment portfolio obviously would not classify him as wealthy by any stretch of the imagination, but he nevertheless was definitely what might have been de-scribed as very "comfortable."

The *1850 Census* also lists an indi-vidual by the name of Samuel Hicks, as a "miller," residing on the Mosteller prop-erty. Since the gristmill of Daniel's for-mer property today dates from 1857, the presence of Hicks in 1850 suggests that another mill quite possibly preceded the one extant on the property today.

Though they were minor industrial-ists – even for the 1850s – the Mostellers nevertheless commonly employed pro-fessional millers to operate their facili-ties. In 1857, the spouse of miller F.M. Costevens – yet another of the millers at the site – was buried in the Mosteller family cemetery.

The U.S. Civil War

The destruction accompanying the U.S. Civil War finally reached Mo-stellers' operations in the spring of 1864. Members of the Union Army's Twenti-eth Corps arrived at the site on May 18. The 23rd Corps used the mill grounds for an encampment. The Federals made use of some of the food stores on the premises, and used the gristmill brief-ly as a headquarters for Maj. Gen. J.M. Schofield.

Local folklore maintains that the Mosteller family hid salted pork in the space between the ceiling and roof of the front porch. A Mr. B.P. Scott (1904-1967), of Cartersville, Georgia, recalled as a child, that he had seen rock salt in the space above the Mostellers' porch and was told the reason the salt was there.

In 1981, Ida Edwards of Baton

Rouge, Louisiana, a long-lived descendant of Daniel Mosteller enjoying her one-hundred-and-second year, reportedly stated that the Mostellers and other families in the community dug graves in local cemeteries and then deposited salted meat and other foods in the pits, explaining to Union troops that the graves contained the bodies of "our boys killed at Resaca and the skirmish of Adairsville."

Miss Edwards also explained how the Mostellers hung up some smoked meat without removing the hog bristles. They then rused the Union troops into believing the meat was spoiled and not fit to eat. They told the soldiers they were saving it to make soap. The boys in blue reportedly bought the story "hook, line, and sinker," leaving the meat untouched.

It is unknown today why the Mosteller Spring milling operations were not burned by the Federal troops upon their departure from their encampment there. The Mosteller operations certainly produced items which would have been of strategic use by the Confederacy, and it was a rare thing indeed for any Southern milling facility to escape being burned to the ground, especially since Federal troops were right there on the site.

The avoidance of destruction of the Mosteller milling operations by the Union Army is inexplicable today. Did the Mostellers have secret Union allegiance which became known by the Federal troops? Was it because the Mostellers hailed originally from the North? Were the Mostellers in fact associated with the Fraternal Order of Masons which often allowed exemption from destruction? These explanations all seem unlikely in the face of their struggles to hide and preserve their foodstuffs, but the actual reason(s) probably will never be known for certain.

Ironically, despite the preservation of their property and milling operations, the Mosteller livelihood in Cass County was destroyed nonetheless. The Civil War wrought such devastation upon the people, the commercial infrastructure, and economy, that there was virtually no commercial enterprise or activity for a number of years following the war, a situation which plunged the Mostellers into poverty with the rest of the South.

Like his brother Daniel, Jacob Mosteller also erected mills. His creations were located approximately two miles northeast of his brother's property near Pinelog Creek. In 1864 – at the height of the U.S. Civil War – Jacob's modest milling operation consisted of a gristmill and a wool products factory.

Jacob's milling properties also strangely escaped the torch, but even though they survived the war, it, again, was the impoverishment of the South and its citizens which caused Jacob to make the somewhat surprising decision to simply abandon his milling enterprises completely in Cass County after the close of the war and move to Tarrant County, Texas, to begin anew.

Later Ownership

David Mosteller, Jr., Daniel's grandson, apparently learned well at his grandfather's knee, and went on to establish a small enterprise of his own farther up in north Georgia near the Tennessee state line. His 1889 *Last Will and Testament* lists 480 acres of land in Walker County, Georgia, which featured a grist mill, a saw mill, and a cotton gin.

David Mosteller, Jr.'s *Will* is an interesting and beneficent document. It lists the old Mosteller property in Bartow County (formerly Cass) in which David also owned an undivided half-interest. The Bartow property is described

Mosteller Spring has been encircled by a stone retaining wall for well over a century. It was a popular gathering spot for civic and religious groups in the early 1900s. (Photo by Olin Jackson)

as 800 acres of land, a gristmill, sawmill, and a wool carder.

This same *Will* also indicates that all debts owed to David by members of the family were to be forgiven, even those debts secured by notes stolen by the Union Army during the war. The *Will* further provided that David's orange grove in Florida was to be sold, and, after debts, funeral expenses, and bequests were settled, the residue of his estate was to be given to the *Mission Board of the Southern Baptist Convention for Cuban and Mexican Missions.*

Berryman Mosteller (1825-1898), David Jr.'s nephew (who subsequently inherited the Bartow County property) constructed a sash sawmill which manufactured much of the lumber used for construction in the nearby community of Folsom. Later, in 1910, this mill was improved by Berryman's son, Andrew J. Mosteller, who developed a general contracting business in conjunction with the sawmill.

The most prominent business and landmark still extant at the old Mosteller property today – and that for which the property is widest-known (aside from the large spring) by most individuals today – is the gristmill which was built in 1857 and 1858. It has a deep fieldstone foundation and a two-story upper construction of wood. It was powered by an overshot waterwheel with a raceway which ran from the stream fed by the big spring.

In 1901, a roller plan sifter system – modern for that time – was installed at the mill. In 1908, a new wheel built by the Hanover Foundry and Machine Company of Hanover, Pennsylvania, was set in place. Interestingly, all the mills at this site had interior gears made – amazingly – of hand-carved hickory which had been seasoned under water.

According to Reba Mosteller Anderson of Naples, Florida, this chimney remnant is believed to be the remains of one of the slave quarters at Mosteller Spring. As is obvious, the chimney has more recently been converted to other use. (Photo by Olin Jackson)

Remnants Today

As of this writing, the Daniel Mosteller house still stands across the road from the gristmill, facing west. The road runs south to Mosteller Spring, the source of the endless water-power that once energized the various mills and operations at the little complex.

Daniel's house is an example of the style common in the area in the mid-1800s. It essentially is composed of four rooms – two upstairs and two downstairs, with a central hall on both floors. This type home often featured four small rooms on each floor and a wing built on the back of the house as is the case with the Mosteller home.

One aspect of Daniel's home which was NOT standard in homes prior to the Civil War is its "indoor plumbing." This special feature – rare in that day and age – was made possible by a stand tank in the back yard which was constantly filled by a hydraulic ram-pump – a truly unique advancement in the 1850s.

Impressive ancient oak trees still grace both sides of the now private road that runs between the old mill and the house. One evening in 1893, James H.F. Gaines, a court bailiff from neighboring Gordon County, was returning home from serving court papers in the Pleasant Valley community. He, however, never made it home. His mutilated body was later discovered among the majestic Mosteller oaks north of the house.

James had served in the Confederate Army during the war and had lost a leg in the conflict. Folks at the time of his unexplained death surmised that his artificial leg had become entangled in the reins of the horse, causing him to lose his balance and fall from his two-wheeled cart. The frightened horse must have dragged him a significant distance, for his ear was later discovered in the road two miles from the body.

The ancient spring, from whence all the stability of the Mosteller operations flowed, still bubbles up vibrantly from deep in the earth today, just as it has since time immemorial. It was a popular gathering spot for the Folsom community in the nineteenth century. Its popularity continued on into the twentieth century with Cedar Creek Baptist Church using the spring's waters downstream for baptisms, with families holding reunions, neighbors gathering for picnics, and travelers along the road simply stopping for a drink. One can easily imagine Union soldiers standing around the spring during their encampment in the 1860s, talking about war, home, and the goodness of the cool tasteful water.

Today, the heydays of the old Mosteller property have been eclipsed by time. The gristmill is in miserable condition; no trace of the sawmill or carder remains; and time and vandals have left their marks upon the old cemetery. The slave cemetery has been lost completely.

Surprisingly, the old Mosteller home which housed so many generations of the family, still survives, as do some of the old out-buildings, all in various stages of disrepair at this writing. The home has been repaired from time to time in recent years, so it seems its life has been extended – at least for the foreseeable future. It stands today in mute testimony to the once-thriving little industrial and agricultural enterprise that was begun so long ago by pioneer Daniel Mosteller.

(Note: The Mosteller Mills property is privately owned, and as such, is not open to the public. Grateful appreciation is extended herewith to Father Phillip Paul Scott for information provided in this article.)

North Georgia Civil War Ghost Town

It began as a stagecoach stop at a refreshing mountain spring. Later, when the new Western & Atlantic Railroad was routed through the site, the town of "Kingston" sprang up – named for the railroad's founder. For many years, it blossomed as a vital mercantile center – until the U.S. Civil War reached its doorstep. Today, it barely survives as little more than a ghost-town.

One would not know it today, but the tiny burg of Kingston, Georgia, was once an up-and-coming community with daily rail passenger and freight service, at least 40 commercial businesses, four substantial hotels, and commerce growing almost by the hour. It had begun with travelers on a pioneer stage route stopping at a sparkling mountain spring, but its real growth occurred when the newly-chartered Western & Atlantic Railroad (W&A) was routed through the site.

"Kingston" gained its name from the founding president and financier of the W&A – John Pendleton King – since it was "King's town."

Construction of the W&A had begun in March of 1838, and by 1845, it had reached Kingston. Since it was routed well beyond the confines of the important nearby community of Rome, yet another rail development – the Rome Railroad – was constructed between Kingston and that city in order that its important commerce not be inhibited.

There sadly is no historic Civil War-era railroad depot or associated buildings still extant in Kingston today. A fellow by the name of Sherman made certain of that. However, the remains of the former depot and the former rail yard's right-of-way can still be seen as of this writing (2023).

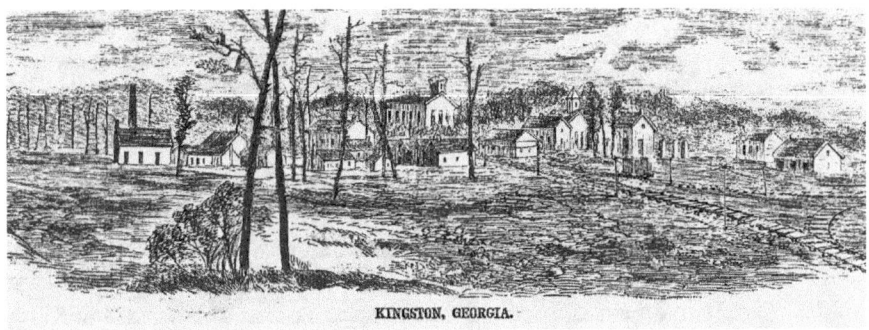

KINGSTON, GEORGIA.

Both Confederate and Union forces controlled Kingston at different times during the U.S. Civil War. The community was considered a strategic site on the Western & Atlantic (W&A) Railroad. The sketch above, which shows the Rome Railroad branching off the W&A, was published in nationally-circulated *Harper's Weekly* magazine on July 2, 1864.

Among other commodities, it was the iron ore deposits and the sea of white cotton which ultimately provided the impetus for much of the growth of Kingston... and grow it did. And as one form of commerce was developed, associated aspects of commerce followed it. Hotels and businesses seemingly sprang up overnight.

Kingston is perhaps most famous for its role in the April 12, 1862 "Great Locomotive Chase," when Union Army raiders organized by James J. Andrews were stranded in the yard for 64 minutes waiting for south-bound freights to pass during the U.S. Civil War. If not for the lengthy delay suffered at this site which allowed the party pursuing the raiders to dramatically close the gap of miles separating them from the thieves who had stolen their locomotive, the incident with Andrews and his men might have turned out quite differently – possibly even with the much more damaging destruction of numerous bridges and trestles along the Western & Atlantic.

Today, the former rail yard at Kingston is still noticeable and a majority of the area is a public park. Two historical markers recognize the Rome Railroad and the city's role in the Andrews Raid. It, however, is a quiet existence today at best, with the alterations in rail traffic.

Kingston's commerce was altered dramatically in 1943, when the Rome Railroad ceased its passenger service and the tracks were abandoned. Likewise, passenger service on the Western & Atlantic Railroad continued to decline in the 1950s, ultimately ceasing there in the early 1960s. By that time, the line had been leased by the Louisville & Nashville Railroad.

Despite declining services, the role of the railroad to post-Civil War Kingston remained significant. Trains would stop at the downtown railyard and passengers and crews alike would pause to conduct commerce in the numerous shops and businesses in town.

Churches in the community were also an important segment of life. Fame came to some of the ministers of these churches ... Church-goers from as far away as Atlanta would often take an excursion train to Kingston just to hear some of these men of God speak.

Today, CSX operates the trains through Kingston. Dozens of trains still pass through the town, but none of them stop – or even pause – there any longer, since there is no need. They speed on through to more important destinations.

Today, trees literally grow through the deteriorating roofs that once sheltered some of the businesses in the old downtown area. The brick walls of some of the buildings are crumbling, and the only things that now thrive there are the honeysuckle and morning glories.

Mrs. Mary Lee Harper witnessed the tide turning. In 1930, she came to Kingston from Rome as a bride when she "married a Kingston boy."

"I remember when Kingston was hot – people coming and going all the time," she explained in an interview in 1992, with sadness in her voice. "It's dead now though – pitiful really."

"Used to be we'd come to town about every day to see the trains and to be seen," she smiled. "Things changed,

rather gradually, and now there's no reason even to go downtown."

Indeed, Railroad Street in the sparsely-populated community appears almost totally abandoned as of this writing. There are no people milling about any longer – no one awaiting the next train, or a turn in the barber's chair, or to dine in what once were many local restaurants, or to check into a hotel for overnight accommodations, or to deposit money in a bank or read a local paper. No newspaper for the town even exists any longer – the former owners and editors having long-since departed for more commercial climes.

Preserving The Past

There would probably be nothing left of the old downtown district at all were it not for the efforts of a few preservation-minded individuals who have clung to the community.

Kingston was born as a site on the Western & Atlantic Railroad (W&A), and as rail passenger service diminished, so also did the commerce of the community. The historic town includes some 18 buildings and sites listed on the National Register of Historic Places.

Photographed in 1900, Railroad Street in Kingston was a muddy thoroughfare. The Kingston Inn (far left) which burned in March of 1911, stood on the site occupied more recently by the Ranson Mercantile building.

The century-old Desoto Hotel – one of the few original downtown businesses still somewhat intact, is far from the showplace it once represented. Owners have come and gone over the years. The late Charles Vernon Ayers, a former resident, was successful in steering through the listing of the Desoto in the *National Register of Historic Places*. When he was mayor of Kingston in the early 1980s, he also designated Railroad Street as a historic district.

Ayers was a railroad and history enthusiast, and once stated that the Desoto had been built in 1890. It survived a disastrous town fire in 1911, and was well-known for its food in the early part of the century before it was closed in 1947.

Mr. Ayers, sadly, passed away in 2010 at the age of 82, after a short stay at the Cartersville Heights Nursing and Rehab Center.

Born in 1928 in Blue Ridge, Georgia, Ayers was a long-time resident of Bartow County, where he was a former editor of the old *Bartow Herald*. After moving to Kingston with preservation in mind, he was instrumental in prolonging the life of numerous aspects of the faded community while assisting his wife, Helen S. Ayers, in operating a fine antiques shop there for many years.

Today, Ayers and his wife are gone. The abandoned downtown suggests that Kingston is home to many secrets, and no doubt many untold stories. Twelve historic markers are scattered over the town, a testament to the outstanding moments which have transcended the history of this north Georgia community, and no doubt even helped shape the future of a nation. Some 18 buildings and sites in the town are listed in the *National Register of Historic Places* today.

The Early Days

The historic markers reveal much of Kingston's rich past. It was established

Railroad Street in Kingston was photographed here in 1991. The corner of the old Masonic Hall is partially visible to the left. The Desoto Hotel is visible in the center, and the structure in the distance with the corner entranceway is the former Ranson Mercantile building.

in 1832 and named in honor of John Pendleton King, president and financier of the *Western and Atlantic (W&A) Railroad*. King was a lawyer, and served in the Georgia State Legislature and later in the U.S. Congress.

Even before the state of Georgia authorized the building of the *W&A Railroad* in 1836, businessmen and travelers had begun journeying by horseback and stagecoach to the site to trade at the newly-formed cotton market there, to drink from its delicious freshwater spring, and to pass time at a new resort to escape the heat and mosquitoes of the state's southern plains.

Ironically, Kingston's fate was sealed on the day its real growth began – in November of 1849, when the *W&A Railroad* was completed in Georgia, hailing the state's entrance into the national railroad transportation system connecting the Mississippi River Valley with the Atlantic Ocean. It's location on the rail line

made it a natural target for destruction by Northern military strategists in the later U.S. Civil War.

The Chattanooga-Atlanta trains often stopped in Kingston to take on water, fuel and passengers. With the completion of the Memphis branch railroad from Kingston to Rome in 1850, Kingston became an important distribution point on the W&A, connecting it with the riverboat transportation on the Coosa River. When the terrible war reached the interior of Georgia, Kingston could not be allowed to survive as a town.

The Civil War

Because of this strategic location on the railroad, Kingston became a busy supply and hospital center during the war. In the fall of 1861, so many soldiers in need of care were being transported through the town on the railroad that the women of Kingston took it upon themselves to establish temporary quarters for the wounded troops in churches, vacant stores and private homes. Several of these homes still exist in good condition today, most notably the Reynolds House, built in 1846 by Benjamin Reynolds, and the home built in 1854 by the author and inventor of the sewing machine - Dr. Francis Robert Goulding.

On two occasions, Kingston took center-stage in the unfolding drama of the war, both times sharing the spotlight with famous Civil War generals.

In April of 1862, the aforementioned Andrews' Raiders seized the locomotive *General* at Big Shanty (present-day Kennesaw, Georgia) with the intention of hijacking it to Chattanooga and destroying all the bridges along the length of the route, thus crippling the *W&A* and the Confederate Army's ability to move soldiers, munitions and other supplies indefinitely. James Andrews

and his men, however, suffered a set-back when they rolled into the busy hub of Kingston on the *General*.

According to James C. Bogle, a leading authority on the *"Great Locomotive Chase"* as historians have dubbed it, Andrews and his men spent a very long and frustrating hour and five minutes in Kingston before they were able to pull out. As explained, the community by this time was a busy commercial center, and delays in access to switch-tracks and supplies were commonplace. It is the consensus of historians that the delay in Kingston caused the raiders' mission to fail.

Another famous general in the Civil War, William T. Sherman of the Union Army, is also forever linked with Kingston. Sherman was headquartered at the Thomas Van Buren Hargis home in Kingston May 19-23, 1864, and returned in November to plan his now-infamous "March to the Sea." There were eight

The Desoto (New Kingston) Hotel is pictured here circa 1918. In an effort to "freshen" the image of the structure following World War I, it was renamed the "New" Kingston Hotel. Then-owner Tom Bryant stands in front.

One of the beautiful antebellum homes built in Kingston. This one was constructed by Benjamin Reynolds in 1846.

separate skirmishes in Kingston during this time, and it was here that Sherman received permission from General Ulysses S. Grant to carry out his fateful destructive march through Atlanta and onward to Savannah.

According to the late Mr. Ayers, the Hargis home burned in 1947, but the field desk that Sherman used while in Kingston survived. It was in Mr. Ayers' possession for many years. Its location today is unknown. "I was aware of its existence for many years," Ayers once stated, "and when the opportunity came to acquire it, I couldn't resist."

As described, Sherman's troops destroyed much of Kingston. The only church remaining after he departed was the Kingston Methodist Church. It opened its doors to all denominations and was also used as a schoolhouse.

When the war ended in 1865, the last remnant of the Confederate Army east of the Mississippi was paroled in Kingston. Brig. Gen. William T. Wofford (C.S.A.) arranged with Brig. Gen. Henry M. Judah (U.S.A.) for the surrender of some 3,000 to 4,000 Confederate soldiers, mostly Georgians not paroled in Virginia, North Carolina and elsewhere.

While the Federals and Confederates gathered in Kingston for the surrender, the people of Kingston observed the first Confederate Memorial Day in the nation.

The Ladies Of Kingston

Local folklore maintains that in the spring of 1865, the ladies of the town wanted to use the "profusion of spring flowers" to decorate the soldiers' graves. As irritating as it may seem today, in order to achieve this humble task these ladies were first required to seek the permission of the Union Army commandant of the area. The identity of this officer is unknown today, but he reportedly assented to this request with one stipulation – that being that the ladies decorate *all the graves*, not just those of the Confederate casualties.

At that time, there were more than 275 Confederates and many Federals buried in the Kingston cemetery, but some have since been removed. Today, there are 249 unknown Confederate graves, one known Confederate, and two unknown Federals buried at the spot.

The tradition of honoring the men who died in and around Kingston during the Civil War continues today. Each spring, Kingston residents have staunchly observed Confederate Memorial Day, due largely to the Woman's History Club there, but their numbers have steadily declined.

Founded in 1900 the club began as a monthly afternoon tea, designed primarily for the entertainment of members. They, ironically, have become almost as much a part of the history of Kingston as the history they originally set out to document and preserve.

According to one of the elder members of the organization, the club has provided many services to the town and the state of Georgia over the years, including the maintenance and observance of the Memorial Day celebrations each year without a single lapse.

The Woman's History Club is also responsible for establishing and maintaining the Confederate Memorial Museum of Kingston. Opened in 1971, the museum houses a substantial collection of Confederate artifacts, including swords, bayonets, cannon balls and civil war script money, and is open to the public on special occasions. Other items in the museum include a case of Indian artifacts; the bulletin board, a desk and bench from the Kingston Depot; exhibits on cotton, saltpeter mines, and various other natural resources found in Bartow County.

Remnants Of The Past

Scrap books and photographs attesting to Kingston's prosperity at the turn of the century are also on display. Pages from the *Kingston Times*, a newspaper circulated around 1915, reveal a prospering community with 40 businesses, several banks and hotels. There are also stories about the massive fire of 1911 in the town, and the subsequent rebuilding of the downtown area.

The *Kingston Times* was short-lived, as were Kingston's good times. The community lived – and died – by the railroad, subsequently being stranded and strangled as passenger and even freight service dwindled and died.

Many photographs of the old downtown Railroad Street in Kingston have been meticulously preserved in the museum, and, ironically, many of the actual buildings in the photographs still exist, but have been allowed to fall into disrepair. By the 1950s they were

> *The community lived – and died – by the railroad, subsequently being stranded and strangled as passenger and even freight service dwindled and died.*

Hallowed graves are honored and decorated each year in Kingston as Confederate Memorial Day is observed. There are 249 unknown Confederate graves, two unknown Federal graves, and one known Confederate grave.

on the decline, headed toward abandonment, and an era had ended.

In the more than 70 years (as of 2023) since the town ceased to function as a scheduled stop on the railroad, little has changed in Kingston. Attempts to attract industry have failed, and dissension among the community's leaders stymied other efforts for progress.

There are still a couple of gas stations and a store or two in the town, but Mr. Ayers and his one-time contemporaries who were once so vital to the preservation efforts are now a part of that history themselves.

In more modern times, Interstate 75 to the east and U.S. Highway 411 to the south both bypassed Kingston. As stated, the rail line is still in active use, but not in a functioning freight or passenger service capacity for the withering town.

Kingston's future is uncertain at best. The town's fate has been so closely linked with the railroad, it is doubtful it will ever prosper again without the revival of passenger train service.

As for Vernon Ayers, who grew up in another railroad town - nearby Blue Ridge - which has also lived and died by the railroad, he once stated he wasn't waiting for the resurrection of passenger rail service, and indeed he didn't – taking that big train ride to Glory.

Perhaps with the resurrection of travel destinations such as nearby historic Barnsley Gardens (five miles away), and the completion of the new Anheuser-Busch Brewery east of the city, Kingston will obtain some "bleed-off" positive development from those sites, but locals aren't holding their breaths.

Whatever lies in the future for Kingston, its success or failure may hinge once again upon the railroad, especially if a rapid rail system extending into the outlying areas of metropolitan Atlanta is ever completed.

Wild & Wooley Robberies Of Old Taylorsville Bank

Taylorsville Bank has been a mainstay in the farming community of southeastern Bartow County almost since the days of the pioneers. The fertility of these rich alluvial soils attracted farmers who in turn needed banking facilities to carry on their profession. Due to its locale, the small bank founded here has enjoyed almost no competition over the years, but its isolated nature also caused it to become a target of bandits, many of whom, surprisingly, proved to be comically inept.

It was during the desperate years of the 1930s and '40s, when gangsters first came into vogue as a result of the Great Depression that the small banking facility in tiny Taylorsville, Georgia, rose to fame as a target of bandits. It, amazingly, was robbed time and again, but due to the Federal Depositors Insurance Corporation (FDIC) and other assurances, coupled with its status as a bank with very limited competition, the Bank of Taylorsville not only weathered the storm, but thrived. And in 1976, the last bandits discovered the little bank isn't such an easy hit anymore.

Interestingly, the events which often transpired during the various robberies at this bank many times resembled a comic opera rather than vicious and violent acts, and many area residents still chuckle in remembrance of some of the circumstances of one or more of these occasions.

Over the years, the little bank learned to "roll with the punches" imposed by inept bandits and continued doing business in the hard times until progress and better finances allowed it to upgrade its defenses to a quality exceeding most larger banks now. Today, intensive security precautions and beefed up law enforcement have eliminated many of the bank's vulnerabilities, making it a much less enticing target for criminals.

Tiny Taylorsville remains a very rural and slow-paced community. It also is quite historic, although little focus is made upon this aspect of the community. Though native aboriginals had villages on and near this spot in prehistoric times and Union Army troops during the U.S. Civil War passed through and camped in the vicinity, locals pay scant heed to these historic trivialities. Farming is the business at hand, and

Bartow County Sheriff Jim Wheeler (l) confers with several FBI agents following a robbery at the Peoples Bank of Bartow in Taylorsville in 1976. (Photo reprinted with permission courtesy of Golden Memory Photos, Cartersville, GA)

Taylorsville Bank plays a major role in this commerce.

It therefore can only be viewed as paradoxical that this community is still known today not for its history, but as a repeated target for bank robbers.

Early Bandits

One manager – Mr. M.A. Perry – who came to the Taylorsville bank in the early 1930s, was forced to endure two such robberies under his watch. His son, W.J. "Bill" Perry, was six or eight years of age at the time, and despite his young age, recalled the incident quite clearly.

"The first robbery Dad experienced at Taylorsville was about 1933," the younger Perry explained. "The gunman locked Dad in the vault and he was lucky to have survived it with the lack of oxygen in there. Dad was the only person

in the bank in those days, so he was all alone.

"Fortunately, an individual named Mr. Bob Taylor (no doubt one of the namesakes of "Taylorsville), who was a bank director, made it his business to check on the bank every day," Perry continued. "He was the only other person in town who knew the combination to the vault, and he just happened to stop by shortly after the robbery. He heard Dad banging on the inside of the vault, and he hurriedly opened the large door.

"The second robbery during Dad's time in Taylorsville occurred sometime around 1936 or '37," Perry added. "Dad had a .38 caliber 'Police Special' that he had begun carrying to defend the bank. One day, a man drove up in a 1934 or '35 Chevy. He walked in and quickly pulled a gun on Dad and ordered him back inside the vault yet again, only this time, Dad wasn't locked inside. The gunman took all the money and put it into a washtub, then told Dad 'You get on the floor. If you come out, I'll kill you.'

"Well. . . Dad laid on the floor until he heard the motor start in that old Chevy. He then grabbed his gun and ran outside and emptied all six rounds at the fleeing car. The car never slowed up though.

"A few days later, that thief was brazen enough to phone in and cackle about how Dad 'couldn't hit the side of a barn.' It sure wasn't from a lack of trying though."

A Run On The Bank

The 1930s in the United States during the height of the Great Depression were indeed very desperate times. Bread lines were long and "soup kitchens" were constant providers of nourishment for a penniless and hungry populace. The nature of this desperation gave rise to outlaw "celebrities" such as Charles "Pretty Boy" Floyd, John Dillinger, Bonnie Parker and Clyde Barrow, "Baby Face" Nelson, and many others.

"Pretty Boy" Floyd, who died October 22, 1934, in a hail of bullets in Wellsville, Ohio, ironically was born and grew up just a few miles down the road from Taylorsville in Adairsville, Georgia. His family home still stands there on Railroad Street.

Aside from having to deal with the outlaws of that day, banking institutions had to be concerned with "a run on the bank" as well. The Taylorsville Bank was no different. In 1932, it also suffered a "run" on its funds, where depositors, suddenly fearful that the bank was about to fail, lined up at the door demanding the facility "cough up" their money.

Few were the banks who successfully weathered such a threat to survival. Once depositors begin collecting en masse at a bank to withdraw their funds, very few such institutions had enough cash reserves on hand to pay out such sums. When this situation arose at the Taylorsville Bank, however, a simple clever strategy allowed it to survive the storm.

"Many of the farmers in the area got the idea the bank was about to fail," Perry continued. "When people started lining up to withdraw their money, Dad called Mr. W. D. Tripp, who was a stockholder and on the board of directors.

Tripp was a seasoned financial expert, and though he no doubt was highly concerned after receiving the phone call from Mr. Perry, he did not panic. He didn't hesitate a moment in applying a quick remedy to the situation.

"Mr. Tripp told Dad to stall as long as possible and pay out just as slowly as possible until he (Mr. Tripp) had a chance to get there," Perry added. "He then went quickly to another bank with which we were associated in Bartow County and borrowed $2,000 – all in one-dollar bills – and put it all in a big bag. He then rushed down to the Taylorsville Bank, walked calmly inside, dumped the $2,000 in bills out on a counter and announced 'I understand some people want their money.'

"Well, in 1932, that $2,000 looked like a million bucks today," Perry smiled. (In actuality, it was a great deal of money, being the equivalent of approximately $39,854.00 in 2023 dollars.) "A large number of the accounts in the Taylorsville Bank were only eight and ten-dollar accounts. Before you knew it, people just began walking away, and that was the end of the crisis."

A Move To Rockmart

Crises at a little bank, however, were not the foundation upon which Mr. Perry wished to build his career. After all, he had worked long and hard to become a banker in order to obtain a steady and lucrative income, so that he could avoid the stresses of life. After he had experienced a second bank robbery in Taylorsville, he began looking around for employment elsewhere.

M.A. Perry soon moved to what he considered to be a much more secure situation in nearby Rockmart in Polk County. A person today can only imagine Perry's shock and dismay when, two years later (about 1939), the Rockmart Bank also was robbed. Even worse, it was the only robbery ever experienced by the Rockmart Bank. Luckily, however, the elder Perry had gone home for lunch that day, and thankfully missed all the excitement of the hold-up.

Interestingly, the Rockmart robbery involved a somewhat comic element – something with which the Taylorsville Bank personnel would soon become familiar. After the Rockmart hold-up, the bandits leapt into their getaway car and were prepared to race away from town, when, to their utter dismay, they discovered their car would not crank.

Just as the robbers were about to flee the scene on foot, one of the friendly Rockmart citizens – completely unaware of the circumstances into which he had stepped – actually assisted the criminals in starting the troublesome vehicle and kindly waved as the bandits – smiling broadly – drove away. It was like a scene from a comic movie.

Yet another episode of comedy also survives – undoubtedly with some embellishment – from a 1940 Taylorsville robbery. The bank manager at that time, William Dorsey, was victimized one morning just as the bank opened for business. The bandits unceremoniously tied Dorsey to an old pot-bellied stove, an act to which the banker strangely took great umbrage, considering it a tremendous humiliation for reasons still unknown.

Even years later, Dorsey continued to react angrily – to the amusement of anyone around him – whenever reminded of the event. "There wasn't no need for that," he would quickly growl. "They had no business tying me to that stove." (Just why the bandits decided to tie him to the stove is unknown today. And no, the stove wasn't hot.)

Today, bank robberies which went awry and in which no one was injured can be subjects of considerable amusement, but the situation is anything but funny for a bank teller gazing down the business end of a loaded revolver. Long after one particularly disturbing robbery, one bank official expressed his feelings thusly: "I was always thankful that they did get away, especially after I found out who they were."

Planning A Robbery

It is the last robbery – in 1976 – inflicted upon the little bank in Taylorsville that is remembered

A person today can only imagine Perry's shock and dismay when, two years later (about 1939), the Rockmart Bank also was robbed.

The 1976 robbery of the Taylorsville bank was planned with a diversion in mind – that being the demolition of nearby historic Euharlee Presbyterian Church. The explosives' detonator fortunately was defective, rendering the device harmless.

most vividly by many area residents today, mainly because it was one of the most unusual – and potentially deadliest. It was also the first robbery of that facility which emphasized the fact that the Taylorsville Bank was no longer "an easy mark."

The two "masterminds" of the '76 hold-up reportedly were experienced professionals despite their ineptitude. According to later courtroom testimony, they arrived in the Cartersville area from their home base in Indianapolis, Indiana, and settled into a multi-purpose truck-stop/pool hall/boarding house on U.S. Highway 41.

One of the men, Leon Johnson, walked with a distinctive limp. The other, Donald Anderson, had "rotten teeth," both of which were very distinctive identification features. The bank employees at Taylorsville would remember these "tells" years after the crime.

The duo became a trio when they met up with Marvina Satterfield, described as an individual who was exceptionally masculine in appearance, more nearly resembling a man with long hair than a female – a not altogether flattering identity. Those three still later were joined by a fourth accomplice – an attractive blonde named Charmaine Garrett – who witnesses would also easily recall and later identify.

The four partners in crime all had one thing in common: They all needed money and intended to obtain it illicitly – violently if necessary.

It wasn't long before the quartet began forging a plan to accomplish their ill deed. They no doubt took their time, observing the rural countryside, plotting which bank would surrender the most loot with the least risk.

Clayton J. Harris, bank manager at the Taylorsville Bank in 1976, says the initial plan of the gang was to rob the First National Bank of Cartersville.

Their scheme involved kidnapping bank manager Russell Archer, taking his family hostage, then threatening harm to them unless Archer opened the bank vault. This plan was squelched, however, when Marvina Satterfield objected, explaining that she might be recognized by the Archer family.

The crooks therefore had to cast about for a new target bank. Taylorsville, with its isolated location soon drew their attention. Its well-known history of robbery and burglary may even have been a contributing factor in their choice.

Despite an obvious lack of security and law enforcement personnel in the vicinity of the bank, the bandits decided a diversion would increase their margin of safety. Their plan called for the creation of an emergency situation – such as a bombing – a short distance away, to draw away any police in the area.

The conspirators located a church several miles away in the little community of Euharlee in Bartow County. They decided to blow it up with dynamite, using a delayed fuse.

"Fortunately for the church and the community, their plan didn't work," recalled church member Bill Thomason thankfully. "The fuse wasn't attached properly and had actually fallen out. The dynamite remained unexploded."

The newspapers of that day reported many details of the robbery, as well as the subsequent manhunt, but there was not a single word describing the deadly explosives at Euharlee. Bank manager Clayton Harris, however, does recall the FBI informing him of the discovery of the dynamite three or four weeks later.

One can only imagine the somber congregation singing and praying in the little church on Sunday, completely unaware of the deadly explosives poised for destruction beneath the church floor.

Harris says he was infuriated when he learned of the proposed wanton destruction of the historic religious structure. "I really didn't get mad about that robbery – you know, angry, angry mad – until I found out about that church deal. The money they stole from the bank was unimportant compared to the (possible loss of life) in the church."

To make their plan as effective as possible, the conspirators reportedly scouted the back-roads and made practice driving runs for a number of days prior to the crime. They had to time the driving routes; select a discreet rendezvous point where they could abandon their "hot" car; and select a drop-off point where the men could hide out with the money overnight while the two women evaded roadblocks.

The criminals decided to steal a car for their getaway vehicle which they would abandon as soon as possible following the robbery. This tactic ultimately proved successful in temporarily delaying police who were hot on their trail in pursuit.

The stolen car – a 12-year-old Ford Galaxie – was snatched in Marietta. The criminals "hot-wired" the ignition to start the car. Before traveling back to Taylorsville, they stopped in Kennesaw where they stole a Michigan license plate, using it to replace the Georgia plate on the Galaxie.

Now the group had two vehicles: the Galaxie for the actual robbery, and a 1970 or '71 "dirty-brown" Ford or Chevrolet, owned by one of the members and which would be used for an escape after abandoning the Galaxie.

The Hold-Up Day

Thursday, March 11, 1976, was the appointed day for the crime. The thieves' first act was to set the explosives beneath the Presbyterian Church at Euharlee and then return to the bank.

At approximately 10:00 a.m., the thieves arrived in Taylorsville, and parked the stolen car directly in front of the bank. Charmaine Garrett remained at the wheel with the engine running, while the others quickly prepared themselves for the robbery.

The two men – Johnson and Anderson – were packing revolvers, and had pulled ski masks over their faces to disguise themselves. They had taken pillow cases to use in the collection of the bank notes.

The men burst through the front door of the bank anticipating a quick "score," when to their unmitigated surprise they discovered themselves facing tellers who were protected behind bullet-proof glass (since the bank management had obviously begun taking precautionary measures after the numerous previous robberies). Ironically, despite the protective glass, the door leading to the interior of the "teller cage" was quickly and easily penetrated by the gunmen due to a flaw in the protective system, according to Clayton Harris.

Harris explained he was escorting two Boy Scout executives out after a meeting in his office. "I was still chatting with them as I opened the door, when these robbers came bouncing in the front door and got the drop on us." It was a lucky break for the bandits – one that the bank personnel would make certain never happened again in the future.

Harris said Johnson pushed him

The men burst through the front door of the bank anticipating a quick "score"

back inside the secure area, then went from one teller to the next with his pillow cases in a villainous sort of "trick-or-treat." Tellers Glenn Williams and Shelva Campbell scooped up the greenbacks and dumped them into the bags.

Johnson reached one flustered teller and reportedly yelled "Big money!" She dropped a handful of hundred-dollar bills into the bag then froze in fear. Johnson promptly prodded her for more with his gun.

Meanwhile, the other bandit, Donald Anderson, stationed himself next to the security door. Assistant Vice President Jackie Smith was sitting at her desk beneath Anderson's gaze, desperately trying to think of what she could do to save the diamonds she was wearing. She stealthily slipped them into the garbage can at her desk. The robbers, however, were not bothering with jewelry or coins that day. They were too busy bagging what turned out to be little more than $22,000.

Harris remembered that one customer in the bank, Marron Haas, began to edge slowly towards the front door. Anderson turned his gun on him and stated matter-of-factly that if he took one more step, he would blow him in half.

"That got me right back up to the counter and got both my hands on the counter just like they were supposed to be," Haas later recounted. "I didn't make another move."

Calling In The Cavalry

It was about this time that the gunmen's luck began to fade. Ray Hughes, a repairman, was working on a faulty air conditioner next to the bank's side door. He had been making frequent trips in and out of the bank, and had wedged a small screwdriver in the side door to keep it from locking.

It was on one of his trips from the air conditioner back into the bank that he suddenly noticed the masked men with guns, and he quickly and quietly backed out the door, unseen. He ran across the street to Wolfe's convenience store, instructing them to call the police and report the robbery.

Next in the fast-moving sequence of events, a bank customer drove up and parked around the corner from the front door. He was near Ray Hughes who had run back to the side of the bank. Either Hughes or a bystander reportedly shouted, "They're robbing the bank!"

When he learned the circumstances unfolding around him, the newly-arrived customer – Charles Ford – ran to his pickup truck and grabbed a .22 caliber, two-shot derringer. He looked around quickly and thought he recognized the getaway car in which Charmaine Garrett sat. He started toward the getaway car, intending to confront the driver with his derringer, but thought better of it (which may have been wise, since Garrett had a sawed-off shotgun in the car with her).

Just as Ford returned to his pickup, the masked bandits dashed from the bank and jumped into their car. Garrett gunned the stolen Galaxie around the corner past Ford and his derringer, past Ray Hughes, the air conditioner repairman, and down the road leading to a rendezvous site three miles east of town.

As the vehicle roared past Charles Ford, he fired two shots at the front tire of the getaway car. The fleeing bandits

The Ford Galaxie used as an escape vehicle in the 1976 robbery is pictured. The right front tire was flattened by .22 rounds fired by Charles Ford, a bystander at the bank during the robbery. (Photo reprinted with permission courtesy of Golden Memory Photos, Cartersville, GA)

According to later court testimony, it was at the rusted bridge (above) that Leon Johnson and Donald Anderson were picked up by their accomplices after hiding out overnight during a cold winter rainfall.

fired back as they sped away, but the shots were poorly aimed and no one was hit. When the car was found later, the right front tire was flat with two bullet holes.

Meanwhile, the planned diversion – the detonation of the explosives beneath Euharlee Presbyterian Church – never happened. And with no diversion, the forces of law and order were able to collectively focus upon the bank theft. More bad luck for the bandits.

The charming 1853 Presbyterian Church, unchanged in almost 175 years, was spared. It was weeks, however, before anyone even knew of the existence of the hidden dynamite. All this time, church members were lifted spiritually as they sat in their lovely old sanctuary each Sunday morning. Little did they know at that time how close they had come to being lifted "physically" by the dynamite into eternity. Prayers in this house of worship undoubtedly took on

a new dimension following discovery of the explosives.

Hot Pursuit

Meanwhile, the alarm had gone out to law enforcement contingents in a three or four-county area following the report from the convenience store. Police forces quickly mobilized and concentrated on the shaken little community as well as on every back road in the county. Within ten minutes, Georgia State Patrol aircraft, including a helicopter, were overhead scouring the area.

According to press reports of that day, "Every available road leading out of Bartow County was covered. Shortly after the robbery, nearby Georgia State Patrol officers from Cartersville, Canton, Rome, Cedartown and Polk County, plus the Cedartown and Cartersville police departments, assisted in the investigation."

In a race with destiny, the stolen

getaway car careened down the road from town, crossing GA Highway 113 and ignoring the stop sign. The bank robbers headed along Davistown Road for their appointed rendezvous.

R.C. Free was traveling in the opposite direction on Davistown toward Taylorsville. He noticed the reckless driving of the bandits and he was able to get a good look at the occupants of the car. He later assisted in their identification.

The bandits eventually reached their pre-planned rendezvous spot where they awaited the second car driven by Marvina Satterfield. During all the excitement, Satterfield had been constantly circling the back roads.

A nearby resident noticed that Satterfield stopped beside the getaway car, picked up its occupants, then drove off. The bandits' carefully laid plans did not take into consideration the attentive eyes of curious bystanders.

An hour later, area police discovered the abandoned getaway car, its engine still running. They took fingerprints and searched for other incriminating evidence.

The bandits meanwhile had continued to follow their plan, with the two men hiding out in the woods overnight, and the two women driving on alone to pass through the road-blocks. That night, weather forecasters had predicted scattered showers by morning and a low in the mid to upper 40s.

As a result of the inclement weather,

Despite the suffering they had done overnight, the criminals undoubtedly were feeling a little better about their odds for escape after being picked up.

both Anderson and Johnson, no doubt, were soggy and suffering from severe exposure by the time the women returned in the early hours of Friday morning to the little creaking bridge over Floyd Creek to pick them up. Despite the suffering they had done overnight, the criminals undoubtedly were feeling a little better about their odds for escape after being picked up. They headed south on GA Highway 61, and reportedly stopped to hide in an American Legion building for the remainder of the night.

Upon arrival in Paulding County, Donald Anderson, amazingly, focused not upon furthering his escape from a capital crime, but rather upon vanity – getting his decayed teeth repaired by a local dentist. He even mindlessly used a portion of the stolen money to pay this bill, because the bank notes were soon traced by the FBI, and Anderson was the first of the gang arrested.

In a continuing comedy of errors, the remaining bandits apparently boldly traveled back to Bartow County and Cartersville where they – also mindlessly – purchased a brand-new Lincoln Continental at City Motors. According to Clayton Harris, Johnson, Satterfield, and Garrett brazenly made a down payment on that expense with some of the stolen money as well, then had the audacity to visit the First National Bank of Cartersville (their original robbery target) where they sought a loan to finance the car.

The bandits' movements in Georgia after that point are unknown, but several weeks later, Charmaine Garrett was located and arrested by FBI agents. Following an intensive interrogation, she confessed to her part in the crimes. A few weeks later, Johnson also was caught, as was Marvina Satterfield. All, except Johnson, were quick to plea-bargain in exchange for lighter sentences.

The Trial

At this time, a federal trial for armed bank robbery in Cartersville, Georgia, would have taken place in Rome, but the defendants were considered too dangerous for the Rome jail. Also, Leon Johnson's brother, Morris, who was in the custody of federal agents in New Orleans at the time, was subpoenaed by the defense to testify on his brother's behalf.

Both of the Johnson brothers had previously escaped from jail. Morris Johnson, amazingly, had twice escaped from the Atlanta Federal Penitentiary, a feat which remains a record to this day.

Morris Johnson also was the proud owner of yet another milestone for criminals – that of making the FBI's "10 Most-Wanted" list. Atlanta, therefore, with its more secure incarceration facilities, was chosen as the site for the trial.

Five months after the bank robbery, Leon Johnson was tried for his part in the crimes. He was the only defendant to plead "Not Guilty." Morris Johnson and five witnesses testified that Leon was home in Indiana at the time of the holdup.

Interestingly, Morris claimed it was he, not Leon, who had masterminded the Taylorsville job. His comments were carried in an article in the **Atlanta Constitution**:

"When the prosecutor asked Johnson if he committed the robbery, he answered, 'I pulled it. Yes.'"

The jury in the trial, however, was unmoved by the subterfuge. The trial lasted only a few days. On August 6, 1976, the jury took just 33 minutes to return a verdict of *"Guilty"* for Leon Johnson.

In September when the bandits were sentenced, Johnson drew a total of 50 years, Satterfield six years, Garrett ten years, and Anderson 15 years.

Bank robberies in recent years have increased at a pace not seen since the 1970s. One FBI official offered a surprising explanation for the increase:

"Lots of bank robbers convicted in the late 1970s and early 1980s are now back on the streets (because of liberal parole policies in use at the time)."

If Leon Johnson was paroled after serving a third of his sentence, the entire Taylorsville Bank robbery gang may all be freely circulating again someplace in Georgia.

Meanwhile, back at the Taylorsville Bank, the window tellers in the tiny facility say they still keep a nervous eye on the front door as each customer enters today. . . . and nobody – nobody – dares to leave the door to the teller cage ajar anymore.

(Period photographs courtesy of Golden Memory Photos, Cartersville, GA. Reprinted with permission)

(Grateful appreciation is expressed herewith for the accumulation of information necessary for this article by the late Gordon Sargent.)

He Sang Back-Up Vocals for the "King," Then Was Banished from the Kingdom

In a quiet country church cemetery in rural northwest Georgia's Cherokee County, a modest – though colorful – tombstone marks the final resting place of a man who once sang back-up vocals for the "king of rock & roll" – Elvis Presley – for almost three years before being strangely dismissed.

Few people will deny that Elvis Presley was – and still is in the minds of most – the king of rock & roll worldwide. There just has never been, nor is there likely ever again to be a musical performer with the charisma, physical attraction, and charm of Presley. When he passed away on a hot August evening in 1977, the world lost an irreplaceable icon, and the members of Presley's entourage were suddenly elevated in status – somewhat to their surprise – as Elvis fanatics searched frantically for anything associated with the departed star. One such individual rests peacefully today himself in a solemn grave and quiet graveyard in northwest Georgia.

Hugh Thomas Jarrett was born on October 11, 1929. While bouncing around in a variety of jobs mainly associated with the radio broadcast world, he was offered an opportunity in 1954 to join the Jordanaires gospel vocal group. The Jordanaires were already a very prominent group of performers who were providing backing vocals for Eddy Arnold on stage and in his television program, so this opportunity was quite the feather in Jarrett's hat.

At this same time, Elvis Presley was a rising star who happened to notice the Jordanaires in a concert at Memphis, Tennessee. He reportedly told them that if he was able to obtain a big-time record deal, he wanted the Jordanaires to provide backing vocals for him on a permanent basis.

In 1956, Presley obtained just such a contract, and, true to his word, he immediately contacted the Jordanaires. On March 15th and 16th, 1956, they performed in a series of initial concerts with Presley in Atlanta, Georgia. Ironically, though Jarrett was a massively-important cog in the Jordanaires, he nevertheless suddenly and inexplicably disappeared from the group in 1958, never to return. This disappearance was never explained nor discussed openly by Jarrett or anyone else until shortly before he died.

Hugh Jarrett passed away at the age of 78 on May 31, 2008, from injuries he had suffered in a tragic automobile accident the previous March. Compared to his earlier days at the peak of his career when he was earning a substantial income as a member of the Jordanaires, touring and appearing with "the King" in his motion pictures, concerts, and national television extravaganzas from 1956 to 1958, Jarrett lived extremely modestly in his later years. His grave in the small country cemetery northwest of Atlanta bespeaks the humble status to which his life had been relegated.

Just as some years can be richly rewarding financially, others can be a sad departure from "the glory years." Even Elvis had years shortly prior to his death when his financial circumstances were becoming dire. But just as did Elvis, Hugh Jarrett soldiered on.

Even in his "down years," particularly when he suddenly was banished from the Jordanaires, never to appear with Elvis again, Hugh Jarrett – though obviously disappointed – was never thunder-struck into paralysis. He just moved on to "the next big thing." He also fell back strongly upon his foundational religious beliefs during those years, and his Christianity shined like a beacon for all to see. Gospel music replaced rock and roll.

Presley had also grown up in a devout Christian family and was a huge proponent of gospel music as well. It is a little-known fact that Elvis won all three of his GRAMMY Awards not in rock & roll or country music categories, but rather in gospel music. In 1967, he landed his first GRAMMY win for *Best Sacred Performance* singing "How Great Thou Art." In 1972, he took home the award for *Best Inspirational Performance* for "He Touched Me," and two years

The late Hugh Jarrett's Cherokee County home was a virtual museum of Elvis memorabilia from his days as a back-up singer for the king of rock & roll. (Photo courtesy of Hugh Jarrett. All Rights Reserved.)

later he won that category again for a live version of "How Great Thou Art."

The Jordanaires therefore were a "natural fit," becoming an important aspect of Elvis's blossoming career in his many concerts across the United States, as well as in his nationally-broadcast television appearances such as the renowned *Ed Sullivan Television Show* in New York and in virtually all of his early major motion pictures. Elvis Presley himself once reportedly quipped, "If there hadn't been a Jordanaires, there wouldn't have been an Elvis Presley."

While dazzled by the early idolization of Presley by his growing legion of fans, the Jordanaires nevertheless also shined in their performances with the king. They, however, were soon literally in disbelief at the fervor being demonstrated by these fans at his early concerts.

They quickly realized that they were about to be a part of something big – very big.

"We came to Atlanta with no idea of what songs Elvis wanted to perform," Jarrett related in an interview by Atlanta writer and publisher "Doc" Lawrence in *North Georgia Journal* magazine in 1998. A day prior to the concert at historic Lowe's Grande Theater on Peachtree Street (the same venue where the world-famous movie *Gone With the Wind* had premiered some 18 years earlier), Elvis reportedly handed Jarrett and the Jordanaires a list of obscure songs – mostly rhythm and blues numbers by singers with wonderful names like "Big Bill Brumsey," "Arthur Crudup," and "Willie Mae Thornton," – and told them that was what he wanted to sing.

As a gospel vocal group, the Jordanaires simply were not familiar with

The Jordanaires vocal group accompany Elvis Presley as he sings one of his favorite Christian hymns. According to the late Hugh Jarrett (far right), the crooner enjoyed relaxing during recording sessions by playing the piano and singing. This photo was taken during a session at RCA Victor Studios in Los Angeles. (Photo courtesy of Hugh Jarrett. All Rights Reserved.)

this new boy's preferred music, and they initially were dumbfounded. *"We finally found a great record store in Buckhead* (an Atlanta suburb) *called 'Jim Salle's,' and bought those records,"* Jarrett explained. *"We learned the songs that way and then rehearsed them with Elvis at Lowe's only a few hours before curtain call."* (Sadly, Lowes Grande where so many historic events had occurred over the years was mysteriously destroyed by a major fire in 1978, approximately five months after Elvis's tragic death.)

"Elvis changed everything," Jarrett added, obviously still excited in the 1990s about this early association even almost half a century later. *"We were accustomed to improvising and we blended our 'do-wahs,' 'ya-yas,' hand-clapping and the like with his singing. We fit together almost perfectly."*

Jarrett said it was shortly after this Atlanta concert that he and the Jordanaires knew instinctively that they had caught a magical ride on a history-making freight train to stardom. Their status as minor celebrities was swiftly becoming a thing of the past as their notoriety with Elvis mounted. Their amazing career-making experience with the star advanced to a hugely-successful series of concerts across the South and then headed straight for New York and, shortly thereafter, Hollywood, where international stardom awaited them all.

"After our first tour through the South, Colonel Parker (Elvis's manager) *negotiated a recording contract with **RCA Victor** and we went to New York to record,"* Jarrett smiled in remembrance. The early ride wasn't quite as smooth as Hugh and his fellow singers had anticipated, however, because Elvis turned out to be a perfectionist with his music, particularly when it came to "recording," and a lot of patience had to be exercised before the young performer was able to get a "take" that he felt was good enough to release to the public.

As his popularity increased, more and more composers began bringing their music to this exciting new performer. *"People brought their songs to him and if he liked them, we would work through lots of versions until we found one he was satisfied with,"* Jarrett revealed. *"One of Elvis's earliest hits, 'Don't Be Cruel,' went through over 50 different versions in an all-day recording session before he found a version he liked."*

*"During the New York recording sessions, Colonel Parker arranged for an appearance for Elvis on the **Milton Berle Show**,"* Jarrett continued. *"The live performance was enormously successful with high viewer ratings.*

"Ed Sullivan, a huge television force as well, surprisingly had expressed no interest in Elvis's appearance on his show," Jarrett said, *"but the Milton Berle success couldn't be ignored."* Jarrett added that they did the **Sullivan Show** and performed their two new RCA recordings, and the crowd went nuts.

"We finished the show with a Southern hymn – 'Peace in the Valley,'

> *As his popularity increased, more and more composers began bringing their music to this exciting new performer.*

47

and the performance was given rave reviews."

The passage of time has a unique way of dulling the memory regarding many details, and the stature of the **Ed Sullivan Show** is a case in point. Back in the day, it was perhaps the most popular performance venue of its kind in America for well over a decade. It introduced not only Elvis to the world, but many other future stars such as the **Beatles**, the **Doors**, the **Rolling Stones**, and on and on, all of whom went on to superstar status.

Hugh Jarrett's resonant sonorous bass can be clearly heard on many of Presley's greatest early hits of the 1950s such as *Hound Dog*, *Don't Be Cruel*, *Teddy Bear*, *Jailhouse Rock*, and *Hard-Headed Woman*, to name just a few. Knowledgeable sources therefore are at a loss to explain what happened to cause Jarrett's sudden inexplicable departure from the group during its greatest years. There obviously was a reason, but the specific incident which precipitated it has remained shrouded in mystery.

Of the eight men on stage for all but one of Elvis's 28 concerts in 1957 [Elvis, bass player Bill Black, lead guitarist Scotty Moore (listed as #29 on the list of all-time greatest guitar players), drummer D.J. Fontana, and all four of the Jordanaires (Hoyt Hawkins, Neal Matthews, Gordon Stoker, and Hugh Jarrett)], all are now deceased. There is no one left alive who might actually be able to explain the exact circumstances of Jarrett's sudden departure from

In 1958, Hugh Jarrett not only was dismissed from Elvis's entourage, he also was permanently banished from the famed Jordanaires.

the group – and he didn't just voluntarily leave for a different career either. . . In 1958, Hugh Jarrett not only was dismissed from Elvis's entourage, he also was permanently banished from the famed Jordanaires.

In two somewhat cryptic explanatory emails in 2004, Gordon Stoker stated *"Hugh Jarrett was released from the group in 1958, so he is not included in any of the festivities relating to Elvis. . . He was replaced by Ray Walker – a fact that Hugh has never gotten over, but we remained friends all these years."*

Though his departure from his fellow crooners was not of an acrimonious nature, the momentous incident nonetheless would have been a bitter pill for most people to swallow, and Jarrett was no exception. In 2004 when the Jordanaires were inducted into the **Country Music Hall of Fame**, Hugh Jarrett sadly and unfairly was completely excluded from the induction, and was allowed no recognition whatsoever. What could possibly have happened to cause so much pain and ostracization?

Even worse, as a result of Jarrett's exclusion from induction into the *Hall of Fame*, his work therefore also was not honored. The line-up of Gordon Stoker, Hoyt Hawkins, Neal Matthews, and Ray Walker received all recognition as "the vocal group" backing Elvis Presley through the associated years, even though it was Jarrett, not Walker, who sang bass during the most spectacular portion of Elvis's career. Hugh took

Hugh Jarrett (far left) and the Jordanaires performed with Elvis during movie productions in Hollywood. Pictured is a scene from the major motion picture *Loving You*. (Photo courtesy of Hugh Jarrett. All Rights Reserved.)

solace in the fact that he was at least accorded membership in the *Gospel Music Hall of Fame*.

After being appraised of these circumstances by the editor of *North Georgia Journal* magazine in 1998, Georgia Governor Zell Miller nominated and spearheaded the effort to have Jarrett inducted into the *Georgia Music Hall of Fame* in Macon, Georgia, where no less than the *Allman Brothers*, *Otis*

Redding, *Little Richard*, and so many other musical legends are enshrined. Though he was hugely grateful for this recognition, Jarrett no doubt considered it small consolation for his being blackballed from the larger, more prestigious Nashville enshrinement.

Regardless of his banishment from the Jordanaires and any further involvement with Elvis Presley, Hugh Jarrett, surprisingly, bore no malice whatsoever

49

toward the Jordanaires or Elvis. He never allowed any bitterness whatsoever to creep into any interviews or subsequent discussions regarding his former life with the Jordanaires. In short, Hugh Jarrett was a prince among men, and will be remembered in that regard.

To the surprise of many, Hugh also remembered Elvis very warmly. *"Elvis was kind, good-humored and thoughtful,"* Jarrett stated wistfully. *"He was generous to a fault too. When we asked him to put the Jordanaires name on his records, he arranged for that to happen despite the fact that the Jordanaires recorded professionally for a competitive label."*

Following his release from the Jordanaires, Jarrett moved on to other careers. Lesser men would have been crushed at the loss of such a lucrative income opportunity, but not Hugh Jarrett. His attitude was simply "onward and upward." He was undeterred, and never faltered in his dedicated pursuit of other income opportunities elsewhere.

In replacement of his singing career, Hugh moved back to radio. He eventually was hired to do his own radio show on Nashville's WLAC where he became known as *"Big Hugh Baby,"* a moniker which would follow him on to other professional pursuits later in his career. He also later became a familiar voice on WPLO and WSB radio stations in Atlanta, continuing his trend of upward mobility in radio.

And just as with others such as the famed **Dick Clark**,

Lesser men would have been crushed at the loss of such a lucrative income opportunity, but not Hugh Jarrett.

Hugh Jarrett was a natural with young people, regularly organizing dancing events which he dubbed *"Hugh Baby Hops."* After relocating to the burgeoning young adult mecca of Atlanta in the 1960s, Hugh purchased a nightclub on U.S. Highway 41 in Marietta, Georgia, just north of Atlanta, which he dubbed *"Big Hugh Baby's Hoparoni."*

A short time later, Hugh was able to parlay his acting chops in Elvis's movies into additional performing roles. He appeared regularly in serial television programs and variety shows. His familiar face also occasionally turned up in programs such as **In the Heat of the Night** being filmed in Atlanta in the mid-1990s starring Carroll O'Connor and Howard Rollins. He also appeared in the made-for-tv movie, **Murder in Coweta County**, starring Johnny Cash. In 1985 he appeared on the big screen as "Arthur" in **The Annihilators**, also known as **Action Force**. In 1989, he portrayed John Sinclaire in the "Sister Sister" episode of **In the Heat of the Night**. His final acting credit was 1992's **The Nightman**, in which he portrayed "Mr. Peabody."

Never one to be out-done energetically, Jarrett also lent his voice as emcee at the popular **Lanierland Country Music Park** where he became a celebrity in residence hosting the greats in country music such as **Waylon Jennings**, **George Jon**es, **Loretta Lynn**, **Tammy Wynette** and many others. He also remained close to his Christian roots as well, hosting a Sunday morning gospel radio program each week in Cumming, Georgia.

After "the King's" sudden departure in 1977 and the later demise of most of the remainder of his retinue, the relationship between Hugh Jarrett and "Graceland" finally began warming once again. In 1997, he was even invited to Graceland to perform with the Jordanaires on the 20th anniversary of Elvis's death. *They had Elvis on this huge screen at a large outdoor concert and we performed live music synchronized with Elvis's image and voice,* Hugh smiled wistfully in remembrance once again. *The ovation was wonderful and very emotional. We were treated like royalty.*

In the summer of 2007 when they were the last remaining performers who had been on-stage with Elvis in the 1950s, Hugh, Scotty Moore, D.J. Fontana and Gordon Stoker were interviewed for television. Though it was a little late in arrival, Hugh at last was finally being allotted some of the credit due for his former association with Presley. The timing at that point was fortunate too, because only a few years later, they all were gone.

So what was it that could have been such an unpardonable sin by Hugh Jarrett as to cause his release from the Jordanaires way back in 1958? In a conversation with R. Olin Jackson, former publisher of *North Georgia Journal* some 40 years later in 1998, Jarrett intimated that he had been present at an event at which he had made a callous remark to which Elvis took umbrage. *"I'm not going to say anything further,"* Jarrett stated at the time. *"I shouldn't have said it, and that was all there was to it. End of story."*

Today, no one who was present in 1958 is still alive to know about the remark – or even care anymore. It's all done and forgotten, and Hugh Jarrett is

remembered today as the kind, generous, and happy-go-lucky soul who, once upon a time long ago, sang back-up vocals for one of the greatest performers of all time. And up in quiet Cherokee County in the tiny graveyard with the modest headstone emblazoned with his "Big Hugh Baby" moniker, the mortal remains of the famed former back-up singer for the king of rock & roll lie in quiet and peaceful repose.

Hugh Jarrett, a devout Christian, finally found peace in a small graveyard at Big Spring Methodist Church in north Georgia's Cherokee County where he was a member - far from the decadence of Hollywood and the rock & roll arena in which he once found fame. Today, he no doubt sings backup for Elvis in a considerably different capacity. (Photo by Judy Jackson)

The Amazing Life & Times Of Mule-Trader Gus Coggins

Fortune smiled often on his early business endeavors which eventually became an enterprise of national proportions. Fate, however, was waiting in the wings, as changing times and intrigue lingering from the U.S. Civil War ended the career of one of Cherokee County's most promising favorite sons.

Driving northward today along Georgia Highway 5 in Canton, travelers often notice the very impressive Georgian Revival-style home set back off the road on a crest above the Etowah River. And on the opposite side of Highway 5, a large and imposing stone barn immediately impresses the senses as a site also of historic note. To the unenlightened, these two structures might arouse little more than a second glance, but to natives of the area, they are the remnants of the once-proud enterprises of one of the most successful and yet tragic figures in Cherokee County history.

Following the onslaught and devastation of the U.S. Civil War – an important portion of which was fought through Georgia all the way to the coast at Savannah – the former plantation lifestyle and economy had been completely destroyed. Most Whites formerly associated with the planter economy were totally disenfranchised by the war, and became a desperate segment of a thoroughly desperate society. There was little if any food, opportunities for livelihood, or anything else. . . . just total devastation.

Negroes who formerly had been slaves on farms and plantations, suddenly found themselves free men, willing – indeed eager – to accept paid laborer positions, many of which formerly had been the exclusive domain of Whites. Opportunities for a livelihood for most people had simply vanished almost overnight.

And even in those laborer positions which traditionally had been occupied by Blacks, the desperate disenfranchised Whites could find no opportunities either, because Negro laborers could be employed at much lower salaries and subsistence levels than could Whites. In a backlash against this depressed economy and paucity of employment opportunities, angry Whites formed vigilante and outlaw groups whose sole purpose of existence became that of punishing the Whites who were hiring the Black laborers.

Lawless Land

It was into this maelstrom of lawlessness, destroyed lifestyles and devastation that the Coggins family settled in Cherokee County. They, however, were an exception to the norm. They were among the few who were able to persevere and "make lemonade from lemons."

Augustus "Gus" Lee Coggins around whom this story is based, was born in Gilmer County on September 24, 1868. His father, Alfred B. Coggins, was a Confederate veteran and the father of nine children.

In the years immediately following the U.S. Civil War, north Georgia was a lawless and desolate locale. Roving criminals added a constant danger to the region; jobs and employment by and large were nonexistent; educational opportunities for children were a thing of the past; and life in general was barely tolerable by the state's populace. For these and other reasons, Alfred Coggins made the decision to move his family from Gilmer southward to Cherokee County's Canton, hoping the relocation would offer an escape from the lawless and undesirable circumstances farther north in the state.

The move proved to be fortuitous in many regards. Alfred became a successful Canton merchant, and the seeds for the entrepreneurial genius of his son, Augustus, were sown. Unfortunately, when it comes to lawlessness, "one can run, but one cannot hide." The same lawless renegades that Alfred had sought to escape in Gilmer persisted in Cherokee

County as well, and despite his son Augustus's amazing business acumen later in his life, these same evil forces would be at least partly responsible ultimately for his tragic professional demise.

The property on which Gus Coggins centered his enterprises enjoys an amazing history all its own. It includes broad fertile river bottomlands most of which are encircled by the Etowah River in a substantial crescent shape, a circumstance which gave life to the site's moniker: "Crescent Farm."

Ancient Site

Rising above these fertile fields is a promontory called Mount Etowah, a spot known to have been occupied (with villages) by aboriginal natives dating back to pre-history. The first known inhabitants of this spot for which any record exists were the Cherokee Indians, but signs of even earlier inhabitants were regularly witnessed in the broken shards of pottery, arrow points and other tools of the ancients which turned up with regularity on the promontory.

Elizabeth Coggins Jones, the daughter of Gus and wife Daisy Coggins, remembers her childhood at the family home intimately. In an interview conducted prior to her death, the historic significance of the home and the business endeavors of her father were recalled with vivid clarity.

"According to legend, the area around Mount Etowah was a Indian village site, and records appear to confirm this," Mrs. Jones explained in the late 1980s interview. *"A 'Chief Still,' sometimes referred to as 'Old Still,' is mentioned as an inhabitant of this site."*

When the first frame house was built upon Mount Etowah in the 1880s by Robert F. Maddox, family tradition maintains that an Indian grave was discovered during the excavation of the cellar of the home. The artifacts discovered therein reportedly were sent to the Smithsonian Institute in Washington, D.C.

"Looking back, it's easy to believe there was a village or community of some kind there," Mrs. Jones continued. *"Two paths from the top of the hill led to the Etowah River below. The one on the right passed a pile of loose flat rocks* (Possibly one of the countless unexplained prehistoric stone cairns which still dot the north Georgia landscape even today in the backwoods.). *Another path on the left led down to connect with the larger path that descended to the river from the Rock Barn. This path veered left across fields and a stream to connect with the road crossing the bridge over the river. A large rock projected into the river at the base of Mt. Etowah and a fish trap was located there."* (The Native Americans often constructed "fish traps" in the rivers and streams to conveniently acquire substantial quantities of the food source when desired.)

White Pioneers

The first known structure built by Whites on "Crescent Farm" is believed to have been built by James McKinney who purchased the property in 1840 from Felix Moss. Deeds to this property in 1868 and 1877 refer to it as *"The McKinney Plantation."*

Robert F. Maddox was the next owner of the Crescent Farm property, and it was he who constructed the first frame house (circa 1880s) on Mount Etowah. He and Major Campbell Wallace were instrumental in bringing the railroad to Canton in 1879. A newspaper clipping from August 21, 1884, states in part that *"Col. R.F. Maddox and family are spending the summer at their lovely villa across the river at Mount Etowah."*

Maddox ultimately sold the plantation to Major Wallace in 1887. Gus Coggins leased the farm from the Wallace estate in the mid-1890s, and then purchased it outright in 1903.

Due to his adept business acumen, Gus Coggins immediately hired large numbers of Black workers for his many businesses. He provided exceptional housing and living conditions for his workers, paid a fair wage, and therefore had no problem attracting some of the best talent in the region. However, as a result of these business practices, he also became a target of White terrorists. He was constantly plagued by inexplicable losses due to fire, which almost certainly were the work of angry area Whites bitter with his employment solely of Black workers.

Virtually the entire financial foundation of Coggins' enterprises – businesses which leaned heavily in the direction of livestock breeding and sales – was based upon the "housing" of livestock. And it is the huge old structure which still stands today on Highway 5 in Canton, which, more than anything else, bears mute testimony both to Coggins' acknowledgement of this fact and his resolution to the problem he faced. Known simply as "the Rock Barn" by most locals today, this immense building was constructed by Coggins in 1906 to help counter his growing losses to arsonists.

A *"barn,"* according to ***Webster's New Dictionary,*** is *"a building used especially to store farm products and to shelter livestock."* Gus Coggins knew this better than most men, and stored a fortunes-worth of these items in his barns at any given time. It, quite likely, was for this reason that when re-building one of his larger livestock barns following one of these devastating fires, Gus decided a "stone" barn would be a much better investment than a wooden one.

The Coggins Family

On January 3, 1894, Gus Coggins married Daisy Ryman of Nashville, Tennessee. Her father, Thomas Green Ryman, owned and operated the Ryman Steamboat Lines. He also constructed a large auditorium in Nashville which is familiar to millions of people today as Ryman Auditorium, the original home of *The Grand Ole Opry*.

Daisy's younger sister, Pearl Ryman, married Thomas Raleigh ("Rol") Coggins, Gus's younger brother. Shortly thereafter, Gus and Rol entered into business together under the name *"Coggins Brothers,"* and the stage was set for one of the most prolific business enterprises ever developed in Cherokee County. Gus Coggins proved to be a talented and productive Canton farmer, horse-breeder and businessman who possessed an uncanny knack for entrepreneurial success.

The 7,000-square-foot Rock Barn is just one example of Coggins' persistent and determined desire to succeed in whatever he pursued, regardless of the circumstances. It is, quite likely, the only stone barn of its age remaining in the state, and its historic significance has been duly noted by its enlistment on the *National Register of Historic Places*.

And to the Coggins family, their home on Mount Etowah was no less important. It, unfortunately, was originally constructed of wood, and therefore also became a target of the arsonists – a terrorist organization which knew no bounds.

"This was my parents' home when I was born in 1899," remembered Mrs. Jones. *"The house was a one-story Victo-*

rian with a porch on three sides. The north side opened onto a court. On one side of the court was the kitchen and on the other side was the carding and quilting room. A screen porch connected the two and was full of shelves with cedar water buckets, lamps to be cleaned and filled, kindling wood, and coal bins."

In 1917, the beautiful Victorian Coggins home on Mount Etowah also fell victim to the arsonists. Miraculously, none of the Coggins family were injured in the fiery maelstrom which once had been their happy home. *"We found the silver flatware in a melted lump in the cellar,"* Mrs. Jones lamented.

But just as the lyrical Phoenix rises from the ashes of destruction, so also did the new Coggins home on Mount Etowah, but this time, Gus adjusted once again to fire-proof materials. *"Father built our two-story home* (which is on the site today) *this time out of red brick in 1922,"* Mrs. Jones said, as she broached a smile.

Coggins built his domain steadily over the years. Crescent Farm was a working plantation with departmental heads managing each segment of its operations.

"In my day, Pete Green, a Black man with a very imposing appearance was in charge of mules and livestock," Mrs. Jones continued. *"John Heard, another Black man, was in charge of the vegetable garden and orchard. He also attended to the personal riding horses and family buggy and surrey.*

"A White overseer was responsible for planting and raising crops. The first one I remember was Mr. Ruth Collins from Salacoa and the last one was Bill Richardson. He coordinated with the livery stable in town which was headed by a manager. Turkeys, guineas, sheep, pure-bred Jersey cattle, hogs, dogs, walking horses, and race

horses were raised with crops of hay, cotton, corn and some molasses cane."

Creating an Empire

Gus Coggins traveled extensively – mainly by railroad – to almost endlessly pursue growth opportunities for his business enterprises. He was perhaps best-known for his engagement in the sales and marketing of mules and other livestock.

This aspect of his business empire carried him to Missouri, Texas, Tennessee, and numerous other states where he purchased large numbers of mules and additional livestock. He also owned livery stables not only in Canton, but in Atlanta as well – regularly herding the animals down Interstate 75 (Just kidding! Just kidding! Couldn't resist.). He also eventually maintained a large mule brokerage business extending across the United States and even to foreign countries.

"A white man, Mr. Harve Barnes, was the office manager and was in charge of the office and business operations at the livery stables on Main Street in Canton," Mrs. Jones continued. *"The office was known as 'The Tack Room,' and this was the place where many of the farmers, businessmen and other citizens would gather to swap stories and keep up with cotton and livestock prices and current events.*

"The men of our community were interested in horseback riding, and my father and many of our farm workers were great enthusiasts of harness racing and the training and showing of fine horses," Mrs. Jones continued. *"There, however, was also a very strict code of conduct for the people living in Cherokee County, as well as most of north Georgia back then. Some people were known as 'Round Heads' and others as 'Cavaliers.' The Round Heads were opposed to horse racing and they*

thought that this pursuit was accompanied with gambling and other types of misconduct."

Gus Coggins constantly lived and managed his businesses within the whirling vortex of these opposing social strata in the Canton environs. *"My father did not belong to any church although he did join the Methodist Church shortly before he died,"* Mrs. Jones added. *"He had a strict code of ethics, but his lifestyle did not conform to that of many people of that era.*

"He was a very practical person, and had good ideas," she smiled again. *"I remember that he once said 'If you want to lay out and plan a good road, then watch where the cows go. Follow their paths, because they always select a path that is well-drained, has a firm foundation, and that is not too steep and has a good grade.'"* It, in fact, is a matter of record that many of the present-day roads and highways across Georgia and elsewhere follow what once were ancient Indian trails which had in turn followed the ancient migratory routes of hoofed wildlife (deer, antelope, buffalo, and others) who had the same compulsive and instinctive habits described by Coggins.

Early Happiness

Aside from their good business sense, both Gus Coggins and his brother, Rol, apparently had a sense of humor too. Lee Rol and his cousin Tom Coggins, according to Mrs. Jones, had a **pet monkey** named "Sally Gal" which they kept around the old Rock Barn for many years. It, understandably, was not only a novelty in the area, but an endless source of entertainment for all involved.

"Rufus Childers had a grocery store on Railroad Street in Canton, just across the river from our home," Mrs. Jones related. *"He'd get in a supply of bananas,*

and the monkey invariably would escape and later be found on a banana stalk that was hanging in front of the Childers Store. We'd retrieve the monkey and bring it back to the barn."

It was another pet, however, with which Gus had the most fun. *"Yes, father also kept a **pet bear**,"* Mrs. Jones chuckled in memory. *"It was a rather large animal, and it could terribly frighten an unsuspecting person just by its presence. It was kept at times at the Rock Barn, and sometimes at the livery stable in Canton. It was probably a better protector of property than any watch-dog; even better than an armed guard, because the bear seemed to enjoy making sudden appearances when no one even knew it was around."*

The last overseer or superintendent that worked for Gus Coggins at Crescent Farm was William E. "Bill" Richardson. In an interview in the late 1980s, his son, Jack, recalled an incident involving his father which the elder Richardson undoubtedly remembered the rest of his life.

"My father went into the barn one night about dusk, and there, of course, were no lights. It apparently was very dark in the barn. My father said he was feeling his way around looking for some gear, when all of a sudden, the bear pounced on him, and gave him a big bear hug. My father always said he wasn't hurt by the bear, but he was so scared, and lunged so violently to escape, that he injured himself in his fear." One can only imagine the terror which must have been struck into the heart of Bill Richardson on that undoubtedly horrifying night.

Race Horse Fame

Fun and games aside, it was the raising of horses for harness racing which gave Gus Coggins the most pleasure. Crescent Farm was perhaps best-known in racing circles for *"Abbedale,"* its world-class race horse. Abbedale brought fame and fortune to Crescent Farm, and has been listed in the *Harness Racing Hall of Fame* in Goshen, New York. Abbedale also earned recognition in the book, **Harness Racing** by Phillip Pines.

Sunday afternoons were especially pleasurable times for Coggins and his family. Gus had laid out and constructed a one-quarter-mile race track not far from Crescent Hill. When horses weren't being run on this track, Gus and other members of his group were traveling about the Southern circuit, trading and racing horses across the Southeast.

A Mr. George Stiles in Rome, Georgia, owned a prominent training track. A Mr. Walter Candler also had a beautiful and elaborate track at Lullwater Farms in Atlanta (present-day home of the president of Emory University in Atlanta). These facilities were frequently used by the Coggins trainers and horses.

Gus Coggins was a firm believer in the value and beauty of many forms of livestock, not the least of which were his fine race horses and the mules which he traded and bartered over much of the United States. It was for the housing and care of these great numbers of livestock that he constructed the numerous barns in the Crescent Farm enterprises, not only in Canton, but in Atlanta as well.

The "Night Riders"

It was the "wooden" barns which proved to be one of the main weak links in the Coggins Brothers' business affairs. Devastating fires plagued these and other wooden structures owned by Coggins throughout his career. One of the first Coggins barns for which there is a record of destruction by fire occurred in February of 1900. In this conflagration, the fine race horse *"Queen Nab"* was destroyed, as well as seven head of cattle. The cause of this fire was never discovered.

"All the other horses in this barn were saved except Queen Nab," remembered Mrs. Jones. *"She had won the $6,000.00 derby in Macon in 1891, and had taken purses in Knoxville and at the state fair in 1891."*

A newspaper account published in the **Cherokee Advance** in Canton described the event as follows: *"It's often been said that you cannot get a horse out of a burning building, but 'Hannah,' Mrs. Coggins' buggy horse, broke out of her stable, jumped over the lot fence, and ran all the way over to town, and had to be carried back to the farm. 'Queen Nab,' the mare that was burned, was one of the best race horses in the state, and was considered the best animal in the barn."*

Gus Coggins lost a lot of barns and livestock before he came up with a solution to his problem. After a period in which three separate barns were burned on three separate occasions, Gus reportedly was nevertheless determined to persevere, but he responded by constructing yet another "wooden" barn. On December 3, 1915, both this new barn as well as an adjacent barn were burned to the ground once again by arsonists, destroying some 162 mules and approximately 15,000 bushels of corn.

Interestingly, with these fourth and fifth barn and livestock losses, a vigilante group known as *"The Night Riders"* blatantly took credit for the terrible destruction. It was ultimately discovered that this organization was terrorizing employers of Blacks throughout north Georgia.

According to the Atlanta newspapers, *"In two instances, notes had been left by 'Night Riders' and in two other instances, no word had been received. The 'Night Riders' operating in Cherokee County are charged with destruction of property valued at approximately ninety thousand dollars during the past two days, following the receipt of mysterious unsigned notes, cautioning employers of Negroes against the pretension of these employees.*

Heavy Losses

"The heaviest sufferers in a series of fires were Coggins Brothers whose immense barns and granaries, located less than a mile west of Canton, were destroyed with a loss of about seventy-five thousand dollars," the newspaper continued. *"Rol Coggins of Atlanta, one of the men interested in the business Monday was unable to state the amount of insurance carried, although he did not believe that it would cover the loss. A message from Canton, however, was to the effect that insurance amounted to less than twenty-five thousand dollars."*

The newspaper accounts explained that other barns and livestock had been similarly destroyed at the property of Otto Sherman, located six miles east of Canton, and at the Freeman Bell farm. The news accounts stated that all of the fires seemed to have been started from the interior of the buildings, since the fires were always well-advanced prior to being discovered. On the side of one of the burned buildings, a five-gallon oil can was discovered.

Speaking of the loss in this fire by Coggins Brothers, the newspapers stated that *"It is learned that 162 horses and mules were burned, together with a large quantity of foodstuffs and farming implements. All cattle were saved by the employees of the concerned owners. Coggins Brothers deal extensively in horses, mules and cattle, and operate a large farm in connection with their barns. . . . . They also employ a large number of workmen, about 75 of whom are Negroes."*

Yet another Coggins barn which was a mule barn, burned in the 1920s. It was located just south of the intersection of Highways 5 and 140, across from the spot where, as of this writing, the present-day McDonald's, Hardee's and several other restaurants are located. A large number of mules were lost in this fire.

Over the years, virtually all of the wooden barns built on the Coggins properties were destroyed by fire at one time or another. As a result of these terrible losses, Gus Coggins came up with the idea of building stone "fire-proof" barns, and built the Rock Barn which still exists today for the protection of his highly-prized race horses. It apparently was a wise precaution too, because the Rock Barn is one of the few Coggins structures which never fell victim to fire. This sturdy historic edifice is used today (as of 2022) as an events venue.

The Rock Barn's existence today is directly attributable then to the violence and fear which was woven into the fabric of life in post-Civil War north Georgia. The valuable race horses housed in the Rock Barn almost certainly would have been the target of the *Night Riders* in 1915, had not the barn been constructed of stone. This structure stands today not only as a monument to a determined entrepreneurial spirit, but also as a reminder of the social injustice which existed in north Georgia at that time.

Despite his perseverance against the arsonists, Gus Coggins was no match for the combination of events which finally felled his businesses. Many of the culminating events were simply beyond

his control. More than anything else, Coggins was a victim of the times - swiftly changing social and industrial practices and trends.

More Heavy Losses

As explained above, the Coggins practice of exclusively hiring Blacks was very unpopular in north Georgia, and Gus suffered as a result. The destruction of the huge mule barn by the *Night Riders* in 1915 was a severe blow. The loss of horses, mules, and grain was estimated at $75,000.00, an immense sum in that day and time. That amount alone in 2022 dollars would be the equivalent of approximately $2,134,000.00.

It was also at approximately this same time that the cotton market collapsed. Cotton was a major commodity produced on Crescent Farm. The loss of this income stream was almost irreplaceable.

And as if the losses to arsonists and the collapse of the cotton market weren't enough, another event proved to be even more devastating – the totally unanticipated loss of the mule market. Just prior to this down-turn, Gus and Rol had obtained huge government contracts to supply Allied troops in Europe with mules during World War I. German U-Boats controlled the shipping channels to Europe however, leaving no available transportation for the immense stock of Coggins mules which Gus was therefore forced to maintain idly in stockyards.

Following the Armistice for World War I in 1918, not only was the war-time market for the mules for the troops suddenly eliminated, a sudden technological advance – the automobile and automotive power – essentially replaced the market for horses and mules entirely. Coggins Brothers, as a result, was forced to absorb unfathomable losses in this market as well.

The fourth and final blow came in the form of the banking system – particularly the chain system of banks to which Gus's bank – The Bank of Cherokee – belonged. At that time, there was no Federal Depositors Insurance Corporation (FDIC) or any other safeguards to protect against the possibility of heavy losses suffered by large inventory businessmen such as Gus and Rol Coggins. Before they knew it, the Coggins brothers' enterprises were ruined financially.

Bankrupt!

The factors described above, combined with an economic panic of the early 1900s, completely destroyed the Coggins financial empire, throwing it into bankruptcy in 1928. All the Coggins holdings, including Crescent Farm and Edgewater Hall, were forced to be sold at auction to satisfy creditors. That quickly, the Coggins financial enterprises simply ceased to exist.

Over the years since 1928, rumors to the effect that Gus Coggins escaped from this disaster as a wealthy man have persisted. Nothing, however, could have been further from the truth.

Gus Coggins, as a result of the humiliation of bankruptcy and the danger brought on by his former hiring practices, was forced to relocate out of the state. He moved to Colorado, where he lived until the last few months of his life. While there, several of his friends visited him over time, and all confirmed that his financial and living circumstances there were exceptionally simple and humble, and in no way indicative of a wealthy man.

During Gus's final year of life, he struggled against leukemia to survive.

Mrs. Jones, his daughter, brought him back to Georgia on the L&N Railroad to live out his final months. The San Francisco-Chicago run connecting with the L&N made a special stop for the man who at one time had shipped more mules by rail than any other customer.

On the Sunday that he arrived back in Canton, Georgia, Gus Coggins was greeted by one hundred sixteen old friends who came to welcome him home. He died only a few months later at age 84, and was buried in the family plot in Canton.

Since 1928, much of the acreage which formerly comprised Crescent Farm has been redeveloped with various new commercial enterprises. Cherokee County High School, Canton Elementary School, a Georgia State Patrol office, the National Guard Armory, just to name a few. Edgewater Hall and the Rock Barn remain as the lone sentinels to the glory days of Gus Coggins and some of the finest harness and race horses ever produced in Georgia.

The Rock Barn which was donated to the *Cherokee County Historical Society* in the late 1980s for renovation was used as a combination museum and conference center for many years. In 1989, the Society received a substantial grant from the *National Trust for Historic Preservation* for maintenance of the Rock Barn. Other grants and gifts followed. As of this writing in 2022, the structure continues to be used as an events venue.

Only time will tell what the future holds for Edgewater Hall and the Rock Barn. Regardless of the circumstances, Gus Coggins has gone down in history as one of the most remarkable businessmen ever produced by Cherokee County.

The Virginia Hill Story

Though gentle and kind to friends and family, life was less rewarding to the attractive young lady from Cobb County, Georgia, who grew up to become the kept woman of Chicago mobsters. She ultimately died a lonely death far from home, and later was immortalized upon the silver screen in her life of crime with Benjamin "Bugsy" Siegel.

Down through the years of its storied history, north Georgia's Cobb County, has produced a number of individuals who have gone on to achieve national – if not international – fame and fortune. Who could forget, for instance, Academy Award-winning actresses Joann Woodward (Mrs. Paul Newman) and Julia Roberts, or country music singer, songwriter, actor, and music hit-maker Travis Tritt, just to name a few. There is, however, another "celebrity" from Cobb who, perhaps, is even more famous than these individuals, but her name must first also be qualified with the adjective "notorious." Her name was Virginia Hill.

Virginia was actually born a few miles away in Lipscomb, Alabama, on August 26, 1916, to Margaret and Mack Hill, spending her earliest years in Bessemer, Alabama. Mack was an itinerant blacksmith and horse-trader back when horses were still a marginal form of public transportation. When Virginia was 8 years of age, Mack moved his growing family to what then were the rural confines of Acworth, Georgia, just north of Marietta, possibly as a result of the multitudes of horses and mules being regularly marketed in that vicinity. At some point the family moved down to Marietta.

Virginia was one of nine or ten children fathered by Mack. According to later stories, Virginia's father was anything but a model parent, often beating her during her childhood . . . that is . . . until the day she threw a hot skillet at him following his latest abusive actions. That got his attention, and sent the message that Virginia was not one with whom to be trifled.

An early "bloomer," young Virginia reportedly was sexually active with boys at age 12, and doubtless contributed more than her share to the acrimonious relationship with her father by regularly publicly flaunting her sexuality. As she reached her higher teenage years, Virginia came to the attention of growing numbers of the male population in the nearby

Virginia Hill sits uncomfortably, possibly in advance of the U.S. Senate Hearings on Organized Crime in which she was called to testify.

Marietta environs. "Miss Virginia," you see, was quite the "looker," and she knew it and used it to every advantage.

The late Bill Kinney, a long-time Cobb resident and former reporter and editor of the *Marietta Daily Journal* apparently knew Virginia quite well, and once described her as "a saucy, curvaceous, red-headed bombshell, who burst upon Marietta's serenity during the hard times of the Great Depression.

"In those days, women were just getting around to wearing one-piece bathing suits," Kinney recalled, "but Virginia (routinely) wore a halter-top and 'short' short-shorts." Dressed provocatively as such and barefooted, she, according to Kinney, would ride her horse down Church Street into Marietta and

around the town square, and then back up Cherokee Street to her house. She was the talk of the town among the adolescents, and apparently was everything but "Lady Godiva" riding naked, and the young men absolutely loved it.

On Her Own

Virginia attended the public schools in Marietta until she was 14, when she allegedly married a mysterious man named George, in order to escape her abusive father. In 1933, at the height of the Great Depression and at the tender age of 17, Virginia moved with George to Chicago, where she promptly ditched him and set out on her own. Back in Georgia, Mack Hill abandoned the remainder of the family, leaving Margaret and the children to fend for themselves.

Ever resourceful in the use of her sexuality to gain the things she needed – or wanted – Virginia shortly found employment as a "shimmy dancer" at the *1933 World's Fair* in Chicago, and it was there that she made the acquaintance of an individual by the name of Joe Epstein, who was to figure prominently in her life for the remainder of her days. Epstein was employed as the bookkeeper and close associate of notorious Chicago mobster Alphonse "Al" Capone.

Virginia Hill may have had little in the way of a formal academic education, but when it came to "street smarts," she was *Phi Beta Kappa*. In short order, she had leveraged her beauty and beguiling personality into an apprenticeship to Epstein who, accordingly, facilitated her move up the ladder within the Mob hierarchy and became her constant source of income.

Through Epstein, Virginia tapped into a tutelage for a lifestyle of crime and graft which gave her easy access to huge sums of Mob-related money. After demonstrating that she could be a loyal and reliable courier for laundered funds and narcotics to and from Mob-controlled income centers like Havana, Cuba, New York, St. Louis, and Chicago, she graduated to Mob maven, and never looked back.

Always well-dressed and bejeweled, Virginia – though certainly not included within inner circles of the Mob – was eventually considered to be a very valuable employee, since she not only was trustworthy, but also far less-likely to become a target of searches and frisking by law enforcement than the typical male Mob foot-soldier. And, as a result of Epstein's loyalty and endless financial support, she became a devoted follower, willing to do virtually anything.

Virginia was a fast-study in graft too.

She was often given thousands of dollars to bet on pre-arranged horses at the race tracks. She followed Epstein's precise instructions, brought back the winnings from fixed tickets and got a 10 percent share of the proceeds. Epstein also showed her how to lure unsuspecting men into "sucker" bets – pure profit for bookies – such as for fixed boxing matches. She was a natural for these illicit activities.

"Joe Epstein ran the gambling business around Chicago," Kinney added. "Of course, things like the races at the tracks were fixed, and Joe Adonis and the other racketeers at those locales not only made a lot of money placing bets there, but so also did Epstein and Virginia."

With incredible ease, using her intoxicating beauty, sexual liaisons and talents for laundering money and stolen

A publicity print of Virginia Hill during her days as a Hollywood starlet. (Associated Press photo courtesy of Bill Kinney, *Marietta Daily Journal*)

merchandise, Virginia rose higher than any other woman in the nation's underworld, associating with the most infamous male racketeers of that era, including Meyer Lansky, Charles "Lucky" Luciano, Joe Adonis, Frank Costello, Johnny Rosselli, Charles and Joe Fischetti, Tony Accardo, Frank Nitti, William "Ice Pick Willie" Alderman, Jack Dragna and, most famously, Benjamin "Bugsy" Siegel.

Despite her growing notoriety in Mob activities, few people back home in Marietta were even vaguely aware of Virginia's involvement with the underworld in Chicago. She often returned

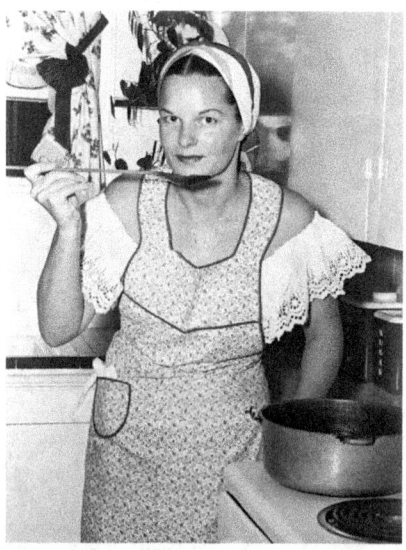

Joe Epstein, a prominent bookkeeper and associate of Alphonse Capone, became acquainted with Virginia during her days in Chicago. She made it clear that she was trustworthy and dependable, and was soon tapped by the mob to transport large sums of illicit cash between Miami, Florida, and Chicago. Virginia reportedly was quite fond of cooking for her friends, and is pictured here in a home purchased for her in Florida by mobster Benjamin Siegel. (Associated Press photo courtesy of Bill Kinney, **Marietta Daily Journal**)

home to Marietta during the early 1930s, but when she did, she always had enough money to bankroll Elvis, and no one could figure out where she got it. Her Marietta followers just knew she was very attractive, had "lots" of money, and freely shared whatever she had with her friends.

"When Virginia came back to town to visit," Kinney smiled in remembrance, "all the women would warn their husbands and boyfriends 'You stay away from that hussy!' But all of we young fellows stood there on the (Marietta town) square at the corner of Hodge's Drug Store anyway, waiting on her... We were all on 'Virginia watch.'

"We just thought by that time that she was an actress, or rich heiress, or that she had married very well into money," Kinney continued. "Nobody asked many questions, because she was so good to us."

Benjamin "Bugsy" Siegel

It was Virginia's association and brief relationship with hitman, hustler and racketeer Benjamin "Bugsy" Siegel which earned her the greatest measure of notoriety and renown within the annals of Mob history. The two began seeing each other as early as 1937, and despite his reputation as a heartless killer, Siegel was drawn to Virginia like a bee to honey, completely infatuated and overwhelmed by her womanly charms.

Siegel was one of Mob boss Joe Adonis' main earners in the 1930s, and with his equal charm, handsome good looks and blue eyes, he was just as attractive to Virginia as was she to him. The two reportedly began a sexual relationship almost immediately upon meeting each other, an action which both hurt and enraged Adonis who was equally smitten with Virginia.

In one of his police mug-shots - this one following an arrest in 1928 - Benjamin Siegel offers a hostile gaze to the camera. It was during the period in which she lived in Chicago that Virginia Hill began her association with mobsters such as Siegel, and her role as a courier of large sums of illicit cash from mob-controlled casinos in Havana, Cuba, sent northward to Chicago and New York.

As a result of this jealousy, Adonis made his anger known to the Chicago Outfit. Since Siegel was virtually untouchable and uncontrollable, it fell to Virginia to suffer the punishment for her perceived amorous transgression, and her financial stream via Joe Epstein was cut dramatically to send her a message. Unfazed, Virginia merely moved back to Georgia for a brief spell to allow her Mob friends time "to find another courier as trustworthy as she" – if that was possible. She also wished simply to visit with her mother in Marietta, so she took some time off.

This period of separation from Siegel, however, was anything but long-term, and they both knew it. It wasn't long before they were an item yet again. Despite the heat they generated together, Virginia's overall relationship with Siegel was nevertheless known to be "stormy" at best. Beneath her sweet exterior veneer and earthy female attraction, Virginia was very independent-minded, and didn't hesitate to speak her mind to Siegel, nor did she allow herself to be controlled, a scenario which often resulted in fierce fighting between the two.

To the already-married Siegel, Hill was his ideal woman in many respects. Their intense pairing and Mob business eventually led them to the West Coast and actor George Raft's Hollywood home in 1939. Raft and Siegel had known each other as kids and remained closely associated throughout their lives.

It no doubt was through Raft that Virginia learned how to acquire an agent and to work her way into the acting world as a starlet. Her beauty and smoldering sexuality were undeniable, and she no doubt made frequent use of the "casting couch" in her efforts to gain admission to Hollywood.

The years 1939 and 1940 would be busy ones for the actress-wannabe.

Photographed in a sport jacket of which he apparently was quite fond since it appears in a number of photographs, Benjamin "Bugsy" Siegel was captured here on film circa 1946. He has assumed his usual posture with his patented hostile stare.

Other Conquests

While Siegel was cooling his heels in prison from August to November of 1940 after being charged with murder, Virginia, surprisingly, took up with a Mexican nightclub dancer named Miguelito Valdez. She even married Valdez during this period in order that he might gain readmission to the United States so that he could resume his lucrative performing career.

Virginia returned with Valdez to Chicago, then shortly departed for Georgia, where she met a 19-year-old college football player at a bar, then married him on the spur of the moment, just as she had done with Valdez. But barely six months later, she had the marriage with her athletic conquest annulled and returned to Valdez. To say the least, Virginia Hill got around.

According to speculation, Virginia may also have taken Louis Dragna's top associate, Johnny Rosselli, as a lover as well. With her credibility within the Mob in high gear, she invested Outfit cash into a nightclub called "The Hurricane" in New York, and appeared at the opening, dancing the rumba in her bare feet with Valdez before news cameras.

After the opening at the nightclub, Virginia tricked the hapless Valdez into signing a contractual agreement which he foolishly thought was a booking for The Hurricane. In reality, it was an uncontested divorce agreement. Virginia was moving on again.

Fluent in Spanish by that point, Hill had also become involved in drug trafficking – specifically heroin – out of Mexico for her Chicago patrons. To curry favor and obtain important information for the Outfit south of the border, she reportedly had affairs with the son of a Mexican finance minister and a connected politician.

Meanwhile, since the day he had first helped her obtain work inside the Outfit, Joe Epstein was still regularly funneling cash through the mail to Virginia – virtually whenever she requested it. It was an income stream which would continue well into the mid-1960s.

Both Luciano and Meyer Lansky used Hill to distribute Mob cash, likely realizing her double attraction as a Mob money courier who not only made financial deliveries, but also provided sexual favors to the recipient on the opposite end. In addition to her other services, the seductress was a spy for and confidant to Mob bosses, exchanging verbal communications with underlings and then reporting back to Epstein, Lansky, Luciano, and others on whatever might have been transpiring "under the table."

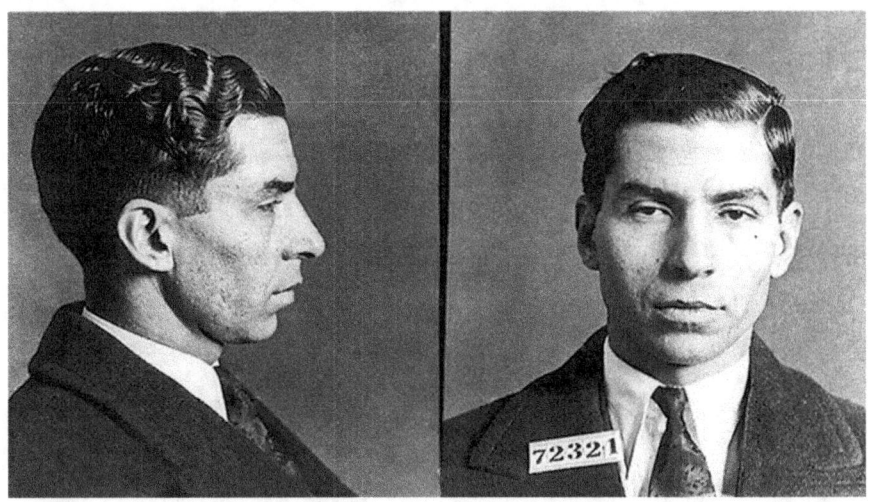

Charles "Lucky" Luciano was a close associate of Virginia Hill's love-interest, Benjamin Siegel. Luciano is pictured here in a mug-shot from one of his arrests. If Siegel's death was in fact a mob-hit, it quite possibly would have been Luciano - in association with mob leader Meyer Lansky - who ordered the termination. Other potential perpetrators of the crime, however, have also been suggested over the years, and the truth likely will never be known.

Virginia received steady income from these pursuits as well.

Show Biz Dreams

By the early 1940s, Virginia was pursuing a career in Hollywood in earnest. She and brother Chick took acting lessons, and she yearned for a serious opportunity in the acting world, not necessarily for the money – for she had plenty of that – but for the glitz and glamour which it would afford. She reportedly spent thousands of dollars on her appearance, buying furs and jewelry, renting suites of rooms at the Beverly Hills Hotel, and hosting lavish parties, and even dropping $7,500 on one celebrity event which was a small fortune in those days. In the end, however, it was all for naught, as all her work resulted in barely one bit part in one movie.

It was in 1941's *Manpower*, a film noir directed by Raoul Walsh and starring Edward G. Robinson, Marlene Dietrich, and George Raft, in which Virginia appeared momentarily as a hatcheck girl. The movie did quite well at the box office, but it did nothing for Virginia's Hollywood career.

Ironically, Virginia would soon find great fame on television – but of an undesirable type – during the U.S. Senate investigation into organized crime which was broadcast into homes around the nation. She had the misfortune to be subpoenaed for her testimony on what she knew about the organized crime figures with whom she associated. Though almost always testy, she was never at a loss for sensationalism and fiery responses to the questions she was asked.

When Ben Siegel was acquitted – for lack of evidence – of the murder for which he had been charged, he renewed his underworld crime activities in the horse-racing and gambling rackets on the west coast of which New York Mob boss Luciano wished to gain control. He also renewed his relationship with Virginia at that time. Her association with the Chicago Outfit's Charles Fischetti and Fischetti's Los Angeles boss, Jack Dragna, allowed them to use her to monitor Siegel's actions.

Meanwhile, during her trips back down to Marietta, Georgia, even though she knew that her activities were nefarious at best and highly illegal at worst, Virginia eventually ceased trying to conceal her involvement with the Mob from her friends at home. A big part of the reason for her return to Marietta was to visit her mother and family, but she was also still highly invested in her illicit

activities as a courier to Miami and Havana, Cuba, for the Mob.

"Virginia was sort of our economy back in those days," Kinney smiled again. "She was our roving branch bank. She carried a roll of hundred dollar bills at a time when you could throw down a twenty dollar bill and ring every cash register on the square in Marietta."

As a result of her meager circumstances as a child, Virginia had grown up being snubbed in her early life. She therefore didn't hesitate to throw her support to her poorer friends when they needed it. "One time Virginia decided to carry us all night-clubbing in Atlanta,"

At a cost in excess of $6 million (originally estimated to cost $3 million) the 105-room Pink Flamingo Hotel & Casino finally opened on Boxing Day 1946. The rainy night was an absolute disaster and the Flamingo suffered huge losses requiring it to close for several months before re-opening. It was discovered that the brain-trust for the huge development in the Nevada desert - Benjamin "Bugsy" Siegel - had considerably underestimated the building costs of the Flamingo. He also reportedly had the temerity to "skim" several million dollars for himself from the construction funds provided by his Mob bosses. As can be seen from this photo, at the time of its construction, the Flamingo was virtually the only resort in the desert at that time. Ironically, Siegel's concept of a gambling resort in the Nevada desert ultimately proved to be successful beyond anyone's wildest dreams, culminating in what today is known as "Las Vegas, Nevada."

Kinney recounted. "We drove down the four-lane (old U.S. Highway 41) stopping at roadside inns along the way. We would just pay a little visit and leave.

"We ended up at the Paradise Room at the Henry Grady Hotel in downtown Atlanta. There we were," Kinney smiled again in remembrance, "just a bunch of rag-tag country boys from Marietta. The maître de refused to seat us, but Virginia just heaved her hefty bosoms and showed him a roll of hundred dollar bills. It wasn't long before we were sitting down 'in front.' And to top it off, while we were there, Virginia introduced us to the performer – Red Skelton. She knew him because he had previously appeared at her club in New York."

Flamingo Folly

Though she loved to visit and party with her Marietta friends and admirers, Virginia never dallied long. Her forays back to Georgia rarely extended beyond a few days before it was quickly back to work for the Mob for her. Her involvement with Siegel also had not cooled at all, despite their continued frequent arguments and fights.

In 1945, Siegel became a partner with Hollywood nightclub owner and publisher Billy Wilkerson, whose planned resort project in Las Vegas had run out of money after he had gambled away his cash. Siegel, sensing an opportunity, obtained about $1.5 million in financing from, among others, Meyer Lansky and Chicago's Fischetti brothers and Murray Humphreys, then took over Wilkerson's project, expanding upon it greatly. Ben Siegel didn't believe in doing things in a small way.

Though the desert casino idea – which Siegel dubbed *The Pink Flamingo,* reportedly after Virginia's long legs – ultimately made millions of dollars for

the Mob, it was initially viewed by Mob bosses as a "white elephant" after construction costs began skyrocketing. Despite the unique idea on which he had sold his Mob boss investors with glowing descriptions of the income possibilities, Siegel had no experience whatsoever in the development business, and was soon being buried by unimaginable expenses, and huge cost over-runs. He was spending far more of the Mob's money than he had originally stated would be necessary in the idea he had pitched to them.

Even worse, by 1947, though there was no proof, rumors had begun swirling that Siegel had skimmed $2 million off the top of the funds intended for the Flamingo's building expenses and given it to his inveterate cash-carrying girlfriend to hide in a Swiss bank account. Just to provide an idea of the import of this "rumored" graft by Siegel, in 1947, $2 million was the equivalent (in buying power) of approximately $24,601,000.00 in 2021 dollars – a breath-taking amount of money, both then and now. And the fact that the building expenses for the Flamingo had already topped $6 million with the end still nowhere in sight certainly didn't help matters.

And if that wasn't bad enough, by 1947, Ben Siegel's luck apparently had just flat run out. Aside from the fact that his expenditures had far exceeded the original estimates, the huge complex finally opened during a rare summer deluge of rain, severely curtailing attendance by patrons. With dwindling operation funds, Siegel was forced to close the casino, then re-open it months later, then endure months of losses before it actually began making a little money. It was also at about this time that it unfortunately was discovered that Siegel had indeed been skimming from the construction funds, taking $600,000.00

The Beverly Hills, California mansion rented by Virginia Hill in the mid-1940s. It was here that mobster Benjamin "Bugsy" Siegel was assassinated, supposedly by a mob hitman, on June 20, 1947. Days prior to his murder, Siegel and Hill reportedly had argued and fought, and she had departed for Europe on more mob courier business in early June. After learning of Siegel's assassination, she, understandably, never returned to this home.

in cash which he had instructed his buddy "Fat Irish" Green to hold for him (Green later wisely returned the money to Lansky). By that point, Benjamin Siegel was a marked man with terminally-numbered days.

Bugsy's Final Hours

According to later revelations by Mob insiders, in early June of 1947, after the above-described problems had reached a fever pitch, Virginia was ordered to leave Las Vegas, and to tell Siegel that she was going to Europe to buy exclusive wines for the Flamingo. Still spending money that was not his to spend, Siegel reportedly chartered a plane to fly her solo back to Los Angeles.

A few days later, Siegel also flew back to Los Angeles, returning to Virginia's Beverly Hills home at 810 North Linden Drive which she had rented (with Siegel's money) from her friend, Juan Romero, her former Hollywood movie agent. Siegel was so confident of his importance to the Mob and the clout that he believed he carried, that he took absolutely no precautions for his personal safety. He drew no drapes on the windows at night as he sat in the lighted room reading. He didn't bother with hiring any security personnel for his protection. He took no precautions whatsoever. Under the circumstances, it is surprising that he actually lived as long as he did.

According to the Los Angeles Police Department's report on the incident, while relaxing and reading the newspaper inside Virginia's Hollywood mansion late in the evening on the warm night of June 21, 1947, Siegel was

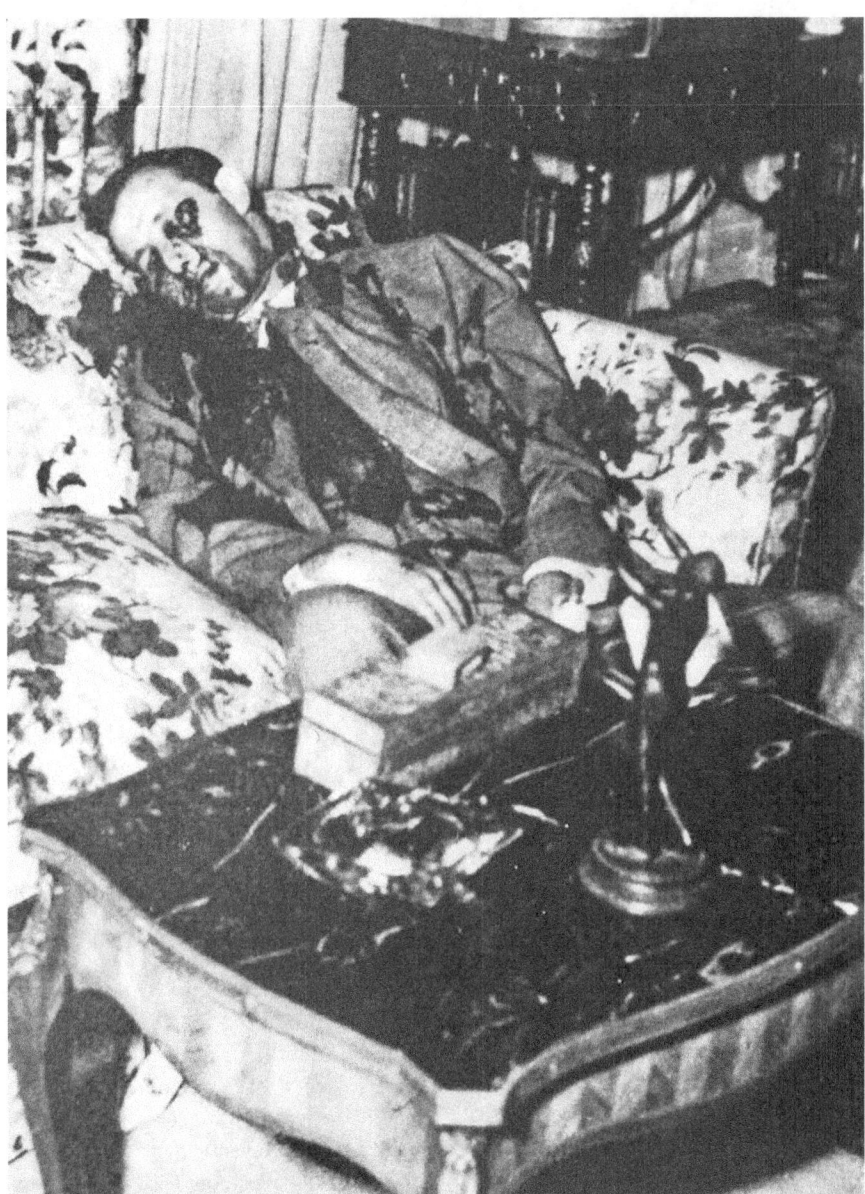

At then-Hollywood starlet Virginia Hill's 810 North Linden Drive residence in Beverly Hills, mobster Benjamin Siegel was assassinated at 10:45 pm on the warm summer evening of June 21, 1947. His executioner, who many presume was Mob-connected, fired seven rounds through the window of Hill's rented mansion. According to the Los Angeles Police Coroner's Report, two of the rounds struck Siegel in the head and two in the torso, killing him instantly. The Los Angeles Police Department's homicide report indicated one of the .30-caliber projectiles passed through Siegel's skull striking the bridge of his nose as it exited his head, ejecting his left eyeball out of its socket and 14 feet across the room where it was later discovered intact by investigating officers. No one was ever charged with the murder.

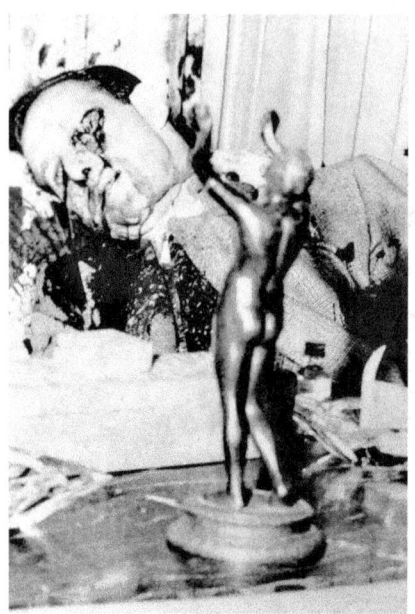

A Los Angeles Police Homicide Division close-up photograph of the deceased Benjamin "Bugsy" Siegel.

Another Los Angeles Police Department photo of the 1947 death scene with Benjamin Siegel in Virginia Hill's home in Beverly Hills, California.

suddenly struck by four rounds (a total of seven were fired) fired through the window from a .30 caliber M-1 carbine. Two of the rounds hit him in the head, and two hit him in the torso, killing him instantly.

The identity of his executioner was never known. The final report by the Homicide Division indicated one of the .30-caliber projectiles had struck the bridge of Siegel's nose, ejecting his left eyeball out of its socket and sending it 14 feet across the room where it was later discovered intact by investigating officers.

Virginia reportedly learned of Siegel's death from a fellow reveler during a party on a boat in Paris. In the coming weeks in Europe she apparently descended into a deep depression and attempted to commit suicide on three separate occasions. Even after returning to the States, she tried to kill herself a fourth time in Miami where Siegel had purchased her a home.

As if she didn't already have enough problems, by this point federal authorities were investigating Hill for income tax evasion. Virginia had long since ceased laundering the illicit funds she received, and had no means to explain the source(s) of her income. From that point forward, it was easy pickings for the Internal Revenue Service. After all, how could a person with no employment nor any visible legitimate source of income have so much cash to spend on a regular basis?

Virginia's New Man

Virginia inevitably began searching for a place to hide. In early 1950, records indicate she traveled to the popular ski resort of Sun Valley, Idaho, where she met and fell in love with a ski instructor named Hans Hauser, a former world champion downhill racer from Austria. By that point in her life, Virginia was still only 33 years of age, but her hard living had robbed her of her charm and beauty. Hauser's friend and fellow ski teacher Otto Lang described Hill as *"far from pretty, a bit short and dumpy"* who compulsively pulled out her eyelashes *"hair by hair."*

Lang also eventually made note of the questionable associates with whom Virginia still involved herself, penning *"some shady and ominous characters began to drift in and call on Virginia, then leave again without skiing."* Despite her by-then virtually nonexistent role in the Chicago Outfit's "business,"

Virginia reportedly still regularly received deliveries of cash on which she subsisted from the ever-reliable Joe Epstein. With the Kefauver Hearings already focusing intensely upon the Mob, they no doubt wished merely to keep Virginia quietly satisfied by this point – even though she was nevertheless fast becoming a problem – in order to avoid drawing any more attention to themselves.

When the FBI began investigating her at the lodge in Sun Valley, the resort's management abruptly asked her to leave. Despite her background and reduced beauty, Hauser sprang a surprise on family and acquaintances by suddenly asking Virginia to marry him. Lang reportedly immediately advised his friend

The body of Benjamin Siegel is removed by the county coroner from the Beverly Hills home of Virginia Hill where he had been assassinated.

against such a rash action, but Hauser ignored him and eloped with Virginia the next morning.

Not only did the marriage last, Virginia and Hans, to the surprise of many more, soon became the proud parents of a son, Peter, on November 20, 1950, in Brighton, Massachusetts. But the severe bouts of depression continued to haunt Virginia Hill constantly.

In 1951, the Kefauver Committee ultimately subpoenaed Virginia, now 34, to appear in New York to testify regarding her Mob-related activities and associations, and the proceedings were nationally televised. She arrived on March 16, 1951, several months after giving birth. She entered the Foley Courthouse in a $5,000 mink cape, broad-brimmed hat and silk gloves, and though she was crippled emotionally, she somehow summoned an inner strength, and she didn't pull any punches with her tormentors either.

Though some hoped and believed that her testimony would open the door for mass-arrests of organized crime figures, Virginia Hill artfully evaded every question from committee counsel Halley about her organized crime associations. She "denied," "denied," "denied," and gave nothing but vague answers to very pointed questions. When asked to explain the source of the hundreds of thousands of dollars she had spent – and continued to spend – she merely responded that all her money came from her winnings on race track bets. She explained her expensive home and possessions by saying they were simply gifts which had been provided for her by Siegel and others.

"Bought me everything I wanted, when I was with Ben. He paid for everything. And he gave me some money, too, bought me a house in Florida," she stated

matter-of-factly. She also admitted recently receiving $10,000 in cash from friends in Mexico. What did they expect her to do? Return it???

As far as her long-time association with known criminals was concerned, Virginia merely stated, "I never knew anything about their business. They didn't tell me about their business. Why would they tell me? I didn't care anything about business in the first place. I don't even understand it."

In the end, little Virginia Hill from Marietta, Georgia, gave the all-powerful Kefauver Committee absolutely nothing they could use against her organized crime friends. That was just the way the Mob wanted it, and it probably lengthened her life by a number of years.

Unbearable Life

Her later life nevertheless, was just as mentally-distressing as had been the 1950s. As a result, Virginia's mental status spiraled steadily into a destructive oblivion.

Virginia and Hans did not remain in the United States very long. He flew to Chile to teach skiing and took their son, Peter, with him. The IRS continued its incessant pursuit of Virginia, indicting her for tax evasion, serving her with liens, and seizing her possessions wherever possible such as automobiles, homes, jewelry and furs, and auctioning them off to the highest bidder. Though Virginia still had some funds squirrelled away with Joe Epstein, they were fast being expended. Virginia simply had never been much of a money-manager, because for most of her life up to that point, she had had more money than she could spend.

Virginia ultimately moved with Hans and Peter to his native Austria, but her residence there was just as unhappy. She wished desperately to come home to America and just be left alone. By the mid-1960s, she wearily began to openly express a wish to simply die.

In 1965, Hans discovered her comatose once again after an overdose of sedatives. He rushed her to the hospital where her stomach was pumped yet again to save her life. From all appearances, Hans Hauser was a remarkably devoted husband in extremely-trying circumstances.

After she had recovered, Virginia flew next to Cuba to attempt residence there, but her identity and reputation had preceded her and she was denied entry. The locus of Hans at this point is unknown.

Finally, in 1966, with her funds completely depleted, even her old faithful friend, Joe Epstein finally turned his back on her. Whether she at that point threatened to reveal what she actually did know about the Mob if they did not provide her with a continued source of income is unknown today. It is known, however, that she spoke via telephone on March 20 of that year to Joe Adonis, who was then living in Italy.

Barely four days later, on March 24, 1966, passersby walking on a footpath beside a small brook near Salzburg, Austria, discovered a body beside a tree that was later identified as Virginia. Her coat reportedly was neatly folded on the ground beside her. Also discovered was a note which stated simply that she was *"tired of life."*

An Austrian official concluded the 49-year-old Virginia had died of a self-administered overdose of sedatives, which did not come as a surprise, since she had made identical attempts at suicide many times previous to that date. One obviously cannot completely dismiss the possibility of a Mob-associated death either.

Sadly, her husband, Hans Hauser, also died from an apparent suicide eight years later in Austria in 1974. His brother, Peter Hauser, a decorated U.S. Army veteran of the Vietnam War, died in a car accident in Toulouse, France in 1994. All three are buried together in a cemetery in Salzburg, Austria.

In the end, the kind but flamboyant temptress not only lost everything, she was denied the ability to return to the one place she had truly called "home" – Marietta, Georgia, where the carefree and happy days of her youth were now long gone, but certainly not forgotten.

On March 24, 1966, passersby walking on a footpath beside a small brook near Salzburg, Austria, discovered a body that was later identified as Virginia Hill. Also discovered was a note which stated simply, *"tired of life."* Following her mysterious death which ultimately was attributed to a drug overdose, Virginia was buried in Salzburg, in the family plot of her Austrian husband. A portion of her name is faintly visible in the extreme lower portion of the headstone in this photo.

Vinings: The Spot Where Sherman First Glimpsed the City of Atlanta

It originated as a ferry crossing built by pioneer entrepreneur Hardy Pace prior to the U.S. Civil War. When the war arrived, Gen. William T. Sherman climbed Vinings Mountain to glimpse the final object of his desperate warfare – the city of Atlanta. Though the community of Vinings was once a quaint and refreshing fiefdom north of Atlanta, the former pioneers to the scenic site undoubtedly would not recognize it today.

I t once was a scenic getaway, as well as one of the major fording points across the Chattahoochee River in pioneer days. Quaint and historic, it is older than Atlanta and includes a mountain 1,170 feet above sea level once used as a signal post by the Union Army. Much of its history and charm, however, is threatened with obliteration by modern development today.

Located essentially along Paces Ferry Road between the Chattahoochee River and Interstate 285, Vinings is bordered by the Chattahoochee, U.S. Highway 41, Georgia Highway 3, and Interstate 285. The historic center of the town covers less than a square mile, yet it is some of the most coveted real estate in the state of Georgia.

First Residents

Artifacts recovered from the soil indicate that nearly 7,000 years ago, primitive hunters and fishermen lived in this area. The height of Vinings Mountain would have provided a secure village site and the river below a source of food and fresh water.

Although no large earthworks exist at Vinings, Mississippian Period "Mound-builders" undoubtedly lived in the present-day Vinings vicinity around 900 A.D., according to researchers. Following the mound-builders, Creek Indians lived in the area until about 1,700 A.D.

In the early 18th century, Cherokees came into north Georgia from North Carolina and Tennessee, pushing the Creeks southward and east of the Chattahoochee. At least one Cherokee village site has been documented in the Vinings area.

A fierce enmity existed between these two tribes, often erupting in bloody battles. Following the American

After ascending Vinings Mountain, Gen. William T. Sherman (US) looked upon the city of Atlanta. Pictured here is a view of the immense fortifications he witnessed which had been built to help defend the city.

Revolutionary War, the Cherokees remained in north Georgia until 1838, when they were herded westward in the now infamous "Trail of Tears" debacle.

First White Settler

"Hardy Pace, the first settler of Vinings, was born in 1785 in North Carolina," said the late Franklin Garrett, former director of the Atlanta Historic Society and known genially as "Mr. Georgia History" prior to his death. "Pace came to DeKalb County from Putnam County in the 1830s and built a home on what is now West Paces Ferry Road."

When Pace heard about the Western & Atlantic Railroad coming through Cobb County, he undoubtedly recognized an opportunity in the making, and decided to move over to Cobb. He began by buying up land from the Indians west of the Chattahoochee.

According to records, Pace once owned 10,000 acres – from Buckhead to Smyrna. He established his now-famous Paces Ferry – namesake of numerous roads and other landmarks in the vicinity – in the 1830s, and began offering an important portage across the Chattahoochee (at the spot where Paces Ferry Road spans the river today).

In 1832, Pace built the 17-room house which first stood on the Paces Mill Road site in the center of what is known today as "Old Vinings." Slaves undoubtedly hauled the huge flat stones used in the construction of the house from nearby Rottenwood Creek.

In addition to his other endeavors, Pace also operated a profitable gristmill on Rottenwood Creek which empties into the Chattahoochee. He had a large cotton plantation as well.

The enterprising pioneer eventually

added a tavern to his thriving business complex. Among other patrons, it serviced the many drovers who herded hogs, cattle and other livestock, and even turkeys to the growing rail center of Atlanta which was barely a town of 2,000 people in 1850, but growing fast.

Pace originally called his little village *"Crossroads,"* but other more direct travelers referred to it simply as *"Pace's Settlement."* Later, the name was changed to *"Vinings"* ironically in honor of a Mr. Vining, an individual whose full name has been lost through time. It is difficult to see how his identity with the community could have exceeded that of Hardy Pace.

Some historians today believe Vining was the civil engineer who built the Western & Atlantic Railroad through Crossroads in 1845. The little depot for the railroad eventually became known as "Vinings Station," later shortened simply to "Vinings."

Dr. Rufus M. Rose, a New Yorker who had moved to Georgia and who interestingly fought for the Confederacy in the U.S. Civil War, became one of the best-known of the early Vinings citizens. A successful businessman, he produced "Four Roses Whiskey" on Little Nancy Creek behind Stillhouse Road.

Rose sold his rye whiskey – *"the best in the territory,"* – for a dollar a quart. The business later was moved to Chattanooga. Rose ultimately moved to a mansion at 537 Peachtree Street in

> *"... The country is high, mountainous, with splendid water and considerable forage in the nature of growing wheat, oats, and corn."*

Atlanta, a structure which later became the Atlanta Museum in 1938.

Civil War Invaders

Following the battles of Resaca, Allatoona Pass, Kennesaw Mountain, et alle, General William Tecumseh Sherman climbed to the top of Vinings Mountain in order to view Atlanta prior to the attack on that locality by his Union forces. He wrote his wife: *"We are now on the Chattahoochee in plain view of Atlanta. ... The country is high, mountainous, with splendid water and considerable forage in the nature of growing wheat, oats, and corn."*

An aide to Gen. Sherman also wrote – almost maliciously – to his wife in Illinois of his view from that same summit: *"Mine eyes have beheld the promised land. The domes and minarets and spires of Atlanta are glittering in the sunlight before us."*

Federal troops soon were making considerable use of Hardy Pace's fording spot – swarming across the Chattahoochee at the ferry site on a pontoon bridge built right beside it. *(Sherman himself crossed at a spot upstream known as "Power's Ferry.").* Their trip proved to be difficult; Sherman wrote after the war that the Confederate fortifications he had viewed at Vinings were some of the most formidable he had ever encountered.

The ubiquitous general used the original Pace home as his headquarters during the 11 days he was in

Vinings. It reportedly was the longest he remained at any one site in the Atlanta area. Union forces later used the home as an ammunition dump, and still later as a hospital as casualties mounted at the nearby Battle of Peachtree Creek. Upon leaving the site, the Union troops torched the historic house, just as they did virtually everything else in the towns and cities of Georgia they invaded after they had looted and pillaged the contents.

Vinings Station continued to be an important site for the Union forces until the fall of Atlanta in September of 1864. The Union Army maintained a signal station for a number of months on top of the mountain. It was an important strategic site since signals both to and from it could be seen for a great distance.

The army also kept a railhead at Vinings. A small garrison remained there for several months as well after Sherman's departure from Atlanta. Probably no other single place during the siege of Atlanta was the hub of such intense activity or was visited by so many high-ranking Union officers as was Vinings.

Pace himself had seen the handwriting on the wall in advance of the destruction of his property. He fled with his family to Milledgeville, just as did many other plantation owners and businessmen. No doubt to his chagrin, Sherman did not overlook Milledgeville in his "March to the Sea," since it was the capital of Georgia. Although one modern reference to Pace's history indicates the venerable entrepreneur rebuilt his home at Vinings in 1865, this conflicts with other accounts, since Pace died in Milledgeville at the age of 79.

War Ruins

When Pace's widow and children returned to Vinings after the war, to see what remained of their once-productive

enterprise, they found that Sherman had burned the family home to the ground – as well as most of the rest of his possessions. Despite this fact, the family returned Hardy Pace's body back to Vinings and buried him in the family cemetery on top of Vinings Mountain.

Historian Franklin Garrett once recalled pedaling a bicycle out to the Pace Cemetery in 1931. He recorded what he discovered for posterity.

"I've always sort of liked the epitaph on Hardy Pace's tombstone," he smiled. "It reads: *They need not the moon in that land of delight; They need not the pale, pale star. For the sun is bright by day and by night, where the souls of the blessed are.*' That indicated he went up," Garrett reportedly added with a flourish, pointing skyward.

Today, though much else in the Vinings arena is expensive real estate, the cemetery, at least, cannot be sold. Twenty descendants of the Pace family were eligible to be buried there if they wished, and some have taken advantage of the offer.

The present-day Pace house, built after Mrs. Pace returned to Vinings in 1865, is believed to have been constructed by Solomon Pace, Hardy's son. It interestingly was made from three slave cabins positioned together and covered with a common roof.

The old Hardy Pace desk in the present house had been taken to Milledgeville prior to the Union troops' occupation of Atlanta. Pace's widow returned the desk and other furnishings back to the site of her husband's original earthly endeavors and successes when she returned to Vinings after the war.

Reconstruction

Following the war, an immense rebuilding effort was underway in the

The rail yards in Atlanta were photographed here in 1864 just prior to the invasion and burning of the city by the minions of Gen. Sherman who was safely headquartered at Vinings. The building at right in the photo is the railroad station. The long line of covered wagons is part of the evacuation of the city.

Vinings area, just as in Atlanta proper. The vast majority of the region had been maliciously burned by Sherman and his "bummers," and the thieves and opportunists who followed in the Army's wake. They were well aware that virtually all males large enough to defend Southern properties were either in other locations fighting the war, retreating and refugeeing ahead of Sherman, or dead. Any Southern possessions in the homes and businesses were easy pickings.

By the 1880s, Vinings had cast off most effects of the war. The railroad still played an important role in the development of the community.

During Reconstruction, Gov. Joseph Emerson Brown leased the Western & Atlantic Railroad and ordered the construction of five open-air pavilions along the route to encourage train excursions.

In 1883, the Pavilion House (the most popular of all the pavilions) was built in Vinings to encourage Atlantans to take advantage of a day's outing beside a spring that still bubbles forth on Mountain Street near Vinings Mountain. Atlantans came in buggies, as well as by train for all-day picnics. Chaperoned picnic dances remained popular throughout the 1920s.

Because of its famous waters, Vinings Mountain eventually witnessed the construction of a "health spa" which were popularized around the turn-of-the-century. For many years, the Boy Scouts of America operated a camp (discontinued in the 1960s) on the mountain too.

Vinings Today

Mrs. Earle Carter, great-great-granddaughter of Hardy Pace, was called "the unofficial mayor of Vinings" for many years. In the 1940s, she purchased the by-then famous Pavilion built decades earlier by Gov. Brown on Mountain Street, enclosed it, and converted it into antique shops.

Feisty Ruth Carter Vanneman, one of the last descendants of Hardy Pace and dubbed "Duchess of Vinings," ironically married three Yankees (some say five), supposedly to gain control of their money "to buy back my land." She restored the Pavilion House as an antique shop in the late 1960s when bus tours came to Vinings to visit the many shops there. Visitors enjoyed the shopping and dining opportunities, as well as the history of the site.

The *Vinings Teahouse* was closed in 1976, after 24 years of business, and Mrs. Vanneman secured Bernard Stricker, owner of *Bernard's on Collier Road* in north Atlanta, to take over operations in the Teahouse. He subsequently opened the tremendously-popular *Old Vinings Inn* at the site, managing it for 18 years.

The *Old Vinings Inn* also closed in January of 1993, but was soon purchased by Tom and

For many years, the Boy Scouts of America operated a camp (discontinued in the 1960s) on the mountain too.

Bill Turrentine, two brothers who reopened the landmark as *Old Vinings Inn Grille*, an intimate bar and full-service restaurant. The old bar upstairs was retained in the comfy, cozy atmosphere which made it so popular over the years. As of this writing, it continues to serve classic Southern fare such as its famous Buttermilk Fried Chicken, and Shrimp & Grits, as well as a line-up of other popular Southern dishes prepared with locally sourced ingredients. By the time one reads this, however, these dining opportunities may have gone the way of Hardy Pace.

Expensive Real Estate

Lying within the trajectory of Atlanta's northwest development, the current intense negotiations for property in and around Vinings might lead one to believe that gold had been discovered at the site. The amazingly rapid development of "The Platinum Triangle" (Galleria Specialty Mall, Cumberland Mall, and Akers Mill Square) adjacent to quiet, quaint Vinings, suddenly infected the community with hungry developers.

Dallas, Texas developer Trammell Crow built three office buildings atop historic Vinings Mountain, land he purchased from Ruth Carter Vanneman. "Man came up here and said he'd give me 15 million dollars for 20 acres of my land," she said. That was an offer she simply couldn't refuse.

When preservationists and fans of the community asked

her what Hardy Pace would think of her sale, she quickly answered "I think he'd love it. The only thing he would say is 'Why in hell did you let Mr. Trammell Crow come out and build a skyscraper when you could have done it yourself?'"

Though her real estate wheeling and dealing made her extremely wealthy, much of Mrs. Vanneman's wealth undoubtedly went to her heirs, since she passed away in 1992.

And what would Hardy Pace, the original white settler on this property, say in response to all the present-day development?

To build the 10- and 12-story buildings in Overlook office park, developers sliced off the rear portion of historic Vinings Mountain. They ejected the longtime black community and demolished the black Methodist Church. They replaced the old Boy Scout camp with a 600-unit apartment complex.

Nearby homeowners were understandably upset with all the "destructive" construction activity. They feared that their quaint town would soon be ravaged beyond repair by commercialism.

"I can sympathize with them," Franklin Garrett commented at the time. "They don't want Vinings to get all paved over and bricked up with truck routes and greasy spoons."

Visitors to Vinings today who expect to dine at the old Vinings Inn and shop at many of the old antique shops which once dotted the community will probably be disappointed. Much of the scenic flavor of the site has also departed.

Items of historic note which do still exist in the community as of this writing include the Old Vinings Inn Bar on the corner of Paces Mill Road and Mountain Street (It apparently will survive due to popular demand and a strong clientele.); the circa 1865 Pace home (scheduled to become a museum according to the dictates of Ruth Carter Vanneman's Last Will & Testament); the old Pavilion which was constructed postwar by Gov. Joe Brown so many years ago; the sparkling spring which attracted travelers in horse and buggy days; and Patio By The River restaurant on Paces Ferry Road at the Chattahoochee River. It is at this former ferryboat site that visitors may also see where Pace's ferry once provided passage across the Chattahoochee.

Condominiums now drape the hillside between Vinings and Highway 41. The once sleepy and quaint community is a far-cry from that originally envisioned by pioneer Pace.

And what would Hardy Pace, the original white settler on this property, say in response to all the present-day development? Well, judging from his personal penchant for development, he, unfortunately, would probably be tickled with the concept.

"Lookout Mountain Hotel" Once Played Host to Hollywood Celebrities

In the late 1920s, the Dinkler Hotels Company, headquartered in Atlanta, Georgia, was one of the largest hotel chains in the South. A landmark structure high in the Blue Ridge Mountains hinterlands of northwest Georgia was once the crown jewel of Dinkler, providing luxury accommodations for such celebrities as Hollywood legends Elizabeth Taylor and Eddie Fisher.

A northeast Georgia mountain-top isn't exactly the type of place one would expect to find a "castle," but visitors approaching Lookout Mountain, Georgia, on a clear day will encounter just such a structure with quite an interesting story. Built at the staggering cost of $1.45 million in 1928, the "Lookout Mountain Hotel" was appropriately dubbed the "crown jewel" in the Dinkler Hotel chain.

Though $1.45 million seems a paltry amount for capitalizing a major hotel, that amount would be the equivalent of $23,374,000.00 in 2023 dollars.

With 200 guest rooms, the largest ballroom in the central South, and wide porches around three sides with spectacular views, the luxury resort offered lavish accommodations for its day and time. Its most unusual feature was a 412-foot-high castle topped with an observation tower and beacon light visible for 150 miles.

Since clouds frequently hover over this somewhat high altitude area, the imposing edifice on this eminence was often referred to as the "Castle in the Clouds" during its hotel years. However, due to ill timing, ill luck and other unfortunate problems, the "castle" began suffering a litany of financial woes only a few years after being completed.

Despite its problem-prone heritage, the immense structure's charm and magic often captivated area residents and VIPs alike. The facility retained enough renown in 1959 to serve as the secret honeymoon accommodations of Hollywood legends Elizabeth Taylor and Eddie Fisher, who were ensconced in Room 531 after their Las Vegas wedding.

The undeniably impressive 40-room structure was originally envisioned and built by Garnet Carter and Oliver B. Andrews as an exclusive luxury hotel and clubhouse for VIP residents and visitors.

It was constructed from local mountain stone and features an English Tudor Revival exterior of stucco and exposed timbers and sits impressively on the east brow of Lookout Mountain.

Situated on Jackson Hill, the highest point on Lookout Mountain, the hotel's breath-taking mountaintop views once attracted VIP guests from all over the country. Its luxurious design wasn't just expressed in its appearance either. Its accommodations included a grill room, a beauty salon, a barber shop, a gift and specialty shop, a bookstore and newsstand, and writing rooms. Outdoor facilities included a swimming pool, tennis courts, and endless mountain trails and gear for horseback riding. Motion pictures were screened regularly in the facility for patrons.

On Saturday, June 23, 1928, guests from throughout the South flocked to the formal opening of the Lookout Mountain Hotel. Chartered trains filled with attendees of the event pulled into the Chattanooga railroad station. Local newspapers hailed the hotel's opening as the area's most exciting social event in years.

Approximately 570 dinner guests attended the opening banquet, including a group of nearly 200 Atlantans headed by the late Georgia Senator and Mrs. Hoke Smith. One of the dinner menu items – squab – was shipped directly from South America specifically for the grand occasion. Another dinner specialty for the guests was "Lookout Mountain Trout," fresh from local waters.

Opening night featured star-studded entertainment. Singer Geneva Butler, a vocal star, headlined the event. George and Irene Marshall, a noted dance team, and "Sleepy" Hall with his orchestra, also provided entertainment.

During the summer, festive dinners and dances were held each night at the hotel. "Dancing under the Stars" on the outdoor patio became a popular pastime. Nationally-known bands crooned

A dramatic aerial view of the Lookout Mountain Hotel, circa 1930s. The extensiveness of its luxurious accommodations are suggested by this photo.

popular melodies while guests danced the latest steps, including the "Charleston" and "Black Bottom."

A brochure from the 1928 operating season advertised single daily rates ranging from $6.00 to $9.00 dollars; daily rates for doubles cost $10.00 to $16.00. All prices included meals and amenities such as swimming and tennis.

One of the most elaborate social events held at the hotel was a testimonial banquet for the owner and publisher of the *New York Times* and *Chattanooga Times* newspapers – Adolph S. Ochs. Held on July 2, 1928, the dinner was a portion of a celebration honoring Ochs' fiftieth year as publisher and owner of the Chattanooga paper. A special chartered train of 150 New Yorkers arrived for this event.

Interestingly, it, ironically enough, was Ochs who first perceived the financial instability of the grand hotel, according to Dr. Marion Barnes, a friend of the late hotel owner Paul Carter. Ochs was being provided with a guided tour of the huge facility's grounds when he made his grave suspicions known to his host, Carter.

"You're going to go broke with this hotel, Paul," Ochs reportedly informed the owner matter-of-factly. "If you ever need a job, come see me in New York," he added, apparently trying to lighten the mood following his prediction. "After driving me around these mountain curves today, I'm convinced you could make a wonderful chauffeur."

Unfortunately for Carter, Ochs' pompous forebodings concerning the hotel proved to be dead-on accurate. Although the "crown jewel" sparkled like gold, its financial stability was not nearly as shiny, and the resort – just as many businesses – simply was unable to survive the Depression years. Celebrations,

Elizabeth Taylor, Eddie Fisher and Debbie Reynolds offer a hint of the intrigue always playing behind the scenes in their intermingled lives. Though married to Reynolds in this photo, Fisher would soon be spending his "new" honeymoon with Taylor at the Lookout Mountain Hotel.

dinners, and dances at the hotel came to a sudden standstill after only two years of operations.

By 1930, the facility had ceased operations entirely as a hotel, and had been converted to a private club with exclusive national membership. Within only a few months, however, the Lookout Mountain Hotel was the center of bankruptcy court proceedings, a repetitive vicious cycle from which it was never able to fully extricate itself. True to his word, Ochs later offered Carter a position as his chauffeur – employment which Carter politely declined.

Instead, Carter requested and was granted a $1,000.00 loan from the publisher to begin rebuilding a financial base. The Chattanoogan proved his financial acumen too. He invested the money wisely, exercised good business judgement in future endeavors, and eventually recouped his losses, to the admiration of those around him.

Despite its set-backs, the hotel continued to operate spasmodically following the Depression years. It, however,

Another view of the Lookout Mountain Hotel photographed circa 1930s

remained a "white elephant" for virtually everyone involved with it. A series of owners with insufficient operating capital, a string of foreclosure sales on the site, and periods of neglect and abandonment took their toll on the once-proud structure over the next 30 years.

In 1964, however, brighter days dawned upon the "Castle in the Clouds." Covenant College purchased the hotel building and 22 acres of surrounding property for the remarkable cut-rate price of $250,000. Dr. Barnes, former board chairman of the college and school president from 1965 to 1979, says the school has attempted to retain much of the original atmosphere of the hotel.

"The outdoor terrace, famous as the site for dancing under the stars in the late twenties, has changed very little," Dr. Barnes points out. "And a common dormitory area which once served as the hotel's honeymoon suite – the same suite once occupied by Elizabeth Taylor and Eddie Fisher – also remains basically unaltered."

As of this writing in 2022, approximately 1,000 students attend the four-year Reformed Presbyterian Evangelical Synod college. College facilities above and beyond the immense former hotel include a student center, library, a physical education building, and an impressive array of athletic facilities for many sports including soccer, basketball, tennis, baseball and others.

Dr. Barnes notes it is ironic that small aircraft pilots in more recent years have used the huge former hotel building as a landmark. He believes that the Depression and the sudden emergence of air transportation were directly responsible for the demise of the hotel. "It was built originally to cater to railway passengers. And unfortunately, air transportation bypassed the site," he explains.

Dr. Barnes is philosophical about the demise of the hotel however. After all, the hotel industry's loss is obviously the education system's (and conversely, Covenant College's) gain.

Why Railroads Went "Belly-Up" In Lumpkin & Dawson Counties

Following the collapse of the very substantial gold mining industries in Lumpkin and Dawson counties in the mid-1800s, area leadership sought to re-ignite commercial growth with the construction of railroads, but the idea just never seemed able to gain any momentum. Though road-beds – some of which still exist today – for railroads across these counties had been graded and partially constructed by the late 1800s, very few rails were ever laid in Lumpkin, and none in Dawson. Today, neither county has an inch of functioning railroad, a fact which continues to mystify the curious.

Even today, the absence of railroad lines across Lumpkin and Dawson counties continues to mystify newcomers and long-time residents alike. The very grand and promising commercial idea in the mid-1870s which had swept into most every other north Georgia county in some form or fashion, just never "took root" in these two locales, and no one seems to know exactly why.

Though a short side-track (which no longer exists) was once constructed into Lumpkin to provide access to the copper and nitrates deposits north of Dahlonega, and a temporary logging track (which also no longer exists) was constructed to the area known as "Turner's Corner" in north Lumpkin, both of these short rail lines (which were side-tracks from the former Gainesville-Northwestern Railroad) were in existence for only a brief period of time. Lumpkin and Dawson are two of the few counties in the state which have no railroads whatsoever today.

Since virtually none of the railroads across Georgia offer passenger transportation any longer (and haven't since the 1960s), most of today's residents consider the absence of the railroad in Lumpkin and Dawson counties to actually be a blessing. Freight trains are noisy, often transport dangerous materials, often delay automobile traffic at crossings, and often cause property values to be depreciated, to name a few of their detractions.

The absence of rail transportation across these two counties – at least to a minor extent – has also helped to restrain the development and over-population of these regions (despite the growth afforded since the 1980s by modern highways such as Georgia 400), much to the additional relief of long-time residents grown cautious and fearful of the crime and congestion resulting from urban sprawl elsewhere.

However, to the residents of the 1870s, the railroad represented all that was good (instead of undesirable) in modern society, such as access to employment, increased access to domestic household and farming products, and dependable transportation. It offered a sense of increased civilization for what had long been a backward, semi-pioneer region.

What then happened to the construction of railroads in these two counties? Rights-of-way and rails for a major line were constructed most of the way from Gainesville to Dahlonega, and similar efforts were expended for road-beds across Dawson County, but before either of these two projects were productively operational, they strangely simply withered and died.

Were these projects an altruistic endeavor, or just another bold scheme to parlay invested stockholder monies into a fast buck? Few records exist today, and most persons involved with the projects or persons who might even remember them, have long since departed this earth.

The late Madeline Anthony, a long-time native and Lumpkin County historian, had, prior to her death, remembered what was called the "Gainesville & Dahlonega Railroad" (G&D RR) from old newspaper clippings she had once preserved, but was not certain of the actual circumstances surrounding the line. The late Ida Phillips – yet

another long-time resident and source of county history – had remembered excited talk during her childhood of the railroad's eminent arrival in the outskirts of Dahlonega, but little else. Yet another fount of information regarding most subjects in Lumpkin County – the late J.B. Jones – who, prior to his death, almost always was a well-stocked reservoir of details involving historic issues in the county, was equally at a loss.

The most notable and reliable source of such history involving Lumpkin County – the late Professor Andrew W. Cain's meticulously-documented *History Of Lumpkin County, 1832-1932* – unfortunately lists no more than a smattering of references on the subject of railroads. Cain described the initial planning and construction of the railroad to the "outskirts" of Dahlonega, but his book provides little more than brief details and the fact that financial support for the line eventually collapsed.

Prior to her death, the late Sybil McRay – long-time archivist/writer/

Col. W.D. Price was a distinguished and highly-respected lawyer, businessman, investor and civic leader. His prominent association with the problem-plagued Gainesville & Dahlonega Railroad venture nevertheless attracted few if any investors. (Photo courtesy of the GA Dept. of Archives & History)

The Price Building in which Col. W.D. Price maintained his substantial law practice still stands on the old town square in Dahlonega, Georgia. It was from this site that the attorney conducted his business affairs and no doubt planned and haggled with investors in the failed Gainesville & Dahlonega Railroad project. (Photo courtesy of the Georgia Dept. of Archives & History)

librarian at Chestatee Regional Library in Gainesville – also offered information on the Gainesville & Dahlonega Railroad, but had no actual explanation for its demise either.

"Yes, I have several references to it," she replied matter-of-factly, when, in the 1980s, she was asked about the rail line. "At one time, you could still see the pilings across the river for the railroad trestle there. It (the railroad) never made it any further to Dahlonega than that point."

Whatever the circumstances, when the first railroads were being constructed across America, it apparently was not unusual for speculation and excited enthusiasm to cloud the realities of the actual financial requirements of a venture of this nature. Such was probably the case with the Lumpkin and Dawson

railroads, but didn't other counties which were successful in attracting railroads also face these same issues?

The two railroad projects, although entirely separate and distinct from each other initially, apparently became collectively associated later in their development as promoters of the lines sought to stave off financial collapse. They both originated in the late 1870s, and several newspaper accounts eventually discussed the combination of the two projects.

The railroad across Lumpkin County was initiated first in 1877-78. According to *Cain's History*, on March 7, 1879 at about 4:00 p.m. in the afternoon, a group of Dahlonega residents "marched out" to where the depot was to be located (never stating exactly where), to witness the completion of the G&D railroad.

Cain's description of the day states: *"When the cannon had performed its part in the joyous occasion, Col. (W.P.) Price came forward with an appropriate little speech; Col. R.H. Baker set the last stake which was driven deep down into the ground by Miss Willie Lewis amid great applause. The crowd then dispersed, with plans to meet on the same spot when the first train arrived, which was apparently expected in the near future."*

Today, one can only speculate at the site of the Gainesville & Dahlonega Railroad depot. Accounts indicate that the railroad ended at that time somewhere in the vicinity of the western side of the Chestatee River at what was known as "Leather's Ford" (just east of the present-day Ford automobile dealership at the intersection of Georgia 400 Highway and Burnt Stand Road in Lumpkin County). Since there was no known construction beyond that point, that would have meant that the "depot" would have been quite a hike from Dahlonega.

Logic dictates that this planned depot would, almost by necessity, have been located farther north near Dahlonega since that was its original planned destination, but later news accounts of the venture indicate that contractors ultimately changed their plans, deciding instead to extend the line to Auraria south of Dahlonega. The reality of the situation meant that the rails would be graded to Auraria and then Dawson County, rather than to Dahlonega, since the most cost-effective route from the Leather's Ford termination would have followed (the already-graded) Burnt Stand Road directly to Auraria Road, which in turns leads directly to Auraria. Due to the necessity of adjoining the Gainesville & Dahlonega with a Dawson County line, the prospect of a depot at or even near

Dahlonega apparently at some point fell out of favor and consideration.

It will likely never be known today whether it was a main line or a spur line (or no line whatsoever) that the G&D planners had originally conceived for construction from Leather's Ford to Dahlonega. Accordingly, the actual planned site of the Dahlonega depot on the Gainesville & Dahlonega Railroad (if one was ever planned at all) will remain shrouded in mystery.

Any further accounts of the Gainesville & Dahlonega Railroad are sketchy at best. According to **Cain's History,** the project suffered almost continuous financial problems and set-backs which ultimately proved insurmountable.

Dahlonega attorney Col. William P. Price was a major financial backer, underwriter and fund-raiser for the G&D Railroad. An interview with him by a reporter from the **Gainesville Eagle** newspaper in the February 21, 1879 issue (as subsequently recorded in **Cain's History**) indicates some of the uncertainty and mystery surrounding the project.

". . . . You are the president of the Gainesville and Dahlonega Railroad?"

"Correct."

"Well, ...I want some facts, and you are going around with them hid away in your bosom. . ."

". . . . Well," said the colonel, as he settled himself in a chair, "we did not want to raise any fuss about it, or excite hopes, until we knew what we were about; but since you force me, I will give you all the facts in my knowledge."

"What then are your plans?"

"The road can be graded by convict labor," Col. Price continued. "On the first of April, there will be some changes in existing arrangements, and then I can get what convicts I want."

"But you know they must be fed and clothed," the reporter countered.

"The farmers of Lumpkin, Union and Dawson and other counties will advance me the provisions. One man alone said he would advance $500.00 and more if necessary in this way."

"Precisely," said the doubting reporter, *"but they must eventually be paid."*

"Well, you see, with those advances, we will issue scrip, good for freight and passage. These we will make in various denominations. The consequence will be that that will be as good as money anywhere contiguous to the (rail)road, and the merchants of Gainesville and Dahlonega will take them (the scrip) because they will be cash to them. Why, one man – Mr. Hand, of my town (Dahlonega), pays $2,000 a year to get his goods here to Dahlonega."

"Then you will have no stock?" asked the reporter, as he looked ruefully at the nicket which he had saved up to invest.

"None whatsoever," the victimized answered promptly. *"All we ask of the people of your city is to buy enough of the scrip, good for freight or passage, no matter into whose hands the road may fall, to give me a few thousand dollars to pay incidental expenses, guarding the convicts, etc. If they will do this, the road will be built."*

The circumstances of the railroad as they transpired from this point are unknown today. With no stock, and the apparent lack of funds and backing, the construction of the Gainesville & Dahlonega Railroad no doubt continued temporarily under Col. Price's leadership, since he was widely-known and highly respected, but it was a precipitous existence at best, a reality which must eventually have assisted in its downfall.

On July 4, 1890, an advertisement describes the outright sale of the rail line venture to Col. Price. Up until this point, Price had apparently been involved in the endeavor with other individuals, but they perhaps had defaulted on their promised support.

Whatever the actual circumstances, Price reportedly purchased the railroad outright for $4,000. A newspaper account of the incident stated that he *"owned judgements and other liens on the property amounting to more than $40,000, and he was compelled to protect this large interest."*

A significant problem in the project seems to have been centered around the prospective Gainesville investors, from which a substantial portion of the railroad's funding was to have been raised. The March 4, 1879 issue of **The Eagle** (as recorded in **Cain's History**) carried a letter to the editor from W.P. Price, which, among other things, stated *"There is no indifference to this enterprise, except in the city of Gainesville. The people of Lumpkin and Hall counties, outside of Gainesville, so far as I could judge, are all favorable to it. A few only of the citizens of Gainesville have expressed any desire for the road. This ought not to be so, and perhaps will not be so, after they fully understand their interests in the premises."*

Other references to the railroad through the remainder of the 19th Century are few and far between. The few which exist indicate that it actually provided service for the region for a short while; others suggest that it was never completed.

At some point in the construction process, a decision apparently was made to construct the railroad solely to Auraria, bypassing Dahlonega entirely, possibly in an effort to provide renewed legitimacy to the project as a connector to a similar railroad under construction through the prosperous Etowah River Valley section of Dawson County. The May 7, 1880 issue of **The Eagle** carried

The road-bed for one of the railroads planned across Dawson County in the late 1800s is still faintly visible through the trees along the right side of the Etowah River in this photo which was taken in 1988. Though the route was graded, the rails were never laid for this line. Sketchy records indicate this construction project was the work of an enterprise known as the Gainesville, Dawsonville and Cartersville Railroad. (Photo by Olin Jackson)

an article announcing the fact that *"After several experimental surveys, Col. Sage (a surveyor for the Gainesville Airline Railroad) has located the line of the Gainesville and Dahlonega Railroad to Aurora* (sic).*"*

On May 20, 1899, *The Eagle* carried a notice indicating that Col. Price had apparently admitted the obvious – Gainesville, for the most part, simply was not interested in investment in a railroad venture to Dahlonega. Gainesville and Hall County already had several railroads and perhaps saw little reason for investment in still more of the steel rails.

The *Eagle* article, however, provided a somewhat convoluted explanation of the lack of support: *"Application was made for charter for the Dahlonega Railroad Company* (as opposed to the 'Gainesville' and Dahlonega Railroad). *It is to be 30 miles in length, and is to be built from Dahlonega to Gainesville or Lula. The capital stock of the company is to be $300,000, all of which is to be common stock. It is the intention of the company to go forward at once with the work."*

And then on June 1, 1899, *The Eagle* carried this brief notice: *"We are reliably informed that the promoters of the Dahlonega Railroad scheme have been tendered by Col. W.P. Price, free of cost, the right-of-way of the old Gainesville and Dahlonega Railroad."* Due to the use of the descriptive term "scheme" in the newspaper article, the railroad venture apparently had obtained a disreputable reputation, perhaps impacting the potential for the attraction of investors.

Regardless of the actual circumstances, the death-knell for the Gainesville & Dahlonega Railroad apparently had been sounded. The full financial losses of Col. Price are unknown today, but they must have been considerable.

With the advent of electricity, the age of the "electric" railway was soon ushered in. The opportunity for water power via a dam and electricity generator at Leather's Ford, coupled with the opportunity to inexpensively obtain the then defunct "Dahlonega Railroad" rights-of-way/etc. apparently gave rise to the creation of an electric railway system which operated for a short while on the existing portion of the by-then abandoned rail line.

The October 15, 1903 issue of the **Atlanta Constitution** carried an article describing that situation: *"The power now used in the city of Gainesville comes from the dam on the Chestatee River, 15 miles northwest of the city. This dam is no little one, itself. It is owned by the Gainesville and Dahlonega Electric Railway Company, and furnishes 1200 horsepower, this company being a twin companion of the North Georgia Electric Company* (which also furnished electric power for Gainesville via a dam and generator at the Chattahoochee River near present-day Riverside Military Academy), *General Warner being at the head of both.*

"The Chestatee dam is two hundred feet long, and twenty-seven feet high. The power is brought to the city on heavy copper wires strung along the right-of-way of the old Gainesville and Dahlonega Railway, an enterprise which ex-Governor Candler headed, and over which road trains at one time ran from Gainesville to a point beyond the Chattahoochee River. The old road-bed has been reworked by the new company, and it is the intention to have cars running over this line in another year to Dahlonega. The road is graded

as far toward Dahlonega as the Chestatee dam and power house, leaving only eight miles of grading necessary. The Chestatee dam cost $100,000, and was completed more than a year ago."

Interestingly judging from this news account, plans were still in the offing as late as 1903 – albeit from a different set of owners/operators – for construction of a rail line to Dahlonega. How long and to what extent the Gainesville & Dahlonega Electric Railway Company operated is unknown. It apparently was not cost-effective however, because it was only operational for a few years before it too was abandoned.

Following the demise of this final reincarnation of the planned Gainesville & Dahlonega Railroad, the railroad rights-of-way eventually reverted back to ownership by the original titleholders of the real estate along the former route, and the rest, as they say, is history.

In Dawson County, the story was much the same, although many of the problems with this rail line seem to have centered around "too much" rather than "too little" interest in the railroad.

An article in the **Dawsonville Mountain Chronicle** of January 27, 1880, announces: *"If our people would grade a railroad and lay the ties to intersect the Gainesville and Dahlonega at Auraria, there would be no difficulty in finding capitalists who would lay the iron and put the road in operation... Owing to the natural advantages, a railroad bed can be graded from this place in Auraria at a less cost than has ever been the case with any railroad for the same distance."*

Contrary to circumstances involving the Gainesville & Dahlonega Railroad, investors for the Dawson County railroad were more numerous, and

Dawson County apparently was a more desirable destination than Lumpkin County, because not one, but several outside railroad companies considered the extension of a rail line to it from the late 1800s up to the early 1900s.

One of the first was the Macon and Cincinnati Air-Line Railroad. An article in the February 24, 1880 issue of *The Mountain Chronicle* announces *"We received yesterday a letter from a gentleman of Brunswick reminding us of the projected Macon and Cincinnati Railroad, which will pass directly through this section. It passes Monticello, Covington, Lawrenceville, Cumming, Dawsonville or Dixon, up the Amicalola and on to Knoxville. Whilst this may not be the very best road for our people, there is more probability of it than any other now. A strong company has been organized for a long time, and have only waited for the Macon and Brunswick Railroad matter to be settled, as there was some contingency connected with that road that would affect this. But the M&B road matter has been satisfactorily settled . . . . and may now be set down as a probability."*

Another account on June 14, 1881 in *The Mountain Chronicle* proclaims: *"Less than $400,000 will grade and lay cross-ties and iron for a narrow gauge railroad from Dawsonville to Atlanta via Cumming and Alpharetta."*

In March of 1882, the *Articles of Association* for the *"Gainesville and Dalton Short-Cut Railroad Company"* were carried in *The Chronicle*. The Gainesville and Dalton was intended to operate in Hall, Dawson, Gilmer, Murray and Whitfield counties.

Stockholders for this venture were: Robert F. Williams (Auraria), Jacob P. Imboden (Dahlonega) and John L. Summerour (Amicalola, Dawson Co.). It (the railroad) was to connect Gainesville and Dalton, a distance of about 85 miles, and provide a shorter route between Cincinnati and Charleston.

In September of 1884, the rights-of-way for the Gainesville, Dawsonville, and Cartersville Railroad Company in Dawson County were also announced, and are carried in Deed Book D in the Dawson County Courthouse records. This railroad, based upon the land lots cited in the records, would have followed roughly the route of present-day State Road 53, east from inside the city of Dawsonville, turning northeastward in the vicinity of the Etowah River, then following the river north into Lumpkin County. Portions of the Gainesville, Dawsonville, and Cartersville Railroad (GD&CRR) were graded and are still visible (as of 2022) at various sites along State Road 53, and along the northern bank of the Etowah River.

By December of 1884, the exact location of the GD&CRR and its depot appear to have been decided; subscriptions to the railroad had been made by some Dawson Countians, and some reservations among the subscribers had developed. The date of the completion of the line had been set as January, 1886, which, interestingly, was the same completion date as that which had been planned for the Dahlonega railroad venture.

In 1886, in fact, not one, but three separate railroads are mentioned in news accounts for construction in Dawson County:

1/ The "Augusta and Chattanooga Railroad Company." This project reportedly had a capital stock of $4 million, however, the board of directors, as a group, had agreed to purchase only $6,000 of the corporation's stock. It appears that the directors expected most of the money to come from *"subscriptions at the county level"* (which in today's language would be known as "a highly leveraged deal").

2/ A second railroad was described as *"another railroad to Cartersville, perhaps by Georgia Marble Works. . . ."* This reference could possibly have been in reference to the Cartersville, Dawsonville, and Gainesville Railroad.

3/ A third rail line was a branch railroad from Auraria to Dahlonega.

Judging from the amount of space dedicated to articles in the ***Dawsonville Mountain Chronicle*** on the possibility of railroad construction to Dawsonville, much of the talk was mere speculation and idle chatter, possibly in hopes of drumming up support for any number of several potential opportunities. Dawson County was much more accessible from several different directions than was Lumpkin, and as such, had more suitors.

The editorials, speculation, and wishful thinking may have achieved their purpose too, since by August 26, 1911, the Etowah Valley Railway Company had actually become a reality - at least on paper. The ***Dawson County Advertiser*** of August 26, 1911, carried the petition for incorporation by ten men: *G.R. Glenn, H.D. Garley* (sic) *(Gurley), John H. Moere* (sic) *(Moore), T.J. Smith, J.M. Brooksner* (sic?), *J.F.* (sic) *(J.E.?) Tate, H. Head, J.F. Sargent, W.H.* (sic?) *(W.B.?) Townsend,* and *Craig R. Arnold.* Interestingly, at least five or six of these investors were residents of Dahlonega, not Dawson County.

The corporate description reads as follows: *". . . shows that they desire for themselves their associates successors and assigns to be incorporated for the period of 101 years with the privilege of renewal as a railroad company under the name of Etowah Valley Railwsy* (sic) *Company, the*

In 1886, three separate railroads were planned across Dawson County. The two individuals in this photo stand at the end of one of the graded roadbeds for one of these lines. A trestle originally planned for this site would have extended this railroad across a deep ravine (foreground) near the Etowah River in Dawson County. The trestle, however, was never built. Due to a lack of funding, bad economic times and other factors, no railroads were ever completed across Dawson or Lumpkin County. (Photo by Olin Jackson)

length of said road will be about 75 miles, as nearly as can be estimated. The general direction of same will be from a point on the Louisville & Nashville R.R. at or near Ballground (sic) *Cherokee County, Ga., thence along the Etowah River thru Creighton, Cherokee county, Ga. to the Northern State line of Ga. in Towns County passing thru the counties of Cherokee, Forsyth, Dawson, Lumpkin, White, Towns all in the state of Ga. Said company proposes to construct and build or purchase and acquire a railroad between the*

With the advent of electricity, the age of the "electric" railway was soon ushered in. The opportunity for abundant electrical energy via a dam and water powered generator at Leather's Ford in Lumpkin County, coupled with the availability of the partially-completed roadbed from the defunct "Dahlonega Railroad," gave rise to the new "electric railway" system which operated for a short while on the abandoned rail line. The October 15, 1903 issue of **The Atlanta Constitution** stated: *"The power now used in the city of Gainesville comes from the dam on the Chestatee River, 15 miles northwest of the city. This dam is no little one, itself. It is owned by the Gainesville and Dahlonega Electric Railway Company, and furnishes 1200 horsepower, this company being a twin companion of the North Georgia Electric Company* (which also furnished electric power for Gainesville via a dam and generator at the Chattahoochee River near present-day Riverside Military Academy)." One of the electrically-powered railway transport cars – probably powered by the Chattahoochee River dam and generator, is pictured. (Photo courtesy of GA Dept. of Archives & History, Atlanta)

points above named along private right of way and on public roads, either or both."

Although the Etowah Valley Railway Company was one of the few which were officially incorporated for business (at least on paper) in Dawson County, the actual owner of the rights-of-way and railroad line constructed in Dawson is questionable today. Some references refer to

ownership as belonging to the Etowah Valley Railway Company, and some refer to the Gainesville Dawsonville and Cartersville Railroad as owner.

Although there was considerable Dawson County interest (as there had been in Dahlonega/Lumpkin County) in bringing a railroad to Dawson, three major factors ultimately combined to deny completion into this county. These included a strong inclination for bickering and competition among the prospective builders; an inherent lack of available capital on the local level; and a fundamental lack of stable commercial industry necessary to lend legitimacy to the project and its construction. The only industry of any significance at this time in Dawson was gold mining, and it had peaked in intensity a number of years in advance of any plans for any railroads.

One of the sections graded for a railroad in Dawson ended not far from the point at which Highway 136 crosses the Etowah River today. If one stands on the bridge today during winter (when the leaves have departed the trees), this grade is clearly visible.

In the waning years of the late 19th Century, the once-explosive growth of the Lumpkin and Dawson County areas had been reduced to a fraction of that enjoyed prior to the California gold rush. The Lumpkin and Dawson County railroad ventures – however ill-conceived and mismanaged – presumably were envisioned as a means to staunch this negative growth trend, and reignite commercial development in the region. Interestingly, today, most land and home owners in the vicinity are, to say the least, probably thrilled that the aforementioned highly-anticipated railroad projects all ended in failure.

Fannin County Pioneers:

The Pioneering Woody Family And Skeenah Valley Grist Mill

No one knows today what motivated Willis Raburn Woody to relocate from North Carolina with his wife and family to the stark wilderness of north Georgia in 1839. It had been barely one year since the native Cherokees had been herded out of the state, and for a man who was already settled and stable in North Carolina, it seems on the surface to have been a risky move. His decision, nevertheless, turned out to be fortuitous, ultimately resulting in the creation of a landmark which has persevered for almost 200 years.

Perhaps Willis Woody's motivation for his move to Georgia involved the land lottery of those days following the removal of the Cherokees, and the opportunity for significant tracts of inexpensive property. It may likewise have been simply the pioneering spirit of these early Americans, who seemed driven to seek out new unexplored territory over the next mountain and around the next bend for no good reason. We will never know for certain. What we do know is that when Woody decided to depart from Rutherford County, North Carolina, and settle on a 192-acre tract in what was then known locally as "Skeenah Valley" at the present-day intersection of Georgia Highway 60 and Skeenah Gap Road, he indelibly stamped his family name upon the spot, and laid claim to a legacy which has persevered to the present day.

According to family lore, Willis had scouted out the area in north Georgia in an earlier trip, and had contracted to purchase the land from a Mrs. Mary Crawley for $1,000.00, a substantial sum in the days of the pioneers. Depending upon which valuation and rate of inflation one uses, the value of $1,000.00 in 1839 was the equivalent of approximately $30,663.00 in 2022. Any way one cuts it that was a considerable amount of money in 1839.

Willis Woody, however, apparently was a cautious and extremely industrious individual. He hadn't come by his money easily, and having painstakingly accumulated it over some 20 years in hard labor and prior investments, he certainly wasn't one to spend it frivolously. He was making a serious investment in north Georgia.

Woody understandably didn't trust the postal service of those days either. According to further family lore, in making his payment for the property from North Carolina, he reportedly severed the currency bills in half, mailing first one half to Mrs. Crawley, and then finally the remaining portions of the bills after he was assured that she had received the earlier portions.

Woody (born in North Carolina on June 6, 1798) and Mary (Polly) Cancelor (born in North Carolina on December 29, 1804) were married on April 4, 1822, in North Carolina. By the time they moved to Georgia, they, at 41 and 35 years of age respectively, were middle-aged, particularly in the hard life of pioneer days in Georgia. Despite Woody's caution and prudence in the investment of his money, this relocation was a gamble.

Prior to their migration to Georgia, eight children had been born to this couple, six of whom arrived when they had lived in Burke County, North Carolina: James (January 13, 1823), John (October 25, 1824), Robert (October 5, 1826), Nancy E. (July 27, 1828), Conrad (October 8, 1830), and Elizabeth Ann (July 26, 1832). After moving to Rutherford County, North Carolina, two additional births came along: Carolyn (or Caroline)

(August 27, 1834), and Willis (December 1, 1836).

The Woody family, with possessions loaded upon a heavy wagon drawn by four horses, reportedly set out from Rutherford County in the fall of 1838. Older children, no doubt, walked alongside the wagon, or rode on horseback as they progressed southwestward. Inside the wagon, smaller children and Polly were safely transported.

The family brought household goods, clothing, staple foods, seed for crops, and tools for carving out trails as they traveled and for clearing virgin forests from their purchased tract when they arrived in Georgia. Also included in the entourage was livestock: cows to provide milk along the way; sheep to provide wool for clothing at their new home; chickens for both food and eggs, and to insure a beginning for a flock; and a few hogs for meat. Some quacking ducks and geese no doubt completed the barnyard menagerie. Dogs, needed for hunting and for protection from wild animals along the route, had been well-trained to serve the Woody family enroute.

The older children helped care for the livestock during the journey, and assisted their father by hunting for game to supplement the family's food supply. At the time they left North Carolina, James was almost sixteen, John fourteen, Robert twelve, and Conrad eight. Of the girls, Nancy was ten, and Elizabeth Ann was six, and they both were

> *Dogs, needed for hunting and for protection from wild animals along the route, had been well-trained to serve the Woody family enroute.*

needed by their mother to help mind Caroline who was four and Willis who was two.

Throughout most of the route from North Carolina to their new property in Georgia, the Woodys had to blaze their own trail, clearing passages over rough terrain when the scant Indian trails did not follow the direction they wished to travel. As with all early pioneers, the Woodys were vulnerable to the elements, and to attacks from the wild animals of the deep forest, particularly large hungry black bears. The predators in Appalachian region in those days also still included wolves and mountain lions which had not yet been hunted to extinction. There was also the danger of renegades and outlaws, who were frequenting the region more and more as the Georgia gold rush gained momentum.

Despite their precautions, the Woody family was unable to avoid early tragedy. As they were passing through Wilscot Gap in Georgia, fourteen-year-old John became very ill, apparently from an infection and high fever. Herbal medications administered by a distraught Polly failed to relieve his malady. He tragically died – much to his family's remorse – on a cold December 28, 1838, as the family neared their new home. Willis Woody, heart-broken, left the family to proceed on their own, as he went ahead to Skeenah Valley to prepare

As with all early pioneers, the Woodys were vulnerable to the elements, and to attacks from the wild animals of the deep forest, particularly large hungry black bears.

a grave for his son's body.

According to family records, the Woodys arrived at Skeenah on a snowy day during the first week of January, 1839. The family's first act at their new home was to lay to rest the body of John Woody (1824-1838) in a plot which ultimately contained one other grave. This site was known for many years thereafter as Woody Cemetery, and later as Sugar Hill Cemetery.

The migration of the Woody family was something short of a miracle. They had made their way to their new home unassisted, utilizing little more than Indian paths and their own travel skills. They had withstood the rigors of exposure to freezing weather with sleet and snow, illness and death, and the privations of the trail during the short days and long nights of winter. But they were of hearty stock too; pioneers in the truest sense.

The new land they claimed called "Skeenah" by the native Cherokees, was also later spelled "Skeniah" by pioneer residents. Translated in Cherokee, it supposedly referred to "Big Bear Valley," and it did indeed – just as it still occasionally does today – include substantial black bears.

The Woodys lived first in a log cabin which had been built by the recently-vacated Cherokees who had departed the previous year during the forced removal now known and remembered as the "Trail of Tears." Unknowing individuals have often associated the Native Americans with habitations such as the "tipis" characteristic of the Plains Indians, but the Woodlands Native Americans of what today is the eastern United States for hundreds of years used clay and wood-composed lodges – sometimes underground – for shelter, and during the last several hundred years, they evolved to the use of simple cabins constructed of downed wooden logs.

Born to Willis and Polly as they settled into life at Skeenah were: Jane Mary (February 8, 1839; little more than a month after their arrival); Lewis Cass (February 25, 1849); and William (October 10, 1851). Two children born in the valley were either stillborn or died in infancy: Merritt (January 3, 1842), and Margaret (June 14, 1844).

With no neighbors in the valley to welcome or comfort them, the Woodys gained strength from each other, and set about the tasks of making a home and a productive farm on Skeenah Creek. Soon, two more log rooms were added to the Indian cabin, and a shed room the length of all three was attached to cover tools and a wagon. Shortly thereafter, a smokehouse, a barn and a gristmill were constructed.

With 13 living children, the Woody family was as active as an anthill. It is unknown today where or how enough room was created in the small cabin for 15 people. Even more amazing is the fact that a couple could find enough privacy to continue procreation for further addition to that family in such close tight quarters. The Woodys apparently were anything if not resourceful.

As indicated previously, Willis Woody was also an enterprising individual. In his original assessment of his prospective property, he had noticed that the waters of Skeenah Creek offered water power for a gristmill – a valuable commodity both as a livelihood for him and as an opportunity for refined food for his neighbors.

The average individual today takes construction for granted, but in Woody's day, any construction project was a tremendous undertaking for a pioneer who had only very limited and rudimentary tools and equipment for any project – small or large.

According to records, Willis Woody built the first mill on Skeenah Creek in 1839, transporting a tremendously-heavy hand-hewn millstone all the way from North Carolina himself. It was a considerable task, but once accomplished, Woody enjoyed the rewards which flowed from his prominence as the only miller in the area. And it was his entrepreneurial skills which had made it possible.

The mill, powered by a unique turbine system which Woody had installed in his new facility, initially ground only corn, but later began grinding wheat and rye on an additional millstone imported from England. The mill eventually began serving customers from a wide area, and it became a popular gathering site for settlers who came to obtain products such as cornmeal, flour, and animal feeds.

Skeenah Mill also served as a means of communication between Suches on the east, Blairsville on the north, Morganton on the west, and settlements to the south. At the mill, settlers learned the latest news of scattered families, exchanged ideas about politics and religion, and began gathering there on Saturday nights for parties and community get-togethers where further news was shared.

It wasn't long before a sawmill was

added further along Skeenah Creek. Despite Woody's numerous successes, life for his neighbors in what today is the Fannin-Union-Gilmer County region of the north Georgia wilderness of pioneer days was extremely physical and difficult, at best. Most settlers met the challenges of mountain frontier living with the power of invention. The adage "Necessity is the mother of invention" was never more applicable.

The Woodys were no exception. They built a springhouse over their spring, but it was built nearer the road than their cabin, so that weary travelers would feel welcome to stop for refreshing water, and to rest or visit "a spell" at the Woody homestead. However, to remedy the inconvenience of the location of the springhouse for his family, Willis devised a wooden trough from the spring down to his cabin, so that the family would have "running" water.

Life eventually began to take on new dimensions, as vestiges of "progress" began to appear in the area. Willis donated the land for Sugar Hill School in 1842, no doubt in order to provide for a better education for his children. A log building was erected on the spot, and became the meeting house for both the school and the church. In an official deed drawn April 6, 1869, recorded in Book E of the Fannin County Deeds, the land and building were officially deeded by a somewhat elderly Woody to Sugar Hill Baptist Church. The deed was signed by

Life eventually began to take on new dimensions, as vestiges of "progress" began to appear in the area.

John Harris, Elijah Petty, W.G.L. Butt, and Willis R. Woody, and notarized by Johnson Brown, Justice of the Peace.

In 1885, Sugar Hill was officially named Salem #1 Baptist Church, but Woody descendants today still fondly refer to it simply as "Sugar Hill." The Woodys have a family reunion there every year on the last Saturday and Sunday in August. In 1989, some of the clan re-enacted the arrival of the Willis Raburn Woody family to Skeenah Valley and their settlement into the pioneer rigors of 1839.

At Sugar Hill School, the children studied from **McGuffy's Reader** and the "Blueback" Speller. Each Sunday, people gathered at the log building for **Bible** study, prayer and hymn singing. Occasionally, an itinerant minister came to hold preaching services or a protracted meeting in the summer, after crops were "laid by."

Willis Woody, according to records, eventually was a slave-holder. When the wooden timbers used in the construction of the dam on Skeenah Creek rotted, slaves labored to build a stone dam.

Thirteen-year-old Lewis Woody reportedly was an avid reader, and kept abreast of North-South animosities through the **Congressional Record**. Where he obtained a copy of such a tome of political news is unknown today.

Son Willis, about twenty-four at the time the U.S. Civil War began, enlisted in the Confederate Army (probably at Fort Nelson near Morganton) on March 4, 1861. He was killed in Mississippi at the Battle of Baker's Creek on May 8, 1863.

Son Conrad, according to records, enlisted in the Morris Company near Dalton on July 3, 1863. He was wounded and discharged on September 11, 1865.

James enlisted at Morganton, Georgia, in Company A, 5th Georgia Infantry, and served in Co. E, 25th Battalion. He died in Rock Island, Illinois, as a prisoner of war (POW).

Unfortunately, death in POW prisons in the North happened far more often than they should have. Even though warm clean accommodations, food, clothing and good medical treatment were available for Confederate prisoners in Union POW camps, these necessities were routinely denied due to the poor treatment reportedly being received by Union prisoners in POW camps in the South. The difference was that by 1863, death from malnutrition, disease and other deprivations was rampant in both the civilian and military populations of the South. There was little if any food to provide even to the guards at the Confederate POW camps in the South, let alone to the Union POWs.

Fannin County experienced its share of divided loyalties during the U.S. Civil War; many area residents supported the Union due to the fact that they simply saw no logic in secession and resented being inducted into the Confederate Army. Those evading service in either Union or Confederate armies hid out in the mountains during the day, and terrorized local families at night, especially the Confederate sympathizers.

The Willis Woody family hid their last horse in the smokehouse in an effort to save it from marauding bandits. A faithful household servant - Suzannah - reportedly protected the Woody boys - Lewis (about twelve) and William (about ten) - the day the outlaws forced them to unlock the smokehouse door and release the horse. The next day, as the story goes, the boys were attempting, in desperation, to plow a garden for the planting of food with a team of unbroken oxen when these same men returned to taunt them from the road.

At some point during the war years, a man was shot near Woody mill. The wounded fellow called out for Ann, one of Willis Woody's daughters, to come and pray for him. She did so, but the man, severely wounded, soon passed away. Ironically, following his death, silverware which had been stolen from the Woody household, was discovered in the man's pockets.

"Aunt" Suzannah, free to leave following the surrender at Appomattox, chose instead to remain with the Woodys, as did many slave families. The claim that all slaves were persecuted and abused by their owners and joyfully all

> *The wounded fellow called out for Ann, one of Willis Woody's daughters, to come and pray for him.*

departed, has been played out year after year to perpetuate the myth of Southern depravity, crimes, and abuse of slaves, but it simply was not accurate.

Aunt Suzannah was an excellent cook, spinner, and weaver. She attended church at Sugar Hill where she was baptized into the fellowship the same day as Martha Murray, who later married Lewis Cass Woody.

Willis Raburn Woody died on August 31, 1870, at age 72, and was laid to rest in the Sugar Hill Cemetery in a grave beside his son, John, who had died all those many years earlier during the family's struggle to reach the new land in Georgia in 1838.

After Polly Woody's advancing years caused her to become forgetful, she entrusted the family money to faithful Aunt Suzannah. Polly Cancelor Woody died June 18, 1878, at age 74, and was also interred at Sugar Hill. Following Polly's burial, Suzannah devotedly and honestly divided the remaining family funds equally among the Woody children, just as she had been instructed by Polly to do.

Suzannah lived with Martha and Lewis Cass Woody until her son in Tennessee returned to Skeenah Valley to take her home in her final years to live with him.

The Woody Mill at Skeenah Valley remained in the family until 1916, when it was sold to J.A. Vandiver. In 1932, Mr. Vandiver installed an overshot waterwheel to replace the Woody turbines.

D.A. Vandiver, son of J.A. Vandiver, succeeded his father as miller. The son operated the mill for approximately twenty-five years, but lost his life in a tragic fall from the dam.

Wanda Vandiver Akins, niece of D.A. Vandiver, recalls fondly that the mill in Skeenah Valley remained a favorite gathering place during the "Vandiver" years.

Saturday nights were times of music and community gatherings. The mill continued to provide a place for grinding grains and for getting caught up on the latest news.

In 1969, a flood destroyed the rock dam Mr. Woody's slaves had built. James Morgan bought the land and mill about 1975. He replaced the stone dam with a concrete retainer, and repaired the mill-race and overshot wheel. A clubhouse was added to the millhouse and a recreational vehicle campground built to attract tourists to "Black Bear" Valley.

The most recent transfer of the Skeenah Gap Mill and land was to Black Water Management Group, Inc., which made the purchase in June, 1989.

Now included on the *National Register of Historic Places*, the mill stands as a monument to the industry and vision of hardy pioneers. The peaceful atmosphere and breath-taking mountain scenery are reminiscent of days long ago, when stealthy Cherokees passed through on whisper-soft moccasins as they went about their tasks of hunting, fishing, growing maize and enjoying life in the beautiful Skeenah Valley.

The gap in the mountains is a reminder of the early settlers who followed their love of independence, carving out a self-sufficient niche for themselves on land which became a part of Fannin County in 1854.

Today, the Woody name lives on in this county. The nurturing efforts of the Willis Raburn Woody family have born fruit, yielding a solid legacy for the family's descendants, just as certainly as the water which flows by the old mill where it all began for the Woodys on a cold day in January, almost 200 years ago.

The Odyssey of Jacob Pettyjohn

*Though he sought a normal, low-key, law-abiding life,
Jacob Pettyjohn's existence turned out to be anything but ordinary.
In 1859, at the age of 42, he was convicted of murder for failure to render
assistance to a victim in need. After winning a "Stay of Execution,"
however, Jacob didn't hang around hoping for a reversed judgment.
To the contrary, he had "seen the handwriting on the wall," and
quickly struck out for Texas, never to return – or did he?*

The Pettyjohn family from Virginia – just as with most families – is not without its unusual characters and events, even to the point of being implicated in a documented murder. Though the Pettyjohn lineage reportedly hails from early royalty in France, this stature was anything but obvious in the Georgia branch of this family.

James D. Pettyjohn (b. 1790 in VA) married *Temperance Rogers* (b. 1800 or 1806 in Jackson Co., GA) in 1815 or 1818. This group of Pettyjohns – either through the Pettyjohns themselves or through relations with the Rogers family – quite possibly included Native American heritage. And this "wild streak" eventually became obvious.

The children of James and Temperance, all of whom were born in Jackson Co., Georgia, were: Nancy (b. 1816); *Jacob* (b. 11/01/1817 in Jackson Co., GA); Sarah Ann (b. 1819); Oliver Perry (b. 1821); John Rodgers (b. 1824); Elizabeth (b. 1827); Mary Evaline (b. 1828); Adaline Permilia and Addison Bainbridge (b. 1832); *Arabella (Arabel Ellen) (b. 1834)*; James Decatur (b. 1836); William Franklin (b. 1837); Thomas Jefferson (b. 1840); and Marion Gates (b. 1843).

Jacob Pettyjohn was destined to live a most unusual life. He had lived an exemplary life for the first 42 years, even serving as a deputy sheriff at one point. A decision to move to Forsyth County, Georgia, however, almost proved to be a fatal step in this life.

Jacob made the move to Forsyth sometime between 1840 and 1845, with his wife *Mary Mariah Whitmire* and their five children. His initial life there proved uneventful until a hot afternoon in August of 1858.

Crime Participants

On that day – August 7 to be exact – Jacob, along with *Isaac Freeland, Levi Q.C. McGinnis, William R. Brannon, James McGinnis, Abraham Buice, William Buice, Claiborn Vaughan and his brother* were involved in a violent incident which ultimately resulted in Claiborn Vaughan's murder.

According to most accounts of this incident, *Jacob was not directly involved with the murder*, but by the simple fact that he was in the vicinity, aware of the situation, and did not render aid to the victim, he also was charged with and ultimately convicted of the crime of "Second Degree Murder" of Vaughan.

According to Forsyth County records, *Isaac Freeland was charged with the actual slaying of Vaughan*, using a knife with a one-by-four-inch blade – essentially a small hunting knife – to cut a large gash on the left side of the victim's neck, severing the jugular vein. The other four defendants – Pettyjohn, Levi McGinnis, James McGinnis and William R. Brannon – were accused of *"feloniously, willfully, unlawfully, and of their malice aforethought. . . . aiding, helping, abetting, comforting, assisting, and maintaining the said Isaac Freeland"* in the commission of this violent crime.

The problems began when court was held by the Justices of the Peace of Forsyth County for the Wildcat District on the first Saturday of August, 1858. The McGinnises, Vaughans, Buices, and several of their companions were in attendance at the courthouse. Like church camp meetings, "Court Week" was a very popular opportunity to meet and socialize with friends, relatives and neighbors.

By noon that day, several others – Isaac Freeland, Jacob Pettyjohn, Pinkney Lindsey, Ransom Barnes, Freeland's older sons, and others – had congregated on the court grounds to watch the proceedings. Court week not only was a big event, it literally was the entertainment medium of that day, especially when serious trials were being heard in court. Little did these men know that they would themselves become the focus of intense attention in a Court Week of the not-too-distant future.

The Devil Water

One of the standard "side attractions" during Court Week was a "liquor wagon" where corn and rye whiskeys were dispensed by the pint or quart for sale to the public. It was, in fact, a time-honored tradition which invariably – and ironically – led to trouble for the participants, and even though it was questionable legally, that circumstance was far outweighed by the custom and popularity of enjoying some "spirits."

Out of this practice of imbibing grew other "sideline events" – such as competitive shooting matches – and the first Saturday

According to most accounts of this incident, Jacob was not directly involved with the murder

in August, 1858, was no exception, with Abraham Buice and Archibald Martin competing against each other in one of the initial matches, and William Buice and Clayborn Vaughan placing side-bets against Jacob Pettyjohn and John Brannon, Jr.'s bets on the Buice-Martin match.

In order to find a place for the marksmanship contest, the group walked about a quarter of a mile southwest from the court grounds to a roadside clearing halfway between Wildcat Courthouse and Freeland's home. These events served as lead-ups to the later observation of whatever capital punishment might be meted out that day to the county's convicted criminals.

Though Abe Buice won the first match fairly, Martin was declared the initial winner of the second match before a loud argument from Buice declared that he had actually won that match also. With the outcome of the second match in question and a quarrel quickly in the making, the men decided to just return to the Wildcat Court ground, but that didn't help matters – not by a long shot. The ubiquitous whiskey which was readily available at the courthouse, along with several individuals who were particularly argumentative that day, served only to fan the flames of a quickly-building murderous conflict.

The Argument Grows

Buice continued to insist he had won both matches, and demanded that Pettyjohn and Brannon turn over their illegitimate winnings from their side-bets to him. According to reports, Pettyjohn ultimately complied, stating "If I didn't win the money, I don't want it," and took the money out of his pocket and handed it to Buice.

According to the late Don Shad-burn's *Pioneer History of Forsyth County*, *"Billy Buice, Jim McGinnis, Levi McGinnis, and Thomas Stone were standing nearby listening and watching. Several of the men soon fell into an argument, instigated by Jim McGinnis who sidled up to Pettyjohn and told him to knock Buice down. McGinnis then began walking around swearing under his breath.*

It was clear by this point that McGinnis was well-inebriated and growing more quarrelsome by the moment. The relationship between the two McGinnises and the two Buices is unknown today for a certainty, but they quite likely were brothers.

"Overhearing the remarks, Billy Buice started cursing both McGinnis and Pettyjohn, and Levi McGinnis quickly stepped forward to offer his support. 'Jim (McGinnis), say what you please (to Buice),' he stated emphatically, rolling up his sleeves. 'If you can't whip him, I can.'

"At this point, cooler heads attempted to take control. Jacob Pettyjohn (to his credit) tried to calm the men and ease their tempers before serious trouble could erupt, but his efforts were in vain. (Why these actions of Pettyjohn were not taken into serious consideration at his trial is unknown today.)

"Sometime later, not long before sundown, Levi McGinnis suggested they 'go get something to drink and make friends.' Several of the men walked down to Ransom Barnes' wagon, tied up 'a little piece below the courthouse, and got a quart of liquor.' – each man contributing a few cents toward the purchase. The quart jar was passed quickly from hand to hand among the few who were eager to take it. The whiskey, however, only aggravated the still unresolved quarrel.

"Levi McGinnis, finding courage from the bottle, grew louder and bolder with his remarks about 'the South

Carolinians.' Suddenly, he jerked Abe Buice's gun from his hand and hit him in the head with the breach, making Buice stagger."

The Fight

According to later testimony, a general scuffling quickly ensued, with McGinnis grabbing Buice by the hair of his head and racing down the hill screaming "G__ damn you! I'll jerk you as bald-headed as I did Pink Lindsey!" The two soon fell to the ground panting and cursing, clawing, and ripping at each other like wild animals. After the fight was broken up – possibly once again by Pettyjohn – Buice apparently decided it best to leave while he still had hair on his head. He gathered his gun and hat and made ready to leave.

About 15 minutes after the fight had ended, the evening was quickly approaching. The court had been adjourned an hour or more earlier. Both the Buices and Vaughan walked away. At this point, Levi McGinnis, still full of fight and eager to tie into someone, began weaving about with a bottle in his hand, loudly admonishing the Buices and Vaughans that they had better leave before he killed *every last damned South Carolinian of them.*"

Witnesses said that at this point, Billy Buice, in his own drunken stupor, made the mistake of bragging that he had been the bully in North Carolina and South Carolina, and that he would be the bully in Georgia too. He apparently intended to clearly indicate he was

> *He was particularly frightened of another confrontation with the drunken Freeland*

not intimidated in the least by McGinnis.

Up to this point, Claiborn Vaughan had managed to stay clear of this quickly-escalating and totally-illogical situation. The Vaughans and Buices departed in the direction of Billy Buice's house. Billy Buice, McGinnis and Freeland were all still fighting among themselves, with none of them really knowing or understanding what they were fighting about, or why. They were all just mad as hornets in a drunken state, and nothing short of unconsciousness was going to alter their lust for conflict.

By this point, still headed down the trail, Abraham Buice – no doubt still stunned from the blow to his head – was not only confused, but also fearful of the way the situation had so quickly gotten out of control. He was particularly frightened of another confrontation with the drunken Freeland whose actions were increasingly of an insane nature.

Watching the Murder

According to later court testimony, in order to collect himself and avoid further conflict with Freeland, Abraham Buice said he *ran off about forty yards from the place where Claiborne Vaughan later would be killed and sat down upon a log to hide.* As he sat in his hideaway, Buice later testified that he *saw three men race down the darkened hill and hollow, toward the second branch across the old Mill Road.* Buice said it was much too dark for him to be able to make out the identity of the three phantom figures, and that soon, yet another individual gave a brief chase before suddenly stopping just short of the creek and turning back in the direction of the court ground.

According to further court testimony, after even more confusion and fighting and cursing and totally irrational accusations, Levi McGinnis, Freeland, and Brannon, in the presence of Pettyjohn – for what could only be described as totally illogical reasons – confronted the unfortunate Claiborne Vaughan who was mounted upon a mare. This, no doubt, was precipitated solely by the fact that Vaughan, peaceable as he had been, had nevertheless been identified and associated with the Buices as a "South Carolinian." Brandishing pocket knives, one or more of the men began dragging Vaughan off the mare, and, as evidence would later indicate, one or more of them also began slashing at Vaughan with a knife in what could only be termed as a deadly manner.

At the trial for this incident, Abe Buice further testified that while he was hiding nearby in the undergrowth and brush, he heard more scuffling sounds, shouting and cursing involving his friend, Vaughan. He stated that he distinctly recognized Vaughan's voice when the victim called out desperately to his attackers *"I surrender! I surrender!"* Then in a louder voice

He witnessed Vaughan raise himself on his hands and slowly crawl to the edge of the road moaning "I'm a dead man . . . . dead man."

Buice next heard Vaughan scream *"Murder! Murder!"*

Vaughan, after falling from his horse, continued to kick and struggle in vain, as his wails of anguish and pain grew weaker by the moment. Jeremiah Freeland who had been following the group saw the silhouetted figure of Vaughan lying in the road. He witnessed Vaughan raise himself on his hands and slowly crawl to the edge of the road moaning *"I'm a dead man . . . . dead man."*

Stunned into Inaction

Meanwhile, Pettyjohn, Jim McGinnis and Bill Brannon all stood nearby – no doubt in shock at what had transpired. They, however, had made the tragic mistake of being frozen in their shock, either unable or unwilling to render assistance to Vaughan who by this point was in dire need of medical attention.

Later, after being identified as a suspect and being arrested and put on trial, Jacob Pettyjohn testified that he had gone along with the crowd as an "idle spectator," at first merely to watch the drunken Freeland and Buice fight. He stated under oath that *"while following the Buices* (who took to concealment) *to the creek, he had heard the fighting and returned to the place where he earlier had passed Claib Vaughan."*

Pettyjohn added that he saw William Brannon again at that

spot and that Brannon – so intoxicated that he could barely walk – had staggered over to Vaughan, kicked him a few times, and demanded, *"Are you dead G__ damn you, old man? If Freeland has not whipped you, I can."*

The east-headed old Blackstock Mill Road on which the murder occurred was intersected north-south with what today would be old U.S. 19, an ancient Indian and game trail in pre-history. The Mill Road passed through three north-south flowing streams – which combine south of the road to form the main tributary of Dick's Creek.

The Trial

Levi McGinnis and Isaac Freeland who had also been arrested and placed on trial for Vaughan's murder were both ultimately convicted of the crime and sentenced to *"Death."* They were both later hung on a gallows at the Forsyth County Jail. Freeland had the distinction of being the first person in recorded history to be hanged in Forsyth County.

William Brannon and Jim McGinnis were likewise found *"Guilty,"* but drew the lesser penalty of *"Involuntary Manslaughter,"* and were sentenced to three years of hard labor at the state penitentiary in Milledgeville. By comparison, they "got off easy."

Meanwhile, a by-now totally crestfallen Jacob Pettyjohn who had heretofore been accustomed to being on the opposite end of the legal spectrum, was, on April 16, 1859, being tried for the capital crime of *"Murder"* of Claiborn Vaughan for his presence and failure to intercede in the matter. On the 23rd day of April, a jury shockingly found Pettyjohn *"Guilty"* of *"Second Degree Murder"* and sentenced him as well to be *"publicly hanged by the neck on a gallows until he is dead."* The reason for his being charged with and ultimately convicted of Second Degree Murder instead of Involuntary Manslaughter is unknown today.

To his great fortune, however, Pettyjohn – no doubt at least partially as a result of his previous unblemished record – won a *"Stay of Execution"* written by Judge Rice on May 21, 1859. The case was bound over to the State Supreme Court of Georgia, and, also as a result of his otherwise sterling record and former law enforcement background, Pettyjohn was released on bail to await his new trial. Everyone fully expected him to just remain in the vicinity until he could be re-tried.

The thunder-struck Pettyjohn, however, had "seen the handwriting on the wall." After having not only been accused of a crime for which there was no evidence that he directly committed, but then being charged not with *"Manslaughter,"* but *"Second Degree Murder,"* Jacob Pettyjohn had no intention of waiting around for yet another trial.

Flight to Texas

In the mid- to late-1800s, the state of Texas was a magnet for young men seeking their fortunes. It was huge and wild, with abundant land available to anyone willing to come and take it. Though most people don't know it, two separate nations once existed within the confines of what today is the continental United States – the Republic of Texas being the oft-overlooked entity. In 1845, that all changed as the great republic entered the Union as a state.

Jacob Pettyjohn quite likely did not waver a moment in his decision to strike out to that wild land of adventure. He quietly and immediately departed Georgia for Texas in 1859, where he began life anew. He ultimately joined the

Confederate Army sometime around 1862, where he reportedly *"served his country heroically during the war years in the Confederate Army."*

According to the Texas State Archives, *"Jacob C. Pettijohn enlisted in the Confederate Army on April 20, 1861, for a period of 12 months."* He was *"a private in Company A, 1st Regiment, Texas Mounted Riflemen,"* commanded by Henry E. McCulloch.

Interestingly, according to his final mustering out information, *"Private Jacob Pettijohn left Ft. Pemberton April 11; arrived at Snyder's Bluff April 13, camped until the 19th when they reached Camp Timmins; 1 muster & payroll combined dated December 31, 1862 to February 28, 1863; 1 muster roll dated February 28, 1863 to April 30, 1863; Absent, left sick in hospital at Vicksburg February 18. Last paid August 31, 1862; bounty due him of $50.00; due him for clothing $33.83; Service 6 months at $11.00 = $66.00 plus $50.00 bounty, plus $33.83 commu. due him for 6 months & clothing. Total: $149.84."*

In 1863, $149.84 was the approximate equivalent of $3,300.00 in 2023 dollars, which was quite a bit of money in those days if Jacob had ever collected it in a commercially-viable form of payment. Unfortunately, the value of the Confederate dollars in which this mustering out payment almost certainly would have been made was dropping like a rock in 1863, and valueless by 1864 – unless Jacob could have been fortunate enough to have been paid in gold or silver, which is doubtful. Since there are no further military records on him, it is unknown today if he ever even collected the funds.

The full story of the life of Jacob Pettyjohn may one day come to light, but his days in Texas currently are somewhat sketchy at best. The one "known" final aspect of his life in that state is that it appears he was fruitful and multiplied in his residence there, since many Pettyjohn descendants reside there today.

The Final Years

Interestingly, on November 19, 1892, Mary Mariah Pettyjohn, Jacob's Georgia wife, filed an application for Jacob's "federal" pension for his service in the Seminole "Indian Wars." This application indicates Jacob served in *"Holland's & Buffington's Company, Georgia Volunteers, Florida War."*

In order for Mary to have filed for Jacob's pension, she would understandably have needed some proof of her husband's demise. This would appear to indicate that he possibly had died in Georgia. Whatever the circumstances, the Pension Application required that there be witnesses to his death, a verifiable death certificate, and a burial plot holding his body.

As a result, according to this evidence, Jacob quite possibly secretly returned to Georgia to live out at least some portion of his final years – or else Mary Mariah was aware of his Texas site of domicile. The actual site of his grave, however – just like many other aspects of his life – remains a mystery.

The full story of the life of Jacob Pettyjohn may one day come to light

Crabapple, GA: The Early Days

As has often been the case with many present-day communities in Georgia (and elsewhere in the U.S.), these sites of commerce often originated from the intersection of two or more Native American (nee "Indian") paths. The present-day cities of Rome, Gainesville, Clayton, Macon, Atlanta, and Roswell are just a few such municipalities. So also is the case with the still tiny but rapidly-growing burg of Crabapple, Georgia.

This north Fulton County community actually lies at the intersection of five roads which once were prehistoric paths: Crabapple Road, Birmingham Highway, Mayfield Road, Mid-Broadwell and Broadwell Roads.

Because Crabapple Road extends south into Roswell, Georgia, the name "Crabapple" is attached to a number of commercial enterprises – even shopping centers in Roswell. A newcomer just might think that the community of Crabapple is miles long, if not miles wide. Though it actually is still quite small, it, nevertheless is rapidly growing in both commerce and citizenry. If those Native Americans who once trod the trading paths which intersected in "downtown" Crabapple could see it today, they no doubt would be in shock.

In The Beginning

The origins of Crabapple may be traced to a number of families who acquired land adjacent to or quite near the aforementioned Indian trails (the intersections of Birmingham Highway/ Mayfield Road, etc.). These pioneer families and their common interests led to the establishment of a church, which eventually became Crabapple Baptist, and a school.

When the log school house was built between Charlotte and Broadwell Roads circa 1892, it had no name. As the story goes, when the mothers of the area began to talk about the need to name the school, the crabapple trees which once proliferated in the area were in lustrous full bloom. Mary Jane Broadwell of one of the pioneer families there simply suggested "Crabapple," and the name stuck.

As time passed, residents of the area not only began to refer to the school as Crabapple, but the community as well, and thus the name of the town was born.

Most of the original Crabapple families – all residing there prior to about 1832 when Whites and Indians lived side by side (or at least fairly near one another) – bore the following names or married into the following families: Albertson, Broadwell, Crisler, David, Dorris, Oliver, Rucker, Rainwater, Mosteller, Gillispie, Bates, Mayfield, and Jameson.

The origins of some of these families prior to their relocation to Milton County, Georgia, have been maintained by their descendants and by groups and organizations in the area. The Broadwells – after emigrating from Europe – came next from North Carolina; the Dorrises from Holland; the Ruckers from South Carolina and Virginia (after Europe); and the Crislers from Philadelphia, and Virginia (after Germany).

Most of the people in Crabapple in antebellum days would have been classified as belonging to "the yeoman class," since they were farmers. Wheat, corn, and tobacco were raised on their farms, but the main livelihood for most of the early families eventually came from "King Cotton."

The social life in Crabapple during this period centered around square dancing, hen roasts, "singings," quiltings, and wood cutting.

There were also a number of other agricultural endeavors in the community, including sheep farms which provided wool for woolen articles. Geese and ducks were raised for feather beds, and wheat straw for the more common bed "ticking."

The social life in Crabapple during this period centered around square dancing, hen roasts, "singings," quiltings, and wood cutting.

Pioneer Dorris Family

James Dorris, an early settler in the area, had a store near Crabapple, and "customers" listed in his ledger from 1835-1844 number some 140 surnames, including: Alberson, Algood, Arwood, Baker, Bates, Batey, Beach, Bentley, Berry, Bishop, Blalock, Blythe, Bramblett, Bradford, Broadwell, Brown, Butler, Camp, Caroll, Chaffin, Cogburn, Cockburn, Conley, Coker, Cook, Cox, Crisler, Davidson, Deen, Dempsey, Densmore, Dinsmore, Devore, Dobbs, Dorris, Doss, Dudley, Duncan, Edwards, Emerson, Everett, Felton, Fields, Findley, Ford, Fowler, Freeman, Gant, Garner, Gazaway, Gentry, Glover, Grimes, Hamilton, Harden, Harris, Harrison, Hayes, Hestler, Hodges, Holland, House, Hinkle, Hubbard, Huggins, Huss, Hutcheson, Ingram, Jackson, Jones, Killgore, Kitchen, Kuzkendall, Land, Landrum, Lee, Lowrey, Mansell, Martin, McConnell, McDanield, McMickene, Middleton, Miller, Morley, More, Morris, Nailer, Nix, Narn, Oliver, Owens, Pain, Pendley, Perry, Payne, Pharris, Phlemmone, Phillips, Pinion, Quarles, Randall, Rainwater, Ray, Reynolds, Roberts, Robinette, Rucker, Rush, Sampler, Scott, Shaw, Simpson, Sims, Slaton, Smith, Stancell, Stevens, Stewart, Swetman, Thompson, Tuton, Vales, Vaughn, Waiter, Walker, Walraven, Waters, Watts, Weaver, Webb, White, Whitley, Whitmire, Williamson, Williams, Willson, Worthy, Wright, and Young.

The Dorris Ledger also contains the names of a number of Indians of the area trading at the store. James Dorris's wife – Nancy Cook Dorris – was an Indian, as is obvious from her time-worn photograph which is still in existence.

James was born in 1801, and died in 1877. Nancy was born in 1799 and died in 1887. Eight children – four of whom died young – were born to the couple. Those who survived to adulthood were W.C. Dorris, who married Mary Galehaugh; Permelie Dorris, who married W.D. Rucker; Elizabeth Dorris, who married N.W.H. Cook; and J. Newton Dorris, who married Fannie Gillispie.

The children of these Dorris family members were as follows: PERMELIA DORRIS RUCKER: Robert Rucker, James Rucker, Joseph Rucker, N.J. Manning Rucker, Roxie Rucker Watkins, Dora Rucker Gillispie, Newton Rucker, Innis Rucker Reed; W.C. DORRIS: Nannie Dorris Rickerson, Missouri Dorris, Louisiana Dorris Gilleland, Julia Dorris Earney, Davis Dorris, James C. Dorris, J.G. Dorris, J.R. Dorris; ELIZABETH DORRIS COOK: J.L. Cook, Callie Cook Fraser, Mollie Cook Buice, Lilla Cook Reece, and J.J.H. Cook; J. NEWTON DORRIS: Charlie B. Dorris, Lula Dorris Lackey, N.P. Dorris Jameson, J.G. Dorris, Isodore Dorris Broadwell, L.N. Doriss, J.L. Dorris, Ida Dorris Rucker, W.G. Dorris, and Nettie B. Dorris Blackwell.

Descendants of J. Newton Dorris's family married another Rucker, a Reece, an Ellington, a Lane, a Seidenstricker, a Reeves, a Dempsey, and two Mansells.

The Rucker Family

One of the more well-known families in Crabapple – both in pioneer days and today – is still active in the community. There are few old-timers in the area who do not remember or have not heard of George Rucker and his *Alpharetta Free Press*, a newspaper well-known throughout the state in times past; Nap Rucker who played professional baseball for the Brooklyn *Dodgers* and was once

"By the grace of God, a deck of cards, and a keg of rum, you are here today."

honored by being featured on the cover of *Life* magazine; and Johnny Rucker who also played professional ball as a centerfielder for baseball's New York *Giants*.

In years past, the Ruckers have held an annual reunion. At one of these affairs in recent years, Edith Copeland Rucker, as the recognized historian of the family, prefaced her speech for that reunion by saying, *"By the grace of God, a deck of cards, and a keg of rum, you are here today."* It doesn't take a wizard to suspect there probably is an interesting story behind those words.

It seems that Thomas Rucker arrived in America on a ship that was wrecked just before reaching the shores of Virginia in the 1600s. There were two potential survivors of the disaster, and they supposedly gambled in a game of "Seven-Up" to determine who would win the remaining keg of rum to use to float to shore. (One has to wonder how they found the time to be involved in a "game" during an ocean gale destroying the ship in which they were passengers, but it nevertheless makes a good story.) Anyway, according to the tale, Rucker won, and "keg of rum" has, over the years, been used as the password of Thomas Rucker's descendants.

Thomas Rucker's grandson, George Rucker, and his wife, Catherine Ehart Rucker, were the first Ruckers to live in Georgia, having moved from Virginia to the Georgia coastal region. Their son, Simeon Bluford Rucker, was the first Rucker to live in the part of Georgia known today as Crabapple.

Simeon ultimately settled in Crabapple with his wife, Jane Barnwell Rucker, but he almost put down roots in another community. He initially moved to Alabama where he became dissatisfied with his circumstances. He kept remembering his trip through the Crabapple area on his way through Georgia to Alabama on a pioneer trail known as "the Alabama Road," a branch of which passed through Crabapple. (*Readers please see "Retracing the Historic Alabama Road" in Mystery & History in Georgia, Volume I*).

One day, Simeon decided, somewhat suddenly, to leave Alabama. For reasons unknown today, he had an anxious desire to return to that beautiful spot he remembered on the Alabama Road in north Georgia. There, in the early 1830s, he settled in to begin raising the Rucker family that has persevered in the area for generations.

The children of Simeon Bluford Rucker and Jane Rucker were: George Elsie, William David, Simeon L., Russell, Nancy, Joel, Julia Ann, and John. John married a widow, Sarah Hembree Jameson, whose son, Thomas Jameson, was reared with the Rucker children as one of them. John and Sarah had the following children: Robert Lee, Julia, Mary, William David, Harriet Jane, John Simeon, Joel Jackson, George Napoleon, and Frankie.

For reasons unknown today, he had an anxious desire to return to that beautiful spot he remembered on the Alabama Road in north Georgia.

The original Joel Rucker (son of Simeon and Jane) and his wife were the parents of George, whose newspaper accomplishments were mentioned earlier in this article. Nap Rucker was the son of the first John Rucker.

Remnants of Yesteryear

If one visits the Crabapple of today, beginning with the old buildings at the crossroads, the past is very evident in the present. There at the crossroads, several aged buildings from Crabapple's early days still survive; there are also many roads named after the pioneers of the area; and there are still a number of houses of the original families dotting the landscape.

Many of the historic old homes have been renovated and restored by new-comers, who today recognize the monetary value of the historic structures. In some cases, the new owners have changed these hallowed homes almost beyond recognition as one of the original structures of the community. There are several historic Rucker homes, a Broadwell, and a Crisler home today, to name a few.

In addition, there are cemeteries in the area that go back to the days of the pioneers. Probably best known is the old Rucker cemetery, now surrounded by Wallace Woods, a modern subdivision at the juncture of Broadwell and Rucker Roads.

The Famous and Not-so-Famous Fill Up Historic Oakland Cemetery

*From its earliest days right up to the present-day,
historic Oakland Cemetery has been the final repository
for Atlantans from every walk of life.*

In 1850, as the small railroad crossroads town was undergoing substantial growth, the city of Atlanta began searching for an adequate repository for the city's "departed," ultimately purchasing six acres a short distance east of town. Over the next seventeen years, "Atlanta Cemetery" (as Oakland was initially known) grew when and where it could, eventually becoming the final resting place for many Georgia celebrities and dignitaries.

The essentially unplanned nature of Oakland also allowed it to avoid the cold and linear characteristics of modern "facilities" of this nature. Its peaceful confines and shady reposes offer gracefully-curving pathways, and convenient benches on which visitors may pause amidst much greenery. Together with the grand marble monuments and intricate statuary, this free-flowing design reflects the Victorian concept that death is not a cold, abrupt end to life, but a chance to rest - to sleep blissfully – until the angel "Gabriel" blows his trumpet.

Like Mount Auburn Cemetery in Cambridge, Massachusetts, and other famous Victorian burial grounds, Oakland is a peaceful place. It is also the third-largest expanse of greenery in the city next to Grant and Piedmont parks. Unlike those spots, however, Oakland is filled with beautiful sculptures, majestic trees . . . . and the remains of 40,000+ Atlantans from all walks of life.

Margaret Mitchell Marsh, famed author of the monstrous best-selling tome ***Gone With The Wind*** which won the *Pulitzer Prize for Literature* in 1937, is just one of the numerous celebrities buried here. Her one and only book has sold more than twenty-one million copies – and counting. Mrs. Marsh's stately grave seems perennially adorned with flowers from her many admirers.

Those more athletically-inclined may be inspired by the grave of Robert Tyre Jones, Jr., better known as "Bobby Jones," easily considered the greatest amateur golfer in the history of the sport. Jones earned the moniker *"The Emperor of Golf"* by winning 13 major golf championships, including his uneclipsed

"Grand Slam" of golf, winning the British Open, the British Amateur, the U.S. Open and the U.S. Amateur.

Despite his prowess with his clubs, Jones chose not to continue the sport of golf as a professional occupation. Instead, he retired to his law practice, never again to compete as a professional. His accomplishments have never been equaled.

Jones grew up only four miles from Oakland at Eastlake. The stately clubhouse there which was often frequented by Jones was renovated by noted Atlanta real estate developer Tom Cousins who purchased the course and clubhouse for $4.5 million.

Many other celebrities lie in peaceful repose at Oakland as well. Strolling beneath the trees and along the shaded pathways, visitors will also find the graves of twenty-four former Atlanta mayors and six former governors, as well as the graves of members of many of the city's most prominent families of yesteryear.

Aside from the beauty of the landscaping in this virtual park, it is also adorned with an amazing array of memorial art-forms. The mausoleums and tombs in this realm are accented with bronze doors, stained glass, and almost infinite sculpture. They all have something to say too if one is listening.

Prior to his death in 1918, Jasper Newton Smith commissioned a sculptor, Oliver W. Edwards, to engrave his likeness – complete with top hat – for placement atop his tomb. When Mr. Smith went to the artist's studio to examine the plaster model, he found one flaw. The statue wore a necktie. Mr. Smith hated ties and never wore them, so he reportedly lifted his cane and smashed the plaster tie into little bits. Today, his likeness faces the cemetery gate, resting comfortably in a large chair – no necktie in sight.

Of course, many graves are marked with simple headstones which speak just as clearly in their austerity. Walking through the Confederate soldiers' section, Scarlett O'Hara's immortal words come quickly to mind: *The monotonous rows of soldiers' graves at Oakland Cemetery stretch longer every day.*

Before the War Between the States was concluded, almost 2,400 Confederate soldiers were laid to rest in Oakland. For many, it was their second interment too, having been hurriedly covered initially in a trench following a terrible engagement on the battlefield. The graves that "Miss Scarlett" bemoaned no longer bear the white wooden crosses, hand-lettered by Major Joseph Morgan and his wife. Those were replaced in 1890 with more permanent cement markers.

It also isn't difficult to hear Mrs. Eugenia Hamilton Goode Morgan chatter with the Confederate widows who saw to the burial of their dead. Their care did not end when the last cross was hammered into place. In 1874, the Atlanta Ladies' Memorial Association began raising money for a sixty-five

Mr. Smith hated ties and never wore them, so he reportedly lifted his cane and smashed the plaster tie into little bits.

foot obelisk to honor the Confederate dead. Four years later when the monument was erected near the graves of five general officers, it was the tallest structure in Atlanta.

In Confederate Section C, one can find the graves of twenty Union soldiers who were captured and then died in Confederate hospitals. They were given military funeral rights and their headstones proudly display the U.S. Army insignia.

Six other Union soldiers, however, weren't quite so fortunate. They weren't buried in Oakland, but they did die there – at the end of a Confederate rope.

On April 12, 1862, a Union spy named James J. Andrews and over twenty of his men dressed in civilian clothing, slipped behind enemy lines into Marietta, Georgia. Their plan was to steal a Confederate locomotive from Big Shanty (Kennesaw) on the Western & Atlantic Railroad and drive it northward, destroying the bridges they passed and dismembering the Confederate transportation system along the route.

The locomotive they seized – *General* (which is displayed today in Kennesaw, Georgia, where it was originally seized) – quickly attracted considerable attention. The General's conductor – Captain William Allen Fuller – initially gave chase in a small hand-car, before commandeering another locomotive for pursuit of the raiders. Ninety miles and three different locomotives later {the *Yonah*, the *William R. Smith*, and the *Texas*, (which is currently on display at the Cyclorama in Atlanta)}, Andrews and his men abandoned the *General* and fled into the countryside. They all were captured by a number of different people over the course of the following week, and taken to Tennessee to stand trial.

Because they were captured in civilian attire, the raiders were tried and convicted as spies in accordance with military law. Following the trial, they were returned to Atlanta. Seven of the men were hanged in the ravine near Oakland, then interred outside the cemetery walls without a military burial. After the war, their bodies were exhumed and moved to the U.S. National Military Cemetery in Chattanooga, Tennessee. There, they each became the recipients of the first *Congressional Medal of Honor* ever issued. Today, a plaque on Oakland's southern wall, near the spot of their original interment, commemorates *"Andrews' Raiders."*

Contrary to the raiders, Captain Fuller, the man who initiated their capture, was interred inside Oakland. His burial plot may be found in the northwest corner, about as far away from the Andrews' Raiders plaque as he could possibly be, and still be inside the cemetery.

Not far from the memorial to Andrews' Raiders lie a number of Jewish plots which bear testament to this facet of early Atlanta society. Some of the city's most successful businessmen were laid to rest in this section, including Morris and Emanuel Rich, founders of the long-time Rich's department stores; Jacob Elsas, the owner of historic Fulton Bag and Cotton Mill; and Joseph Jacobs, the pharmacist who invented and first served a little refreshment called *"Coca-Cola."*

And still they come, the most recent VIP entry being world-famous actor, entertainer, and Grammy Award-winning musical artist Kenny Rogers, who, though a Texas native, took Atlanta as his home in his later years and chose to be buried here near his Georgia family. Rogers had more than 20 solo #1 hits during his lifetime and was beloved by millions.

The Day the Railroad Came to Roswell – Well, Almost

*It was a landmark at the edge of the town for 40 years,
and just as is the case with most beloved short-line railroads,
railroad enthusiasts continue to study and enjoy the
details involving this historic line. Interestingly, though it
was officially identified as "The Roswell Railroad," it was
never actually constructed all the way to its namesake city.*

In 1863, the city of Roswell obtained a charter which provided for the organization of *"the Atlanta and Roswell Railroad Company (A&RRR)"* which would be constructed from downtown Atlanta (actually as a branch-line of the Western & Atlantic Railroad) to what then was the quiet country burg of Roswell. No action, however, was ever forthcoming from this charter until 1870, when the Atlanta and Richmond Air-Line (A&RA) railroad was constructing a line from Atlanta to Charlotte, North Carolina.

The original charter for the A&RA was amended to consolidate the Atlanta and Roswell Railroad Company with the Atlanta and Richmond Air-Line, in the process providing for the creation and attachment of the Roswell rail line thereto. Despite this action, construction still was delayed, and the topic became one of frustration for the citizens of Roswell for many years, most of whom were eager to have their own railroad line for commercial and transportation needs.

A letter from the President of the Roswell Manufacturing Company dated July, 1880, stated the circumstances fairly succinctly: *"The question of securing for this Company a better connection with Commercial centres and a quicker and more economical method of transportation than by wagon, for production, supplies and merchandise, has received the serious consideration of every President who has charge of your interest at this point."* This document is the clearest indication available of the frustration felt for almost two decades by the merchants of the up-and-coming town.

Founded in 1839 by Roswell King who had moved to the area in 1836, the sleepy township of Roswell had grown in bursts and halts since its earliest days due to its somewhat isolated location and the absence of rail or any other mode of dependable transportation. Located on one branch of the pioneer *"Alabama Roads"* at the *"Shallow Ford"* across the Chattahoochee, Roswell enjoyed a steady supply of citizenry who

"Old Buck" on the Roswell Railroad provided reliable service for many years. The Roswell train depot was on the south side of the Chattahoochee River near present-day Roberts Drive. The plaque in the photo identifies "Chamblee Station" on the route.

nevertheless were constantly frustrated with the rough roads into and out of the town which became virtually impassable in wet weather.

Up to the year 1880 as stated in the Roswell Manufacturing Company President's letter: *"All freights to and from Roswell have to be transported to and from Marietta or Doraville* (both of which did have railroads) *over common, and in winter, very rough roads by wagons, which require ten mules, five wagons, five teamsters, one smith and helper."*

A proposition eventually was made by the Roswell Manufacturing Company's president to the effect that it would pledge a payment in the amount of $10,000 to the owners of the railroad for construction of the line to Roswell, but *"only when the road is completed and in operation."* Ultimately, $7,000 of the stated amount was raised, and the president asked the company's board to authorize payment of the remaining $3,000, with the stipulation that *"not one dollar shall be paid until the road is finished and in operation."* The emphatic nature of the statement underlines the frustration which had been endured year after year by the town fathers in obtaining the much sought-after railroad.

Following a number of legal proceedings during 1881 which included liens, foreclosures on liens, judgements, inheritances, various legal decrees, sales of interests, conveyances of properties, etc., a reorganization occurred, and the *"Roswell Railroad Company"* was formed. The new corporation renewed its relations with the Atlanta and Richmond Air-Line which had also been newly reorganized as the Atlanta and Charlotte Air-Line.

The Atlanta and Charlotte received 201 out of a total issue of 400 shares of capital stock of the Roswell Railroad Company, and thus secured control of the rail line. The road – much to the unbridled delight of the town's citizenry – was then finally completed as a narrow-gauge line from Chamblee to the Chattahoochee River in Roswell – at which point construction again was halted. Despite the fact that a road-bed for the railroad had been graded beyond the river almost all the way up to the Roswell Manufacturing Company in "downtown" Roswell, neither a trestle over, nor rails beyond the river were ever completed. This railroad just seemed to be constantly plagued by "obstacles," but completion of the railroad to a station just across the river at the edge of town was nevertheless a huge improvement over the sole previous option of travel over the dirt trails of the area.

Before the Roswell Railroad was

Roswell Railroad was in operation for 40 years (1881-1921). Ike Roberts - pictured here - served as engineer for the entire duration of the railroad. His former home still stands (as of this writing in 2022) on Roberts Drive, which was named in his honor.

opened for operation, the Roswell and Doraville Railroad had succeeded to all the rights of the Atlanta and Charlotte Air-Line, and had begun operation on the earlier-completed lower portion of the line. This relationship continued until 1894, when the Southern Railway Company succeeded to the same relationship because of its assumption of the Atlanta and Charlotte Air-Line.

The Roswell Railroad officially began service on September 1, 1881, with Isaac "Ike" Martin Roberts at the throttle as engineer of the steam-driven locomotive pulling the train which made the twice-daily trip up and down its route. With Ike at the helm, a unique era in Roswell history began. *(Editor's Note: To add perspective to the time-period, this was approximately two months prior to the famed gunfight at the rear of O.K. Corral in Tombstone, Arizona Territory at which Wyatt Earp and his brothers earned lasting fame.)*

Ike Roberts had been born in Gaston County, North Carolina, on February 28, 1853. He was the son of John Morgan Roberts (1827-1865) and Lucinda White Roberts (1823-1895).

When Ike was 19, he left home and walked 45 miles to Spartanburg, South Carolina, where he joined a construction gang building the Atlanta and Charlotte Air-Line. When the road was completed, he secured a job as "wood-passer" on one of the locomotives.

In 1874, Ike "went on the road," working as a fireman on a freight train between Atlanta and Charlotte. In the span of three short years, he rose to the post of engineer on that line.

Early-on, Ike became involved with the construction work for the road-bed of the line being built to Roswell; he also worked as an agent to secure the rights-of-way for the Atlanta and Charlotte Air-Line. Since the headquarters of the new Roswell line was located at the railroad's junction near the south bank of the Chattahoochee River, Ike took up residence in that vicinity, living in boarding houses for a number of years.

The right-of-way of the Roswell Railroad was just under ten miles (9.8 miles to be specific) in length. Its former route (on what today are paved streets through Sandy Springs, Chamblee, and Dunwoody) began at the Chamblee Depot (known earlier as the "Roswell Station"). From there, the route continued to Peachtree Industrial Boulevard before angling up North Peachtree Road and passing through Dunwoody to Roberts Road, where it was graded up a long incline before ending just short of a juncture with present-day Roswell Road near the Chattahoochee.

During its days of operation, the Roswell Railroad train would leave Roswell at 7:00 a.m., and arrive back at 10:00 a.m. Then it would leave again at 3:00 p.m. and arrive back at 5:00 p.m. The train to which most area residents fondly referred as *"The Dinkey"* (and *"Old Buck"* by others), was gratefully accepted into the community.

If "flagged," The Dinkey – as was the tradition in those days – would stop at any place along the line to pick up passengers or to let them off. Aside from these flagged stops, there were four regular stops between Roswell and Chamblee: "Powers," (near what today is the intersection of Pitts Road and Spalding Drive); "Morgan Falls Junction" (where Roberts Drive crosses Spalding Drive); "Dunwoody Station;" and "Wilson's Mill" (near Peeler Road). A branch line was also built from the Morgan Falls Junction to what today is Morgan Falls, to carry materials to construct the Georgia Power Company dam and electrical generation plant at that site.

The train had an engine with tender, a combination baggage car and coach for passengers, freight cars, and flat cars. The passenger compartment had a rest room, a heater, and a water cooler. A glass case at one end held a saw, an axe, a crow-bar, and tools for emergencies.

On the run to Chamblee, the train customarily transported a number of cars loaded with lumber, stove-wood, vegetables, and fruit. On its return to Roswell, the cargo would often consist of supplies, manufactured goods, and fertilizer. Horse-drawn buggies ("taxis") would meet the train at the depot near the Chattahoochee River, and take passengers across the wooden covered bridge into "downtown" Roswell.

In addition to engineer Ike Roberts, the Roswell line had a crew consisting of a fireman, a conductor, a brake-baggageman, and a flagman. Though these former employees enjoy a footnote in history in their association with the rail line, it is Ike's name which inevitably is the topic of discussion when the subject of the Roswell Railroad is raised by the few-remaining old-timers in the area.

In 1893, Ike married Nancy Turley (1869-1924) from Roswell. In 1895, after their first two children were born, they moved into their own house, newly built for them, on Roberts Road, handily-located across from the train depot. Ike, amazingly, owned about 700 acres of land in that area which today is crowded with commercial and residential development.

Ike and Nancy had five children, all girls: Lula, Laura, Edith, Sarah, and Alda. It has been said that, even though Ike had no sons to carry on his name, he had eternal connections with many

Roswell Railroad depot (later a Southern Railway depot) is pictured here near Roberts Drive just south of the Chattahoochee River. Following the railroad's demise in 1921, the depot was purchased by engineer Ike Roberts and used as a hay barn for many years.

of the prominent families of Roswell through his daughters' marriages to a Foster, a Lyon, a Wing, and a Bowden.

At one time or another in Ike's lifetime, he owned two of Roswell's best-known antebellum homes – Bulloch Hall and Primrose Cottage. He also owned a lumber company, a dairy, and, in a partnership, the Civil War-era Laurel Mill complex [including the manager's office (which still stands as of this writing in 2023) halfway up busy Roswell Road between the river and town.] He was also at one time chairman of the board of the Roswell Bank.

In 1905, when Ike owned Bulloch Hall, an event of unsurpassed historic significance occurred in Roswell. The president of the United States – Theodore "Teddy" Roosevelt – traveled to Roswell to pay a visit to Bulloch Hall which was originally his mother's home where she and his father had been married. Teddy, traveling to the site on "The Dinkey" with Ike Roberts at the helm,

was traveling to this historic landmark (which also still stands as of this writing in 2023) where his mother had been born.

In 1903, in an effort to update and make the line more serviceable, heavier rails were installed on the Roswell Railroad, thus eliminating the original narrow-gauge tracks. This allowed the railroad access to larger rail cars and the ability to transport more gross weight.

Despite its progress and upgrades, the Roswell Railroad – as inevitably was the case with most short-lines – eventually literally worked itself out of a job. The times they were a'changing. Rail passenger service had been relegated to the junk heap by all the new-fangled "automobiles" in circulation. Motorized tractor trailer rigs now transported gross tonnage of merchandise and refrigerated items, and the industrial sites under construction which had required the transport of heavy-grade equipment – such as the Georgia

Slightly to the left of the covered bridge (present-day Roswell Road Bridge at the Chattahoochee River) on the opposite bank (as one views this photo), the completed Roswell Railroad ended a short distance from the south river bank. The "un-completed portion" of the road-bed for the railroad (which ironically is the only portion still in existence today) was graded on the near (north) side from the river a short distance to the left of the structures pictured lower-left, and this short section of the grade may still be viewed today. The buildings pictured lower left are a section of the Ivy Woolens Mill complex built in 1857 and operated by James R. King, son of Roswell King. The structure at lower-right was the Roswell Hotel. (Photo courtesy of GA Dept. of Archives & History, Atlanta)

Power Generation Station at Morgan Falls – were completed.

The little railroad struggled along in its last years, and finally, in 1921, the Roswell Railroad simply ceased operations, much to the disappointment and sadness of Roswell's citizenry. Just as had the old Tallulah Falls Railroad in Tallulah Falls, Georgia, and so many other short-line railroads in other towns, the Roswell Railroad had become a staple of life in the community, and area residents were stunned by its loss.

Ike Roberts made a trip to Washington, D.C., and somehow came away with the deed to the Roswell Depot property, paying only $1.00 in the transaction. Thereafter, he used the historic

structure as a barn. It can only be considered a shame today that this structure was not preserved for posterity as a visible reminder of the history of Roswell.

Ike continued on in the railroad business until his death. He went from The Dinkey to the "Air-Line Belle," a line with daily runs between Atlanta and Toccoa.

When he died in 1930 at the age of 77, Ike Roberts was the oldest engineer in the Charlotte division of Southern Railway, both in age and in length of service. The heart attack which felled him occurred at old Terminal Station in Atlanta soon after he reported for work one morning.

Ike's obituary claimed that he was *"one of the fastest and smoothest engineers*

This view, looking north toward downtown Roswell, circa 1914, offers an idea of the muddy boggy streets the town's residents were forced to endure prior to concrete paving, which was a number of years in the future. This was one of the reasons the railroad was so eagerly anticipated. (Photo courtesy of GA Dept. of Archives & History, Atlanta)

in the service of the road." It wasn't necessarily true, but it sounded nice, and Ike was a beloved member of the community. The obit continued by explaining that even in his last years, Ike *"would set a passenger train in motion without a perceptible jar, and he would nurse it to a stop again with the smoothness of an automobile slowing down."*

During his 58 years of service on Southern locomotives, Ike was never involved in a single major accident.

As of this writing, reminders of Ike and the Roswell Railroad still exist. Well-known Roberts Drive on the southeast bank of the Chattahoochee River was the site of Ike's residence for many years, and bears his name. His imposing home on that road still stands, well-preserved and in continuous use since it was built.

Occasionally, during the past few decades, new home builders and/or road construction crews have unearthed a piece of track or some other artifact from the Roswell Railroad.

And perhaps, if it was an old-timer from the area who came upon the bit of railroad memorabilia, Ike Roberts and "The Dinkey" were remembered in a nostalgic moment or two.

References

Fairfax Harrison, *A History of the Legal Development of the Railroad System of Southern Railway Company*; Washington D.C.: Southern Railway Company, 1901

Elizabeth L. Davis and Ethel W. Spruill, *The Story of Dunwoody, Its Heritages and Horizons, 1821-1975*; Atlanta: Williams Printing Co., 1975

Lois Coogle, *Sandy Springs - Past Tense*; Atlanta: Decor Master Co., 1971

Darlene Walsh, *Roswell: A Pictorial History* and *Roswell, Georgia*: Roswell Historical Society, 1985.)

(Grateful appreciation is expressed herewith to Dr. Caroline M. Dillman who provided most of the information used in this article.)

The Fayetteville, GA Home of "Doc" Holliday's Uncle

As of this writing (2023), John Henry "Doc" Holliday has been dead for almost 135 years, but his legend today is more profoundly and widely-known than ever before. He was born in Griffin, Georgia, and spent a fair amount of time in the Atlanta area, visiting with his uncle's family and later practicing dentistry.

Many Southerners have often claimed that historians – particularly historians from the North – were little more than myth-makers when it came to documenting "factual" information about the South. Invariably, these "Northern" historians – rather than sticking to writing about the history of their own region – choose instead to "document" Southern history, where, instead of sticking to the facts, they all-too-often write from a jaundiced perspective, "creating" and re-writing Southern history.

In fairness, even though Northern writers and documentarians all too frequently write inaccurately about Southern history, Southerners, while not re-writers of their own history, nevertheless invariably choose to embellish that history. When the two forces are combined, a myth of epic proportions is quite often the end product.

Victoria Wilcox, one-time chairwoman of the Holliday-Dorsey-Fife House Association of Fayetteville, Georgia, once asserted that the "Doc" Holliday of Western lore is in many ways just such a myth.

"I don't think John Henry (Doc) ever wanted to be a gunfighter," Wilcox asserted in an interview. "I believe what he really wanted was the kind of (refined) life his uncle lived right here in Fayetteville. He was even named after his uncle – Dr. Holliday – who was a medical doctor."

The "Atlanta" Hollidays

Doc's uncle was Dr. John Stiles Holliday, a Fayetteville physician. "John Stiles was the first of the Holliday family to obtain a college degree. John Henry was the second," Ms. Wilcox added, as she quickly ticked off facts about the famed gambler/gunman. Over the years, Wilcox stockpiled a wealth of information about the Hollidays, growing to be known as an authority on the subject.

"The Holliday House is the 'most intact' ante-bellum home in all of metro-Atlanta," Wilcox noted proudly. "What I mean by intact is that when you walk in, you stand on the original Georgia heart-pine floors that have been there since the house was first built. Very little has been altered in the home since Dr. Holliday first lived here. Plumbing wasn't even added until the 1940s."

The Holliday home, as it exists today, has been around since 1855, but the original structure was probably built even earlier than that, perhaps as early as 1846 when John Stiles Holliday first purchased the property.

"In the vernacular, the original dwelling would have been considered an 'I-frame home,'" explained Wilcox. "A formal entry flanked by two rooms, one on each side with a stairway leading to two more rooms upstairs."

Prior to moving in with his family, Dr. John Stiles Holliday remodeled the house. Without aid of an architect, he added six massive Greek columns to the front verandah. He also added four more rooms to the rear of the home, making a total of four rooms downstairs and four upstairs. And nearby, he cultivated a vegetable garden and a small orchard to provide some of the family's foods.

Famous Connections

The old home has other interesting roots beyond that of the Holliday family. Prior to occupation of the home by his family, Dr. Holliday agreed to allow students at the new Fayetteville Academy to use the then-new home as a boarding house. The Hollidays therefore did not actually take up residence in the home until 1857.

Annie Fitzgerald, the grandmother of Margaret Mitchell, famed author of the international best-selling novel *Gone With The Wind*, attended Fayetteville Academy as a young girl. As a result of this family experience, Mitchell would later send her *Gone With The*

John Henry Holliday is pictured from a tinted daguerreotype, 1852. The precocious toddler offered no hint of the famous – or infamous – life he would later lead. (Karen Holliday Tanner Photo Collection; Reprinted with Permission).

Wind heroine, "Scarlett O'Hara," to the "Fayetteville Girl's Academy," modeled after Fayetteville Academy in Mitchell's imagination.

The esteemed author's writings in association with her family experiences did not stop with Scarlett either. Her cousin from the Fitzgerald clan – Martha Anne "Mattie" Holliday – was the prototype for Mitchell's character of "Melanie" in the famed novel.

Mattie spent her childhood in Fayetteville and nearby Jonesboro. The Hollidays were a close-knit Irish clan, and family gatherings at the Holliday home were common.

It was during these and other such gatherings that a strong bond between young Mattie and John Henry (Doc) Holliday was established – a relationship about which there has been much speculation and romantic intrigue over the ensuing century.

Cousin Mattie

Only twenty months older than Doc, Mattie Holliday was his playmate and companion during assemblies at the Holliday house in Fayetteville. The secrets the two shared as children formed the basis of an intimacy that lasted throughout their lives. The depth and

His oft-times painful future still worlds away, the infant Holliday was photographed with his mother, Alice Jane McKey Holliday, circa 1852. Even as a small tyke, John Henry demonstrates a gaze which might be unsettling to some. (Craig Fouts Photo Collection; Reprinted with Permission)

This impressive home built by Dr. John Stiles Holliday, the uncle of John Henry "Doc" Holliday of western fame, still stands in Fayetteville, Georgia, as of this writing (2022). It has been in existence at least since 1855, and quite possibly was built as early as 1846 when Dr. Holliday first purchased the property. John Stiles Holliday diagnosed the tuberculosis in his nephew circa 1873. It was at this home that young John Henry spent much time in his youth forming a bond with his cousin Mattie which ultimately had a profound impact upon both their lives. (Photo courtesy of Holliday-Dorsey-Fife House)

breadth of this relationship and its exact details are not known today, and perhaps have been lost to posterity, but the subject nevertheless has been fodder for much myth-making over the years.

In the 1993 major motion picture *Tombstone*, starring Kurt Russell and Val Kilmer, a mythical Doc confesses to Wyatt Earp that an affair with a cousin caused her to enter a convent and him to leave his home in disgrace. This, quite possibly, is a somewhat accurate portrayal of the actual circumstances.

Cousin Mattie, born December 14, 1849, was raised a Catholic, and became a nun at the age of 34. She took the name "Melanie" in honor of Saint Melaine, who, after marrying a kinsman, sought a life of complete devotion to God. Did Mattie take the name Melanie

because she was in love with her own cousin, Doc?

"Family members in the past have been reluctant to admit that any such relationship actually existed between John Henry and Mattie," confessed Wilcox, "but the myth that he left Georgia simply because of poor health is questionable. John Henry supposedly left Georgia for a higher and dryer climate to combat the tuberculosis with which he had been diagnosed, but he traveled to Dallas, Texas, which is actually a lower elevation, geographically, than even Atlanta, and is almost as humid.

"In all likelihood, the Doc-Mattie relationship probably did in fact play a role in his decision to leave Georgia," Wilcox added. "After all, many people with advanced cases of tuberculosis

This artist's rendering of Dr. John Stiles Holliday was created circa 1860, and, even in the most generous of descriptions, has to be considered just a bit unsettling. His demeanor was characteristic of the Holliday men. (Collection of Morgan DeLancey Magee)

Mattie (later "Sister Melanie") Holliday, was John Henry Holliday's first cousin, and has been the subject of much speculation concerning his life down through history. Some historians have maintained that a love affair between the two caused him to abandon his native Georgia forever, and her to be relegated to a convent. (Susan McKey Thomas collection; Reprinted with Permission)

such as was suffered by Doc were going to Florida for treatment in those days."

In fairness, many travel decisions made by Holliday the last ten or fifteen years of his life were not logical ones, and seem to have been little more than aimless wandering in search of adventure and yet another gambling opportunity. To attach any special significance to his travels from 1873 and later would be pure folly.

Summer Love

It is entirely plausible that Doc fell in love with his favored cousin the year he turned sixteen. In 1864, in an effort to escape the Union army which was advancing into north Georgia, Doc's father had moved the family from Griffin (in north Georgia) to Valdosta (in extreme south Georgia).

After the war, around 1867, Doc spent one summer with Mattie's family

in Jonesboro, and it quite possibly was during this period that their romance blossomed. Even long after she became "Sister Melanie," Doc maintained a strong bond with his cousin, often writing to her of secrets only the two of them shared.

Who knows today if these letters and missives were love letters? In point of fact, it will probably never be known now to a certainty. Mattie considered the letters ultra-private, and later burned them to avoid any revelation of the details within them in the future.

According to family legend, Mattie later regretted the destruction of the letters. *"Had I not destroyed most of his letters, the world would have known a much different man than the one of Western lore,"* she later confessed.

Henry Burroughs Holliday, Doc's father, was photographed circa 1852, while the family yet lived in Griffin, Georgia, south of Atlanta. Interestingly, not only is Doc Holliday's gravesite a mystery today, but so also is that of his father's which is highly unusual for a person of his former prominence.

Sophie Walton was a female slave born in January of 1856 on a farm owned by the Walton family. Sophie enjoyed a higher status than the other slave children because she had been fathered by Mr. Walton. During the Federal occupation of Georgia, Mr. Walton could no longer care for all of his "ex-slaves," and arranged for Sophie to go live at the home of Dr. John Stiles Holliday, Doc's uncle. Among her many skills, Sophie was extremely adept at cards, and taught Doc many of the skills he later used as a professional card player out West. Sophie was photographed here in 1895 in Atlanta.

According to records, Doc went on to study dentistry at the Pennsylvania College of Dental Surgery, graduating in 1872. He was planning happily for his future, totally unaware he would be gone in a scant fifteen years.

After graduation, Doc practiced dentistry briefly in Atlanta. It was at about this time that he was diagnosed with tuberculosis, a dreaded disease for which there was no cure at that time.

A Move To Dallas

It was shortly after learning of his disease that Doc departed for Texas, quite likely sometime in 1873. One can only imagine the pain and despair his fate must have caused him. He probably had suffered a tragic love affair from which there was no recourse, and then shortly thereafter had been informed that he had contracted a fatal disease.

After arriving in Dallas, Doc must have needed funds, for he set up a dental practice there. At this time, the West was still a wild frontier in many respects. In short order, Doc had become a part of this wildness, picking up the traits of drinking, gambling, and carrying firearms. He, however, also continued to practice dentistry.

According to O.K. Corral chronicler Paula Marks, Doc soon garnered a reputation as *"one of the touchiest drunks in the West."* Wyatt Earp himself declared *"Doc's fatalistic courage . . . gave (him) the edge over any out-and-out killer I ever knew."*

Doc was arrested January 1st, 1875, for shooting at a saloon-keeper in Dallas. According to the January 2, 1875 issue of the **Dallas Herald**, *"Dr. Holliday and Mr. Austin, a saloon keeper, relieved the monotony of the noise of fire crackers by taking a couple of shots at each other yesterday afternoon. The cheerful note of the peaceful six-shooter is heard once more among us. Both shooters were arrested."*

Doc apparently decided at that point that it was time to leave Dallas, and drifted on to Fort Griffin. There, he was indicted by a grand jury for *"gaming in a saloon,"* along with Hurricane Bill, Liz, Etta, Kate, et alle, and charged with keeping a *"disorderly house."*

"Kate," "Bat," and Wyatt

This "Kate" named in the indictment was the first published link between Doc and the female who eventually became known in Western lore as "Big Nose Kate." Along with Doc, Mary Katherine "Kate" Harony would become widely known for her "adventures."

From 1875 to 1878, little is accurately known about Doc's wanderings. It is known, however, that he eventually traveled with Kate to Denver, Colorado, where he began dealing a popular card game called faro.

By late 1877, Doc and Kate were back in Fort Griffin. It was here that he first met another drifter who would gain fame in the West by the name of Wyatt Earp. Doc's illness and frail health no doubt caused him to prefer New Mexico, Texas, Kansas and Arizona in the winter months, saving the gambling

opportunities in the gold and silver mining towns in Colorado and parts northward for the summer months.

By 1878, Doc had arrived in Dodge City, already preceded by a rather substantial reputation as a dangerous man. It was here that he played poker in the Long Branch Saloon, and rode in posses with Wyatt Earp and Bat Masterson. Masterson, who disliked Doc and later became a writer of sorts, penned a number of articles – after Doc's death – which portrayed the Georgian in a negative light.

According to an article Masterson wrote in a 1907 issue of **Human Life** magazine, Doc *"went from Dodge to Trinidad, Colorado, where, within a week from the time he landed, he shot and seriously wounded a young sport by the name of Kid Colton over a very trivial matter. He was again forced to hunt the tall timber and managed to make his escape to Las Vegas, New Mexico, which was then something of a boom town. . ."*

Masterson later wrote that *"Holliday had few friends anywhere in the West. He was selfish and had a perverse nature – traits not calculated to make a man popular in the early days on the frontier."*

Whatever the circumstances, the John Henry Holliday described by William Barclay "Bat" Masterson did not match the description of the Southern gentleman of record back in Georgia. And in retrospect, it is famously-easy to ridicule and criticize an individual when that individual isn't around to defend his good name.

Interestingly, though highly critical of Holliday's "perverse nature" as Masterson described him, it was Masterson himself who, after becoming so unpopular and troublesome, was run out of the city of Denver, Colorado, and told never to return.

The Mystery & Marvel of Historic Roswell Mill

Founded in 1839, just one year after the Cherokee Indians were removed from the youthful state of Georgia, the Roswell Manufacturing Company embarked upon what ultimately became a hugely-successful commercial endeavor. Its success, however, unwittingly set it on a collision course with the Union Army juggernaut in the terrible U.S. Civil War, which resulted in the mysterious disappearance of the mill's workers whose fates have remained unexplained to the present day.

In 1830, two years after gold had been discovered in what today is the north Georgia mountains, businessman Roswell King traveled from Darien on the Georgia coast to check on investments he had made in several of the mines in the uplands of the growing state. As he made his way northward through Cherokee Indian Territory into the area known today as "north Fulton County," he paused along a stream – later named "Vickery Creek" – which emptied into a large river to which the native Indians referred as "Chattahoochee." When it came to business investments of that day, King was "a quick study," and he quickly noted the site's potential for water-powered industry.

At the time that King passed through this spot, a half-breed Cherokee named Charles Wofford, interestingly, was already operating a gristmill on the very stream mentioned above. Pausing at the spot, King reportedly envisioned a much larger operation – ginning cotton, carding wool, and sawing wood – all powered by the waters of the somewhat substantial stream feeding into the great river.

Even at this early date, King's dream quite possibly also included the eventual development of a town, as well as a site of peaceful beauty to which his extended family could relocate to live and work in a productive factory environment, raising their children and leading prosperous lives at this attractive site.

Never one to rest upon his laurels, King had soon made arrangements to purchase property at this site in order to secure his dream and convert his idea into a reality. Today, despite all the unbridled growth and development in Georgia's north Fulton County, remnants of King's original milling operations at this site amazingly still exist.

The town itself – "Roswell" – created an enduring legacy for the pioneer

A rare early photograph from the 1880s of the Roswell Mill complex after it had been reconstructed from the devastation of the U.S. Civil War. Notice the many different mill buildings clustered along the banks of Vickery Creek and the hillside above. A water flume extends from the uppermost top-left building to the structure below it which is believed to have been an early electrical power generation plant.

businessman's name which has otherwise disappeared from the realm. Though King and some of his descendants lived for many years in this community to which he gave his name, no other aspect of his former presence at this site – aside from his grave – exists today. His last direct descendant still living in the historic town – Katherine Simpson – passed away in 1994.

Cherokee Lands

By the 1820s, a number of the wise leaders of the Cherokee Nation once located in present-day north Georgia, had realized they and their people must in some way co-exist with their white invaders – or they simply would perish. The numbers of the settlers and the power of their weapons were far too great to overcome by the warfare which had previously been practiced by the Cherokees and their predecessors since the dawn of time in the area. Their wise leaders sought a new strategy.

As history has recorded, the Cherokees responded heroically to the challenge, adopting a democratic form of government modeled after the White man's, with the goal of assimilating into his culture. They began operating businesses, creating a court system, setting up their own law enforcement, and some privileged few even gained enough wealth to live in mansions and own plantations rivaling their White invaders.

The Cherokees also amazingly created an important tool in a very short period of time which continues to astound historians and sociologists alike

Pictured is the 1882 Roswell Mill building (Mill #2) as it appears today. After many years of productivity, it fell victim to cheaper labor available in developing countries abroad. (Photo by Olin Jackson)

even today – an alphabet which the average Cherokee was able to master in little more than a week. All previous written and spoken languages of cultures throughout the world had required not weeks, but eons of time for their creation, development, and refinement. Some primitive cultures in the world still do not have a written language even today.

With the alphabet, the Cherokees were able to create their own written form of communication and, also amazingly, a newspaper, which very nearly enabled them to peacefully and diplomatically overcome the enormous odds against their retention of their native lands in what today is the southeastern United States. Had it not been for the state of Georgia's and the President of the United States' "thumbing of their collective noses" at an official edict of the Supreme Court of the United States,

the Cherokees might well have retained ownership of at least a portion of this homeland to the present day.

One of these bright innovative Cherokees was a well-educated female named Sharlot (Charlotte) Vickery. She was a half-blood who had married a White settler named Daren Cordery. The couple were part-owners of a ferry which traversed the Chattahoochee in what today is known as Forsyth County.

Sharlot lived at the headwaters of the large stream (a.k.a. Big Creek) near this spot which later bore her name. It was the same creek that Roswell King had witnessed in his travel northward to his gold mine(s), and along which he envisioned the milling operations of his dreams.

Although the Cherokees – including Sharlot Vickery – were legal owners in the eyes of the White man's law (including much of what today is north

Located above the ruins of the 1854 Mill (Mill #1), this dam on Vickery Creek diverted water to power an early generator at the mill.

Georgia by virtue of the *Cherokee Cession Treaty* of 1817 and 1819), White settlers nevertheless continued to pour into the area, staking claims to the land for the precious yellow metal recently discovered there. Though the tide of new settlers was endless, the state of Georgia – via troops from the federal government – initially attempted to protect the Cherokee lands.

On May 29, 1820, General Andrew Jackson, acting under orders from U.S. Secretary of War John C. Calhoun, reportedly posted a notice upon a tree on the south side of the Chattahoochee at a spot known as "Shallow Ford" a short distance west of the present-day Roswell Road Bridge. The official announcement read: "(Intruders of the Cherokee) *lands, beware. I am required to remove all white men found trespassing on the Cherokee land not having a written permit from the agent* (Cherokee Indian Agent) *Colo.* (Colonel) *R.S. Meigs. This duty I am about to perform.*"

In 1832, however, due in large part to the immense value of the gold quickly being discovered there, the state of Georgia, in a bold and utterly unconscionable move, unceremoniously reversed itself, and illicitly laid claim to much of the Cherokee lands which fell within the boundaries of the state as decreed in that day. Despite the fact that a decision by Chief Justice John Marshall and the U.S. Supreme Court had officially ruled that the new Georgia law laying claim to the Cherokee lands was unconstitutional, the Cherokees were nevertheless evicted. American folklore supposedly maintains that Andrew Jackson, president of the U.S. by this time, arrogantly countered the court's ruling by stating "John Marshall has made his decision. Now let him enforce it."

In fairness, by this point in history, Jackson had been fighting marauding Indians for much of his life, and had simply decided that in order to maintain a peaceful transition as "Manifest Destiny" and settlement of the "New World" from coast to coast took its course, the "uncivilized" Indians must go. He not only refused to protect the Cherokees' interests with federal troops, but instead used the troops to permanently expel the Cherokees from north Georgia, and portions of Tennessee and the Carolinas.

As most students of Native American history now know, the Cherokees were rounded up and herded out of what today is the state of Georgia in the infamous "Trail of Tears" in 1838. Sharlot Vickery – owner of the ferry across the Chattahoochee near Vickery Creek – was among those Indians forced to forfeit their businesses and leave their native land behind forever. From that time until the present day, the creek below Roswell Mill has borne this unfortunate Cherokee's name, and is still referred to today as "Vickery Creek."

Following the Indians' removal, Roswell King returned to the spot along Vickery Creek to begin the fulfillment of his dream. With the able assistance of numerous manual laborers, King and his son, Barrington, built a substantial dam to capture the waters of the creek so that they could be harnessed into kinetic energy to turn a large millwheel which in turn powered his many operations at this site.

King also built a sawmill for the production of lumber and a kiln in which to make bricks for the construction of homes and businesses. With the help of his slaves, he began the construction of a large cotton mill, and by 1839,

the Roswell Manufacturing Company was well on its way toward becoming a major enterprise.

Despite his enormous and ingenious efforts, Roswell King died in 1844 before realizing the full completion of his dream. His son, Barrington, took over management of the milling endeavors and eventually doubled the size of the venture.

By 1853, a new four-story factory constructed of bricks had been built. This new mill doubled the work force and eventually tripled the revenues generated by the Roswell Manufacturing Company which had been developed into a hugely successful and innovative production line for cotton products.

By 1854, Roswell Manufacturing Company consisted of two cotton mills and a flour mill. A facility for the production of woolen products known as "Ivy Mill" was built in 1857 slightly downstream from the main mills by James R. King, Barrington's son. This mill was a separate facility distinctly independent of the Roswell Manufacturing Company.

In 1842, Barrington King had also built an impressive mansion called Barrington Hall for his family on a promontory above town. *(In 2005, this breath-taking antebellum home which had most recently been the private residence of Lois Simpson, the adopted daughter of Katherine Simpson, was opened to the public for daily tours. It is included on the **National Register of Historic Places** today and is an integral portion of the captivating tours of the historic community of Roswell.)*

By the time Barrington King had built the four-story brick factory at the mills in 1853, the Roswell Manufacturing Company's estimated net-worth was in excess of one million dollars. In 2023 dollars, that would be the equivalent of approximately $36,000,000.00, but does not do justice to the actual value of that sum in 1853, since at that time, $36,000,000.00 could have purchased far more than in 2023. As an example, the entire geographic realm of the present-day state of Alaska was purchased in 1867 for only $7.2 million.

The King family, to put it mildly, was fabulously wealthy in that day and age, but dark clouds were gathering on the horizon. Jealous eyes to the north were watching with ever-mounting unease, the burgeoning commercial growth of an independent-minded South bent upon development of an industrial realm which would compete with the industrial North.

The *Tariff of Abominations*

By the 1820s, two very separate business segments had developed in the youthful United States. In the northern states where an early foundation of industrial development had originated, factories and mills steadily appeared upon the landscape. In contrast, those states south of the Mason-Dixon Line had developed into an agrarian society which basically functioned as a wholesaler of inexpensive raw materials such as cotton, flax, rice, pig-iron, tanned leather and the like – supported by the institution of slavery – for the factories in the North.

It was a routine which was very profitable for Northern industrial capitalists. They bought raw materials from the South at a very inexpensive rate – since Southern producers had no place else to sell their products – and then turned around and sold back the finished products made from those raw materials at an excessively expensive rate

to Southern markets – since Southern retailers and consumers, once again, had no other option for purchasing those products.

As the years passed, this exceptionally unfair market situation became more and more intolerable for plantation owners and other producers of raw materials in the South. Businessmen and prospective industrialists in the South therefore began seeking better opportunities from Europe rather than from Northern suppliers.

When, by the late 1850s, substantial commercial enterprises had begun appearing in the South to also produce finished products from Southern raw materials, and when these independent-minded Southern commercial enterprises thereby began actively competing with the New England industrialists by selling not only their raw materials, but their commercially-finished products to European buyers at a substantially more profitable rate, Northern capitalists were both alarmed and outraged. This dramatic change in the business dynamic of Southern capitalists was very quickly becoming very expensive to the North and it could not be tolerated.

In order to control the South and keep it "in harness" to the New England manufacturing monopolies, Northern industrialists and capitalists sought and obtained protective tariffs from Congress on raw materials and finished goods the South was obtaining from the European markets which were causing so much consternation to New England industrialists.

One new tariff in particular – called the *"Tariff of 1828"* by the federal government and the *"Tariff of Abominations"* by Southern industrialists – was particularly egregious. It was an extremely high tax

(38% on foreign finished products and 45% on foreign raw materials) which had the effect of converting the formerly inexpensive European goods into products which were even more expensive than the already expensive goods being manufactured in the North. To say the least, Southern industrialists now were outraged, and rightfully so.

Even worse, this elimination of Europe as a source of inexpensive goods (as a result of the *Tariff of 1828*) to markets in the United States conversely virtually eliminated the sales of Southern products such as cotton to these European buyers, since the balance of trade had been severely upset, limiting the funds available to European buyers for the purchase of Southern products. It was a situation which "re-crippled" the already struggling Southern economy.

As a result of this Northern "price-fixing" and associated unfair restrictive tariffs, Southern industrialists and buyers eventually rebelled by simply ignoring the unfair law and tariffs in order to continue conducting profitable business arrangements with European markets. When Northern industrialists and their political leaders realized the Southern industrialists and the growing industrial South would not be controlled, they were outraged anew, and the issue eventually reached a flashpoint.

Though this strategy by Southern businessmen and industrialists was successful in the short-term, it eventually sowed the seeds of the South's destruction. The Roswell Manufacturing Company was just one such example. In the years immediately prior to the U.S. Civil War, Southern industrialists such as

Also built in 1854, this structure which still stands as of this writing (2023), was built as the company store for Roswell Mill. It was one of the few mill buildings in Roswell not burned during the U.S. Civil War. (Photo by Olin Jackson)

the Kings of Roswell had erroneously assumed that if the ignorance of Northern price-fixing and punitive tariffs by Southern businessmen did ultimately result in war, the conflict would be of short duration and the South would be quickly victorious, so there was no cause for concern.

War Reaches Roswell

As a result, production at facilities such as the Roswell mills increased steadily as the years passed. The Kings sold their products not only to foreign buyers, but to local purchasers as well. Cotton fabric produced at the Roswell Manufacturing Company was sold to the state and taken to Atlanta for use as hospital bandages, sheets on bedding, and manufactured into other commodities such as clothing and uniform items, all of which ultimately became important to the eventual war effort.

Aside from the materials eventually produced for the war effort, the Roswell Manufacturing Company also produced yarn, rope, flour, leather goods and other products for sale to the area's civilian population. This substantial commercial endeavor continued unimpeded until 1864.

By late 1863 and early 1864, at least six separate mill buildings had been built along the hillside above Vickery Creek. Included in the complex was a dye building, a picker building, a tannery, one warehouse, and the main mill structure which is estimated to have been 140 feet long, 53 feet wide, and four stories in height. The mill was powered by a 16 x 20-foot water wheel turned by the force of the water flowing down a substantial millrace from Vickery Creek.

As federal gunboats began blockading Southern ports of entry to thwart the importation of inexpensive European commodities and federal officials initiated strict programs for the collection of the despised trading tariffs, the sparks of rebellion finally ignited the bonfires of war.

When the U.S. Civil War began with the firing upon Fort Sumter in South Carolina, Barrington King was 62. By this time, yet another generation of Kings – Barrington Jr., Thomas, William and James – had all reached manhood and begun pursuing professional careers of their own.

James had been sent to New Jersey in the mid-1850s to learn the basics of managing a mill operation. As the commercialized center of industrial America, New England was a rich training ground in the arts of industrial creation and management.

When young James had returned at the conclusion of his "apprenticeship" in the North, he assumed management of the operations of Ivy Mill (*described above*) which produced woolen products. As the war gained momentum, Ivy Mill was tasked with the production of – among other things – Confederate uniforms, which were commonly fabricated from wool, a much longer-lasting and more durable clothing than cotton.

During the war, James reached the rank of captain in the Confederate Army, and continued operation of the woolens mill on Vickery Creek. He remained in this capacity until just prior to the arrival of Union Gen. Kenner Jarrard's cavalry troops in Roswell in 1864, at which time, he departed for points southward.

Thomas also supported the Confederacy and was wounded at the Battle of Bull Run, returning to Roswell for a short period of time before departing again for battle at Chickamauga. He was killed in battle there.

Barrington Jr. fought at Bentonville, North Carolina, and was killed as well in 1865, in one of the last attacks of the war.

William lived on a plantation in Marietta *(the mansion of which still survives today and was known to Atlantans in the 1980s and 1990s as the "1848 House Restaurant," a highly popular dining establishment)*. He maintained a diary of his experiences on this plantation during the advances of Union General Sherman at nearby Kennesaw Mountain just north of Marietta, recording the chaotic events of that day, including the Battle of Bushy Park *(as the plantation was called at that time)*. Bushy Park also served as a hospital for the Union forces after the battle.

Though many have argued vociferously that the U.S. Civil War was ignited by the issue of slavery, many other students of the war argue just as vociferously that the true catalyst was the constant and growing burden of price controls and punitive tariffs imposed by Northern industrialists and political leaders of the 1820s through the 1850s. Southern capitalists and consumers eventually were simply unable to tolerate the system any longer.

In point of fact, slavery already existed in the South at that time. As wrong as it was, it was legal and very viable in the late 1850s, and the South did not have to go to war to either obtain

> *Southern capitalists and consumers eventually were simply unable to tolerate the system any longer.*

or retain it. Lincoln did not even issue his *Emancipation Proclamation* until January 1, 1863, almost two full years after the war had already begun, and even then, it was not intentionally issued to "free the slaves," but rather as a tool of war, to deprive the South of a huge cost-free source of labor.

In July of 1864, as General William Tecumseh Sherman's Union Army advanced ever nearer to its primary objective of Atlanta in the South's heartland, the Kings of Roswell, including Barrington King, Sr., and other prominent families in town departed for points southward to evade capture.

The Kings, though no doubt heavily invested in the Confederate economy and its by-then worthless paper currency, apparently were not as unprepared for war-time losses as were most, for after the war, they would quickly re-build – with dependable funds based upon currencies other than Confederate dollars – which apparently had been prudently deposited outside the South (possibly in European banks) following the onset of the war.

Interestingly, a Frenchman by the name of Theophilus Roche' had arrived in Roswell in 1863, seeking work as a journeyman weaver. He ultimately was hired by James King. When the King family fled Roswell in the summer of 1864, James, in a last ditch effort to save his woolens production mill, temporarily transferred ownership of the operation to Roche', who, in turn, hoisted a French flag above the mill, naively hoping it would be considered as "French soil," and spared. It, of course, was not, as Sherman and his minions clearly demonstrated over and over that they intended to destroy anything and everything even remotely associated with "commercial industry" in the independence-minded South.

It was into the vortex of this industrial trauma that the Roswell Manufacturing Company was thrust in 1864. Monopolistic-minded Northern industrialists were convinced they were entitled to the exclusive right of industrial production in the United States, and that the South should be required to remain an agrarian society providing a constant stream of cheap raw materials for Northern factories.

Industrial operations such as Roswell's mills represented a direct threat to Northern capitalists and therefore had to be destroyed. During the war, these industrial operations weren't torched by Sherman and his minions solely because they produced clothing for the war effort. To the contrary, they were torched because collectively they provided the possibility of independence for the South.

Mystery of the Mill Workers

Over recent years, much controversy has arisen among historians concerning the events which transpired during and after the destruction of the Roswell Mill site by Sherman's foot-soldiers and the "bummers" which followed in their wake partaking of the spoils of war. Sherman was well aware of the facilities at Roswell through his

Erected in 1839 for workers at the Roswell Cotton Mill, these apartments – known as "The Old Bricks," – enjoy status as the oldest apartments in the South. (Photo by Olin Jackson)

Brigadier General Kenner Jarrard, commander of the Union Army's Second Cavalry Division, was given the command to destroy Roswell Mill during the U.S. Civil War.

intelligence operations, and had sent Brig. Gen. Kenner Garrard to the town primarily to secure the shallow ford across the Chattahoochee River just south of Roswell.

Over the ensuing years, a story has been perpetuated that Garrard "accidentally" discovered Confederate insignia in items being produced by Ivy Mill in Roswell, and that all the milling operations in the town were therefore suspect and destined for destruction. However, in all likelihood, Garrard traveled to Roswell no less specifically to burn any and all industry therein, than he did to secure the shallow ford.

Sherman, in fact, was instructing all his generals to make certain in particular that all manufacturing facilities – whether they produced nothing more than bandages or not – were destroyed. In Roswell, he went a step further, instructing General Garrard to capture and imprison anyone associated with the milling operations there in order to completely destroy any man-power possibly available to re-start future milling operations – such had been the success of the Roswell Manufacturing Company. Just as it could not be allowed to assist in the war effort, the Roswell enterprise and its abilities to independently produce and sell its finished products to European and other buyers at a profit – instead of to Northern capitalists and industrialists at a loss – also could not be tolerated.

It is a matter of record today that the majority of the workers at Roswell Mill were women and children, and the fact that he had been ordered to capture and imprison them troubled Gen. Kenner Garrard on a moral perspective. He, accordingly, forwarded a message to this effect to Sherman requesting further instructions.

William Tecumseh Sherman not only was unsympathetic, he was brutal in his response. He ordered Garrard to have the women and children transported immediately to Marietta and then locked inside bare rail boxcars in the horrendous July heat in Georgia, and shipped – without toilet facilities, food, water, sleeping space, or even a seat other than the hard floor – more than 250 miles to Nashville, Tennessee. From there, they were then sent under the same circumstances an additional 175 miles to Louisville, Kentucky, where those who survived the terrible ordeal were locked in a prisoner-of-war camp.

To say the least today, this treatment of innocent women and children was heartless, not to mention outrageous, and was eerily similar to the horribly inhumane treatment which would be experienced some 70 years in the future by women and children at the hands of another unspeakably brutal army in the 1930s and '40s in Germany. It is unknown today just how many of the Roswell mill workers survived the horrors of the 425-mile trip and their imprisonment in Kentucky, since no records of this incident – very conveniently – exist today. It is, however, a matter of record that these women and children were shipped to that destination under the circumstances described, and that they never again returned to their homes in Roswell, nor was any communication from them ever received by loved ones back in Roswell. This action today at the very least would be considered a "War Crime," punishable by death.

It is also a matter of record that Sherman was, at the very least, a conscienceless individual. He fully intended to decisively destroy the state of Georgia, its citizenry, its industrial and commercial capability and its military potential, and re-populate it with immigrants from elsewhere. In the process, he clearly cared not who suffered nor how much they suffered in achieving this goal. His letter in October of 1864 to Grant clearly demonstrates these intentions:

Allatoona 7:30 p.m.

Oct. 9th 1864

Lt. Gen. Grant

City Point

It will be a physical impossibility to protect this road now that Hood, Forrest, Wheeler and the whole batch of Devils are turned loose without home or habitation. I think Hoods movements indicate a direction to the end of the Selma and Talladega road to Blue Mountain about sixty miles south west of Rome from which he will threaten Kingston, Bridgeport and

Decatur and I propose we break up the road from Chattanooga and strike out with wagons for Milledgeville Millen and Savannah.

Until we can re-populate Georgia it is useless to occupy it, but utter destruction of its roads, houses, and people will cripple their military resources. By attempting to hold the roads we will lose a thousand men monthly and will gain no result. I can make the march and make Georgia howl. *We have over 8,000 cattle and 3,000,000 pounds of bread but no corn, but we can forage the interior of the state.*

W.T. Sherman

According to military records, the Mill prisoners were held under Garrard's guard in Roswell from July 6th until the 10th. On July 9th, the general had promised his men – who numbered in the thousands – a special whiskey allotment for their successes. One Union soldier who experienced this event later wrote, *"We had never seen so many pretty women in one place in all our lives."*

Prior to departing Marietta, the Roswell Mill workers met their counterparts from a similar water-powered manufacturing facility west of Atlanta called Sweetwater Creek Mill. These workers had similarly been taken prisoner and were also shipped under the same circumstances to POW camps in the North.

Little more than speculation is available today regarding the events surrounding the journey to Louisville. The complete circumstances of this tragic episode and the story of the lives of the workers from that point forward may never be known.

From 1864 until well into the 1880s, most areas in the devastated South were lawless towns and forested expanses where criminals and cutthroats roamed at will, murdering, robbing, raping, and pillaging in abandon. These wolves of war took what they wished from whomever they wished. It was an unimaginable Hell-on-earth in the South during these years where survival became the only objective in life for the majority of the citizenry, since law enforcement was non-existent. It therefore should not be surprising that the fate of the Roswell Mill workers has remained an unsolved mystery since 1864.

Those government entities and officials who normally would have been the keepers of records and knowledgeable of the ultimate circumstances of unfortunates such as the Roswell Mill workers were overwhelmed themselves in their own efforts to survive the terrible times and rebuild their lives. As such, the mill workers and their ultimate fates were simply dismissed as "casualties of war."

Sketchy initial records for the facilities where a handful of the Roswell Mill workers were imprisoned are extant today in Louisville. The few men that were included were sent to a male prison and separated from the women and children. The women were imprisoned in a separate facility.

Once imprisoned, no sympathies or kindnesses whatsoever were extended to any Confederate prisoners in these Northern POW camps, even though ample food, medical supplies, and clothing existed there. The reason for this harsh treatment of their former fellow-Americans is unknown today, but it in all likelihood was done in retaliation for the poor treatment of Northern prisoners in Southern POW camps.

The difference in this circumstance was that by the second or third year of the war, the South was starving. All the coastal shipping ports had been blockaded by this point, so there was no way to obtain a supply of food in retail markets, and virtually all of the men and boys were away fighting in the war so there was no one at home to plant or maintain even simple vegetable gardens or to raise livestock. The little food that existed was distributed to the soldiers – who also went hungry most of the time – so there, in turn, was virtually no source for food for Union Army prisoners in the Southern prisoner-of-war camps.

As a result, very little sympathy was shown to the women and children – and certainly not to the men workers – from Roswell Mill. Records in Louisville indicate some of the women died of typhoid and measles outbreaks, since they were so closely confined in such poor conditions. A lucky few – following a swearing of an oath of allegiance to the federal government – reportedly were released with no shelter nor means of support or food, and they simply vanished from the public record.

The extant prison records in Louisville include the names of only 16 of the women workers and 17 of the children from the Roswell Mill workers that were confined there in the female prison. Some of the children – if they survived at all – undoubtedly became orphans.

The women prisoners in particular – without food, money or means of transportation – simply were permanently stranded in the North where, if they were lucky, they married a returning soldier. If unlucky – as most undoubtedly were – they were forced to settle for "other means of support" for themselves and their children. That, of course, is assuming they survived the terrible ordeal.

The possibilities for survival of the children were even more bleak.

Barrington King Returns

At the age of 67, Barrington King traveled from the Georgia coast – to which he had refugeed – back to Roswell where he began rebuilding his father's dream. Sherman and his minions, however, had been efficient. The only mill buildings that had survived the war intact were the worker residences, known today as "The Bricks;" the outer shell of the machine shop; and the company store, which faced the old Roswell town square. All of these structures continue to stand as of this writing (2023).

Since there were ample building materials – and since it is very difficult to destroy a natural resource such as a major stream – the mill complex was completely rebuilt and in complete operation once again shortly after the war. It is unknown today from whence came the financial capability for the regeneration of all this infrastructure, but as pointed out above, the Kings were very astute businessmen.

In contrast, the huge mill at Sweetwater Creek was likewise completely destroyed, but it was never re-built, its owners obviously either capitalized solely with Confederate dollars, or else killed in the war. The stark chimneys and remnants of this facility still stand today along the creek southwest of Atlanta, silent sentinels to the war's destruction.

Barrington King's efforts at Roswell, however, lasted but one year. He died in January of 1866. He, ironically, had survived the onslaught of the war, becoming a refugee to the coast of Georgia, and then the long trip overland back to his home in Roswell where he successfully regenerated the source of his wealth, only to be kicked in the head by a horse and mortally wounded.

George W. Camp was elected to succeed King as chairman of the board of the Roswell Manufacturing Company, and he worked vigorously at rebuilding the complex.

Barrington King's property was divided among his family. His widow sold most of her stock in the Roswell Manufacturing Company to the newly-named president of the company – Andrew Jackson Hansell.

Hansell hired a clerk named F.J. Minhinette, who followed his employer as president of the company in 1882. Minhinette made many improvements and additions to the complex, continuing as controller of the company for ten years.

By this point, the Roswell Manufacturing Company complex had grown substantially, with numerous mill buildings. A new identification system therefore had become necessary. The factory which had been built in 1854 and rebuilt after the Civil War became known as "Mill No. 1." A factory built in 1882 [which still stands as of this writing (2023)] became known as "Mill No. 2."

By the late 1890s, the available water power at the Roswell Mill complex had become insufficient for the needs there, so the 1854 mill was converted to steam power and the 1882 mill to electrical power via generators which made more efficient use of the water power. The complex became more productive than ever.

Despite all this productivity, on June 12, 1926, Mother Nature dealt the business yet another fateful blow. On that day – sixty-four years after Sherman had burned the factories – lightning revisited the flames of destruction upon the 1854 structure, reducing it once again to ashes.

Instead of again rebuilding the 1854 brick structure, the company chose instead to expand the 1882 wooden building. A new dye building was also constructed west of the mill. These additions were completed in 1929.

By this time, the Roswell Manufacturing Company had been in operation for almost 100 years, constructing and reconstructing over 26 buildings. Soon after the new construction was completed, the company again changed ownership. This time, it was renamed "Southern Mills."

Death Knell of the Cotton Mills

An abundance of cheap labor and raw materials had transformed the South into a region dotted with fabric mills by the 1930s. The commercial endeavor now called "Southern Mills" was one of these.

The Southern Mills factory in Roswell operated successfully for forty years following the disappearance of the Roswell Manufacturing Company identity. It was a main source of income for many of the city's residents during this period, and specialized in laundry netting and carpet backing. It also continued manufacturing cotton cloth, the material originally envisioned by Roswell King.

Despite all its progress and growth, by 1975, the mill complex in Roswell finally succumbed to the erosion of profits brought on by a cheaper labor pool in developing countries abroad. The products manufactured at Southern Mills, where the worker salaries were now mandated by employee unions, could no longer be profitably produced. As a result, the mill was closed permanently and all but forgotten for a number of years.

In 1989, using location information provided by a local Roswell historian, an archaeological dig funded by the Roswell Historical Society was conducted at the presumed site of the Roswell Manufacturing Company's first (1839) cotton mill. The dig was conducted by Southeastern Archaeological Services in Athens, Georgia.

In their work, the archaeologists discovered that the Roswell cotton mill complex is one of the most intact textile sites still in existence in Georgia. In their report, they name only five other mills of equivalent archaeological significance.

"It is a unique opportunity for the public to be able to visit and view the evolution of water power use in the textile industry," writes Karen G. Wood in her *Archaeological Survey Of The Presumed Location Of The First Roswell Factory*. Through her research, Wood discovered that the Roswell Mill was one of the earliest cotton mills built in Georgia, and its history offers a unique opportunity to witness the evolution of the textile industry in Georgia for a period spanning 125 years.

> *The archaeologists discovered that the Roswell cotton mill complex is one of the most intact textile sites still in existence in Georgia.*

Demorest, GA: The Early Days

The roots of this small college-town in north Georgia lie in a group of investors from New England immediately following the dark days of the U.S. Civil War. It later produced major league baseball Hall of Famer Johnny Mize.

The present-day site of Demorest, Georgia, isn't exactly what one would describe as a metropolis. Despite all the growth and development to the south toward Atlanta, Demorest maintains a "sleepy" disposition somewhat reminiscent of a small 19th Century mountain town.

In 1889, the "town" was actually little more than a plantation owned by Dr. Henry Rossingnol. It included a two-story summer home – known appropriately enough as "the Rossingnol place." This structure later became one of the first structures comprising Piedmont College.

Eastward, down on Hazel Creek, a sawmill which produced lumber and a gristmill producing flour – both water-powered – existed. Little other industry existed at this site at that time.

In the 1880s, much of north Georgia still bore a strong resemblance to primeval wilderness. It was pierced by a few very rough "corduroy roads" formed by laying saplings horizontally across the roadbed. The saplings provided a short-term measure of stability against the mucky mire for buckboards, stagecoaches and other conveyances, but the slender trees and branches inevitably sank into the quagmire themselves, necessitating the repeated harvesting and laying of new saplings until the "road" was quite bumpy, but at least navigable, *most of the time.*

Servicing the educational needs of the children in and around Rossingnol plantation was a small, one-room schoolhouse which provided education in "readin', writin', and figgerin.'" The site at which this schoolhouse once existed eventually became the vineyard of the late Miss Lillian McKee. The school year consisted of a six-week session in the summer (between cultivation and harvest), and a two to three-month session in the winter, dependent of course upon the disposition of the weather.

"As early as 1890 a group of real estate promoters from a number of northern states in New England and the Midwest, became interested in Habersham County," Ms. McKee once related in an interview. "Its pleasant climate and primitive condition apparently suggested the possibility of a 'prohibition town' with high moral standards to the Northerners."

No one seems to know today exactly how these visitors from up North

This early structure in Demorest eventually became the main building of Piedmont College, photographed here circa 1920s. Piedmont added considerable prestige to the tiny town of Demorest, helping to attract commercial enterprises to the community.

happened upon this remote site. Suffice it to say, that in the 1880s and 1890s, a lot of Northern investors – known euphemistically as "carpet-baggers" by many Southerners – were traversing the South seeking investment opportunities in the countless severely-depressed properties. These countless investment opportunities were available for the having for little more than the taxes owed upon them during those post-war times of abject Southern poverty and despair.

The investors organized what was known as the "Demorest Home Mining and Improvement Company," with a capital stock of $1,500,000. The shares were issued at a par value of $25.00 and in 1890 were sold at $15.00 each. Even though the property was available for virtually nothing, these Northern "investors" were still creatively making use of standard techniques to use "OPM"

("Other People's Money") to gain wealth for themselves.

Demorest achieved its name from W. Jennings Demorest, who was an outspoken "Prohibition" advocate and leader of the 1890s. Mr. Demorest never found the opportunity to respond to the honor by gracing the town of Demorest with his presence. When he died in New York in 1895, the flags of Demorest reportedly floated nevertheless for a week at half-mast.

A good rock dam was built at some point circa 1890s across Camp Creek just to the north of Piedmont College campus. The dam was responsible for flooding the valley, and creating "Lake Demorest" and "South Lake," the latter of which was located above the trestle for the now-historic (and gone since 1961) Tallulah Falls Railroad (TF) which once passed through the town on its 58-mile

The Demorest Cornet Band posed for this photograph at Piedmont College circa 1900. Though it would appear this was an adult group, at least three youngsters also apparently were participants. Entertainments such as this small musical group were highly popular around the turn of the century.

journey from Cornelia, Georgia, to Franklin, North Carolina each day. In earlier times, South Lake reportedly was as large as Lake Demorest, which was it-self twice its present-day size.

Interestingly, the waters behind the dam impounding these lakes built up to such as degree that a steamer named "the Estes" was used to ply the lake wa-ters. The conveyance, surprisingly, could accommodate up to sixty passengers. There were also many row boats for rent-al on the lake as well. From the rear of a substantial "boathouse" were sold ice cream and other confections during the heat of the summer months. It was a classic backdrop – almost Norman Rockwellian in style and appearance.

On the lower side of the dam, a sub-stantial natural spring – strong with iron and sulfur – existed. The water from this spring was claimed to be a better tonic than one could get from a doctor. Spring Park in the center of the city boasted no less than five medicinal springs used by patrons right up until the close of World War I, when Mayor Butler had four of them sealed due to impurities which ap-parently had invaded the water – possi-bly from someone's cesspool or a local pigsty.

The "Prohibition" nature of the town in which its leaders were so in-vested was plainly visible in the Demor-est Mining and Improvement Compa-ny stock which included in its original deeds the provision that *"No spiritu-ous, vinous, fermented or other intoxi-cating liquor shall ever be made, stored, sold, or given away for a beverage; and no gambling or prostitution shall ever be permitted."*

The local ladies of the Women's Christian Temperance Union (WCTU) pledged never *"to employ any child who uses tobacco, and to try to influence merchants not to sell tobacco in any form to minors."* The WCTU had been founded in Cleveland, Ohio, in November of 1874, and was a quite-zealous religious organization whose primary goal was to combat the influence of alcohol on families and society. It had found its way into the north Georgia hinterlands via the in-migration of the Northern investors' wives.

The *Demorest Times* founded in 1890, was edited by F.J. Sibley. Several thousand copies of the newspaper were printed each week and were distributed more for publicity purposes, rather than for local news reporting.

The following advertisement appears to have been framed for its specific appeal to a Northern clientele as it appeared week after week:

Altitude of Demorest 1,600 feet above sea level,

-Very healthy

-No malaria

-Water, pure, cool, freestone water in springs, wells or brooks

-Sunstroke unknown

-The summers are more pleasant than in any state north of the Ohio River

-Snakes not common

-Northern men can work out of doors in the summer in safety.

In the January 9, 1891 issue of the *Demorest Times*, a listing of the town's organizations are provided as follows: *church organizations, 2; church buildings, 1; City Hall, 1; school building, 1 (one room); stores, 10; factories, 10; dwelling houses, 68.*

In a January, 1892 issue, the *Times* reported the population statistics: *June 1889, 9; January 1890, 50; June 1890, 210; January 1891, 450; January 1892, 525.* (The publicity seems to have been effective.)

On June 3, 1892 the *Times* reported that Demorest had only two deaths.

The Tallulah Falls Railroad's Demorest, Georgia Depot was constructed in 1903 by master carpenter George H. Cason. This view, looking north, was photographed prior to the railroad's demise. This depot was once one of the more ornate on the line, perhaps due to the elevated status of Demorest as a "college town." Notice the impressive quality of the entrance porch ceiling trim and balusters around the porch, the roof spires and dormer decorations.

The former Demorest Depot of the Tallulah Falls Railroad was photographed here in 1995. It is one of the few stations still intact from the old line, and, while the railroad was still in existence, it was occasionally used as a film site for major motion pictures such as *"I'd Climb The Highest Mountain"* (1950) starring Susan Hayward, Rory Calhoun, and William Lundigan. This more modern view of this depot again looks north, and shows the depot agent's window, beside which the railroad once passed.

One of these, interestingly, was from *"overstrain,"* owing to the lifting of heavy machinery. The other victim had passed away from *"La Grippe,"* which, of course could not possibly have been contracted locally in healthful Demorest. The unfortunate victim, according to the reputation-sensitive newspaper account, had been *"infected in Ohio."*

Also founded in 1890 (as seems to have been most of the commercial enterprises of the town) was the Demorest Manufacturing Company, which occupied a two and one-half-story building, 40 by 100 feet, which constructed furniture and wagon materials.

Another commercial enterprise – the Machine Works – was later known as the "Demorest Foundry and Machine Works" and was in operation until 1931. The proprietor was E.D. Hendrickson. This business produced machines which fabricated wooden shingles. Due to the plethora of pines in south Georgia (from

which many shingles were traditionally made), shingle factories generated by the Demorest Foundry and Machine Works quickly popped up all over the southern portion of the state.

Ten or fifteen years later the building housing the Demorest Foundry and Machine Works was surprisingly literally carried away by a substantial flood – perhaps from a collapsed impoundment dam. When the business rebuilt, the housing was constructed on high ground north of the dam. The Demorest Broom Works stood on this site more recently.

The Demorest Engraving Works – later known as Stambough Novelty Works – was also established in 1890. Here were made a number of various wooden articles. Starting with wooden napkin rings and other novelties, they expanded to shutters for photographers and folding dental chairs. In the 1890s, it was not uncommon for a physician to sometimes pull teeth. Dentists who focused more on drilling and filling deteriorated teeth would travel around with horse and buggy to ply their trade.

There also seems to have been a demand for folding dental chairs overseas. Missionaries ordered them for use at various stations in the field. In World War II – as metal became scarce – Stambough's dental chairs gained even wider use. Quilting frames and drying racks were among other products manufactured by this concern.

Two hundred feet east of what once was the railroad track for the Tallulah Falls Railroad, the Demorest Bath Works – again, built in 1890 – occupied a building 30 by 100 feet and two stories high in town. At that time, few homes were equipped with bathrooms, and the factory advertised *folding bath tubs that would not disfigure a handsome parlor or any other room in the house."*

A Mr. Norton founded the Demorest Hoop Works – *in 1890*. At first the business thrived, operating night and day, but when the usage of wooden barrels was no longer in vogue, the business expired. Children ultimately became the only users of the now-rusting hoops, rolling them along tirelessly with a stick.

Boom and bust applied to other factories in the town as well. The Demorest Frame and Saw Works (again, founded in 1890!), was operated by McClure and Davol. A Mr. Willet founded the Furniture and Millworks for Builders in 1894. Both of these flourished for only a few years.

In 1891, the Edward Flor Saddle-Tree and Collar Factory was established, with appurtenant glue works. Located on the north side of Hazel Creek, it was powered by water. As business expanded, one small building after another was added.

The Edward Flor Company was one of the longest-surviving original businesses in the town for many years, and may still be in business as of this writing (2023). Paul Carpenter established a broom factory in 1907, with a factory near the Demorest Depot of the old TF. As the railroad died, so also did the broom factory. Interestingly, the old depot building – though silent and forlorn at this writing and with no rail tracks to convey a train any longer – still stands today.

George Cason, with his sisters, moved to Demorest in 1889 to take advantage of the school there. They were among the first 50 settlers. At age 16 Cason began a bicycle repair shop and put himself through school repairing bicycles. In 1903 he contracted for and built Demorest's now long-standing Tallulah Falls Depot building.

The pioneer merchandising es-

Central Avenue in "downtown" Demorest was photographed here circa 1914. The two, three, and four-story commercial structures were quite impressive for what then was a tiny community in the hinterlands of the north Georgia mountains, and indicate the importance of the town's college and growing industries. The four-story Springs Hotel no longer exists today, having long since been erased from the landscape.

tablishments were the grocery-hardware business operated by A.A. Stafford and son; Fisher's Photograph Gallery; Starkweather's Shoe and Drygoods; and Mullinax and Mansfield's Meat and Grocery. To accommodate out-of-town shoppers and travelers, a livery stable (later converted into the Piedmont College classroom building) was constructed next door to the San Toy Hotel (later Commons Hall).

One of Demorest's most popular landmarks is the Johnny Mize Athletic Center and Museum, named for major league baseball's Hall of Famer, Johnny Mize who was a native of Demorest. Mize played baseball at Piedmont when he was first honing his craft, and later spent his professional career with the St. Louis Cardinals, New York Giants, and the New York Yankees. In addition to the museum, Mize's childhood home is a Georgia Historical site and is privately owned today.

Demorest's first mayors were George D. Stone (1890-91), A.A. Stafford (1892), W.H. Van Hise (1893), C.C. Banks (1894) and W.F. Chrisler (1895). A six-mill tax was levied in 1895 to support a public school, and a stock law was voted in. Heretofore gardens and produce-fields had been fenced in, and cows, horses and chickens had been allowed to run free. The local farmers – not impressed with the new responsibility of fencing-in and confining their livestock – were rather incensed by this new law.

A bank building was completed in 1892 with J.S. Green as president. Mr. A. Hampton was cashier. In 1895 the bank was bought by C.E. Hendrickson.

In 1891 the "Northern" Methodist Church completed its sanctuary. This structure still stands as of this writing, interestingly serving today as a residence.

A rear view of the Springs Hotel in Demorest was photographed circa 1920s.

The Baptists also built their church, which was subsequently replaced by a modern edifice.

Ten years later in 1901, the "Southern" Methodist Church was built. This structure also survives and served as the Demorest Woman's Club House in more recent years.

In 1908 the cornerstone was laid for the Congregational Church.

Dr. G.W.D. Patterson, an early doctor, was the first postmaster in the town. His office and home were the frame building on Central Avenue, later to become the first Piedmont College library building.

The history of Piedmont College is a complete story in itself. Almost from the beginning, it has been an integral part of the town, not only as a school, but as a social center where the brass band, the stringed orchestra and the Demorest Chautauqua were held in earlier years. The entire countryside regularly gathered in the old auditorium to witness the dramatic presentations of the students and lyceum performers as well as the many competitions of the basketball teams over the years.

(Grateful appreciation is expressed herewith to the Northeast Georgian newspaper, an article in which provided much of the information used in this article.)

Gainesville and "Environs'" Grand Old Inns From Yesteryear

Once upon a time, in the late 1800s and early 1900s, northeast Georgia – particularly the Gainesville area – was a popular vacation destination in the Southeast. Today, the charred and abandoned ruins of some of these hostelries from yesteryear attest to this fact, and can still be seen if one knows where to look in and around the city.

Though it is an "up and coming" mini-metropolis today – and a far cry from being considered a vacation destination anymore – Gainesville, Georgia, in an earlier life was considered quite the resort, offering a plethora of fine hotels, mountain inns, and "getaways" for summer travelers. In 1888, the city published a 68-page promotional piece which prominently described the mountain town as *"The Great Health Resort of the South."*

Though not a modest claim, it, nevertheless was not a claim without some merit either. It pointed out the area's healthful climate, its assorted varieties of sparkling clean, pure, and "healthful" mountain water, excellent cuisine, entertaining activities, and many other qualities which were attractive to vacationers of that era.

It, however, was the quality and variety of the hotels, inns, spas, and other accommodations – particularly those

with healthful medicinally-beneficial natural mountain springs – upon which the publication (and the public) most often focused. Many of the destinations had been constructed at the sites of mineral springs which the publication stated: *"were long used and prized by the Indians, and since the settlement of the country by Whites, they have been resorted to annually by invalids from all portions of the South."*

These claims, for the most part, were not frivolous either, since many of the refreshing natural springs put forth waters containing an array of healthful minerals. Even the clay soils adjacent to some of the springs had been accumulating these minerals since time immemorial, and could therefore be utilized for other healthful medicinal purposes. The native Indians were not unaware of these qualities, and White settlers eventually also learned of their value.

Aside from the mountain springs

Photographed circa 1900, the Arlington Hotel was built in 1882, and was located at the corner of Main and Spring Streets in Gainesville. It was purchased by J.W. Hunt in the 1920s, becoming popularized as the Dixie Hunt Hotel. This hotel was basically destroyed by the terrible Gainesville tornado of 1936. Some portions, however – particularly the basement sections – were still serviceable after the tornado, and were retained when a new Dixie Hunt Hotel was built upon the site in 1937. In recent years, this structure was renamed "Hunt Tower," and still exists as of this writing (2022). It is the only historic hotel remaining in downtown Gainesville today. (Photo courtesy of GA Dept of Archives & History, Atlanta)

and attractive resorts, much of northeast Georgia offered the naturally cool and refreshing conditions favored by vacationers of that era, but it was the grand hotels which had been constructed at these sites – with all their charms, social graces, excellent foods, multitudinous activities and varied amenities – which were also valued by these vacationing travelers who came in a steady stream in the late 1800s.

There were four great "in-town" hotels in Gainesville in the early 1900s. They formed a type of recreational community tied together with a delightful, almost ornamental, street-car line.

THE ARLINGTON, in the very center of Gainesville, was an elegantly-furnished three-story brick building that could accommodate 200 guests. *"This hotel is the great center of the social amusements during the season, having a delightful ball room and a splendid band at the service of the young folks every evening,"* the brochure intones. Built originally in 1882, the Arlington was renamed the Dixie Hunt Hotel in the 1920s and was basically destroyed by the terrible Gainesville tornado of 1936. Interestingly, some portions, particularly the basement sections were still serviceable after the tornado, and were retained when a new Dixie Hunt Hotel was built upon the site in 1937. In recent

The Hudson House, built in 1887, was located on the northeast corner of North Main and Washington streets. It, reportedly, was demolished in 1959 for construction of the F.W. Woolworth Co. building, so it apparently survived the 1936 Gainesville Tornado.

years, this structure was renamed "Hunt Tower," and still exists as of this writing (2023). It is the only historic hotel remaining in downtown Gainesville today.

THE PIEDMONT HOTEL was owned and operated by Confederate General James Longstreet, described as *"Lee's warhorse."* This hostelry was noted as *"cool and comfortable"* in an age that knew no air-conditioning. *"Broad verandas encircle the entire building,"* its literature added. Though most of this hotel disappeared long ago, one wing has survived, and may be viewed today not far from the town square.

THE HUNT HOUSE, which could handle 125 guests, intrigued visitors with its *"electric call bells and other conveniences of a first-class house."* By the 1920s, most cities and towns in America had received electricity from either privately-owned or municipally-provided utility companies, but in the late 1800s in the rural South, it was practically unknown, so this "amenity" added immeasurably to the attraction of The Hunt House.

THE HUDSON HOUSE, like The Arlington, was also located on Gainesville's town square. *"It has double parlors, large, airy rooms, with accommodations for 100 guests,"* its promotional literature boasted.

Within a short drivable distance outside of Gainesville, there also once were numerous mountain inns and boarding houses. Some of these were near enough that they were serviced by the city's street-car line. Even those accommodations farther away in northeast Georgia in places like Lakemont, Clayton, Dillard, and Rabun Gap were easily accessible via the scenic Tallulah Falls Railroad.

Within the near vicinity of virtually all of these accommodations, some type of clear mountain spring and its associated activities were almost always available and used as a drawing card for guests. Indeed, Gainesville itself was originally known as "Mule Camp Springs" for this very reason.

Some of these accommodations outside but near to Gainesville were Gower Spring Resort, and, just a few miles further, Clermont to the north. A few miles beyond Clermont, Porter Springs Resort outside Dahlonega earned quite the reputation for hospitality as well in the early 1900s.

GOWER SPRING and its associated resort hotel were once located at what today is a commercial site on the left as one travels out Thompson Bridge Road toward Dahlonega. Though the Gower Spring site was "outside town"

when constructed, it, of course, is today within the city limits of Gainesville. The Gower Spring Hotel once existed upon the crown of the ridge near the curve of Green Street Circle in an area occupied today by residential homes.

Some archival issues of the old *Gainesville Eagle* newspaper – forerunner of the present-day *Gainesville Daily Times*, report a portion of the history of this former resort destination. The June 16, 1871, issue of the paper states:

"We learn that a Chalybeate Spring has recently been discovered on the lands of Dr. T.C. Gower (a son of E.N. Gower) which is located about a mile and a quarter north of the city. . . it is pronounced by those who have visited as of most excellent quality," the paper announced.

Three months later, the paper reported that even celebrated individuals of that day were patronizing and

Gower Spring Resort, built in the 1880s, was once located between Green Street Circle and Thompson Bridge Road. The spring was in the vicinity of what today (2022) is a large shopping center. The artist responsible for this rendering of the site is unknown today. Green Street, which at that time would have been little more than a dirt trail, is indicated in the foreground.

Built circa 1845, White Sulfur Springs Hotel reached its zenith in the mid-1920s, and was exceptionally popular as a mountain resort. It went into receivership during the 1929 Stock Market Crash, never to re-emerge. It was strangely consumed by fire in 1933.

interested in Gower Spring Resort: *"former Governor Joseph E. Brown spent a day or two in our city, and while here, purchased the valuable property known as 'the Gower place' on the street leading to Clark's and Thompson's bridges."* The lot, according to the report, contained about seven acres, and *"is one of the most handsome locations about our place."*

This news article added that Gov. Brown also purchased 125 acres of land lying one mile and a quarter north of town. However, a search of the deed records in Hall County strangely does not reveal any such property ever in the ownership by Gov. Brown.

Whatever the circumstances, the *Eagle* stated in January, 1877, that Mr. Gower was *"erecting a commodious hotel at his celebrated Mineral Spring, near the northern limit of the city, and is*

making considerable progress, in spite of bad weather." The hotel was to have been ready for the opening of the summer season.

The spring site, denoted originally by several large rock out-croppings, apparently was located just off the circle across from what in recent times has been a shopping area. Though the spring undoubtedly remains at this site today, its specific location appears to have been lost over time. Since the rate of flow from the spring was measured at little more than one gallon per minute, it would not have been difficult for the spring to have been re-routed through culverts to a new outlet (as was the case with Mule Camp Spring near the Gainesville Train Depot) and thus lost to visibility at the original Gower Spring site.

Farther northward above Dahlone-

The Piedmont Hotel was located on Main Street, approximately three blocks from the Southern Depot in Gainesville. It was owned by Confederate Gen. James Longstreet (CSA) who had retired to Gainesville following the U.S. Civil War. A portion of one wing of this structure, "rediscovered" by surprise in the 1990s, still exists as of this writing (2023). (Photo courtesy of GA Dept. of Archives & History, Atlanta)

ga, the PORTER SPRINGS RESORT held sway. Discovered by land agent and Methodist minister Joseph McKee in 1868, this highly-charged mineral spring apparently had also been in great use by the early native inhabitants. In the process of removing the accumulated mud and debris to open up the spring for better access, McKee discovered a wall of thin rocks forming a box around the spring which he stated *"would seem to indicate that the spring had been used for medical or other purposes perhaps a thousand years ago."*

Several years later, after its development into a summer attraction, Porter Springs resort soon became noted throughout the Southeast for its superb and healthful cuisine. A large U-shaped hotel was constructed with long front porches which opened onto a beautifully-landscaped quadrangular court where peacocks freely roamed.

The structure which housed the ballroom and dining room was connected to the main building by a covered elevated gangway. A small orchestral group consisting of a violinist, bassist, and harp player serenaded guests with music during meals and at dances held nightly.

Porter Springs soon became noted throughout the Southeast for its superb and healthful cuisine. A garden, vineyard and orchard kept the kitchen supplied with fresh produce. A herd of thoroughbred Jersey cows which were maintained nearby supplied milk, butter and beef as needed.

The actual spring at Porter Springs was sometimes referred to as "Bethesda Springs" or "Cedar Mountain Springs," but most people referred to it simply as "Porter Springs" after the original owner of the property. Interestingly, Cedar Mountain – and undoubtedly the spring at "Porter Springs" – became a portion of the legend of the Indian princess "Trahlyta," whose fabled grave may still be viewed today at the intersection of U.S. Highway 19 and GA Highway 60 nearby, a site known today as "Stone Pile Gap."

It was WHITE SULFUR SPRINGS resort which undoubtedly earned the Gainesville area its late 1800s-era national reputation. It was located in the rolling wooded hills six miles north of town. Constructed prior to the U.S. Civil War, it attracted the rich and socially prominent from throughout the South, and even had its own private railway station on the Southern Railroad. White Sulfur Springs remained in operation until the stock market crash of 1929 which ruined so many businesses and investors, including the owner of White Sulfur resort. In 1933, the by-then abandoned facility sadly met the same fate as so many of these fabled structures, burning to the ground.

In its day, however, White Sulfur Springs resort thrived. The hotel itself was large, with wide porches to catch the mountain breezes, and cottages dotted shady avenues on the landscaped grounds. The baths and swimming pool were said to have been constructed after a Roman design. The dining room was described as splendid, with ample sterling silver and fresh flower arrangements. And the food – well – it was said to have been unequalled in the travel destination industry.

White Sulfur was, in a word, "sumptuous," as far as accommodations of the 1800s were concerned. In the afternoons, a band played music, and in the evenings, dances were held in the hotel ballroom. And due to the convenient access to the otherwise remote accommodations via the Southern Railroad, the professional bands providing musical entertainment were booked from places as far away as New York City.

Other "distractions" included a ten-pin alley for bowling; a billiards parlor inside the inn; and back outside, tennis courts provided accommodations for the more athletically-inclined.

And while guests undoubtedly came for the social activities, refreshing mountain climate, delicious dining delicacies and so much more, they also took advantage of the *"curative waters"* which reportedly greatly relieved *"rheumatism, blood poisoning, dyspepsia, and other complaints."* How *"curative waters"* could be expected to cure "blood poisoning" is unknown today, but there was even a resident physician in-house during the season.

In short, the travel and tourism industry flourished in the Gainesville area from the late 1800s until the late 1920s, and the town's hotels gained a wide reputation and following as a summer playground and as a romantic honeymoon destination.

A combination of events and trends ultimately ushered in the demise of the heydays of Gainesville's great hotels:

For one thing, the scientific community discovered the cause of malaria – a disease which historically had motivated residents to flee their homes in the swampy coastal and lowland areas which had become associated with the debilitating sickness during the summer months. When it was learned that mosquitoes were the carriers of the malady and that they existed not only in the lowlands but in the mountains as well, some of the luster for travel to the uplands was dulled.

Paved highways and advances in the automobile provided an alternative to rail transportation, a circumstance which caused many more destinations to be within reach of the average traveler. After the *Great Depression* either crippled or forced many of Gainesville's hotels into foreclosure, travel patterns and social customs were altered so dramatically that the city's grand old hotels were never able to recover.

And finally – air conditioning. The cooling confines of affordable air-conditioned rooms caused destinations such as the ocean and beaches and places such as Florida to become very competitive with the mountain destinations.

Today, fleeting remnants of these fine old hotels are still visible in the Gainesville area if one knows where to look. And in the countryside, an occasional traveler or new area resident may also still chance upon the charred ruins of the abandoned mountain resorts of yesteryear, totally unaware of the degree of refinement which once existed in the wilds of north Georgia.

Historic Clermont, GA and the Gainesville-Northwestern RR

It was constructed as a transportation medium for the timber being harvested in northeast Georgia, and became a way of life for residents along the line from 1912 to 1935. When the seeming inexhaustible timber had all been harvested by the early 1930s, the little mountain short-line was necessary no more, and went out of business. When it disappeared, a way of life disappeared with it.

Just as occurred in the 1950s with a sister line – the Tallulah Falls Railroad – the Gainesville-Northwestern Railroad (G&NW) between Gainesville and Robertstown, Georgia, eventually depleted all the products which had originally given it life in 1912, and literally put itself out of business by 1933. The rails were pulled up and sold for scrap iron to Japan and the rights-of-way reverted back to ownership by the local landowners. It was a sad day for residents all up and down the picturesque little rail line into the mountains – but it had been really good while it lasted.

In the years preceding World War I, a group of businessmen had realized the value of the immense stock of forest products available in the northeast Georgia mountains. This same timber products industry also spawned a tiny community which would later grow to a far-greater prominence still in existence today – Helen, Georgia.

The Gainesville-Northwestern was incorporated on February 9, 1912, primarily to provide a viable and dependable mode of transportation for the timber products being harvested in northeast Georgia, and the wood products being produced from this timber by Byrd-Matthews Lumber Company in the present-day Helen vicinity. Passenger, freight, and mail service were provided by the G&NW which ran daily from Gainesville to Robertstown, passing thru numerous whistle- and flag-stops along the way.

Byrd-Matthews Lumber Company was one of the largest lumber mills east of the Mississippi in its day. It produced thousands of board feet of lumber every week which was shipped to Gainesville. After reaching that town, the lumber was transferred to other railroads

The first post office at the community of "Dip," (later renamed "Clermont") was in the home of Mr. and Mrs. William Harvey Keith. The man on the horse in this photograph is Mr. Josiah W. Blackwell, the first mail carrier for the area.

for distribution throughout the United States as well as to a number of foreign countries. Lumber production was big business in north Georgia where virgin timber was still abundant in the early 1900s, and railroads such as the Gainesville-Northwestern Railroad were vital in the effort to harvest this timber.

The "passenger" aspect of the Gainesville-Northwestern Railroad featured what was known as "an excursion service" to and from Gainesville to and from Robertstown (above Helen), and also provided freight and postal service to these areas as well. The run began at the old Gainesville Depot (which still stands as of this writing in 2023) and made stops at Bradford Street Station (removed long ago), New Holland (also gone), Clark (gone), Autry (gone), Dewberry (gone), Brookton

(the ruins of which survived until just recently), Clermont (long gone), County Line (gone), Mossy Creek Campground (long gone), Meldean (gone), Cleveland (long gone), Asbestos (gone), Mt. Yonah (gone), Nacoochee (still exists as of this writing in 2023), Helen (gone), and Robertstown (also gone). Gainesville, Brookton, Clermont, Meldean, Cleveland, Nacoochee, Helen, and Robertstown were what was known as "agency stations," and the train made regular stops at them. The others were known as "flag stops," (where stops were made only if the train was "flagged").

Clermont had existed as a community prior to the construction of the G&NW, springing up in part due to the town's strategic location on an aged travel route for traditional mountain products taken to market each year in Gainesville. When the railroad was constructed through the tiny town, Clermont gained a prime supply line and became a market destination from the more heavily populated cities of Gainesville and Atlanta to the south, factors which further enhanced its growth and fostered the commerce which sprang to life in Clermont from 1912 to the mid-1930s.

Another growth catalyst in Clermont which preceded the railroad was Chattahoochee High School, established around 1890. It became a Baptist Church-supported school which belonged to the Mercer University system of preparatory schools in 1919. It was a four-year school, with records indicating it produced its first graduating class in 1906.

Educational institutions of this nature were few in number in the north Georgia mountains at that time, and facilities such as Chattahoochee High became a strong incentive for the relocation of families interested in higher education for their children.

"My father and mother moved us to Clermont specifically so we could have the opportunity to go to a nine-month school," said the late Essie Hudgins Jordan, who was a graduate of Chattahoochee High. She was also a member of the faculty during the 1923-24 school year.

Miss Essie's father, James Zacheus Hudgins, had moved their family from Sugar Hill in South Hall County to Clermont in North Hall in the spring of 1913 (per Dorothy Hudgins Shaw) when she was thirteen years old. "Despite the fact that it meant wholly relocating a home and a profitable family business, it was important to Mother and Father that we children receive a good education," she added.

Miss Essie's beautiful old family home – built by her father in 1913 – still stands (as of this writing in 2023) on

King Street in Clermont. It is one of a number of elegant turn-of-the-century homes which highlight the architectural beauty and scenic attractiveness of the town even today. While it was being constructed in 1913, the Hudgins family rented a home near Wauka Mountain.

In 1913, Clermont and the surrounding counties were still a very sparsely populated area, a type of pioneer country in many ways. "Father had a general store beside the railroad there in the center of town," Mrs. Jordan continued. "Clermont was a wonderful place for a child to grow up, and I had a large family – six brothers and six sisters.

"All the stories you read about pioneer life which describe the little general store where saddles, sunbonnets, barrels of apples, cheeses, dry goods, traps, and all the other staples of life in the mountains in that day and time, are very descriptive of what was sold in Father's store," she smiled. "On cold winter days, men gathered around an old pot-bellied stove to play checkers. 'Father loved to play checkers,' she stated in a conspiratorial whisper.

The original Concord Baptist Church was photographed here sometime between 1882 and 1919. A brick structure which still stands replaced this building in the early 1920s. (Photo courtesy of Mr. Ralph Hampton, Gainesville)

"Chattahoochee High School was a boarding school at that time," Miss Essie added. "The dormitory which housed both girls and boys was on the campus grounds. It had space for a music room and a library, as well as an apartment set aside for the school superintendent. Some of the students rented small cottages, going home on weekends and in the summer, when school was not in session."

The 1923-24 *"Annual Announcement"* booklet from Chattahoochee High offers a glimpse back in time at the school. It describes the institution as: *". . . located near the little town of Clermont, on the Gainesville-North Western Railroad, 16 miles from Gainesville.... This puts Chattahoochee in a few minutes of Gainesville in one direction, and a few minutes of the mountains going north. For several miles in three directions, may be seen broad fields of corn and cotton and small grain. Much of this plateau section is yet wooded....Clermont is a thriving town, built up since the school was established. The town gives many advantages: one bank, post office, hotel, drug store, furniture store, five general mercantile stores, express office, two blacksmith establishments, and a telephone exchange."*

As might be expected, social codes at the school were strict. Boys and girls were expected to refrain from all communication with each other except *"that which ordinary courtesy demands."* Boys and girls were not allowed the freedom of the town, except by special permission. They were expected to remain in their rooms at night. Boys were required to *"abstain from smoking cigarettes, playing cards, profanity, intoxicating liquors and the keeping of firearms."*

Before the railroad came through,

Griffin Brothers' Cotton Warehouse on King Street was photographed circa 1926. The Gainesville & Northwestern Railroad which supplied Clermont is ever so slightly visible to the right rear of this building. Warehouse owner John T. Griffin (far right, foreground) was remembered by one elderly resident as a stern disciplinarian.

This rare photograph shows Chattahoochee High School, an early education center in northeast Georgia. It once stood across the highway from Concord Baptist Church in Clermont.

and before Chattahoochee High School was constructed, Clermont's primary claim to fame had been its resort identity. The name *"Clermont"* is a shortened version of "Clear Mountains." The scenic location of the town in the shadow of nearby Wauka Mountain and the beginnings of the Blue Ridge Mountains in north Georgia, led to the construction of the Clermont Hotel in 1911-12. This structure, now over 110 years old, still stands on the old town square as of 2023.

Though not luxurious by any means, the Clermont Hotel was elegant for its day. The Gainesville-Northwestern Railroad passed right beside it and had its depot across the street. A tennis court (apparently one of the first in the north Georgia area) was available to the rear of the hotel, for guests.

Up toward what then was the tiny community of Helen, Mr. T.B. Henderson owned a general merchandise store next to the G&NW's Nacoochee Station. Both it and the Nacoochee Station still exist and are original to the community, being well over 100 years old as of 2023. *(Henderson's former General Store is the old brick building at the intersection of Highways 75 and 17, near the Indian mound. The former Nacoochee Station building stands across Highway 75 from the old general store building.)* Mr. Henderson's daughter, Mary Lula Henderson Davidson, provided the following descriptive details concerning early life in turn-of-the-century Nacoochee:

"The Nacoochee Post Office was located in the general store and my father was postmaster there. He also served as rail agent at the Nacoochee Station. His duties included the issuance of tickets and the posting of freight bills. Most of the merchandise in his store came in by rail from Athens or Gainesville.

"Father was one of the few persons in the area who owned an automobile.

The late Essie Hudgins (Jordan) was photographed in 1923 following her graduation from Georgia Normal and Industrial College in Milledgeville, Georgia. Mrs. Jordan was one of the first female faculty members (1923-1924) of Chattahoochee High School in Clermont, Georgia, and an early graduate of the school.

Sometimes passengers coming in on the train would need transportation to one of the 'resorts' in the area or to a friend or relative's house. After arriving at Nacoochee Station, my brother - Bon - would drive the travelers to their destinations."

Mrs. Davidson also described how she helped her father in the store, post office and at the little railroad station. She remembers that in the store, they sold groceries, hardware, men's, women's and children's clothing, seeds and fertilizer, all mostly delivered by rail. She said that Mr. L.G. Hardman *(whose beautiful old home also still stands near the intersection of Hwy. 75 and 17, and was originally constructed by Civil War veteran Col.*

James Hall Nichols) shipped butter and milk from his dairy by rail to Gainesville, and Mr. "Simp" Logan shipped asbestos from his asbestos mine by railroad.

Mr. Henry Davidson, who became the husband of Miss Mary Lula Henderson, was one of the many who helped to build the railroad from Gainesville to Robertstown. His brother, Mr. George Davidson, was an engineer on the train and Mr. Paul Westmoreland was fireman.

The railroad brought many visitors to the White County area. Major resorts included the Alley House *(still in existence as the Old Sautee Inn today)* in Nacoochee; the Henderson Hotel in Cleveland (now long disappeared); and the Mitchell Mountain Ranch (also long gone) in Helen.

The Gainesville-Northwestern continued its 37-mile run from Gainesville to Robertstown until circa 1932. Shortly thereafter, when the once-inexhaustible supply of virgin timber had been depleted almost entirely, the railroad, with its life-blood gone, eventually became insolvent and service was discontinued. The tracks were taken up; the railroad rights-of-way reverted back to private ownership, and the Gainesville-Northwestern Railroad disappeared forever from the Hall and White County landscapes.

Chattahoochee High School Graduates (1906-1923)

1906 - J.T. Miller

1907 - Grover Miller

1908 - A.S. Kytle

1909 - George, Gearin, W.C. Grindle, C.W. Henderson, Fred Staton, W.L. Walker

1910 - H.W. Keith, U.A. Lawson, E.B. O'Kelley, M.K. Staton, Inez Spencer, Ruth Waters

Essie Carroll Hudgins (Jordan) sits (far right) with two of her sisters at the home built by her father, James Zacheus Hudgins, in Clermont, Hall County, Georgia, in 1913. This beautiful home still stands (as of this writing in 2023) on King Street in Clermont.

1911 - F.L. Brown. B.J. Head, H.G. Hudgins, U.S. Lancaster, H.L. Lawson, R.H. Thomas, Minnie Head, Exer Head, Lola Staton.

1912 - H.E. Buffington, A.B. Eberhart, Claude Grindle, Hubert Haynes, W.H. Lord, B.H. Robinson, Beulah Hudgins, Vivian Jarrard, Liccie Payne, Lillie Payne, Nellie Whelchel

1913 - W.T. Evans, Charles E. Hawkins, W.P. Pettyjohn, W.A. Whitmire, John Haynes, A.B. Keith, C.H. Keith, F.P. Lockhart, Lena Hudgins, Mary Hulsey, Florence Ragan, Pink Standridge

1914 - C.J. Broom, H.T. Brookshire, O.G. Lancaster, G.F. Tyner, Salena Jarrard, Anna Belle Lockhart.

1915 - C.C. Jarrard, J.A. Meaders,

M.D. Reed, Irene Bailey, Josephine Grogan, Chester Head, Iris Maddox.

1916 - Chesley Bennett, Harry Garrison, Richard Hawkins, Carl Lancaster, Elmira Grogan, Daisy Hudgins, Ethel Roark

1917 - W.E. Barnwell, R.L. Carter, Ernest Hulsey, J.L. Keith, D.T. Lawson, Y.W. Peck, H.H. Peyton, Beulah Greer, Myrtle Haynes, Ada Highsmith, Ethleen Jarrard, Florida Mauldin, Willie Staton.

1918 - Una Abercrombie, Laurie Truelove, Maude Logan, Esther Langford, Lillie Mac Culpepper, Annie Mae Haynes, Agnes Roark, Etta Chandler, Henry Reed, Clarence Puckett, Glenn Cooper, Edward Brown, Escoe Logan, Garnett Keith.

1919 - Valera Bowen, Bertie Mae

Miller, Lillie Head, Sallie Hix, Hoke Grier, Homer Keith, Roy Martin, Bertha Waters, Essie Hudgins, Idell Haynes, Essie Tanner, Hester Tanner, Lucile Roark, Dewey Patten, Frank Cain, Howard Poole, Vassie Keith, Nell Whitmire.

1920 - Ernest Abercrombie, Clifton Bryson, Wallis Bennett, D.T. Buice, Nita Catlett, Callie Chandler, Adele Head, Vallie Hulsey, Floyd Hendrix, Avie Forrester, Jewell Keith, D.W. Lord, Ralph Miller, Clyde Maddox, Russell Marlow, Nellie Mae Pierce, Charlie Staton, Adelia Joe Staton, Clarence Walker, Julius Whitmire, Paul Whitmore, Edgar Hulsey.

1921 - Jarnet Carruth, Bonnie Carruth, Hugh Brice, Annie Brice, Henry Logan, Hortense Delong, Mabel Haynes, Mae Grant, Lee Grant, Herschel McGee, Seaborn Gilstrap, Y.D. Jones, Fred Moore, Ralph Thompson, J. Henry Lackey, Albert Martin, Nell

Christopher, Mary Brown, Eugenia Rogers, Maudelle Pierce, Sylvia Gailey, Mary Elder, Price Bowen, Ruth Head, Michael McNeal, Texas Wallace, Herschel Davis, Laura Belle Culpepper, June Murphy, Ralph Murphy, Pearl Truelove, Pink Culpepper.

1922 - Ruth Crawford, Lee Buice, David Hudgins, Lucas Griffin, Willie Meaders, Cladith Simpson, Mozelle Marlowe, Hassie Mae Whitmire, Cordia Mullinax, Gertrude Kytle, Clarence Walker.

1923 - Cary Adams, Ernest Brown, Ralph Buffington, Lunie Mae Coker, Winnie Chandler, Kelsey Delong, Otis Dyer, Birdie Gailey, J.E. Grizzle, Clyde Hudgins, Mae Hooper, Mary Belle Jackson, Nina Keith, Vera Keith, Cora Belle Lancaster, Myrtle Moore, Fred Orr, Turner Quillian, Emma Haynes, Marilu Hudgins, Maggie Smith, Tony Walker.

Clermont (meaning "Clear Mountains") once thrived as a tourist resort and was located on the Gainesville-Northwestern Railroad which greatly aided in its access to travelers. The Clermont Hotel (pictured) which now is well over 100 years old, was built in 1912, and still stands as of this writing (2023). The Gainesville & Northwestern Railroad track once existed just to the right of the hotel in this photo, and passed through the town square. (Photo by Olin Jackson)

The Mysterious Disappearance Of Old Gower Spring Resort

Though occupied now by suburban homes and a commercial shopping center, a site in northwest Gainesville which strangely disappeared was once a thriving tourist resort.

Lakes and other bodies of water have long played an active role in the history of Gainesville and Hall County. Of course, today, it's Lake Lanier which is the focus of recreation in the area, but at one time early in the county's history, it was the numerous natural springs which attracted visitors – and they came in droves too.

One such spring, interestingly, was located only a block or two off the present-day public square in Gainesville, and was called "Mule Camp Springs." Though most people are not aware of it today, this spring still exists, covered over and flowing through culverts beneath the city streets.

In its day, Mule Camp Springs was a vital source of clean unadulterated water upon which area residents and thirsty travelers alike could count. The pioneer community which sprang up at this site became the first county seat in Hall County, and later evolved into the community of Gainesville.

Indians, mule traders and travelers alike all once "pow-wowed" and camped around this spring, and present-day "Spring Street" in Gainesville earned its identity from this site. The healthful climate and water of Mule Camp Springs gradually attracted more and more visitors in the summers, and the area eventually became known as a resort center.

One off-shoot of this resort concept in the Gainesville area was Gower Spring. Following the discovery of a healthful spring there, a large hotel was built at the site, and it was reported that *"the hundreds upon hundreds of pale-faced emaciated invalids who came to the site returned to their homes with rosy cheeks."*

Gower Spring and its associated resort hotel were once located at what today is a commercial site on the left as one travels out Thompson Bridge Road toward Dahlonega on the outskirts of town. The hotel itself was located on the crown of the ridge near the curve of Green Street Circle in the neighborhood occupied today by residential homes.

The spring apparently was located in an area denoted by several large rock outcroppings just off the circle across from what more recently has been a commercial shopping area. Though the spring undoubtedly remains at this site, its specific location has been lost over time.

The illustration above depicts the 1880s-era Gower Springs Resort – named for E.N. Gower Sr. – which once existed between Green Street Circle and Thompson Bridge Road in northwest Gainesville. The mountain inn was built near the crown of the ridge in this vicinity above a popular freshwater spring. It enjoyed direct transportation facilities provided by the Gainesville & Dahlonega Electric Railway Line which passed nearby. The inn, however, was short-lived, disappearing only a few years after its construction.

Since the rate of flow from the spring was measured at little more than one gallon per minute, it would not have been difficult for the spring to have been re-routed through culverts to a new outlet (such as was the case with Mule Camp Spring) and thus lost to visibility at the original Gower Spring site.

The history of the Gower Spring resort is interesting. Mr. Eben N. Gower, who migrated to Gainesville from Pendleton District, South Carolina, was reported to have been one of the prominent citizens of early Gainesville, and possibly did more to shape the early destiny of the city than most of his other pioneering contemporaries.

Long before the U.S. Civil War, when Gainesville was little more than a post village, Mr. Gower manufactured horse and mule-drawn wagons and carriages at the site, ushering in the advent of commerce for Gainesville. He eventually realized the true wealth of the area at that time existed in its natural resources, which were virtually unknown to the outside world.

After analyzing the mineral waters at the spring northwest of town, the entrepreneur built Gower Spring Hotel, and advertised it as a summer resort *"where the purest and most exhilarating air and mineral water most conducive to health, can be found."* He was not wanting for customers either – at least initially.

Some archival issues of the old *Gainesville Eagle* newspaper – forerunner of the present-day *Gainesville Daily Times*, report a portion of the history of Gower Spring. The June 16, 1871, issue of the paper states:

"We learn that a Chalybeate Spring has recently been discovered on the lands of Dr. T.C. Gower (a son of E.N. Gower) which is located about a mile and a quarter north of the city. . . it is pronounced by those who have visited as of most excellent quality," the paper announced.

Three months later, the paper reported that even celebrated individuals of that day were patronizing and interested in Gower Spring Resort: *"Former Governor Joseph E. Brown spent a day or two in our city, and while here, purchased the valuable property known as 'the Gower place' on the street leading to Clark's and Thompson's bridges."* The lot, according to the report, contained about seven acres, and *"is one of the most handsome locations about our place."*

This news article added that Gov. Brown also purchased 125 acres of land lying one and one-quarter miles north of town. However, a search of the deed records in Hall County strangely does not reveal any such property ever in the ownership by Gov. Brown.

Whatever the circumstances, the *Eagle* stated in January, 1877, that Mr.

With the advent of electricity, the age of the "electric" railway soon came to fruition in Gainesville. Utilizing the existing portion of the defunct "Gainesville & Dahlonega Railroad" an "electric railway system" which passed near Gower Spring, was operated for a short while. It provided easy rail transportation to the popular site. An 1880 issue of the **Gainesville Eagle** newspaper noted: *". . . . The Gainesville street railroad runs to the Spring from the Air Line railroad."*

Gower was *"erecting a commodious hotel at his celebrated Mineral Spring, near the northern limit of the city, and is making considerable progress, in spite of bad weather."* The hotel was to have been ready for the opening of the summer season.

But all did not remain "peaches and cream." Barely three years later, in 1880, an advertisement appeared in the **Eagle** which, rather than promoting the hotel and all its amenities, instead offered the property for sale. The ad indicated that if the building was not sold, it would be for rent to an early applicant:

"The Celebrated Gower Spring, located just outside the city limits of Gainesville, Ga. The best chalybeate water in Georgia. Hundreds who have drank (sic) of the water can add testimony as to its medical virtue. The hotel has 30 rooms;

the house is all plastered and in good condition; built three years ago; fine mountain view; on the place is a carriage and blacksmith shop, stables, servant houses, etc. 120 acres of land, about 10 in cultivation; a fine young peach orchard. The Gainesville street railroad runs to the Spring from the Air Line railroad. This is a chance for a good investment as this is one of the finest summer resorts in the country. . . Terms made on application to A.B.C. Dorsey & Co., Real Estate Agent, Gainesville, Ga."

It is not clear today exactly what transpired during the 1880s, but whatever the circumstances, E.N. Gower was successful in divesting himself of the resort by the late 1880s. A booklet entitled **Health Resorts of the South**, published in 1888, stated that Gainesville was the gateway to many famous resorts, and *"one mile from Gainesville, and reached by the horse cars, is the noted Gower Spring, owned by P.B. Holzendorff. The hotel stands upon an eminence above the spring, surrounded by oak trees; the house is new and well-kept."*

The resort had all the makings of a successful operation in the early-going. As stated in the above newspaper advertisement, it was even serviced for a short period of time by a rail line which had originally been built for the by-then defunct "Gainesville & Dahlonega Railroad." When financing for the development of the railroad proved not to be forthcoming, the rail line which had nonetheless been laid between downtown Gainesville and the Chattahoochee River was converted to use as an electric railway, made functional by electricity generated by water-power at the nearby dam across the river. An early newspaper report described the rail line servicing Gower Spring as follows: *"The power now used in the city of Gainesville comes from the dam on the Chestatee River, 15 miles northwest of the city. This dam is no little one, itself. It is owned by the Gainesville and Dahlonega Electric Railway Company, and furnishes 1200 horsepower, this company being a twin companion of the North Georgia Electric Company* (which also furnished electric power for Gainesville via a dam and generator at the Chattahoochee River near present-day Riverside Military Academy), *General Warner being at the head of both.*

In the spring of 1896, the local newspaper reported that recreation accommodations had been added, or at least upgraded at Gower Spring: *"The grounds are being improved and beautified. Two dancing pavilions have been erected - one 24 feet by 42 feet, and another 40 feet by 40 feet. A ten-pin alley and tennis courts are being constructed and a bandstand has been erected where the Gainesville brass band and orchestra will discourse sweet music several evenings a week. A handsome ice cream salon has been filled up and a soda fount (sic) will operate."*

And then, for reasons unknown today, the bottom literally fell out of operations at the resort. A *Geological Survey of Georgia, Bulletin No. 20*, by State Geologist S.W. McCallie in 1913 paints a whole different perspective of the once highly-touted and vibrant resort. It, in fact, announces the property as demised: *"Gower Spring, Hall County, located on the Gainesville-Dahlonega public road only a few hundred yards from the corporate limits of Gainesville . . . A few years ago, this spring was a very popular resort, but since the destruction of the hotel nearby, the spring has been neglected and it is now but little used. The flow is about a gallon per minute."*

The method and actual moment of the ultimate demise of now-historic Gower Spring Resort are not known today. The structure possibly fell victim to one of the tornadoes which have tormented Hall County over the years, or, perhaps it was razed by a fire, which also regularly victimized the wooden hotels and inns of that day. The actual circumstances are a mystery today.

E.N. Gower mercifully never lived to witness the total destruction of his beloved resort. He passed away in 1897. Mrs. Gower, according to reports, continued to reside near the spring until her death a year later in 1898.

Some recent reports have indicated that a few fruit trees remain at this site even today – likely as not hold-overs from the resort's orchard – a fitting final tribute to the bloom of life which once existed at this site.

The Mysterious Disappearance Of Old Mule Camp Spring

*It sprang up as a rest-stop around a vibrant natural spring
at the convergence of two ancient Indian trails. Over the years,
as the community of Gainesville grew, the historic spring from
which the town drew its original name was covered over and
obscured by new construction and forgotten. Today – at least
for the present – the spring has been revealed once again.*

A traveler to Mule Camp Spring circa 1799 wrote *"The action was lively but relaxed at Mule Camp Springs. There was laughter. The aroma of cooking food. Serious business talk, and spirited discussion about a rawhide jacket and the importance of comfortable boots. Music from a guitar and a fiddle. Dancing. A pause at the crossroads from the pressures of life."* In those days, not a building, nor a street nor culvert nor anything else of concrete, steel, or glass existed at this forgotten site in old downtown Gainesville, Georgia.

Today, however, the historic spring which originally identified this site which later grew into Gainesville is hidden beneath a concrete cap and the city streets, but the spring site itself was recently "rediscovered." Though the old mule-drawn covered wagons and the pioneers of yesteryear who cracked their whips and traveled the once dusty former Indian trail are long gone, remnants of the site still exist if one knows where to look.

Located at the site of the old Davis-Washington Lumber Company building near downtown Gainesville and the old railroad depot, the spring site once existed in isolation, alongside the northern extension of what was known as "Standing Peachtree Trail," a historic north-south Indian and pioneer trading path through what today is the state of Georgia.

One remnant of the trail and spring may still be discerned in present-day Gainesville's "Spring Street," one of the avenues laid out when the city was originally surveyed in the early 1800s. Though few were still using the spring by that point, the road and its association with the historic spring and former trail were preserved for posterity.

A number of historic 19th century brick buildings still exist at the old Mule Camp Spring site today – early hints of the larger "civilization" which was destined to eventually prevail in the vicinity. These structures are clustered near what was originally a quite active passenger railroad line.

Photographed circa 1890s, the old Gainesville town square is filled with a host of mule-drawn covered wagons which, in days of old, transported mountain residents down to the "big city" to buy and sell their wares and the necessities of life each month. They often drew refreshment from nearby Mule Camp Spring.

The city of Gainesville sits astride the Eastern Continental Divide, a ridge of land through the state which divides the headwaters of the Oconee River on the east – which flows to the Atlantic Ocean – from the watershed of the Chattahoochee River on the west which ultimately empties into the Gulf of Mexico. This strip of land was originally a game trail in prehistory for the buffalo, antelope, and other cloven-hoofed wildlife who instinctively sought out the easiest routes of travel in avoidance of the fording of streams and the climbing of inclines in their annual migrations.

When the aboriginal inhabitants migrated to this area, they also patronized this north-south game trail, adopting it as their own trail for travel and trade. Still later natives made further use of it.

The Indians – and the wildlife before them – also used this particular route through what today is Gainesville because of the vital natural spring which was always valued as a reliable and safe source of thirst-quenching water. Over the hundreds of years they occupied this territory, the Indians came to believe the water possessed magical medicinal qualities, and they weren't far from being correct either, due to the spring's rich mineral content.

In time, when pioneer settlers began arriving in the area, they also patronized the Indian trail and came to appreciate the refreshing, clean, healthful waters from the spring. And since much of the early pioneer travel was accomplished by mule-drawn covered wagons, the site earned the moniker "Mule Camp Spring."

On a very foggy day in the 1890s, goods are being unloaded from a rail car at the Gainesville, Georgia Railroad Depot. Mule Camp Spring was once located in this general vicinity, but as modern development encroached upon this area, it is believed the waters of the spring have been channeled away in underground pipes.

Many of these early travelers trekked to and from the growing community of Augusta, Georgia, because it represented the farthest navigable point northward for riverboats traveling from the Georgia coast up the Savannah River. Augusta therefore became the "jumping off spot" for these pioneers as they traveled, explored, and settled on land on the interior of what today is Georgia.

When these pioneer settlers departed Augusta – which is one of the oldest towns in Georgia – they followed yet another Indian trail which traveled northwestward – again avoiding as many unfordable rivers, streams, and uphill inclines as possible – through Indian Territory up to Mule Camp Spring. This trail intersected the north-south-running "Standing Peachtree Trail," and was responsible for the "crossroads" which

eventually caused the settlement later known as Gainesville.

One of the sites at which this east-west-traveling route did require the fording of a river was just beyond Mule Camp Spring at what came to be known as the "shallow ford" across the Chattahoochee River. A remnant of this route still exists today in Gainesville's "Shallowford Road."

The fur trade became, almost immediately, a major aspect of the economy in the fledgling English colonies in America, and Georgia and the Southeast were no exception. The area became a source of income for American trappers who sold their furs to traders, who, in turn, sold to larger firms which shipped the commodity to buyers in Europe. The east-west trail from Mule Camp Spring to the river-port of Augusta eventually became a major pioneer trading route, mimicking the Indian trade on the route which had preceded it.

As decade after decade passed, the site of Mule Camp Spring gradually grew more and more in importance. As the railroads advanced through Georgia, one route followed a portion of the old north-south Standing Peachtree route into town, in turn passing quite near to the ancient spring.

In actuality, Gainesville has a number of freshwater springs near the downtown vicinity, and over recent years, there has been a lively debate at times about which is the "real" spring for which Mule Camp Spring was named. Nevertheless, the ancient spring near the old downtown section and original train depot is the spot most identified with the name.

Part of the mystery and controversy concerning the spring's location today comes from the fact it was "lost" for more than half a century. As Gainesville and the development thereof increased dramatically following the advent of the railroads in the 1870s, one of the rail lines was laid quite near the spring (or springs), and new development gradually appeared in the vicinity.

With this new growth obviously came new construction during the 1880s when brick buildings were built along the railroad. Davis-Washington Lumber Company, founded in 1919, occupied an even older existing building that had originally been a candy factory.

In later years, Davis-Washington expanded its operations, and in order to allow for construction of a new planing mill, the company's leaders decided to "cap" the spring near the building and re-route its water, an action which had the effect essentially of hiding the spring and blighting it from the collective public memory over time. The only visible clue

that the spring still existed following this "capping" was a small concrete structure adjacent to the planing mill warehouse.

"We knew it was there," said Hubert Deaton, a retired businessman and one of the last owners of Davis-Washington. "You could look about 30 feet down the concrete pipe that housed it and see the water, and hear it flowing. We estimated it flowed at a rate of about 8,000 gallons a day. We actually had a pump on it, but it was out of sight, and most people either forgot about it or just didn't know it existed."

Davis-Washington Lumber Company ultimately was closed permanently in 1990, and the buildings lay empty in downtown Gainesville except for the election season in 1992 when local Republicans used it as their headquarters. A portion of the historic building played host to a campaigning Senator Paul Coverdell, Senate Majority Leader Bob Dole, the advance staff of a visiting President George Bush, and a host of local and national GOP candidates and dignitaries.

It was approximately at this same time that the Davis-Washington building owners made the decision to demolish the old warehouse that had hidden the spring for so long, re-revealing the famous watering hole in all its natural splendor, and in the process, creating a centerpiece for the revitalization of some of Gainesville's most historic real estate.

Today – at least at this moment in 2023 – the action is again lively at "Mule Camp Spring." There sometimes is laughter. There is the aroma of delicious cooking food. There is occasional serious business talk, and maybe even a little music on special occasions from a guitar or fiddle. Life seems to have come full circle for the historic site – at least in some circumstances, and at least for the present.

Last Remaining Gristmill in Hall:

Tales of Old Healon Mill

With the spectacular demise of historic Tanner's Mill in a huge conflagration in 1986, Healon's Mill has now assumed the mantle of sole remaining historic gristmill in Hall County. Hall County administrators are taking careful steps to preserve this last vestige of pioneer mercantilism.

Most people have special feelings where gristmills are concerned. These feelings might be called fascination, or maybe even excessive curiosity. We especially admire the particularly old ones that still grace a few streams across the South, especially the ones that remain intact. Healon Mill represents Hall County's last.

Is it just their beauty and history that appeal to us, or might there be another element? Perhaps we also admire the ingenuity required to create an apparatus, powered by flowing water generating enough power to move huge mill stones and produce an essential finished product from corn, wheat, rice or other grains.

Whatever the reason, more and more travelers like to visit, photograph, tour, and learn as much as possible about these aged devices from yesteryear and their history. This, then, is the story of the last standing water mill (or gristmill) in Hall County.

At one time, many such gristmills dotted the landscape across Hall wherever a sudden change in flowing water elevation offered an opportunity for power generation, but when fire tragically destroyed historic Tanner's Mill in 1986, Healon's Mill assumed the sole mantle of "historic gristmill" for the county.

Healon's Mill was actually constructed prior to the U.S. Civil War by an individual named Billy Head. He is identified in most writings and official county documents of that era as a millwright.

In the years that followed, the mill passed through the hands of a succession of millers and was therefore known by a series of names, including "Broxton," "Carter's," "Old Hyde's," "Heard's," "Shore's," and "Turner's" Mill. It has been called Healon's Mill for well over 60 years now as of this writing (2023).

Healon's Mill is located in Airline Community, in extreme eastern Hall County, just minutes past Gainesville on Interstate-985 North toward Cornelia. At exit seven, I-985 becomes GA 365 North, and is no longer a controlled-access highway. At the exit for White Sulphur Springs Road, slow down and prepare to turn right onto graveled Whitehall

Healon Mill, originally known as "Head's Mill," was constructed prior to the U.S. Civil War. It has, over recent years, attracted a steady stream of artists and photographers intent upon capturing the beauty of the site on canvass and film.

Road. The mill exists beside the Oconee River, one mile from the highway.

As one reaches the site, he or she must cross a sturdy wooden bridge and park beside the mill. The structure is quite near the gravel road which undoubtedly follows the original wagon trail worn into the earth by farmers in horse-drawn wagons and on horseback many years ago.

Today, there are no organized tours of Healon's Mill, but the owner enjoys talking about its history and the hard work required to restore it and get it listed on the *National Register of Historic Places*.

"When my husband first talked of buying the old place," said Bernice Healon in a recent interview, "I was appalled. He took me to see it one weekend and told me of his plans to purchase it if the owner would sell.

"Well, it was just completely covered with kudzu – the snakiest-looking place I'd ever seen. I wouldn't even get out of the car. It looked so terrible and the old mill wheel was off its spindle and resting on the ground. I didn't see any way it would ever be lifted back into place, even if we did ever get through the kudzu and dirt."

Despite Bernice's reservations, her husband in fact did purchase the mill shortly thereafter, and the clean-up of the old structure began in earnest in the early 1960s.

"Fred loved old machines and buildings and such," she smiled in remembrance. "He also enjoyed fixing them up and restoring them. We worked like dogs every chance we got, cleanin' and choppin' and washin' and fixin'," she continued.

Just as Mrs. Healon expected, plac-

The construction date of the blacksmith shop at Healon Mill is unknown. Either the blacksmithing structure pictured here, or a predecessor, would have been necessary for creation of the metal mechanical portions of Healon Mill.

ing the mill-wheel back on its spindle indeed proved to be a massive undertaking – one which almost defeated them. "My husband and Cal Wilson eventually brought in great big railroad jacks and just lifted that huge wheel right up, slipped it on the spindle, and dropped it right into the track," she smiled.

"Cal was sheriff in Hall County. He built that corner cabinet settin' over there, and he and Fred replaced the flooring and such that was rotted."

One welcomed addition was a large fireplace and chimney which rise out of the heart of the mill. "It gets really cold here at night so close to the water," Bernice grimaces.

Mrs. Healon is justifiably proud of the work she and several other historians did to get the old mill recognized as a historical landmark. "It required a lot of effort by many, many people," she

explains. "Even with the help of the Georgia Mountains Regional Development Center, it took over three years to accomplish."

Since that time, the Healons enjoyed many peaceful hours of retreat at the old mill, working by day and being lulled to sleep at night by the song of the Oconee as it tumbled past just beyond the old shuttered windows.

Once everything was complete, the Healons attempted to convert the old mill into a commercial endeavor. A gift shop in the mill turned out to be more trouble than it was worth according to Bernice.

Today, the stately old mill sits in idle repose, a quiet reminder of a time long past. Research has indicated the mill has stood at the location at the headwaters of the Oconee River for nearly 200 years now.

Today, with the help of a little

peaceful day-dreaming, one can almost imagine the creaking of harness and other tack as wagon wheels lurch down the old dirt road. As the wagon crosses the river, water splashes back into the current from the cups on the wheels.

Intermingled with this activity, the rich musty odors of the river and the lush vegetation along it mingle with the fresh aroma of finely-ground corn and the heady tang of strong pipe tobacco and animal sweat. Tired horses and mules long for a cool drink from the swirling waters of the Oconee, and for the removal of the foam-flecked leather straps which connect them to their burdensome task.

Early community gristmills such as Healon's provided many services in addition to the grinding of grain. They were also the site of important suppliers of other goods and services, as well as the best place to learn the latest news.

The miller exacted a small toll for his services – usually 10 to 12 percent of the milled grain – which he would then re-sell to townsfolk and other non-farmers. He served an area roughly defined by the one-day trip of a wagon loaded with grain.

The majority of his customers traveled to the mill, had their crop ground, and returned to their farms the same day, in order to lessen the risk of damage to their product by inclement weather.

Most mills also served a small number of farmers who traveled a longer distance for the miller's services. They over-nighted at the mill, sleeping in or under their wagons. Sleep, however,

Tired horses and mules long for a cool drink from the swirling waters of the Oconee

came only after sitting around a communal fire with other fellow-travelers, discussing topics of the day, and often sipping another grain by-product for which the mountain reaches have long been well-known.

Through the years, Healon's Mill has offered several other services, in addition to the milling. These have included blacksmithing and wine-pressing. Both buildings from these long-abandoned businesses are still standing adjacent to the mill.

The water-power at Healon's Mill was also harnessed for use as a sawmill for a period of time, but it's unclear today if grain was also being ground during this period.

Bernice Healon says there are many unknown gaps in the history of the old mill today. There are also a number of stories and legends. She is particularly fond of one which involves an early miller – a man by the name of Turner. He and his wife were well-known for having some rather spectacular arguments.

"One ice-cold Saturday morning, a small group of farmers showed up very early to be first in line for grinding," Mrs. Healon explains, with a twinkle in her eyes. "They were going to make a fire in this old stone fireplace that you see here," she says, pointing to a moldering chimney inside the old mill. "They planned to start shelling corn and be ready for the miller when he came over to the mill from that green house across the road there.

"Well, there was a prop against the outside of the door, and when they removed it to go inside, out jumped Mrs. Turner, all wild-eyed and with her hair sticking out every which way. She took off up that hill and they didn't see her for the rest of the day. When the men looked inside the mill, they found a tiny fire in the hearth made from corn cobs. Old man Turner had locked his wife up in the mill all night long without even a piece of wood for a fire, and she had been forced to burn old corn cobs to keep from freezing."

The green house across the road to which Mrs. Healon had referred is known as the Turner house. Healon's daughter, Delaine Quinn, lived there at one time with her husband Hugh and their daughter Melanie Edge.

Billy Head, the original owner of the mill, reportedly hollowed out a log beneath the mill. That was where the Heads stashed their gold and silver during the Civil War. They knew that any gristmill would eventually be visited by marauding Federal troops.

It is not known today how successful the Heads were in avoiding the marauding Yankees. It has been documented however, that they soon lost an equally valuable entity shortly thereafter. Their daughter was taken from them by a returning Southern soldier.

Armor Rucker was serving with the Army of the Confederacy in Virginia when the war ended. He walked the entire 500 or so miles back to his northeast Georgia farm and returned to his labors in the fields.

Arriving at Head's Mill late one day to have corn ground, Rucker decided to spend the night. It was during this period that he reportedly met and fell in love with the miller's comely daughter. Nancy Florida Head agreed to marry Rucker and a goodly number of off-spring ultimately resulted from this union.

Head's Mill, in fact, was visited by a wide range of travelers over the years, some good, some not so good. Bill Miner, a notorious bandit *(Readers please see "The Capture of Old West Bandit Bill Miner," **Mystery & History in Georgia, Volume I**)* was also in the neighborhood for a period of time.

Miner, immortalized in modern-day books and major motion pictures, conducted his last train robbery only a short distance from Head's Mill at White Sulphur Springs. With several accomplices, Miner stopped a Southern Railway train from Atlanta, dynamited the train's safe, and collected an untold amount of freshly-minted silver coins, many of which are believed to have never been recovered.

"Miner and his gang hid out in an old cabin right up there in those hills," Mrs. Healon said. "Folks have been digging around here ever since, trying to get rich quick."

Other extraordinary events occurred at Head's Mill as well. Aeronautical history was nearly made at the side of the old mill when a man named Williams reportedly built one of the first airplanes in America. He, quite possibly also used the little blacksmith shop for the forging of many of his plane's parts.

At the time, there reportedly was little historical recording of Williams' efforts, because the Wright brothers became airborne in their plane at about this same time over Kitty Hawk, North Carolina. Williams, who never did get his plane aloft, reportedly lost interest after he realized the Wrights had stolen his chance to be the first in flight.

Healon's Mill is of the "overshot" waterwheel design. This means that the wheel had no paddles. It was designed with receptacles that caught water provided by a millrace above the wheel. The weight of the water in the receptacles turned the wheel as it filled these "cups."

Among the many unique aspects of Healon Mill is the old wine-press shack (background). Installed by a Mr. J. Heard circa 1900, it represented an attempt at diversification as the viability of gristmills began to wane, following the advent of commercially-produced flour.

Most individuals are more familiar with the undershot waterwheel which looks much like the paddle wheel on a steamboat. The undershot wheel is turned by water passing beneath the millwheel, and is much less efficient than the overshot version.

A combination of metal and wooden gears and other mechanical parts were used to transfer the energy from the turning water-wheel to the grinding stones. Many of these parts are stored today inside and beneath Healon's Mill which is no longer in operation.

With an overshot water-wheel, there was the obvious need to provide water to the top of the wheel. This was accomplished by building the mill at a fall-line or spot where the mill could exist below the level of water upstream. The water was then dammed upstream, and re-routed downstream via a wooden (or sometimes

metal) millrace. The water in the mill-race dropped at a lesser rate than that of the natural stream, allowing the millrace to empty the water at a higher level (above the millwheel) downstream at the mill.

Portions of the old millrace are still in place at Healon's Mill, according to Bernice Healon. "Water just springs from the ground everywhere around here," she laughs.

Despite more modern advances such as steam power and electricity, and the construction of large refined milling operations which no longer required water-power, a number of small gristmills remained in business beyond their day. As late as 1950, some stubborn Southerners continued to insist upon freshly-ground corn for bread, pone and livestock feed, and in fact, were still supporting some 400 community gristmills across the South.

As early as the turn of the 20th century, the owners of Healon's Mill made efforts to continue to find creative uses for the mill's equipment. An individual named J. Heard installed a wine-press to take advantage of the fine crops of grapes being harvested on the nearby hills of Habersham County. A man named Shore converted the mill into a cotton gin, and Braxton Carter hired a Mr. Hyde to run a sawmill in the structure.

Today, the serene beauty of Healon's Mill has not escaped the eye of photographers and artists.

Just when the blacksmith shop entered the picture at Healon's Mill is not recorded. Either it or a forerunner undoubtedly forged metal parts for the mill's construction. The smithy would certainly have found a ready market in the local community for such traditional services as the repair and manufacture of farm implements, as well as horse and mule shoeing and wagon repair.

Today, the serene beauty of Healon's Mill has not escaped the eye of photographers and artists. Bernice Healon says she welcomes the visitations of both.

Noted area painter James Darnell popularized the site for painters around 50 years ago with his award-winning painting of the mill as viewed from the bridge.

Readers planning a day-trip to the mill will be interested to know that many artists forsook the beautiful old mill and chose instead the old blacksmith shop or wine-press as their subject. Still others were so taken with the flora and the stream itself that they ultimately elected to exclude everything "man-made" from their paintings.

The pump house, which sits just north of the Turner House, marks the spot of the original spring which likely supplied drinking water to Billy Head as he constructed the mill.

Minor alterations were made to the mill by the Healons over time, but much of the original design-work is still visible in the hewn timbers, old stairways and ancient shutters. The millstone is still in place and intact within the structure, and other machinery necessary to operate the mill is stored within the building.

Bernice Healon firmly maintained that the old mill could be made operational again "if ever the occasion should arise."

In 2003, Hall County purchased the Healon's-Head's Mill property and four acres of surrounding land using grant funding. After several years, the County, along with a group of interested citizens, known as *"The Friends of Healon's-Head's Mill,"* began the process of restoring and re-opening the pre-Civil War structure to the public. Since it is the only remaining gristmill in Hall County, county administrators are taking careful steps to preserve this uniquely-historic site for posterity.

Gunman "Doc" Holliday's Former Valdosta Home

His legacy as a gambler and fearsome gunfighter in the old West are secure. Lesser known, however, are the details of John Henry Holliday's life during his adolescence in Valdosta, Georgia.

If there is one sure thing that can be said of the legacy of John Henry "Doc" Holliday, it is that there is virtually no agreement whatsoever about many aspects of his life. No one was more aware of this than author Susan McKey Thomas of Valdosta, Georgia, the legendary gunfighter's first cousin once removed, who spent the better part of three decades trying to sort through competing popular mythologies for the truth.

"I have no ax to grind, and I have no one to protect," said Thomas in an interview in 1999. Her sharp wit and elegantly groomed appearance offered only a small hint of her age. "I'm just trying to get to the truth," she stated matter-of-factly.

Thomas's historical odyssey began in 1972, when members of the Lowndes County Historical Society were asked to submit summaries of their family backgrounds for inclusion in the society's records. Wading into waters fraught with hear-say and legend, Thomas and Albert Pendleton, secretary of the Society's newsletter, discovered what Thomas called "many shocking inaccuracies" about her famous forebear.

Research Discoveries

"One of the first things we found out was that Wyatt Earp was little more than a pimp," explained Pendleton. Indeed, historians support the claim that several of the Earp brothers and their wives – some of whom were prostitutes themselves – ran brothels across the Old West, but then that was not unusual at all at that time. In fact, it was more the norm than the exception.

Doc Holliday himself "took up company" with a prostitute – Katheryn Haroney – also known as "Big Nose" Kate Elder. Holliday's adventures in the West, however accurate the re-telling of them may or may not be, are reasonably well-known. Less-known, however, is the story of the Holliday family in Valdosta, where John Henry spent much of his adolescence.

Even here, Thomas and Pendleton ran into a myriad of conflicting stories, enough so that it took 18 months of painstaking research before Thomas felt she could reliably submit her family story to the historical society for future readers and researchers.

The work of Thomas and Pendleton,

Major Henry Burroughs Holliday moved to Valdosta, Georgia, circa 1863, to escape the onslaught of Gen. William T. Sherman's devastation in the state. Pictured above is the Holliday home in Valdosta, where a young John Henry spent his adolescence attending Valdosta Institute and hunting and fishing in the surrounding countryside.

in fact, turned up so much information that their contributions took the form of a book, *In Search of the Hollidays*, published in 1973 by Little River Press. "We found out so many things that it just seemed like we needed to write them down," Pendleton said.

The book turned out to be something of a local sensation, and in the years that followed, copies were sold to history buffs from almost every state and several foreign countries. From that effort, the desire to know more about her famous cousin drove Thomas to an on-going investigation of much of the Holliday mystique, including the eight years in which John Henry lived in Valdosta.

Early Valdosta Days

The story of John Henry Holliday in Valdosta, Georgia, begins early in

1864, when his father, Major Henry Burroughs Holliday, brought his family to a settlement of about 1,500 people in what then was a virtual wilderness in extreme south Georgia. It was far from the Holliday family home in Griffin, Georgia, but it was a safe haven from the looming Federal siege of Atlanta and the advancing Union Army of Gen. William T. Sherman.

Major Holliday, a veteran of the Creek Indian wars, the Mexican War and the U.S. Civil War, had retired from military service and found refuge in a large tract of land northeast of Valdosta, near a tiny fiefdom known as Bemiss. By that time, the Hollidays had already reared to manhood a young orphan – Francisco Hidalgo – brought home by a compassionate Major Holliday in 1849 after the Mexican War.

In earlier years when he had lived in Griffin, Georgia, Major Holliday – as he was formally known – had worked as a druggist. In the largely unsettled south Georgia countryside, however, he became an entrepreneur, opening a plant nursery, planting vineyards and promoting the production of pecans, an undertaking which today has grown into a major agricultural industry stretching from Valdosta westward across the clay hills of southwest Georgia and on to the north of the state. Indeed, Georgia now produces more pecans than peaches. It, in fact, produces more pecans today than any other state in the Union.

Ms. Thomas said the young John Holliday, 12 years old when he arrived in Valdosta, was remembered by area residents as being nice looking and slightly built, with piercing blue eyes and blonde hair.

Later biographies recorded John Henry's gracious manners as well as his unpredictable temperament, but Valdostans remembered only a well-mannered adolescent who dressed neatly and grew into a young man known for his ability on a dance floor amidst the musical talents of his McKey relatives.

The McKey Family

History correctly records that young John Henry was well-educated. He was schooled at the private Valdosta Institute which, as reported by Louis Pendleton in his *Echo of Drums*, stressed classics and taught *"advanced branches."* Headmaster Samuel McWhir Varnedoe (how's that for a name?) set up a challenging curriculum including Greek, Latin, French, advanced English, mathematics and history.

Following the end of the Civil War, the Holliday/McKey family clung to a semblance of affluence when most other Southern families and former businessmen were relegated to poverty. The young Holliday's three McKey uncles – James, William and Thomas – bought a large tract of land in the lakes area along the Georgia-Florida border south of Valdosta in an area known as Bellview.

The McKey property, known as "Banner Plantation," is said to have been a favorite haunt of John Henry, who reportedly spent much of his adolescent years hunting and fishing on the property. His favorite uncle, Tom, who was only 10 years older than John, often accompanied him.

Years later and a world away out West, John Henry assumed the alias Thomas "Mackey" (as the family surname was then spelled) for a short time, presumably because he had encountered legal problems or conflicts of another nature, and needed to disguise his identity.

"I don't know why he did that," Susan Thomas said in her 1999 interview. "He wasn't famous, really, until the O.K. Corral." Many historians would reply, however, that despite the fact that he hadn't yet been involved in the famous gunfight in Tombstone, John Henry was, nevertheless, becoming known as a testy gunfighter even by the time he reached Dodge City, and had already reportedly been involved in more than one altercation.

Whatever the case, back in south Georgia, what seems to have been an idyllic childhood for John Henry was shattered by tragedy in the form of the unexpected serious illness of his mother. Alice Jane McKey Holliday gradually lost her strength and endured a lingering and torturous state of health until September 16, 1866, when she finally passed away from the same illness – tuberculosis

– which would later haunt and prematurely-destroy John Henry. The youngster, who had dearly loved his mother, reportedly was devastated.

As if his mother's death was not bad enough, family stories maintain that John Henry was shaken even worse by the almost immediate remarriage of his father to another woman a mere three months after his mother's death. Major Holliday married Rachel Martin, 23, a young lady who was less than half his age and only nine years older than John Henry.

Reconstruction Trauma

Other outside factors also impacted the Holliday family in Valdosta. Following the U.S. Civil War, the turbulent years of Reconstruction took a serious toll on the Holliday family's financial fortunes. An abusive Federal occupation with its associated retributive and punitive legalities for anything "Southern" set the Holliday circumstances back even further.

Rachel Martin's family owned farmland which adjoined the Holliday property. Records indicate that the Martins purchased the Holliday tract, and that Major Holliday's father-in-law gave to his daughter a house in Valdosta at 405 Savannah Avenue. The Holliday family – including young John Henry – soon relocated to this new address.

Never one to take defeat easily, Major Holliday immediately began working to recover the family fortune. He opened several businesses, including a furniture

store. The *1870 Census* lists him broadly as "general agent." Eventually, Thomas says, Holliday regained all of his former properties, but he never fully recovered financially.

Major Holliday also gained some acclaim in the political arena in his community. He served four terms as Valdosta's mayor.

While his father was beginning to prosper once again, the younger Holliday began pursuing the behavior for which he would become more widely known later in life. Local tradition maintains – incorrectly – that he eventually fled town after running afoul of Federal officials.

Young John Henry was in fact accused of being associated with – and indeed may even have been the mastermind of – a plot to destroy with explosives the then-Federally-operated Lowndes County Courthouse. In the Reconstruction South, the county courthouses often were taken over by occupying Federal forces in order to set up a legal sanctioning body for the doling out of punishments of White Southerners. Though a subsequent newspaper account of the incident (in which John Henry supposedly was involved) lists the names of five participants who were accused of the crime, John Henry, was not one of those identified or even implicated in the crime.

Major Holliday was one of five men appointed by the Valdosta City Council to draw up a plan to deal with the unrest in the area during

Major Holliday also gained some acclaim in the political arena in his community.

Valdosta Institute, a private 19th century school, provided young John Henry with an excellent education in the classics. The date of this rare and recently-discovered photo is unknown, but it quite likely was taken circa 1870s, possibly even during the time-period in which it was attended by John Henry.

Reconstruction according to Ms. Thomas. One could surmise that John Henry's family connections could have protected him from prosecution in the courthouse incident, but any such conclusion, like so many others involving Doc Holliday, would be pure conjecture at this late date.

Swimming Hole Incident

Ms. Thomas said young Holliday was also involved in a shooting incident reportedly prompted by his discovery of a group of Blacks in a riverside swimming spot he and his friends often frequented near the confluence of the Withlacoochee and Little rivers at the old settlement of Troupville. In reality, however, what modern America wished to conveniently convert into yet another "racial issue" perpetrated by a "racist" Southerner, actually amounted to little more than young Holliday defending himself after being attacked by the Blacks when he had demanded that they leave the property.

Once again, this "racial incident" occurred during the Reconstruction years, when tensions were extremely high. At that time, many Blacks reveled in their new-found superior social status, often intentionally inflaming a situation by flaunting their ability to violate long-standing Southern social mores. Rather than calm the circumstances, Reconstruction-elected officials often fanned the flames of divisiveness with abusive penalties for trumped-up (and often completely false) charges against Southern Whites.

Ms. Thomas said the story involving John Henry was confirmed by Thomas McKey, John's uncle. In the late 1920s, Thomas says McKey related the incident involving John Henry to writer Stuart Lake who was working on what later would become a controversial book about Wyatt Earp.

"He told the story of (McKey and Holliday) going to a swimming hole which Whites had traditionally used as a spot for swimming and leisure activity, and that was when they discovered a group of Blacks in the water," Ms. Thomas related. "[John Henry] first ordered the trespassers out of the water, and after being abusively spurned and threatened, he then turned to retrieve his pistol." One of the Blacks, however, had quickly armed himself when he saw that Doc was turning for his gun.

According to local tradition, a Black federal officer was killed in the incident, but in the interview with writer Stuart Lake, Thomas McKey firmly denied anyone was wounded or injured in any way. Here again, the supposedly "murdered Black Federal officer" was nothing more than a complete fabrication designed to conveniently paint Holliday as a racist in order to fan the flames of divisiveness in a conquered South.

Today, there is no microfilm available for the *Valdosta Times* newspaper during the period in question, but McKey's assertion of John Henry's innocence is given some credence by the fact that there is no evidence of any such incident in the records of the Lowndes County Superior Court for the years 1866 through 1873, and the occupying Federal authorities, as well as Reconstruction-elected officials (as explained above), were always quick to take advantage of any opportunity to punish any White Southerner involved in any incident or even the slightest infraction which held even a hint of a racial edge.

On To Dental School

Despite the trouble John Henry may or may not have initiated as a teen, he went on to graduate from the Valdosta Institute in 1870. Later that year, he applied and was admitted to the Pennsylvania College of Dental Surgery from which he was graduated during the 16th annual graduation ceremonies of March 1, 1872.

During his studies in Pennsylvania, John Henry occasionally returned to work his required "preceptership" with Valdosta dentist Lucian Frederick Frink. Ms. Thomas said there is some evidence that Holliday performed dental work in Valdosta in October of 1871, and it is believed he returned home for a brief visit after his graduation, but a short time later, he struck out for Atlanta to open a dental practice in that newly-rebuilt city which was just then recovering from the destructiveness of the Union Army forces in Georgia.

Though he did not know it at the time, even as he left Valdosta, the newly anointed "Dr." Holliday was no doubt already a doomed man. Within a year, he would be diagnosed with tuberculosis, a disease for which there was no treatment until the mid-20th century. It was the same disease which had killed his mother.

This diagnosis was a fate that possibly sent John Henry to the drier climate of the West for health reasons, and, within the space of four more years, found him becoming a playfully subversive gambler who had a "very short fuse" when larger and much stronger individuals sought to bully him or physically take advantage of his slight stature.

Historians and researchers today maintain that John Henry almost certainly had been infected with the tuberculosis bacterium years prior to the diagnosis of his disease. He might possibly have contracted it from a dental patient upon which he trained early in his college education. However, in reality, he more than likely contracted it from his mother, although Thomas says there obviously is no way to prove that today. Each day, his advancing illness robbed him of still more of this strength.

Interestingly, Francisco Hidalgo, the Mexican youth raised by the Hollidays is also known to have died of the dreaded disease as well in 1873, providing still more strong evidence that the seeds of Doc Holliday's eventual demise in a Colorado hotel in 1887 were sown long before that time, either in Griffin or in Valdosta.

Leaving Home Forever

Once he left Valdosta, Doc Holliday apparently considered his break with south Georgia to be permanent. There is no evidence that he ever returned to visit, even though there is evidence that he strongly yearned for a reconnection with his family.

A legend within the Holliday family maintains that Major Holliday arranged a meeting with his son while in New Orleans at a Confederate veterans' convention in 1885, and begged the ailing John Henry to come home to his family. Whether the meeting ever took place or not is, predictably, unverifiable today.

What can be said with certainty, however, is that if the estranged father and son had such a meeting, it was their last. Doc Holliday did not return to Georgia, and by 1885, he was so sick that he could barely manage to support himself in the gambling profession any longer – and to him, it was literally a profession, not a game. After he ceased practicing dentistry, gambling was his full-time occupation, and when healthy, he was quite adept at it.

Though often merry – and sometimes even comical in nature – John Henry's otherwise testy nature caused him to be involved in more than one serious altercation shortly after his migration to the West. In a locale which thrived upon reputations, the legend of Doc Holliday as a gunman quickly became established, and any return to his home in Georgia where his family's reputation might be tarnished by his disreputable identity became impossible for the wandering former dentist to even consider.

During her research of John Henry Holliday, Susan Thomas did make one very interesting – and very unexpected – discovery. The orphan – Francisco Hidalgo – left behind a legacy of his own in neighboring Berrien County in the form of the "Edalgo" family, of which he was the progenitor.

After more than a century, that piece of information came as a complete and total surprise to the Edalgos who continue to live in this south Georgia county even as of this writing, and who previously had been unable to trace their ancestry beyond their local community.

Remnants In Valdosta

Today, the Holliday legacy is alive and well in Valdosta, even if the Major and Doc are long gone and the Holliday name itself has all but disappeared in the community.

Major Holliday, in addition to serving as mayor of the city, rose to additional prominence in that town. He served as secretary of the Lowndes County Agricultural Society, secretary of the Confederate Veterans of Camp Troup, census enumerator, and superintendent of local elections. He even had a street named for him near the original site of the Holliday house off Savannah Avenue.

The Holliday house in Valdosta – John Henry's adolescent home – lives on as well as of this writing (2023). In the 1970s, the aged structure was purchased by Valdosta businessman Dick Davis and moved to a new location off U.S. Highway 41 South. A few years later, the home was given a new lease on life when it was purchased by a local couple and moved to one of the new subdivisions which sprawl far to the northwest of town.

After its relocation, the house was extensively renovated, although many of its original aspects were preserved and incorporated into the new additions to the structure. It was later purchased and occupied by Dr. David Johnson and his wife, Susan, at 2605 Pebblewood Drive in Valdosta. Its disposition beyond that status is unknown today.

Amazing Howser Waterwheel, And Early Electricity in Dahlonega

Though he had little more than a 5th grade education, Robert Howser, Sr. was "Phi Kappa Beta" when it came to water power and mechanical manipulation. In 1920-21, he demonstrated his prowess in this regard by providing electricity all by his lonesome to the entire city of Dahlonega, Georgia.

The giant waterwheel designed and assembled by Robert Howser, Sr., stood 40 feet high and weighed approximately 30 tons. It was a marvel in its day, and provided the first electricity for the city of Dahlonega.

Cane Creek Falls, on the outskirts of Dahlonega, has been one of the best-known picnic grounds in north Georgia for well over 150 years. Beginning in 1921 and for many years thereafter, the little waterfall amazingly supplied the town with electricity for street and home lights through a small business venture that displayed individual initiative to a degree seldom seen today. The water-power at Cane Creek Falls was converted into electricity by the second-most powerful overshot wheel ever used in the United States.

Robert B. Howser, Jr. of Smyrna, recalled the old days when a man could organize, build and operate his own power company. The Dahlonega plant belonged to his father.

Robert B. Howser, Sr. had grown up in a little water-power empire at nearby Dawsonville, where he and his father and brothers had operated a sawmill, flour mill, cotton gin and electric plant, all powered by water. After World War I, Robert D. Sr. decided to branch out on his own and become the power king of Dahlonega.

Bob Jr. recalls that his father paid $1,000 for Cane Creek Falls and 40 acres of surrounding land. "Then he made some drawings on brown wrapping paper, because they were the only large sheets he could get, I suppose," said Mr. Howser. "Dad had a country school education, which probably would rank around the fifth grade, but he was post graduate in water-power and simpler forms of machinery."

The drawings Howser made were the design for the great Dahlonega

In 1921, Robert D. Howser, Sr. paid $1,000.00 for Lumpkin County's Cane Creek Falls and forty acres of the surrounding land. He then proceeded to erect the huge millwheel pictured here, to utilize the water-power from Cane Creek for the generation of electricity. It provided the first electrical current to the city of Dahlonega, Georgia, from 1921 to 1935. In the 1930s the property was sold to the Georgia Power Company who subsequently sold it to the Methodist Conference which created Camp Glisson at the site and continues to own the property as of this writing. The mill-race is faintly discernible in the center of this photo. (Photo courtesy of the GA Dept. of Archives & History, Atlanta, GA)

waterwheel and connecting machinery he intended to use to bring electricity to the town. He took his drawings all the way to a waterwheel firm in Hanover, Pa., and the great wheel was built to his specifications, at a cost of $5,555.

It should be noted here that in 1921 when this transaction was made, $5,555.00 was a great deal of money. It had the purchasing power equivalent to $83,883.00 in 2023 dollars. Where Robert, Sr. was able to acquire this amount of money as well as the courage to risk it on a venture of this nature is unknown today. At the very least, it would be safe to say that he must have had great confidence in his mechanical capabilities.

The large waterwheel Howser had designed was made of steel with considerable copper content in order to inhibit rusting. According to records, it was 40 feet in diameter, eight feet wide and weighed about 30 tons.

After the great wheel had been manufactured and shipped to Gainesville, Georgia, Howser then was faced with a problem. How does he get that huge waterwheel up the mountains to its final destination?

Dahlonega has never had a railroad. According to the younger Howser, a flat car carrying the wheel in eight separate sections had been parked on a sidetrack north of Gainesville. That was as far as the manufacturer could get it.

Though he was only a few miles from his destination, for anyone else it would have seemed like a thousand miles – but not for Robert Howser, Sr. He merely examined the problem and plotted a solution.

Motor trucks of that era were not designed for huge loads such as the waterwheel, and certainly not for hauling big tonnage on the kind of roads that climbed over the mountains from Gainesville to Dahlonega. Wagons of the era creaked mightily under four bales of cotton (approximately one ton), and the eight sections of the waterwheel each weighed nearly four tons.

Undeterred, Howser, Sr. was anything if not resourceful. "At that time, there were two steel-wheeled drays in Gainesville, and my father rented both of them," Bob Jr. explained. "Eight horses were hitched to each, and they brought the sections overland. I was too small to go on the long hauls, but I remember watching the drays pass through Dahlonega. It was like a parade. Nearly everybody in town turned out for the sight.

In order to coalesce the individual pieces of his waterwheel into a single unit once he had reached his destination at Cane Creek Falls, Howser demonstrated his resourcefulness yet again. "Local men set up a large pole derrick and raised and assembled the wheel with blocks and tackle," Bob, Jr. continued. "Water from the pool above the dam ran through a flume along the hillside and across a little bridge to the top of the wheel," Howser, Jr. added. "The generator was in a small clapboard building that stood in the shadow of the wheel."

Even after he had achieved the impossible and transported and assembled the huge water-wheel, yet another huge task still lay before the elder Howser. Dahlonega had never previously had the magic of electricity, and no one therefore had any electric wiring in their homes. There wasn't even wiring for streetlights!

Howser, Jr. recalls that his father – amazingly – personally assumed the task of wiring the city of Dahlonega and the North Georgia College campus for street lighting as well as house lighting, using chestnut power poles that were about as durable as the later creosoted pine poles. Imagine assuming the chore of wiring one house, let alone an entire town. It was a daunting task at best. One has to concede at this point, however, that the wiring for the small homes in that day and time in Dahlonega was not a complicated matter – but still a big job.

Then, even after he had completed the chore of wiring – and footed the bill for all that expensive wire – Howser, Sr. was confronted with yet another obstacle. In the summer of 1925, Lumpkin County and environs experienced a severe drought. To put it simply, there was no rainfall to speak of for months on end. All the streams dried up and water was in short supply.

As a result, Cane Creek, only eight or nine miles long and fed entirely by mountain springs, dwindled to little more than a trickle of its former volume. As the stream dried up

In the summer of 1925, Lumpkin County and environs experienced a severe drought.

and the terrain became powder-dry, Howser's great water-wheel slowed dramatically, and power was reduced accordingly. For most of the long hot summer, the lights of Dahlonega faded from incandescent to a dull red.

The wintertime, however, brought a different set of circumstances to the water-wheel entirely. Mr. Howser recalls that in freezing weather somebody had to stand by with a hammer to crack the ice off the cog-wheels. With water pouring out of a flume which was elevated 40 feet up in the air, the resulting mist, spray and leakage caused ice to form on most everything in the vicinity of the water-wheel, particularly on cold, windy days. Left untended, the ice could cause the equipment to fail.

As the seasons changed, so did the rainfall, and the waterwheel generated full power. The pool below Cane Creek Falls was Dahlonega's unofficial swimming pool in summers. Ever the good-natured civic-minded individual, Howser dragged out sand with mules and a slip scrape, then ran a low dam across the foot of the large pool to raise the water about three feet. One of the most popular features was a smooth slide down the granite wall at one side of the falls. The children of Dahlonega were delighted.

Running across pictures of the old wheel recently, Mr. Howser, Jr. wrote to the manufacturers – the Fitz Company of Hanover, Pennsylvania – for any information available about the wheel.

As the seasons changed, so did the rainfall, and the waterwheel generated full power.

He received an immediate reply stating that the Dahlonega wheel was the second most powerful over-shot wheel ever set up in the United States, producing over 100 horsepower. The manufacturers said it ran on a shaft that was 8 $7/16$ inches in diameter and 16 feet long. The power was transmitted by a large gear-wheel 35 feet in diameter bolted to the spokes, and the speed was stepped up again by a pulley 116 inches in diameter by 20 inches wide.

The Fitz Company also built the wheel that out-performed this one, for the Burden mines. Since the location was not mentioned, it is presumed the mines were in Pennsylvania. This wheel was 28 feet in diameter, but more than twice as wide as the wheel at Dahlonega.

When Dahlonega's electrical requirements out-grew the capacity of the water-wheel in 1935, Robert Howser, Sr. sold out to the Georgia Power Company, which then supplied electric current to Dahlonega from its network of plants. In 1942, the company gave the great wheel to Lumpkin County for the scrap drive, and it, sadly, was melted down for the war effort.

Today, Cane Creek Falls where the little power plant once existed is included among the property of Camp Glisson of the North Georgia Methodist Conference Assembly Center, and has been improved as a recreation area. It continues to be exceptionally popular as a playground for children in the lazy summers in the mountains.

Dahlonega's "Hall's Block" and Frank Hall's Secret

"Hall's Block" in Dahlonega was built in the late 19th Century, only eighteen years after the surrender of Confederate forces at Appomattox Courthouse in Virginia. Despite its age, this dominant structure continues to hold sway today over much of the architecture on the town square. Its builder, however – once a prominent businessman in town – was then, and continues today to be an enigma in the community.

The imposing brick building on the northwestern corner of the Dahlonega town square is faintly reminiscent of a faded fortress from yesteryear, still boasting heavy iron bars over some of the windows even today. Completed in 1883, it was designed as a mere general store, but in the lawless years following the U.S. Civil War, extra measures were required to protect one's assets. Its original owner, Frank W. Hall, was believed to have acquired his wealth through constant caution of this nature, possibly even into "moonlighting" as an illicit gold miner.

Hall, a native of Vermont, had relocated to Dahlonega in 1868, being employed by the Boston Massachusetts Company to oversee several local gold mills and mining operations in the Lumpkin County vicinity owned by the company. Though he was virtually penniless when he arrived, Hall was eventually numbered among the most influential and wealthiest men in the county, acquiring many businesses, tracts of land

and a substantial general merchandise store in addition to his fine home near the town square.

Aside from his other qualities, Frank Hall was also very obviously an astute entrepreneur who was quick to understand that the real money was made not from mining gold, but from selling merchandise and equipment to the men who did. But did Frank Hall conscientiously practice this philosophy? Maybe. Maybe not.

About fifteen years after he arrived in Dahlonega, Hall opened what then was a huge mercantile center on the town square, emblazoning the name of his enterprise *"Hall's Block"* across the top of the new structure so that his prominence in his community was unmistakable. The original two-foot letters on the cornice which Hall installed all those years ago still remain intact today on the impressive structure which is now included on the **National Register of Historic Places**.

So prolific in fact was Hall, that he

is something of a legend today to those familiar with the history of Lumpkin County. While digging the cellar for Hall's new home on South Chestatee Street just off the town square in 1899, his workmen made the surprise discovery of a substantial gold vein on his property. When, however, he sought to mine his new-found wealth, the town fathers refused his request for a mining permit. Their reasoning was simple. Hall's lot was located within the town limits, and mining simply was not allowed there.

Hall honored the legal mandate and abandoned – at least temporarily – the precious yellow metal buried on his lot – but it wasn't without a fight....

An excerpt from the November 3, 1899 issue of the **Dahlonega Nugget** newspaper by Editor W. B. Townsend confirms the discovery: *"Captain Hall's workmen, while excavating the cellar for his new warehouse on the corner of Chestatee and Waters Street, just across from R.H. Webb's lot, struck a rich gold-bearing vein several feet wide, depth not known."*

Editor Townsend went on to note that Capt. Hall had informed him that he would not develop the vein since it ran under his building and was on a town lot. Townsend also noted that Hall had stated that he didn't have any time to spend working a gold mine anyway!

This was a strange comment indeed from a man who had originally relocated

Hall converted the structure into an "Assay Office" for use during the day, while he secretly and illicitly mined the gold beneath his home during the wee hours of the mornings

to Dahlonega specifically as a mining superintendent with expertise in gold mining and who had ultimately been involved with numerous local gold mines in the area for almost three decades. So was his claim that he did not intend to mine the gold on his town property an honest statement – or merely a ruse?

It is known today at the very least that Hall did not initially just immediately volunteer to ignore the rich gold vein on his property. He in fact waged a bitter six-month legal battle with the City of Dahlonega – which he ultimately lost – in a vain attempt to gain the right to mine the gold on his town lot. After losing the lawsuit, it was reported that he had covered up his gold vein and simply continued construction of his "home" on that site – but the real truth recently came to light – much to the surprise of many.

It is now known that after the verdict on his suit to gain the right to mine the gold on his town lot, Frank Hall continued the construction of his "home" on that lot (which later became the *Smith House Restaurant*), but from that point forward, he actually had no intention whatsoever of residing in the home. Instead, Hall converted the structure into an "Assay Office" for use during the day, while he secretly and illicitly mined the gold beneath his home during the wee hours of the mornings

Though emblazoned with the signage "Moore's Store" in this circa 1921 photo, the pediment at the roofline of this structure – which still stands in Dahlonega as of this writing (2023) – clearly identifies it as one of Frank Hall's early creations, built by him some 40 years earlier circa 1881 as a general store in Dahlonega. The multi-talented Hall ultimately owned numerous businesses in the Lumpkin County area. (Photo courtesy of GA Dept. of Archives & History, Atlanta)

for several months. Though he was a law-abiding and highly respected citizen of Dahlonega, Frank Hall, it seems, was not about to allow something like a little city ordinance to deny him the riches to which he felt he was rightfully entitled.

Much to the surprise of modern-day residents of the city, it was discovered that Hall had quietly opened a shaft in the basement of his new home and mined the gold therein at least for numerous months, and possibly for several years. When the gold in the vein was exhausted, Hall simply sealed the opening to the shaft shut with concrete, disguising his illegalities for well over 100 years. Perhaps this bit of illegal philandering was at least part of the reason that the businessman – despite all his

real estate and investments in Lumpkin County – just suddenly pulled up stakes one day and left town forever.

Today, this now-historic gold mine beneath one of the rooms of the Smith House Restaurant *(Readers please see "The Secret Gold Mine Beneath the Smith House" in the Lumpkin County section of this publication.)* is a much-visited attraction at the famous eatery. One may peer down into the shaft from a glass-enclosed viewing area and see where Frank Hall – all those years ago – illegally and secretly mined gold from a substantial vein beneath his home. Now we know how the somewhat mysterious businessman was able perhaps to afford some of the many businesses and real estate he purchased in the county – including Hall's Block!

The Hall House constructed next door to Hall's Block was another of Frank Hall's investment projects. It also was constructed circa 1881 and is the second-oldest building on Dahlonega's historic square. Frank Hall originally built the Hall House as both his initial home and a boarding house in the town. (Photo courtesy of GA Dept. of Archives & History, Atlanta)

Despite its age and the thousands of individuals who have passed through its doors over the years, Hall's Block has known only a handful of owners (if one considers the Moore family – several members of which owned the property from 1919 to 1984 – as a single ownership). After possessing the building for 65 years, the late Mrs. Robert M. Moore ended her family's association by selling to the late Dahlonega entrepreneur Jon Stone in 1984.

It was during his renovations of the historic building that Stone uncovered some interesting relics from previous owners. He found a faded and crumbling ledger book full of receipts dating back to Hall's ownership in the 1890s. He also uncovered two dusty vintage appliances, at least one of which was a marvel in its day: a unit which doubled as both a dishes and clothes washer with a sink, and a six-burner kerosene stove which was stored next to the washer.

"I think they were accidentally shoved together with a lot of other things that needed to be repaired, and were just forgotten," Stone remarked at the time. "They both still had the original sales tags on them and were even operational." Though he was offered hundreds of dollars for these items over the years, Stone declined to sell. They were considered antiques and "collectors' items" at that time, and that was over 30 years ago as of this writing in 2023.

The Moore legacy runs deep – much deeper than Frank Hall's – in the aged store building. It was in 1881, while employed as a water and brick boy helping in the early construction of Hall's Block, that John H. Moore, according to

Historic Hall's Mill Bridge – The advent of automotive travel – along with other changes – took away almost as many new customers as it created for north Georgia travel destinations. This well-dressed gentleman pauses at Hall's Mill Bridge in Lumpkin County, circa 1920s. The ruins of this now-historic heavy iron bridge still exist (as of this writing in 2023) near the juncture of the Chestatee River and Highway 60 just south of Dahlonega. A heavy iron bridge identical to this landmark once spanned the Etowah River nearby at present-day Castleberry Bridge just west of Auraria, Georgia, suggesting the same builder may have built both structures. The original iron Castleberry Bridge disappeared years ago, and was replaced by the more modern concrete version now located at that site. (Photo courtesy of GA Dept of Archives & History, Atlanta)

family tradition, set his sights on his future. "Build her good, boys," he reportedly stated during the building's construction, "because someday, I'm going to own it."

At the time, Moore was making barely 30 cents a day in wages, but he obviously had much higher aspirations. Some 38 years later (in September of 1919), he achieved his goal, purchasing Hall's Block, the small adjoining brick office, and Hall House (the inn next door) for a total of $3,000. That seems like a paltry sum today to pay for such a substantial collection of town real estate, but in 1919, the sum of $3,000.00 was the

approximate equivalent of $49,199.00 in 2023 dollars. In 1919, that was a substantial sum.

In 1921, John Moore decided to share ownership of Hall's Block, entering into a partnership with his brother, G.H. Moore. The family-run enterprise (a general store similar to that originated by Hall) eventually passed to John W. Moore's eldest son, Robert Hughes Moore in 1944. Robert continued the business until 1962, when "Moore's Store" closed its doors permanently, and the space in the building was rented out to a series of businesses.

When the subject of Hall's Block

is broached with long-time Dahlonega residents, it is often the experiences of the colorful Robert H. Moore – rather than Hall – which are remembered most fondly by many. For many years, Moore reportedly provided most of what was needed for life in small-town Dahlonega. He was never far from the fabric of life in the community.

As quoted in an *Atlanta Constitution Sunday Magazine* article in the 1960s, Moore – through the relation of one of his many experiences in the community – demonstrates why he was such a colorful personality:

"One day a man came in and told me he wanted a dress for his wife," Moore stated. *"I asked him what size and he said, 'Hit don't make no difference.' He asked for some stockings and when I asked what color he said, 'Hit don't make no difference.' Then he told me he wanted some drawers and I asked if he wanted ones that buttoned in the front or the back, and he said, 'Hit don't make no difference. She won't be using 'em no way. She's dead as a door-nail.'"*

The family traditions and legacy of Hall's Block (or Moore's Store, depending upon how one wishes to identify it) run true and deep in Dahlonega, and were never relinquished without trepidation. Though she professed no strong feelings for the property on the day of its sale to Jon Stone in 1984, Mrs. Robert (Ola) Moore did shed tears at the closing, according to Stone, relinquishing

> *The long-departed businessman would no doubt still be quite proud of his former signature asset*

control of an enterprise which had been in the family for some 65 years. As the **Bible** states, however, *"All things must pass."*

Despite the passage of ownership, the future of the building has remained bright. The interesting shops and historic décor inside it make maximum use of the structure's historic architecture to attract tourist traffic. In renovating the structure in 1984, Stone returned it to its original design of four entranceways in front. One doorway leads upstairs; one doorway leads downstairs; and two doorways lead to the main floor.

To accomplish his renovation, Stone hired electricians, carpenters, a brick mason and others. The original pine flooring was uncovered. The manually-operated service elevator (similar to a large dumb waiter) was resurrected and put back into use. New heating, ventilation, plumbing and wiring were installed, and a general face-lift was provided for the entire structure.

Today, the flags often fly colorfully on the front façade of Hall's Block, and the 2-foot letters on the cornice still prominently proclaim the structure as having originally been owned by the enigmatic Frank W. Hall. The long-departed businessman would no doubt still be quite proud of his former signature asset, despite the fact that the illicit nature of at least a portion of his once-famed wealth is now publicly known.

The Secret Gold Mine Beneath the Smith House

As of the year 2023, the inexplicable gold mine had secretly existed beneath the basement of the famous Smith House Restaurant in Dahlonega for almost 125 years. It is unknown today why the original owner – Capt. Frank W. Hall – did not mine all the gold in the vein, or why he chose to seal it up as a secret in perpetuity. It is known, however, that he mined this gold surreptitiously, in violation of Lumpkin County law.

On February 14, 2006, a mysterious mine shaft was amazingly uncovered by workmen in the basement of the historic Smith House Restaurant in Dahlonega, Georgia. Interestingly, there had been, for many years, a legend concerning the structure's original builder and his discovery of a rich vein of gold beneath his home, but the 2006 revelation of a large concealed mine tunnel with un-mined gold came not only as a surprise, but a complete shock to the present-day owners.

Capt. Frank W. Hall had moved from Vermont to Dahlonega in 1868 shortly after the end of the U.S. Civil War. He was employed by The Boston Massachusetts Company to oversee several local gold mills and mining operations in the Lumpkin County vicinity owned by the company.

Despite the fact that Hall was almost penniless when he arrived in Dahlonega, he, supposedly – as a result of his sharp business acumen – eventually became one of the most influential and wealthy men in the county, acquiring numerous tracts of property and businesses, including a fine home which he constructed just off the Dahlonega town square.

The discovery of the secret gold mine beneath Hall's former property indicates that though he may have indeed enjoyed a sharp knack for business, he also enjoyed a secret source of income for the accumulation of at least a portion of his immense wealth.

Hall had purchased the property on which he built his home (later known as the Smith House) in 1895. By 1899, having already made his mark in the Dahlonega community, Hall had completed construction of his rambling farmhouse abode just off the town square, and had been busy with his assaying business inside the structure for a number of months.

The structure which later became the well-known Smith House Restaurant in Dahlonega was constructed in 1899 by Capt. Frank W. Hall, a native of Vermont. Though built specifically for him and his wife as a residence, the Halls never lived in the structure. It instead was strangely only used as an assay office (one of Hall's numerous professions) during the day, and apparently was used surreptitiously in the evenings to conceal the illicit mining of gold in the substantial illegal mine shaft beneath a wing of this building. The inn and restaurant are pictured (l) and the former carriage house which today houses administrative offices is visible (r).

Hall's mysterious mine shaft was later discovered beneath what once was the old dining room of the Smith House Restaurant in which the late Fred and Thelma Welch had served thousands of guests from the 1950s right up until the 1990s. The immense opening of the mine shaft had been sealed up with a concrete cap at some point in time, but, surprisingly, probably NOT by Hall prior to his departure in 1900.

The Welchs' son – Freddie – eventually assumed the reins of ownership and management of the renowned Dahlonega eatery in later years, and maintains he had heard rumors of a gold mine somewhere on the property all his life, but no one had ever known the actual location of the mine. It was Freddie who initiated the renovation at the Smith House which ultimately uncovered the secret mine.

News of the gold-mining shaft apparently had leaked out back in Hall's day, because the rumors had persisted through the decades since Hall's departure, but even those "in the know," apparently did not know exactly where the mine was located – or, if they did, they weren't forthcoming with the information.

Origin of the Mine

Hall had originally discovered the gold vein beneath his property in 1899 as he was digging the cellar for his new

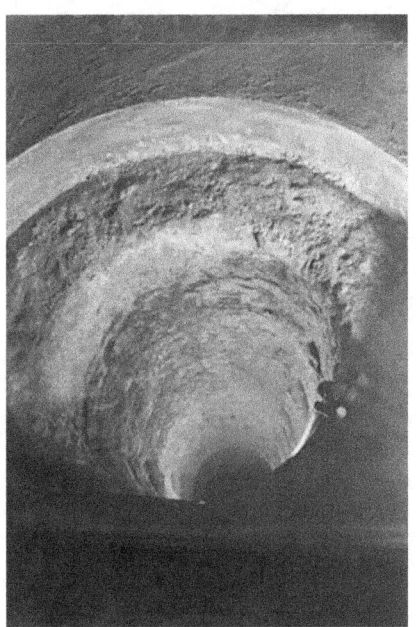

The immense shaft of the gold mine opened by Frank Hall in the lower level of the Smith House Restaurant circa 1898, was discovered (or re-discovered) beneath a concrete cap in 2006. It indicates the degree and depth of Frank Hall's surreptitious mining endeavor in the late 1890s.

An excerpt from the November 3, 1899 issue of the *Dahlonega Nugget* newspaper by Editor W. B. Townsend reads as follows:

"Captain Hall's workmen, while excavating the cellar for his new warehouse on the corner of Chestatee and Waters Street, just across from R.H. Webb's lot, struck a rich gold-bearing vein several feet wide, depth not known."

Editor Townsend went on to note that Capt. Hall had informed him that he would not develop the vein since it ran under his building and was on a town lot. Townsend also noted that Hall had stated that he didn't have any time to spend working a gold mine!

Today, Hall's claim must be considered – at best – to have been subterfuge. His public proclamation of his lack of interest in pursuit of the substantial gold on his property is simply unbelievable, particularly since it emanated from a man who had originally relocated to Dahlonega specifically as a mining superintendent with expertise in mining and who had ultimately been involved with numerous local gold mines in the area for three decades.

It is known today that, in fact, at the very least, Hall did not initially just volunteer to ignore the rich gold vein on his property. He in actuality waged a six-month legal battle with the City of Dahlonega – which he lost – in a vain attempt to gain the right to mine the gold.

After losing the lawsuit, Hall supposedly covered up his gold vein with the fine structure known today as the Smith House and simply walked away from the riches. At least this was the image he presented to the town fathers.

Today, however, we know to the contrary, that though he may in fact have begun construction of the edifice – which later became the Smith House

home, but had either agreed to placate the town fathers by not mining the gold in the vein, or, had been forbidden by the town fathers from pursuit of the gold in the vein because it was located within the city limits and would therefore violate city codes.

In the early days of mining in the Dahlonega area in the mid-1800s, Lumpkin County was pock-marked with mines. In "downtown" Dahlonega, mines once even existed in the middle of town streets. Town fathers eventually realized they must forbid mining within the city limits or risk the collapse of untold numbers of real estate into the shafts dug in the rabid pursuit of the precious metal.

Restaurant – initially as a home, he ultimately had no intention of actually residing in it after losing his court case. It would simply have been too difficult to do so and simultaneously conceal his illicit gold mining activities – which he had obviously made up his mind to pursue.

In point of fact, Hall had decided to use the new structure officially as an assaying office during the day, while maintaining it as a shelter to surreptitiously mine his gold in the cellar – probably during the evening hours. Though he was a law-abiding and highly respected citizen, Frank Hall apparently wasn't about to allow a little city ordinance to deny him the riches to which he felt he was rightfully entitled.

The May 18, 1900 issue of the *Nugget* reported on Hall's new digs: *"Frank W. Hall moved his office last week into his new building and is living in what is known as 'Hope House.'"* The office to which the quotation refers was Hall's professional assay office for testing gold which was located in the present-day Smith House Restaurant building. This business operation no doubt made it very convenient for him to assay the ore of *other miners* during the day, while also openly processing as well – under the same auspices – the gold-bearing soil from his own concealed gold mine. After all, the process of assaying the gold-bearing soils of other individuals was the same as processing the soil from his own mine. It was so simple, and none of the town officials apparently suspected a thing was amiss.

The Mystery Deepens

Interestingly, this raises yet another question. How was Frank Hall actually able to mine and process his gold ore single-handedly? The answer undoubtedly is, he didn't. He almost had to have had an accomplice – or accomplices. After all, it would have been an almost overwhelming chore for him to have mined all that gold bearing soil and then to have hauled it up out of his mine shaft beneath the floor of his home himself.

So who actually mined and hauled the large quantities of gold ore? Did Hall use someone nearby who he paid off to remain quiet? This undoubtedly will remain yet another part of the mystery of this unusual enterprise. In retrospect, it perhaps should not be considered such a surprise that a secret of this magnitude could have been maintained for so many years. After all, those assisting Hall in the surreptitious illicit project were just as guilty legally as was he, so they had good reason to remain silent.

There are a number of other unexplained aspects of Hall's secret venture as well which few if any investigators and speculators of this mysterious mining endeavor have entertained. These include:

1/ Who labored the many hours it must have required to secretly dig the immense mine shaft beneath Hall's home?

A later view of the Smith House (following Hall's departure from the area) photographed circa late 1930s.

The Smith family who first operated the structure as an inn and restaurant are pictured here. Ben, Bessie, and young Verne. If one did not know any better, one might suspect that *"someone"* had just made a donation to a diaper. One parent looks mortified; one looks absolutely disgusted; and young Verne appears absolutely "relieved."

2/ Who actually removed all the spoil and gold ore from that deep shaft?

3/ Where, in fact, was all that gold ore secretly processed if not right there on Hall's residential property?

4/ How much did his accomplices profit from this venture?

5/ Were these accomplices bribed, or did they participate in this task purely motivated by profit?

6/ What became of these accomplices?

7/ How did Hall successfully achieve these substantial tasks without any of his business associates, friends, or family knowing of his actions, particularly since these actions were obviously illegal?

All of these questions continue to add to the mystique of Frank Hall. They quite likely will never be solved.

The Historic Hope House

Interestingly, the *"Hope House"* to which the **Nugget** article referred above, was a structure which once stood in the vicinity of the present-day parking lot of the Smith House Restaurant. Even though the Hopes only lived in this structure for a brief few years, it has been forever associated with them as *"the Hope House."* Mule skinner A.A. Hope purchased the abode as a residence for his family in 1884.

As Dahlonega's oldest surviving domestic structure still in its original location, the historic Hope House, unfortunately, was removed in 1985 from its location at the Smith House property when the decision was made that more space was needed at the highly-popularized Dahlonega eatery. It (the Hope House) was transported to what once was known as Mountain Music Park on south side of nearby Crown Mountain, and its disposition at the time of this writing is unknown.

Due to stringent efforts more recently at preservation of the historic structures and sites in and around Dahlonega, any effort today toward the removal of a structure such as the Hope House would undoubtedly receive more careful consideration by a more preservation-minded town leadership. A number of recent attempts at the removal of historic structures for the erection of new developments have been met with strident opposition by preservation-minded officials for understandable reasons. After all, it is the historic charm of Dahlonega which makes it such a popular travel destination today.

Frank Hall's Departure

It is unknown today why Frank Hall did not completely mine all the gold in the rich vein beneath his home, or why he chose eventually to seal up and conceal the opening to the shaft. Smith House owner Freddie Welch has stated that he had samples of the gold ore from the mine assayed shortly after its discovery, and the results indicated that the gold from the vein therein not only is far from depleted, but is quite rich as well.

When queried why he would not pursue the mining of the gold in the secret shaft himself, Welch apparently indicated that there is much more "gold" in a thriving tourism and dining destination such as the Smith House, than there would be in a small gold mine.

So why did Hall just "pull up stakes" and pull out of town in 1900? Perhaps he had simply accumulated all the wealth he felt he needed from his secret mine and investments in order to be able to comfortably live out the remainder of his life.

Perhaps he just decided that "enough is enough" and sealed up the mine to hide his illicit endeavor.

Speculators have also suggested that perhaps Hall had come to the realization that he or his wife was suffering from a serious health condition, a circumstance which may have altered forever his priorities in life. Just as with many of the other mysteries of Hall's life, these riddles now will also never be solved.

Though Hall's substantial home just off the Dahlonega town square was relatively modern for its day and time and designed to be the "new quarters" for him and his wife, Esther, the couple never occupied the premises as a home. Instead, after Hall had sealed up and hidden the mine shaft, he and Esther quietly moved to an area known as "Ingleside" near Atlanta – departing Dahlonega forever.

Interestingly – and sadly – despite what may have been immense illicit riches, Hall did not live long enough to enjoy much of the wealth he had accumulated. Shortly after his move to Atlanta in 1900, he died suddenly and unexpectedly at age 56 from typhoid fever, no doubt contracting the disease – ironically – from an impure water source in the over-crowded circumstances of the swiftly-recovering city which had risen from the ashes of the U.S. Civil War some 35 years earlier.

According to his obituary in the **Dahlonega Nugget**, Hall was described as *"the richest person in Lumpkin County long before he decided to take up his new place of abode."* He was also a public-spirited citizen who represented Lumpkin County in the Georgia State Legislature, Dahlonega in the mayor's office, and North Georgia College as a member of the Board of Trustees.

Had the secret gold mine never been discovered, there might always

This bucolic and scenic photograph captures the beauty of "Hall's Mill" which once existed on the Chestatee River near Dahlonega. The ruins of this structure - also one of Frank Hall's businesses - still stand a short distance from the abandoned Hall's Mill Bridge. (Photo courtesy of GA Dept. of Archives & History, Atlanta)

have been a mystery surrounding the question of why Hall would have built such an impressive and inviting residential structure just off the town square in Dahlonega, only to take up residence instead in a smaller and much lesser-quality abode such as the Hope House. Today, Hall's impetus is quite clear.

Another Departure Motivation?

According to the late Dahlonega historian Madeleine K. Anthony, another run-in with the city fathers may also have had an impact on Hall's decision to leave the city. According to Ms. Anthony, historic records indicate that the town fathers not only refused to grant Hall the right to mine the gold on his property, but also to install a new-fangled convenience known as "indoor-plumbing" to which he was accustomed.

In that day and time in the South, indoor toilets were actually understandably considered unsanitary, since they consisted of what was known as a very odorous and unhygienic "out-house." The location of such a structure within the confines of one's home – particularly in the hot and humid climate of the

South – was so unacceptable as to be inconceivable. The odors and other prevailing detestable aspects of this option alone simply made it unthinkable.

Hall, however, had been born and raised in Vermont where it was far too cold in the winter months for one to use an out-house, particularly if one had another option, and the Vermont Halls apparently had solved the problem by somehow moving "the throne" indoors to "heated" space while somehow also dealing with the detestable aspects of the circumstances.

Perhaps Hall had acquired one of the first "flush toilets" in the area and had intended to set up his "indoor john" with that "commodious" device. Whatever the successful circumstances he had developed for the indoor device, it apparently was a practice Hall had doubtless hoped to recreate in his Dahlonega home – and apparently had even specially set up his new home for such use – only to be denied once again by the city.

Those days in the late 1800s in Dahlonega were a time when the town offered no city water or sewage service whatsoever – right up even to the day the late Ben and Bessie Smith opened the original Smith House in 1922. The inn, however, did have its own well, with a pump powered by electricity generated by a giant water-wheel at nearby Cane Creek Falls, and at least part of this infrastructure was courtesy of Frank Hall.

"There also were woodstoves in the lobby and in some of the rooms for winter guests," the Smith's son, the late Vernon Smith recalled prior to his passing. "One of my jobs was to cut and split wood to keep the stoves burning. I also had to milk the cows which we kept so our guests could have fresh milk and butter."

The Carriage House, once a vital aspect of the Smith House operations in the early 1900s when the horse and buggy was still the basic mode of travel, is pictured here. Buggies and small conveyances were housed in the upper front portion and the horses were taken around to the rear of this structure where they were housed in stalls. This structure still exists to the front-right of the Smith House complex today. Price Memorial Hall of present-day University of North Georgia is visible to the right rear.

Pictured in his traditional white coat and high cook's hat, long-time Dahlonega resident Virstee Howell once prepared delicious meals at the Smith House during the 1930s and '40s. Patrons traveled from miles away to enjoy Virstee's "ham patties" and "banana fritters" which were dishes he invented himself. When he retired, patrons mourned his departure for years.

Vestiges from Yesteryear

Unbeknownst by most guests today at the Smith House, the "carriage house" which once sheltered the livestock (horses) used by guests to pull their buggies and other conveyances to the popular inn and eatery in the early days still stands in the courtyard (to the right as one walks into the Smith House). The vehicles (buggies and carriages) were housed on the ground (front) level of the carriage house, and the livestock were taken to stalls in the rear lower level. Hay used to feed the horses was stored in the rear upper level.

Yet another surprise "uncovered" in the secret gold mine in its recent "discovery" were items such as a 1940s-era light

bulb, indicating a later owner of the property apparently had earlier discovered the secret gold mining shaft and then, for reasons unknown today, also had covered it back over with a concrete cap.

What explanation might one draw from this curious occurrence? Did the individual who tossed in the 1940s-era light bulb assume he had simply discovered an old dry water well? We'll never know the answer to that question either. Lots of unsolved mysteries.

Though Frank Hall is long gone today, the evidence of his former existence in Dahlonega – with historic "Hall's Block" and "the Hall House" on the town square, the Smith House just off the town square, and the remnants of Hall's Mill down on the Chestatee River – is still very visible today. And the mysterious circumstances surrounding the hidden mine shaft will no doubt live on in perpetuity.

Grandpa Was An Outlaw

Jeff Anderson was the leader of a notorious band of outlaws who terrorized Lumpkin County during the U.S. Civil War. After escaping prison in the second of several jail-breaks, he lived a hidden life for the next few years in Dalton, Georgia, before heading west in 1901. According to records, he settled first in Texas, but soon moved to Oklahoma - which was still a frontier without statehood status - to avoid being recaptured by the authorities. Anderson family records indicated Jeff never returned to Georgia, and never married, but recently discovered evidence has revealed the former outlaw lived his final years near Chattanooga, Tennessee, . . . and even more interestingly, that he had a wife and children there.

Thomas Jefferson "Jeff" Anderson didn't necessarily "start off bad." It just seemed to be in his blood. He apparently came from a respectable family. No one really knows when he took "the road less traveled," but at some point, he obviously just decided that a law-abiding life was not the life for him.

Jeff's father, William H. Anderson, and uncle, John Anderson, moved to Dahlonega, Georgia, from Habersham County in time to be listed in the ***1834 Federal Census of Lumpkin*** not long after Dahlonega and Lumpkin County were established. These Andersons settled in Crumby District, east of Dahlonega in the Philippi Community (present-day Cavender Creek vicinity).

"John and William must have been prosperous due to the numerous records one may still find documenting their activities at the Dahlonega Clerk of Court's Office,"

wrote family researchers who provided information about the pioneer brothers in the ***Heritage of Lumpkin County, Georgia, 1832-1996***. Among other pursuits, the brothers farmed, bought and sold land, and owned stock in the Spring Place Mining Company in Fannin County.

William H. and Margaret Anderson were the parents of seven sons and two daughters. Thomas Jefferson was their sixth child, born in 1839. There is no way of knowing today whether Jeff showed violent tendencies in his earlier years or if his criminal pursuits were a product of family divisiveness created by the Civil War.

Census records reveal that William H. Anderson owned one slave. Military records show that Jeff's brothers, William M., Isaac, Henry, and Benjamin, fought for the Confederacy. Those records also show that their brother – Thomas Abraham – abhorred slavery (apparently honoring his given middle name) and enlisted in the Union Army.

Jeff initially enlisted in the First Georgia Volunteer Infantry, but, true to form, soon deserted, perhaps because of the influence of his older brother Abraham's anti-slavery stance. More than likely, however, it was just another example of his developing lawless nature.

Just as is Jeff's early character development hazy and obscure today, so also is any explanation as to why he ultimately morphed into the blood-thirsty leader of a band of outlaws known as *"the bridge burners"* who terrorized the citizens and soldiers of north Georgia, and used guerrilla tactics to constantly harass local Confederate units.

According to research conducted by the late Dahlonega historian Bill Kinsland, Jeff Anderson was arrested by Lumpkin County Sheriff John Early in February of 1862, and tried for *Assault and Battery*, *Assault and Battery with Intent To Rape*, and *Misdemeanor*. He was also arrested under an order from Captain William Martin and charged with desertion from the First Georgia Volunteer Infantry.

Dahlonega Escape

Considered a very dangerous man, Jeff was confined to the "common jail" in Dahlonega with his legs securely fastened to the wall with a heavy logging chain. The sheriff no doubt was convinced that chain was all it took to lock down the criminal.

Early on March 9 of 1862 – the day that Jeff Anderson was due to be picked up by military authorities to be returned to his unit – his brothers Henry and Benjamin "Dock" Anderson, accompanied by a friend named Bart Edge, rode into town and tied their horses in front of the jail.

An uneasy Jeff Anderson was photographed here, probably in his late 20s or early 30s in a long frock coat. This may have been a prison photo, due to the position of the hands which is strangely reminiscent of the position required when one is wearing handcuffs and attempting to hide that fact. (Photo courtesy of George Anderson)

Back in the 1860s, the good Lord simply made men "tough." They had to be, just to survive. The ambient temperature in the un-heated calaboose in which Jeff was incarcerated undoubtedly was well below freezing that cold March morning, and Jeff had survived in it all night long.

Historians today believe this jail quite probably was the one which once existed on the east side of Chestatee Street one block south of the old Baptist Church building in Dahlonega. In this facility, the main cell was accessed from the upper story of the jail through a trap

Mary "Mollie" Rebecca Dilbeck Anderson (1862-1952), wife of Civil War outlaw Jeff Anderson, lived to a ripe 90 years, and died in Tennessee.

door. Prisoners entered the enclosure by walking down a ladder.

When jailer John McCoskey arrived to bring Anderson his breakfast that cold March morning, Bart Edge reportedly approached the lawman and asked to visit the prisoner. McCoskey – apparently unfamiliar with the men and sensing little if any danger in the request – obligingly led Edge and one of the Andersons into the jail where he opened the dungeon door.

Jeff immediately complained that he was *"powerful sick"* and begged for "Doc" Howard to come attend to him.

Caught completely off guard, McCoskey went to the front door to send someone for Dr. Howard, but before he could take a step back, Jeff Anderson was *"halfway out of the dungeon, coat and boots off"* sprinting for freedom.

McCoskey later testified in court that Anderson *"pitched through the jail door, I after him, and down the steps."* The jailer's nephew Walter McCoskey gave testimony that the escaped prisoner hit him in the head as he ran by and that he saw one of the men step in front of his uncle (McCoskey) to delay his pursuit of the jail-breaker.

Whatever the circumstances, by the time McCoskey could manoeuver around the obstructing relative, Jeff Anderson, reportedly, was already fading from sight up the street, ironically toward the courthouse. According to an account of the incident, he ran *"across the square, past the Mustering Grounds and down Wimpy Mill Road,"* before disappearing.

Bart Edge, Dock and Henry Anderson were later arrested and charged with the crime of *Rescue*. Sheriff Early testified that Anderson, amazingly, had used a rasp to cut himself loose from the heavy log chain. How his no-doubt numb fingers had been able to saw through a thick logging chain with what no-doubt was at best a second-rate worn-out rasp is anybody's guess today. As previously stated, the outlaws of the 1860s were mighty tough hombres.

Edge and the Anderson brothers later testified that they had not helped Jeff to escape at all, and *"would have caught him if they could."* Despite the obvious prison-break and other charges, there is no record today of the case ever coming to trial.

Henry Anderson, who was two years younger than Jeff, was 21 at the time. He enlisted in Smith's Legion of the Georgia Volunteers two months later. He was transferred to Company C, 65th Regiment, Georgia Infantry a year later. He subsequently died in the Loudon, Tennessee hospital on March 29, 1863.

"Dock," whose real name was Benjamin F. Anderson, was Jeff's youngest brother and only 17 years of age at the time. He served in Company C of the 52nd Regiment of the Georgia Volunteers, Barton's Brigade. Bart Edge had enlisted in the same unit, and was captured at the Battle of Vicksburg in July of 1863.

Re-Captured & Re-Escaped

After his escape in Dahlonega, Jeff Anderson remained on the run for several months before finally being recaptured. An article in the October 4, 1862 **Atlanta Southern Confederacy** noted, *"Yesterday a mounted escort, detailed from Captain Tillet's Artillery Company, arrived here in charge of a large amount of Gold from the Mint at Dahlonega, belonging to the Confederate government. They also brought with them in chains a desperado named Anderson, whose outrages in Lumpkin County and the vicinity have been intolerable for some time. He is a deserter from the 1st Georgia Regulars, and has been hiding himself in the caves and dens of the mountains for the last five or six months, harboring runaway negroes, stealing, robbing widows and helpless women and children whose husbands and fathers are in the war, and had become a terror to the whole country. He will be properly cared for."*

It is difficult to imagine today how one could survive more than a few weeks in a cave in the mountains above Dahlonega, Georgia – much of that time in the dead of winter – but somehow Jeff Anderson managed just such a feat for almost eight months.

Author Harold E. O'Kelley relates in his book, **Dahlonega's Blue Ridge Rangers in the Civil War**, that Jeff Anderson was imprisoned in the Atlanta jail along with *"fellow Bridge Burners, Yankee POWs, and some 'Engine Thieves' who were captured during the failed Andrews' Raid."* The story of how Union spies stole a train and attempted to destroy the Confederate rail line between Atlanta and Chattanooga was portrayed in the Walt Disney major motion picture **The Great Locomotive Chase** filmed in northeast Georgia in the 1955. An article describing this incident appears in *Mystery & History in Georgia, Volume I* by author Olin Jackson.

According to O'Kelley, some of the incarcerated *"Engine Thieves"* and *"Bridge Burners"* subsequently made a daring escape from the Atlanta prison. Some of Andrews' men later described one of their party as a *"Rebel Deserter"* who stayed with their group for a few days before leaving them somewhere north of Atlanta. This may well have been Jeff Anderson, who was known to have returned to the mountains of north Georgia where he continued his guerilla war tactics.

After the war was over in 1865, Jeff, who was still a *"Wanted"* man, reportedly hid out on his older brother Abraham's farm in Whitfield County near Dalton for a number of years. Abraham, the Union sympathizer, was described as *"religious and kind-hearted"* and perhaps thought that his wayward brother could be reformed by providing him with a safe haven and kindness.

NW GA Residence

If these were Abraham's thoughts and hopes, they ultimately were vanquished. Jeff, though remaining with his brother for over two decades, ultimately could not shake the demons which apparently possessed him, and departed for parts unknown sometime in the mid-1880s, apparently as a result of a serious family rift.

The details of Jeff Anderson's life from the mid-1880s to the turn of the 20th century remained a mystery for approximately a century before a distant relative – Bill Smyth – appeared in Dahlonega searching for information about his unique forebear. In the midst of his inquiries, Mr. Smyth explained to Dahlonega historians that his notorious

grandfather Jeff had married Mary "Mollie" Rebecca Dilbeck (1862-1952) from the Jack's River area in Fannin County in 1886 when he was 47 and she was 24. They had eight children – four boys and four girls.

The first child was Bill Smyth's mother, Mary Georgia Ann Anderson, who was born in Rockmart, Georgia, on January 29, 1887. Mary Georgia Ann's parents must have been among the first settlers in Rockmart, since that town was only incorporated in 1872. Whether Jeff himself was living in Rockmart when his children were being born is unknown today, but he quite likely also resided there.

In the 1880s, Rockmart was still a wild backwoods crossroads town located near the historic "old Alabama Road," a branch of which passed through Dahlonega and continued across Georgia, passing between Rockmart and nearby Cedartown, Georgia. It was one of the primary routes westward for pioneers, and would have been a natural avenue for a criminal to use in flight. Rockmart was an area in which a *"Wanted"* criminal could easily hide, since law enforcement – particularly in post-Civil War north Georgia – was virtually nonexistent.

Rockmart, in fact, was a haven for criminals during this time-period. It had been borne out of the advancement of the railroad through northwest Georgia. Prior to that time, little more than a rough-and-tumble community called Van Wert had existed in that vicinity. It was inhabited by thieves, marauders, cut-throats and other desperados.

Van Wert had been founded in 1837, while native Cherokee Indians still resided in the area. A documented Cherokee village once existed there near the confluence of Euharlee and Fish creeks. Even in the early days of its development, Van Wert was reported to be so filthy and degenerate that area residents referred to it derisively as "Clean Town."

At approximately that same time, Van Wert was named the county seat of Paulding County (in which it was located prior to the creation of Polk County), causing it to experience a jump in growth. The discovery of gold only a few miles outside the town added to the growth.

Van Wert soon had a population in excess of 100, a courthouse, a church, two hotels, several commercial shops and businesses, a county courthouse, a blacksmith shop, several saloons, an array of prostitutes, and even an academy. Today, nothing remains of any of the above-described commercial aspect of Van Wert except the historic church and a remnant of what may have been the town's old jail.

It seems some things die hard too. As of the year 2023, the Rockmart/Van

Bill Smyth, grandson of Thomas Jefferson "Jeff" Anderson. (Photo courtesy of Anne Amerson)

Wert vicinity still reported one of the highest crime rates per capita in the entire United States.

From Rockmart to The Cove

The other Anderson children sired by Jeff Anderson in Rockmart were Maud Josephine (b. 1889); Mattie (b. 1891 and married Oscar Hunter, a policeman); Charles Martin (b. 1893); William Arthur (b. 1896, and known as "Clint"); Henry Franklin (b. 1899); Benjamin Harrison (born 1901) and Viola (born 1904). William, Henry and Benjamin bear the same names coincidentally as three of Jeff's brothers. It quite possibly was the increased growth of Van Wert – and subsequently Rockmart – which gave rise to Jeff's "itch to move on."

"Mama told me about moving to McLemore Cove between Pigeon Mountain and Lookout Mountain when she was six years old," Bill recounted. "They moved in three covered wagons, and Mama slept in the one that held the barrels of Grandpa's whiskey. When she woke up, she couldn't walk from breathing the fumes!

McLemore Cove in extreme northwest Georgia, was another secluded locale which offered refuge to those who wished to avoid law enforcement authorities, and was a natural hide-out for Jeff. Due to its inaccessibility caused by the high surrounding peaks of the Blue Ridge Mountains south of Chattanooga, "the cove" continues to be lightly populated even today.

It was spots such as Rockmart and McLemore Cove which allowed Jeff to avoid recapture by law enforcement authorities for all the remaining years of his life. He lived a life generally of avoidance and disguise.

"Mama said they returned to

and and foot. Had
ed Maryland, they
once recruited to the
n arms. Let it not
id is unwilling, cold,
not so.
still throwing up the
de of Washington.—
rom the Potomac to
an is reported to have
he creek of Antietam.
It 15,000. It was de
Halleck, and Mac,
es require desperate
c, was to take all the
o that he saved Mary-
fice the most of them.
is time that we were
elming numbers.
t Sharpsburg, 40,000
ew recruits, left Al-
o surprise Richmond,
proceeded far South
fearing that McClel-
defeated and Wash-

een heard from Mc
ent those dispatches
General Lee states

The news from the Continent is unimportant. Garibaldi is worse.
The Opinion Nationale, of Paris, Prince Napoleon's organ, condemns the idea of an
emancipation proclamation for the negroes in
anticipation, and in very severe terms, while
the Dublin Freeman's Journal (a Union paper)
points out the inutility of such a measure for
the negroes themselves.

Arrival of Gold—A Deserter.

Yesterday a mounted escort, detailed from
Captain Tiller's Artillery company, arrived
here in charge of a large amount of Gold from
the Mint at Dahlonega, belonging to the Confederate government.
The also brought with them in chains a desperado named Anderson, whose outrages in
Lumpkin county and the vicinity have been intolerable for some time. He is a deserter from
the 1st Georgia Regulars, and has been hiding
himself in the caves and dens of the mountains for the last five or six months, harboring
runaway negroes, stealing, robbing widows
and helpless women and children whose husbands and fathers are in the war, and had become a terror to the whole country. He will
be properly cared for.—*Atlanta Confederacy.*

Notice.

QUARTERMASTER'S DEPARTMENT, }
Columbus, Ga., Sept. 13, '62. }
I have been charged with the important duty of providing Shoes for our Soldiers, and I
must appeal to the patriotism of our people to

them promptly. A
for Subscribers ha
for delivery. They
Receipts, and we w
may direct. We ho
owners.
The Cotton of Sui
the market price b
change for Bonds.
A G E
Savannah—R. Ha
Columbus—D. A
Macon—N. C. Mu
Newnan—J. J. Pi
LaGrange—Jesse

oct4-2m

SAW MILLE
WE have on han
we will excha
oct3tf

NOTICE TO

I AM authorized.
ed from my Regi
Smith, to raise a co
be attached to Maj
Artillery. All pers
rolled will be recei
are subject to be c
President in consec
the Conscript act.
Persons wishing t
names at once. I l
Virginia and Fast

Beneath the sub-headline *"Arrival of Gold - A Deserter,"* an article in the **Columbus** (Georgia) **Sun** newspaper of October 6, 1862, documents in its second paragraph outlaw Jeff Anderson's transport from the Dahlonega, Georgia Jail to the Atlanta Jail. Interestingly, he was incarcerated in Atlanta with a group of captured Union spies known in history as *"Andrews Raiders,"* who had recently stolen a locomotive in Big Shanty, Georgia. Several of these men later escaped from the Atlanta Jail with Anderson to hide out in the north Georgia mountains. Several others – including leader James J. Andrews – were hung in Atlanta, earning them a footnote in history, as well as even more fame from a 20th Century major motion picture – *"The Great Locomotive Chase"* – filmed in 1957 in northeast Georgia and starring Fess Parker, Jeffrey Hunter, Slim Pickens and others. (Period news clipping courtesy of the Digital Library of Georgia Newspapers and Robert S. Davis, Jr.)

Dahlonega one time when she was young," Bill continued. "She always wanted to come back (to Lumpkin County) too after that, but she said there was no good way to come because there simply were no bridges or even a real road back then."

Another reason Bill's mother may not have returned with her family to Dahlonega, was that her father not only was persona non grata, he quite likely was still a *"Wanted"* criminal in Lumpkin County. There is, however, evidence

to indicate Jeff Anderson did return to Dahlonega in the 1880s when his mother died.

Smyth said his mother described the house in which she had grown up as being on stilts and having a metal roof. She remembered how frightened they were when they heard mountain panthers jump on the tin roof. When that happened, a hot fire reportedly would be built in the fireplace to keep the wild cats from coming down the chimney. This described home quite likely was the one in which they lived in McLemore Cove. It represented still more of Jeff's life of avoidance out in the wild countryside beyond the reach of law enforcement.

Mary Georgia Ann ultimately grew into womanhood and married Robert Henry Smyth in 1905. The couple raised six boys, one of whom died in childbirth. Lewis was born in 1906, Chester (known as "Chub") in 1908, Jack in 1916, Robert Lee ("Bud") in 1919, and William ("Bill") in 1927.

Jeff's wife, Mary "Mollie" Rebecca Anderson reportedly lived in Tennessee until 1952 when she was 90. According to her grandson Bill, she was still working in her garden and cooking at that time, even though she weighed only 76 pounds. She also reportedly did not have a gray hair on her head, and was said to have been a full-blood Indian.

"Grandma was the sweetest person you'd ever meet," Bill said. "Mama was just like her too. She and her sisters were very hard-working and religious. You'd never suspect that their father was an outlaw. The boys were hard-working too, but I've heard tell they were about as rough as their father."

Bill remembers his mother describing her father as having red hair and pale blue eyes that "looked like they were looking right through you."

"I've been told Grandpa was quite a fiddle player too," Bill smiled. "His son, William Arthur, whom I called 'Uncle Clint,' learned to play by watching Grandpa. When Grandpa would call the steps for people to dance, they said you could hear him a mile away."

A Secret Wife?

According to information about Jeff Anderson in the **Heritage of Lumpkin County 1832-1996**, he, for unknown reasons eventually migrated westward to Bonham, Texas (near Dallas) in the autumn of 1901. Anderson descendants of Thomas Abraham wrote, *"We are certain Jeff was in Texas during this period because his nephew, Henry, and his wife Cordelia, went to Texas to find Jeff. While they were there, their third son William was born on October 19, 1901.*

"Jeff later went to Oklahoma because there was no law there in order to avoid being captured. Oklahoma was Indian territory at this time. . . . We are certain Jeff was in Durant, Oklahoma around April 1905, because Henry and Henry's wife Cordelia went on a second trip in a covered wagon to find Jeff.

"While they were there, their fourth son, Clint was born on April 29, 1905. Henry and Cordelia spotted Jeff at a distance, but he left with some men on horseback and they never caught him. The family received messages from Jeff on two occasions, once from Durant and another time from Hugo. Jeff never returned."

That information about the outlaw Jeff Anderson was submitted by George Anderson of Maryville, Tennessee, the grandson of Abraham's son, Henry Clay Anderson, and his wife Cordelia, who went to Texas and Oklahoma looking for Jeff. George was astonished to learn that Jeff had married and fathered a number of children.

"I'm not sure we're talking about the same man," George puzzled, even after speaking by phone with Bill Smyth, possibly a cousin of whom he had known nothing until recently. "There are lots of Andersons, and there may have been two Jeff Andersons. Some of the dates just don't seem to correspond."

Could there possibly have been two different "Jeff Andersons" who were both Civil War-era outlaws who originated from the same locale? Possible, but not likely.

Nevertheless, if Bill Smyth's grandfather was the same man as George Anderson's great-great uncle, why did he keep his marriage a secret from his family and why did he not inform them of his whereabouts? Why indeed did he leave his Georgia wife – Mary Rebecca – in the first place?

A possible explanation may lie in the fact that the alienation between the brothers at the time Jeff left Abraham's household may have been so bitter that Jeff simply chose to permanently cut all ties and disappear forever. Worse relationships have existed throughout history. The simple lure of a new life with a new wife could have provided all the motivation an individual like Jeff Anderson needed.

Still More GA Children?

If the man believed to be in Texas and Oklahoma for several years following the turn of the century was in fact Bill Smyth's grandfather, he must at least have traveled back to Georgia on occasion, because he reportedly sired additional children there in 1901 and 1904 with Mary Rebecca.

Interestingly, prior to his move to the West, Jeff Anderson had made his home near the Tennessee border (probably at or near the aforementioned McLemore Cove), less than forty miles northwest of Abraham Anderson's farm near Dalton. Despite the nearness of their residences, they apparently never encountered one another again following their final separation, possibly due to the mountainous terrain separating them.

According to stories Bill described about his grandpa Jeff Anderson, the outlaw apparently mellowed at least to some extent with age and a family, but remained feisty even into his later years.

"(I've been told) Grandpa (Jeff's) dog went missing one time," he laughed again. "When he heard a dog barking that sounded like his, he followed the sound until he came to a fenced-in yard. He opened the gate and walked in and started to untie his dog. When a man appeared and demanded to know what he was doing, Grandpa calmly ignored him.

"Don't you know you can get into trouble coming into a man's yard and stealing his dog?" the fellow demanded.

"Grandpa - according to the story - pulled out his gun and replied, 'Well, son, don't you know it works both ways?' He then turned around and walked back out the gate leading his dog."

Bill Smyth says he has information showing that his grandfather died in 1913, and remembers his mother showing him the outlaw's unmarked grave at Strawhill Cemetery, "down the Dalton pike" from Cleveland, Tennessee. Could it be possible that his body was returned there from Texas or Oklahoma for burial following his death? Or had he returned to live out his later years in that vicinity with Mollie?

Bill Smyth's grandmother, Mary "Mollie" Rebecca Anderson lived a number of years longer (until 1952) and was buried at Red Hill Cemetery just outside Cleveland, Tennessee. She did not want to be buried beside Jeff because she thought that cemetery was too far from where she was living near some of her children.

Bill added that he has heard that his grandfather died from being "bled," which once was a popular medical treatment for numerous ailments. It seems ironic that in an age when maverick behavior was often blamed on "bad blood," the notorious "black sheep" of the family should meet his end by a treatment thought to rid the body of "bad blood" even though he apparently went "straight" later in his life.

Famous Associations of Historic Castleberry Bridge

As one of the first byways in Lumpkin County, Castleberry Bridge Road has witnessed the comings and goings of numerous historic figures over the years. Its builder's family is also connected to countless historic aspects of both Lumpkin and Hall counties.

Castleberry Bridge Road which crosses the Etowah River and extends between Auraria, Georgia, and Highway 9 South in Lumpkin County, commemorates the name of one of the first settlers in the area. Elisha Castleberry and wife – Jane – undoubtedly arrived soon after gold was discovered in what then was part of the Cherokee Nation, since their daughter – Fannie – was born there in 1830.

The gold mining community which was developed at this site was without a name until the summer of 1832, when Nathaniel Nuckolls built a hotel that was soon overflowing with rooming occupants. People began calling the town "Nuckollsville" after the enterprising innkeeper until it was officially christened "Auraria" the following November. Senator (and former Vice President of the United States) John C. Calhoun, a well-known politician from South Carolina who owned gold-mining property in the Auraria area had insisted upon the new name since he considered

"Nuckollsville" to be too vulgar a name. Auraria is derived from Latin and means "gold" or "golden area."

Progenitor Elisha Castleberry

When the state of Georgia held a land lottery in 1832-33 to distribute the four million acres of land ultimately taken from the native Cherokees, Elisha Castleberry drew Land Lot 673 of District 12, which was located just west of Auraria. An old land lottery map shows the Etowah River running through the center of his new property. By 1850, Castleberry had acquired fifteen 40-acre gold lots in and around Auraria and many city lots as well.

Aside from being present for the north Georgia gold rush, family stories maintain that Elisha was also one of the "Forty-Niners" who traveled to California when gold was discovered there twenty years later, but he apparently didn't remain very long, since he died in Lumpkin County in April of 1850. He was buried at Antioch Baptist Church in Auraria, an appropriate final resting spot, since he had donated the land for both the church and cemetery.

In his will, Elisha left slaves, stock, blacksmith tools, furniture, and land lots to his wife Jane. When she died in 1873, she was buried beside him.

Elisha and Jane Castleberry had five sons (Edmund, Richard J., Jackson, Samuel Guerry, and Frank) and five daughters (Phoebe, Eliza, Samantha, Fannie, and Sarah). Both Edmund and Jackson listed their occupation as "*miner*" in the *1850 Federal Census of Lumpkin County*. Edmund is buried at Antioch near his parents under a tombstone inscribed "*Rev. E.G. Castleberry*."

Eliza was never married and was still living with her mother in 1870, according to the *1870 Federal Census*.

Eliza's Famous Ears

Eliza's eyesight reportedly failed in her later years, but her hearing reportedly was extremely acute. At some point in her life her neighbors apparently realized Eliza possessed this unusual capability, and began taking advantage of it to keep track of their cattle.

Prior to the days of the stock laws, livestock were allowed to freely roam the mountains and river valleys, except when the cows were brought home in the evening to be milked. Since their owners never knew from one moment to the

The original Castleberry Bridge, an aged heavy iron structure (pictured) spanning the Etowah River just west of Auraria, Georgia, disappeared years ago, and was replaced by a more modern concrete version. Since the property on each side of the road at this site was owned by Elisha Castleberry, the original bridge commemorated his name, and the tradition continues to the present day in the name of the road. It appears that the contractor for this bridge was the same as that which constructed historic Hall's Mill Bridge which still exists (though abandoned today) near the juncture of the Chestatee River and Highway 60 south of Dahlonega. (Photo courtesy of the GA Dept. of Archives & History, Atlanta)

Photographed circa 1900 in Auraria, Georgia, near Castleberry Bridge Road, a black family by the name of Castleberry paused on the former gold rush community's dusty main road. The two elderly individuals in this photo quite possibly were former slaves once owned by Elisha Castleberry. (Photo courtesy of GA Dept. of Archives & History, Atlanta)

next where their cattle actually were, it almost always required hours to locate the wayward beasts.

After Eliza had reached an elderly age, her neighbors in Auraria who owned the free-ranging cattle began bringing their cowbells to "Granny" Castleberry to allow her to listen to the tone of each cow's bell prior to the time it was hung around the animal's neck. When an individual's cow then needed to be located, Eliza – who by that point knew the tone of each owner's cowbell – reportedly could almost always send that owner in the correct direction of his or her cow based upon the sound (which only she could hear) of that cow's respective bell. Years after she died, Auraria residents continued to mourn Eliza's departure – not only because she was such a likeable person, but also because of the

many hours she saved them when they needed to locate their cows.

Samantha Castleberry married Thomas Christian who owned an interest in the Whim Hill Mine and other mining property in the area. Their son – Benjamin Franklin Christian – had a teaming business which hauled freight between Gainesville and Auraria by mule train. He later opened a general merchandise store and mail-order business in Auraria.

Howser Family Connection

Sarah Castleberry married Henry Howser in 1864 following the death of her first husband, L.R. Williams. Howser was a builder as well as a miner. He laid the foundation for the Dawson County Courthouse in 1858.

Howser also built the first schoolhouse as well as a 40-room hotel in

Dawsonville. Constructed circa 1887 just south of the courthouse, the elaborate Howser Hotel unfortunately burned to the ground in 1904.

In the late 1860s, Henry Howser, his brother Thomas, and Sarah's nephew – Josephus Castleberry – built another prominent landmark in the county – Howser Mill – on Shoal Creek. At last check (2023), this historic landmark was still standing a short distance from downtown Dawsonville on Howser Mill Road.

Richard J. Castleberry, the second son of Elisha and Jane, married Martha Thompson in 1843. The *1860 Federal Census of Lumpkin County* shows them living there with five children (sons Josephus, 15; Zachery Taylor, 14; Marcus, 12; Richard C., 10; and a daughter, America, nicknamed "Merrica," 6).

When Martha died in 1868 at the age of 43, she was buried at Antioch Church near the graves of her husband's parents. A year later, Richard married Cynthia Thompson, whose grandfather, Andrew Thompson, was one of the first White settlers in adjacent Hall County.

Origin of "Thompson" Bridge

Andrew built a home in Hall beside the Chattahoochee River (just across the river from Dawson County) as early as 1819 and established a trading post there for Indians and the few other White settlers in the area. His three sons – Guilford Green, Ovid, and Andrew Jackson Thompson – built and operated a toll bridge across the river and established a mill nearby.

Over the years, covered wooden bridges, a pontoon bridge, an iron bridge, and a modern concrete-and-steel bridge have replaced that original toll bridge, and each one was called "Thompson Bridge."

Even though Richard Castleberry was 48 and Cynthia Thompson was

In the late 1860s, Henry Howser, his brother Thomas, and Josephus Castleberry built Howser Mill on Shoal Creek in Dawson County. At last check (2023), this historic landmark was still standing a short distance from downtown Dawsonville on Howser Mill Road.

only 21 at the time of their marriage, he outlived her by nine years. They did not have any children and both are buried in Alta Vista Cemetery in Gainesville, Georgia.

Richard's son by his first wife – Josephus (born in 1845) – is believed to be the J.F. Castleberry who operated two of Dahlonega's large hotels in the early 1900s. An item in the June 22, 1900, issue of *The Dahlonega Nugget* announced that J.F. Castleberry had *"recently opened out the old Burnside House now known as the Dahlonega Hotel. Mr. Castleberry used to run the Hall House and his manner of feeding and treating people are too well-known to receive any comment from us."*

Richard's second son – Zachery Taylor Castleberry – married Nancy E. "Nannie" Palmour in Hall County. Zach undoubtedly was named for the national hero of that day who became the 12th U.S. president.

First National Bank Founder

Z.T. Castleberry was one of the founders of the First National Bank of Gainesville and served as the bank's president from 1891 to 1917. He, along with Col. S.C. Dunlap, was also one of the organizers of the Gainesville and Chattahoochee Power and Manufacturing Company, a business which generated electricity for the city of Gainesville and operated an electric railroad in town.

Marcus Ferdinand Castleberry married Margaret Frances Graham in 1866. They had nine children.

Richard C. Castleberry married Mary Catherine "Kate" Prater, the daughter of Joseph and Martha Ann Hope Prater. They lived in Gainesville, where Richard C. ran a general merchandise store in a building belonging to his father-in-law.

In 1889, Richard was vying for appointment as postmaster in Gainesville. The man doling out such patronage positions was none other than former Confederate General James Longstreet, a leading Republican who had made Gainesville his home after the Civil War.

Richard and three other individuals coveting the postmaster position were all nevertheless disappointed when Longstreet selected another individual. Richard and the other three applicants protested Longstreet's selection, but their objections were to no avail. Though there reportedly was no evidence of arson, Longstreet's expansive home in Gainesville suspiciously fell victim to a raging fire several days later.

The Texas Castleberrys

A few years later in 1894, Richard C. apparently had soured on life in north Georgia. He and wife Kate, her mother Martha Ann Hope Prater, and their first six surviving children, departed Gainesville to move by covered wagon to greener grass in Texas. Richard may have been

Thomas Howser (1835-1916) married Easter Brown on August 4, 1878, and, along with Josephus Castleberry and Thomas's brother, Henry, built - among many other edifices - Howser Mill in Dawson County. Notice the immense gnarled hands and fingers, signs of the wear and tear imposed by extreme physical labor. The Howsers were noted as builders and entrepreneurs in both Dawson and Lumpkin counties. (Photo courtesy of GA Dept. of Archives & History, Atlanta)

enticed by the promise of good, cheap farmland being opened up in the state by the railroads. He farmed until his retirement in 1923, and died six years later in Meadow, Texas, in 1929.

Interestingly, Richard C. Castleberry's Texas-bred grandson – Paul John – later remembered hearing stories as a child about his great-grandfather (described to him as a "mountain man" who lived near a river with a strange-sounding Indian name). He subsequently visited relatives in Georgia when he was 12 years old and was shown the home of Richard J. Castleberry whose father was the namesake of a pioneer byway in Lumpkin County whose historic roots are almost forgotten today.

Memories Of Old Yahoola Lodge

It was originally built by early settlers of north Georgia and later relocated to its current site by the grandson of one of the "Forty-Niners." Down through the years, this charming and intriguing log cabin just north of Dahlonega, Georgia has served as home for several appreciative families, and has quite a history.

Will Reese left Dahlonega shortly after the turn of the century to seek his fortune in the big city of Atlanta. He and his partner, R.E. Benson, established a successful restaurant on Piedmont Avenue near Grady Hospital which catered largely to streetcar conductors. The restaurant was open twenty-four hours a day and even provided a barber shop and shower baths. And though he remained very busy with his Atlanta enterprises, Reese never ceased longing for the mountains of his Lumpkin County home.

Will's family roots ran deep into the soil of Lumpkin. His father, Andrew Jackson Reese, had been a lieutenant in the Confederate Army, and later became superintendent of the fabled Calhoun Gold Mine in Dahlonega. Both Will's father and mother were orphaned at an early age and raised by Mr. and Mrs. A.G. Wimpy who were among Dahlonega's earliest settlers.

Will's grandfather, Solomon Reese, had been one of the "Forty-Niners" who headed for California in search of gold after his wife, Mathilda, died at the age of 39. It is unknown today in whose care he left his children, but when word was received that he had died along the Platte River in Nebraska in 1850, "Uncle Archie" and "Aunt Nancy" Wimpy amazingly adopted all eight of the Reese children as well as two orphans, including Andrew's future bride, Fannie O'Connor.

Though his business in Atlanta kept him constantly buried with work, every time he could tear himself away, Will returned to the mountains with his wife and twin sons, Bob and Bill. They frequently camped out at Cane Creek Falls, but Will realized that if he wanted his family to enjoy their trips to the mountains as much as he did, he was going to have to provide some of the comforts of home.

Will had talked so much about the north Georgia mountains to his partner, R.E. Benson, that in 1930, the two of them decided to go in together to build a mountain hideaway where the two families could relax as well as work together; a retreat which would be rustic enough to suit Will, and yet comfortable enough to please the women-folk.

Instead of buying lumber and building a cabin on their land overlooking the Yahoola River two miles north of Dahlonega, the two men decided it would be more interesting (and economical) to find and restore an original pioneer log cabin. Armed with maps given to them by Forest Ranger Arthur Woody *(Readers please see Mystery & History, Volume I, "The Life and Times of Ranger Arthur Woody" in the Union County section)*, the two men spent many days traveling over abandoned and almost impassable mountain trails in search of cabins worth moving. In those days, the hills and mountainsides were dotted with the old abandoned cabins, and instead of only one, they found four!

Dismantling the cabins and moving them to a new site proved to be a much more monumental task than the men had anticipated. The ends of the eighteen- and twenty-foot-long hand-hewn logs were cut in such a way that they were *"locked in a grip of steel when joined together,"* according to Will Reese's own description. *"We had to begin at the top and work down. The logs were also cut in such a manner that the water drained from the joints, which were still bright like fresh-cut lumber when we lifted them from their century-old resting place."*

For accurate and easy reassembly, each log was carefully numbered, then stained an old weather-worn grey to protect it from the elements, then loaded onto a truck and hauled over the mountains to its new location.

The first structure they moved had been known as the McDougal cabin. It became the left half of a composite structure which they dubbed "Yahoola Lodge."

When Mr. A. McDougal later chanced to visit the lodge, he related some fascinating history which reportedly took place within this cabin where he said he was born. According to his account, shortly after the U.S. Civil War, his mother was alone in the cabin when a band of carpetbaggers burst through the door and threatened to kill her if she didn't give them the gold they somehow knew that she and her husband had panned in a nearby stream. Pioneer women didn't scare easily, however, and she refused to reveal the hiding place of the gold, even when the bandits dropped a noose around her neck and threw the end of the rope over the low-hung rafters. The cut-throats in the north Georgia region in the years following the war had killed for a lot less.

Mrs. McDougal, according her son, nevertheless was still defiant when the rope tightened and her body was pulled upward to dangle above the floor. The outlaws apparently gave up after they realized Mrs. McDougal was not going to reveal the secret. They left just as quickly as they had appeared, letting a severely-weakened Mrs. McDougal fall harshly to the floor where she laid, gasping, but still alive.

Interestingly, the outlaws never suspected that the gold they had sought was hidden in a groove cut into the very log rafter over which they had hung their rope! The tallest outlaw could easily have reached his hand into the hiding place had he known of its existence.

Although the original rafters had

rotted and been replaced, Mr. McDougal's daughter located the wall where her grandmother's warping bars (a series of pegs driven into the logs for use in weaving home-spun cloth) had been broken from the logs.

The McDougal cabin became Yahoola Lodge's guest or "preacher's room" and was furnished either with original mountain-made furniture or accurate reproductions. A waist-high bed with posts reaching almost to the rafters concealed a trundle bed which was pulled out at night to provide additional sleeping space. The pine floor boards were dotted with authentic rag rugs.

Another log structure – the Collins cabin – became Yahoola Lodge's living room and was separated from the McDougal cabin by a wide hallway called a "dogtrot." This cabin originally had four doors because it reportedly was originally constructed by a moonshiner who apparently wanted plenty of exits in case the "revenooers" paid him an unexpected visit.

Mr. Reese discovered that a chair-maker had once inhabited the Collins cabin. The pegs over which he bent the wood to shape the backs and rockers were still visible in the logs. Mr. Reese maintained the tradition of keeping an old musket and powder horn hanging on pegs over the main doorway and a coonskin tacked on the outside of the door as a sign of welcome.

A third structure – the Gaddis cabin – became the kitchen and dining room for Yahoola Lodge and was separated from the main house as was common during pioneer days, to keep from losing everything in case of a fire. To maintain the atmosphere of a pioneer kitchen, Mr. Reese kept an old crane with its ancient pot swinging over the log fire in the large fireplace, and strings of red peppers and

"leather breeches" (dried beans) hanging from the fire shelf.

A long oak table put together with pegs provided eating space for as many as ten people on benches of like construction. Split-bottom chairs constantly invited family-members and visitors to sit and enjoy the warmth of the crackling fire.

A fourth structure – the Lingerfelt cabin – was used for spare parts whenever a rotten log was discovered in one of the other three structures. A trapper had once lived in it, and one end was full of holes where he had nailed up pelts to dry.

Will and R.E. did much of the work of "reconstructing" Yahoola Lodge themselves, and what they didn't actually do, they carefully supervised.

At first, mountain workmen who completed some of the repairs for the partners were convinced that the two men from Atlanta were crazy, and made frequent reference to the "foolishness in moving worthless old logs." They finally concluded however, that Reese and Benson were "sot in their ways," and resigned themselves to completing the project as instructed.

The original occupants of the log cabins had used oil lamps, carried water from a spring and cooked over open fires in the fireplaces. However, knowing their wives wouldn't settle for life as pioneer women, Will and R.E. quickly decided electricity and running water would be very worthwhile improvements.

To accomplish these conveniences, a well had to be dug, and in those days, such a task was accomplished with manual labor – by hand, with a pick and shovel. Sometimes, the use of dynamite was even necessary to break large rocks loose from deep in the well. (This, of course, was back in the days before seriously dangerous items such as dynamite were regulated by the government.)

On one occasion when dynamite had been used, one of the men doing the digging descended back down into the well a little too soon after a charge had been detonated, and passed out from the fumes and lack of oxygen. When they realized what had occurred, one of the other workers had been required to descend into the well to bring him out. One reportedly hasn't lived until he has attempted to haul out an unconscious man from the depths and close quarters of a freshwater well.

Despite all this work on the well, and even though it was at least 75 feet in depth, it never provided much water. The partners eventually were forced to install a water ram-pump in a freshwater spring near the river 300 to 400 yards behind the house.

Will and R.E. wanted Yahoola Lodge to be a surprise to their families, and though their wives and children knew that the men were building some sort of cabin up in the mountains, they were not allowed to see it until it was nearly completed. The wives reportedly were pleasantly surprised to see the happy blend of rustic atmosphere with modern conveniences which their husbands had created. (However, having done this myself in a cabin in the mountains, I can vouch for the fact that once exposed to the ultra-modern conveniences of "civilization," females can never really be

> *"I remember one old lady who enjoyed the refreshments until the music began. Then she got up and left, saying it was 'the work of the devil.'"*

coaxed to drop back in time just a bit and "rough it" in a mountain cabin. Like water and oil, the two just don't mix, no matter how hard the poor male struggles.)

Both families nevertheless became frequent visitors to Yahoola Lodge. Mr. Benson did much of the cooking. Everybody helped pick blackberries and huckleberries for pies that were the highlight of every mealtime.

Bob and Bill, Will Reese's twin sons, loved to roam the woods around the lodge and go fishing in the Yahoola River where they kept a small motorboat. The Benson family frequently gathered around an old-fashioned pump organ to play and sing old favorites.

"Dad loved to show the place to visitors too," Bob later recalled, "and he would frequently get up from the dinner table when curious guests arrived wishing for a tour of the lodge. On one occasion, he moved the furniture out and brought fiddlers in for a square dance. I remember one old lady who enjoyed the refreshments until the music began. Then she got up and left, saying it was 'the work of the devil.'"

As was his custom, as soon as Will Reese walked through the doorway of the lodge, he took off his city shoes and popped an old clay pipe into his mouth. He never lit the pipe. It was just part of his image of being at home in the mountains.

Another part of that image was driving his ox cart into town. He also drove it in Dahlonega's annual Gold Rush parades and he was even part of the wagon train that carried Dahlonega gold to the Georgia State Capitol to be used in gilding the Capitol dome. Buck, the ox, couldn't have endured the entire trip, however, so Will hauled him and the wagon in a truck to Piedmont Park where they then joined the wagon train.

A barn was built at Yahoola Lodge to house Buck and Prince, the horses. At one time, it also housed sheep, but sheep-raising proved unsuccessful because dogs from nearby farms killed so many of the docile defenseless animals.

Will Reese was a member of the Methodist Church in Dahlonega, and was largely responsible for the beautiful stained glass windows which were installed in the structure built in 1930. Other family members later purchased the windows as family memorials except for the one which Will dedicated in loving memory to his parents and the Wimpys who had raised them.

Following Will's death in 1961, Yahoola Lodge was closed up and stood vacant for many years. Even though a caretaker was looking after the place, there still were break-ins, and many things disappeared from the by-then historic site, including the pump from the old well.

In 1965, Jack and Bonnie Chapman happened to visit the lodge on a weekend when Mrs. Reese and her son Bill and family were visiting in Dahlonega. Jack, a division superintendent with Mid-Western Gas at the time, is the son of Lela Chapman, sister to Dahlonega native Guy Wimpy. Lela grew up in Dahlonega, and attended the local schools there, including North Georgia

College (now University of North Georgia).

Bonnie remembers that she fell in love with Yahoola Lodge the day they visited, and vowed that one day she would call it home. Jack discouraged her from getting her hopes up, however, because he didn't think the Reeses would ever sell it.

Two years later, Bonnie started thinking about the old lodge again. She felt an inner prompting to get in touch with Mrs. Reese, but didn't know her address or phone number. Bonnie eventually reached her through a number supplied by the telephone operator, and discovered to her surprise that the lodge was for sale.

It took about a year to get all the complications involving the sale resolved, but eventually, Jack and Bonnie were able to buy Yahoola Lodge. Since they were not yet ready to retire and move to Dahlonega, they decided to rent the lodge in the meantime.

In 1970, when Verne and Linda Smith returned to Dahlonega (Verne had been a student at North Georgia College and was a lieutenant-colonel in the Army at the time), rental property was very scarce, and they were having a tough time finding a place to live. When Verne learned of the availability of Yahoola Lodge, he mentioned it to Linda, expecting her to want to keep looking for something more modern. She agreed, however, to go look at the structure, and it was love at first sight. "Let's take it," she reportedly said before they had even ventured inside.

The lodge had previously been rented for a short time, but Jack's Dad, Leonard Chapman (who was serving as caretaker), was at first hesitant to sign a lease with the Smiths because "Jack and Bonnie might be coming back soon." An agreement was reached, however, and the Smith family spent four happy years at Yahoola Lodge.

Like the Reese and Benson children before them, the three little Smith children loved roaming the woods with their dog and playing in the creek. They also had secret places to hide small treasures in the knotholes of the logs of their rooms.

Linda enjoyed having a place to garden. Leonard Chapman became a good friend who brought them eggs and firewood and helped Linda plant her garden. Verne held Cub Scout meetings in the Gaddis cabin where the Reeses and Bensons had cooked and eaten together years earlier.

Like Mr. Reese, Linda always kept her door open to visitors and frequently gave impromptu tours to unexpected guests who drove up wanting to see the lodge. She frequently shunned her modern cookstove in favor of cooking in a pot over an open fire just as Mr. Reese had done.

Although they could see through the gaps between the logs in some places (where the chinking had been depleted), Linda remembers the house as being warm in the winter and cool in the summers, a fact which is understandable since log walls are known to have an excellent insulation capability – better even than many modern homes.

Linda says one of her fondest memories of her experiences at the lodge is of sitting on the back porch and listening to the rain falling on the tin roof above them. "It was totally relaxing," she recalls.

Its charming aspects aside, the lodge did have inconveniences. There were no closets; the lodge had but one small upstairs bathroom; and there was a shortage of parking space for guests. The Biblical adage: *"the first shall be the last and the last shall be first,"* was literally true for visitors at the lodge, because the first guests to arrive could not leave until the late-comers had departed! Verne, who was attached to the Military Science Department at North Georgia College, volunteered his home for many NGC Alumni Association functions, and well remembers being out many evenings directing traffic with his flashlight.

Despite these drawbacks, the Smiths, just as their predecessors, loved the atmosphere at Yahoola Lodge, and remember their years there with great fondness. When the family revisited the lodge years later, one of their children checked his secret hiding place in one of the old knotholes and found the contents still intact. Verne and family say they have lived in many places around the world during Verne's military career, but when they think of "home," it's always Yahoola Lodge.

In 1984, almost twenty years after visiting Yahoola Lodge for the first time, Bonnie Chapman's dream of living there finally came true. She and husband Jack were able at last to put their name on the mailbox.

Bonnie set about artfully furnishing the lodge with the antiques she had been collecting over the years. She also treasures the antiques which the Reeses left with the house.

She and Jack enlarged and modernized Yahoola Lodge without detracting from the original rustic decor. They also enclosed most of the huge screened-in porch to create a kitchen and eating area inside the main house. A large deck was created to replace the original porch.

Following the addition of a bedroom and bath, the Gaddis cabin – which originally had housed the kitchen - was converted into an apartment for Jack's mother, Lela, who lived there until a fall necessitated her admission into a nursing home where she lived until her death in January of 1990.

Closets were not part of the architecture of early homes, including Yahoola Lodge, but Bonnie had too many clothes to hang on pegs on the wall. Fortunately, the lodge had plenty of unused space under the eaves that could be transformed into storage space.

A bathroom was added downstairs, and the tiny upstairs bathroom was enlarged and modernized. It was a good thing Bonnie wouldn't part with the huge claw-footed bathtub either, because it was too heavy to move, and it would not have begun to fit down the narrow stairwell.

Skylights were added to the low ceilings to create more light and space. The fireplaces were closed up with the addition of central heat and air, but the Chapmans seldom turned on the air-conditioning. "There was almost always a cooling breeze from the creek valley, even when it was uncomfortably hot in Dahlonega," they maintained.

One of the things Jack and Bonnie liked to show visitors was the hollow log which forms the mantel in the living room. In the early days, Will Reese kept a stuffed alligator in this compartment - its head sticking out one end. To the shock and eventual delight of unsuspecting visitors, Reese would manipulate the head with a string at the opposite end of the mantel, causing the alligator to appear to be alive!

During the time they owned Yahoola Lodge, the Chapmans were visited not only by the Reese and Benson children and grandchildren who came back to reminisce, but also by people who were born in one of the log cabins which had stood in the area where Camp Wahsega (a present-day cabins and camping retreat just north of Dahlonega built in the 1930s for the Civilian Conservation Corps troops who once worked in the area) is now located.

Another visitor was Duffie Grizzle, who was born in 1894 and helped Will Reese reconstruct the log cabins in the 1930s. Bob remembers that Duffie continued to take an interest in the Reese family by taking him and Bill squirrel hunting.

In clearing off the undergrowth around the lodge, Jack and Bonnie discovered rocks that Mr. Reese had laid to make trails down to the river and through the woods. He enjoyed rockwork and built a twelve- by fifty-foot rock terrace across the front of the main cabin. A large flagstone shaped like the state of Georgia lies just outside the front door. The massive stone chimney outside the living room contains a rock which resembles a huge arrowhead.

Jack and Bonnie once pointed out to me an ancient road marker that Will Reese had found and nailed to the side of the barn. Carved into it is a "D" for Dahlonega with the number "12" underneath. They delighted in the same things he enjoyed, and had a strong sense of communion with him as they walked the trails and lifted the old-fashioned latches on the doors of the cabins.

One of the Chapman treasures was a gas lamp post which Will Reese had brought from Atlanta. "I can just see him finding this," Bonnie smiled in relating the story to me. "Though I never knew Will Reese in person, I know him from living here at Yahoola Lodge. His presence here is still very strong."

(Grateful appreciation is expressed herewith for collection of the information in this article by the late Anne Dismukes Amerson of Dahlonega)

Mysterious Dredge Barges Of Lumpkin & Dawson Counties

Over the past century, many techniques - some quite unusual -
have been used to recover the precious yellow metal
from the soils of Lumpkin, Dawson and White counties.

When research is conducted today involving the pioneer riverboat traffic of Georgia, it is often the Savannah, or Altamaha, or lower Chattahoochee or Coosa rivers which immediately spring to mind. One never considers large vessels navigating the narrow and usually very shallow headwaters of the north Georgia mountains, but in areas along the Etowah, Chestatee, and Chattahoochee Rivers and in even smaller waterways, large "dredge barges" excavated great areas in a commercial quest for the precious yellow metal.

These huge vessels, actually huge floating factories, were created as an alternative method of mining gold in Dawson and Lumpkin counties after the easily obtainable ore had been panned and dug from the hills and mountainsides of this region. Several entrepreneurial businessmen apparently realized that a significant quantity of gold remained for the taking in the river bottoms and along the banks of the waterways. All they needed was an economically-feasible craft to mine it.

Hikers and sightseers in these two counties today may still observe the remains of some of these ventures if they know where to look. Remnants of the huge floating barges – several of which eventually sank to the river bottoms after being abandoned – can still often be seen during dry-weather periods.

These innovative mining relics occupy a unique place in Georgia history. One oddity – a type of early diving bell – believed to have been constructed as early as the late 1830s, was discovered in the 1980s still containing rudimentary mining equipment and other implements used in the days of the early gold rush in this region. Sadly, the relatively easy accessibility of these sites has also allowed treasure hunters to pillage and destroy these early vessels as they were probed for relics. Some individuals have even intentionally damaged the vessels at these historic sites, erasing forever the historic remains.

Dredge-barge mining was practiced most extensively in the early 1900s in Dawson and Lumpkin counties in Georgia. The barges – with their huge metal shovels, conveyor belts and ore separation devices – were developed after the easy gold mining opportunities had been

Large "dredge barges" which scoured the river bottoms for gold, once plied the waters of the Chestatee River in Lumpkin County in the early 1900s. These craft were so immense and powerful that they often altered the routes and configurations of the rivers on which they operated. This craft was photographed on the Chestatee in the vicinity of the present-day Highway 60 bridge south of Dahlonega. (Photo courtesy of the GA Dept. of Archives & History, Atlanta)

exhausted in north Georgia. There was still a significant amount of gold in the region, but it was expensive and difficult to reach. The barges were created as a solution to that problem.

One of the most accessible sites today with the remains of one of these huge boats existed at last check in Dawson County, not far from the Georgia Highway 136 and Etowah River Road intersection. The late Arch Bishop, a life-long resident and long-time historian of Dawson County, remembered the old Etowah River dredge barge from his childhood.

"This barge, at a length of approximately 90 feet and a width of approximately 30 feet, pulled its great weight up the Etowah by being harnessed to trees along the route and then using the great steam-powered winches on board to winch the craft upstream," Bishop explained."

At a promising mining site, the men on the barge used a large steam-powered dredging bucket and other conveyances to scoop up tons of dirt from the river bottom and banks, processing the rich soil for gold right there on the barge in a large floating factory. After the gold had been separated from the soil, the conveyor belt automatically dumped the "spoil" back into the river behind the barge.

"You can still see that the end beams of the barge are 24' x 24'," Bishop explained in an interview in 1989, pointing out the remnants of the craft in the Etowah River, "so they were from huge trees. I was told that many men in this area made a living back then cutting up pine trees and stacking the wood along the river bank ahead of the barge, so the wood could be burned as fuel in the barge's steam engine."

Bishop explained that in winching itself upriver, the barge was tied off from all four corners to trees along the bank, to keep the great barge from turning sideways in the river. When it wanted to move up-stream, the winches - powered by the steam engine - easily accomplished the cumbersome task.

The huge barge literally dredged its way up the river, digging into the river bottom and river banks with its shovel to a depth of about 18 feet. "It apparently was a moveable drag-line type dredge," Bishop added.

When the weather was unusually dry, the barge captain reportedly would order the shovel operator to pile up huge walls of mud and sediment behind the barge, in effect damming up the river, and creating a deep pool in which the barge could float.

Ironically, it eventually was the unique premise upon which the huge boat operated that initiated its demise. In order to make its way upstream by winching onto the trees along the way, the company owning the barge was required to obtain easements from the property owners along the way. The barge owners apparently never anticipated that an owner along the route might deny them the use of their trees, no matter the price, but eventually, that's exactly what happened.

"That old barge sits today only a few feet from where it was abandoned in the 1920s," Bishop continued. "A lawsuit stopped the barge in its tracks, and forced the owners out of business."

Bishop said that the barge company probably could have induced (bribed) the landowner in question to allow the barge to continue, but it must have become apparent that other owners farther up the river would then follow suit, probably even increasing the "ante" as the barge

Winched from the Chestatee River just east of the Highway 60 bridge in 1983, this craft was one of many devices used to supposedly reach "unreachable" gold on the river-bottoms around the turn-of-the-century. It was designed to be lifted from the deck of a large barge, deposited within the river, then the water from within it pumped out to allow men with extremely short-handled shovels to descend inside it to access gold deposits. Generations of fishermen in the Chestatee had lost fishing lines ensnared by this rusty hulk lying in a deep spot in the river. (Photo by Olin Jackson)

moved along, depleting the barge company's profits to the point of no return.

Oddly enough, very little additional information concerning this dredge barge is known today, despite the fact that it was in operation as recently as 1916. It is unknown today how successful the dredging operation was in recovering gold in this manner, but it must have been at least marginally profitable.

In contrast, in neighboring Lumpkin County, far more is known about the huge boats which operated to a larger degree on the Chestatee River. In fact, a newspaper account as far back as the 1830s records the Chestatee River's mining traffic.

In an issue of the *Western Herald* newspaper published on April 9, 1833 in Auraria, Georgia, an interesting account of the village of Auraria is provided, as well as a description of a strange "diving bell" which was used on a vessel in the Chestatee for dredging gold from the river bottom there.

The article reads as follows: *"Mr. McCollum, late of Tennessee, a gentleman of character for enterprise and mechanical genius, has just constructed in the neighborhood, a boat with a diving bell attached to it for the purpose of raising gravel, and collecting gold from the bed of water courses. The boat was launched in the Chestatee River on Friday evening last, in our presence, and we feel confident in saying that we believe the example will be followed by many, and that the projector will be richly compensated for his laudable and useful experiment."*

How this diving bell was to be used to obtain gold from the river bottom is unclear to many historians today, but in 1983, modern-day dredge miners discovered

what may be the remains of this structure. A riveted metal craft very similar to the "diving bell" described above, was discovered in a deep water pool near the Highway 60 overpass on the Chestatee.

The hulk was dragged from the river with a diesel-powered grader. Inside the heavily-rusted solid-metal craft, small short-handled shovels and other mining implements were discovered – most of them still serviceable.

This diving bell quite possibly was the first such device used to dredge the river bottom for gold. And since it probably was both dangerous and not cost-effective in the 1840s, it probably had a short lifespan.

Later dredge barge mining however did become profitable around the turn of the century, after the value of gold had

Photographed circa 1912, the use of the "Long Tom" is demonstrated by these two young ladies in the vicinity of Findley Ridge in Dahlonega. Special canals had been constructed from streams and rivers north of Dahlonega to channel abundant water long distances up and down inclines in the topography to generate the water power necessary to wash great quantities of gold ore-rich soil into sluices for processing. (Photo courtesy of the GA Dept. of Archives & History, Atlanta)

risen, and the easily mined quantities had been obtained from the hills and valleys of Lumpkin, Dawson, White and other counties in the gold belt.

Unfortunately, this historic piece of mining equipment, technologically innovative in its day (considering the assumption that the device appears to have been an underwater craft designed and constructed while the Cherokee Indians still resided in the region), was abandoned near the point at which it was dragged from the river, and left unpreserved and unprotected for years. Today, this curious vessel is permanently exhibited in Hancock Park at North Meaders and Warwick streets in downtown Dahlonega.

Also in this April 9, 1833 issue of the *Western Herald*, an interesting description of the community of Auraria is provided which gives an idea of the time-frame concerned: *"The town population is estimated at one thousand, and that of the county, at ten thousand, and constantly increasing, with a rapidity almost too incredible to relate. The Indian population is small; their right of occupancy to the soil, having in most cases been extinguished previous to the survey and distribution of the country."*

In 1909, in an article in the *Dahlonega Nugget*, Editor W. B. Townsend wrote: *"We noticed at the Tate House latter part of last week, Mr. W. P. Seawell and his son, of Kansas City. The gentleman is interested with his brother, who has been here for some time, in the construction of a big dredge that is going to be built for the Chestatee River, to work the Hollifield property recently purchased by them. The excavation of the pit for the boat was completed last week. . ."*

The Seawell dredge boat was nearing completion in construction by the latter part of 1909. Apparently, it also was the largest such river-going craft ever seen by much of the population of Dahlonega at the time, because there was much speculation as to its ability to float once completed.

The October 15, 1909 issue of the *Nugget* provides a glimpse of this speculation: *"With favorable weather, the constructors of the Seawell boat hope to complete it by Christmas. It is an up-to-date very large boat, far greater than any that has ever been built in this country. It will have 71 dippers, each weighing five hundred pounds. Though modern, it is no experiment, as Mr. Stanton has already built a number of them for other mining countries. Some of the natives say that the boat will be too large to float, which tickles those who have seen still larger ones of the same kind built and in operation."*

It appears that this craft initiated by the Seawells was among the first of several mining ventures on the Chestatee during this period after the profit potential of this mining method was realized. Some individuals became even more innovative.

In the February 19, 1909 issue of the *Dahlonega Nugget*, the following passage provides an example: *"After getting misplaced and being on the road for about two months, the clasp for the new mining boat of Gilbert and Lutz in the Chestatee River was received last Saturday, which was put in position and the boat started. It is said that everything moved off like clockwork, handling tons and tons of sand and gravel daily at small expense, as only four hands, including the night watchman, are required to operate it and later on a night shift will be added, making their expenses still less. The boats heretofore operated with dippers, and when deep beds of sand were struck, work was somewhat retarded. It will not be the case with this boat, as it works with a suction pump that brings up everything clean as it goes - unless it is a stone that is too large to pass through the nozzle. In addition to this, they have a diving suit which enables a man to safely go down, walk about on the bottom of the river, and see just what there is on it. . ."*

Some ideas worked well, and some didn't. Apparently, the ingenious device described above, turned out to be more of a problem than a money-maker, as the April 2, 1909 issue of the *Nugget* explained: *"The Gilbert and Lutz dredge has been moved back up the river from the Burns place, and it may be that the dredge will be enlarged and converted into a dipper boat as the suction is so strong, that large rocks and roots are drawn to the nozzle, clogging the entrance so that nothing can pass. . ."*

One of the drawbacks to the huge dredge-barges was the fact that they had to be operated in an area in which there was plenty of water for floatation. If the barge settled onto an uneven river bottom, its heavy equipment would be torn apart. The Seawell boat apparently suffered from both this type of damage and that inflicted by vandals. The December 16, 1910 issue of the *Dahlonega Nugget* describes such an incident:

"They have had a lot of trouble down at the Seawell boat. As stated some time ago, the dam bursted letting the vessel down on the bottom, and after working some time in getting it in position again, it was found that a big two-inch rod had broke right square in two on account of the strain being so great. This rod has been welded, and they hope to be able to begin work next Monday."

The dredges usually were in operation day and night, since the ebb and flow of waters in the rivers required that the huge barges constantly keep damming the river behind them to keep enough water pooled to maintain floatation. And since they were in operation

during the hours of darkness, they required lighting which was extended to them by rudimentary power lines extended from nearby generators at damsites along the river.

It was at such a site that one of the occasions of robbery was reported in the *Dahlonega Nugget* on March 31, 1916: *"About the middle of last week, it was discovered that quite a lot of the copper wire on the power line from the New Bridge plant* (Note: New Bridge Plant is believed to have been near the present-day site of the Highway 60 overpass on the Chestatee River.) *to the Seawell mining dredge in this county, had been taken down and carried away.*

"The entire wire or power line was not taken. Only that which could be removed by the light of the moon in places far enough from the thinly settled country residences as to cause no alarm.

"The wire, sold as old junk, is estimated to be worth $205.00 If bought new, it would cost over three hundred dollars. The boat had not been running for some weeks which gave the thieves a good chance to get in their work.

"Manager Cowan, of the boat, upon learning that a lot of old junk had since been shipped to Atlanta from Gainesville in barrels, got Sheriff Ray and the two left for Atlanta last Monday afternoon to see if they can find where these barrels went to. If they can, then Mr. Cowan will swear out a search warrant in order to have the proper authority for a personal inspection.

"Later - The Sheriff got the wire, has returned, and you will hear of some arrests being made soon."

Editor Townsend at this point, apparently had a rudimentary understanding of the suspected crime which had taken place, but had decided to postpone the publication of the news until he had obtained all the facts, and quite possibly to promote sales of the little weekly newspaper too. The following week, he continued with his news report of the incident:

"We told you last week about the copper wire on the power line running from New Bridge to the Seawell or Bunker Hill dredge in this county, being stolen recently. Superintendent F.C. Cowan, of the mine, and Sheriff Ray began an investigation last week, finding in an Atlanta depot where some wire had been shipped by Rotchtien, a dealer in old junk at Gainesville, addressed to a concern in that city. It was in barrels. Mr. Cowan procured a search warrant and the barrels were opened and in them were found 505 pounds of the company's wire..."

Apparently, equipment failures, vandalism, and expenses in general eventually became the nemesis of the huge dredge boats, because one by one, they all ultimately discontinued their operations and were abandoned. World War I also was reaching a peak at this point, and American involvement, with its need of man-power and raw supplies, also are suspected of having taken a toll on the operation of the dredge boats.

In the June 27, 1917 issue of the **Dahlonega Nugget**, foreclosure proceedings against the Seawell barge are announced, probably signaling the end of its operations, since no further mention of it has been found in future issues of the **Nugget**.

Though other dredge mining operations undoubtedly were on-going in Lumpkin County at this time, the Seawell dredge is the only one discovered. It apparently was in operation, off and on, until 1917.

It is significant to note, that despite the attraction of Lumpkin and Dawson counties today as sites of residence, they represented locales of quite the opposite dimension during the days of heavy

mining operations. The practice of hydraulic mining - which involved the use of huge water cannons which literally washed down the mountain sides - coupled with the endeavors of the tremendous dredge barges, took a terrible toll on the environmental quality of life in this region. Rivers, streams, lakes and other reservoirs of water were voided of aquatic life as a result of the tremendous pollution from uncontrolled siltation and sediment run-off. The Lumpkin County hillsides, which today are covered in lush growths of hardwoods and other vegetation, were a virtual wasteland in the early 1900s.

It was only after the uncontrolled and unregulated industrial gold mining had ceased in the tri-county area of Lumpkin, Dawson and White counties, and nature was allowed to recover for a period of some 75 years, that the scenic beauty and natural resources of this district returned.

The late Anne Amerson, a writer from Dahlonega, Georgia, examines the remains of one of the large dredge barges in the Chestatee River which once scooped up great loads of the river-bottom soil to process it for placer gold in the early 1900s.

Gold Rush Town Dahlonega Once "Hollywood" of the South

Dahlonega, Georgia, gained renown in the 19ᵗʰ Century after gold was discovered there. However, in the early 1900s, a motherlode of a different type was discovered when New York film-makers came south in search of Western-style scenery.

The precious yellow metal discovered in the hills of what today are Dahlonega and Lumpkin County created an instant sensation, as well as an industry of immense proportions attracting almost worldwide attention in the 19ᵗʰ Century. Substantial gold mining enterprises in the vicinity endured from the early 1800s to well into the 1900s, and from these endeavors, numerous "spin-off" enterprises ultimately came into existence. One of these, to the surprise of many, was professional movie-making.

Dahlonega, and indeed much of north Georgia, was once referred to as "The Hollywood of the South," but that identity occurred in more recent times, when such major motion pictures as *I'd Climb The Highest Mountain, The Great Locomotive Chase, The Long Riders,* and *Deliverance* were filmed on location in the area. Unbeknownst to many is the fact that professional movie-makers came to Dahlonega much earlier, even before "Hollywood" existed.

Initial film-making efforts in the United States were originally headquar-

tered in New York, for obvious reasons. It was here that inventors such as Thomas A. Edison perfected the "moving picture," and New York with its many major theaters and legions of acting troups made it a natural pool of talent and production equipment.

As the "Western" film genre came into vogue in the early 1900s, New York-headquartered film-makers were forced to travel long distances across the country before reaching the arid western states where they could obtain a "backdrop" of obvious "western" appearance. This of course was prior to the days of modern and convenient air-travel, and as such, a train-ride from New York to Arizona, New Mexico, or Colorado to obtain the proper western scenery for film-making was extremely burdensome.

When producers and directors accidentally discovered that areas in Georgia at which the gold-rush – and all it involved – had denuded the hills and mountains of that region to an appearance very similar to the western United States, film-makers were thrilled. They suddenly were able to reduce their expenses and production

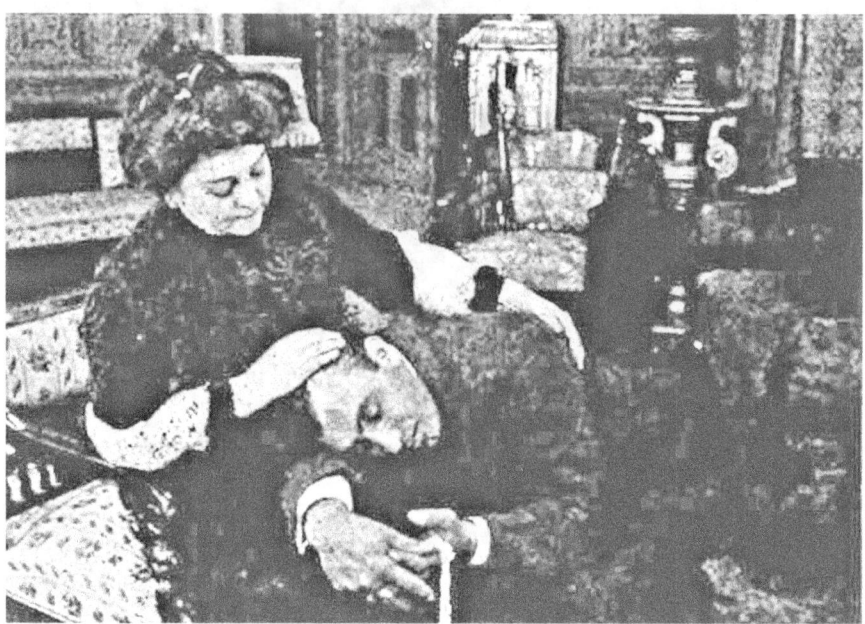

Bill Matthews (portrayed by movie star William Farnum) owner of the "Croix D'or" mine, is beset on all sides by a trusted colleague who is plotting to steal away his claim in the 1915 silent film *"The Plunderer."* Matthews (Farnum) is consoled by his co-star, Claire Whitney, portraying "Joan," his love interest and daughter to the dishonest scheming miner.

times dramatically, and they began flocking to north Georgia.

A Golden Opportunity

Due to years of extensive mining activities and a naturally mountainous terrain, Dahlonega, in 1915, very closely resembled the landscape of the arid western states, offering an ideal filming location. Even better, the vicinity's many abandoned gold mines, discarded mining equipment, mining cuts, and rugged mountain scenery provided a setting that truly looked "Western," and which was much more accessible than the real thing in the western United States.

As a result, a number of silent movies were filmed on location in and around Dahlonega during this period. The area probably would have received even greater early attention had not a group

of film-makers and actors ultimately moved to southern California shortly thereafter, where the pleasant weather and abundant actual scenery offered a permanent filming opportunity which shortly was dubbed *Hollywoodland*, later to be shortened to *Hollywood*. Prior to that time, however, Dahlonega, Georgia was very much on the minds of movie-makers, and offered the best and most feasible film-making location.

On March 15, 1915, the Fox Film Company's then-famed motion picture director, Edgar Lewis, set out from the company's headquarters in New York to begin filming a new motion picture entitled *The Plunderer*, which was based upon the best-selling novel of the same name by Roy North, a celebrated author of Western stories. Accompanying him were leading man, William Farnum – a $100,000-a-year screen star who was the "Hopalong Cassi-dy" of his day – and about twenty other actors and actresses, including leading lady, Miss Claire Whitney.

In those days the trip from New York City to Gainesville, Georgia, required just over a day's travel-time by rail. After overnighting in Gainesville, the actors, director, film-crew, equipment and baggage had to be transferred to rented wagons that could convey the load the remaining twenty-five miles through the mountains to Dahlonega.

The director and leading cast members undoubtedly were able to arrange transportation in the new-fangled automobiles of that day, although horses were still considerably more reliable in the muddy and often forbidding mountain terrain. In the early 1900s, the more easily accessible Georgia Highway 60 between Gainesville and Dahlonega did not exist. The route to Dahlonega from Gainesville proceeded by way of what was known (and is still remembered by many locals) as "Quillian's Corner," up what later would become U.S. 129 which continued over Neel's Gap to Blairsville. In the early 1900s, the Quillian's Corner route was a narrow, winding, and dusty (or extremely muddy, depending upon the weather) dirt trail which could be a challenge in inclement weather, particularly for the narrow automobile tires used in that day.

Southern Hospitality

When the weary travelers finally arrived in Dahlonega, no doubt thinking that they had come to the end of the earth, they rested and recuperated at the Mountain Inn, a large hotel overlooking the town. This hostelry was owned and operated by the always genial Dr. Craig Arnold, one of the local officials in a large mining endeavor – the

William Farnum as "Bill Mathews" (far right), Claire Whitney as "Joan Presby" his love interest, and Dick Townsend as "Harry Spingler" (far left), sporting as much drama upon their faces as is humanly possible in a silent film, provide a promotional scene from *"The Plunderer,"* filmed in Dahlonega in 1915.

Consolidated Gold Mining Company – which had ceased operations in 1906 for a variety of unusual reasons. Later known as the Mountain Lodge, the hotel was built shortly after the turn of the century as a type of "club house" and residence for Consolidated officials.

Dr. Arnold always treated his Northern guests to a lavish table of Southern cooking, not all of which was always appreciated. When the *Plunderer* movie crew overheard local folks discussing how good 'possum meat was, they expressed a desire to try it. "Doc" Arnold obligingly had his kitchen prepare what then was considered a Southern delicacy – a fat 'possum cooked and served with sweet potatoes. It was later reported that film-making literally had to be abandoned the following day because all the actors were deathly sick from the meal! (If would appear that their digestive systems simply were not on par with Southern cuisine.)

On another occasion when spare ribs were served for supper, Elizabeth Eyre (who portrayed one of the leading

Another scene from the *"The Plunderer,"* filmed in Dahlonega, with William Farnum (center) and Claire Whitney (background). One of many confrontations depicted in the movie in order to give it life.

feminine roles) commented that she never knew that pork could be cooked in "so many obnoxious ways." Again, "different goose, different gander," with elevated noses.

In addition to housing and feeding the actors, Dr. Arnold assisted the director in locating suitable filming sites, as well as local "extras" for "bit-parts" in the films. Movie extras in those days were paid $1.00 per morning and $1.50 if they worked into the afternoon. Doc Arnold himself had a role in the movie, portraying Mr. Thomas Presby, a rich mines and timber owner.

Film Sites

Much of the footage of *The Plunderer* was filmed at the Consolidated Gold Mining facility on Yahoola Creek in Dahlonega. The huge chlorination plant and its 120-stamp mill had

been abandoned since the Consolidated Company had suffered bankruptcy some nine years earlier. The commissary, an old wooden building once used as a store-house, was converted into a "Western dance hall" for the film, and was the setting for a rip-roaring scene in which a fight breaks out between drunken miners.

According to the April 1, 1915 issue of the *Dahlonega Nugget*, *The Plunderer* is *"a true, wild mining play and requires the use of large mills, pipe lines, underground workings and power plants, all of which were found here, just as desired and these within the corporate limits of the City. This picture will spread the fame of Dahlonega over the entire world and show the natural beauty of our mountains, the many large open cuts where gold was taken in years past and create a renewed interest in gold mining. Mr. Edgar Lewis, the inimitable Director, is untiring in his efforts to make this picture his master- piece, and in this effort he is bound to suc- ceed. He has a kindly word for every one and creates the acts without apparent ef- fort and with great patience."*

The *Nugget* also had high praise for the assistant director, Mr. George De- Carlton, and the financial manager, Mr. John Zanft, who did advance scouting in Dahlonega for a filming site. It was on their recommendation that the Fox Film Company decided to shoot the film in Dahlonega instead of in Arizona as had been originally planned. The newspaper noted that the photographer, Mr. Frank Kugler, had established a national rep- utation with the quality of his filming, *"sufficient proof that these pictures will be of the very best."*

Film Cast

The film's leading man, Mr. William Farnum, was described as *"the noblest Ro- man of them all' when it comes to real act- ing."* Farnum had achieved prominence several years earlier when he starred in the title role in *Ben Hur*, described as the finest stage production ever presented up to that time. In *The Plunderer*, Far- num portrayed Bill Matthews, a partner in a fabulous mine known as "The Cross of Gold." It is amusing that the editor of the *Dahlonega Nugget*, one William Benjamin Franklin Townsend, could not resist noting that *"one of the actors* (obvi- ously referring to Farnum) *gets a salary higher than that paid the President of the United States."*

Claire Whitney, the leading lady, was described as *"a cross between Pearl White and Dale Evans, who was every inch a platinum bond."* She obviously had earned Editor Townsend's rapt at- tention as well.

Margaret Meaders who penned an article for the June 4, 1950 issue of the *Atlanta Journal & Constitution Mag- azine* entitled *"When Bill Farnum Rode in a Dahlonega Western,"* described watching the filming of a scene in which Miss Whitney rode *"hell-for-leather"* on a white horse down a mountainside min- ing flume, one jump ahead of the villain pursuing her. Meaders said she remem- bered it well, despite her tender age, be- cause Miss Whitney made about twen- ty-five such head-long flights before the director finally yelled "Cut!"

Since nearly all of the actors and ac- tresses of that day did their own stunts, and since movie-making was in its infan- cy in development, accidents were not uncommon. In fact, they were more the norm than not. On one occasion, Whit- ney's horse ran away with her and threw her roughly to the ground. Fortunately, her injuries were only minor, and, always the "trooper," she climbed back up upon her mount to re-shoot the scene. An- other member of the cast was also hurt slightly in one of the cave shots.

The livestock used in the filming also suffered, since there obviously was no "American Society for Prevention of Cruelty to Animals (ASPCA) in those

A cabinet card used to promote *"The Plunder- er"* in movie theaters across the nation in 1915. This promotional photo was taken inside one of the multitude of dilapidated and aban- doned mine shafts in the Dahlonega vicinity.

William Farnum as "Bill Mathews" (left) is photographed in yet another action scene from the **"The Plunderer."** This shot is believed to have been filmed in one of the buildings at the by-then abandoned Consolidated Gold Mine in Dahlonega, remnants of which still exist today in a tourist attraction of the same name at this site.

days. One of the mules being used as a pack animal in one of the scenes met an unfortunate end when he shied at a camera, then plunged headlong to his death off precipitous Findley Ridge. From that day forward, that particular spot on Findley – which was a steep cliff created by hydraulic mining – was always referred to thereafter as "Dead Horse Cut."

Reviews

When filming on *The Plunderer* "wrapped," the cast and crew packed up and returned to New York. The June 11, 1915 issue of the *Nugget* provided the following glimpse of the finished production as seen through the eyes of a viewer at the Strand Theatre in Atlanta:

"The play opens with Mr. Farnum and Spingler (his partner) with their burros at the tunnel entrance to Findley Shoot (Chute). They lead their burros up the side of the cut into Dead Horse Cut and then out to the point overlooking Yahoola Creek. This is a beautiful scene and fully equal to anything to be seen in Colorado.

"Many scenes were shown of the Consolidated Mill, Night Cut, Hand Tunnel, the tube line, and also an underground scene in the Pruett Stope showing local people at work.

"Several pretty scenes are shown at the Toledo Mine office and blacksmith shop where Frank Christy is at work at the forge and Jess McDonald slaps him on

242

the back in passing. The dinner scene in which Garner Huff rings the triangle and the hungry miners rush into dinner is very amusing and realistic.

"A number of scenes are shown both inside and out at the Crown Mountain Assay Office. The scene in which Miss Whitney denounces her father for stealing the gold from her sweetheart's mine is exceptionally good.

"At the machine shop, Mr. Gross as the old engineer is very natural. The air compressor is shown in operation.

"The explosion at the New Bridge Dam and the damage it was supposed to cause at the Gorge Dam are both good scenes, and required a lot of work and expense to produce. However, the explosion of the dam taken while the company was here failed to show up as well as desired, and Mr. Frank Kugler, chief cameraman, with Andy Culp to assist, came back to retake this and also the scene at the night (Knight) cut in which 'Henry the Villain' blows up a lot of rocks closing the tunnel

entrance while Farnum and Spingler are inside.

"Rufe Ed Baker's night ride is one of the best acts in the show. The scenes in front of Dr. Arnold's garage are very distinct. John Worley shows up as natural as life.

"The fight at the Abercrombie house between 'Bully Presby' and the local miners is very realistic. Paul McDougal, John Worley, Bev Brooksher, William Tolbert, and others are easily recognized.

"At the Consolidated, Billy Adams, Lige Satterfield, John Tolbert, Shorty Watson and several others looked very natural.

"The birthday scene, taken in the front room of the Mountain Inn, showing Miss Whitney playing with the three little rabbits and a canary bird, is very pretty. . . Miss Whitney is very charming and graceful in every act. The love scenes are pretty, and the rock which nearly strikes her horse in rolling down the mountain is terrifying. Miss Ayres' riding is a feature of the

The Consolidated Gold Mining Company in Dahlonega, Georgia, photographed here in this poor print from 1915, was the scene of much of the filming of *"The Plunderer."* Notice how reminiscent are the mining buildings and terrain in Dahlonega to such scenery as often appeared in westerns which were filmed in southern California (and elsewhere) from the 1920s through the 1960s.

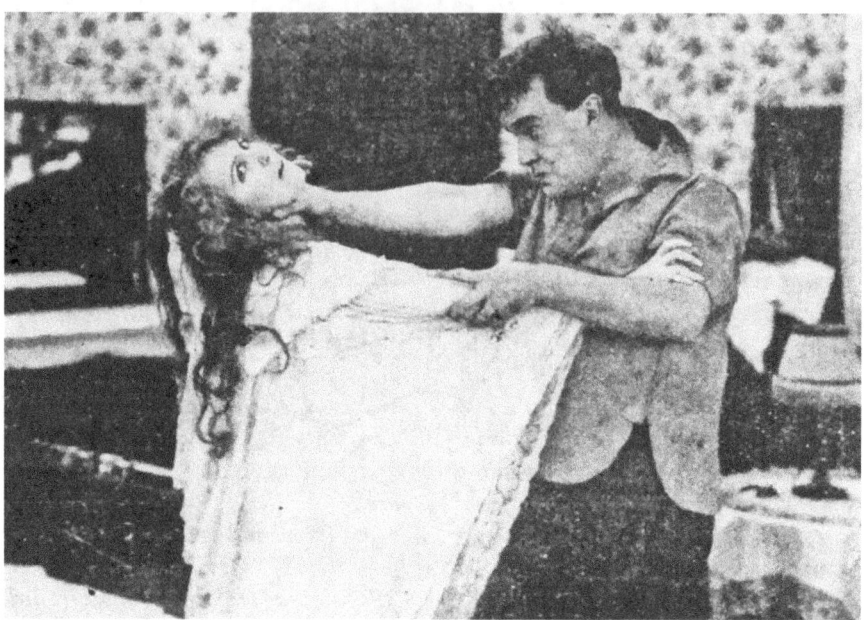

In *"Life without a Soul"* a silent film which also was filmed in Dahlonega in 1915, actress Pauline Curley portrays Claudia Frawley and Percy Standing *"the Creature."* This film was an early rendition of "Frankenstein" based upon Mary Shelley's best-selling book.

play and is more splendidly done. When the play comes to Dahlonega, it will be a night of real enjoyment."

Remembrances

The final comment in the newspaper article above begs the question: "Was *The Plunderer* ever shown in Dahlonega?" Evidence suggests that it was shown in the chapel of North Georgia College (present-day University of North Georgia), but strangely, there is no indication in any records that anyone recalled having seen it. As of this writing (2023), only a handful of Dahlonega residents can even still recall any aspects of the film-making at all.

The late Vernon Smith remembered watching the filming of a night scene made at "Doc" Butler's store across from the old Pruett house near Wimpy Mill Road. "Carbide flashlights were used," he explained.

Virstee Howell recalled that his mother cooked at the Mountain Inn where the movie cast was lodged. "When they departed, they gave her a pair of real leather chaps to give to me because I was so cowboy-crazy as a lad," he added.

Elizabeth Moore had not yet come to Dahlonega when *The Plunderer* was filmed, but she recalled that her late husband, Henry, had driven the movie cast out to a log cabin on Black Mountain Road to do some filming. Henry was a camera buff and took many snapshots of the actors and actresses.

Ola Moore's late husband, Robert, had a horse that was used in the film. She related that he was paid $5.00 a day for its use, which included saddling and currying it.

Ethel Adams' brother, Hardy Price, drove a team of oxen in the movie, and her brother-in-law, Charlie Free, unfortunately owned the mule which fell to its death off Findley Ridge.

Marion Boatfield's father, Jess Mc-Donald, played the part of the blacksmith in the movie. Ms. Boatfield recalled the time her father related an amusing experience involving the film-making. "The director told everybody to go home and put on their oldest clothes so that they'd look as normal as possible for mining families," McDonald reportedly explained with a smile. "When one old mountaineer asked the director if he should go change too, Mr. Lewis shook his head sadly saying, 'No, I don't see how you could look any worse than you already do.'"

The person with the most vivid memories of the filming of *The Plunderer* had both pleasant and painful recollections of the experience. Pearl Ray, the daughter of former Lumpkin County Sheriff T.M. Ray, had gathered with several other town children to play at the Consolidated Mines area and watch the "picture men" engaged in their work. Pearl says she was sitting on one of the old abandoned ore carts when it began rolling down a steep grade, passing close enough to another loaded car to catch her leg in between the two. The crushing blow gashed her leg to the bone.

William Farnum reportedly picked Pearl up and took her to Dr. Head who sewed up her leg as best he could. It was understood at the time, however, that her leg would probably require amputation.

While she was recuperating at home, Pearl says William Farnum visited her several times, bringing her a box of candy and movie magazines. These apparently were a pretty good remedy, because Pearl's leg eventually healed completely. "I never saw the film, but I'll never forget William Farnum," she says.

Pauline Curley was a Vaudeville and silent film actress from Holyoke, Massachusetts. Her film career spanned much of the silent film era, from 1915 to 1928. She lived a long rich life, passing away at the age of 97 in Santa Monica, California, in 2000.

Other Films

The next movie to be filmed in Dahlonega (in November of 1915) was not a Western, but Dahlonega was gaining a reputation as an excellent film-making site, so it was drawing all callers. There is no indication today why Dahlonega was chosen for the Ocean Film Company's production of *The Life Without a Soul*, a movie version of Mary Shelley's book - *Frankenstein*. There were only eight members in the cast of this production. Perhaps the many mining tunnels offered a ghoulish back-drop for filming.

In one of the scenes, the script called for the actor portraying Frankenstein to enter into a terrible rage, knocking out windows, tearing up furniture, and playing general havoc with the movie set. The actor reportedly played the

One of a number of ghoulish scenes from **"Life Without a Soul."** The actress in this scene is unknown, but her eyes would give one pause in turning out the lights at night. Actors in silent horror films, by necessity, went for as much "shock value" in their work as possible, since they were so limited by the absence of sound.

Ethel Clayton portrays "Ruth Jordan" and House Peters portrays her uncompromising suitor "Steve Ghent" in this silent movie, **"The Great Divide,"** intentionally filmed in Dahlonega, Georgia, due to the bare mining terrain which resembled that of Arizona. It is interesting to note here that the "Grand Canyon" behind the actors is actually one of the numerous mining gulches cut by hydraulic gold mining on Dahlonega's Findley Ridge, not the famous Arizona canyon being hawked on this promotional literature.

"Dead Horse Cut" was just one of many mining sites on Findley Ridge south of Dahlonega, Georgia, and demonstrates the interest the landscape engendered for filmmakers due to its resemblance to Western topography. It was photographed here circa 1920s.

The silent film *"Big Jim McGarrity,"* yet another work of the western genre making use of the Dahlonega scenery, was filmed in 1916 by Pathe Freres Company. It starred Robert Edeson.

After being used as a "stand-in" in a pinch by one director, Dahlonega resident Dr. Craig Arnold gained a quick reputation as a go-to guy when a scene required it. He was called upon on more than one occasion by directors thereafter to take on roles other than "bit-parts." In this scene from *"Big Jim Garrity"* an actual abandoned and flooded Dahlonega gold mine shaft is used for part of the action. Arnold portrays the mine doctor (far right) who was called upon to resuscitate twenty-five trapped and drowning men - quite an undertaking, considering the fact that the skills of a doctor in real life would be preoccupied with the resuscitation of but a single individual.

part so well that the company had to re-furnish part of the hotel (quite possibly Doc Arnold's "Mountain Inn") in which the scene was being shot.

Yet another silent film done in Dahlonega in 1915 is a movie entitled *The Great Divide* by Lubin Manufac-turing Company. In the plot of this film, Ethel Clayton is an Easterner who, for reasons unknown, wishes for a rough and unrefined man to marry (they al-ways want the "bad boys" until after the marriage!). She, unhappily, gets her wish when she is abducted by a drunken pros-pector played by House Peters.

A portion of the plot in this film includes a gold-bearing ridge hon-ey-combed with mining shafts, and scenes in which the villain is killed in a landslide - supposedly in the Grand Canyon, no less - but since artificial landslides were not permitted there (as they still are not today), filming was moved to Georgia, and a site in Dahlone-ga known as "Preacher Cut." This site - a well-known landmark in Dahlonega

even in recent years - was erased from the Dahlonega landscape circa 2000, by residential development on Crown Mountain.

Another Western was filmed in 1916 in Dahlonega by Pathe Freres Com-pany. It was entitled *Big Jim Garrity* and starred Robert Edeson. Dahlone-ga resident Dr. Craig Arnold again had a role in this film, portraying the mine doctor who was called to resuscitate twenty-five men (did he have his hands full, or what?) caught in a flooded mine.

Arnold also played the innkeeper in *The Life Without a Soul*, another of the horror movies which were coming into vogue, and which again took advantage of the dark and forbidding mining land-scape in and around Dahlonega.

A film entitled *Driven* was produced in 1923 by Brabin Productions, Inc. of New York. It portrayed an old mountain-eer and three moonshining sons.

According to the plot of this film, Essie, a mountain girl, moves in with a family of neighboring "moonshine"

"Driven," starred Elinor Fair and Charles Emmett Mack.

"Driven," filmed in Dahlonega in 1923, was directed by Charles Brabin, who was married to sexy movie "vamp" Theda Bara. When a local rumor began circulating in Dahlonega that Ms. Bara was traveling to the north Georgia community to visit her husband on-set, it was pandemonium on the old town square. This cabinet card of his beautiful wife in one of her performances offers an explanation.

bootleggers when her father, also a bootlegger, is killed by federal agents. She falls in love with Tom, one of the family's brothers, but another brother, the violent and brutal Lem, decides he wants her for himself, and beats Tom badly. What the girl doesn't know is that it wasn't the feds who killed her father – it was Lem. Complications ensue.

Background scenery for this movie included Amicalola Falls, Brasstown Bald, Blood Mountain, and Mount Yonah.

Interestingly, Charles Brabin, who directed this film, was the husband of

sexy theater "vamp" Theda Bara. When it was rumored that the famous actress might be traveling to Dahlonega to visit her husband, the whole town reportedly turned out to inspect every strange woman who appeared on the town square!

The Daughter of Devil Dan produced by Buffalo Pictures Company in 1921, created some excitement not in the script. One of the scenes took place in a cove on Yahoola Creek where a mountain moonshining still was set up as a portion of the movie set. Irma Harrison, the leading lady, was beseeching her father, "Devil Dan," portrayed by Kempton Greene, to give up his illegal trade. The script called for Irma to then dynamite a dam upstream, to remove all traces of the still before her sweetheart could arrive to arrest her father.

The script, however, did not call for real bullets to be fired or a real U.S. marshal to arrest the entire party, both of which occurred. No amount of explaining could convince the confused lawman

Pictured are two versions – side by side – of the bridge across Yahoola Creek one mile east of downtown Dahlonega. These offer an idea of the extremely rough and often impassable nature of the roads into Dahlonega in the early 1900s. The film crews making the trek to the town during that time period had only the lower covered bridge in this photo to reach town. The more modern upper "Heroe's Bridge" (demolished long ago for a still-more modern bridge) was not constructed until 1922.

(who apparently thought he had made a whale of an arrest) that he had made a terrible mistake. The whole company, amazingly, was arrested and forced to make bond for their appearance in Federal Court in Gainesville.

Between 1915 and 1920, many permanent motion picture studios from the East Coast had sprung up in "Hollywoodland." By the early to mid-1920s, film-making of silent movies in Georgia had almost completely disappeared.

Vanished Footage

In more recent times, Mrs. Sharon Johnson, a former employee with the Georgia Department of Natural Resources who managed the Dahlonega Gold Museum (old Lumpkin County Courthouse) for many years, attempted without success, to locate copies of these now almost forgotten silent films from days gone by, hoping to be able to show the films at the museum.

Unfortunately, these now historic movies no doubt languish forgotten in unmarked canisters in some vast film library (Turner Network Television?), or have been destroyed or discarded long ago, their value and usefulness assumed to have expired.

Today, even the Dahlonega countryside which was once so reminiscent of the "Old West" to early movie-makers has disappeared, its scarred hillsides now thankfully recovered with timber and greenery.

The 1913 Dahlonega Bank Robbery

*It is but a footnote in history today, but back in the early 1900s,
a group of bandits tried to rob the Bank of Lumpkin County, and met
with a bit more resistance than they had anticipated. The ensuing
blazing gun-battle rivaled a scene right out of the old West.*

The impressive country-style home originally built by the Jones family still sits prominently on the west-northwest corner of the town square in Dahlonega, Georgia. As of this writing in 2023, it is occupied by commercial businesses, but back on the cold night of February 12, 1913, it housed the brood of Dr. and Mrs. C.H. Jones. Its residents didn't know it at the time, but they were about to witness a shocking attempted bank robbery.

Theodocia Jones – recently widowed by the death of her physician husband – had been awakened from her sleep by strangers milling about and muttering on the sidewalk outside her home and she instinctively suspected that something unusual was in the offing. Little did she know that her intuition had sniffed out a major crime in the making.

Just as Theodocia was seriously considering the summoning of help, the men suddenly just disappeared. Though she was eventually able to get back to sleep, it was a troubled slumber. She was still uneasy enough the following morning to go to the little drugstore next door to their home to warn the "coffee-klatch" patrons warming themselves casually around the wood stove, telling them beseechingly that they needed to be concerned; that strangers were hanging about the town square in the middle of the night.

As men typically will do until directly confronted by a dangerous circumstance, they dismissed her concerns as neurotic alarmism. Everyone knew that Theodocia had lost her husband the previous year. The men in the drug store good-naturedly attempted to do little more than console her.

Frustrated and put-out with the men, Theodocia went back home next door and pursued her daily tasks – but with a still-growing feeling of fear. She was so concerned that she sent her daughter – Wanda – to fetch a friend to come spend the next night at their home.

"Boom" in the Night!

That evening, sure enough, shortly after midnight in the wee hours of the morning, a muffled explosion suddenly broke the calm of the winter night. Theodocia was fully awake almost immediately. She tenderly but quickly scooped up her infant daughter, Frances, in her arms, then hustled the other children – Wanda and Charles Harry – into the dining room where they all hid behind the chimney.

In 1913, the tiny and rural mountain town of Dahlonega, Georgia, was composed of little more than 200 households. Many of them also had heard the substantial racket and some were concerned. This, after all, was barely 48 years after the close of the U.S. Civil War, and the more concerned men remembered those types of noises quite well. However, it was also the dead of winter outside, and the noise they had detected simply was not alarming enough to urge them out of their warm beds into the frigid winter weather for an investigation.

Mischievous cadets just up the street at North Georgia Agricultural College (NGAC) were notorious for firing off the college cannon at odd hours and waking the town residents. Most of the awakened sleepers therefore merely wrote off the commotion to more adolescent mischief and went back to sleep.

The explosion had occurred just below the Hall House on the north side of the Dahlonega town square where one NGAC student by the name of Cleveland Duncan was rooming on the second floor. When he stepped out of his room onto the Hall House's second floor porch to investigate the source of the noise, Cleveland was shocked to see a man with a revolver standing directly below him in front of the small Bank of Lumpkin County building. It did not require a super-intellect to deduce that something out of the ordinary was afoot, and the young college student was immediately suspicious.

Interestingly, at about this same time, the stranger with the revolver looked up and discovered young Cleveland witnessing his actions, and he immediately fired a round from his pistol, much to Cleveland's shock. Just as would anyone who didn't want their head perforated – young Cleveland jerked back inside his room.

With the pop of gunfire now joining the unusual noises outside, the boldness – or ignorance – of the bandits soon became responsible for the attraction of still more attention, but this time, it would be a much more serious confrontation.

"Mista Bob"

By 1913 there were over six million telephones in use in the United States, but only a precious few of them existed in what then was the very remotely-located backwoods town of Dahlonega. Fortunately, a phone did exist in the lobby of the Hall House, and Cleveland Duncan had the presence of mind to make use of it.

Across the town square at an angle from where Duncan stood was what was known in those days as "Meaders' Corner." It existed at the corner of Main and North Park streets, and was owned and occupied by Robert C. "Mista Bob" Meaders. The Meaders family lived in the downstairs portion of this structure and the local Dahlonega telephone exchange – which was owned and operated by Bob – was located in the upper level.

Aside from his communications responsibilities, Mista Bob was also the president of the Lumpkin County Bank.

"Meaders Corner" (foreground) photographed circa 1950s, appears exactly as it did on the cold winter night of February 13, 1913, when owner Robert C. "Mista Bob" Meaders slipped out the rear door and then, with the assistance of Sheriff Tom Ray, blazed away with firearms to thwart an attempted robbery of the Bank of Lumpkin County on the north side of the town square. One of the large windows pictured on the upstairs porch of the Meaders home was shattered by gunfire from one of the bandits when Robert's wife, Margaret, illuminated the room to call the sheriff. All of the structures visible in this photo are unchanged from the night of the attempted robbery, and some of them still exist today on the old town square. (Photo courtesy of Margaret Meaders)

Cleveland Duncan knew that if he called the telephone exchange, a special buzzer downstairs used to summon "Central" (the person operating the telephone exchange at any given time) would awaken the Meaders and bring someone to the telephone. *(Author's Note: In the 21st Century, it is somewhat amusing to imagine the telephone operator being awakened from sleep to travel "upstairs" to answer the telephone, but those were the circumstances in 1913.)*

Unbeknownst to young Cleveland, no awakening was necessary at this point for Bob Meaders. We're talking serious consequences for anyone brazen enough to try to steal money from Mista Bob, and any "boom" immediately got his attention. The dedicated town leader was already on his way upstairs to the telephone switchboard when Cleveland's call set off the buzzer.

Cleveland, no doubt, was almost beside himself at this point. He had already been fired upon by the perpetrators on the town square. When he excitedly described the circumstances to Bob, the bank president quickly dressed, retrieved his revolver, and then set out to investigate. Before he left, he instructed his wife, Maggie, to "Call the sheriff and tell him the bank is being robbed."

Bob then didn't waste any time slipping quietly out the back door of his home into the mid-winter chill and easing down behind Will Jones's store and then on to the Sergeant Building. After taking extreme caution to remain undetected by the thieves, Bob next moved through what at that time was a vacant lot to the east end of the Hall House. The bandits had not yet caught wind of Bob's actions as he reconnoitered the situation.

Two of the bandits had been posted as "look-outs" at the courthouse (present-day Dahlonega Gold Museum). The large picture window of the upstairs telephone exchange in the Meaders building had been dark up to this point. Having never previously dealt with a situation of this nature, Miss Maggie thought nothing of turning on the lights to reveal the switchboard in order to summon Sheriff Tom Ray.

When the room lit up and Maggie stepped in front of the picture window to initiate the call, the bandits immediately knew what she was doing and opened fire on her. A totally shocked Maggie Meaders dropped instantly to the floor as the window shattered and broken glass rained all around her as a result of the gunfire.

Though shaken, Maggie was unharmed, and reached up to plug in the appropriate connections on the telephone switchboard to call not only the sheriff, but everyone else of whom she could think to summon. Fingers had never moved so quickly on a telephone switchboard.

"High Noon"

Meanwhile, back down on the square, Mista Bob hadn't taken kindly to his bank being robbed, and when his wife was fired upon, that was the last straw as far as he was concerned. He opened up with a blaze of gunfire of his own. He later explained that it was so dark, he couldn't actually see the bandits, but he knew where they were by the muzzle-flashes from their weapons, and he had concentrated his gunfire upon those locations.

It was about this point that Sheriff Ray hurriedly rounded the corner onto the square, having run the several blocks down Main Street from the Lumpkin County Jail (which also still exists today). Since he was unaware of the actual

circumstances, Ray was incautious in his advance, and Bob shouted a quick warning to him to take cover.

It was at this point that a round fired by one of the bandits shattered a store window directly behind the sheriff, so he didn't require any further urging. It was now very clear that these outlaws thought nothing of killing someone to achieve their robbery of the bank.

Still somewhat confused with the circumstances, Ray reportedly shouted to Bob inquiring about the identity of the men and the nature of their actions. Bob, losing patience with the lawman, reportedly shouted back "You idiot! They're robbing the bank and they've been shooting at you ever since you rounded the corner!"

When Ray finally realized the actual circumstances, he worked his way around the square to where Bob was crouched behind the Hall House. He handed Meaders another handgun. Bob reloaded his own revolver and the two of them then advanced steadily on the criminals, reportedly firing with weapons in both hands, in a scene reminiscent of *High Noon*.

Attempted Getaway

The duo's determined gunfire produced dividends almost immediately as one of the bandits went down with a wound. When the remaining thieves took stock of the situation, they apparently decided that discretion was the better part of valor and they took flight, running for an automobile parked just off the square on South Main Street. They then drove quickly off into the darkness, southward down old U.S. 19 Highway.

Though the thieves had departed, Mista Bob and the sheriff were unaware at this point of their whereabouts, and had taken cover to take stock and then advance upon them once again. A short time later, they were informed by other town residents that the perpetrators had left in a vehicle.

As daylight began breaking over the horizon onto the Dahlonega town square, the sheriff began organizing a posse. Though the thieves had quickly exited the area in a vehicle, the posse was composed of some two dozen men on horseback.

Surprisingly, though the thieves had enjoyed a sizeable advantage in their getaway in the vehicle, for reasons unknown today, they had later paused to grab some sleep – perhaps exhausted from their several continuous days and nights of canvassing the Dahlonega streets and businesses to plan the robbery.

According to accounts of the incident, the men, amazingly, were eventually discovered sleeping in a ditch. The arrests took place near Ellijay, Georgia. Though their getaway had seemed almost assured since they were speeding away in an automobile, it seems surprising today that men on horseback could overtake and capture the criminals seemingly so easily.

In those days, however, all the "streets" – bar none – were no more than dusty mountain trails, and a talented tracker on horseback was easily able to follow the tracks of an automobile on a dirt road little-traveled by other vehicles. By eight o'clock that evening, all the men were behind bars at the Lumpkin County Jail in Dahlonega, under the watchful eye of Sheriff Ray.

Aftermath

Much to his relief, Mista Bob reportedly discovered that the only items the thieves had managed to actually steal from the bank were two pistols.

In more recent times, Bob's son – Robert Meadors, Jr. of Camarillo, California, – stated "They apparently were unfamiliar with (and had been thwarted by) the type of safe used by the bank which had two front doors.

"After drilling through the outer door, they had attempted to blast through the second door," Meaders added, "but the explosion had actually done more to deter than to help them. It sealed the door into the safe to produce what amounted to an almost solid steel box. That safe later had to be placed on the sidewalk outside the bank and cut open with a blow torch."

In an article by writer (and Mista Bob's sister) Margaret Meaders which was later published in the June-July, 1970 issue of *Georgia Magazine*, she explained the outlaws *"gave assumed names throughout most of their trial, but eventually were identified as professional thieves on their way to Knoxville, Tennessee, from Atlanta. Hearing about the two little banks in Dahlonega, they had decided to 'knock off' one or both on their way north and pick up a little 'easy money.'"*

According to an article in the February 28, 1913 issue of the *Dahlonega Nugget* newspaper:

"The parties who gave their names as Charles Miller, John M. Harris, William Thornton and W.M. Flynn, charged with entering the bank of Lumpkin County and blowing open the outer door of its safe on the morning of the 14th inst., at about one o'clock were here last Monday before Justice of the Peace W.B. Townsend, and all bound over to the next term of Lumpkin Superior Court on the charge of burglary, bond of each being fixed at ten thousand dollars, who have been sent to Fulton County Jail by Judge Jones for safe-keeping.

"The parties who entered the bank

Photographed circa 1900, quite near the 1913 attempted robbery of the Bank of Lumpkin County, one of the upper rooms of the Hall House (pictured) was occupied by North Georgia Agricultural College (fore-runner of present-day University of North Georgia) student Cleveland Duncan. After hearing the muffled explosion of the attempted break-in by bandits at the bank, Duncan peered over the railing of the upper level and was immediately fired upon by one of the bank robbers standing directly below. The small bank building (bricked with barred windows) is visible on the left. (Photo courtesy of GA Dept. of Archives & History, Atlanta)

got nothing but a couple of pistols, but they seceeded (sic) in wrecking the front of the safe before they were run off by Sheriff T.M. Ray and R.C. Meaders, president of the bank. The insurance company had to replace the safe with a new one. Neither was there any positive or direct evidence that these men did enter this bank, but the circumstantial proof was strong against them, all of whom beyond a doubt were traveling under false colors by using assumed names.

"The quartette (sic) was convicted of burglary, by the Superior Court of Lumpkin County, and were sent to the penitentiary; but were soon pardoned out by the Governor."

Yesteryear's Buildings

Interestingly, due to preservation-minded residents, much of the old town square has been preserved and still exists just as it did on the night of this attempted robbery in 1913.

One of the few exceptions is the old Meaders building on the corner owned by Mista Bob and in which he and his family lived and operated Dahlonega's first telephone exchange for many years. It, unfortunately, was demolished years ago and a new structure was built upon that site.

The old "Will Jones Store," however, one of the oldest structures in Dahlonega, still stands and has housed a number of businesses over the years. It continues to be a popular business site today.

The "Sargent Building" also still stands and was an automobile dealership for many years. It also continues to be a popular locale for shops and businesses.

The "vacant lot" between the Sargent Building and the "Hall House" is no longer "vacant," having been occupied later by a building which still stands today.

The "Hall House," constructed in the early 1880s (and known as the "Robert M. Moore Building" for many years) was built by early Dahlonega businessman Frank W. Hall, and also still stands as of this writing, and is still used as a residential dwelling upstairs while being occupied by shops and businesses downstairs.

The focus of all the excitement in 1913 – the little one-story Lumpkin County Bank building – also still stands as of this writing. Built in 1881, it originally served as Frank W. Hall's business office. Hall was a mining and real estate entrepreneur who reportedly was the richest individual in Lumpkin County in his day. He also contracted for the construction of and owned "Hall's Block" on the northwestern corner of the square (behind the bank), the aforementioned "Hall House," the present-day eatery known as "The Smith House" restaurant, as well as a number of other edifices in the county.

Hall departed Dahlonega somewhat mysteriously in 1900. Over 100 years later in 2006, it was discovered that he apparently had, for a number of years, been illicitly mining gold ore from a substantial shaft beneath what today is the Smith House Restaurant (*Readers please see "The Secret Gold Mine Beneath the Smith House" in the Lumpkin County section of this volume.*).

Captain Hall was also responsible for the construction of historic Lumpkin

County Jail where the outlaws were imprisoned (and which still stands today) a short distance from the town square. Though it served as a lock-up for numerous figures down through the county's history, including notorious old West outlaw Bill Miner, captured outside Dahlonega in 1911, it has not served as a jail for many years. Today, it is a preserved historic site, serving as of this writing as the site of the Lumpkin County Historic Society.

In 1931, a few years after the 1913 robbery attempt, the Bank of Lumpkin County ceased to exist after it was merged with the Bank of Dahlonega. The combined banks were relocated to the southeast corner of the town square where the business existed for many years. That structure also still stands today.

The historic Jones home – built circa 1885 – is known as "the Conner House" as of this writing and houses several shops today.

The historic Lumpkin County Courthouse – built in 1836 – also still exists and houses the Dahlonega Gold Museum today. Visitors from throughout the world come to view its pioneer-justice interior month after month, year after year, some seeking information about relatives and other aspects of the county's history among the many archives housed in this building. One of its upstairs display cases houses a Smith & Wesson revolver taken from one of the bandits arrested in the robbery attempt.

Also on display in the Gold Museum is a bullet discovered embedded in one of the columns that were an original part of the interior of the old courthouse. The source of the round is unknown today, and since the streets of the Dahlonega town square have experienced quite a bit of gunfire over the years – all the way back to the 1830s – the source of the round likely will never be known.

The Unbelievable Consolidated Gold Mine

It began life in 1898 as a highly anticipated gold milling operation in what then were the backwoods of north Georgia. Despite the immense mine shafts and hugely-expensive milling equipment, the Consolidated Gold Mine was in operation only a very few years before becoming a victim of its own efficiency. There literally was not enough gold ore to keep the huge mill in operation full-time, causing its expenses to be greater than its income.

For almost three-quarters of a century, the gold fields in north Georgia's Lumpkin County were worked by countless prospectors seeking their fortune from the rugged mountain terrain. Some were successful, but most suffered in vain for the precious yellow metal. The Consolidated Gold Mining Company, organized in Dahlonega in 1898, was reputed to have been the largest gold mill ever constructed east of the Mississippi River, but even in this grand venture, failure became inevitable – that is, until the early 1980s, when one entrepreneur discovered that people will pay handsomely just to tour a historic gold mine.

When Bryan Whitfield III purchased the property and mineral rights in 1980, he envisioned reactivating the Consolidated as a working mine. He had already been successful in the coal mining business in West Virginia, employing over 3,000 workers at one point.

Whitfield, however, soon discov-

ered that even with the price of gold today, the process required to recover it from the ore in the north Georgia mountains made it too costly to keep it profitable. The "easy gold" was long gone, and that which remains is known as "sulfide gold" because it is locked up in hard ore from which it is difficult and expensive to extract.

For years, visitors who came to Dahlonega wishing to tour a real gold mine were told that the mines were all on private property and unsafe as well. Whitfield's son – Bryan IV and his wife Donna – came up with the idea that the Consolidated could fill that "tour" interest, and so they set out to see what they could do to make their idea bear fruit.

After several years of cleaning out and reinforcing the Knight Vein at the Consolidated, the Whitfields opened the site for tours in October of 1991. To their amazement, their mine drew almost 20,000 people the first year it was open, and Bryan and Donna realized they may have stumbled upon a "hidden

Photographed in the early 1900s, this view of the Consolidated Gold Mining site includes most of the structures used to process gold-bearing ore at the site. The stamp mill is located in the center of the photo. The large smokestack from the roasting furnace is visible right-rear. And the Assaying Office is visible left-center. The structure in the right foreground is the old Boatfield family home. (Photo courtesy of the GA Dept. of Archives & History, Atlanta)

motherlode." Slightly more than a century earlier however (as of this writing in 2023), their predecessors at the huge mine had not been so fortunate.

When gold was first discovered in north Georgia in 1828, men from every walk of life were soon wading in every creek and branch in search of the mesmerizing metal. Many of these early miners undoubtedly believed that the gold actually originated "in water," little realizing that in actuality, its heavy weight had caused it to be washed down via gravity from the surrounding hillsides to be deposited in the lower-lying stream-beds.

For those who came early, a simple pan was the only tool necessary for the separation of the shining flecks and nuggets from the sandy soil.

Eager to speed up the process, however, some of the hardy men soon began inventing new tools that would allow them to sort more ore in less time. Instead of working with one panful at a time, they began shoveling sand and gravel into a sluice box by the bucket-loads where a greater quantity of the gold was collected much more quickly.

Other, more inventive creations, improved still further on the collection process until large milling operations (with huge vertical crushers or "stamps") were invented to convert the ore into dust. Though it polluted and poisoned the streams unmercifully, the owners and operators of these mills used mercury-coated plates which attracted the gold like a magnet after it was washed from the ore.

To remove ore from deep within the mountains of Lumpkin County, shafts were dug and rails were laid for heavy ore-carts which transported the ore to a "hopper." The miners pictured here were photographed at this mine in Dahlonega in 1913. (Photo courtesy of the GA Dept. of Archives & History, Atlanta)

The Civil War brought virtually all mining to a standstill in north Georgia. It wasn't until the turn of the 20th Century that mining was resumed on a large scale in Lumpkin County, and the largest of these operations was the Consolidated.

The huge site included a 300 x 100-foot, 4-story, 120-stamp mill; a 128 x 128-foot, 4-story chlorination plant; an assay laboratory; and a blacksmith and machine shop. The *Engineering and Mining Journal* described it as *"the first systematic attempt at deep mining and intelligent milling in Georgia."*

The company at the forefront of this operation called itself *The Consolidated Gold Mining Company* because it purchased 7,000 acres of mineral land in and around Dahlonega, which included the Singleton, Mary Henry and Tahloneka and other previously worked mines and veins all "consolidated" into one mining venture. The processing plant was located on Yahoola Creek less than a mile from the town square of Dahlonega.

Dahlonega's enthusiasm for this huge venture pumping great revenue into the community was verbalized on June 30, 1899 by the editor of *The Dahlonega Nugget* who wrote: *"There is no calculating the amount of good the Dahlonega Consolidated Gold Mining Company is doing in this country; every industrious laborer with or without a team is given employment. . ."*

After the land was cleared of timber, construction work began in August and was pushed through with such vigor that the stamp mill was ready for operation by the following May despite the inevitable winter weather delays. All of the machinery and some of the building materials were hauled 25 miles from the railway station in Gainesville to Dahlonega, over narrow and twisting mountain trails which often became quagmires after heavy rains. Some of the heavy equipment had to be carried on specially-constructed wagons drawn by 18 or 20 mules.

Each of the 120 stamps in the mill weighed 850 pounds and fell at the then-incredible rate of 90 stamps per minute, giving the mill the capacity to crush 600 tons of ore every 24 hours. The ore was stored in a 27,000-ton capacity bin on the hillside above the mill.

After being fed into a large crusher, the ore was carried by endless belt bucket hoist to the upper floor of the mill. There, a wide horizontal endless belt conveyed it to the pounding stamps. Free gold was caught with amalgam plates, while tailings were carried by pipe to concentrators on the first floor.

The remaining concentrates were hauled by wheelbarrows or carts through an enclosed passageway to the chlorination plant to be deposited into a roasting furnace and then into steel barrels containing sulfuric acid and calcium chloride.

The filtered solution washed out of the barrels was conveyed by an air-pressure engine into two precipitate tanks where jets of hydrogen sulfide precipitated the gold chloride. Finally, the gold chloride was caught on canvass and filter paper to be smelted, refined, and cast into bars.

The time required for a given mass of ore to go through the entire process was about 36 hours. The inventors of the chlorination process claimed that it

This view of the Consolidated Gold Mining venture was photographed in 1913, approximately eight years after the company suffered bankruptcy. The buildings sat vacant and abandoned for almost 100 years before falling into disrepair and being demolished in the 1990s. (Photo courtesy of the GA Dept. of Archives & History, Atlanta)

This view shows a section of the huge ore crushers in the milling department. Judging from the appearance of the rusted support posts and the debris in this room, this mill had been abandoned for a number of years, and is being inspected by unknown individuals. (Photo courtesy of the GA Dept. of Archives & History, Atlanta)

would save 95% of the gold at low cost, enabling them to work low-grade ore at a good profit.

The stamp mill was run by two 500-horsepower Pelton water-wheels powered by water from a reservoir on a nearby hill. The reservoir was filled with water brought by a 21-mile man-made aqueduct called "the Hand Ditch." The water-wheels not only generated electricity for running the mill, but also provided a number of businesses and homes in Dahlonega with electricity for their use.

The late Dahlonega native Ralph Fitts once recalled the first electric lights he ever saw. "My uncle, Charlie Stargel, worked at the Consolidated, and he had the job of opening the flood-gate every afternoon just before dark," Fitts explained. "It was fascinating to

watch how the filament in the clear light-bulbs would begin to glow as electricity flowed through it. Back then, it cost only ten cents a month to have electric lights."

There was such positive expectation in its potential productivity that no expense was spared in building the massive Consolidated plant. It was designed to be operated by 250 employees and was constructed of the finest materials.

Unfortunately, the success of the Consolidated was short-lived. The company, amazingly, went bankrupt after only a few years of operation, and the property was sold at a tremendous loss at a Trustees' Sale in 1906.

"As it turned out, the Consolidated Gold Mining Company was just too big an operation for the amount of ore that was readily available," the late

Zimmer's Mountain Lodge in Dahlonega was originally constructed as a private club for the management of the Consolidated Gold Mining Company. It was purchased by Zimmer and converted into an inn/resort of sorts following the mining company's demise and prospered for a number of years before being destroyed by fire.

local resident and veteran miner Marion Boatfield once explained. "The company went broke because they just plain ran out of ore to process. You can't run stamps without ore or it will burst the mortars. I remember that whenever the stockholders came down to watch, the (operators of the mill) used to throw rubber boots under the stamps just to make it look like they were in full operation without ruining the stamps."

The late W.R. Crisson, a well-known Dahlonega miner in his own right who died in 1907, once said the Consolidated Mines failed because the operation was too big. He was also of the opinion that the out-of-state mining experts would have done better had they listened to experienced local miners who were more knowledgeable about what methods worked best in their area.

After the Trustees' Sale, the Consolidated buildings and their contents essentially were abandoned and never again used to process gold. Over the years, vandals threw rocks and broke the 5-gallon glass demi-johns of sulfuric acid in the chlorination plant, and the spilled acid hastened the buildings' ruin. "Twenty years later, you still couldn't walk anywhere in the area or the acid would eat up your shoes," Boatfield recalled.

Interestingly, the abandoned ruins provided a perfect setting for a silent movie entitled *The Plunderer*, filmed on location in and around Dahlonega in 1915. Marion Boatfield's father, Jesse McDonald, was hired to portray the blacksmith in the film.

The late Dr. Craig Arnold eventually purchased the old Consolidated property in 1933, and rented it to John and Marion Boatfield the following year. They moved into what had been the assay office where ore had been tested to determine the gold content. The Boatfields acted as caretakers for the property and also mined on a small scale on the side, processing the ore with a small gas-powered "Tom Thumb" stamp mill. "Doc" Arnold got a royalty from the gold recovered, which he shipped to the U.S. Mint in Philadelphia.

Even that small-scale mining was ended during World War II. "You couldn't get mercury to catch the gold anymore, and even if you could, it (the mercury) was more expensive than the gold," Mrs. Boatfield explained.

The Tom Thumb stamp mill used on the property is now on display in the Dahlonega Gold Museum.

Following Doc Arnold's death in 1948, all of the remaining equipment at the old Consolidated Mines was sold at public auction, but the Boatfields were allowed to continue living on the property for the remainder of their lives.

John Boatfield's life-long interest in gold undoubtedly came from his grandfather, Frederick D. "Boartfield," who came to Dahlonega in 1838 to work at the newly-opened United States Branch Mint. He apparently was the only original Mint employee still around when it was closed at the on-set of the U.S. Civil War in 1861.

When the Consolidated Mines chlorination plant was torn down in 1951, Dahlonega resident Henry Moore bought some of the heart pine wood and used it to build a hardware store on the south side of the Dahlonega town square. Ollie Seabolt (father of former Lumpkin County Sheriff Kenneth Seabolt) bought wood from the stamp mill when it was torn down.

Mrs. Boatfield recalls that a man from North Carolina bought fifty of the stamps in the mill, but the other seventy were junked. The concentrating tables were sold as scrap metal to buyers from Japan. After that, little else remained except the old assay office (which became the Boatfields' home) and the large brick smokestack from the roasting furnace.

The road into the old site had deteriorated so badly by this time that John and Marion needed a 4-wheel drive vehicle just to get in and out. Most of the property eventually was reclaimed by nature.

When Dahlonega Gold, Inc., purchased the Consolidated property in the 1960s, the company owners asked Mrs. Boatfield to guide them into one of the old mining tunnels. Mrs. Boatfield, however, had no intention of risking being buried alive in a cave-in. "You can go in if you want to, but I'll stay out here and tell them where you're at," she reportedly replied, knowing how unstable the old tunnels had become over the years.

More years went by, and still nothing was ever done with the property. Finally, in 1980, the Whitfields purchased it, and things began to change.

Today, visitors to the Consolidated don yellow plastic hard-hats to protect their heads against the occasional drips of water and follow a guide down a ramp into a gaping hole in the side of the mountain. Once inside, they find themselves with an awesome view of what is known as "the glory hole," a yawning 250-foot vertical shaft. The gold vein discovered there actually runs through a supporting pillar in the center of the shaft, but it had to be left untouched to provide support for the shaft.

Steep steps lead down into the main

shaft, where visitors follow the old ore car rail tracks deeper into the aged mine. The ore cars were pulled by a DC motor powered by a spring-loaded pole which followed a bare copper wire running along the ceiling of the shaft (similar to the system later used by street-cars in many cities).

Electricity also ran the air compressors which powered jack hammers used in the mine. Guides point out an early drill referred to by old-timers as a "widow-maker" because it generated so much dust. Many miners died of lung diseases caused by the constant breathing of dust from the mines.

Guides in the mine also demonstrate a later "drifter drill" which eliminated the dust problem with a water

Bryan Whitfield, a fourth generation coal miner from West Virginia transferred his mining and management skills into the development of a public attraction called Consolidated Gold Mine in Dahlonega, now one of the top tourist attractions in north Georgia. (Photo by Olin Jackson)

hook-up. Even though the guides operated it at only partial power, the noise reverberating through the tunnel gives visitors a very clear indication of how deafening the device must have been for miners using it at full power.

After drilling holes on either side of a vein, miners packed the holes with dynamite to blast out the ore for processing. Many "drill holes" are still visible today in the walls of the tunnel.

Despite its immense appearance, only approximately one-third of the tunnel had been cleared of debris at this writing (2021) by the Whitfields, and they reportedly were eager to begin work on some of the lower levels, immensely curious of what might be discovered there. "When the pumps were cut off in 1906, the lower section quickly filled up with water, and we think that a lot of the old mining equipment is still down there, Whitfield explained. "We didn't find much in the upper levels because they had been robbed out (by later treasure hunters)."

The Whitfields attempted to locate the 50 original stamps that had been moved to North Carolina, only to discover they had been dismantled and scrapped. Although pounding stamps are no long used to process gold in modern gold mills, Bryan and Donna installed some stamps and other equipment so that visitors could actually see gold being milled on the premises.

The Consolidated Gold Mines site is listed on the ***National Register of Historic Places***, and the Whitfields were awarded the Lumpkin County Historical Society's "*Madeleine K. Anthony Award*" in 1992, for their preservation of this very historic site and remnant of Lumpkin County's golden past.

Historic (1846) Crisson Mine Still Producing Gold Today

Originally opened as the Rider Mine circa 1846, the mining operation known famously today as the Crisson Mine in Dahlonega, Georgia, has been operated by the same family now for well over a century.

The mining site looked promising in 1883, so E.E. Crisson purchased it. Since it wasn't productive early-on, E.E. not only managed his mine with its 10-stamp mill for processing the ore, he also farmed and operated a general merchandise store on the property located two-and-one-half miles from downtown Dahlonega on old Wimpy Mill Road (present-day U.S. 19 Connector).

E.E. Crisson's father, William Reese (W.R.) Crisson, was well-known as one of the more successful miners who had owned and worked a number of local mines in the Lumpkin County area over the years, including the Findley, Lockhart, and Singleton mines. His father, Elijah Crisson, possibly came to what today is Lumpkin some years prior or even to Benjamin Parks, who supposedly accidentally stubbed his toe on a gold-bearing quartz rock in 1828, precipitating the now-famous north Georgia gold rush.

Family tradition maintains that W.R. was born in 1818 in a cabin which once stood where Tanyard Branch runs into Yahoola Creek, an area where several rich mines were later opened. Family members today suspect that Elijah knew about the gold and was busy panning out the placer deposits on the sly, keeping the existence of the site a secret.

Things apparently started getting too crowded for Elijah though once the gold rush began in earnest, and he reportedly traveled out West with his oldest son, planning to send for the remainder of his family after settling in a new location. However, as was often the case with travelers of frontier times venturing across Indian country, Elijah and his son simply vanished, never to be heard from again. Perhaps their bones laid upon the prairie for years, bleaching in the sun, before disappearing completely.

According to family tradition, W.R., who was 12 years of age when his father and brother disappeared, helped clear the land and build Lumpkin County's first log courthouse in 1833. Apparently tiring of his life in Lumpkin County, W.R. also traveled out West to California in 1850, successfully crossing Indian territory.

He, however, apparently fared no

better in California than he had in Georgia, because W.R. returned a few years later. Having had the opportunity to compare and observe the gold mining skills in both locales, he reportedly decided that one could do better mining for gold in Lumpkin County than California. According to members of the family, they still possess the tools he took with him to California, although one has to wonder why someone would personally drag heavy mining tools all the way across the country.

When W.R. and other miners returned from out West, they possessed knowledge and experience little-known back East. It allowed for faster processing of gold ore, which was a major advancement.

Up to that point, miners had been forced to haul their ore to the nearest stamp mill by the best conveyance available – usually a mule-drawn wagon. The new method utilized by miners out West was called "hydraulic mining," and W.R. is credited with being one of the first to use it in north Georgia.

Hydraulic mining essentially made use of the power of water which was plentiful in the streams of north Georgia. A long raceway was constructed from the head-waters of a creek upstream from a mining site. The raceway conducted the water at a steady drop in elevation to the mining site, all the while building up momentum gravitationally in the downhill flow of the water.

At the site at which the miner desired to process ore, the water was either captured in holding ponds at the top of a mountain and then periodically released down the mountainside to wash gold-bearing ore across sluices, or, it was conducted through powerful water cannons known as "Little Giants," or "Long Toms," which were also used to wash

gold ore from mountainsides down into and across sluices to capture the gold.

In one example of the above, the head-waters of the Yahoola Creek in Lumpkin County were dammed and a 20-mile alternate ditch was dug to convey the water down to various mines which all purchased the water by a measure known as "the miner's inch." The water was stored in reservoirs at each mining site and used, as explained above, to wash gold-bearing ore across sluice boxes in which the precious metal was captured.

The dam across the Yahoola was only seven miles from Dahlonega ("as the crow flies"), but the lengthy aqueduct was forced to follow the contours of the mountainous terrain a much greater distance in order to maintain the necessary gradual drop in elevation required to continuously increase the gravitational flow of the water.

Gold receipts were light at the Dahlonega Branch Mint during 1859 and the early part of 1860, when many of the local miners were occupied with digging the Yahoola Ditch and building the trestles and flumes to carry the water over ravines which couldn't otherwise be circumvented. All mining in Lumpkin County came to a standstill, however, when the U.S. Civil War began in 1861.

By the time the war had ended in 1865, a substantial portion of the Yahoola conveyance (the flumes of which were constructed of wood at various spots along the canal) had either rotted away or been vandalized. Other portions of the Yahoola Ditch, however, which were constructed with earthen canals sometimes lined with stone, may still be seen even today if one ventures out into the countryside north of Dahlonega and knows where to search.

For many years, the Dahlonega, Georgia, area was over-run with numerous small mining operations functioning with crudely-built stamp mills such as the one pictured here. The Crisson Mine was begun as a venture similar to this. The lad in this photo quite obviously posed grudgingly. (Photo courtesy of the GA Dept. of Archives & History, Atlanta)

It wasn't until a decade later that Col. N.H. Hand, president of the Hand Gold Mining Company, repaired the ditch, flumes and trestles, allowing the water to flow once again to the mines. W.R. Crisson reportedly was a member of the surveying party that re-worked the flumes, ditches and dikes.

With water available once again for the operation of a stamp mill, W.R.'s son, E.E., purchased the Rider Mine and began working it successfully. By 1920, however, maintenance on the Yahoola Ditch had again been so neglected that most of the water being transported along the line was leaking out before it ever reached the mines.

Without water, all work at the Rider/Crisson Mine came to a halt except for a small one-man operation maintained by E.E.'s son, Charlie Crisson.

The abandoned mill deteriorated over time and ultimately collapsed.

E.E.'s other son, Reese, moved his family to Atlanta in search of work during the lean years of the Great Depression. Reese's son, John, was thirteen years of age at the time. He took with him many memories of slipping off to the family's property in Dahlonega to climb the abandoned stamp mill and watch his Uncle Charlie mine for gold.

Instead of one of the many professions which his ancestors had pursued, John chose a life in the U.S. military. All the years that he was serving, however, he never ceased dreaming of moving back to Dahlonega and reactivating the old Crisson Mine.

"I never figured on going anywhere else," he once stated in an interview. *"I*

Miners venturing to California during the 1849 gold rush returned to Georgia with an entirely new extraction technique called "hydraulic mining." The wooden flumes in this photo ingeniously channeled water from local streams to sluice boxes and also to a powerful device (held by the individual pictured in this photo) known variously as a "water cannon," a "Long Tom" or "Little Giant." This water cannon was capable of easily washing entire hillsides down into sluice-boxes for the mass collection of gold and gold ore. These destructive devices often reduced the hillsides to deep valleys, and filled area streams with silt devastating much of the native wildlife. (Photo courtesy of the GA Dept. of Archives & History, Atlanta)

remembered Dahlonega not only for its gold, but also for having the finest people I had ever met anywhere in the world."

After returning from a tour of service in Vietnam, John was assigned to the U.S. Army Recruiting Station in Atlanta, and was finally near enough to Dahlonega to begin working the mine on weekends. He made good with the opportunity too.

The old iron stamps used by his grandfather had long since been taken from the mine while the family was away, and John feared they might have been sold for scrap metal. He was overjoyed when he finally tracked them down and put them back into place at the mine.

At the time, John says his plans in-

volved nothing more than a limited commercial operation at the old mine site. However, local television productions featuring the mine attracted so many tourists that he was soon persuaded to put in panning boxes to take advantage of all the traffic.

The mine was initially open only on weekends, and no office or other structures even existed at the mine at that time. John's wife – Dorothy – remembers literally sitting at a folding table under an umbrella (to escape the heat of the sun), taking in money from tourists in a cigar box. The hopeful prospectors could pan all day for $1.00. John's sister, Maybelle Barrett, showed the prospective miners how to swirl their pans to discard the water and sand, leaving flakes – and sometimes even nuggets – of gold in the bottom of the pan.

John also continued his limited commercial operations at the mine during this period. His brother, R.L., operated the stamp mill while John was working in Atlanta.

In 1970, the price of gold was still fixed at a paltry $35 an ounce, but even at that low price, the mine proved profitable. On an average eight-hour day, the plant reportedly processed 500 tons of ore, requiring 650 gallons of water per minute to move the ore from stage to stage.

After retiring from the Army in 1972, John was able to move to Dahlonega permanently and operate the Crisson Mine on a full-time basis. He and Dorothy built a home next door, putting white quartz rocks from the mine to attractive use in the construction of their walls and fireplace.

"Most of the rocks have gold in them, but not enough to make it worthwhile to process them," Dorothy smiled in explanation. "You can actually see the

The Crisson family, photographed circa 1910, included (L-R) Ben Crisson, Reese Crisson, Rachel Lee Crisson and Irene (wife of W.R. Crisson).

gold glittering in the rocks in our fireplace."

The stamp mill is silent today, since John had to retire from active mining after a heart attack in 1990. The gold panning operation, however, continued under the capable management of long-time employees Tony and Tammy Ray.

"People come here from all over the world to try their hand at panning," Tammy stated with enthusiasm. "We see 200 to 300 people every day during the summer. That includes a lot of large groups from schools, day-care centers, churches, and senior centers. Handicapped groups enjoy screening for gemstones, since they're larger and easier to sift out than tiny flakes of gold."

Few people depart the site without finding flakes of the shining metal in their pans. "If you don't find at least fifteen pieces of gold, it's just a bad bucket," Tony explains.

Some folks are even fortunate enough to find nuggets. Everyone who does so is photographed, and the picture is posted in the gift shop. By the end of the year, the space is usually filled with nearly a hundred photos, and the collection is started anew.

One particular photograph shows John Earler, a railroad engineer from Marietta, holding a case containing the collection of nuggets he discovered over the years panning at the Crisson Mine. Collectively, they add up to almost 3 ounces of gold. He also has a vial filled with 5 ounces of gold flakes. A German tourist once offered him $600 for one of his larger nuggets, but John kindly declined his offer. Good thing he did. They're worth much more today.

As of this writing (2022) the price of gold is approximately $1,800.00 per ounce, a far cry from the $35.00 per ounce when John Crisson re-opened his family's mine in 1970. Many prognosticators maintain the price of gold will continue to rise as a result of the unstable circumstances which prevail in the world today.

John Earler says he tries to drive to Dahlonega to pan every week. Weather isn't a problem at the Crisson Mine where a heated sun room offers a comfy spot for panners to work "rain or shine" in summer or winter. Even additional outdoor panning boxes are covered overhead so that panners don't get more than their hands wet when it rains.

John says he buys five buckets of ore per visit, but he doesn't process it one pan at a time. Instead, he puts it through a small sluice box purchased from the Crisson Mine Gift Shop, speeding up the process enormously.

John also says he sometimes pans for gold in some of the rivers in Lumpkin County. "It's cheaper, but it's also a lot harder work, because the water is deep and fast and *cold*," he smiles. "It's easier in the branches, but more difficult to obtain the required permission from the people who own the surrounding land over which you have to cross to reach the stream.

"Most of the gold I've found in the branches has been coated with mercury too," John adds. "It looks more like silver than gold. It apparently escaped while being processed back when mercury was used to collect the gold before people knew how dangerous it was. The mercury has to be burned off."

At last check, the Crisson Gold Mine was open seven days a week year-round, with indoor winter panning facilities. Visitors can buy the mine's rich ore by the pan or the bucket, and guides will instruct them in the art of panning.

The Crisson Mine is located two-and-one-half miles northeast of Dahlonega on Highway 19 Connector. For more information, contact the Dahlonega Chamber of Commerce.

Photographed in the early 1900s, a portion of the 20-mile aqueduct known as the Yahoola Ditch, is pictured. This unique system conveyed water to various mining sites throughout Lumpkin County. The large waterline was composed variously of graded earthen ditches, trestled wooden conveyances, and enclosed culverts near the end of the line, all of which followed the natural contours of the terrain to reach a final destination. Since the water inside the pipelines gradually increased in velocity as it traveled on a continuous gravitational downhill grade from high in the mountains, it could even travel up steep inclines as pictured here without any pumping or other assistance. (Photo courtesy of the GA Dept. of Archives & History, Atlanta)

Vanished Treasure of Gold From Dahlonega's U.S. Mint

One of the most compelling mysteries of the U.S. Civil War involves the disappearance of a treasure which today would be worth millions of dollars. In 1861, a huge cache of gold comprised of specie (coinage) valued at that time at almost $17,000.00 and gold bullion valued at approximately $10,000.00, simply vanished after being transported by Confederate officials to Atlanta from the U.S. Branch Mint in Dahlonega. This golden hoard – the approximate equivalent of $890,000.00 in 2023 dollars – would be worth tens of millions of dollars more today on the collector's market due to the rare and historic nature of these coins.

Gold! The very mention of it perks up the senses of virtually anyone within earshot, and any tale or – even more importantly – actual documentation of the ultimate circumstances involving these riches will always be an immediate attention-grabber. Such is the case with the gold which once resided at the U.S. Branch Mint in Dahlonega and mysteriously disappeared during the opening days of confusion in the U.S. Civil War.

In the weeks and months following the declaration of war and the secession of the state of Georgia from the Union in January of 1861, confusion reigned. As tensions mounted from the growing military engagements, the immensely-valuable gold coinage and bullion housed in the U.S. Branch Mint in Dahlonega, Georgia, was somehow overlooked by Federal, Confederate, or state of Georgia officials, but came under intense scrutiny by local residents. What was to become of all that gold? Who really owned it at that point, since it obviously no longer existed within the geographic confines of the United States?

To be specific, in those confusing times, no one really knew who owned the gold, and attempts to lay claim to it were therefore being initiated by numerous interlopers. Federal officials had departed the Mint shortly after Georgia's secession, strangely just abandoning the golden hoard. The heavy sacks of gold coins and cases of bullion couldn't merely be bundled up and hauled out by mule-drawn pack-wagons without a sizeable armed detail of security to accompany the riches. . . So, in the short-term, the gold just sat there while the war effort was ratcheted up and lawless local residents plotted their strategy to take possession.

Pictured is a rare view of the U.S. Branch Mint in Dahlonega, Georgia. This photograph, discovered accidentally in 1983 in a disused filing cabinet at North Georgia College (present-day University of North Georgia) in Dahlonega, is the only known actual print of the former Mint building. This structure was abandoned by the U.S. Mint personnel in 1861, and sat vacant until donated for use as a branch of the University of Georgia in 1871. The seven years it was used by college students (1871-1878) were the poverty-stricken dark days immediately following the U.S. Civil War when funds for student uniforms did not exist and weapons were not allowed. Many of the individuals pictured in this photo therefore quite possibly are either Confederate or Union troops (instead of college students), since many of them appear to be in uniform, standing at attention, some with shouldered arms. This building burned to the ground on December 20, 1878, and Price Memorial Hall of North Georgia Agricultural College (present-day University of North Georgia) was constructed upon the Mint's original limestone foundation that same year.

According to a report by Mint Assayer Mamie L. Folsom (1861) published in Andrew W. Cain's seminal *History of Lumpkin County, 1832-1932*, *"There were some rough characters in the mountains in those days. When the state seceded, one of them by the name of Harrison Riley* (Readers please see *"The Gunfights and Mysterious Life of Lumpkin Pioneer Harrison Riley"* in the Lumpkin County section of *Mystery & History in Georgia, Volume I*) *threatened to organize a crowd and make a raid on the Mint, as he declared that the money belonged to nobody in particular, and that he was as much entitled to it as anybody. We heard of the threatened raid and armed*

ourselves, closing the vaults and putting the keys in a place of safety. Riley evidently thought better of the matter, for he never put in an appearance."[1]

The Mint with its stocks of gold bullion and coinage existed in what then was a mountainous, remote and virtually lawless former gold rush region of Georgia's Lumpkin County. Though the state of Georgia had quickly instructed its General Assembly to pass legislation which declared that all *"United States property"* within the state's boundaries now belonged to *"Confederate Georgia,"* no one really seemed to know how to "legally" proceed with management and/or dispersal of the funds in the Mint

Even after the declaration of war and foundation of the Confederate States of America, fully 1,597 gold "half eagles" ($5.00 gold pieces) were coined at the Dahlonega Branch Mint which bore the imprint of *"United States of America."* In 1861, the Dahlonega Mint – at the value of gold at that time – held almost $17,000.00 in specie (coinage) and approximately $10,000.00 in gold bullion. In 1861, $17,000.00 was the equivalent of approximately $571,180.00 in 2023 dollars and $10,000.00 was the approximate equivalent of $319,486.00, so collectively, the Mint had funds in 1861 with a 2023 value of almost $900,000.00, a sizeable sum even today, and a breath-taking amount of money in 1861.

– and no one seemed particularly anxious to press the issue which might perhaps place them in a position of having committed high theft, and possibly even treason, if the Confederacy's secession effort ultimately failed.

Loosely organized in its initial creation in 1861, the top leadership of the Confederate States of America either were not immediately aware of the assets in the Branch Mint in Dahlonega, or else they had too many other more pressing matters of concern to focus upon the Dahlonega facility. As a result, George Kellogg, superintendent of the Mint was caught between the proverbial "rock and a hard place." What was he to do?

A Question of Loyalty

Obviously conflicted, Kellogg sought instructions from the only su-periors he thought appropriate. He began first with his immediate supervisor – Superintendent James Ross Snowden at the Philadelphia Mint. Snowden was treasurer of the United States Mint from 1847 to 1850, and director of the Mint from 1853 to 1861.

Though known as an exceptionally astute individual, Snowden, at best, responded to Kellogg's inquiry in a most curious and vague manner, stating: *"It appears. . . notwithstanding the revolutionary proceedings in the State of Georgia, the Branch Mint in Dahlonega continues to recognize itself as a branch of the Mint of the United States."* Really? "'The Mint' recognizes itself?" Snowden's response remains a "head-scratcher" even today.

At the same time that he was corresponding with Snowden, Kellogg also sought advice and instructions from Georgia Governor Joseph Emerson Brown in Milledgeville, as to how he should proceed. It would seem that Kellogg was "hedging his bets" with these inquiries to both Union and Confederate authorities, obviously taking pains to avoid any actions which might later be interpreted as "treasonous" on his part by either side.

Brown, interestingly, proved equally vague and even mysterious in his response as to the procedure Kellogg should take. He (Brown) appeared almost reticent at that early juncture in the youthful Confederacy to make a declaration upon a Federal institution, no doubt knowing full well that it was not out of the realm of possibility that the Confederacy could in time fail and be returned to the control of the U.S. Federal government. He therefore also apparently did not wish to place himself in a compromising position for charges of treason this early in the war.

Unable to receive any explicit instructions on how to proceed, Kellogg,

aud and foot. Had
ed Maryland, they
once recruited to the
n arms. Let it not
id is unwilling, cold,
not so.
still throwing up the
de of Washington.—
rom the Potomac to
au is reported to have
he creek of Antietam.
It 15,000. It was de
Halleck, and Mac,
es require desperate
e, was to take all the
o that he saved Mary-
fice the most of them.
is time that we were
elming numbers.
t Sharpsburg, 40,000
ew recruits, left Al-
o surprise Richmond,
proceeded far South
fearing that McClel-
defeated and Wash-

een heard from Mc
ant those dispatches
General Lee states

The news from the Continent is unimportant. Garibaldi is worse.
The Opinion Nationale, of Paris, Prince Napoleon's organ, condemns the idea of an
emancipation proclamation for the negroes in
anticipation, and in very severe terms, while
the Dublin Freeman's Journal (a Union paper)
points out the inutility of such a measure for
the negroes themselves.

Arrival of Gold—A Deserter.

Yesterday a mounted escort, detailed from
Captain Tiller's Artillery company, arrived
here in charge of a large amount of Gold from
the Mint at Dahlonega, belonging to the Confederate government.
They also brought with them in chains a desperado named Anderson, whose outrages in
Lumpkin county and the vicinity have been intolerable for some time. He is a deserter from
the 1st Georgia Regulars, and has been hiding
himself in the caves and dens of the mountains for the last five or six months, harboring
runaway negroes, stealing, robbing widows
and helpless women and children whose husbands and fathers are in the war, and had become a terror to the whole country. He will
be properly cared for.—*Atlanta Confederacy.*

Notice.

QUARTERMASTER'S DEPARTMENT, }
Columbus, Ga., Sept. 13, '62. }

I have been charged with the important duty of providing Shoes for our Soldiers, and I
must appeal to the patriotism of our people to

them promptly. A
for Subscribers ha
for delivery. They
Receipts, and we w
may direct. We ho
owners.
The Cotton of Su
the market price b
change for Bonds
AG
Savannah—R. Ha
Columbus—D. Ad
Macon—N. C. Mu
Newnan—J. J. Pi
LaGrange—Jesse

oct4-2m

SAW MILL E

WE have on han
we will excha
oct3tf

NOTICE TO

I AM authorized.
ed from my Regi
Smith, to raise a c
be attached to Maj
Artillery. All pers
rolled will be receiv
are subject to the
President in conse
the Conscript act.
Persons wishing t
names at once. I
Virginia and Fast.

The **Columbus** (Georgia) **Sun** newspaper of October 6, 1862, documents the arrival in Atlanta of the assets from the U.S. Branch Mint in Dahlonega, GA. No further record of this gold shipment has ever been discovered, and the ultimate disposition of this shipment of gold remains as one of the great mysteries of the war. (Period news clipping courtesy of the Digital Library of Georgia Newspapers and Robert S. Davis, Jr.)

according to records, apparently decided that he had no choice but to merely
continue as usual with operation of the
Dahlonega Mint, accepting the reality
that he now was "behind enemy lines"
without even the benefit of a subsistence
payroll for his employees at the Mint.

Since there obviously would be no
further salaries paid via the "home office" in Philadelphia, and since Governor Brown had been as unspecific as had
Superintendent Snowden as to how he
should proceed, Kellogg apparently simply made what might be termed "an executive decision" on his payroll plight.
From all indications, he proceeded at
that point to pay his employees *in gold*

from coinage which existed at the Mint. In
retrospect, he really had no other reason-
able choice other than to just walk away
from a fortune in gold.

Though the "in-house" payroll strategy was workable for the short-term, it
nevertheless still left Kellogg in an un-
enviable position. To whom should he
devote his loyalty, and what was to become of the gold stocks in the Mint?
How should he defend those valuable assets, and from whom even should he defend them? How should he even recon-
cile the gold stocks he was using to pay
his employees?

Uncertain of his next step with the
bullion which had already been prepared

for coinage, Kellogg again wrote to Georgia Governor Brown inquiring if there would be *"any impropriety in continuing to coin with the present dies* (engraved metal plates used to "stamp" individual coins) *until there is further action?"* (With that action, Kellogg, interestingly, was shrewdly providing a legitimate alibi for himself, no matter the outcome of the secession issue.) Brown responded that it would not be improper, but reminded Kellogg that he was responsible nevertheless to the State of Georgia and *"not at all to the U.S. government."*[2]

U.S. or Confederate Coinage?

Kellogg's next most pressing problem obviously existed in the actual coins he would be producing. They all would obviously still be stamped as *"United States of America"* (and not as *"Confederate States of America"*) coins. It is for this reason that even after the declaration of

Confederate President Jefferson Davis and his staff were caught up in the early machinations of the U.S. Civil War, and too busy to realize the fortune which existed in the abandoned United States Branch Mint in the backwoods of tiny Dahlonega, Georgia. (Illustration courtesy of GA Dept. of Archives & History, Atlanta)

war and foundation of the Confederate States of America, fully 1,597 gold "half eagles" ($5.00 gold pieces) were coined at the Dahlonega Branch Mint which bore the imprint of *"United States of America,"* and which were dutifully reported as such to the Philadelphia Mint.

In his book ***Gold Coins of the Dahlonega Mint, 1838-1861***, Douglas Winter notes that the Confederacy ultimately used some of the Dahlonega Mint bullion to strike gold dollars and half eagles, although *"there is no way today to positively distinguish between Union and Confederate strikings* (since the only dies were still those for U.S. coins; no coins were struck after 1861; and the loyalties which were maintained by Kellogg and his staff during this period of time are entirely unknown today). *The remainder of the bullion was not converted into coins due to a lack of die-making materials and qualified personnel."*[3]

Of important note at this point is the fact that despite his normally meticulous and very timely reports to Philadelphia and the U.S. Treasury regarding the coinage at the U.S. Branch Mint at Dahlonega, Kellogg's 1861 records do not include any details whatsoever of the coinage of any *$1.00 gold pieces* in Dahlonega, yet there nevertheless are in existence even today rare (and quite valuable) $1.00 gold coins for that year bearing the Dahlonega mint mark.

Could Kellogg and his men have minted the $1.00 Dahlonega coins for the continued payment of their salaries? Or could perhaps one or more of the men – possibly even including Kellogg himself – have been taking advantage of the unstable times and surreptitiously minting coins for their own personal gain? The truth, as well as any knowledge of how many of these $1.00 gold coins from 1861 were actually struck, undoubtedly will never be known.

At the very least, however, correspondence from Kellogg to the Philadelphia Mint acknowledges receipt of the 1861 United States $1.00 coin dies, so it is a documented fact that Kellogg – via the Dahlonega facility – had the capability of striking coins for that year. The total number and quality of those coins, however, must be added to the many mysteries involving the Dahlonega Mint.

It is due to these circumstances that the 1861-D $1.00 gold coin from the Dahlonega Branch Mint is so rare and valuable today. Very few are known to be in existence. It is considered the most famous and valuable of the Dahlonega Mint coins.

Most experts today agree the number of the 1861-D coins of $1.00 denomination actually produced probably ranged from 1,000 to 1,500 coins, of which less than 60 are known to still be in existence. According to Jack Hancock of Hancock & Harwell, an Atlanta firm dealing in rare coins and precious metals, aside from the number of these coins which were actually minted, *"The mystique surrounding them lies in the question, 'Were they minted under the auspices of the Federal government, or the Confederate government?'"*[4]

It was no doubt due at least in part to the totality of the circumstances described above that Dahlonega Mint Superintendent Kellogg abruptly tendered his resignation from the Mint on April 25, 1861, an action which engenders a certain amount of suspicion today among researchers. His letter to President Lincoln no less, read as follows: *"Under the present circumstances together with the action taken by the Confederate States government, I conclude it is proper that I resign as Superintendent-Treasurer of this Mint. Therefore I tender my resignation... to take effect on the fifteenth of May next."*

Could Kellogg have decided discretion was the better part of valor and that he should abandon his post after having minted too many coins for which there was no legal accounting to the Federal government? Or, was he simply taking what he deemed to be the more logical and proper course of action and service to the Confederacy? We'll probably never know the answers to these questions either unless some obscure correspondence is one day discovered.

Vanished Dahlonega Gold

Despite Kellogg's resignation and the apparent lack of leadership at the facility, the Dahlonega Mint, according to records, strangely continued somehow to receive deposits of gold for coinage through April of 1861. At that time, according to the superintendent's report

While Georgia Governor Joseph Emerson Brown also was made aware of the fortune in gold coins abandoned in the U.S. Mint at Dahlonega, he nevertheless apparently was reluctant to take possession of the tremendously-valuable assets for fear of later being brought up on charges of treason should the Confederacy fail. (Photo courtesy of GA Dept. of Archives & History, Atlanta)

for the first quarter of the year (made this time to officials with the Confederate government), the Dahlonega Mint – at the value of gold in 1861 – held almost $17,000.00 in specie (coinage) and approximately $10,000.00 in gold bullion.

Adjusting for inflation, that cumulative $27,000.00 at the Mint was the equivalent of approximately $890,000.00 in 2023 dollars. That, however, does not begin to do justice to the vastness of the $27,000.00 in 1861, since, at the "street value" of $890,000.00, it would have carried almost unlimited purchasing power. Though it continues to carry great purchasing power even today, $890,000.00 was a breath-taking amount of capital in 1861, and would have been indescribably tempting to whomever might have had access to it. Even a small portion of it could have been a handsome retirement for all the Mint employees.

The above valuation of course, is also only made based upon the 2023 "market value" of the gold. If made based upon the gold *and* the extremely-rare nature of the coins themselves, this golden hoard could be worth tens of millions of dollars today if discovered squirrelled away someplace in a secret stash.

So what actually happened to the remainder of the gold coins and bullion at the Dahlonega Mint? Even if coining dies for any years following 1861 had existed (which they didn't), an apparent severe shortage of gold and silver bullion in the South precluded any further coinage after June 1, 1861, at which time the Confederate government officially closed both the Dahlonega and New Orleans branch mints.

In May of 1861, the Confederate Congress had passed legislation which provided that *"all monies and bullion in the hands of any (Mint) officer shall forthwith be transferred to the Treasurer of the Confederate States."* George Kellogg's final Dahlonega Branch Mint inventory report which was submitted June 26, 1861, noted that the amount of gold and bullion on hand as of June 1, 1861 was $25,389.86 (down some $1,610.14 from the $27,000.00 which Kellogg had reported as existing through the end of March, 1861). *"I forwarded to Mr. Pressley the funds & bullion in the mint there,"* Kellogg stated.[5] *(Author's Note: Benjamin C. Pressley was the Confederate Assistant Treasurer at Charleston, South Carolina.)*

Is one therefore to assume the gold coinage and bullion housed within the Dahlonega Branch Mint were actually shipped to Charleston? Maybe. Maybe not.

Adding still more confusion to this matter is the fact that after New Orleans fell to Federal naval forces in the spring of 1862, "Confederate" gold bullion and funds at New Orleans reportedly were transferred to Jackson, Mississippi, for safe-keeping. According to reports of this incident, in July of that same year, Confederate Assistant Treasurer A.J. Guirot shipped *973 ounces of gold and 17,736 ounces of silver* from Jackson to "Dahlonega," with instructions to Dahlonega Mint Assayer Lewis W. Quillian to assay the bullion.

So aside from its original gold which had been on hand at the outset of the war, the Dahlonega Mint gained yet another substantial treasure in gold bullion when assets were transferred from Jackson, Mississippi in 1862. It is unknown for certain today just why this gold would have been shipped from Mississippi to the wilds of Lumpkin County, Georgia, or if the original gold at the Dahlonega Branch Mint reported by George Kellogg's final inventory of June 26, 1861, also still resided therein at this time.

Quillian's reports do not describe the

assayed precious metal from Jackson, Mississippi, in any manner other than "gold" or "silver." However, almost all of the assay reports indicate a gold fineness of <u>exactly</u> "900," which, curiously, is the <u>exact same degree of fineness of gold and silver which had been coined in the original gold bullion at the Dahlonega Mint</u> in that era.

In his article *"The Dahlonega Mint: A Civil War Mystery"* published in the Summer, 1984 issue of **North Georgia Journal** magazine, the late Dahlonega writer and researcher Bill Kinsland raised the possibility that the Jackson, Mississippi, bullion shipped to Dahlonega may actually have been *"a large hoard of gold and silver coins."*[6] Whatever the nature of the treasure, Kinsland reported that the bullion *"was melted into bars (17 of gold, 196 of silver, and 3 of gold and silver mixed) and packaged for shipment."*

Instructed then to ship the bars from Dahlonega to the <u>Confederate Depository in Augusta, Georgia</u>, Quillian explained in a letter dated September 15, 1862, that the shipment weighed about 1,800 pounds and would require *"two spans of horses"* to draw it, even if he could find responsible authorities to deliver it to Atlanta (which he apparently could not at that time).

On October 1, however, Quillian reported anew that *Confederate military authorities* from Atlanta had arrived in Dahlonega and taken possession of the shipment. This shipment <u>almost certainly did at least reach Atlanta</u>, since its arrival there was duly reported a few days later in the **Southern Confederacy** newspaper of Atlanta, and reprinted in the October 6, 1862 issue of the **Columbus** (Georgia) **Daily Sun** newspaper, which noted *"a mounted escort detailed from Captain Tiller's Artillery Company arrived here in charge of a large amount of gold from the Mint in Dahlonega."*

Although Quillian had specifically requested that the officer in charge of this military detail deliver the bullion to the <u>Express Agent in Atlanta</u> (from whence the bullion would then supposedly be shipped to the Confederate Depository in Augusta), <u>the shipment, for reasons unknown today, was held indefinitely in Atlanta</u> after reaching that destination.

From that day forward, no further record has ever been located which indicates any disposition of the shipment of this Dahlonega gold and silver any further than Atlanta, nor has any documentation to indicate if it ever made it to the Depository in Augusta ever been discovered. In fact, the ultimate destination of this immense golden treasure remains today as one of the <u>great unsolved mysteries of the U.S. Civil War.</u>

(Grateful appreciation is expressed herewith to writers/researchers Bill Kinsland, Anne Dismukes Amerson, Ray Chandler and Robert S. Davis, Jr., who collectively and separately researched various segments regarding the mystery surrounding the vanished gold assets from the U.S. Branch Mint in Dahlonega, Georgia.)

Footnotes:

1/ Cain, Andrew W., **History of Lumpkin County, 1832-1932,** (1932), reprinted, (1978, **The Reprint Company**)

2/ Head, Silvia Gailey and Etheridge, Elizabeth W., **The Neighborhood Mint**, Mercer University Press, (1986)

3/ Winter, Douglas, **Gold Coins of the Dahlonega Mint, 1838-1861**, (1997)

4/ Hancock, Jack, Hancock & Harwell Precious Metals

5/ Birdsall, C.M., **The United States Branch Mint at Dahlonega: Its History and Coinage**, Southern Historical Press, Easley, SC (1984)

6/ Kinsland, Bill, "The Dahlonega Mint: A Civil War Mystery," **North Georgia Journal**, (June, 1984)

The Heydays of Old Madison Springs Hotel

When a leper accidentally fell into mineral-enriched mud below a natural spring welling up from the ground near present-day Danielsville, Georgia, a miraculous cure seemingly occurred. Soon, the refreshing spring water became a much-visited site around which a vibrant resort was constructed in the early 1800s. However, following the tragedy of the U.S. Civil War, a vicious fire in 1871 raised the resort to the ground, erasing the popular destination from the landscape.

The arrival of Dr. John Atkinson Hunnicutt marked the beginning of yet another era at the ghostly site of what once was known as Madison Springs Resort approximately seven miles from Danielsville, Georgia. In order to reach his newly purchased mineral spring in 1872, Dr. Hunnicutt had to pass 28 ghostly blackened brick columns which were all that remained of the once-grand resort.

The hotel had burned on a cold January night the previous year, and citizens in Athens, 23 miles away, reported seeing *"the whole sky far to the northward aglow."* According to citizens in Danielsville, *"a person could have read a newspaper from the light of the burning structure."*

When the conflagration had died to glowing embers, a glorious (though some say frivolous) era at the prominent resort came to an abrupt and sad conclusion. The resort had been a place where the antebellum planter elite had danced the Virginia reel – all dressed in costume for the "grand fancy ball" – and walked down "Euclid Avenue," a broad, white sand-covered path which led from the hotel to the mineral spring which gave the resort its name. At night, the avenue was lighted by "pine knots" atop stands and some recalled seeing as many as one hundred couples at a time moving up and down this glowing pathway.

Despite its remote location in Madison County, Dr. Hunnicutt had purchased the property almost exclusively due to his belief in the curative power of the mineral waters in the famed spring.

An illustration of Madison Springs Resort created in 1850, just a few years prior to its demise.

His first-born child – Martha "Mattie" Hunnicutt – was sickly, and Dr. Hunnicutt had been unable to cure his own child through normal medical procedures. He was placing all his hope in the bitter water which flowed from the "iron mineral spring" at the site.

According to family tradition, Mattie's health did indeed improve in the late 1870s. Whether this should be credited to the curative value of the iron spring water or merely to Mattie's healthy growth from youth into a young lady is unknown today. Whatever the circumstances, the Hunnicutt family believed in the "spirit of the mineral waters," and for generations thereafter, continued to visit the spot regularly.

Madison Springs Today

Today, this area in Madison County is still barren of the sprawl of civilization, and is yet a somewhat remote corner of the state. A private dirt road ends at the former site of the old Madison Springs Hotel. One can only imagine the hardships a 19th century stagecoach traveler must have been required to endure in order to participate in the activities at Madison Springs at the height of its glory, but participate they did – in droves.

As of this writing, the cement foundation from the old hotel is still visible, and bricks still line what once was the entrance to the grand structure where guests exited the stagecoach which ran from Augusta to Athens to the Springs as early as 1817.

One can imagine Daniel Morrison as he directed the construction of the hotel's 28 columns in 1839 – fourteen feet of brick at the bottom and fourteen feet of wood at the top. All that remains of the antebellum resort today are the large marble urn from which an iron-tasting water still flows, and one columned summer cottage which somehow has survived all these years.

If one uses his or her imagination, he or she might visualize the comings and goings of former visitors to the Springs, because of a brief recorded history of the resort (*Madison Springs, Madison County, Georgia*, written in 1933 by the Rev. C.P. Willcox who married Martha "Mattie" Hunnicutt). Prominent Confederate Georgia firebrand Robert Toombs and the sickly Alexander Stephens, former vice president of the Confederacy, both spent time at the resort. They were among many of the prominent residents of Georgia and elsewhere who flocked to this once-popular destination.

Early Denizens

Three different legends concerning the discovery of the first mineral spring at this site have been handed down through time, but most people adhere to "*the John Vinyard story.*"

In 1814, Vinyard reportedly lived on a bluff above the spring and suffered from leprosy. One day, in a state of delirium, he accidentally fell down a steep hill and into the water and mud which had always collected below a natural spring. Unable to climb out alone, Vinyard remained in his muddy sinkhole until pulled out hours later by his wife.

The next morning, Vinyard noticed that his condition amazingly was showing signs of a definite improvement. He attributed his recovery to his unexpected bath in the spring. From that day forward, not only did Vinyard bathe daily in the spring water, he also drank the mineral-laden liquid each day.

This belief in the magical powers of mineral waters extends far back in history, even to pre-history. Colonial Americans, like their European counterparts before them, were often drawn to natural springs due to the dependable purity of the water.

George Washington visited Saratoga Springs in New York for rest and "*the cure,*" and early writers reported that some visitors actually lost consciousness from "*the exhilarating quality of the waters*" at Saratoga. It was from this landmark that Madison Springs soon earned the moniker "*Saratoga of the South.*" Pioneer residents in the early 1800s in what today is Madison County, Georgia, needed little proof beyond Vinyard's recovery to convince them of the power of the Madison Springs waters.

James Alexander was convinced too. In 1816, he purchased 1,035 acres from Vinyard, including the land containing the springs, and converted the area into a health resort. He began construction of a village with "*a central hotel or tavern which was intended to draw guests from far and wide.*" Prominent families from Wilkes County built cottages at the Spring and Alexander completed his impressive hotel in 1817.

Eight years later, however, Alexander lost the property, and when a U.S. Post Office was established at the site, Alexander even lost his namesake, for "*Alexanderville*" was officially renamed "*Madison Springs*" in 1825.

The property changed hands several more times after 1825, once even coming under the ownership of prominent Civil War-era politician Robert Toombs. However, it was when Daniel Morrison purchased the property in 1839 for $7,000, that Madison Springs entered its golden era of development.

Alexander's hotel was described as "*an unsightly, ugly barn-looking concern*" by a writer of that day, so Morrison was faced with a dilemma. He no doubt realized his hotel was in desperate need of a serious architectural face-life. He therefore spent some $30,000.00 on enlivening the site, and when completed, it was then described as *"one of the best-built and most beautiful structures in the state."*

Construction Specifications

The new hotel contained a dining room 40 by 92 feet, a ballroom 40 by 40, and 30 chambers for guest accommodations. It had two levels and an attic, and both stories were completely surrounded by piazzas 14 feet wide and flanked by 28 "immense square columns" which were 28 feet high. The colonnade around the structure was said to be *"near four hundred feet long."* Thirteen strolls around this colonnade therefore would be the equivalent of a mile, an exercise which allowed the ladies to walk and yet protect their long skirts on rainy days.

The development also included two rows of cabins with piazzas all whitewashed and forming an impressive vista with the hotel at the end. An annex called "The Long House" or "Stag House" accommodated gentlemen only. By 1854, Morrison stated in an advertisement that he could accommodate 300 guests.

To continue the refinement of his resort, Morrison had china made especially for the hotel with *"Madison Springs, D. Morrison, Proprietor"* etched in black along with drawings of the hotel and the pavilion located next to the spring. Morrison also commissioned the creation of an impressive embossed marble urn from an Augusta craftsman and placed it at the iron spring.

In the dining room, fans – square wooden frames enclosed with sheets of cloth – hung vertically from the ceiling and were joined by a cord. The fans were swung back and forth by an attendant, creating air currents and scattering flies from the food-laden tables.

The *"best of wines, liquors and cigars"* were made available when the season began on the first of May. One hundred chickens were killed, battered, and fried in the kitchen every day.

It is amusing to note that Morrison – an aggressive entrepreneur – felt compelled to "discover a new spring" occasionally in order to compete with

Martha "Mattie" Hunnicutt, daughter of Dr. John Hunnicutt, was a teenager when this photo was made. She was born in 1874.

other similar resorts such as nearby Ca-
toosa, Porter Springs (above Dahlonega), and newcomer White Sulphur
Springs (above Gainesville). In 1843, he
announced the discovery of one *"of great
strength."*

Eventually, a total of three springs
were located in the Madison Springs vicinity: Number One or *"the iron spring"*;
Number Two or *"the sulfur spring"*; and
Number Three, *"the freestone spring"*
which contained no minerals.

Antebellum Madison Springs

Under the direction of James Alexander, Madison Springs had become
known as *"the seat of health,"* but by the
late 1830s, Morrison, to attract the planter elite, changed the advertisements and
emphasized the *"amusements"* available
at Madison Springs.

By the late 1850s, Morrison was
promoting every known form of amusement, and listed the health aspect of the
resort at the end of the advertisements.
Visitors could join in horse-back riding, carriage trips to Currahee Mountain (near Toccoa, Georgia), to Toccoa
Falls and to Tallulah Falls. They could
play nine pins, ten pins, billiards, checkers, chess, or backgammon. Some visitors put on plays and other dramatic performances.

Dancing, forbidden in 1824 at the
Springs, was the most popular amusement at the resort by the 1850s, and music was provided by bands like The Battery Band, an eight-piece German group
from Charleston. One University of
Georgia student said he danced *"every
night until 12 or 1 o'clock,"* and that after
that he got the band and serenaded some
of the 'ladies' that he liked. He also reportedly returned to Athens with a lady
by his side, so his escapades may have
been just a bit extreme.

University students, after com-
mencement exercises and just before departing Athens, Georgia, to go out into
the world to "seek their fortunes," went
to the Springs with their parents, school-
mates and friends. It was a special occasion each year. Informal parties of students often rented wagons and camped
out at the Springs when accommodations were filled. One group after three
days and nights at the Springs returned
to Athens and reported that they had
*"never seen so large a number of beautiful
women together."*

The young ladies, and even their
mothers, agreed that attending a dance
at Madison Springs, especially the annual ball, was an extremely important social occasion – one that eligible ladies
and gentlemen of that day just did not
miss. On one occasion, Mary Smythe of
Augusta had planned to attend the ball
in 1854. Mary's mother was helping her
dress when a letter arrived by stagecoach.
The letter advised that George Smythe,
Mary's uncle, had just died. Mary's mother, however, put the letter away and did
not tell Mary of the impending funeral. Bad news could wait till another day.
The socially-vital annual ball at Madison
Springs simply could not be missed.

In the 1840s and 1850s, the annual
ball was attended by as many as 400 and
the hotel hired 10 extra managers weeks
in advance. Costumed participants entered the ballroom with or without
masks. They dressed as characters from
history, mythology, fiction, and folklore.
Men might choose Sir Walter Raleigh,
Rob Roy (a Scotch outlaw), an Indian
chief, or even a "Bloomer Girl" (a take-
off on bloomers which were in vogue
and often ridiculed).

The newspapers recorded the dress
of young ladies, but not their names. It
was considered poor taste to mention

a young lady's name in the paper, so females were identified merely as "Miss M. of South Carolina," or "Miss B. of Mississippi." The ladies impersonated Queen Elizabeth, Mary (Queen of Scots), a Scotch lassie, a peasant girl, an Indian maiden, a bride, etc.

The Hunnicutts

Following the conclusion of the U.S. Civil War, Georgia – and indeed most of the South – was a lawless and extremely-dangerous environment for a decade or more. Also, since there was no longer "a planter elite" at that point, Madison Springs was virtually abandoned. The Southern aristocracy at that time was fighting poverty as earnestly as was the yeoman farmer and the freedmen. By 1869, the by-then virtually forgotten Madison Springs Resort was being offered for sale.

It was in 1871 that a lantern reportedly tragically overturned in a barn at the resort. A brisk wind quickly spread the fire to the immense hotel. In a matter of only a few hours, the impressive resort and the lifestyle it had supported for well over half a century had vanished in a breath-taking fire.

In 1872, a group of Athenians purchased the property as a private summer resort for their families. A few years later, Dr. John Atkinson Hunnicutt bought out his partners one by one, and eventually became sole owner of the property.

During their summer hiatus every year, the Hunnicutts occupied two of the old hotel's adjacent cottages which had somehow miraculously survived the fire and which dated from the 1830s. The Hunnicutts eventually added a screened "sleeping porch" across the top floor of one of the structures. The other cottage was torn down and a log cabin was erected on the site.

Two 19th Century cottages on the grounds at which Madison Springs Resort once was located survived the disastrous fire and destruction of the hotel in 1871. One of these cottages was later demolished in the 1930s when the Hunnicutt family constructed a log cabin on the site. Pictured above is the remaining cottage from the former resort. The lower floor dates from the 1830s. The upstairs portion was added in the early 1900s.

Of the few aspects of old Madison Springs Resort which remain at the site today, one is an old graveyard. In the days of stagecoach travel, a death at a site often meant burial at that site, particularly if there was no nearby railroad. In the Madison Springs graveyard, James Willis's headstone indicates he died in 1825. Elizabeth M. Hill, age 6, died in 1828 – the year gold was discovered in north Georgia.

There is evidence that aboriginal natives also camped and perhaps lived near the springs along the Broad River. They quite possibly also drank from the freestone spring from time to time. According to tradition, they didn't care for the bitter-tasting water from "the iron spring." Visitors to the site have occasionally discovered beautiful arrowheads at the site, as well as broken pieces of the Madison Springs china from days long ago.

The Strange Crime of Cherokee Corn Tassels

The epic trial and execution of George Corn Tassels in Gainesville, Georgia, in 1830, unerringly set the stage for the Cherokees' heart-breaking "Trail of Tears," and one of the darkest chapters in U.S. history. All official records of the Corn Tassels incident have, unsurprisingly, been completely lost from the public record.

One of the most enduring, and indeed compelling criminal incidents in the history of the United States is today essentially a matter of mystery and controversy, and undoubtedly will remain that way forever. At a tiny Cherokee Indian town in what today is north Georgia – the specific site of which is also a mystery today – a native Cherokee named George Corn Tassels murdered another Cherokee. Tassels' precedent-setting trial and execution for this crime by the state of Georgia had civil rights and legal implications which still resound today through the U.S. halls of injustice.

The specific criminal proceedings involving Tassels – as serious as they were and which ultimately rose all the way to the Supreme Court of the United States for a decisive verdict – pale to insignificance within the outrageous politics surrounding his case.

Ironically, in all likelihood, Tassels' trial should have been conducted solely within the court system of the Cherokee Nation, since the murder physically occurred in what then was still legally Cherokee territory, but the state of Georgia chose to ignore that fact in order to establish a precedent of "control" over the tribe by "hijacking" the criminal justice proceedings to conduct them instead in the courts of the state of Georgia.

Aside from its immense lust for the gold recently discovered in the Cherokee Nation in 1828, the state of Georgia also coveted the new geographic boundaries it wished to establish which would usurp those lands currently controlled by the Cherokee Nation. In order to illicitly achieve those objectives, Georgia officials knew they first must require the Cherokee Nation to submit to the laws of the state of Georgia, so that the indigenous peoples could ultimately be legally removed to reservations in the West.

Corn Tassels' amazing and confounding episode in history actually is originally rooted in the American Revolution where the Cherokee Indians unfortunately threw their support and loyalty to the British who they hoped would remove the invading colonists from the New World. This strategy of course "back-fired" terribly against the Cherokees when the colonists' vengeful retaliations forced the Native Americans to move south-westward from their homelands in the Carolinas to escape the decimation being inflicted upon them.

As a result, the remnants of the Cherokees now facing extinction migrated downward into what today is north Georgia, particularly northwest Georgia, in a quest for survival. Though the lands there at that time were claimed – at least in part – by the neighboring Creek Indians, the Cherokees had little choice in the matter, even though it meant exchanging warfare with the Whites for warfare with the Creeks. At least the Creeks were far fewer in number and weapons.

In 1802, after the close of the Revolutionary War, the United States government and the state of Georgia finally reached an agreement for the removal of the remaining Indian nations – the Creeks and the Cherokees – from within the boundaries of the land being claimed by Georgia. In exchange for removal of the Indians, the state of Georgia in turn agreed to relinquish its claims upon the lands to the west, which ultimately became the states of Alabama and Mississippi as "Manifest Destiny" began unfolding in the young nation.

Georgia Governor George R. Gilmer fought for the removal of the Cherokees from what today is the southeastern United States. He lost his political support (and his elective office) for promoting state (instead of private citizen) ownership of gold mines as a means of reducing property taxes for wealthy Georgia planters. (From Gilmer, Annals)

"State's Rights" Issue

The removal of the indigenous tribes in the Southeast however, proved to be a much more difficult task than those in charge of Georgia's state government had anticipated. As the issue evolved, the justices of the Supreme Court of the United States surprised the young state by becoming "strange bed-fellows" with the Cherokees, ruling that Georgia was in fact forbidden from expelling the natives from their own lands.

During this same period throughout the South, an extreme and oppressive tax – known as the "*Tariff of Abominations*" – had been levied in 1828 by the federal government upon Southern goods which had been destined for more profitable sale in foreign markets instead of northern U.S. markets. This action

Augustin Smith Clayton ultimately lost his judgeship for ruling that the state of Georgia could not constitutionally arrest a Cherokee for mining gold on the Indian's own land. Clayton later apologized to Cherokee Chief John Ross for his part in the Tassels case and other actions against the Cherokees. (Painting courtesy of Hargrett Rare Books & Manuscripts Library, University of Georgia Libraries)

had inflamed the already swiftly-growing issue of "*State's Rights*," – particularly in the South – which maintained that each state, by virtue of the **U.S. Constitution** and the "**Bill of Rights**," had the legal authority to "nullify" and/or overrule certain federal laws if those "laws" were deemed to be unfairly oppressive and illicit. This movement, which came to be known as "*the Nullification Crisis*," had quickly grown to such proportions that it had raised the real specter of secession of many Southern states thirty years prior to the actual U.S. Civil War.

Rolled up within the vortex of this

"State's Rights" controversy was the issue of legal control by state governments such as Georgia over the indigenous Indian tribes within or adjoining those states. By the 1830s, the states' presumed right of control over indigenous peoples – including the native Cherokee and Creek Indians in Georgia – had joined the Nullification Crisis as a dominant issue in national politics.

Georgia Initiatives

Not surprisingly, debate upon the institution of slavery was also an incendiary aspect of the "state's rights" issue. The conflict between Georgia and the federal government over the Indian removal issue carried much of the same "state's rights" rhetoric that would later accompany the Southern arguments in support of slavery.

Following the establishment by the Cherokees of their formal government in 1827, Georgia subsequently began combining the issues of Indian removal and "state's rights." It had no choice if it was to achieve the state's desired goals in these realms.

The state of Georgia realized it had to move quickly too, since it was being literally out-maneuvered societally and politically by the Cherokees who had finally realized that their only chance for survival in the Southeast was to assimilate with the White culture – a task which they were swiftly successfully achieving. This not only would allow the native Cherokees to remain in the state, controlling and governing their native lands, but also controlling the gold which existed in Cherokee territory.

By an act of the state legislature on December 26, 1827, the Georgia General Assembly therefore expanded the legal jurisdictions of Carroll and DeKalb counties to include the Cherokee Indian lands adjoining those counties. Two years later, the state also extended the legal boundaries of Gwinnett, Habersham, Hall and Rabun counties as well into the neighboring lands of the Cherokees.

In order to establish further control, the new law, as written, further declared all legal actions and enactments of the Cherokee government to be null and void. In the fifteenth and final paragraph of this legislation, the state of Georgia also banned any testimony by an Indian in a state court suit involving a White man, unless the White man resided in Indian territory. This law, amazingly, remained officially on the books and "in force" until the advent and success of the Civil Rights movement in the United States in the 1960s.

By 1830, these acts and other issues had heightened tensions between Georgia and Cherokee officials almost to the breaking point. Because gold had been discovered on Cherokee lands in 1828, hundreds of White miners had illicitly moved into the territory in a voracious search for the precious yellow metal.

In a quest to control the trespassers and the associated abuse, Georgia Governor George R. Gilmer asked for and received federal assistance in the form of troops which were used to arrest anyone of any race found mining on the Indian lands. Georgia residents, however, ultimately rebelled against this federal oppression, threatening the tenure of

A newspaper advertisement at the Georgia state capital in Milledgeville announces the lotteries being conducted for the former lands of the Cherokees in north Georgia.

The actual site of the murder committed by Corn Tassels has been lost to history. Scholars and researchers for many years have believed the offense may have been committed at the Taloney / Mt. Carmel Indian Mission which was once located in the present-day mountain community of Blaine in Pickens County. However, the missionaries at Carmel Mission who normally were very meticulous records-keepers did not record any details whatsoever of George Corn Tassels or his murder of Cornelius Dougherty in any of their writings, which, at best, is highly unusual. One of the mission buildings at Carmel was photographed above shortly before the site fell into complete ruin. (Photo courtesy of Charles O. Walker)

Gilmer, and compelling him later that same year to have the troops replaced with soldiers employed by Georgia – the "Georgia Guard." This diminishment in enforcement opened the door for gangs of outlaws to rob, kill, burn-out, evict and otherwise abuse the Cherokees mercilessly, particularly since Georgia law now prevented any Indian from acting as a witness against a White man in state court.

The Cherokee leadership – described by critics as far more "White" than "Indian" and advised by missionaries from the North scheming to control a quarter of Georgia's territory – fought back in the federal courts. And despite being successful in these legal endeavors, it, nevertheless, was a vain success as history has shown.

Cherokee Initiatives

Former Western Circuit Judge William H. Underwood and his partner, Thomas H. Harris, as well as William Y. Hansel and Samuel Rockwell, were hired by the Cherokee Nation to represent any Cherokees brought before a Georgia court. These attorneys served as legal representatives for their Native American clients in dozens of court cases over several years. Though often suffering the threat of violence from White Georgians, these attorneys nevertheless persevered.

The Cherokees also hired former

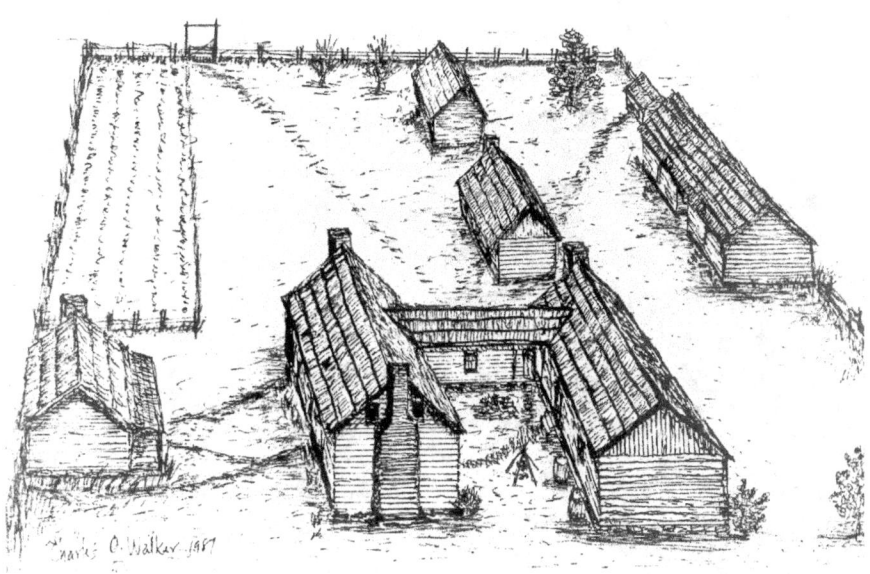

The late Charles O. Walker of north Georgia's Pickens County sketched this recreation (based upon period descriptions of the site and several rare photographs) of historic Taloney / Mt. Carmel Indian Mission which once existed in the present-day community of Blaine. (Drawing courtesy of Rev. Charles Walker; reprinted with permission)

United States Attorney General William Wirt of Baltimore, Maryland, to represent their interests in Washington. As attorney general, Wirt had twice offered the opinion that the Indian nations existed as independent nations beyond the authority of the states.

Wirt, Underwood, and the Cherokees searched earnestly for strong court cases to use to test the Georgia law before the United States Supreme Court, but struggled in vain to find the right case to use to set precedent – that is, until George Corn Tassels murdered a fellow Cherokee on Indian land in 1830. Wirt learned at almost the last moment that Georgia authorities had arrested Tassels, but after studying the incident, he knew he had finally found the legal case for which he had long been searching. In January of 1831, the case for Tassels' defense became a vital part of the

nationally-known **Cherokee Nation vs. the State of Georgia**.

Interestingly, the most obvious source today for primary information on Tassels' case not surprisingly no longer exists. The Georgia State Supreme Court records for the year of 1830 in Hall and Gwinnett counties have disappeared completely. No official copy of any of those proceedings is known to exist today – not in the official records of the State of Georgia, nor the Georgia Department of Archives & History in Atlanta, nor within the University of Georgia's Library system (not even in the *Hargrett Rare Books and Manuscripts* section), nor anywhere else. This, however, does not mean that no description of this incident has survived.

At some point in later years, legal scholars ironically discovered details of the crime reported in a story recorded

William Wirt, as United States Attorney General, made some decisions which favored Cherokee Indian sovereignty, and others which did not. As attorney for the Cherokee Nation, however, he fought for George Corn Tassels and for the right of the Cherokees to keep their nation in Georgia. (Painting courtesy of Hargrett Rare Book and Manuscripts Library, University of Georgia Libraries)

by a Ms. Belle K. Abbott in 1889. Ms. Abbott was a local historian in Georgia who was also a correspondent for the Atlanta press, and according to her report, Tassels had murdered a fellow Cherokee in the small Indian community of Sanderstown (known in general today as Talking Rock) in a neighborhood called "Taloney" in Pickens County, Georgia.

The Murder

According to Abbott's description of the murder carried in the **Georgia Journal** – a Milledgeville, Georgia

newspaper of that era – there were a number of confusing sources of information on the incident.

To begin with, Letty Proctor who, according to the article, was present at her home in Sanderstown, reportedly testified that Indians George Corn Tassels and Cornelius Dougherty were drunk at her home on the morning of July 15, 1830. She said the two men seemed amicable enough initially, although Tassels at some point suddenly announced that he was "going to shoot" Dougherty, but that Dougherty merely took the statement as a joke.

In the report, Ms. Proctor went on to state that she *"felt safe in leaving the men for a moment"* while she was otherwise engaged. She said that while she was absent, she heard a gunshot at ten o'clock and rushed back into the house as a wounded Dougherty staggered out through the front doorway announcing that George had shot him in the right side.

Ms. Proctor further stated that she immediately sent for the nearest constable – Mark Castleberrry. John Dougherty (relation to Cornelius is unknown) eventually arrived at Proctor's home and took care of the victim who nevertheless subsequently died two days later.

John Dougherty later stated before Constable Castleberry that he had heard Tassels state – somewhat psychotically – that he had no grudge against Cornelius, but only wanted to guarantee that he and his friend from boyhood would "share the same grave." Castleberry later testified that George nevertheless had stated there had also been a previous quarrel over a woman.

Yet another source – a member of the Georgia Guard – later testified that Tassels spoke in English and admitted that he and Cornelius had been arguing.

Tassels himself never denied commission of the murder, even openly admitting it.

Historian James C. Flanigan published yet another account of George Corn Tassels and his victim having a dispute over a woman who later appeared in court to tearfully plead for "her lover." Whether or not the woman to whom he referred was Letty Proctor is unknown today.

The actual site of the Cornelius Dougherty murder is yet another mysterious aspect of the long list of controversial details involving this matter. Reverend Isaac Proctor headed the Taloney or Carmel Mission at Talking Rock where Belle Abbott supposedly heard – more than 50 years later – that the murder had occurred, but no record of the murder at this site actually exists. The missionaries at Carmel – who normally were very meticulous records-keepers – did not record any details whatsoever of George Corn Tassels or his murder of Cornelius Dougherty in any of their writings, which, at best, is highly unusual.

No record of a resident at Taloney named Letty Proctor has ever been discovered either.

Murder Site Mystery

That much being known, it is today considered quite possible that this incident actually occurred someplace other than Taloney. In the 1830s, at what was known as "Big Savannah" in the present-day adjoining county of Dawson, there existed a Cherokee community by the name of Dougherty. The large household of James Dougherty, Sr., actually lived at this site.

The Dougherty family at Big Savannah quite probably was descended from a White man – probably not coincidentally also named Cornelius Dougherty

U.S. Supreme Court Chief Justice John Marshall argued in favor of the sovereign rights of the Cherokees regarding the state of Georgia in *"Cherokee Nation vs. Georgia"* (the George Corn Tassels case) and in *"Worcester vs. Georgia."* Marshall, according to some sources, did so to help President Andrew Jackson's efforts to stop state secessionism in the Nullification Crisis, and he reportedly did it in a manner which would spare the president from being forced to enforce federal laws in favor of the Indians. Other quarters maintain that following the court's decision regarding the Cherokees, President Jackson nevertheless merely ignored the mandate which ruled in favor of the Native Americans. (Photo courtesy of Hargrett Rare Books & Manuscripts Library, University of Georgia Libraries)

– who lived among the Indians before Oglethorpe founded Georgia in 1733. Even more interesting is the fact that these Doughertys of Big Savannah were neighbors to a household headed by one John "Proctor."

U.S. President Andrew Jackson refused to enforce the decisions of the U.S. Supreme Court regarding the protection of the rights of the Cherokee Indians. In this manner, he was able to stave off the secessionist tendencies arising within the Southern states.

Also living nearby in Big Savannah were Cherokee families that used their native names – translated into English – of which "Corn Tassels" could serve as an example. It is also a matter of historic record that George Corn Tassels told a guard that he would prefer to face trial at "Savannah" before the Cherokees. He subsequently appeared before Mark Castleberry of Hall County, who was the nearest constable, and who, incidentally, also lived much nearer to Big Savannah than to the far-off Carmel Mission at Taloney. A large extended family by the name of Castleberry lived in nearby Auraria, just a few miles away from Big Savannah.

In late November of 1830, the Tassels trial was finally held. Historian Flanigan wrote that a change of venue caused the trial to be moved to Lawrenceville in Gwinnett County, but no contemporary source supports that claim.

William H. Underwood served as defense counsel while Turner H. Trippe represented the State. On November 22, 1830, a Georgia court found Tassels "*Guilty*" of murder and sentenced him to death.

Judge Clayton not only delivered the jury's verdict, but, interestingly, also seized the opportunity for a long public discourse on the "*State's Rights*" issue, and the need for the removal of the Cherokees – perhaps to get it in the public record of the trial. In a later letter to Governor Gilmer, Clayton denied that he sought a confrontation with the federal government over "State's Rights." His record, however, indicates otherwise.

Georgia newspapers subsequently reported that the Tassels' trial would likely go to the United States Supreme Court. On December 22, a *Writ of Error* arrived for Gilmer from United States Chief Justice John Marshall. It was dated December 12. This document announced that the authority of Georgia in the case of Tassels and other matters in Wirt's petition would be heard before the high court.

Accordingly, Governor Gilmer suddenly found himself "between a rock and a hard place." He had fought to avoid a federal challenge to the Georgia laws as he feared such action only favored the Cherokees. Wirt had a tremendous reputation not only in political power, but as a legal mind.

The governor subsequently took the matter of the Writ before the Georgia State Legislature which was then in special session. According to one source, he arrived at the State House out of breath and in a panic. He urged defiance of the court.

The Georgia House and Senate both quickly passed a resolution ordering Sheriff Jacob Eberhart of Hall County to carry out the sentence immediately as handed down. Gilmer's letter – dated that same December 22, 1830 – which he sent to Eberhart with this resolution, traveled the 120 miles to Gainesville and reached the sheriff before December 24 – an amazing feat which likely could not be equaled even by today's plodding U.S. Postal Service in motorized vehicles on modern highways.

Tassels's Execution

On a cold winter day, as sleet fell, George Corn Tassels rode in his coffin – no doubt shivering – to a scaffold in a large open field near present-day Cotton Avenue in Gainesville, Georgia. As with all public hangings, a substantial law enforcement contingent was present to make certain the sentence was carried out without interruption. Crowds of men, women, and even children clogged the roads to reach the site of the hanging which had become a substantial public event.

When Tassels and his guards reached the gallows, Eberhart ordered the prisoner to stand up. He then tied the Cherokee's hands and pulled a cap over his face before securing the rope around his neck.

Though it is not known for certain today, Tassels was probably hung from the branch of a tree after having a wagon or cart pulled from beneath him. Whatever the circumstances, he was hung by the neck – for approximately 20 minutes – until he ceased movement.

Death by strangulation is an extremely traumatic manner of execution. Normally, the noose of a gallows is positioned to the side of the neck in order to snap the vertebra and spinal cord

after the convicted has fallen suddenly through a trap door, killing the victim immediately.

This method of execution, however, was not used on Corn Tassels. He was simply strangled painfully slowly to death.

When his body ceased moving, doctors approached Corn Tassels to examine him. They then pronounced him dead and the rope was cut to release his body.

Often repeated accounts of this incident maintain that hundreds of Cherokees silently witnessed this hanging. A correspondent to *The Athenian* newspaper of Athens, Georgia, however, reported eighteen to twenty Indians present.

The Cherokees, interestingly, did not transport Tassels' body back to his home for interment, but rather buried him somewhat unceremoniously in a vacant area in the middle of what later became South Broad Street in Gainesville. The actual site of his burial is unknown today, since no historic marker has ever been erected to mark the sad spot.

Some twenty years later, Tassels' body was exhumed. The reason for this exhumation is unknown today. Perhaps the burial site had come into general use as a travel route by that point, requiring a street or road to be laid out. The site of Tassel's reburial is unknown today, adding to the long list of mysterious aspects of this incident.

A traveler by the name of William Jasper Cotter, according to records, witnessed the exhumation of the body. In his writings, Cotter recorded that coagulated blood was still visible around Tassels' neck even after the 20-year point.

Effect of the Execution

Tassels' execution ultimately had widespread implications. John Ross

Palmer Gristmill, built circa 1906, once existed beside the original bridge across the Etowah River (located approximately 100 yards north of the present-day State Road 53 Bridge) at Dougherty, Georgia, Dawson County. In the 1830s, this was a Cherokee town composed greatly of the extended family of Cherokee James Dougherty, Sr. It is believed by some researchers that the murder committed by George Corn Tassels may actually have occurred at this site instead of at Taloney Mission in Murray County.

and the Cherokee leadership reported the hanging to the U.S. Congress, where their friends used it to adamantly denounce Georgia's actions in extending its authority over the Cherokees and executing an Indian in defiance of existing treaties. Nevertheless, the case that brought George Corn Tassels to his end – *State vs. George Corn Tassels* – became the primary court citation for state authority over Native Americans until 1831.

In the year following Tassels' death, the United States Supreme Court heard *Cherokee Nation vs. Georgia*. Wirt represented the Cherokees but the State of Georgia simply ignored the case and provided no representation.

The U.S. Supreme Court subsequently handed down a divided and somewhat confusing ruling. Chief Justice John Marshall and one other justice ruled strangely that the Cherokees were not a foreign nation – as stated in Wirt's petition – and as such, could therefore not sue in the Supreme Court. (One could conceivably therefore argue that the Cherokees' non-status as a foreign nation would in fact therefore grant them the ability to sue in the U.S. Supreme Court since one would logically assume at that point that they were therefore U.S. citizens.) Two other justices agreed with Wirt's petition. The remaining two justices argued that the Cherokees were neither a domestic nor a foreign nation, but a conquered people without rights (which many people would confess rings more logically).

Four of the justices, however, did agree that Georgia had no authority over the Cherokee lands, laying the groundwork for yet another suit (which many Americans would also agree rings logically). In that case (*Worcester vs. State of Georgia, 1832*), concerning Judge Clayton's trials of White Northern missionaries arrested for resisting Georgia's laws, the Court ruled that the State of Georgia had no legal authority in the Cherokee lands, a verdict which should have granted great power to the Cherokees in their quest to retain their homeland. Unfortunately, in the end, it had little effect.

Today, legend maintains that following this decision, U.S. President Andrew Jackson cynically stated that *"Marshall has his decision. Now let him enforce it."* In all likelihood, Jackson never actually made such a statement, but his administration also nevertheless took no actions either to threaten or contest the Georgia laws, and, instead continued to encourage Indian removal to reservations in the West.

Federal soldiers, in fact, enforced the final removals of the last organized Native American peoples in the southern and mid-western states east of the Mississippi River in the late 1830s. With no federal intervention in support of the Cherokees' sovereignty, (despite their success at the U.S. Supreme Court), their situation steadily declined.

So also followed the fortunes of other indigenous Native American societies. In 1833, the State of Georgia divided the lands of the Cherokee Nation into eleven new Georgia counties. State authorities completely ignored the existence of the Cherokee judicial system and the rulings of the United States Supreme Court.

Similar Cases

The same summer (1830) that Tassels had committed murder, the Cherokees' own court at Coosawattee tried Cherokee Indian James Graves after he boasted, while drunk, of murdering an unknown White man. The Cherokee court found Graves "*Not Guilty*" due to a lack of evidence, and therefore not liable, according to treaty, for his surrender to the federal Indian agent and the State of Georgia for re-trial.

The State of Georgia, nevertheless, took Graves into custody anyway, and re-tried him for the presumed murder in the newly-created county of Murray in northwest Georgia. This time, a White jury found Graves "*Guilty.*"

Judge John W. Hooper postponed the execution of Graves in a vain hope for federal intervention. The Georgia State Legislature, however, again in defiance of the U.S. Supreme Court, passed yet another resolution ordering the execution proceedings to continue without

delay. On November 21, 1834, Graves met the same fate as had Tassels.

In a similar set of circumstances, Cherokee John Hogg Smith was hanged in Walker County in 1834, supposedly for murdering two Indians.

Following his arrest for the murders of everyone in the James L. Bowman family at Salacoa, Georgia, in 1832, Cherokee George Tooke (known to the Cherokees as "Une'ga-tehee" or "White Man Killer") escaped from the DeKalb County, Georgia jail. A White Cherokee County posse wounded and recaptured him in 1835 and a Cass (present-day Bartow) County jury found him "*Guilty.*" He also was hanged. By then, an act of November 12, 1834, even provided state funds to counties for the prosecution and punishment of Cherokees.

Ironically, Georgia's advocates for "*State's Rights*" won such legal battles in the 1830s against Native Americans, only to literally "lose the war" for the same cause in the U.S. Civil War.

As a result of the incendiary political climate of the 1830s, the details of George Corn Tassels' ordeal had begun to vanish even while he yet lived. They were literally buried beneath the overwhelming issues of "*State's Rights*" and Indian Removal politics.

Though his crime was murder for which Tassels did not deny his guilt, his trial nonetheless became an important lynch-pin in the quest of Native Americans for treatment as a sovereign nation within a nation – conquered or not. It would be many years in the future, however, before the rights of Native Americans in the United States – despite the fact they were a conquered people – would be legally established within the U.S. courts. In the interim, there was much suffering and despair.

Early Northwest Georgia Railroad Disasters

In the early 1900s, the railroads were evolving into a huge business enterprise, much of it based upon the observance of strict time-tables as to when products and people reached a specified destination. As the speeds of the behemoths hurtling down the ribbons of rail increased to keep these arrival times, the caution of the engineers at the helm wasn't always adequate. The rail accidents in northwest Georgia which sometimes occurred as a result of this lack of caution were almost always terribly disastrous, and sometimes breathtakingly so.

"They were goin' down grade making ninety miles an hour,
When the whistle broke into a scream -
He was found in the wreck with his hand on the throttle,
Scalded to death by the steam."

- From "The Wreck of Old 97"

On the crisp autumn morning of October 23rd, 1903, there was no hint of the unfolding disaster waiting ahead. All witnesses to that terrible event have now passed on into eternity, but the written records of the incident describe a calmness which belied the onrushing horror. *"Train Number 81, southbound on the Southern Railway, had a few minutes to get in the clear at Dallas for Number 18 northbound vestibule Sunday morning,"* according to a news report in a 1903 issue of the ***Dallas New Era***. The men on board did not know it at the time, but a sizeable disaster was only a few moments away. . .

The article continued by explaining *"Engineer Jim Nichols opened the throttle of his monster engine on the summit one mile south of McPherson. Engine 345 never acted better. The big machine moved forward at a terrific rate with twenty-five cars behind. The engineer looked at his watch and knew that time was precious."*

Pumpkinvine Creek Trestle

The disaster which broke the stillness that quiet Sunday morning occurred approximately one mile north of the tiny community of Dallas in northwest Georgia. It was the type of accident that, unfortunately, was not unusual on

For reasons still unknown today, Pumpkinvine Creek Trestle collapsed beneath the weight of Southern Railway's Train #81 on October 23, 1903, killing the fireman of the train. (Photo courtesy of Duane Mintz & Jack Howell)

lonely mountain trestles in the early days of railroading. It was also the type of accident which immortalized the trainmen who traveled these dangerous routes – often at excessive speeds – day after day until fate finally overtook them.

Train Number 81 was a very heavy train. It included some twenty-five cars, and was hurtling down the track at approximately 60 miles an hour when the huge locomotive rolled onto the high steel bridge over Pumpkinvine Creek. The engineer later said he felt the trestle lurch from the weight, and he quickly throttled back, but it was too late. Behind him, six spans of heavy steel trestlework began collapsing with a thunderous roar into the creek-bed seventy-seven feet below, taking thirteen freight cars, the engine tender and the fireman with it into eternity.

Then, just as suddenly as the hor-

rifying accident had begun, it ended, bringing a deathly silence to the spot. As he brought his locomotive to a screeching stop, Nichols reportedly turned and looked desperately for his faithful fireman, John Fagala (also reported as *"J.M. Flagler"* in the news article), who had been standing on the tender when the collapse began. After a quick but futile search around the tight confines of the locomotive, Nichols next went back to the edge of the broken trestle high above the flowing creek below, where his eyes landed upon the sight he feared he would find in the ravine below.

The tender had been ripped from the engine coupling as the track collapsed beneath it. It was lying far below in a tangle of trestle steel and freight cars. John Fagala (Flagler?) undoubtedly never felt the impact when he struck the bottom of the chasm. He may have

The trestle over Pumpkinvine Creek was photographed above by the late Gordon Sargent in 1997. Very little has changed at this site since the 1903 disaster.

and highest in northwest Georgia. It had safely carried hundreds of fast trains in the late 1800s. Today, no one knows what caused the bridge to suddenly collapse, but many individuals knowledgeable of rail accidents have speculated on the cause. One report indicated the large locomotive had simply been traveling too fast and had jumped the rails on the curved trestle, leading the cars behind it to devastation.

"The first time I heard of the Pumpkinvine trestle collapsing was from Mr. Paul McDonald, Southern Railway's third trick operator at Rockmart," explained the late Duane "Cowboy" Mintz, a former conductor on Southern Railway, who said he passed back and forth across the Pumpkinvine Creek trestle continuously himself during his career.

"Later, after I went to work for Southern, I mentioned the incident while dead-heading to Chattanooga on (Train) Number 32, Rockmart's four o'clock train in the afternoon. I was rebuffed by some of the veteran railroaders who seemed to be irritated at me for passing on tales of which they had never heard. The old head conductor, Mr. E.E. (Emmett) Whittle, however, came to my rescue. 'The boy's right,' he told them. 'It happened not long after I went to work (for Southern). I almost quit the railroad on account of that accident.'"

jumped free of the tender, hoping for the best, or maybe he had simply been tossed off the precipice as the tender was snatched from the engine. Whatever the circumstances, his body was found in the wreckage, his neck and leg broken. He had been killed instantly.

Miraculously, the last cars of the train had somehow remained intact upon the track on the opposite side of the chasm. Consequently, the conductor and flagman in the caboose survived the devastation without a scratch. The reason for the salvation of this portion of the train is unknown today.

The 360-foot bridge across Pumpkinvine Creek was one of the longest

The Pumpkinvine Creek trestle is located on the rail line between Atlanta, Georgia and Chattanooga, Tennessee on the route once known as the "Georgia Division" of Southern Railway. Even today, trains still pass over a steel trestle (one of the longest and highest on the division) at this same site above the creek many times a day. "I, as well as a lot of others, never did like crossing it," Mintz

The old Southern Railway depot in Rockmart, Georgia, a few miles from the Pumpkinvine Creek trestle was photographed circa 1905. Train #81 stopped regularly at this station. A locomotive quite similar to Train #81 idles in front of the depot. (Photo courtesy of Rockmart Library)

added. "I personally don't like any trestle that is built as part of a curve, especially like that one is."

Braswell Mountains Culprit

The Dallas to Rockmart portion of the Georgia Division has long been a dangerous one. As a part of the Atlanta to Chattanooga line in Southern Railway's network it was completed on July 1, 1882. There have been at least four major disasters on the Dallas to Rockmart segment alone in the past 90 years, and possibly numerous other lesser ones.

Break-neck speed and a tight railroad time-table undoubtedly were major factors in several of the incidents. In 1902, Southern Railway obtained a contract to haul the mail between Washington, D.C. and Atlanta, Georgia, on the New York to New Orleans line. The U.S.

government wanted the best means possible for quick transport of the mails, and fast locomotives were the answer. In return, Southern Railway earned $140,000 a year for this service. In those days, that was big money – the rough equivalent of $4,483,000.00 in 2023 dollars.

But it was a double-edged sword. If Southern Railway couldn't keep up with the schedule, it was penalized $100.00 for every thirty minutes the mail was late at every destination. That was more than enough incentive for rail management to impose heavy, heavy pressure on trainmen to maintain schedules. This almost always meant exceeding the speed limit by many miles an hour more than the speed at which a stretch of rails and their supporting components such as trestles were designed to be used. And the fact that some trains were traveling on dangerous stretches of track to begin with, only added to the propensity for disaster.

One such example is the stretch of tracks between Dallas, Georgia and Rockmart. On the evening of December 23, 1926, on the outskirts of Rockmart, the Ponce de Leon passenger train, traveling in excess of 50 miles per hour, collided head-on with the Royal Palm passenger train because of confusion exacerbated by excessive speed.

This disaster resulted in at least 19 – and possibly 20 or more – fatalities (the exact number is unknown today), and at least 113 passengers, 4 Southern Railway employees and 6 Pullman employees were seriously injured. This wreck remains as one of the worst disasters in the history of the railroad in the United States.

At least part of the reason for these accidents outside Rockmart stemmed from the fact that trains have long been able to build up considerable speed coming down out of the Braswell Mountains outside Rockmart, and engineers were loathe to cut this speed once having built it up along this stretch. It has happened time and time again, and even today, the big freight trains hurtling toward Chattanooga often pass through Rockmart at far higher rates of speed than necessary and safe.

Big Raccoon Creek Trestle

Another accident (on that same dangerous stretch between Dallas and Rockmart) which caused the death of several individuals occurred nearby at Big Raccoon Creek trestle in February of 1883. The bridgework at this site was practically new at that time, and railroad historians have long pondered the reason for its collapse. "It's just another of the many puzzling events in the annals of

railroading in the early days," Mintz continued matter-of-factly.

The 44-year veteran of the rails served on the Georgia Division Safety Committee of Southern Railway for ten years. "I wrote, printed and distributed a safety newsletter, and one of the articles I carried in the newsletter was a description of the Big Raccoon Creek accident," he smiled.

The trestle at Big Raccoon Creek is seven miles north of Dallas. The creek itself is just a small stream, but the heavily eroded creek-bed is significantly deep with high bluffs on either side. At the time of the accident, the trestle at this site was a three-deck trestle, spanning 1,480 feet from bluff to bluff and rising 94 feet from the creek-bed.

Mr. Mintz's newsletter article of this disaster, reprinted from a news report in the February 22, 1883 issue of the **Dallas New Era** newspaper, described the accident as follows: *"Last Saturday morning, about 10:30 a.m., as Train Number 59, a through-freight of the E.T.V. & G. R.R. (East Tennessee, Virginia & Georgia Railroad) was leaving the switch at the tunnel, south-bound. Conductor Bob Shoemaker boarded the engine, as it was convenient for him at the time, and (he) remarked to his engineer that he would ride with him down to Dallas rather than drop back to his caboose.*

"All went well until the train, running at the rate of 7 or 8 miles an hour, ran upon Big Raccoon Trestle. . . Having passed across to within a few yards of the south side with his engine, Mr. Neeley gave her a little more steam in order to pull over the grade in front. Almost immediately, a severe shock being felt, Mr. Shoemaker, (comprehending) the cause and looking back, shouted, 'Pull her open! Pull her open! The bridge is going!' . . . The terrible crash that followed left them standing

upon the very brink of a yawning abyss - the bottom of which was covered with ruins, all within a moment of time.

"The (collapsed) section consisted of ten or eleven cars laden with merchandise, and the caboose. There were three men in the caboose and a Negro brakeman about midway of the train. . . The unfortunate brakeman was killed outright. Mr. R.P. Kidwell . . . was on board, enroute to Atlanta to visit his family. He too was so fatally injured that death came as a relief to his sufferings very soon after being removed from the debris to the car in waiting. Mr. John Cox . . . also in the caboose, sustained injuries that proved fatal to him as well, living until Saturday night totally unconscious all the while. Mr. Charles Camp, flagman . . . remained unconscious for several hours, then awoke to the realization of his remarkable escape . . . (He had) a scalp wound, a crushed ankle, and a dislocated elbow, (but he was alive!)."

The heavy train had passed across the trestle until the caboose was immediately over the creek. At that point, according to the news account printed in the *New Era,* section after section of the trestle began giving way somewhere near the center of the train. The general collapse of the trestle was very similar to the collapse of the trestle just six or seven miles away at Pumpkinvine Creek in 1903.

Common Cause For The Disasters?

The 360-foot trestle across Pumpkinvine had safely carried hundreds of fast trains over the years. The cause of its collapse is still unknown also, but the news account in the 1903 *New Era* speculates upon the possibilities. *"Some think train wreckers had removed a rail causing the wreck, while others believe that the high rate of speed caused the terrible disaster,"* the newspaper intoned.

On December 23rd, 1926, a horrendous collision between the Ponce de Leon and the Royal Palm passenger trains just south of Southern Railway's Rockmart Depot resulted in one of the worst rail disasters in U.S. history. This accident occurred only a short distance from the Pumpkinvine Creek trestle disaster site. The heavy-metal cab of the Ponce de Leon visible in this photo was completely crushed and twisted in the horrendous collision. Had the Royal Palm – which was almost stationary on the tracks at the time – been moving at the same speed (in excess of 50 mph) as the Ponce de Leon, the resulting devastation would have been indescribable. (Photo courtesy of Atlanta Historic Society)

Duane Mintz said he didn't think a missing rail had caused the accident at all. "If a rail had been missing, the whole engine would have gone over the side of the trestle, and it wouldn't have caused much trestle damage either," the trainman explained. "I think simple structural weakness caused both the Raccoon Creek and Pumpkinvine Creek disasters."

A very similar accident, which was highly publicized across the United States, had occurred on the Southern Railway just three weeks earlier. The wreck of the "Old 97" which occurred in Danville, Virginia, became the subject for a popular ballad which is still remembered by many railroad enthusiasts today:

Steve Broady, the engineer of the Old 97, was pushing the mail train faster

The financial success of early railroads could be made or lost in relation to the road crews which serviced them. Photographed here on what appears to have been a foggy day, an L&N (formerly Southern Railway) crew posed in 1910 at Crandall, Georgia, near Chatsworth. Jim Howard (seated, left) was section foreman in charge of repairs from Crandall to Ramhurst. (Photo courtesy of the Georgia Dept. of Archives & History, Atlanta)

and faster to make up lost time. Witnesses claim the train reached ninety miles an hour as the 80-ton behemoth swept down a grade and struck the "curved" timber trestle. A flange on one of the wheels reportedly broke off, and the engine with its cars plunged seventy-five feet into the creek below.

Twelve of the nineteen individuals on board Old 97 were killed. The engineer and fireman were found with the skin flayed from their bodies by the super-heated steam from the crushed boiler. It was a fate from which the engineer at Pumpkinvine Creek had mercifully been spared, but there's no arguing that the Danville, Virginia and Pumpkinvine Creek, Georgia disasters were eerily similar in nature.

Whatever the cause of the wreck at Pumpkinvine, rail officials were determined not to allow the accident to keep the line out of service any longer than absolutely necessary. Service between Chattanooga and Atlanta was

temporarily rerouted through Rome, while a huge work crew labored feverishly to repair the damage. Every hour the line remained out of service represented a great financial loss for Southern.

"Two wrecking crews reached the scene about 12:00 p.m., six hours after the occurrence, and more than two hundred men were clearing away the debris," the **Dallas New Era** explained.

Even this amount of man-power, however, apparently was not enough, and still more men were dispatched to the site to help. Working around the clock, the men had the track and trestle repaired three days after the disaster. By Wednesday morning, the first train steamed safely over the repaired bridge, heading north to Chattanooga.

Once the wreckage had been cleared away and the repairs had been made, the scene at Pumpkinvine Creek quickly returned to normal too. Previously on that fateful Sunday, sightseers had streamed out of Dallas to view the site of the disaster. And with the crowds came scavengers who dug through the wreckage in search of booty.

The atmosphere, no doubt, was somewhat like a country carnival. The crushed freight cars had spilled their cargoes of corn, oats, cotton, and apples, and according to one wag, a load of Bull Durham tobacco. It was reported with some mirth, that virtually every boy in Paulding County learned to smoke as a result of this wreck.

Meanwhile, in sleepy Varnell, Georgia, near the Tennessee state line, the festivities were not quite so lively. . . A railroader – the poor fireman at the Pumpkinvine Creek Trestle accident – had been killed. The grieving wife – with her two small children – received their loved one home from the railroad for the last time.

Famous Paulding County Civil War Site:

The Bloody Battle at Pickett's Mill

It is a Georgia State Historic Site today, but back in the summer of 1864, it earned notoriety from an extremely sanguineous battle which shocked both sides in the U.S. Civil War as Gen. William T. Sherman threw his men unceasingly into the fray in the Atlanta Campaign.

In 1864, Little Pumpkinvine Creek (known today as Pickett's Mill Creek), was the center of a small settlement which had arisen in Georgia's pioneer days. The site drew its identity from a gristmill built and owned by Benjamin Pickett. Known in recent years as Pickett's Mill State Historic Site, it was the location of a particularly grisly episode in the history of the U.S. Civil War.

Pickett's Mill exists about two miles northeast of New Hope Church in present-day Paulding County. This relatively new state historic site, was opened in May of 1990 by preservation-minded individuals. It had become necessary for the site's protection after legions of relic hunters had plundered the vicinity mercilessly for scores of years. It now attracts growing numbers of visitors each year under a much more protected mode.

Today, an interpretive ranger and/or self-guided tours for the preserve explain in detail the importance of the events of that day in 1864 – almost 160 years ago as of this writing in 2022 – and their impact on the little community in which the battle occurred.

State preservationists have determined there may originally have been as many as eleven homes at this site which became a particularly vicious engagement during the war. The owners of the homes had earlier departed the area when it became painfully obvious that a large destructive battle was about to take place. When they returned after the conflict – those that actually bothered to return – discovered by and large that little remained of the homes and lives they had once enjoyed there.

A precious one or two structures which had been designated as officer headquarters sites have managed to survive into the 21st Century. All the other homes were destroyed in the fighting, and it quite often was not the shot and shell which destroyed them.

The Confederate defenders in the Atlanta Campaign had learned that if

A modern bridge extends across Pumpkinvine Creek today, but in 1864, this covered bridge, located three and one-half miles north of Dallas, provided fordage across the creek. This photo shows a view of the bridge from the Dallas side of Pumpkinvine Creek.

they wished to fight effectively and at a more deadly rate, then they would have to build entrenchments for concentrated – and yet concealed – fire-power against the enemy. And as they dug their trenches, the soldiers had learned to use logs on the facing side of the trench, beneath and between which they could pour out deadly volleys of fire from protection.

As such, if there were ready-made logs in the vicinity for quick usage in the trench constructions, that, unfortunately was the route that would be taken, and many – if not most – of the homes, barns, churches, and other structures at Pickett's Mill had been constructed of logs which were quickly but methodically dismantled and their logs installed in the trenches.

Sherman's Strategy

General William T. Sherman who commanded the Union forces moving down through Georgia was not the brightest of Grant's generals, but he had ample resources – well over 100,000 men in three separate armies (Army of the Cumberland, Army of the Tennessee, and Army of the Ohio), substantial munitions, rapid-fire weapons, and

plentiful food via the recently-repaired Western & Atlantic Railroad all the way from Chattanooga – which far exceeded the resources of the Confederates defending Georgia who numbered approximately 65,000 men starving and in rags, and most of whom were armed with little more than single-shot muskets.

Despite his numeric and resources advantage, Sherman's armies often simply could not dislodge the stubborn Confederates who were desperate and generally more adept at war. His only strategy – used since Chattanooga and all down through northwest Georgia – had been to fight until he reached the point at which he could advance no further, then, due to his numeric superiority, he would flank the Confederates, sending an army to either side of the Confederate line, at which point, the out-numbered Southern troops would have no option other than to fall back to another defensive position.

According to the memoirs of Sherman, published in 1876, *"On the other side of the Allatoona Range, Pumpkinvine Creek flowed north and west; Dallas* (Georgia), *the point aimed at, was a small town on the other or east side of this creek.. . Its possession would be a threat to Marietta and Atlanta,"* Sherman stated. . . . *"My movement was chiefly designed to compel Johnston (Gen. Joseph, C.S.A.) to give up the Allatoona. . . .*

"On the 25th,*"* Sherman continued *"all the columns were moving steadily on Dallas – McPherson and Davis away off to the right near Van Wert; Thomas on the main road in the center, with Hooker's Twentieth Corps ahead, toward Dallas; and Schofield on the left rear. This leading division (Hooker) struck a heavy infantry force which was moving down from Allatoona toward Dallas, and a sharp battle ensued. I came up in person soon after,*

and as my map showed we were near an important cross-roads called 'New Hope,' from a Methodist meeting house there of that name, I ordered General Hooker to secure it if possible that night.

"The woods were so dense and the resistance so spirited, that Hooker could not carry the position, though the battle was noisy and prolonged far into the night," Sherman added. *"This point, 'New Hope,' was the accidental intersection of the road leading from Allatoona to Dallas with that from Van Wert to Marietta. . . . From the bloody fighting there for the next week (it) was called by the soldiers 'Hell-Hole.'"*

Following the sanguinary fighting at Dallas and New Hope Church, Sherman decided once again to flank the out-numbered Confederates, to attempt to maneuver his troops between them and Atlanta. On May 27, 1864, he committed around 14,000 troops to the fateful venture.

Unexpected Disaster

In a heavily-wooded landscape with foliage-choked ravines, the Union troops met with absolute disaster. Although they again enjoyed numeric and weapons superiority, the Federals were no match for the battle-seasoned Confederates in the dense undergrowth of the ravines. One particular spot was especially devastating.

A small contingent – about 5,000 men – from Pat Cleburne's Confederate division were waiting atop the Little Pumpkinvine ravine. This lovely little mini-canyon was "the hell-hole" to which Sherman referred in his memoirs, and was also remembered by the Confederates by that name as well.

The Union troops attacked in column formation. Though this maneuver was known to be virtual suicide for the initial participants, it usually meant

Two unidentified Federal soldiers pause in a field for a meal shortly before the terrible engagement at Pickett's Mill. It quite likely was the last food consumed in their young lives. A canteen carried water or coffee which was boiled in a tin cup or an old tomato can. A tin plate served as a frying pan and serving dish if they were fortunate enough to have fresh food which required cooking. A green stick split at one end and forced over the rim of the plate made a handle to hold it over a fire. Following their meal, the men would routinely shed most of their non-combat equipment in order to move more easily and quietly through the underbrush. One soldier wrote *"We went stripped of every unnecessary thing. . ."*

an attacking army would be delivering a series of successive blows with enough force, eventually, to break through the enemy's lines, forcing them to fall back in disarray and confusion. However, in this instance in "the hell-hole," the disadvantage to this type of attack was that the attackers' front was so small and the terrain so shaped, that the attackers could be fired upon by both flanks of the defenders. This draw-back, coupled with the unusual terrain at the battle site, spelled abject doom for the men in blue. Not only was it suicidal for the initial men in this case, it was suicidal for ALL of them.

Three times, the Federals stumbled and cursed their way down the steep

The ruins of Pickett's Mill are faintly visible to the left in this photo. In May of 1864, thick vegetation such as this represented a portion of the many problems culminating for Union troops in the disastrous attack in what came to be known by the men and history as "the Hell Hole."

ravine, only to be pinned down at the bottom by fierce fire. Today, where a quiet little brook flows – one of a number of small tributaries feeding Pickett's Mill Creek – the dead and wounded piled up in unbelievable numbers in 1864. One would have thought that at some point, the Union troopers would have realized the futility of their mission and fallen back, but they just kept coming and dying.

Although Civil War lore is filled with descriptions of waterways "running red with blood," the small stream at this site undoubtedly literally did just that. One resident from this vicinity who lived to a ripe old age into the 1950s claimed that, as a little boy, he witnessed the battle being fought at Pickett's Mill. He explained how he personally saw the stream running bright red with blood.

With men who are wounded, their natural inclination – if possible – is to move to the nearest source of water, since wounded individuals usually suffer from a fierce thirst from the loss of body fluids. The source of the water they sought was the little stream into which they all were

dying and their bodies eventually were piling quite high all down the ravine.

A Coup de Gras

The fiercest fighting ended in the early evening, with the surviving Federal troops still pinned down at the bottom of the ravine. Dead and wounded also littered the adjacent wooded landscape as darkness fell, and one final act in the drama remained.

Around 10:00 p.m. that night, the Confederate line, whooping and hollering – as had their Scots-Irish ancestors eons before them in their ancient homeland – in the manner that had become so terrifying over the past several years to the Federals, charged the by-now totally dispirited Union troops. It was one of the few examples of a night charge during the Civil War. Confederate troops stumbled down the ravine and flushed out the remaining hapless Federals, annihilating those within reach, and capturing those who chose to surrender.

The dawn of May 28 revealed the carnage from the previous day's madness. When the sun had chased the shades of night away. . . . it revealed a sight on that hillside which was horrifying even to the battle-hardened Confederates, according to later accounts of the incident.

All along the front of the center and left of the Confederate line, the ground was literally massed with dead Union soldiers. Federal casualties at this site were later numbered at approximately 1,600 men. The Confederates, in comparison, had themselves lost around 500, so they had not escaped unscathed.

Pickett's Mill probably was burned by Federal soldiers in the days after the battle, as much in retribution as in an insane obsessiveness with the destruction of every fabric of civilized life in Georgia as Sherman had noted he intended to do.

In recent years, Federal diaries of soldiers at the battle have been discovered which describe the men catching "fish and turtles in the millpond," so it is obvious they definitely had control of the ground following the fight. The Confederates had pulled out hours earlier on the evening of June 3rd, to fall back to Kennesaw Mountain and Peachtree Creek and elsewhere to thwart the continuous flanking movements of Sherman's troops.

Pickett's Mill, in many ways, was the story of the entire Atlanta Campaign. Following fine battlefield performances, the Confederates were forced to withdraw again and again due to Sherman's numeric advantage which allowed him to forfeit untold numbers of his men and make endless flanking movements to achieve his goal of destroying Atlanta and a huge swath of Georgia.

In Later Years

After the war, some farming was resumed in the Pickett's Mill area. Then timber companies purchased the property, ultimately harvesting the timber in the 1920s and '30s. According to reports, the timber saws of the loggers frequently were dulled and broken by the countless Minie balls and other projectiles from the battle lodged in the larger trees.

New vegetation and trees rapidly reappeared in the ensuing years, reestablishing the thick undergrowth and forest over the infamous ravine and battlefield area. A consortium of interested preservationists, led by Dr. Philip Secrist of Cobb County, purchased the site in 1973, holding it until the State of Georgia purchased it for preservation.

Today, the park's Visitors Center offers an excellent multi-media presentation which explains the battle. It also houses related exhibits and a small selection of pertinent books and materials for sale.

Three separate trails of up to 1.5 miles allow visitors to hike to the former Federal and Confederate battle positions. Earthworks, thrown up just prior to the battle, are still visible today, as are the ruins of the pioneer gristmill which jut out over the creek. The trails are well-marked, and by reading the Trail Guide obtainable at the Visitor's Center, a self-guided tour is possible.

Visitors to Pickett's Mill should bring sufficient bottled water in warm weather and wear shoes suitable for the terrain, since the trail can be rugged and steep in spots. None of the trails are handicapped accessible, nor are strollers recommended.

(Pickett's Mill State Historic Site in Paulding County can be reached by traveling approximately 12 miles west on Highway 120 from the Square in Marietta. Turn right onto Highway 92 for four miles. Go left on Due West Road, continuing for almost two miles to Mt. Tabor Road. After turning right onto Mt. Tabor Road, the entrance to the park will be within half a mile on the right.)

Old Pickens County Jail

*Built in 1906, the criminals it held and the incidents
experienced therein were many and storied.*

An ancient stone prison built in 1906 on Main Street in Jasper, Georgia, is often assumed to be the county's first jail. Though it is indeed an old jail by comparison, it is not the oldest jail ever used by the town – not by a long shot. It is, however, the one noted in the county's history as experiencing the most sensational incidents.

The first Pickens County jail was built in the 1850s. It was two stories tall and made of logs, and was burned during the chaos of the U.S. Civil War. Seems one of the first objectives of outlaws during the dark days of the 1860s was to destroy the methods of confining them.

The second Pickens County jail was made of rock and existed to the rear of the present-day courthouse. It held a number of individuals sensationalized in early trials. After being abandoned for prison purposes it housed a portion of a sewing plant for a short while, and then was demolished in the 1960s. The large stones from this "old jail" now shore up the courthouse parking lot.

Much of the discourse regarding the Pickens County jails in the past has focused upon the exceedingly poor construction used in the edifices. This can only be viewed as ironic, since the construction of jails historically has received a remarkably low priority by the Pickens taxpayers, a circumstance which has been duly reflected in the ability (actually the lack thereof) of these jails to successfully confine inmates.

The situation involving the second jail eventually reached such a sorry state that even the Pickens County grand juries began assailing it as *"unsanitary, unsafe, uncomfortable, and in a deplorable condition,"* but this nevertheless was not enough to spur its replacement until the spring of 1906.

The prime mover in building what was then "the new jail" was Dr. William B. Tate. He served as foreman on the final two grand juries to condemn the rock jail as inferior and uninhabitable, and as a leader on a citizens' committee appointed to oversee construction of a new jail.

J.W. Coluke and Company were the 1906 jail's architects and the contractors were William Landrum and Son. The sophisticated marble work on the front of the jail was done by Lee W. Prather, a local stone mason, and the marble came from the Delaware Quarry in Marble Hill, the first marble quarry in Georgia (originated circa 1836 by Henry Terry Fitsimmons).

Most old buildings have at least one love story and the 1906 Pickens County Jail is no different. When Luther Cartright of the Pauley Jail Company of St. Louis, Missouri, came to Jasper to put the bars in the jail, he roomed at the Lennings Hotel (present-day Woodbridge Inn). He reportedly fell in love with and married the innkeeper's daughter.

When Cartright retired from the jail business, he and his wife and their family returned to Pickens County to live. At last check, descendants of this family still lived in the area – a family that owes its beginnings to the jail. Luther Cartright also worked on the pink marble mansion in Tate in the 1920s, which happens to be the county's only other *National Register Historic Site*.

The Cartrights were not the only non-criminal family to be associated with the jail. The sheriffs (later the deputies) and their families were required to live on the first floor of the jail and for that reason many of the county's more prominent families have spent more time in the jail than any criminal!

For some of the sheriffs this was a minor inconvenience; for others it was a drudgery. Indeed, according to former Pickens County Sheriff Billy Wofford, he and his family, by having to domicile in and tend to the jail, were more prisoners than the inmates, since the inmates eventually got to leave.

The first floor of the jail has but four rooms into which the sheriffs had to squeeze what was sometimes their somewhat large families. For this and other reasons, it wasn't long before the brick and marble "new" jail on Main Street became outmoded itself. The new conveniences which were all modern in 1906, had ultimately become antiquated and outmoded once again.

For starters, the jail originally had no plumbing of any kind. Water from a well off the back porch had to be hauled inside the jail each day for the sheriff and his family and the inmates. This well also served the huge crowds that periodically gathered in Jasper for singing conventions.

Cooking in the jail was conducted on a wood-burning stove, although the jail did have a coal furnace in the basement. And an always odoriferous outhouse out back served as – well – an outhouse.

Conditions were worse for the prisoners. Until more recent times, the jail had no cells whatsoever. The only cell door was the first floor door at the stairs leading to the second floor, where the prisoners lived in a general population, meaning the sheriff and his family were constantly in close contact – and potential danger – with the prisoners.

It was under these circumstances that a notable jail-break occurred in the 1920s. At 5:00 P.M. on May 23, 1923, Pickens County Sheriff D.P. Poole climbed the stairs to the cells on the second floor of the jail to bring his prisoners the usual bucket of fresh water for the evening. A seasoned lawman such as Sheriff Poole normally would have exercised more caution in such a situation. On this day, however, Poole apparently misjudged the criminals consigned to his care.

Among the "guests" on the second floor that day, was an individual by the name of Ralph King, accused of *"assault with intent to commit murder,"* and his accomplice, Fred Hill. The latter had escaped from this same jail hardly a month earlier via a route which surprisingly had been used by several previous prisoners. The bars in the windows of the cells apparently had not been sturdily installed, and Hill had found it quite simple to loosen and remove one of the bars, and then slide quietly down to the back porch roof.

On the day that Fred Hill escaped

from the jail for the first time, he had been visited by his wife earlier that morning. For reasons unknown today, she had mentioned in passing to one of the guards that she would be staying with her parents, so the pursuing lawmen had a relatively good hunch where they might re-capture Hill.

Interestingly, despite being surprised by lawmen on the premises of his wife's parents' home, the determined fugitive nevertheless eluded his captors once again as he lit out across a swamp. He was later apprehended some 50 or 60 miles away in Rome, Georgia, and had been back in jail only a week, when he and King decided to attack Sheriff Poole in order to escape once again.

Despite the background of these two men, Poole, for reasons unknown today, apparently did not consider them dangerous. He didn't have a deputy nor a sidearm as he ascended the stairs to tend to the prisoners for the night.

At the top of the stairs, the two men jumped Poole. One of them had a brick which he had worked loose from the jail wall, and the other reportedly had a bottle. Poole fell to the jail floor, temporarily stunned, after being repeatedly struck by the men.

While the duo searched Poole for a weapon, the lawman recovered and began fighting back. With exhaustion near at hand, the two men finally decided flight was their best option, and abandoned the determined sheriff.

They turned to run down the stairs to Poole's living quarters on the first floor of the jail, but the sheriff was anything if not a brave lawman. Never one to be easily conquered, he latched onto the two prisoners with all his might, apparently hoping to slow them down long enough for help to arrive.

By this time, Poole's wife had heard the commotion and obvious struggle taking place upstairs, and had run to the bottom of the stairs, screaming like a banshee. Though obviously in shock, she at least was raising enough of a ruckus to draw attention to the situation from outside the jail.

Jasper resident Oscar Champion lived next door to the jail at that time. Mrs. Poole's screams had been effective, for Champion had been alerted and had run onto the back porch of the jail. Realizing that a prisoner escape was in progress, he ran into the sheriff's living quarters and found Poole's pistol.

By this time, the two prisoners had finally reached the bottom of the stairs and were only inches away from freedom. King finally broke free and leaped from the jail porch, heading towards a cotton field (a site occupied today by the Jasper Elementary School) and freedom.

Oscar Champion had never fired a weapon at anyone before (or since) in his life. However, on this day, he closed his eyes, pointed the pistol at the escapee, and ordered the fleeing man to stop.

When the man failed to halt, Poole yelled at Champion to shoot. Oscar squeezed off a round from the big pistol and the countryside around the normally peaceful mountain community resounded from the discharge.

According to Mr. Champion, despite the fact that King was running at an incredible clip across the cotton field, he almost fell backwards in his immediate effort to halt and raise his hands. He then marched quietly back to the jail as the sheriff subdued the other man.

This, however, was not the conclusion of this tale. Things were just beginning to get interesting. . . .

The sheriff, as one might imagine, assumed the desperate attempts at freedom were at an end, and that he would simply return his two escapees to the lock-up with the rest of the prisoners on the second floor. By this time, however, the general population of remaining prisoners had been exposed to a taste of freedom as well, and were reluctant to acquiesce so easily.

According to reports, the detainees began raining a shower of bricks, soft drink bottles and disinfectant upon anyone who attempted to reach them, refusing to allow the sheriff access back into the facility. By this point, Poole's patience was exhausted, and he responded to this revolt with another heavy round from the revolver.

The prisoners, however, were not so easily deterred. Many of them had been fired upon previously – some of them many times. They responded with still more bottles and bricks.

By this point, however, some fifty or sixty men, most of them armed, gathered around the jail and one of them – Felix Allred – directed the prisoners to give up or die *(In those days, prison revolts and namby-pamby negotiated settlements simply were not part of the plan.)*. In 1923, Pickens County was barely beyond frontier status, and frontier justice therefore still prevailed. The disgruntled prisoners, realizing they had little choice, finally succumbed, but remained restless and agitated.

Ironically, the two escapees from that day were eventually found *"Not Guilty"* of the original charges for which they were being held, but were each sentenced to two years in prison for the attack on Sheriff Poole. So instead of a clean record, they both became convicted felons with all the delights which go with that station in life.

Poole, by this time, had decided discretion was the better part of valor, and opted out of the law enforcement profession. He had had enough. He chose not to seek re-election to his position, no doubt strongly encouraged to depart by his wife whose nerves undoubtedly were shot.

The late Oscar Champion subsequently decided to put some distance between himself and the jail as well, moving to nearby Tate, Georgia, and living to be over 100 years of age. Before he passed away, he would discuss the 1923 Pickens County jail-break and riot only if specifically asked, and even then a fair amount of coaxing was necessary.

There were a number of other escapes from the 1906 jail, a fact which did nothing to diminish the obvious need for a newer, more secure facility. One popular means of exit was through a second floor window above the back porch. With a cable attached to a mule team or truck, the bars and window could be ripped out and the inmate could escape to the roof and from there to the ground. This, admittedly, required determined criminals for success to occur, but the mountains were full of them in those days. Several sheets of metal welded to the roof of the second floor of the jail attest to yet another avenue of escape during the last years of the jail's operation.

Despite its failures, the jail also capably served its purpose to some degree. It successfully confined a number of highly-notorious individuals who attracted state and nation-wide attention for their crimes.

Among the persons held there were the men accused of murdering and then dismembering U.S. Revenue Agent Lee Cape in 1929. The testimony in that case was so gruesome that the presiding judge was forced to clear the courtroom of women and children.

Also confined in the 1906 jail was the man who was convicted of murdering cab driver Earl Holbert in 1948. Despite conviction of the guilty party, the motive for this murder has never been fully determined. It remains as one of the more mysterious crimes in Pickens history.

The 1906 Pickens County Jail building also boasts one of Georgia's few remaining gallows, an item not to be missed on any tour of the old building. Despite its intended purpose, however, no one was ever hanged at this site. Amazingly, when the gallows was installed, the trap was constructed backwards, rendering the device useless, so even if its use had been necessitated, the punishment would have required application elsewhere.

There have been at least two suicides in the jail, and at least one infant was born in there to an inmate. (The inmate, incidentally, later returned for a tour of the old facility in which she was once incarcerated.)

The 1906 jail continued to deteriorate over the years, despite the addition of modern improvements such as electricity, plumbing, and extra cells. When the number of necessary bunks, mattresses, and other necessities became too few to service the inmates being housed in the facility, circumstances at the jail had reached the breaking point.

One individual, held for only a minor violation, remembered being imprisoned in the same room with a murderer and a rapist. Sheriff Wofford remembers instances when mischievous inmates plugged up the water drain upstairs in order to flood the sheriff's quarters below.

Plans for a new jail were discussed in 1960, and a 1965 grand jury called for the sale of the existing jail property to raise money for a new county prison. New construction however met with delay after delay, and conditions at the jail grew even worse.

By 1980, circumstances at the jail had reached an absolute impasse. The Atlanta newspapers eventually got wind of the deplorable circumstances and described the lock-up in a news story as *"the worst jail in Georgia."*

Finally, in the spring of 1980, two inmates filed a class-action lawsuit in federal court, claiming that confinement in the jail violated the 1st, 4th, 6th, 8th, and 14th amendments of the **U.S. Constitution**. The jail, subsequently, was ordered closed by the state. In 1982, the present Pickens County jail was opened near the county airport.

After the old 1906 jail was closed, it next became necessary to decide what to do with it. If the decision had been left to the former inmates, sheriffs, sheriffs' families, and many of the county's taxpayers, the structure undoubtedly would have been destroyed.

However, Ms. Kathryn Downes, one of the founding members of the *Marble Valley* (Pickens County) *Historical Society*, was preservation – not demolition-minded. She managed to persuade two successive county commissioners to allow her to save the dilapidated but historic building.

Following the Historic Society's initiation of restoration efforts on the old jail, the building was nominated and ultimately accepted for placement on the **National Register of Historic Places**, and a historical marker was placed in front of the building. Others were obviously preservation-minded as well, because $10,000 in cash and $30,000 in labor and materials ultimately were donated to and expended upon the historic structure.

The entire building was subsequently permanently preserved for posterity. And much of the old jail has been preserved just as it was in the days in which it saw active service, a reminder of what life was like for the criminals in days of yore in old Pickens County.

Pickens County In The Civil War

There is no topic concerning Pickens County which has spurred more debate over the years than the circumstances of its participation in the U.S. Civil War. It has been reported variously that Pickens residents "were all Republicans," "seceded from the Confederacy," and "raised a Union flag in defiance of the Confederate authorities." It has also been reported that somewhere between one-eighth and one-sixth of the county's 1860 population served in the Confederate Army, and that the county strongly supported the Southern cause. The truth, as usual, lies somewhere between the two extremes.

Yes, a Union flag was flown in protest to secession in Pickens County after the South seceded. Lemuel Allred, the member of the Georgia State Legislature who had pushed for the bill to create Pickens County in 1853, later took credit for the flag in his claim for compensation from the federal government. The flag flew from the courthouse, and in a weird bit of irony, was torn down, not by the local townspeople, but by a sudden storm. This incident represents a microcosm of the strange Civil War history of Pickens.

Despite the storm's destruction of the emblem, Allred maintained that a local mob threatened to burn down his cabin in retribution for his "Unionist" activities. State authorities, however, were surprisingly sympathetic to his cause.

Governor Joseph Emerson Brown, formerly of Canton and one-time judge of the Superior Court in Pickens County, supported his friend Lemuel, even though Brown himself was a rabid secessionist.

"Let it float," wrote Brown. *"It floated over our fathers, and we all love the flag now. We have only been compelled to lay it aside by the injustice that has been practiced under its folds. If the people of Pickens desire to hang it out, and keep it there, let them so do."*

After the war, Lemuel's flag was displayed in the courthouse in a place of honor. Shortly thereafter, a community and a number of the children in Pickens were named for the otherwise despised Union General William T. Sherman, whose name has been held in contempt from that day to the present among many Georgia residents.

Luke Tate who penned his seminal *History of Pickens County* in 1935 calculated that one-eighth to one-sixth of the county's population served in the Southern forces, but that statement is misleading and in need of qualification. Many of his "Confederates" were draftees who otherwise didn't support the Southern cause at all, and the members of the county militia were required to serve in it no matter what their political sympathies may have been. Many boys enlisted for no other reason than to leave their mountain farms to see something of the outside world and to enjoy what they believed would be a "lark." They ultimately were incredibly disappointed.

Early War Attitudes

As in many wars, most participants sorely underestimated the circumstances. Most Southerners were convinced the fighting would not last more than a year, and that the matters of disagreement between residents of the North and the South would be resolved before the leaves even fell that autumn. They too were horrifyingly disappointed.

Luke Tate correctly interprets the Pickens County Grand Jury Presentments to indicate that the area's support for the South rivaled any county in the Confederacy. This support from the Grand Jurists also was not limited to the men either. Miss Henrietta Cunningham of Jasper, a school teacher, presented Company E, 23rd Georgia Volunteers – the first company raised for the Confederacy in Pickens County – with a battle flag.

Interestingly, in September of 1861, a poem by "Kate" of Jasper which urges her love to volunteer for service – even if it should result in his death – was published in an Atlanta newspaper. *"Ere you return, we'll meet again in that blest world on high!"* she penned. Perhaps her interests lay with someone other than her "beloved."

Pickens County had no shortage of Confederates or Democrats, then or since. In point of fact, Pickens County stands out as "Republican" in the history of the Civil War in Georgia not because of widespread opposition to secession but because it had an active pro-Union element that was often, but not always, missing in other counties.

Truth be told, it is quite likely that a majority of Pickens residents were not active supporters of either cause, and mainly preferred merely to be left alone. Unfortunately, they were not to have their way.

Reasons for War

In the popular mind, the Civil War was simply suddenly sparked to life by cannon-fire at Fort Sumter in April of 1861. The reality was quite different. In 1832 South Carolina threatened secession in the *Nullification Crisis* – which, contrary to popular belief, was much more relevant as a cause of the war than was the issue of slavery – though one would be hard-pressed to convince many quarters of that circumstance today. The slavery issue is a convenient hook upon which to hang the cloak of war, but Lincoln did not even issue his *Emancipation Proclamation* until early 1863, almost two full years *after* the war had begun.

As early as 1837, British traveler G. W. Featherstonhaugh (pronounced Fanshaw) found people in what later became Pickens County hotly debating secession in their local taverns. He left unmistakable notes to this effect in a diary he kept as he traveled across what today is Georgia.

South Carolina failed to ignite a Civil War in the 1830s, however, largely because of a lack of support for *Nullification* by Georgia. During yet another similar crisis of 1850 South Carolina again threatened to secede and again failed largely due to Georgia's unwilling-ness to support them. In North Georgia at that time, political rallies were held by two competing groups – one which sup-ported circumstances as they existed in the Union, and one which supported a state's inherent right to nullify federal laws which were unfairly oppressive and unacceptable, and to secede if such nulli-fication was disallowed.

By that point in the 1850s, a sub-stantial number of the hardy residents of the mountains in Georgia had a reputa-tion for being "Union men," so attitudes regarding the Nullification issue cut both ways. Various reasons have been given for this lack of enthusiasm for se-cession, but one of the most glaring was the lack of slave ownership among the poor mountain residents.

In 1860 only Samuel Tate (grand-father of the later marble magnate/mil-lionaire of the same name) was recorded in the Federal Census as owning enough slaves to be considered as a planter in Pickens County. It was only after the railroad later advanced into the county's realm that it was able to take its place as the northern-most Georgia frontier of the cotton kingdom.

Not only were there very few slaves in Pickens County, the isolated nature of the mountaineers caused them to be much less dependent upon Northern goods, and therefore much less exposed to the excessive Northern prices demanded for those goods than were the planters in the cotton belt. Many White mountain families even feared that slavery might in time be expanded to include them.

These same mountain families had moved into the Pickens County area af-ter 1832 from the Carolinas and Virgin-ia, from which many had been forced to move – in some instances more than once – by the encroachments of the planters

with their money, slaves, and political power. Small independent farmers sim-ply could not compete against "cotton barons" with large forces of slave labor.

In the final *Nullification Crisis* in 1860 that did ignite the U.S. Civil War, many Pickens voters elected the county's delegates to the Secession Convention on the assurance that those delegates would vote "No" to the very end re-garding the issue of secession. Delegate James Simmons, a former Indian trader whose home, the Simmons House, still stands as of this writing, made just such a promise, and he kept it, but the die had already been cast.

The Georgia Convention was com-posed of a substantial number of pro-Union supporters from across the state, but in the end all but six of them voted for secession in a traditional show of uni-ty. Among the six abstentions was Sim-mons, who did sign a statement to *"here-by pledge our lives, our fortunes, and our sacred honor to the defense of Georgia, if necessary, against hostile invasion from any source whatsoever."*

The Civil War

The war that followed certainly was not finished "before the leaves fell." The Confederacy remained almost com-pletely intact for over two years, until the disastrous defeats at Vicksburg, Gettys-burg, and Chattanooga, but even prior to those defeats, the Confederacy had se-rious problems. Volunteers could not be enlisted fast enough to meet the Con-federate Army's needs, and an extreme-ly unpopular draft law was therefore passed by the national government and impressed upon the citizenry.

As a result of their forced participa-tion in service in the Confederate Army, many poor mountain families were left almost to starve after the men and boys were conscripted. However, special exemptions were allowed for the planter elite, to insure that enough White men remained to supervise the slaves and avoid any production slow-downs.

As a result, desertions rose steadily, encouraged as the war continued, by shortages of supplies, mounting casualties, and Confederate defeats. Soon many of the South's military-age and capable men - draft or not – were back at their farms, with or without official sanction.

One very devastating aspect of the South's war strategy (or lack thereof) is that the Confederate planners had not taken into consideration the fact that the South had historically imported much of its foods and other basic necessities of life from the industrialized North prior to the war, and when the Northern blockade of the South began taking effect, the cotton kingdom was reduced to starvation. Bread riots broke out even in the early days of the war.

Pickens County was a major supplier – interestingly through agent Lemuel Allred of all people – of alcohol to the Confederate hospitals in Atlanta and presumably to the ordinance bureau as well. To ease the food shortages, the first laws against illicit liquor production ("moonshining") were passed in the South and, consequently, the first indictments of Pickens County residents – doing what they and their forebears had been practicing for centuries – quickly followed. The net result was that even more dissention was generated among the mountain folk.

Salt was the basis of another shortage issue. It, in fact, was the most famous item of shortage in the war and it was not uncommon for many Southern families to go to the extreme measure of digging up smokehouse floors in order to boil the "salted" soil to regain the precious

commodity which had dripped out of salted meats. Iron, leather, lead, coffee, and many other products also disappeared as the war progressed, except for that which could be bought from profiteers. These shortages and problems are documented in letters to Governor Joseph E. Brown by such Pickens County officials as James Simmons.

Pickens County residents did actively serve in the Confederate Army, but so also did some in the Union Army, both groups seeing service in all of the major campaigns. They could be found on almost every battlefield and many can be found in the cemeteries there today.

Fortunately for their families – and for the men and boys lucky enough to return – most of the fighting did not approach their homes back in Pickens County. It was conducted in places far from the mountains of Pickens.

War and Lawlessness

Following the Battle of Chickamauga and Gen. William T. Sherman's troops' entry into Georgia, however, things suddenly changed for the worse. The fighting – at least from the perspective of the onslaught of the thieves and renegades from both Union and Confederate troops – brought the war to the doorstep of virtually every Pickens County home. From that day to well into the 1880s, a time of arson, thievery, assault, rape, murder, starvation, and general horrendous misery settled over not only Pickens County, but the entire northern half of the state.

North Georgia in particular became a popular refuge for Confederate deserters, where concealment was easier in the mountainous terrain, and where persons could be found who supported the Union and would help deserters as a means of helping to defeat the

Confederacy. As a result, several expeditions of Georgia state troops were sent into the mountainous terrain to ferret out and punish the deserters and pro-Union contingents or "Tories." Regular patrols by "Home Guard" units also routinely searched – and abused – the Union-supporting mountain residents. Torture and hangings of perpetrators were commonplace.

Union sympathizers began leading foraging parties from Sherman's army to plunder the farms of Confederate families to feed the Union army. Since these Union sympathizers were "irregulars" wearing no uniforms, they could be treated as spies and executed by the Home Guard units. However, many critics of the state troops contended that they and the "Home Guard" units were little more than bandits and murderers themselves, who used their presumed affiliation with the Confederate Army as official sanction to plunder anyone they chose, even families that were supporting the Confederacy.

The Pickens County Grand Jury Presentments for those years are filled with indictments against the Home Guard, and specific incidents such as the "Covington Hang" have become legendary. In an attempt to bring a halt to the lawless Home Guards, Rev. Elias Allred, Lemuel's brother, obtained help from the only source available to him – the Union army of Gen. Sherman.

Captain Joseph P. Cummings, commanding the 3rd Kentucky Cavalry (U.S.), entered Pickens County in July of 1864. The 3rd Kentucky defeated the Confederate Home Guard near present-day Talking Rock and formed, under Elias Allred, a 125-man defense force to prevent further depredations. Cummings and his men also brought a number of families out of Pickens County to the safety of the federal forces. Under such circumstances, the gratitude of the people of Pickens County to Gen. Sherman – murderous as he was to the Confederacy in general – is somewhat understandable.

Few records of the last days of the Civil War in Pickens County are available today, and those that are available are found mainly in what remains of the Grand Jury Presentments of that day. At some point in the confusion and lawlessness of those times, the jail in Jasper was burned and the locks from the courthouse were stolen. As a result, Pickens County's official records were at first presumed to have been destroyed, only to later turn up in bits and pieces in other counties, with local officials who had removed the records and themselves to safety.

The grand juries lamented the fact that public education had ceased to exist and called upon ministers and local churches to take on this task, remedying this shortcoming. That the citizens felt the need to carry guns as they walked the streets was also noted.

A Union flag again flew in Pickens County, that of the federal garrison of Capt. Levi M. Hess, Company I, 29th Indiana Volunteer Infantry, who helped the Grand Jury to meet. The Civil War brought division, shortages, feuds, crime, heroism, and a great deal of confusion and misery to Pickens County before matters improved years later. No simple answers or explanations existed then nor are they easy to obtain even today, after the passage of more than 160 years (as of 2023) of those terrible events.

(Grateful appreciation is expressed herewith to Robert S. Davis, Jr., who provided portions of the information used in this article.)

Historic Pioneer Inn From Yesteryear. . .

It began life in 1880, obtaining customers from the travelers on the old Federal Road which passed immediately beside it. Later, as the railroad reached Pickens County, it passed directly in front of the inn, providing still more customers. Today, tourists and sight-seers into the Blue Ridge Mountains from Atlanta continue to be enthralled and captivated by this unique vestige of hospitality from yesteryear.

According to Luke E. Tate's seminal *History of Pickens County* (c. 1935, Atlanta, GA), Edmund E. Lenning was among the stampede of miners in the *California Gold Rush* of 1849. *"Before leaving home, Lenning had made the statement that he was going out there and make ten thousand dollars in gold, then come back to the 'red hills of Georgia,' marry, and not work anymore,"* Tate wrote. *"He kept his word all the way through."* And thus, all those years ago, the seeds of what later became the Woodbridge Inn were sown.

Some 27 years later on June 4, 1877, Lenning reportedly purchased seventeen acres just up the old Federal Road from the growing burg of Jasper, Georgia, along with a two-room log cabin divided by a dog-trot. The inn on this site was still a few years into the future, however, as Lenning originally intended to be involved in no laborious activity whatsoever other than a bit of "gentleman farming."

Lenning set up his Pickens County farming enterprise originally as a headquarters for his dairy and chicken farm, where he also intended to grow peaches. Shortly thereafter in 1880, he replaced his cabin with a two-story heart-pine frame building which, beneath an exterior of modern siding, is the same structure which still stands on the site today.

Taking advantage of each opportunity as it presented itself, Lenning also eventually designed his new structure to take in boarders and railroad travelers, as "side income." He added a restaurant early-on to accommodate his clientele.

Whether he had anticipated it or not, his "stand" – as the early inns were called in that day – was ideally located to take advantage of the traveling public.

In 1805, the Federal Road – extending from what today is Flowery Branch, Georgia (in present-day Hall County) to the Tennessee state line – had been surveyed and constructed by the fledgling state of Georgia, and passed right beside Lenning's inn, providing a steady stream of potential customers.

The native Cherokees had granted the U.S. government the right to construct the road across what at that time was Indian territory in north Georgia, and a number of their more opportunistic members had constructed taverns (inns) along this first real Georgia state highway. Edmund Lenning – whether accidentally or intentionally – also decided to take advantage of this opportunity.

The old road was still in use in the Pickens County area as recently as World War II. Even today, a portion of it – known as Chambers Street – is yet in use in Jasper where it passes beside the Woodbridge Inn.

As if that were not enough of an opportunity, in 1883, the Marietta and North Georgia Railroad being constructed into the north Georgia mountains arrived in Jasper, and the first depot (which burned in 1905) was built directly across from Lenning's property, providing him with still more customers seeking food and shelter from the elements. The depot replacing the one which had burned was located just slightly down the hill and to the right of the old bridge out front which crosses over the railroad and which ultimately became the calling card of the inn.

Aside from its ideal location, it has been the excellent food at this inn which attracted return-customers year after year, particularly the railroad passengers. Prior to the early 1960s, the Marietta & North Georgia Railroad (or the L&N Railroad, depending upon the time-frame), offered both passenger and freight service. Upon arrival in Jasper, travelers to that destination would automatically trudge up the hill for food and accommodations at the inn, and if these travelers didn't know about the inn in advance, the passenger car conductor on the train almost certainly would inform them.

During construction of the house, Lenning had built four main rooms and a central hallway on each floor. On the rear of the building (facing south onto Chambers Street), a kitchen was later added, giving the original building an "L" shape.

Most of the original building is constructed of hand-hewn beams and crudely-sawn boards. Only the elaborate front door (which is still in use today, although it was considered the "side door" in Lenning's day) demonstrated any extravagance whatsoever, with its beaded-cut wood in the frames.

Guests to this early inn over the years included jurors and lawyers (who regularly traveled to the county courthouse up the street during "court-week"), teachers, drummers (salesmen), governors, congressmen, and many others, most of whom were either traveling via the railroad or along the old Federal Road. By 1900, a visit by rail (and shortly thereafter in a new-fangled device called an automobile) to the scenic mountain community of Jasper had become a popular pastime, and the "Lenning House," as a result, developed into a popular tourism destination – probably more popular even than its namesake preferred, since he was so averse to "labor."

On July 16, 1919, Edmond E. Lenning passed away, leaving the Lenning House to his two widowed daughters.

Historic Woodbridge Inn in Jasper, Georgia, photographed in the 1990s. (Photo by Olin Jackson)

By the 1930s, the sisters had moved from Jasper and the building had all but been abandoned.

Edmond's son – James E. Lenning – finally purchased the property on February 4, 1937. He added eight rooms (four on each floor) to the rear of the building, including the large dining room. Bathrooms and electricity were also installed, windows replaced and the porch extended.

Although he was a disabled World War I veteran, Jim Lenning was blessed with an exuberant and welcoming personality, according to the late Jasper resident Ora Cox Little, his sister-in-law. "He could draw crowds simply by talking," she laughed in remembrance.

Jim's wife, Mary, operated what had become known by that point as the Lenning Hotel, and she continued to manage and maintain the business after Jim's death in 1942. In 1950, having no children, she bequeathed the hotel property to her sister – Ora – with the stipulation that the business be known thenceforth

as the "Jasper Hotel," since it no longer would belong to a Lenning.

Ora reportedly knew the old hotel well, just as she did all of the Lennings. She had operated a little telephone office next to the old wooden bridge across from the hotel. She and her sons had also helped out at the hotel after her sister had assumed ownership.

In 1970, state legal requirements for a hotel compelled Ora to return the "Jasper Hotel" to status as a boarding house. Her restaurant remained open for three meals a day, Monday through Friday, and all but the evening meal on Saturday and Sunday. A basic menu of meats and vegetables was offered at a cost of $1.50 (later $2.50) per meal.

"We regularly offered fried chicken, roast beef or ham; candied apples; brochelle; cream potatoes; English peas; asparagus; pear salad; and cake," she stated with a fond twinkle in her eyes. "Many a Sunday, our dining room was filled to capacity (200), and I have turned away as many as

300 on some Sundays," she stated proudly. "They'd come from Atlanta, Gainesville, Chattanooga and everywhere."

It was Ora Little who added the large picture windows in the dining room which today still offer the dramatic view of the mountains to the northeast. Her cooking was also renowned, earning her plaudits in the *Atlanta Journal Sunday Magazine* .

By 1971, however, after 21 years, the work had become too much for Ora, and she, in turn, decided to retire. Her sale of the inn began a rapid succession of owners thereafter, as well as a dramatic decline in the property. Each new proprietor took out proportionately larger loans to pay off what had been owed by the previous owner.

By this point, there were no boarders, and the restaurant was operated only sporadically. It finally became painfully obvious to all concerned that what once had been a vibrant, popular, and profitable inn and dining business had now fallen upon hard times.

Enter a new owner with true hospitality business acumen and a determined resolve to revitalize the old inn. On December 27, 1976, Jochem (Joe) and Brenda S. Rueffert began a new era for the aging inn/restaurant. They also began a dramatic face-lift of the sagging old structure, and its star slowly began to rise once again – slowly.

"I made them an offer I was sure they would refuse," the late Joe Rueffert remembered in an interview in the 1990s with pained amusement upon his face, "but they surprised me and accepted."

Even with the modest cost, Joe explains he and Brenda and their two children worked a hundred or a hundred and ten hours every week to keep the struggling business afloat, and it still lost money in the early days. "Brenda was the waitress and cashier. I was the sole cook, dish washer, repairman - whatever was needed," Joe laughed. "We eventually reached the point that we tried to give it away, but nobody would take it," he smiled in resignation.

As weeks turned into months and months into years, Joe and his family – over time – were thrilled that no one did take them up on their offer, because the business today reportedly is more popular than ever. Literally a gold mine.

Though there have been improvements to the original building over the years, the basic structure erected by Ed Lenning in the 1880s remains intact, and in addition to attracting curious inquiries, it continues to occasionally surprise the Ruefferts.

"When I tried to have a sprinkler system installed, the workmen found that the building was not built with the standard two-by-four construction," Joe explained. "Instead, they found oldtimey four-by-four beams made of solid oak - hard as rock today. The workmen literally were breaking all their drill-bits on the wood, and almost gave up on me."

The floor joists in the old building are just as unique. Lenning simply used half an oak tree for each joist, placing the entire foundation upon square pillars of marble. It is anything but standard construction today, but it's also rock-solid. Joe had to add a tunnel beneath the building in order to be able to maintain the plumbing for which Edmond Lenning never planned.

"Today, it's our home, and I'm most proud of the fact that it's a family-owned-and-operated business," Joe summed up at the time. "The fact that my children – Hans and Sonja – are a vital part of this operation is the most rewarding part of all to me."

It is the entrepreneurial spirit of individuals such as the Ruefferts that resurrected the town of Jasper in the 1980s and 1990s. Buildings all along the city's Main Street such as the Davis Building (circa 1880); the historic 1906 Pickens County brick jail (recently placed upon the National Register of Historic Places); the town's now-historic movie theater (circa 1920s and an abandoned relic in most small towns today); and numerous other structures, have been renovated and preserved.

Though the early years at the old inn were filled with seemingly insurmountable problems, Brenda and Joe ultimately were able to laugh about their youthful experiences. "When we bought it, it had this old imitation-brick tar-paper siding," Joe scowled "It was hardly insulated at all and the roof leaked terribly.

"On a rainy day, we'd put out pails to catch the water while we served what little customers we had," he continued. "I could not afford a plumber, so I learned how to repair pipes myself – sometimes in sub-zero weather."

The back-breaking labor of the Ruefferts however eventually paid handsome dividends. The couple and their two children – Hans and Sonja – converted the old inn into one of the most charming aspects of the entire community of Jasper.

Above and beyond the attractive grounds and accommodations, however, it is the cuisine which has attracted so much attention over recent years. "I instructed all of my employees," Joe continued with a flourish, "that if any dish whatsoever is questionable in quality or taste, it is to be thrown out. Questionable food which is eliminated, will more than pay for itself in satisfied customers who will return again and again."

As the **Bible** states, *"All things must pass,"* and so also did Jochem "Joe" Rueffert who passed away Friday, March 19, 2010 surrounded by friends and family. Joe had undergone several operations for kidney transplants over the years, and eventually, his tired body just gave out. He also had been pre-deceased by his daughter, Sonja. Joe had been born Jochem Rüffert in Frauenwaldau, Germany on July 15, 1940. One of four brothers born to homemaker Dora and veterinarian Werner Ruffert, Joe's childhood saw his family having to make many sacrifices during the post-World War II years.

So much of what Joe did to survive as a child shaped the man he ultimately became. He never wasted anything, from chicken bones to bent nails, Joe knew how to re-use and recycle way before it became a trend.

As a young adult in East Germany, Joe was assigned the duty of guarding the notorious Berlin Wall during his required military service. Instead, Joe decided to escape and come over the wall to the West. He dodged bullets and land mines to escape to his freedom. This rare story of bravery and determination was featured in many publications and television interviews, including one on CNN.

Once in the West, Joe attended hotel and catering school in the Bavarian city of Tegernsee. This experience granted him the opportunity to travel to work in the United States at O'Hare Airport in Chicago. Joe spoke no English when he first arrived, but said he learned the language, amazingly, by watching *The Three Stooges* daily on television.

Eventually, Joe ended up working in the South where he met a pretty Georgia girl named Brenda Sewell. Brenda and Joe married and began their family having Sonja in 1969 and Hans in 1972.

Today, the amazing Woodbridge Inn continues on (as of this writing in 2022) under the Rueffert banner.

The Mysterious and Terrible Whitestone Disaster Of 1938

One of the most devastating floods in Georgia history occurred in a little community in Pickens County called Whitestone, where record rainfall fell in an extraordinarily short period of time. The community of stone-working mills, gristmills, and sawmills which used retention dams suddenly became the site of a horrifying nightmare.

"Their screams were heard by people, who stood and watched them go, and saw the light in their house, as it swung to and fro."

From *The Whitestone Tragedy*
by Mrs. Mark Forrester

April 7, 1938, was one of those rare days when the weather moved from the back page to the front page of many newspapers in the nation. On the morning of April 8, the *Atlanta Constitution* reported that Georgia had been fortunate in suffering no serious weather-related damage. However, the *Constitution* is a morning paper, and at that time of day, no one had yet been able to reach an operating telephone to report the horrendous tragedy in what then was far-off Pickens County, Georgia.

In the previous 24 hours, savage storms had raged over half of the continental United States – from blizzards in Texas to destructive winds in Massachusetts. On the previous eerie night, tornados in Alabama killed eleven people while floods drowned another fifteen.

Floods in Rome, Georgia, had trapped 250 families who were later rescued; in Cornelia, Georgia, hen egg-sized hail had damaged homes and property; in Douglasville, Georgia, houses had been leveled by high winds; and at Fairmount, Georgia, eighteen of forty-two railroad cars loaded with coal had been de-railed by the rising waters of the Coosawattee River. Across the country, the Red Cross estimated 150 communities suffered significant damage, but none of this damage approached the level of that in Pickens.

On the Pickens-Gilmer County line, the marble mining mill community of Whitestone had a population of approximately 200 people in 1938. It was a quiet little backwoods town where people set out fish hooks to catch their dinner from Talona Creek, and where the night-life became exciting when a game of Rook commenced.

Deadly Location

Located in the Talona Valley and surrounded by high hills and mountains, Whitestone exists in an area resembling a giant soup bowl, a geographic characteristic which finally proved to be deadly on the night of April 7, 1938. This valley was the site of a number of stone-working mills, gristmills, sawmills, and the like, almost all of which were water-powered, making use of sizeable retention ponds to store and provide the water used to power the mills.

Many of the dams at these retention ponds were man-made, or at least "manually-improved" to raise the barriers on the lower "dam" ends of the ponds, in order to raise water levels in the ponds. Compounding this disastrous formula was the fact that up and down Talona Creek (which supplied the water for these ponds), mill workers and residents had constructed homes and businesses in the vicinity.

Under normal conditions, none of this would have been – and for many years had not been – a problem. The circumstances during this week of April, 1938, however, were anything but normal.

The Reverend Walter Payne lived at Whitestone, and in his memoirs, he wrote that the day began as any other overcast day. However, a heavy hail-storm and rain

Rain came down so heavy that it sounded like huge barrels of water were being emptied upon the roofs of the houses from the heavens above.

began at 4:00 p.m., followed by more thundershowers and *down*-pours from 6:00 p.m. to 8:00 p.m. Then the weather turned really bizarre.

The clouds at this point, according to reports, suddenly became unbelievably thick. Rain came down so heavy that it sounded like huge barrels of water were being emptied upon the roofs of the houses from the heavens above, and the sky became a continuous electrical storm, so bright, that one could almost read by the lightning.

The rainfall was so intense that Talona Creek quickly began rising and spilling over its banks, and suddenly, the whole valley simply began filling with water - just like a huge bowl being filled by a huge pitcher. A loud crash was witnessed by Rev. Payne and his family, an occurrence later identified as a series of simultaneous "cloud-bursts" on the hilltops around the valley. Rev. Payne later noted in his memoirs that he initially thought an entire mountainside had come crashing down.

The destruction was swift and devastating. Mill dams that had stood for almost a century began to collapse one by one throughout the valley. People awakening at home realized very quickly that their only hope to avoid the awesome power of the water from the horrendous rainfall and collapsing mill dams lay in a quick retreat to higher ground. However, they soon learned that any escape had been eliminated by the devastatingly-swift rise of the area waters.

One group which had been to a "singing" at Talking Rock School, literally was forced to quickly abandon the vehicles in which they were riding and swim for their lives as the surging waters rose frighteningly-swiftly above the vehicles, drowning out the engines. A number of these perished.

Will Ponder, a night watchman at the Willingham-Little Stone Company, was punching in his time card at 9:00 p.m. when he witnessed a tremendous cloud-burst on the mountain above and behind his house and the combined house/dry-goods grocery of Forrest Carter Conner. He instinctively sensed a disaster was eminent, and hurried to go warn the Conner family, but the window of opportunity for that effort had already been closed as well.

A Rescue Attempt

Will later explained that when he reached the Conner house on the banks of what was quickly becoming a very deadly Talona Creek, the waters were already far too dangerous to cross. On this particular night, Will's two young step-daughters were over-nighting with the Conners, spending their first evening away from home. Despite his repeated and desperate attempts to awaken them by yelling and throwing rocks at the windows, there was no response whatsoever from those inside.

Will next went to his own house, and brought back Howard Lindsey and C.W. Owensby. Despite the terrible dangers involved, the two boys bravely risked their lives to swim through the raging waters to a railroad boxcar on a siding between them and the Conner House. From there, in death-defying desperation, they literally had to then swim to the Conner porch, such was the rapid rise of the waters of Talona Creek. They immediately banged upon the door until the family was awakened.

With tension rising and the situation growing more perilous by the moment, the young children in the house began screaming. The water quickly even became knee-deep inside the Conner house, and panic began setting in.

In his later report of the tragedy, Will explained how he had desperately attempted – unsuccessfully – to throw a rope and chain to the porch of the home. At one point, he was pulled into the swirling waters dangerously close to the point of no return.

Meanwhile, upstream, the sudden cloud-bursts and rising waters began sweeping away property everywhere, including a substantial saw-milling operation. One by one, the retention dams in the ponds all failed. Logs from the sawmill quickly jammed into a narrow gap through which the creek normally passed, damming and obstructing it completely as debris collected between and among the logs, causing the water level to rise to a terrifying height.

As the awesome body of water rose in height, it suddenly rushed over an adjacent embankment, washing out a new channel and then unleashing the immense lake of water upon the valley. The resulting malevolent onslaught was horrifying to those who witnessed it first-hand, and in less than ten minutes the on-rushing wall of water – which initially was approximately six feet in height – had grown substantially higher, and had spread across the entire breadth of the valley.

Forrest Conner, his son James, and brother-in-law Carl Lindsey (Howard's brother) emerged onto the front porch of the Connor House with Howard and C.W. With total destruction now imminent, they, in abject desperation, were about to try to swim for the rope Will Ponder had thrown, when suddenly, the deadly wall of water from upstream broadsided the house.

"Whatever happens, it will happen to all of us."

The porch of the home, reportedly, was cleanly washed away. The house itself was quickly literally lifted off its concrete block foundation and swept down the valley, floating crazily upon the terrible waters.

Howard and C.W., amazingly, were somehow yet able to swim to the safety of a group of nearby railroad boxcars. Will Ponder found refuge in the nearby train station. Another person reportedly escaped by climbing the station flag pole.

Thrust Into Eternity

Forrest, James, and Carl however, had shared the fate of the rest of the family. Forrest Conner's last words above the roar of the waters were, "Whatever happens, it will happen to all of us."

Witnesses to the tragedy said that the house floated crazily away with its lanterns still visible through the windows and swinging wildly. Others reported that the screams of the children could be heard above the noise of the water, but Mr. B.L. Green who had retreated to high ground near the swelling maelstrom, later said that no sound whatsoever emanated from the ghostly structure as it rushed past him.

The house ultimately traveled a quarter of a mile before crashing into a group of trees and then breaking up into splinters and boards which disappeared into the swirling waters.

Later that night, almost as suddenly as it had begun, the raging storm ended, but it took longer for the water in the valley and the swollen creeks to subside. Rescue efforts began almost immediately, but in the dark, with mud and debris strewn all across the valley, little could be accomplished before daylight.

Howard and C.W., despite being injured, wet, and exhausted, were among the first to begin searching for survivors. The task of relaying the message of the need for emergency assistance proved to be just as difficult, since the roads had been washed away or were still submerged, and the steel bridges in the area had all collapsed.

Recovery of Bodies

As the bodies were located, they were carried by hand to ambulances at the nearest passable roads. When the news of the catastrophe did reach the media in the outside world, it was carried nationally, and thousands of people reportedly came to the little valley to offer help, including 150 Works Progress Administration (WPA) and Civilian Conservation Corps (CCC) personnel from Cartersville, Georgia.

All thirteen persons in the Conner House that night were drowned. Oleta Conner, age 6, and Claude Conner, age 8, were found at 6:00 a.m. the next day, a mile from where the house had stood. Their bodies were discovered across the creek and the railroad track, tangled in debris. Eugene Conner, age 1, was found shortly thereafter, a mile and a half from Whitestone. Forrest Conner, age 41, was found next, hanging grotesquely from the limbs of a tree where the wall of water had deposited him. In the afternoon of the same day, the bodies of Mildred Conner, age 11, and Mrs. Martha Conner, age 33, were also finally discovered.

On April 11, the CCC workers discovered Harold Bud Conner, age 9, in an old mill dam a mile and a half from Whitestone, and Flora Sue Conner, age 4, in a drift five miles from Whitestone. On April 15, at 9:00 a.m., the body of Carl Lindsey, age 21, was found wedged in a trestle approximately two miles from Whitestone. Thelma Abercrombie, age 9, was discovered shortly thereafter, buried in the mud a mile and a half from Whitestone. Her sister, Bonnie Abercrombie, age 4, was found next in a drift, and then James Conner, age 14.

Every possible effort was made to locate the final and still missing body - that of Forrest Conner, Jr., age 16 - in time for the family's mass funeral. The search, however, proved unsuccessful.

The other ten members of the Conner family laid in state at the Lawson and Poole Funeral Home prior to being taken for funeral services to the auditorium of the old Jasper Elementary School. A crowd estimated at 10,000 attended the funeral, and state troopers were necessary to assist with traffic (which numbered over 2,000 vehicles) in the tiny mountain community.

The coffins were carried to nearby Philadelphia Church for burial in a mass grave thirty-three feet in length. A photograph of the grave was featured in *Life* magazine. The funeral was a military funeral, and the burial a Masonic burial,

since Forrest Sr. had been both a World War I veteran and a Mason.

Thelma and Bonnie Abercrombie, Will Ponder's step-daughters, were buried at Mt. Pisgah Cemetery in nearby Gilmer County on the same day.

Final Mysteries

As for the body of Forrest Conner, Jr., it was Ed Chester, a local house painter in Talking Rock who ultimately solved the mystery of the location of this body. Ed explained that he had had a dream concerning the location of Conner.

With his friend – Zeb Haygood – Chester went to the site he envisioned in his dream. It was an extremely deep hole in Talona Creek. There, almost completely submerged beneath sand and gravel, searchers actually found the body. Young Forrest Conner, Jr. was buried beside the rest of his family that same day.

As a footnote and a final unsolved riddle in the tragedy, the heavy steel safe from Forrest Conner Sr.'s store was one of the many items tossed about by the terrible waters in the Whitestone flood. Whether the safe was ultimately buried beneath the sands in a deep recess in Talona Creek or was somehow whisked away by a resourceful looter, is unknown today. It is known, however, that since the day of the flood, the immensely heavy device has never been located.

The Mystery of How Talking Rock Was Named

For well over 150 years as of this writing (2023), residents and researchers alike have pondered the origin of the name of this town. Speculation continues.

The mystery concerning the origin of the name of the Pickens County community of "Talking Rock" is, at the very least, no nearer being solved than it was over a century and a half ago. Despite a great deal of research and study over the years, the source of the name continues to elude even the ablest historians.

This research problem is compounded by the fact that the tiny community at this site had a dual-identity in pioneer days. The resident Cherokees called it "Sanderstown" (after a prominent local Indian family). Following in-migration to the spot by White settlers in the 1830s, it, at some point, later earned the moniker "Talking Rock" – at the same time as the native Cherokees continued referral to it as Sanderstown. Both names appeared on early maps of the region for forty years as two distinctly separate communities – at the same site.

One of these "Talking Rocks" – presumably the Sanderstown version – is the present-day community of Blaine. The other was a small industrial village which was located where present-day Highway 136 crosses Talking Rock Creek. Confusing matters even further is the fact that the present-day incorporated town of Talking Rock is neither of the above-described sites, but rather a community that was created a few miles further east around the railroad station on the railroad which crept into the region in the early 1880s.

Despite its curiously-conflicted identity, the area to which the original White settlers referred as Talking Rock has a rich heritage. At Talking Rock Ford (site of the

The area to which the original White settlers referred as Talking Rock has a rich heritage.

330

present-day Highway 136 bridge), the now-historic Federal Road was surveyed in 1805 to give Georgia and Tennessee a highway through the Cherokee Nation. Unbeknownst to many today, numerous historic figures often passed down this roadway, including President James Monroe and Gen. Andrew Jackson to name a few.

Wealthy Cherokee head-man James Vann also used this route to and from his home at Spring Place near present-day Chatsworth in Murray County when traveling to his inn and ferry crossing in present-day Forsyth County at the Chattahoochee River. It was on this road that he paused at Buffington's Tavern near the present-day county line between Cherokee and Forsyth Counties when he was murdered and buried on a cold winter night in 1809. (*Readers please see Mystery & History in Georgia, Volume I*, "*The Mysterious Murder of Cherokee Chief James Vann.*")

The wealthy Cherokee Sanders family which once lived at Talking Rock allowed the American Board of Missions to establish the Carmel or Talona Mission there in 1819. The historic Mission building still stood until circa 1918, when it sadly was demolished – an unfortunate historic loss.

At Talking Rock (Ball Creek) Ford, George Corn Tassel murdered another Indian in 1829. In a political quandary of great import, the state of Georgia chose to "test" the legal latitude to which it deemed it was entitled by exercising authority over the Cherokee Nation, placing Corn Tassel on trial for his actions. Though perfectly legal according to Cherokee law, the murder Corn Tassel committed was a capital-felony in the state of Georgia for which the Cherokee was found guilty and hung at what today is the middle of a downtown street in Gainesville, GA.

This inability of the United States Supreme Court to stop the state of Georgia in the trial of Corn Tassel revealed just how impotent that branch of the federal government could be, especially in the early days of its existence. This glaring impotence subsequently heralded the end of almost any hope entertained by the resident Cherokees of remaining in their north Georgia homeland.

The one person who could have enforced this matter and set a legal precedent – Andrew Jackson – chose, as history has recorded, to turn a deaf ear. The fate of the Cherokee Nation in the eastern United States turned with Jackson's decision – or lack thereof.

At the site of nearby present-day Blaine Masonic Lodge, Fort Newnan – one of the stockades where the Cherokees were incarcerated prior to their relocation to the West on the now-infamous "Trail of Tears" in 1838 – once stood. No sign or remnant of this stockade exists today – only a fading memory.

In the late 1850s – also at Talking Rock

Unbeknownst to many today, numerous historic figures often passed down this roadway

Ford – English immigrant William C. Atherton, in partnership with his brothers James and Thomas, pioneered water-powered manufacturing in north Georgia. The ruins of the dam and the 1,000-foot raceway which he constructed to power his operations, are still visible today. The raceway was roughly fifteen feet wide and four feet high. It eventually powered a cotton factory, two cotton gins, a wool carder, a gristmill, a sawmill, and a blacksmith shop.

He will be rewarded for his efforts by an inscription on the opposite side reading: Now turn me back over you idiot, so I can fool someone else.

Nearer to modern Talking Rock was the community of Lebanon, where the only Presbyterian Church in Pickens County had existed until recent times. Here Pickens County's only Civil War battle was waged in 1864, when Union troopers of the 3rd Kentucky Cavalry defeated the local Confederate Home Guard, putting a temporary halt to the depredations being committed against the pro-Union families of the county.

By the late 1880s, the Athertons were gone, their manufacturing domain was in ruins, and the Lebanon Church had collapsed under the weight of snow from an unprecedented heavy snowstorm. The now-historic church cemetery still exists at this spot, and was in fact still being used as a depository until recent years.

The more modern community of Talking Rock which grew up around the local railroad station continued to prosper and, in fact, grew into a larger and wealthier community for a while than even the county seat of Jasper. Talking Rock eventually became an incorporated community in 1883.

This growth in Talking Rock was only temporary, however. With the development of better roads, automobiles, and the corresponding decline in the importance of the railroad, the town in recent times has declined to little more than a shadow of the prominence it once enjoyed. One needs only to witness the decayed and abandoned remains of the old hotel and other once-prominent buildings to understand the level to which the little community has been diminished.

It's not the history, however, which most intrigues local residents and visitors to the community today. It's the origin of the name of the nearby creek for which Talking Rock is believed by some to have gained its name.

Popular folklore in the area today maintains that there is a large boulder in the creek with an inscription which reads: *Turn me over.* And if some gullible newcomer is ever miraculously able to overturn the rock, he will be rewarded for his efforts by an inscription on the opposite side reading: *Now turn me back over you idiot, so I can fool someone else.*

Another popular explanation for

the name maintains that the creek is named for the local pastime of sitting in rocking chairs and talking with friends.

Finding a serious answer to the question of the origin of the name of Talking Rock Creek is more difficult. No petroglyphs (prehistoric engravings in local stones and boulders) have ever been found in the area. According to Indian historian James Mooney, famous for his *Myths of the Cherokees*, the Indians called the creek "Nunya-Gunwani'ski", which is believed to mean "rock that talks."

According to tradition, an old trader reportedly once told Mooney that the creek was named for a rock where the Cherokees held councils. Mooney didn't believe this story, but in modern times, the late Rev. Charles O. Walker of Jasper, GA, once located what appeared to be just such a site on Wild Cat Creek, a small tributary of Talking Rock Creek near the ford.

Also at the Talking Rock ford is "Ball Creek," an identity possibly assigned to the site by early pioneer trappers for Cherokee Indian ball games once played at the aforementioned council ground. Ball Ground in neighboring Cherokee County is named for yet another such ball field/council ground.

A.S. Furcron, editor of *The Georgia Mineral Society Newsletter*, believed that the name Talking Rock could have indicated the presence of an "echo rock," a natural reverberation created by cliffs, caves, and mountain coves in the vicinity.

On October 3, 1948, Furcron set out with friends Charles Wilkins, Sam Knox, Roy Chapman, and Charles Webb to find such an echo rock on Talking Rock Creek. They found what they were after near where the creek crosses the county line, although far better echoes were later discovered in the nearby cliffs of the Talona Valley near Whitestone.

Furcron believed that the name Talking Rock originally applied to the whole area, but eventually came to mean only the creek. A popular local speculation maintains that the *real* meaning of the Cherokee name for the creek was "babbling brook." Since the translation of Cherokee words and meanings into English has always been a "sticky wicket," this theory cannot be dismissed out of hand.

One last premise for the origin of the name, Talking Rock, might also be extended: In the collections of the Georgia Surveyor General Department, a *Map of North America,* showing portions of north Georgia and North and South Carolina is on file. This map was compiled around 1820, and identifies the present-day Talking Rock Creek as *"Rolling Stone Creek."*

Along Talking Rock Creek, at the Talking Rock Ford, there are sheer rock cliffs, and the danger of a falling boulder or rock striking a traveler moving down the pioneer trace – Federal Road – was very real. Perhaps the Cherokee name for the creek was actually only the Indians' equivalent of our present-day yellow road signs which read: *Watch for Falling Rocks.* Who knows???

The real meaning of the Cherokee name for the creek was "babbling brook."

The Alvin Gilmore Jordan Story:

A Polk County Resident And an "Old West" Connection

Samuel Jordan's family immigrated to America during its founding years, settling in the vicinity of what eventually became officially designated by the U.S. Postal Service as "Dutch Hill," a pioneer community in Perry Township, Clarion County, Pennsylvania. One of Samuel's descendants – Alvin Gilmore Jordan – obtained a job with the westward-expanding railroad and embarked upon an adventure which introduced him to one of the most famous families in American history.

The surname "Jordan" has its origin in many different places, most notably from Greek and Hebrew name associations with the Jordan River in Israel. It also was returned to Europe by the Crusaders in ancient times after their reverent remembrances of that historic body of water. Accordingly, the name eventually made its way to America via European colonization there.

Among the first recordings of this surname in England were those of John **Jorden** of Cambridge in 1202 and Walter **Jurdan** of Sussex in 1327. An even earlier branch of adventurers with this nomenclature came to Ireland with the "English invaders" in 1168, reportedly accompanying "Strongbow Earl" of Pembroke and ultimately acquiring lands there in payment for their loyalty to King John.

Interestingly, these "Irish" Jordans – in order to also "acquire" an acceptable (and believable) "Irish heritage" necessary for easier assimilation into the Irish population – hit upon the idea of actually changing their name to "**MacJordan**," a surname still in existence in Ireland today.

In Normandy, France, the name was initially recorded as "**Jordanus**," and eventually became associated with the nobleman's class in that country. For unknown reasons today, the Jordan moniker also eventually emerged as an identity associated with nobility in Italy. Still later, it became a more common name – as explained above – following introduction into Ireland, England, Germany, and Scotland, as well as numerous other locales.

In addition to these variables, the Jordan name eventually began appearing in various guises in the Spanish, Polish, and Hungarian languages. To say the least, though it is sometimes quantified as a somewhat rare name, the surname "Jordan" in actuality has "been around." The task therefore of determining the origin of one's particular branch of the Jordan ancestral pool can be quite tricky, not to mention frustrating. The research requires patience and determination.

It is unknown by this writer just when the father of *Samuel S. Jordan, Sr.* emigrated to America – or, from whence he originated – but the event undoubtedly occurred during the early days of colonial America, since it is a matter of record that Samuel S. Sr. was born in Huntingdon County, Pennsylvania, in 1797. Whether, in fact, his father was the original immigrant to the New World in this family line remains to be seen. Another possible source of entrance into the United States for this branch of the Jordans has been traced in more recent years to Virginia.

Samuel was married twice. His date of birth, as well as the names of his children with wife, *Susannah Truby*, are listed on a legal transaction with his second wife, *Elizabeth Silvers*, in property deeded to her. The union of Samuel and Susannah produced at least seven children, including *George Jordan*, who was born March 31, 1825 in Pennsylvania.

The Pennsylvania "Dutch"

For many years, some genealogists studying this "Pennsylvania-Dutch" branch of Jordans from the Samuel S. Jordan, Sr. family line have believed them to have immigrated to America by way of Holland – and this may even be accurate. Interestingly, the small Pennsylvania town in which most of the Jordans associated with Samuel S. Jordan, Sr. lived (and near which some still live today) in present-day Allegheny County even has an official United States Postal Service address of "Dutch Hill." This identity, however, could be a misnomer.

Beginning in the late 16th Century, Holland gained international dominance in the sea travel-trade industry. Many immigrants to the New World such as the Jordans therefore traveled to colonial America by way of Holland, fleeing as it were, religious persecution which was rampant upon those practicing the Protestant religion in France, Germany, England, Spain and Holland at that time. As such, these individuals fleeing to Holland for transport to the New World frequently became associated with Dutch nativity. Though understandable, this presumption of Dutch ancestry for all of these immigrants is not necessarily accurate.

In point of fact, most of the early "Pennsylvania Dutch" (including many still today) speak not "Dutch," but rather "German," just as do the Mennonites, the Amish, the Moravians, and any number of other similar cultural groups in this vicinity. They, therefore, must be presumed – and accurately so – to possibly be of German or Swiss origin instead of Dutch.

Due to their harsh persecution for their religious fervor, these very close-knit German cultural sects often chose to isolate themselves as much as possible in their new home, assuming in the process a somewhat unusual clannish identity. Ironically, though they sought only simple peace, survival and religious freedom, their clannish behavior earned them a certain amount of abuse even in their new home in America.

Jordan Family Lines in America by Country of Origin

Country	Numbers	Percent
Ireland	1,011	44
England	861	38
Germany	350	16
Scotland	55	2
Total	**2,277**	**100**

Part of the confusion regarding the origin or nativity of these "Pennsylvania Dutch" stems from the fact that they referred to themselves as "Deutsch," which is the German word for "German." English speaking Americans, hearing these Germans refer to themselves as "Deutsch," and knowing they traveled by way of Holland, therefore almost certainly misidentified many of them for generations as "Pennsylvania 'Dutch.'"

As such, if an appreciable number of the original settlers of "Dutch Hill," Pennsylvania, spoke German, this would obviously also lend strong credence to their German instead of "Dutch" nativity and the fact that the town's name had simply been corrupted originally by an otherwise unknowing populace.

Were the Jordans in the Samuel S. Jordan, Sr. family line also of German or Swiss heritage? Possibly. Possibly not. There were founding families in this "Dutch/Deutsch" community other than the Jordans, such as the Gravatts, who might also have been the actual connection with a German heritage. Further study is required before the nativity of the *Samuel S., Sr.* line of Jordans can be firmly established.

The late Goldie Evelyn Jordan of California (1890-1978) stated in correspondence that *"I have always supposed that my great-grandfather Samuel Jordan had come to western Pennsylvania (when that area was first being settled) from England, but (others) thought he had first come to Virginia."*

Samuel's son – *George Jordan* – who also hailed from Dutch Hill, Pennsylvania, was also married twice:

His first spouse was Catharine Horner (b. 03/31/1832 d. 03/12/1859) whom he married on October 18, 1849, at Dutch Hill, the marriage being performed by a "Rev. J. Walker." From this union came: Cassius Wallace (b. 05/02/1851), Alice Jane (b. 08/20/1855), Horace Wesley (b. 12/19/1857), and Harriet Ellen, whose recorded birthdate of 06/20/1859 in some records obviously conflicts with her presumed mother's death on 03/12/1859.

Interestingly, when Catharine died – possibly during childbirth with her final child on 03/12/1859 (also listed as 08/12/1859) – Horace, Alice, and Harriet (for reasons unknown today) went to live with relatives, instead of remaining with George. The *1860 Federal Census* shows them living with Andrew Horner, Sr. (Catharine's parents). It is known that some descendants of these children lived in North Carolina as recently as the 1970s. *(Per information from Essie Hudgins Jordan, wife of*

Mary Melinda "Linnie" Gravatt Jordan is pictured with daughter Goldie Evelyn Jordan in California. Linnie suffered from degenerative heart disease and the debilitating effects of intermittent angina and other maladies which dramatically lessened the quality of her life. The pinched, stern expression on her face in this photo bespeaks her suffering. Her cooperative daughter nevertheless is astonishingly beautiful, growing up to live a long and full life in California. (Photo from author's collection. All rights reserved.)

Guy Wilfred Jordan of Rockmart, Georgia. Some which Essie mentioned as being known are Laufer, Brady, and Hulda Jordan.)

George Jordan's second marriage was to **Barbara (Barbary) Ann Polard/Pollard Ferguson/Feurguson** on 10/20/1861) in Pennsylvania, a widow (b. 06/21/1830, Pennsylvania, d. 06/25/1901) with children by a previous marriage. Barbara/Barbary and George fathered at least one child – *Alvin Gilmore Jordan* – in Dutch Hill, PA on August 12, 1863, but several more "Jordan" children are listed in George's *Last Will*

& Testament. They all lived in the vicinity of Clarion County, PA most of their lives, with the exception of Alvin Gilmore.

Though Alvin had half-brothers and half-sisters by his father's first marriage, it is unknown today if he and they ever lived together or even in the same vicinity – or if they even knew each other. Descendants of Horace, Alice and Harriet Jordan quite possibly still reside in the North Carolina area even today.

Alvin & "Linnie" Marry

Almost from the outset, Alvin Gilmore was an obviously ambitious individual. By the time he and *Mary Melinda "Linnie" Gravatt* – who also was a native of the Dutch Hill vicinity (and also of possible French or Dutch or German extraction) – were married in 1887, Alvin was already gainfully employed by the Santa Fe Railroad and living in Omaha, Nebraska.

The route Alvin took to gain employment with the railroad is unknown today, as are many facets of his life, but he had to have been a part of the original westward-expansion of the rail industry. He had already been employed by the railroad for a number of years by the mid-1880s, residing in the growing rail center of Omaha. The original trans-continental railroad was not completed to California until 1869, so Alvin may indeed have gained his initial employment with that westward rail expansion.

Mary Melinda, curiously, was living in Lincoln, Nebraska, at the same time as Alvin's residence in Omaha. Yet another inexplicable detail of their back-story involves the explanation of how these two individuals, who were born in the same close-knit neighborhood in

The dusty and quiet 8th Street in downtown Colton was photographed circa 1890s. It was in the Colton environs that Alvin Jordan lived and worked on the Santa Fe Railroad which had a rail yard nearby. Son, Guy, and daughter, Goldie, attended school and grew to young adulthood in this community. It was also here that Wyatt, Virgil, Morgan, James, and Warren Earp lived and worked at bars and other enterprises at varying times, often traveling to and from the town by way of the Santa Fe Railroad.

Pennsylvania, would relocate – apparently independently of each other – to two quite separate cities in Nebraska, and then amazingly "find" each other for marriage.

A newspaper clipping announcing the couple's wedding appeared in the Lincoln, Nebraska, newspaper in 1887. It read as follows:

"Married, September 29, 1887, at the Christian parsonage by Elder J.B. Johnson, Mr. Alvin Gilmore Jordan and Miss Linnie Gravatt of this city. The wedding was a quiet one, only a few friends being present. The happy pair will make their home in Omaha, whither our best wishes accompany them."

Alvin Gilmore and Mary Melinda made yet another curious move too. Despite his assumed stable employment with the railroad at a time (circa

1888-1889) when such stable employment was fleeting, Alvin nevertheless left this job to return to the old Jordan home-place in Pennsylvania with Mary Melinda to live for a number of years. Was this move made to allow a pregnant Linnie to be near her parents in the birthing and early childhood of the couple's two children (a son, Guy Wilfred and a daughter, Goldie Evelyn)?

Or was this change of venue made in order to attend to aging parents who needed Alvin's and/or Linnie's assistance (George died in 1892; Barbara Ann died in 1901)? Or, was it made because Alvin had in fact lost his job with the railroad and therefore was without employment? We quite likely will never know the answers to these questions.

Whatever the reason, once the youngsters were up and growing, Alvin and Mary Melinda and family returned to the West where he took yet another job with the railroad – again, the Santa Fe – in sunny Colton, California, which was fast becoming one of the busiest "at-grade" railroad crossings in the United States, a circumstance that town still enjoys as of this writing in 2023. While we don't know the exact date of this relocation to the West, we do know that Alvin and his family appear on the *1910 Federal Census* of Colton, San Bernardino County, California, where his occupation is listed as *"carpenter, railroad."*

It is quite possible that Alvin and Linnie moved to Colton – a suburb of the town of San Bernardino a mile or two away – somewhat earlier. If Alvin's mother died in 1901, and they had no other reason to remain in the East, it would not be unreasonable to assume he and Linnie had returned to the West as early as 1902. If one examines the *Last Will & Testament* of Alvin's father, George, it is clear that Alvin, somewhat

surprisingly, was left no property by his father in Pennsylvania, so perhaps he merely had little incentive to remain back East.

At that time, much of the interior and exterior structures of the "rolling stock" (passenger and freight cars) were, to a large degree, constructed of wood, much of it very ornately built, especially in the passenger club cars. Alvin's skills at carpentry must have been considerable, judging from his long tenure with the railroad (well over 20 years). He apparently found steady employment at this profession.

Colton Crossing outside Colton was the site of one of the more notable "frog wars" in American railroad history. A frog war occurred when one private railroad company found itself in the circumstance of having to construct its rail line "across" the tracks of another major rail line, a situation which inevitably resulted in construction complications and hostilities between the two competing railroads.

Colton High School, pictured here in 1903, was the home of the Colton *"Yellow Jackets"* school sports teams. Guy Wilfred Jordan and Goldie Evelyn Jordan attended this school in their formative years.

He still had his whole life in front of him when this photo of Guy Jordan was snapped with the Colton High School basketball team where he was a senior classman in 1907. To put this in perspective time-wise, the final episode in the Indian Wars had occurred just over 15 years earlier with the Sioux at the infamous Battle of Wounded Knee in South Dakota.

Looking steadfastly at the camera from the third row, third person from the left, Guy W. Jordan was a stalwart on the Stanford University track and field team where, among other activities, he was a record-setting pole vaulter. (Photo courtesy of Stanford University)

In the summer of 1882 (just a few months following the famed gunfight behind the O.K. Corral in Tombstone, Arizona Territory), tensions reached their boiling point when construction of the tracks for the California Southern Railroad reached Colton, California. In an attempt to forcibly prevent the competing California Southern crews from completion of their line which intersected the tracks of the Southern Pacific (SP), a SP locomotive and gondola were parked on the tracks at the location of the planned crossing in order to deny access to Cal Southern. In addition, the SP, believing itself to have the upper hand legally, hired armed men, including the by-then well-known Virgil Earp of Tombstone fame, to guard the tracks. Competition for control of the major east-west routes of the rails was big and valuable business.

Before the growing potential for violence at the Colton crossing could get out of hand, Governor Robert Waterman ordered San Bernardino County Sheriff J.B. Burkhart to enforce a state court order for completion of Cal Southern's route. Waterman informed Earp of the court order, causing the former lawman to acquiesce and instruct the SP engineer to remove its locomotive where it was blocking the intersection. The crossing then was built, ending the Southern Pacific's monopoly in Southern California.

The Earps in Colton

Though Alvin and Linnie Jordan did not know it upon their arrival in the Colton environs, one of their neighboring families in that town was the famed Earps. At that time, however, the Earps were just another family associated with law enforcement in the West, but they

Wyatt Berry Stapp Earp was born 1848 and died in 1929. He and his brothers were involved in numerous business endeavors in the Colton, California vicinity. Wyatt, always the wanderer, later relocated to Idaho, Alaska, San Diego and other sites, always in search of adventure and an opportunity for income.

Nellie "Bessie" Bartlett Ketcham Earp was married to oldest brother James Earp. Bessie was an attractive female who had nevertheless lived a hard life, reflected in her no-nonsense uncompromising gaze. She is pictured here with the youngest Earp brother, Warren. Prior to (and quite probably even after) meeting James, Bessie was a prostitute which was not uncommon in those days in the West. She, died at the somewhat youthful age of 47 in January of 1887, in Colton, and was buried in San Bernardino's Pioneer Memorial Cemetery. Warren was so roundly disliked by virtually all his acquaintances that when he was murdered in 1900 in Willcox, Arizona, he was hastily buried in an unmarked grave and forgotten. The specific site of his grave today in Willcox is unknown.

would nevertheless later become one of the most famous in American history.

Did Alvin and/or Linnie personally know any member(s) of the Earp family? That circumstance cannot be positively confirmed or denied today, but in a town as small as Colton, California, (pop. 6,150 in 1900) it would be fair to say that Alvin Gilmore Jordan almost certainly at least knew of, and possibly interacted with, one or more members of the Earp family during his years of residence in that vicinity.

It would, in fact, have been difficult for Alvin to have avoided the Earps. He not only worked for the Santa Fe – a favored mode of transportation of the Earp family – he also invested in, repaired and renovated real estate in the

Colton/greater San Bernardino area, which put him in constant contact with the public, and quite possibly on occasion with various Earp family members as well.

Nicholas Earp and family had initially arrived in San Bernardino County, California, on December 17, 1864. They remained in the vicinity, living on a small farm for approximately four years until 1868 when they returned to their former home in Lamar, Missouri. The travels of the Earp family back and forth between California and Missouri were made via covered wagon, since there was no railroad or other mode of transportation from the eastern United States (or elsewhere) to California until 1869. These trips were made under extremely dangerous circumstances, since the western interior of the nation at that time was still an extremely wild and remote country largely controlled by hostile native Indians.

In 1877, the Earp patriarch and family returned to San Bernardino with youngest son **Warren** – who was twenty-three years of age at the time – in tow. Warren did not initially share the adventures of his older brothers, choosing instead to remain with his parents in California.

As a result of his very aggressive personality, the family referred to young Warren as "the tiger" in his early years. Unfortunately, this undesirable personality trait would gradually evolve into a bullying and very abusive treatment of almost everyone with whom he came into contact, particularly if Warren was under the influence of alcohol. It ultimately was largely responsible for ending his life prematurely.

According to the **San Bernardino Index** newspaper, *"Warren Earp of Colton, while intoxicated, entered the French restaurant on D Street and called for a supper. While his order was being prepared and before it was served, he became very noisy and tried to break the bottles in the caster. The night steward*

The Colton, California, cement production plant where a young Guy Jordan gained his first employment in the field of geology. He would go on to become Chief Chemist in the Southern States Portland Cement Plant in Rockmart, Georgia, in later years, where he unfortunately perished in a tragic industrial accident in 1946.

spoke to him politely and told him to keep quiet or else go out. At this Earp turned to and began to abuse the steward, raising up and striking him in the face at the same time. Earp struck the steward on the arm with a pickle jar, shattering the bottle and lacerating the waiter's arm and hand in a fearful manner. Officer Thomas was called in and placed Earp under arrest."

Over the course of the next nine years, Warren reportedly was involved in at least three major bar fights at sites in San Bernardino County which were recorded as news items. In one incident, he reportedly drew his sidearm and shot off the right thumb of his antagonist – a man named Jones. In another, he faced off against two Mexicans, waging war against them with a wooden club, reportedly seriously injuring one of the men.

All three participants in this wooden club melee were arrested, but as was often the case, father Nicholas was there to bail Warren out of jail that same night. That fatherly over-protection, it appears, was responsible to a great degree for Warren's dissent into unpredictable and unacceptable social behavior. He seldom, if ever, was required to suffer any consequences for his transgressions.

The other Earp siblings – *James*, *Virgil*, *Wyatt* and *Morgan* – had earlier departed from the family nest in San Bernardino to pursue various other occupational opportunities – usually in law enforcement, saloon operation, or mining – in neighboring states. Wyatt was even a buffalo hunter on the dangerous open western plains for one stretch of time.

In 1880, *Nicholas* and wife, *Virginia*, and *Warren* moved yet again, this time to nearby Colton where the elder Earp purchased a farm outside of town

Alvin Gilmore Jordan (standing) poses with his son, a young Guy Wilfred Jordan in San Bernardino, California, circa 1920.

which became the center of Earp operations for many years. He also purchased a saloon in Colton which he named the "Gem." Both Virgil and Warren managed this saloon for papa Nicholas for periods of time.

Since he had a legal background – having served earlier in Missouri as a judge – Nicholas was able to apply this knowledge to several occupations associated with the legal profession in the Colton and San Bernardino areas, including service as justice of the peace in Colton. As such, he interacted on a regular basis with the Colton populace for many years.

All of Nicholas's sons and their various wives lived on and off in Colton from the 1870s through the 1930s, until their deaths or migrations to other locales eliminated their existence in the Colton environs.

Early in the decade of the 1880s, James, Virgil, Wyatt and Morgan all migrated into lower Arizona Territory to

Though he is believed to have attended Stanford University in California on an academic scholarship, Guy Jordan also appears to have been talented as an athlete. He not only was an outstanding participant in track and field, but also in a number of other sports, including baseball. He stands, far right-rear, with the Stanford team, seemingly all business, almost with a swagger.

seek their fortunes in the gold and silver-mining mecca of what had come to be known as Tombstone. On October 26, 1881, Virgil, Wyatt, and Morgan were involved in the now-famous and epic gunfight behind the O.K. Corral in Tombstone, which resulted in three deaths. Their lives were never the same from that point forward.

Following the Tombstone incident and his later crippling wounds from an attempt on his life in that town on December 28 of 1881, **U.S. Deputy Marshal Virgil Earp** decided a change of venue was in order for himself, and moved from Tombstone to Colton where he took up residence with wife, Allie, at 528 West "H" Street for a number of years. This home still stands in Colton as of this writing (2023).

Despite his devastated left arm which hung useless by his side for the remainder of his life after he recovered from the assassination attempt, Virgil nevertheless was still effective as a law enforcement officer. He opened a detective agency in Colton, and in 1886 he was elected the town constable. When Colton was incorporated as a city, Virgil was elected as the first City Marshal on July 11, 1887. He was paid $75 a month and was re-elected to another term in 1888.

In later 1888, Virgil resigned as city marshal and he and Allie left Colton for nearby San Bernardino. Five years later, in 1893, he and Allie moved yet again to the short-lived mining town of Vanderbilt, California, where he owned and operated "Earp's Hall," a saloon, gambling hall, and meeting place used for public gatherings and even the town's weekly church services. His successes in the political arena in Vanderbilt, however, did not rise to the level of his business successes, since he lost the election for town constable in 1894.

In 1895, the San Bernardino City and County Directories carried the following listings: *San Bernardino Section: Earp, Warren – Capitalist. Earp, Virgil W. – Saloon Keeper. Colton Section: Earp, Nicholas P. – Book Agent.*

Final Days of the Earps

On March 18, 1882, in an attempt to eliminate what remained of the ever-vigilant and rigorous Earp law-enforcement cabal remaining in Tombstone, several members of the "Cow Boy" outlaw group assassinated *Morgan Earp* as he played billiards in Hatch's Saloon and narrowly missed placing a round in *Wyatt* as well as he sat watching the game.

Brother *James* and his wife, "*Bessie*," accompanied Morgan's body back to Colton where he was buried in that town's *Slover Mountain Cemetery*. When, five years later, quarrying operations encroached upon Morgan's remains in *Slover*, he was relocated to the nearby *Hermosa Garden Cemetery*.

Morgan's beautiful wife, *Louisa "Lou" Houston Earp* reportedly had actually separated from Morgan earlier and traveled to Colton to live after discovering he had been "carrying on" with another consort in the Tombstone area, so she never again saw him alive after leaving southern Arizona Territory. Louisa unfortunately also died prematurely herself in 1894 in Long Beach, California, at age 39. She was buried in *Evergreen Cemetery* in Los Angeles.

No doubt sensing his brothers' need for support in Tombstone following the rising tensions there, *Warren* had relocated from Colton to Arizona during this period for a short time, but just as in Colton, his trouble-prone ways continued to follow him as he was involved in incident after incident. He, nevertheless, teamed up there with brother Wyatt and his law enforcement associates to support them as the outlaw element became more determined in their efforts to eliminate the Earp faction.

In later 1882, after ridding the southern Arizona Territory of many of the outlaws residing there, Wyatt and Warren, accompanied by John Henry "Doc" Holliday, "Texas" Jack Vermillion, "Turkey Creek" Jack Johnson, and one or two others departed that vicinity, traveling to New Mexico, Colorado, Idaho, California, and other locales, continuing to search for adventure and sources of income, usually in gold or silver-mining towns.

The home once occupied by Virgil and Allie Earp at 528 West "H" Street in Colton, California, is pictured. Virgil lived here for a number of years while serving as marshal of Colton and engaging in other business endeavors. Though permanently crippled in his left arm and almost killed by an attempt on his life in Tombstone, Arizona Territory in December of 1881, he nevertheless recovered, and was still able to effectively serve in law enforcement for many years.

The San Bernardino - Santa Fe Railroad Depot was photographed in 1915. Alvin Gilmore Jordan was headquartered here in his capacity as a master carpenter with the Santa Fe for many years. This site was one of the busiest rail yards in the Southwest for many years.

The Santa Fe Railroad's "California Limited" was photographed at Cajon Summit. Cajon is the highest point in the rail line between the San Bernardino Mountains to the east and the San Gabriel Mountains to the west in Southern California. Alvin Gilmore Jordan would have been responsible for maintenance of the passenger cars in this train. In 1885 the California Southern Railroad opened the first usable and efficient transportation corridor through the region, which later became the Atchison, Topeka & Santa Fe's (AT&SF) main line.

Warren eventually returned to the Colton/San Bernardino environs to live a short while with brothers Virgil and James, and other members of his family, but he shortly tired of Colton – or else had worn-out his welcome there – and returned, surprisingly, to Arizona, where he was hired by a cattle business near Willcox. In one of the last photos taken of him, he is pictured (either in Tombstone or Colton) with James's wife, Bessie.

In 1900, *Warren*'s penchant for trouble finally caught up with him in a fatal manner, resulting in his shooting death in a saloon in Willcox following a drunken argument. He and range boss Johnny Boyette had engaged in numerous violent confrontations in recent months, and had both become extremely hostile to the opposite party. Finally, following threats of violent harm by Earp, Boyette reportedly drew his revolver without provocation, and simply shot Warren in cold blood, killing him instantly.

Just as he had been in Colton, San Bernardino, and Tombstone, the youngest Earp was so roundly disliked in Willcox that no law enforcement authorities ever even attempted to arrest Boyette, nor were any charges filed against him. Very little was ever even conducted in the way of any criminal investigation of the shooting, such was the apparent relief of the town officials at the youngest Earp's elimination.

Warren Earp reportedly was hastily buried in an unmarked grave in *Willcox Pioneer Cemetery*, no doubt to eliminate the possibility of a coroner's inquest to determine Boyette's guilt or innocence, since it was recorded by a number of sources that Warren was clearly unarmed at the time of the shooting. The exact site of his grave was never marked,

and though the cemetery in which his remains reside is known, the specific site of those remains is a complete mystery today. A similar fate had befallen Earp associate and renowned Old West figure John Henry "Doc" Holliday a few years earlier in Glenwood Springs, Colorado.

In 1901, *Virgil* and *Wyatt* attempted to open a gambling hall in Colton, but the town fathers voted down the enterprise, much to the two brothers' disappointment. The two continued nevertheless with other business endeavors in the Colton/San Bernardino area over the years, as well as in a number of other states and locales.

Guy Jordan was graduated from Stanford University in 1913 with a Bachelor of Science degree in Chemistry. He appears here in his U.S. Army uniform, serving in World War I, where he was a staff sergeant in Ordinance. He, somewhat surprisingly, appears considerably older than in his college photos of but a few years earlier.

The railroad roundhouse at Colton, California, circa 1912.

In 1905, *Virgil's* hard life finally caught up with him when, at age 62, he came down with and died from pneumonia. As an inveterate cigar-smoker, his tobacco affinity had not aided his attempt at recovery from the pneumococcal bacteria which had invaded his lungs. Since his first wife and child lived in Portland, Oregon, Virgil's body was shipped there by rail for burial in that city's *Riverview Cemetery*.

In February of 1907, *Nicholas Earp*, patriarch of the Earp family who had lived to the ripe old age of 94, finally passed away in Colton. As a veteran of the Black Hawk and Mexican American wars, Nicholas was entitled to free burial at a nearby military cemetery.

Nicholas's wife – *Virginia Anne Cooksey Earp* – died in San Bernardino and is buried in the *Pioneer Memorial Cemetery* in that town.

In January of 1926, *James Earp*, the oldest full brother (half-brother *Newton*

being the oldest) who had survived the U.S. Civil War, as well as the troubles in Tombstone, Arizona, where he had been a barkeeper, died quietly in San Bernardino at age 84. He was buried in that city's *Mountain View Cemetery*.

James's beautiful wife, *Nellie "Bessie" Bartlett Ketcham Earp* – just as with Morgan's Louisa – also had died prematurely in January of 1887, at the young age of 47. She was buried in San Bernardino's *Pioneer Memorial Cemetery* not far from her mother-in-law, Virginia Anne Cooksey Earp.

In 1929, despite all the many dangerous engagements and gunfights in his life which he had survived, *Wyatt Earp* finally was himself felled, but not by an outlaw's or assassin's bullet. Prostate cancer took the lawman just short of his 81st birthday in Los Angeles, California. During his life he had been a buffalo hunter, lawman, gambling table manager, saloon keeper, miner, boxing referee, gambler, and brothel keeper, to name a few of his occupations.

Wyatt's famous last words as he passed away were *"Suppose. Suppose."* The cryptic words were never explained. Wyatt was cremated and his ashes were interred in Colma, a suburb of San Francisco, California, in a Jewish cemetery where wife, *Josephine*, was later buried alongside him.

Virgil Earp's last wife – *Alvira "Allie" Packingham Sullivan Earp* – died in November of 1947. She had weathered all the tough years with the Earps, including the shoot-outs in Tombstone and elsewhere, outliving her husband by 42 years. She was one of the last original Earps in Colton, and was buried with a number of the other Earp family members in Colton's *Mountain View Cemetery*.

Alvin & Linnie in Colton

According to the *1920 Federal Census*, Alvin and Linnie Jordan were still living in Colton, where his profession was listed as *"carpenter foreman"* for the railroad. Alvin's talents in carpentry and wood-working for the railroad were well-established by this point. He eventually earned the designation of *"Master Carpenter"* before retiring from his railroad employment.

Alvin and Linnie's children – *Goldie Evelyn* and *Guy Wilfred* – spent the majority of their youth in Colton, attending the Colton schools while various members of the Earp family were active in that town. Guy was graduated from Colton Union High School in 1907. He continued his education at Stanford University where he was graduated with a Bachelor of Science degree in chemistry in 1913.

Guy no doubt was scholastically-inclined, because he almost certainly attended college on what must have been an academic scholarship, since his father's humble income undoubtedly would not have been enough to underwrite the expenses of board and tuition at a major college. Guy not only successfully completed his degree at Stanford, he also reportedly excelled there athletically in track & field sports (where he was very competitive in pole-vaulting) and on the school's baseball team.

During both high school and college, Guy was employed by both the Colton Portland Cement Company and the Calaveras Cement Company as the plant chemist. He also was later employed as plant chemist in a sugar refinery in Santa Domingo in Central America.

Guy's early professional endeavors no doubt became the basis for his later employment with the Portland Cement Company in Rockmart, Georgia, at which he was hired as Chief Chemist in 1919 following his military service in World War I.

Linnie's Death

By June 15, 1934, Alvin Gilmore Jordan's stationery listed his address as *415 North McClay Street, Santa Ana, CA*. On that date he wrote the following letter to Guy in Rockmart:

"Dear Guy:

"Your letter received last week which found your mother somewhat improved. (At this time, Mary Melinda Gravatt, Alvin's wife and Guy's mother, suffered from a continuous debilitating illness, primarily involving heart disease.) *She goes around the house pretty well, but does not go out. Only to the doctor. Goes in a taxi. She has not been down for quite a while until today. She has not been feeling quite as well and has lost her appetite.*

"Our home we had when we left San

Bernardino and which I sold to Mrs. Rebers (sp ?) and took 3 lots as a payment and a mortgage for $2,500.00 came back. The mortgage was due a year ago last February. She had lost all the money she had when the San Bernardino County Bank closed (This of course was during the height of the Great Depression) *and asked to have the mortgage renewed for 3 years longer. She said the taxes were paid to date.*

"We had so much sickness last fall and winter, I never got over to S.B. (San Bernardino) *to see about them* (the taxes on the house sold to Mrs. Rebers). *Did not think it necessary, but in May* (of 1934) *I wrote for a statement of the taxes and found they were not paid for 1932 or 1933, and the place was sold to the state*

for taxes in August of 1933. In fact, all of Mrs. Rebers' was. So I was up there last week trying to fix it up. It cost me about $155.00 (the equivalent of approximately $3,000.00 in 2023 dollars, which was a lot of money in 1934). *I still have the legal costs to pay when we get through with it. I don't know just what it will be. I did not like to take the house back as it is hard to rent, and rents are very low, and it is very hard for me to look after it, but it was the best thing I could do.*

"I guess Goldie (Goldie Evelyn Jordan, Alvin Gilmore's daughter and Guy

Photographed circa 1934 in the rear yard of their home at 215 Bluff Street in Rockmart, Georgia, Essie Hudgins Jordan (seated) admires newborn Patricia Carroll. Daughter Marilyn stands (left). This home, built prior to 1927, retained this appearance until circa 2004, when a substantial rear wing was added to the home by a new owner which concealed this portion of the rear yard.

Guy Wilfred Jordan returned to his home in California with his new family circa 1931. Pictured in his arms is daughter Marilyn.

Wilfred's sister) *is about the same. I have not seen her since about the 1ˢᵗ of March. She said she was coming home awhile after school was done, but I don't know when. It has been quite cool here all through June. Had nearly an inch of rain last week.*

"I have not been able to get away any place this spring except I go once a month to the hospital and was 2 days in San Bernardino last week. There are two bedrooms in the house up there that have to be renovated, but I think I can get it done without going up. I also have to get the house in Fullerton painted. (Alvin Gilmore, putting his carpentry skills to good use, apparently owned several homes which he used as rental properties in the general vicinity around Santa Ana where he was living in 1934.)

"We will be rather anxious about you and **Essie** (**Essie Hudgins Jordan**, wife to Guy) *next month, so write us as soon as all is over.* (Alvin apparently is referring to the impending birth of **Patricia Carroll Jordan**, Guy's second daughter, who was born in Rockmart, Georgia, on June 25, 1934, just ten days from the date of this letter.)

"Love to you all.

"Father and Mother"

On June 6, 1937, Alvin Gilmore Jordan, whose stationery lists his home address at this time as *"Route 1, Box 1721, Tujunga, California,"* forwarded the following sad letter to his son, Guy Wilfred Jordan of Rockmart:

"Dear Guy:

"Just a few words to let you know that we laid your mother to rest on Friday, June 9ᵗʰ (1937), *in the Fairhaven Mausoleum in Santa Ana.*

"She always suffered a lot during all her sickness, but nothing comparable with the suffering during her last illness. She scarcely rested more than one or two hours out of the 24 unless under the influence of opiates, *and the doctor we had nor Goldie were neither much in favor of them.*

"One day we called in another doctor. He gave her relief for five hours. The regular doctor only gave her the hypodermics four times, and with the exception of the first and last one, they had very little effect. The day she passed away, she went to sleep about 10:00 am and passed away about 4:55 pm without ever waking up.

"She was very anxious to go from the beginning because she suffered so. Her sickness first started with angina pectoris, and then edema of the lungs and kidneys. There was a Mrs. Pardick stayed here all night. She, Goldie and myself nursed her through it all. The doctor was here about every day and several times during the

Alvin Gilmore Jordan (r) poses with son, Guy Wilfred (holding daughter Marilyn) circa 1931 in California.

night. Everything possible was done, but to no avail. She was in her usual health when I came home, but took suddenly sick when partly through eating breakfast the 4th day after I arrived home, and kept getting a little worse and weaker until the end came.

"Goldie expects to keep house for me, and as far as I know now, we will remain here where we are. Goldie may write more particulars to you. This is about all I feel able to write at the present time.

"Love to all.

"Father"

Alvin's & Guy's Deaths

The letters above offer a glimpse into the life of Alvin Gilmore following the decline and eventual loss of his wife, Mary Melinda "Linnie" Gravatt Jordan. Though he owned what seemed to be at least one home and two rental properties, Alvin Gilmore appears nevertheless to be struggling to get by on a meager income, just like millions of other Americans during the *Great Depression*.

On one hand, it seems mildly unusual that Guy Jordan did not travel from Rockmart, Georgia, to be with his mother in her last days, but on the other, the circumstances during the *Depression* not only were extremely unpredictable, they were exceedingly dangerous for travelers – particularly those traveling long distances through isolated territory. For this and other reasons, Guy apparently was simply unable to travel back home to California for the death or funeral of his mother.

Even though he was the chief chemist at a cement production facility in Rockmart by that point, Guy, as explained above, was employed from the mid-1920s through 1946, a timespan roughly equivalent to one of the lowest-paying and unstable periods in modern American history. As a result, he certainly was not a wealthy man, a circumstance emphasized by the fact that wife-Essie was required to re-enter the employment world as a teacher following Guy's death.

Guy perhaps also felt the need to maintain constant control of his employment, since there were so many others in desperate straits seeking employment at virtually any payment rate. Regardless of the circumstances, his true worth lay not in the monetary world, but rather in the respect and admiration he enjoyed from his contemporaries, friends, and family.

In the September, 1946 weekly bulletin from the First Baptist Church in Rockmart, these sentiments were perhaps best expressed. It is unknown today who wrote these words, but they read as follows:

"There is no possible way for anyone on earth to measure or rightly value the work of our beloved Guy Jordan. The whole community knew him to be a man of God – unashamed, clean, upright in every respect. . . . None, save those who were closest to him knew the time and energy he spent freely and gladly caring for the things of Christ. When others were too busy and had 'more important' things to do, one could always count on Guy. He worked earnestly and seriously at the Master's business: Deacon, treasurer, Training Union Director. He performed untold numbers of thankless tasks without expecting anyone to cheer or applaud. . . . Would to God all men were so eager to serve and honor as well."

Shortly after the passing of both Guy and his father (who died January 31, 1947, just a few months after Guy), a close family friend – Hazel Dell Thompson of Los Angeles, California – wrote Goldie Evelyn Hill, the sole surviving member of the Jordan family. The letter

A rare early view of the Jordan home at 215 Bluff Street in Rockmart. This structure, built prior to 1927, still stands as of 2023. A rear wing was added circa 2004, and the front porch bannisters have been removed and replaced with a screened porch. Pictured in the right foreground is a "sandbox," once a common "distraction" for endless hours of children's play in the 1950s-1970s.

was composed almost exactly ten years after Alvin Gilmore had written the letter to his son, Guy, announcing the death of Mary Melinda. It reads as follows:

"My dear Goldie:

"Just a few lines to send you my blessing and very best wishes. It will always comfort you to know you were enabled to give your dear father the companionship and love that you and you alone could give. No one but just you could give him what he needed.

"I think toward the last he confused you a little with your darling mother. I kissed him goodbye at the hospital when we left him lying on the bed. Lillian also kissed him, and it seemed to make him

happy and peaceful. I do not think he suffered much. In fact, he tried to get up to see us to the door. It was necessary to coax him just a little to remain quietly in bed.

"Goldie my dear you have what many others lack – a good conscience – and something to look forward to with certainty in the future – a wonderful home with loved ones beyond all this uncertainty and strife. You may be sure that all is well with your dear ones, mother, father and brother Guy (Guy Jordan had been tragically killed in a terrible industrial accident at the Southern States Portland Cement Plant, Rockmart, Georgia, in 1946). All their needs will be supplied.

"The spirit world that lies all about

353

us is no delusion, but a certainty. Many while yet living in the physical body have explored it, though in a quite limited sense of course. I, with my own eyes and other senses have long lived in the consciousness of this inner world. Verily indeed, there is "no dead," and we who are still in the body are in truth the ones who are nearest dead. The very body – or bodies – in which our spirits are confined restrict us every which way we turn.

"So we, who have consciousness of a wonderful future ahead should of all people be the most happy. It seems a little hard at times for us who are seemingly left alone in this world, and yet, we know we are never alone, for round about us on every hand, angelic hands reach out to support us.

"Love and very best wishes always –

"Hazel Dell Thompson"

Interestingly, the Chairman of the California Portland Cement Company in Colton, California, wrote to Essie Hudgins Jordan (Guy Jordan's wife) on September 9, 1946, as follows:

"Dear Mrs. Jordan:

"Mr. Harry Kaiser who was in my office when you visited here recently was out of town last week. He returned today and I told him about Guy. He feels just as I do and he asked me to express his sincere sympathy to both you and your daughters. You will remember that Guy and Harry both worked here with me when they were boys.

"If you can think of anything that I can do, please let me know. With my continued sympathy to you and your daughters, I am

"Sincerely,

"Wilson C. Hanna"

Guy's Rockmart Abode

Following Guy Wilfred Jordan's tragic death in Rockmart in 1946, his wife Essie continued to live in the large aged home which Guy had purchased for the couple circa 1927 at 215 Bluff Street, Rockmart. Guy had remodeled an older home on the site which had partially burned years earlier. Today, if one ascends the stairs to the attic of this old home which is now well over 100 years old, the charred exposed rafters and timbers may still be viewed.

Guy and Essie's first daughter, Marilyn, was born in this home. Though three other daughters were born to the couple, two of them died shortly after birth.

Essie maintained residence in the old home for the remainder of her life, helping to rear many grandchildren born in the 1950s and '60s, and serving as a beloved high school biology and chemistry teacher at nearby Rockmart High School from the late 1920s through 1970. She ultimately passed away peacefully in her sleep at this Bluff Street residence in 1999, one month shy of her 99th birthday.

Many happy gatherings of the Jordan, Jackson and Bradley families for special occasions such as birthday celebrations, Thanksgiving dinners, New Year's Day meals, Christmas Eve and Day events and much more were held over the years at this home. The receptions for the weddings of both of Guy's daughters – Marilyn and Patricia – were held at this site. The countless experiences of the family at this site will long be remembered with strong affection by those who enjoyed them all those years ago.

(The late Guy W. and Essie Hudgins Jordan were the parents of the late Marilyn Jordan Jackson of Rockmart, Georgia, and the late Patricia Jordan Nixon (nee Bradley) of Doraville, Georgia. Many of the Jackson and Bradley children still reside in these areas as of this writing.)

Hightower Falls Mills
And a Legacy of Death

Remnants of this historic landmark – with a history dating to 1832 when the Cherokee Indians still resided in the area – have stood for over 190 years as of this writing in 2023. Despite some good productive years, this structure also has a dark history as well.

The sheer cliffs which rise abruptly from the floor of this lovely corner of Morgan Valley were ancient even when the dinosaurs roamed

Hightower Falls Mills were photographed circa 1905. Pictured (lower right) is the original gristmill constructed by John Wilson in 1832, which Elias Dorsey Hightower converted into a cotton gin. The three-story gristmill built by Hightower in 1850, is visible (upper left). On the first floor, millstones ground wheat and corn; on the second floor, wool carding equipment processed wool from sheep. The third floor was used for storage of wool. (Photo courtesy of Watson Dyer)

the earth. Over eons of time, the small stream has carved a notch into the wall as it tumbles some 60 or 80 feet to a pool at the foot of the precipice before meandering across fields to become Euharlee Creek. It is a peaceful site today – still known to local residents as Hightower Falls. The tranquility here, however, belies the spot's tragic legacy.

Today, the ruins of a pioneer gristmill and associated milling operations stand as silent sentinels, harbingers of the times when water-powered machinery dominated the landscape. Today, it is a peaceful and beautiful setting doing service as a back-drop for special events such as weddings. It, however, was not always such an idyllic location.

Beginnings

Elias Dorsey Hightower, traveling from Greene County, Georgia, arrived at the spot in 1846 when it was still a portion of Paulding County. He purchased a wooden gristmill which had

Photographed in the 1890s, this group of daring individuals is posed precariously on the cliff-side near the falls. Elias Dorsey Hightower constructed a substantial dam above the falls to increase the water-power, and a larger flume (visible, foreground) to carry the additional water to power his mill. (Photo courtesy of the GA Dept of Archives & History, Atlanta, GA)

been erected at the falls by John Wilson in 1832 – a time when Cherokee Indians still inhabited the area.

Hightower converted Wilson's mill into a working copy of Eli Whitney's cotton engine or "gin," to process the fluffy white crop which was swiftly transforming the South at that time into a huge agrarian-based society. Virtually every tillable field, hill, and valley was being planted in the crop, and cotton gins were becoming profitable enterprises.

About 50 feet up the mountainside, Hightower also built a three-story mill in 1850. He used local stone for building materials, and, no doubt, slave labor in the construction and later in the operation of the enterprise.

Due to the sheer size of the historic remnants at this site, one would surmise that the expansive milling operations which once existed here were successful enterprises at one time. On the first floor of Hightower's original building, mill stones ground wheat and corn. On the second floor, wool carding equipment

processed the wool from sheep raised on the property. The third floor was used for wool storage.[1]

About ten years after construction of the mill, operations there ceased as the U.S. Civil War engulfed the nation. Thomas Hightower, the son of Elias Dorsey Hightower and a key element of the milling operations, left his father's business to volunteer for service in the 21st Georgia Volunteers.

Thomas's wife, Lucelia Darden, had recently moved from Polk County to a spot east of Atlanta known as Powelton, to be with relatives for the birth of the couple's first-born. She, undoubtedly, was also eager to move out of the path of a juggernaut from the North known as Gen. William Tecumseh Sherman.

On the 7th of December, 1864, Thomas wrote to Lucelia from New Market, Virginia. His letter expressed concern for his father, stating, "He must be in a considerable fret (as a result of the war and the lack of raw materials and man-power at Hightower Mills)."[2]

War Reaches the Falls

As elements of the U.S. Civil War swept ever nearer to Hightower Falls, Elias Dorsey Hightower had definite cause for concern. Sherman had ordered his troops to destroy, without exception, all factories in Georgia, but he had surprisingly exempted "small flouring mills manifestly for local use." His troops, however, often failed to follow these orders, and many a small gristmill was burned to the ground as a result.

Elias Dorsey Hightower's mill and operations were likewise soon to be put to the test. Hightower had already endured much of the tortures of war. Two of his four eldest sons had enlisted at the start of the conflict. One had died of

Photographed circa 1907 are the barn and corn-crib at the Elias Dorsey Hightower home-place. Charles R. Carter is visible, center. Robert Bulloch is pictured, left. George Hart, a field hand is pictured, right.

wounds at White Sulfur Springs, Virginia (now West Virginia) early in 1863.

Elias undoubtedly was greatly concerned for the safety of his son Tom too. Sherman was progressing steadily down through the Dalton-Atlanta corridor in his notorious "March to the Sea," and in November of 1864, contingents of the right wing of his army under the command of Gen. McPherson razed much of Cedartown.[4]

In mid-November, Lee McCormack, a schoolteacher who lived with the Hightowers, brought the frightening news when he visited Tom Hightower in New Market, Virginia. On November 28th, Tom passed the news to his wife in Powelton.

"They burned everything in town that was not occupied," wrote Tom. "Court House, all the storehouses, grocers,

blacksmith shops and every house that there was no person living in. Burnt old Bill Peek's dwelling and all of his out houses. They take and kill everything as they go. Kill all the stock, ducks, chickens, etc., take all the provisions both for beast and man."[5]

One plantation a few miles west of Cedartown which was reported to have the largest holdings of slaves suffered indignities at the hands of one group of the marauding uncouth strangers which were becoming so prevalent in Sherman's wake. *"They went out to old Mrs. Battles' and tore open all her feather beds and poured them out in the middle of the floor, poured three sacks of salt on them and a sack of wheat bran and a jug of vinegar and stirred them all up together.*[6]

"From Cedartown they went to Van

357

Hightower Home (circa 1907) - Pictured are four members of the Carter family, descendants of Elias Hightower. The female far right is Martha Ann Carter, Elias' daughter and mother of the young Carter killed tragically at the mill. The photo appears to indicate that the family is hard at work replacing worn shingles on the roof.

Wert and it shared the same fate. He had three corps with him there. Two of them went the direct road to Van Wert and the other came on to Antioch. Camped at John Wright's." (Author's Note: The Wright house still stands today little more than a mile from the Hightower house.)

Thomas Hightower, however, was helpless to come to the aid of his family at Hightower Falls. As more detailed accounts began filtering in, he must have grown more worried with each passing day.

According to Hightower's great-grandson, Charles N. Carter, Union troops did visit the mill, and helped themselves to corn meal, baked corn bread, and even "killed one of Grandpa's pigs," to make supper. The hogs had been driven up into the hills beyond the

falls for protection, but one old sow apparently had wandered back down just as the Yankees arrived, and met its fate shortly thereafter.

Possibly mellowed from a full meal and a good night's sleep, the troops spared the Hightower home from the torch, and moved on. The Yankees subsequently departed Hightower Falls – amazingly without even destroying the mills – but not without a parting shot. Tom shared the incident with his wife:

"So the little old lady (his mother) told the Yankees what she thought of them! I guess they were taking some of her tricks (possessions) she did not want to see go off and it roused her. That is the way to treat them. Show them you aren't afraid of them."[8]

After The War

Following the war, the rebuilding process must have been slow and tedious as the lives of Polk County residents slowly returned to a semblance of normality. "Judge" Hightower (as he had become known), served in the Georgia General Assembly in 1873 and 1874.[9] In Cedartown, Elias Dorsey was a partner in the law firm of W.M. Phillips & Company.[10] Where he found the time for a law practice, public service as a state representative, and the owner/operator of Hightower Falls milling operations, is unknown today.

Business undoubtedly picked up at Hightower Falls too following the war. Aside from the cotton gin and wool-carding operations, Hightower also had a tannery, a sorghum syrup mill, honey bee hives and a plantation to manage.[11]

To feed the wool-carding machinery, Hightower imported hundreds of sheep as well as sheep herders from Wales. To house the shepherds, two cabins were constructed above the falls.[12]

Despite all his varied interests and professional endeavors, it appears that it was his grist-milling operation which occupied most of Elias Dorsey Hightower's time. He seemed to have been a student of the subject, visiting mills in North and South Carolina to advance his skills in the profession.

In the process, Hightower was able to improve his mill's power by raising the falls several feet with the addition of a dam at the top of the precipice. The increased power enabled him to install a larger water race with a new wheel reported to have been 18 feet in diameter and six feet across.[13]

The dam described above survived until the 1970s when it was washed

The home constructed in 1857 by A.H. Wood for Elias Dorsey Hightower still stands as of this writing (2023) at Hightower Falls.

out by torrential rains. The ensuing downpour also carried away the foundation remnants of the wooden building which had housed Hightower's cotton gin.

Hightower Homestead

When the Hightowers originally came to the Polk County area in 1846, they lived in a house at the end of what is known today as Hightower Falls Road quite near the mill. In 1857, A. H. Wood built a new home for Elias Hightower further down the road from the mill. According to the custom of that day, the house was built facing south, in order to allow the structure (and its front windows) to take full advantage of the sun's warming rays even on the coldest days of winter.

The old homestead where the Hightowers raised their eleven children stands unchanged today, except for the removal of the front porch. It was originally a large two story house with four rooms downstairs and four up.

All the rooms are 20 by 20 feet with 14-foot ceilings and 12-foot-wide halls on each floor. The back of the house was built exactly like the front with balconies over the double doors. The roof was built with native slate from nearby Rockmart where the specialized shingles were milled. There were also large fireplaces of handmade brick in all the rooms.[14]

There have only been six or seven owners of the Hightower house since it was built in 1857. The known owners are: Elias Dorsey Hightow-

er; his son-in-law E.C. Carter and his son E.R. Carter; I.L. Isbell whose wife is a great-granddaughter of the builder; Warren Gaffard who did extensive remodeling; and Ben Cochran.[15]

Tragedy Strikes

It was within this blissful existence in 1891, some 25 years after the horrors of the Civil War, that real tragedy struck the Hightower family.

At 11:00 a.m. on Saturday morning, September 12th, the cotton gin was in full operation as Elias Dorsey Carter, the first-born grandson, namesake, and apple of his grandfather's eye, was working in the gin. According to reports, a belt disconnected from one of the drive wheels and became entangled in part of the heavy ginning machinery, pulling it over upon young Elias. The heavy device was described as the gin in one newspaper account, and as a cotton press according to others.[16]

Whatever the circumstances, the victim, only 31 years of age and unmarried, suffered two broken thighs and a broken back. Fellow workers carried him to his grandfather's home where he reportedly suffered in agony. By 2:00 p.m. of the following day, he was dead, so his injuries undoubtedly were more severe than broken bones.

Ironically, Tom's death occurred on the 83rd birthday of the venerable family patriarch. The tragedy was a tremendous blow to Elias Dorsey Hightower. He reportedly lost his will to live from that day forward.

Shortly after the death of one son, Elias

The tragedy was a tremendous blow to Elias Dorsey Hightower.

Hightower's daughter, Martha Ann Hightower Carter, lost another son to epilepsy. Then her father...

On May 4th, 1892, after only a few months of grieving for his grandson, Elias Dorsey Hightower passed away himself. His obituary stated that he *"often spoke of his approaching end, saying that he was ready to go."*[17]

"He felt responsible for the death of his first-born grandson, because of that accident," recalled great-great-granddaughter Mrs. Debbie Carter Grogan, drawing upon family tradition. According to a relative's letter at the time, *"he had been aggrieved sick all year."*[18]

Elias Dorsey Hightower was laid to rest in the family plot near his beloved grandson, and next to his wife.

The exact effect of the above tragedies on the enterprises at Hightower Falls is unknown today. The various businesses such as the cotton gin, gristmill and tannery may simply have become victims of time as progress rendered them obsolete antiques.

Whatever the circumstances, all the once-vibrant enterprises at the falls gradually fell into disrepair and disappeared, one by one. Today, only the silent stone ruins of the old mills mark their former existence.

Life could be brutal for pioneer settlers and Civil War-era survivors. They, however, were a rugged lot. They had to be.

A relative in a letter reporting the three Hightower family deaths to her son in Texas observed stoically, *"They have had trouble."*[19]

(Grateful appreciation is hereby expressed to the late Gordon D. Sargent of Cedartown, who compiled the details for this article. The substantial assistance provided by Mrs. Debbie Carter Grogan, Mr. Charles Carter, Mr. Watson Dyer, and Mrs. Kay Morgan in the collection of information necessary for the production of this article is also gratefully acknowledged.)

Footnotes:

1/ National Society Of Daughters Of The American Revolution, Number 8 in a series.

2/ December 7, 1864, *Confederate Letters 1861-1865 of Thomas M. Hightower*, Microfilm Drawer 170, Box 13, Georgia Dept of Archives & History, Atlanta, GA.

3/ Thomson, M.T., "The Grist Mill In Georgia," *The Georgia Review*, Vol. 7 (3): 1-15 (1953).

4/ *PastTimes* "The 125th Anniversary of the Northwest Georgia Campaign," August 1989, p. 88, News Publishing Company, Rome, GA.

5/ *Confederate Letters*, Op. Cit., November 28, 1864.

6/ Ibid.

7/ Ibid.

8/ *Confederate Letters*, Op. Cit., January 13, 1865.

9/ *Journals of the House of Representatives*, Annual Session of the General Assembly, 1873 and 1874.

10/ *Polk County Ordinary Minutes*, Book C, p. 3, November 22, 1894, Office Of The Probate Judge, Cedartown.

11/ Jordan, Ralph, "Tales by Old Timer," *The Cedartown Standard*, no date.

12/ Ferguson, W. Nettles, September 18, 1969, p. 3-B, *The Rockmart Journal*.

13/ Jordan, Op. Cit.

14/ National Society of Daughters of the American Revolution, Number 8 in a series.

15/ Ibid.

16/ *The Cedartown Standard*, p. 4, col. 4, and p. 2, col. 4, September 17, 1891.

17/ *The Cedartown Standard*, p. 2, col. 5, May 12, 1892.

18/ Letter from Mrs. Joanna Carter to her son Thomas in Texas, dated May 9, 1892.

19/ Ibid.

Remembering The "Old Simpson Place"

The grist mills of yesteryear which once dotted the landscape across America from the eastern seaboard to the Mississippi River and beyond, once were an important aspect of community life. Early pioneers and later residents – right up to the mid-20th Century – required the mills to obtain cornmeal, flour, sawed lumber, and a variety of other necessities of life. A tiny social circle usually existed in the immediate vicinity of each of these mills. Polk County's "Old Simpson Place" is one example.

The aged home has been renovated untold times since it was originally built, but it is still recognizable today as a historic structure. A short distance away, the stone ruins of an old mill add even more historic flavor.

On the surface, this former early county enterprise appears much as any other property which was once an active farm, but it is the picturesque waterfall just a few hundred yards away in a crevice in the mountains that captures one's attention. "Simpson Creek" still provides the waterpower that once drove the millwheel of "Simpson Falls Mill," giving life to the little community. It was one of the earliest sites of enterprise in pioneer Paulding (present-day Polk) County.

The site exists only a few miles outside the small community of Rockmart, Georgia, just off Vinson Mountain Road. At this point, the last foothills of the Southern Appalachian Mountains descend gracefully to the flatland.

Verdant forests of hardwoods and cascading waterfalls in rushing streams which slow to a meander in the pastureland below, are a pleasant surprise to the occasional unsuspecting visitor to this spot today. Many would also be surprised to learn that it is actually a biological anomaly with its rhododendron, mountain laurel, granitic stone (instead of shale which predominates in Polk County), and trout-capable cool water quality.

The person or persons who controlled waterpower in the 1800s enjoyed extra status in a community, particularly in an area such as Paulding County where other waterpower opportunities were somewhat limited. Ownership of property of this nature meant a virtual monopoly in milling operations, and for a mill which was surrounded by rich creek-bottomlands supplying an abundance of grain crops such as corn, and orchards of apples, peaches, and apricots, the circumstances were ripe for a crossroads enterprise to develop. Such was the nature of the old Simpson place.

"And on a Sunday afternoon, that road out there was just full of buggies – not cars, mind you – buggies."

William Thomas Simpson [born in Paulding (later Polk) County on August 17, 1849; died at the Simpson homeplace on March 16, 1917] was the son of one of Paulding's pioneer settlers – Rev. William Wesley Simpson. "W.T." became the owner (exactly when or under what circumstances are unknown today, and the few records are sketchy) of this property circa 1875.

The identity of the original owner is also unknown, but the late Addie Randall – who was 92 years old at the time of this interview in 1989, and the granddaughter of William Thomas Simpson – said she knew. She stated without hesitation that relatives of the family had lived in the vicinity of the property since the days of the removal of the Cherokee Indians in the late 1830s, and the father of Rev. Simpson is believed to have lived in a log cabin on present-day Hutchings Mountain Road just a mile or two (as the crow flies) from Simpson Falls Mill.

With an animated personality and a physical agility that belied her years, Miss Randall painted a captivating picture of the site's characteristics from the late 1800s to the early 1900s on this hot August evening when she re-visited the site of her forebears for what proved to be the final time (Miss Randall passed away on October 17 of that year).

"I can remember an awful lot of things from the time I was about five years of age to the present," she explained to a group of attentive listeners gathered around her on this night.

"I remember the orchards the most," she continued. "They were everywhere, all down through the pastures back of the barn and up on the hill behind the house and up through the front pastures to the road (present-day Vinson Mountain Road)."

Despite renovations which have partially altered the home's appearance over the years, Miss Randall vividly recalled the layout of the original rambling two-story "salt-box" farmhouse. "When I was a child," she continued, "this house had the most beautiful white picket fence across the front of it. And it had a big porch across the front of the house too which wrapped around one side where it was enlarged around the well. And rockers – big rocking chairs – all along the porch," she said, her eyes lighting up as she remembered.

"And on a Sunday afternoon, that road out there was just full of buggies – not cars, mind you – buggies. My mother and father lived out in Morgan Valley *(a residential area a few miles to the west)*, and we'd ford all those creeks in our buggy to get here to Grandma's, because we weren't sure our car would make it."

It is not known for certain today, but it quite possibly was because of the existence of the gristmill on the property that two pioneer roads from the nearby community of Van Wert *(pioneer forerunner of present-day Rockmart)* at one time met on the Simpson property near the old home. Visitors to the mill came for a number of reasons in addition to the products supplied by the mill.

One of the pioneer roads – old Vinson Mountain Road – still follows much of its original path from town to the Simpson property, but was re-routed to provide better access over the mountain sometime in the early 1900s. The now-abandoned original trail through the woods and over the mountain can still be located by individuals familiar with its existence.

The other pioneer road – a narrow lane through the countryside – branched off from Hutchings Mountain Road *(crossing Simpson Creek at the spot occupied today by the bridge over Lake Doreen),* following the route of least resistance through the hollows and along the hillsides of what once comprised the old White plantation. This historic trail soon reached the Simpson property where one branch converged with old Vinson Mountain Road (near the old Simpson homestead), and the other branch traveled up Simpson Creek to Simpson Falls Mill.

But since it was located on his property, it would have been highly unusual for someone else to have owned it.

Though completely abandoned today, this early trail is still discernable just beyond the Lake Doreen bridge if one walks back through the poison ivy and rough scrub growth over the hills and then down through the pastureland on the other side of the mountains to the former Simpson property. This route reportedly was originally constructed with slave labor.

Today, no one knows for a certainty that Simpson Falls Mill was actually owned by W.T. Simpson, but since it was located on his property, it would have been highly unusual for someone else to have owned it. Though early property and/or deed records from this time-period do not exist today, the falls have carried the Simpson name since the county's extant pioneer records.

Over the years, numerous relics have been discovered at the site of Simpson Falls Mill. One of the more dramatic in recent times, was a portion of the old wooden millwheel which floated up from the bottom of a deep portion of Simpson Creek during a flood sometime in the 1970s. It is believed that at some point in time – possibly during the U.S. Civil War – the mill was burned and this remnant of the millwheel floated downstream before becoming lodged in the creek bottom.

It is the ruins of the grist mill which attract the most attention at the site today too. The mill's date of construction is unknown, but judging from the antiquity of the design of the stone foundations and the hand-forged iron nails which held together the upper wooden portion, it was almost certainly built prior to the 1860s.

Miss Randall soon informed us that it had been at least 70 to 75 years since she had been up to the site of the old mill. For that reason, we were somewhat eager to return her to the site in order, hopefully, to generate more memories. We all loaded up in a four-wheel-drive vehicle to reach the site which, at the time of this writing, existed at the end of a one-way road which was impassible in a regular two-wheel drive automobile.

Before we even reached the site, Addie's sharp memory was already recalling landmarks which she correctly described to us in detail. "We used to have lots of picnics on a big flat rock which sat out in the middle of the creek there below the falls," she said, with a distant look in her eyes. "It was a big picnic spot." *(Sure enough, as we reached the mill a short time later, the big flat rock, large enough to seat 10 or 15 people, was one of the first sites to greet us.)*

As we approached the half-way point on the trail up to the mill site, Miss Randall surprised us with one of several revelations on this day. "It was right about here that the tanner had his shop. He tanned leather and made leather goods," she beamed, matter-of-factly. "I think it was a two-room shop." *(Note: This author could remember in his youth the tanning pits still visible at this site which were pointed out to him by his father in the 1950s.)*

It had been previously known by only a handful of present-day area residents that a tannery had existed at this spot, and Miss Randall was not finished with her revelations either. She also described where a cobbler's shop had once

existed as well at the mill site. An ancient wooden shoe mold (known as a shoe "last") discovered above the ceiling of the old Simpson home when it was renovated in the 1960s may well be proof of the former existence of this shop.

"I can't believe all this is still here," Miss Randall remarked as we helped her out of the vehicle and over to the old mill's foundations. "This was such an active place when I was a child, and Grandma and Grandpa wouldn't allow us to come up here to the mill much."

When queried about the government-licensed liquor distillery which once operated at the site, Miss Randall replied in the affirmative. "I was always told that there was a distillery here too," she said, "but I never saw it, and I think it (the distillery) was not operating when I was a child. Grandma and Grandpa just wouldn't let us come up here," she explained, as she gazed around her at the ruins of the old structure.

In addition to his agricultural products, the shops and small enterprises at the mill site quite likely generated the income which allowed W.T. Simpson to become the prominent citizen of Van Wert / Rockmart indicated in the records of that day. He was active in the community of Van Wert, particularly as involved old Piedmont Institute which once existed in the vicinity of the old Rockmart High School building (present-day Rockmart City Hall and administrative offices).

"He apparently made plenty of money," Miss Randall continued, "because he had apples growing everywhere, and he never sold any of them. Just used what he needed and gave many of them away. And his apple houses in the cellar of this big house here and up on the hill behind it were filled completely in the autumn. They were constantly making cider in the cellar of this house," she said with a flourish.

It no doubt was the availability of this abundance of apple cider which was the source of a fair amount of acrimony in the Simpson household too. W.T. apparently had a "brewery" on the premises which he put to regular and good use. In a letter to her daughter *(Annie Simpson Waits, who lived in Mississippi)* dated September 16, 1909, Mrs. W.T. Simpson explains the actual extent of cider-making on the premises. *"Willie* (W.T.) *and Wiley* (their son) *have gone to town this morning to get some barrels for cider,"* she states. *"They have already made one hundred gallons, and will make more; there are so many apples on the ground."*

In another letter to her daughter dated December 21, 1907, Mrs. Simpson laments the upcoming Christmas season and the customary abuse of alcoholic beverages during this period. *"I do dread the Christmas holidays,"* she writes. *"I know there will be a great deal of drinking and rowdying in the country. Everybody will try to drink as much as they can, as it will go out of the state the first of January. I sure am glad it is going out, but some will get it, if possible, but it will not be so easy to get."*

Mrs. Simpson refers quite likely to attempts by prohibitionists of the area to eliminate the liquor traffic. Prior to national prohibition in 1919, the Anti-Saloon

League, a powerful evangelically-supported group was organized in 1893. It was maintained by funds its agents were permitted to collect at regular church services throughout the South and elsewhere.

With a budget that by 1903 had reached $400,000 per year, the power of the Anti-Saloon League was far-reaching. It made the issue "wet" or "dry" take precedence over nearly every other issue in state and local politics during the early 1900s.

Also during this time in the early 1900s, the state of Georgia, quite likely had initiated a statewide liquor prohibition. If this in fact was the case, a government-sponsored liquor distillery on the Simpson property at this time also quite likely was discontinued as of 1908. This would have reduced the enterprises at Simpson Falls to the tannery, the cobbler's shop, and the grist mill.

"The mill was run by a Mr. Ross McBride. Yes, that's it – 'Pink' McBride," Addie Randall continued. It was at this point that she surprised us with another revelation. "Mr. McBride lived in a house right across the little dirt road in front of grandma and grandpa's house," she stated emphatically.

Though some details involving the old mill had been known for years, the existence of a separate homesite on the property for the miller was indeed a revelation. It had previously been

It no doubt was the availability of this abundance of apple cider which was the source of a fair amount of acrimony in the Simpson household too.

assumed that he had lived in the mill itself. It, however, had also been previously known that "someone" had lived in a home which once existed across the road from the homestead, due to the existence of a large flat hearthstone from the structure's former fireplace which can still be seen if one knows where to look today.

"Mr. McBride later was the miller at Hightower Falls near my house in Morgan Valley," Addie added, "and he was replaced as miller here at Simpson Falls by a Mr. Carroll" *(yet another piece of the puzzle).*

W.T. Simpson apparently was a highly respected farmer and manager of the little domain at his farm for a number of years. From the distillery, the grist mill, the tannery, the cobbler's shop, and the corn, cotton, wheat and other crops from his 200 to 300 acres of rich bottomlands, he possibly enjoyed a comfortable income.

"Grandma and Grandpa always seemed to do well to me, as far as a child could tell of course," Addie smiled. "And I'll never forget that Grandma kept a big black purse under her bed that she always kept 'her' money in. She had two brothers who owned a lot of acreage in the Mississippi delta country at one time. After they died, she inherited it, and she received paychecks from the crops – I guess it was cotton and other things – that were grown there."

W.T. Simpson had married his wife – Eleanor Heslep – in 1875. It is not known, but is assumed that they moved into the big Simpson farmhouse shortly thereafter. "This house was already here when they married," Addie explained, her mind obviously ticking along like a new Swiss watch. "Grandpa bought the house from a Mr. Davis.

"I used to love the drive out here

so much," she continued, the memories now returning more freely from the recesses of her mind. "In the early days, we'd come in a black surrey. It didn't have any fringe on it," she added deprecatingly. "I always wanted fringe, but never got it.

"And when we got here, I remember the apples most of all. They were everywhere. Them and the chickens. Law, it seemed like everybody in the country had chickens. In later years, we'd drive out in, uh, what was that first car . . . I guess a 'Model A' Ford."

Addie went on to explain that the front left room of W.T. Simpson's house was originally the "parlour." "There was a big black piano in there. There were also mahogany settees. It was an amazing room. The ceiling had been painted by one of those itinerant painters they had then. He had painted a beautiful multi-colored medallion-like image on the ceiling," she said. *(It is suspected that this painting still exists above a new ceiling installed in the 1950s.)*

Numerous children and grandchildren of the Simpsons obviously enjoyed the big, yet cozy farmhouse and all its interesting qualities over the years. William Thomas Simpson had been married first to Harriet Phoebe Barber, daughter of Judge W.C. and Sarah Barber. Harriet died, leaving no children.

W.T. next married Eleanor Heslep, daughter of Judge David D. and Margaret Heslep. From this union were born four children: Margaret (who became Mrs. J. Watts Randall); Annie (who married John M. Waits); Cornelia (who became Mrs. Luther Whitfield); and Wiley (who married Jessie Cole).

From the union of Margaret and J. Watts Randall came: Addie, W.E., Annie Merle, J.W. Jr., Frank, Marjorie, and Mary Jo Jones.

From the union of Annie and John Waits came: Eleanor Cochran, John Marcus, and Hazel Sanders.

From the union of Cornelia and Luther Whitfield came: Luniel Peel, Harry, and Heslep.

And from the union of Wiley and Jessie Simpson came: Paul and Lois Bowman.

Above and beyond his enterprises at the Simpson farm, W.T. Simpson was also a member of the Board of Trustees of nearby Piedmont Institute, and was an active Methodist. The Institute was the pride of northwest Georgia, founded in 1890. Despite its best efforts, however, by 1912, the Institute was forced to close as a result of a large accumulation of debts. The fact that the cost for admission was so inexpensive, coupled with the extremely strenuous curriculum which discouraged all but the most talented students, proved to be its undoing.

In its 22 years of existence, the Institute had graduated some 94 students (with 16 more prospects waiting in the wings when the school closed in 1912). An average of roughly five students per year were graduated from its halls, and the income from such a limited student-body simply could not keep the Institute funded.

W. T. Simpson no doubt racked his brain to find a way to preserve the Institute, but in the end, he came up empty. His talents, undoubtedly lay in agriculture and business.

After approximately 30 to 35 years of farming, growing corn, cotton, wheat, apples and other crops, hard times apparently began to encroach upon the Simpsons as well. Interestingly, this was only a couple of years prior to the demise of the Institute, and may well have contributed to W.T.'s inability to resolve the Institute's problems.

In her letter of March 8, 1908, to her daughter Annie, Mrs. W.T. Simpson provides a glimpse of the farm's and community's decline: *"I went to town and paid off my debts,"* she says. *"My account at Ferguson's was $60.00, but I didn't pay him all the year before. I think everybody ought to buy as little as possible during these hard times... I had to let Willie have some money till he sells his cotton, and John thinks he will never get 15 cents (per ginned lint pound)."*

Though little is known about him today, W.T. Simpson quite likely lived much of his life in a vortex of communal emotions. His father – Rev. William Wesley Simpson – almost certainly was a devout prohibitionist, and has been described as one of the founders of nearby historic Van Wert Methodist Church from which famed evangelist Sam Jones – firebrand in opposition to alcoholic beverages – began his ministry. W.T. – in contrast – lived adjacent to (and almost certainly advocated the use of beverages from) the previously-described liquor distillery at Simpson Falls.

W.T. also quite likely made his own wines, etc., from his apples, and apparently suffered health-wise, possibly from stomach ailments, as is indicated in Mrs. Simpson's March 8, 1908 letter to her daughter Annie:

"We went in the buggy by Van Wert, and your Papa walked through the near way. He had one of his spells with his stomach, and didn't eat a bite of dinner. He came home and took some pills last night and is better this morning. I don't know what is the matter with him. He has spells when he hasn't been drinking at all."

The exact nature of W.T.'s health ailment is unknown today. It could have been a variety of things. Whatever the circumstances, W.T. finally succumbed to his maladies, passing away in 1917, while hoeing in his garden behind the house one afternoon.

"He just collapsed and died right there in the garden," Addie said. He had out-lived his beloved wife – Eleanor – by over eight years however.

"I'll never forget Grandma's death either," Addie added. "She died in the front bedroom *(front-right room as one faces the front door of the old home)* in January of 1909.

"For her funeral they had a black hearse and two black horses. Mr. Harry Ferguson did the funeral. There were no funeral homes back then. We rode in an automobile right behind the hearse, and those two horses were so slow on that old road going back to town through Van Wert. I'll never forget that." *(By this point in 1909, Van Wert, having been bypassed by the railroad, was a dying town. The adjacent new community of Rockmart, founded in the 1870s near the site of the new railroad, had come into prominence.)*

Some present-day residents believe that at some point shortly after the death of W.T. Simpson in 1917, the old mill at Simpson Falls burned to the ground. This is possible, and quite likely, since it is believed that the mill, its government-licensed distillery and other operations were still active up until W.T.'s death.

However, in 1865, a wing of Gen. William T. Sherman's Union Army traveling to Atlanta, burned Van Wert and nearby Cedartown during the U.S. Civil War. Simpson Falls Mill, with its production of wood products, corn meal, and other supplies, and coupled with the tannery at the site, would have made the mill difficult for Yankee firebrands to ignore, particularly since the route

they traveled toward Atlanta passed just a mile or so from the mill. It therefore could possibly have been burned during the war.

By 1917, with progress moving into the region, gristmills fell out of vogue (and need) with the advent of mass-produced commercially-processed corn meal, flour and other products. The mill at Simpson Falls therefore was never rebuilt, and the little crossroads enterprise faded and died.

Today, the beautiful waters of Simpson Creek still spill majestically over the rocky ledge at this site, and the noise from the cascading waters still excites the senses as one approaches the spot. Simpson Creek of course still flows from the mountain down to the bottomlands, and the old Simpson home-place recently received yet another facelift.

And even though W.T., his family, the gristmill and other infrastructure are long gone, the old Simpson home lives on.

The following information sources are acknowledged:

1/ ***A Short History Of American Democracy****,* John D. Hicks, George E. Mowry, 1956, pp. 602-603.

2/ *Interviews with Miss Addie Randall, August, 1989*

3/ *Interviews with Mary Ann Bennett*

4/ *Interview with Ralph Jackson, Jr.*

5/ *The* ***Rockmart Journal*** *newspaper*

6/ *Simpson family letters & records*

Ralph Olin Jackson Sr. Family In Polk County

Ralph Olin Jackson, Sr., never advanced beyond the 4ᵗʰ grade in school, but when it came to investments, "R.O." as he was known, was Phi Beta Kappa.

Ralph Olin Jackson, Sr., born on October 23, 1893, moved from Bartow County to Polk County in 1920, approximately 48 years after the town of Rockmart (1872) was founded. He was the son of William Anthony Jackson and Cornelia Fricks Jackson, and had already been a successful farmer even before moving to Polk County where he sought new opportunity.

Just prior to his move to Rockmart, Mr. Jackson had married Isabelle Neel, and he and his new bride traveled with the couple's possessions via six or seven mule-drawn wagons to a 300-acre farm Mr. Jackson had purchased on the highway between Rockmart and present-day Aragon, near the present-day entrance to a quarry.

Mr. Jackson initially raised cotton – with which he had been very successful in Bartow – in the rolling pastureland opposite his large home. However, following the onslaught of the boll weevil plague of the late 1920s and early 1930s, he converted his business into a dairy farm.

When Goodyear Mills opened a large facility in Rockmart in the 1930s, Mr. Jackson was able to obtain a contract to sell milk to the residents in the mill's associated mill village. He also sold his products to the residents of Rockmart and nearby Aragon.

The farm Mr. Jackson had purchased was not only a productive farm, but a historic tract of property as well. During the U.S. Civil War, a contingent of the troops of General William T. Sherman camped for a period of time on the property. In the years the property was owned by Mr. Jackson, a Union Army bayonet, as well as a bullet mold (both in the possession today of Mr. Jackson's grandson, Olin), were unearthed on a gentle prominence on the property. These relics had obviously been lost or forgotten by the

> *The farm was not only a productive farm, but a historic tract of property as well.*

troops who camped there in the 1860s.

Mr. Jackson had what was known as a "three-team farm" in its early days, keeping up to three teams of mules busy plowing, sowing, and harvesting the crops he grew. His laborious, but perceptive farming practices proved successful once again.

By 1943, assisted by a number of successful real estate investments and a limited but shrewd acumen for stock investments (He purchased shares of a product called "Coca-Cola" a few years before it found markets worldwide), Ralph was able to retire at the age of 50 and live on the income from his investments. He sold the Aragon Highway farm property to Southern States Portland Cement Company, then purchased a residence on Elm Street adjacent to the First Baptist Church in Rockmart.

At about this same time, Ralph also purchased - for taxes - a 700-acre farm south of Rockmart known as "the old Simpson place" at the foot of Vinson Mountain. This property - used by Mr. Jackson to raise beef cattle - also included a substantial residence, a large barn, historic Simpson waterfalls and the remains of Simpson Falls Gristmill, a pioneer-era water mill used to grind corn and other grains into flour. It is believed that a pre-Civil War government-licensed distillery as well as a tannery and a cobbler's shop, also once existed in the vicinity of the gristmill.

In 1947, Mr. Jackson built a substantial lake and lakeside cabin on this property. He and Isabelle used this residence

Ralph was able to retire at the age of 50 and live on the income from his investments.

during the summer months. As of this writing, this 700-acre tract of property is owned by Mr. Jackson's grandchildren, as well as several other private owners.

Ironically, though he never advanced any further than the 4th grade (in an 11-grade school system), Mr. Jackson was destined to become an active participant in the development of Rockmart's education system. He was a member of the Polk County Board of Education for twenty years, serving as chairman for more than a decade. He served on the board which initiated the first county-wide, nine-month school system, and was chairman when the board consolidated the school system, eliminating the tiny sub-standard classrooms which had been used for decades.

Mr. Jackson was also a charter member of both the Cedar Valley Farmers' Club and the Rockmart Rotary Club, serving as a director of the charter Rotary. He was a deacon of the First Baptist Church in Rockmart and instrumental in its development from the 1940s thru the 1960s.

Mr. and Mrs. Jackson became the parents of two girls, Mary Ann (1922) and Julia (1925), and a boy, Ralph, Jr. (1923). All three children ultimately were graduated from high school and college. Isabelle passed away in 1982. Mr. Jackson passed away in 1986, and their children have long since passed away as well. At this writing in 2023, most of the grandchildren had passed away as well.

The Mysterious and Amazing "Polk County Pot Plane"

On a rural wooded hillside in northwest Georgia's Polk County, one of the most unbelievable (and illegal) aircraft landings, coupled with one of the largest drug-smuggling endeavors in Georgia history, occurred on a hot August night in 1975.... and no one was even prosecuted!

As the rural residents of the somewhat isolated region of western Polk County, Georgia, turned in for bed on a hot and humid Sunday evening in August of 1975, they paid little if any attention to the roar, whine, and clank of heavy equipment in the Fullwood Springs area on "Treat Mountain" southwest of Cedartown. After all, it was not unusual for someone to use a grader after hours to open a road for pulp-wood harvesting operations the following day, or to level a tract of property for some other purpose. One FBI agent later explained the public disregard of the strange cacophony by stating "No one ever came by there except the postman. Why should they be concerned?"

What none of these residents realized, however, was that far from being a run-of-the-mill totally-innocuous "legal" work crew, these heavy equipment operators were actually heavy-duty drug smugglers who were literally grading a landing strip on the mountainside for the drop-off of one of the largest shipments of marijuana in Georgia state

history. It not only was a shocking attempt at smuggling a huge amount of the illicit weed, it also turned out to be an unbelievably-amazing landing of a huge DC-4 cargo plane at a site which would shock the aviation world.

Even more surprising, the entire operation was basically carried out by adolescents in their 20s, some of whom were college students. Even the daring aircraft pilot was but 27 years of age at the time, and none of the smugglers were ever successfully prosecuted despite being caught "red-handed" at their crime. Adding to the bizarre nature of this almost capricious crime is the fact that some reports of the incident maintain the landing strip for the huge aircraft in this incident was accidentally constructed *in the wrong state!*

Later investigations revealed that the ground crew had originally intended to construct the airstrip in Cleburne County, Alabama, because their research had revealed the law enforcement in that county to be only a sheriff and two deputies in an extremely-sparsely populated area. Had the landing been made there, it might well have been successful. The reason for their selection of a different construction site or how the pilot even knew how to find the new site are unknown today.

As the Treat Mountain airstrip was being prepared that summer evening beneath a moonless sky, several trucks intermittently turned west off Tallapoosa Road (Highway 100) onto what normally was a virtually-abandoned rough gravel road, their headlights slicing through the thick forest gloom. They were headed for the rough landing strip to pick up the marijuana to forward it to buyers who would then disperse it at other distribution points.

Due to the sparse settlement of this area, the men and their trucks – just as the airstrip grading crew – all went completely unnoticed in the early-going. The few residents in the vicinity had already turned in for the evening, and in those days, there certainly were no law enforcement officials patrolling this backwoods region.

Amazing Caper

By the evening of the scheduled landing of the smugglers on Treat Mountain, the airstrip contractors had been able to clear little more than 1,000 feet of rough runway. According to some reports, this exceedingly short airstrip came as a shock to the pilot of the large four-engine DC-4 aircraft which was to land at the site. Other reports maintain the pilot knew of and even approved the short strip in advance. Whatever the circumstances, rather than the approximate 12 football field-length strip required to safely land the sizeable DC-4, the strip on which the smuggling pilot actually landed was barely the length of 3 football fields. The fact that he was able to successfully "drop" into this small rough clearing at all without crashing still amazes aviation authorities even today.

Interestingly, the entire scheme – despite the numerous set-backs with which the smugglers ultimately were confronted – might nevertheless have been successful had it not been for two insignificant players – a lone truck driver who just happened to be in the right place at the wrong time, and a family who had not been able to get to sleep that evening and therefore also witnessed the plane landing.

Along toward midnight after the construction crew had accomplished what they could do in the time allotted to them, they next had to illuminate the airfield for a night landing. The men quickly installed a long string of electrical lights around the periphery of the strip and then connected the circuit to a gas-powered electric generator. One of the men then yanked on the generator's recoil starter, and as it chugged to life, the lights identifying the small raw earth strip suddenly blossomed out of the forest landscape.

At one end of the clearing, a flashlight bobbed and flickered as a lone smuggler shinnied to the top of a tall pine at the appointed hour. He was to be a guiding beacon for the pilot making this incredible landing. The flashlight he was holding was intended to mark the top of the trees at the end of the runway, in order to prevent the huge aircraft from crashing into the deadly pines.

Shortly after midnight, the droning DC-4 roared in low over the sparse farms in the vicinity. For the first time, the enterprise of the daring criminals began drawing attention. "Some citizens down near Esom Hill called in to the sheriff's office that night," explained Hoyt Dingler, a former detective with the Polk County Police Department who was assigned to the case. "They said that a plane had crashed; that it had

The large DC-4 cargo aircraft which, amazingly, landed successfully near the Fullwood Springs area in northwest Georgia's Polk County was photographed here several days after it was discovered by law enforcement authorities. (Photo courtesy of Dennis Holland)

almost hit their house; and that they saw it go down. That's when the police got involved."

Despite this alert to the authorities, the smugglers still enjoyed a sizeable advantage. The landing strip was securely-hidden in a deep forest in a very remote area, and there was virtually no way for law enforcement officials to find it even if they wanted to – which they desperately did at that point. After yet another witness – a lone truck driver who just happened to be traveling on the lonely Tallapoosa Road that night – also witnessed the dramatic landing of the DC-4 when it roared in over the strip, a search-and-rescue mission began in earnest.

The trucker had been driving along totally unconcerned until he received the shock of this life. The behemoth aircraft suddenly appeared barreling over

the tree-line as it passed directly over the truck driver and, from all indications, was just seconds from crashing. The stunned and shocked driver who almost "crashed and burned" himself in the traumatic event, immediately radioed the Haralson County Sheriff's Office to report the exact location of the aircraft.

A Very Close Call

The huge load of marijuana and hashish had come all the way from Columbia, South America. The smuggling activity represented an unprecedented attempt at using Polk County as a drop-site for the distribution of a major shipment of illicit drugs throughout the Georgia, Alabama, and Florida areas. This DC-4 was the largest aircraft ever to land in the county up to that point in time, and, without a doubt, to accomplish one of the most daring landings ever attempted in the Southeast.

In making his landing, the pilot had homed in upon the somewhat feeble runway lights, roaring in from the west and dropping to tree-top level. No doubt knowing that he wouldn't be able to circle for another attempt at landing should his first attempt go awry, the daring pilot dropped to tree-top level just prior to the end of the airstrip, then dropped even lower as he reached the beginning of the strip in order to use every inch possible of the tiny landing area.

The aircraft's landing lights no doubt horrifyingly illuminated the substantial pine tops and branches rising up a scant few feet below the craft's wings. As it passed over the trees, the craft's propellers were so close to the pines that they chopped double-arm loads of pine needles and new-growth limb tips as the pilot literally dropped onto the strip. Despite the fact that his landing gear also snagged pine branches as he maneuvered to land, he, amazingly, successfully guided the behemoth onto the strip and sat it down in the soft earth, coasting to an abrupt halt.

"The freshly-pushed up dirt in that clearing allowed the plane wheels to sink down and that's what saved it," Dingler added. "I guess 25 feet or more and the plane would have crashed into a ravine."

An admiring Georgia State Patrol chopper pilot later stated "He just locked it down and slid in all the way. He was either a whole lot of an amazing pilot or else a whole lot of "coo coo as coconuts.""

The smuggler who had been perched in the tree-top at the end of the runway had realized at the last minute that the plane was dropping too soon. He had desperately attempted to signal the pilot that he was approaching disaster, frantically waving his flashlight.

The pilot, nevertheless, had ignored the smuggler – knowing every inch of the raw strip was going to be precious – and had dropped right into the very tree in which the smuggler was perched.

"(He literally dove) out of the top of that tree," Dingler continued in describing the tree-top signaler. "He was so horrified, though, that he somehow wasn't physically injured too badly from the fall. . . . but he later told me 'I died up there in that tree.'" Just as with the huge aircraft, the soft earth of the landing strip cushioned the smuggler's fall, and he walked shakily away as the craft taxied to a stop.

Later investigations indicated the pilot astoundingly had landed the breath-taking aircraft in *only 350 feet of space*. The 93-foot giant with its 118-foot wingspan then had be abandoned on the airstrip, because there would be no getting it back into the air from that soft muddy strip that night. Despite its large size, the plane somehow remained undiscovered by law enforcement for the next 14 hours.

One of the arrested suspects speaking later with police stated that when the pilot emerged from the aircraft, he was ragingly furious with the construction crew for making the airstrip so short. Blind with anger, he had screamed at the men that not only could the shoddy workmanship have cost him his life, he was now going to have to abandon his aircraft in order to avoid capture.

As mentioned previously, however, other reports indicated the pilot was fully aware of the short strip, and – no doubt due to his inexperience – had approved the short strip length in advance.

Police Pursuit

Things, meanwhile, were beginning to heat up for the bandits regarding their pursuit by law enforcement officials. Since being witnessed by the local residents and then finally by the truck driver, the plane and its actual location were being narrowed down by law enforcement officials. They just couldn't seem to get to it due to the dense forest undergrowth.

While the surprised officers back at the county police headquarters were scurrying to answer the calls and pursue leads regarding the bizarre incident, the smugglers were hurriedly unloading their valuable cargo in order to make a getaway. Though they had done a reasonably good job at planning the airstrip and the landing of the plane, their actions from that point forward nevertheless resembled a comical Chinese fire-drill.

By this point, sheriff's deputies from Haralson and Polk counties were combing the backroads of the Fullwood Springs area. Shortly after midnight, the driver of one of the patrol cars stopped to examine some debris in the road. Before he and his partner could get back into their patrol car, a Chevrolet Blazer came swiftly around a curve and was only narrowly able to avert striking the two men, speeding away without stopping. The two officers radioed for help and minutes later, the Buchanan Police Department pulled the Blazer over, arresting the driver.

The police officers who had first encountered the Blazer naturally became even more suspicious of other vehicles on that particular road at that late hour. They next encountered a large U-Haul truck on a small secondary road and pulled it over. "We thought it was sort of strange meeting a U-Haul vehicle in that area a little after midnight," one official smiled.

The truck was muddy in appearance and was dragging a number of honeysuckle vines comically from its rear

bumper, indicating it had been driven in heavy undergrowth. "It looked just like a load of 'moonshine' headed for market," another official later added. "We thought it had been loadin' up from a 'still.'" The Fullwood Springs area shared a long reputation with nearby Esom Hill as a site for the production of considerable amounts of untaxed alcoholic beverages (i.e. "moonshine").

The lawmen – contingents of the Haralson County Sheriff's Department – had escorted the truck back to the county jail in Buchanan, reportedly to obtain what was known in police parlance as "a whiskey warrant" to authorize a search of the vehicle and its compartments for moonshine. They then reportedly searched the vehicle – without probable cause. This insignificant-seeming action would later come back to haunt the officers during subsequent stages of the arrests and investigations.

When the arresting officers opened the doors to the rear of the truck, they found, to their surprise, three men sitting sheepishly upon a large load of 60-pound bales in burlap, the contents of which turned out to be marijuana. Normally, this would have been quite a coup for the lawmen, but the now-substantial matter of illegal search and seizure would soon render it worthless.

After they had weighed the bales of illegal weed, the officers learned the truck was carrying 3,260 pounds of marijuana and 84 "bricks" of hashish, all with an estimated street value at that time of over $750,000.00 (the equivalent of approximately $4.3 million in 2023 dollars). Had they been successful in their getaway and then sold the illicit goods at market value, the five men charged with the crime might shortly have become exceedingly wealthy men for that day. As things turned out, however, they ultimately got away with little more than their freedom – and the knowledge they were participants in one of the most dramatic smuggling incidents ever attempted in the Southeast.

Meanwhile, in the fast-moving events unfolding back in the Fullwood Springs area, Detective Dingler was among the numerous law enforcement officials patrolling the area searching for a sign of the wrecked aircraft – but they continued to come up empty-handed. They could find nothing! No debris. No burning aircraft. Nothing.

The following morning, however, when daylight illuminated the northwest Georgia forestland, things changed considerably. The Georgia State Patrol brought in a helicopter to fly over the area – and what to their wondering eyes should appear, but a huge aircraft which somehow had been transported to a tiny clearing in the middle of a dense forest.

"A man by the name of Wilson Weaver was one of the people in the chopper," continued Dingler. "I was in a car on the ground in the area. In those choppers, you've got two buttons on the stick. One is for the intercom in the chopper, and the other is for the area law enforcement radio communications. Wilson got so excited when he saw that huge plane that instead of fingering the intercom button (to talk to his co-pilot), he instead pressed the radio button, exclaiming 'Geez, look at that big S.O.B.'

"Then he started yelling," Dingler laughed. "'There's a person running! We've found the plane!' he said. He could see me on the ground and was shouting 'Take a right! Take a left! There's a person running from it!'"

Illegal Search

The 30-year-old DC-4 on the side of a mountain in the backwoods of Polk

immediately became the talk of the county. Polk County had entered the pantheon of drug smuggling history on a big-time basis, and folks began flocking to the scene of the now-infamous crime. Polk County suddenly began getting a lot of ink in newspapers across the Southeast.

The men being held and charged with the crime included the driver of the *U-Haul* truck and his four accomplices. When the five men were searched, lawmen discovered keys for an Atlanta-area motel.

With their investigations indicating that the crime had wide-spread implications, law enforcement officials widened their dragnet for additional accomplices. Cobb County police promptly staked out the motel identified from the keys.

Their patience eventually paid off. They soon nabbed a suitcase full of money and additional amounts of marijuana, but here again, claims of illegal search and seizure by the attorneys of the defendants would later be used to render the evidence in the case useless. The lawmen, however, saw it differently.

"About the time we set up our surveillance, they (the suspects at the motel) got 'antsy' and took off," explained one of the Cobb County law enforcement officials. "When we stopped them, they were really amateurish. They immediately *consented* to a search... We found a small amount of marijuana and the money. They claimed they didn't have any idea where the $180,000.00 in the suitcase came from." But did the men actually *consent* to the search? That became the question of the day.

"The smugglers on the ground eventually were all rounded up and detained, but the pilot in the huge DC-4 was nowhere to be found. "There was quite a bit of paperwork in the plane,"

Dingler continued. "It had had some work done on it and the receipts were all in the plane, so it was reasonably easy to trace (the plane's owner)."

Aside from the eight men and the suitcase full of money in Cobb County, police also seized a blue pickup truck and a four-wheel-drive vehicle. Some of the law enforcement personnel speculated that the Atlanta men had been waiting at the motel to purchase a large amount of the marijuana from the five who had been captured earlier near the landing site. They also speculated that in addition to the captured marijuana, another two tons of the illegal weed had somehow completely disappeared. Did the pilot successfully escape with the missing pot in payment for his lost aircraft? That question remains unexplained to this day.

"One of the men that cooperated with us gave us a lot of information," Dingler continued. "He told us that it was mostly out West that they were flying in the stuff. He said they had *U-Haul* trucks (waiting at each site). The plane would fly in, throw the dope off, and then fly back out. Then they would put the dope on the trucks. They apparently had gotten away with it for a long time."

And then The Pilot

Despite all the arrests in the case, the pilot of the aircraft was never prosecuted for the Polk County incident (but then, neither ultimately were any of the other suspects). The pilot, however, was quickly becoming quite the folk hero for his daring miraculous midnight landing on the tiny hastily-constructed landing strip and his subsequent Houdini-like escape.

Back on Treat Mountain, a broad red band with the registration number "N67038" ran the length of the white

aircraft. This number led authorities to the owner – a Robert G. Eby of Ft. Lauderdale, Florida.

According to a published report in the August 7, 1975 issue of the *Atlanta Constitution*, Eby, a colorful and resourceful 27-year-old Navy veteran had purchased the DC-4 at a military auction at the notorious giant aircraft storage and "graveyard" facility in Tucson, Arizona, for $16,000.00, and had spent several months and at least $30,000.00 more overhauling it and obtaining his pilot's license.

The paper trail also led to recent activities of Eby at Boca Raton, Florida. According to the August 18, 1975 issue of the *Constitution*, Eby had been flying "touch and go" landings in Boca Raton for several weeks. Then the DC-4 had departed that airport and some twenty hours later was seen going down in Polk County.

According to a 2019 newspaper interview with Martin "Marty" Bert Raulins, one of the participants in the Polk smuggling incident, he had been introduced to Eby in the early 1970s. Raulins stated that after making the DC-4 airworthy, Eby had loaded it with gifts and a dune buggy (presumably to exchange for the illicit marijuana) and then piloted the craft to a clandestine airstrip in Colombia where he picked up the illicit weed destined for Georgia.

Raulins said the smugglers chose to create the strip on Treat Mountain in Polk County for the obvious reasons of the isolated location and the limited law enforcement personnel available to make pursuit if and when the crime was detected. And contrary to popular opinion and previous police reports, Raulins said the airstrip location wasn't altered at the last minute, nor was Eby – the pilot – unaware of the shortness (1,000 feet) of the strip. Raulins said Eby in fact had approved both prior to flying to the location to drop off the shipment of marijuana.

"Eby was forced to abandon the aircraft on Treat Mountain because it was mired too deeply in mud," Raulins added. The contractors apparently had been required to construct the airstrip so swiftly that there had been no time to compact the soil, and a heavy summer thundershower perhaps had further exacerbated the poor circumstances at the site unexpectedly.

"After he abandoned the DC-4, Eby and several others then took off in a separate vehicle with their portion of the 'pot' and 'hash,'" Raulins said. It is believed that Eby drove back to Florida from that point, perhaps recouping all or a portion of his losses for the abandoned plane via sales of the bales of marijuana with which he absconded.

His accomplice, however, wasn't as fortunate. "As I was driving away," Raulins added, "I drove past a police car on the side of the road." The officer, apparently suspicious of Raulins and the truck following close behind him, radioed ahead for them to be stopped and searched – just one of several instances which attorneys later used as *"illegal search and seizure"* leverage to free the men.

Two weeks after the momentous event, Robert Eby, the "suspected" pilot in the surprising landing, turned himself in to authorities in Polk County, since the plane involved in the crime was obviously registered in his name – a fact which normally would have been difficult to explain away (or so law enforcement investigators had presumed). Eby was accompanied by his attorney from Arizona. The lawyer, to the surprise of all involved, completely denied not only

that Eby owned the plane, but that he was the pilot on the night of the delivery despite the fact that registration records clearly did show he owned the plane, his fingerprints clearly were found in the plane, and he clearly had been seen flying it only a few days previous to the Polk incident. His position: "Prove I was there."

Furthermore, the attorney also stated that his client was an entrepreneur with many business interests, including that of the construction of a prototype patrol boat for use by the U.S. Coast Guard in the chase and capture of narcotics smugglers. Why would he be smuggling drugs himself?

Eby, however, was far from the innocent victim he and his attorney portrayed if one believed other news reports, according to Robert C. Hutchinson, former deputy special agent in charge with the U.S. Department of Homeland Security. "He was pending trial for the Polk County smuggling incident when he was arrested for yet another similar smuggling venture in Virginia," Hutchinson stated.

"Eby was also later arrested in 1976 in Clewiston, Florida, after being linked to an aircraft carrying marijuana in an incident there," Hutchinson added. "Law enforcement personnel had received information that a suspicious Douglas DC-3 had landed at Airglades Airport. When they responded, they discovered ten burlap bags of marijuana totaling approximately 287 pounds. This was Eby's third known arrest for air smuggling marijuana into the United States."

Despite the prevailing indications of Eby's guilt, barely a year after the arrests in the case in Polk County, all federal charges against the defendants were suddenly dropped, and the case was completely abandoned by Federal officials. It then fell to Polk County,

Georgia authorities to prosecute the men on state charges. This, however, ultimately never occurred either. The defendants were never brought to trial and the largest drug-bust case in Polk County history literally went "belly-up." So what happened?

According to Hoyt Dingler, there were several reasons the case against the men was foiled, including the above-mentioned lack of "probable cause" when the illegal searches of the men and their property in the *U-Haul* truck and elsewhere were made by law enforcement officials. Their arrest technique apparently was problematic as well. In other words, poor police work.

According to one of the defense attorneys in the case "Under the terms of the U.S. Constitution, a warrant cannot be issued under general terms. You can't arbitrarily search a house or a car just because you want to get in there and see if you can find some evidence. You've got to have 'probable cause.'"

And when the defendants appeared for the initial hearing on their case, they had brought an array of "big gun" attorneys with them to make certain this "probable cause" issue caused the charges against them to "go away." With such stumbling blocks in the prosecution's case, after Polk County District Attorney John Perrin had inherited the task of prosecuting the case on state charges, he decided it also was a fait accompli as well for the defendants.

The largest drug bust in the Polk County's history ultimately came to naught due essentially to "slick attorneys" and "questionable police work."

Despite the dismissals, state and federal authorities no doubt took some solace in the fact that they did retain the aircraft, cash, automobiles, and other personal property seized from the defendants in Polk County and in the Cobb County arrests. One cannot help but wonder why law enforcement officials could even take the men's property at that point if they were completely unable to charge them with a crime. And what happened to the plane??

"De Plane! De Plane!"

Back out in the Polk County piney woods, the huge stuck aircraft was still drawing considerably large crowds of curious lookey-looks but no one really knew what to do with the plane. People were coming from all around to view the novelty. One individual who admitted he had nothing better to do had driven all the way from Michigan to join the throngs visiting the huge craft parked on the mountainside.

Numerous suggestions were eventually made to resolve the problem of the plane which, after all, was stuck on the side of a mountain on private property and apparently now the possession of the federal government. One idea involved the dismantling of the aircraft and air-lifting it in sections by giant helicopters to a site where it would be reassembled and then flown once again. Another suggestion involved the attachment of "JATOs" (jet-assisted take-off) to the underside of the craft to get it out of the forest. The Federal Aviation Administration, however, soon advised that since the DC-4 was not designed for the use of JATOs, they could not approve that procedure.

Perhaps the trophy could be left in place and turned into some type of paying tourist attraction. There was even talk of converting it into some type of monument to marijuana smuggling, but the town fathers were not amused with that suggestion at all.

Federal authorities ultimately de-

The extremely rough condition of the airstrip which had been hastily carved out of the side of Treat Mountain is visible in this view of the DC-4. Experienced aircraft pilots were amazed the pilot of the large DC-4 was able to successfully land in such a confined space.

cided to simply sell the craft at public auction since the only registered owner of record – Robert Eby – denied being either the pilot or owner and no other owner could be located. If sold, the craft could then become someone else's problem.

And that's exactly what they did. When auctioned off, the DC-4 fetched a handsome $20,000.00, with federal officials of course retaining the funds. Now, what was the new owner going to do with the plane? Enter state representative Jim West from Jonesboro, Georgia.

The DC-4 had been trapped for three months in the isolated clearing when West made the winning $20,000.00 bid for the craft. Now, all he had to do was get the aging albatross off the mountain.

Interestingly, of all the players in this bizarre incident, Rep. West may well have been the most enterprising. Following the auction, he declared that he was going to fly his new acquisition off the mountain himself and even film a movie of the entire smuggling incident, using the huge plane as a "prop," literally. Topping things off, the audacious Eby even agreed to cooperate with West in the production of the movie, outrageously documenting the "landing" of the craft on Treat Mountain for use in the production.

Before any filming of the take-off could occur, the 1,000-foot airstrip had to be extended to 3,500 feet. The FAA was firm on the length requirement, but compromised on one aspect. The agency declared it would not block any take-off attempt, but would make the pilot responsible for the violation of any rules.

West proceeded to have the field lengthened, and by March of 1976, he was ready to make his move – and his movie. According to reports, like the great dare-devil Evel Knievel of yesteryear, West arrived very dramatically at "Treat Mountain Airport" with three camera crews, two pilots, and "some spark plugs in his pocket."

Once everything was ready, West, with his pilot and co-pilot at the ready, climbed into the plane and started the engines. After months of forced idleness, the 30-year-old cargo plane thundered to life and lumbered down the runway, lifting into the air seemingly effortlessly, sailing off into the wild blue yonder. Piece of cake.

West later stated that he subsequently sold the plane – no doubt for a tidy profit – "to a guy in Miami" (wink wink), stating that as far as he knows, it is still carrying "freight" someplace. He did not reveal the identity of the buyer.

In explanation of the details of his "movie," West said "Yeah, we did do a movie on it. We released it as *'In Hot Pursuit: The Polk County Pot Plane.'*" Though definitely comical and filmed in the *Smoky and the Bandit* genre, the low, low budget "movie" can still be viewed today on *YouTube* and is even mildly entertaining for the unsophisticated.

And As For Eby?

Pilot Robert G. Eby's destiny with infamy did not draw to a conclusion with the 1975 Polk County incident.

"On March 22, 1977, a Douglas DC-4 landed at the Hanover County (Virginia) Industrial Air Park transporting marijuana directly from Colombia," continued retired DHS special investigator Robert C. Hutchinson. "The arrival of the large four-engine aircraft at such a small rural air park immediately generated unwanted attention, and Robert G. Eby, Franklin M. Phillips, and "Dutch" Robbins were arrested at the airport…

"Co-defendants Eby and Phillips ultimately were convicted of possession of marijuana with intent to distribute, but these convictions were later overturned by the United States Supreme Court due to the relatively small number of women in the master jury pool," Hutchinson added. "The number was judged too small for a fair jury pool of their peers."

In their 1981 re-trial for this overturned conviction, Eby and Phillips shrewdly pleaded *Guilty* to conspiracy to smuggle marijuana and possession with the intent to distribute, hoping for a favorable pre-sentence report from the plea. Their strategy worked. In 1982, a circuit court judge suspended 50-year sentences for Eby and Phillips.

Eby's whereabouts as of 2023 is a mystery. If still alive, he would be 75 years of age – a little "long-in-tooth" for drug smuggling.

Jim Thurman who reportedly actually piloted the DC-4 off Treat Mountain for the *In Hot Pursuit. . .* movie, along with John Nuckolls, Marty Raulins, and Derry Ferris – all of whom were participants in the now infamous smuggling event – returned to Cedartown, Georgia, in 2021 as semi-celebrities to sign copies of author Jim Kitchens' 2020 book *Flying High* which documented the unusual incident.

Thus ended the amazing, strange, and mysterious saga of the "*Polk County Pot Plane.*" Today, the site once known as "Treat Mountain Airport" has been reclaimed by nature, and most newcomers to the area are blissfully unaware of the huge drug smuggling operation which once took place there in the summer of 1975. Area old-timers, however, still check twice these days when they hear earth-moving equipment being operated in the forests under cover of darkness.

Retracing the Former Route of the Blue Ridge Railroad

Planned as direct competition for the Central Railroad between Macon and Savannah, the Blue Ridge Railroad from Charleston was "side-tracked" by the U.S. Civil War and never re-started. Though it never reached fruition, the engineering marvel which was surveyed and partially-built through Rabun County, Georgia, utilized almost indestructible granite in its construction, and undoubtedly would still be in use today, had the line ever been completed.

A portion of an abandoned pre-Civil War-era railroad – much to the surprise of many today – still exists in northeast Georgia's Rabun County. Called the Blue Ridge Railroad (BRR), it was designed to extend from Charleston, South Carolina to Knoxville, Tennessee to enhance the commerce of the Charleston seaport in competition with the Savannah seaport in Georgia. But, just as occurred with many plans made prior to 1860, the BRR died aborning with the advent of the U.S. Civil War.

The Blue Ridge Railroad was originally conceived by fiery U.S. Senator and former vice president of the United States John C. Calhoun of South Carolina. He and the line's financiers promoted it tirelessly, but following Calhoun's death in 1850, a huge and important "political" element of the line entered the grave with him.

Calhoun had watched in frustration as development of the neighboring port of Savannah, Georgia, had threatened to siphon off the cotton product and prestige from the port of Charleston. The South Carolina Railroad connecting Hamburg, South Carolina to Charleston had been built in 1830 in a futile attempt to counter that competition, serving for a short while as a viable alternative for the massive shipments of Southern cotton which had begun flowing to the seaport of Savannah.

To counter the South Carolina Railroad, a group of Savannah officials obtained a state charter, and, by 1843, had constructed the Central Railroad 190 miles to Macon with a connection there to the Western & Atlantic Railroad (W&A) for transport of cotton and other products all the way from Chattanooga, Tennessee, with stops all along the route to Savannah gathering, among other things, the cotton "cash crop." This new railroad took on rapid growth, as did the Savannah rail yards and associated industry.

It is not difficult to imagine the competitive wrath this new railroad undoubtedly re-ignited in Senator Calhoun. This new competitive advantage in Georgia could not be allowed to continue. His counter-stroke had been the Blue Ridge Railroad.

Suffice it to say, that in the 1850s, residents of Georgia's Rabun County – through which the BRR had been surveyed and designed to pass – such as "Colonel" Henry T. Mozeley and James Bleckley were thrilled and captivated with the idea of this railroad and all it represented for the advancement of their mountain county. Mozeley was one of the incorporators in the Georgia Charter of 1838, while Bleckley was a director.

These same two gentlemen also obtained a charter for the Georgia Northeastern Railroad from Athens *"so as to strike the Blue Ridge Railroad at or near the town of Clayton,"* but that venture

Researcher Ruddy Ellis pauses at what has become known to hikers as "Observation Point" in Rabun County. Dick's Creek Falls are visible (right, foreground), as is the mighty Chattooga River (background). The Blue Ridge Railroad (BRR) bridge across the Chattooga, which was never completed, would have spanned the river just downstream from this site, and would have been 450 feet long and 100 feet high.

obviously never came to fruition either. However, interestingly enough, the portion of this railroad from "Rabun Gap Junction" (present-day Cornelia, Georgia) on into Rabun County later of course did become the fabled Tallulah Falls (TF) Railroad. The historic TF, however, was still a number of years into the future at that time.

Though advanced in years, Calhoun over in South Carolina maintained a steady determination to orient the route of the new Blue Ridge Railroad through Georgia's Rabun Gap and then down the Tennessee River, instead of acquiescing to the wishes of fellow South Carolina statesman Robert Y. Hayne, whose vision involved taking the line through the mountains near Asheville and down the French Broad River. Calhoun, of course, ultimately gained the upper hand in that contest, but his death in 1850 coupled with the war in 1860, ended any hope whatsoever for completion of the BRR which was abandoned and forgotten in the dark days of the 1870s in Georgia.

Hiking the old BRR

Today, the now-aged tunnel at Stumphouse Mountain in South Carolina, and the amazingly massive stone masonry works (which the Blue Ridge Railroad used instead of trestles) are some of the more visible reminders of this surprising relic from yesteryear. The builders of this line obviously intended for it to handle a significant amount of freight, and they were building it to last indefinitely.

In retrospect, it is almost shameful that the builders of the later Tallulah Falls Railroad – a tremendously-scenic route passing through Norman Rockwell-quality mountain towns – were not equally dedicated to such construction quality. The TF might still be in

Though the growth of large trees and downed timber obscure it today, the former grade (known in railroading parlance in sites such as this as a "cut") of the Blue Ridge Railroad can still be seen through the forest. (Photo by Ruddy Ellis)

operation today as a wonderful scenic tourist train had that been the case.

Despite the huge investment of time and money, the efforts of the BRR's builders toward this project ultimately were all for naught. Though records indicate it was 80% completed by 1859, the outbreak of the U.S. Civil War interrupted funding and the devastation and poverty of the South were so impactful that construction on the line was never re-commenced.

One massive tunnel (through Stumphouse Mountain) had been a particularly difficult obstacle. By the time other developers (after the war) got around to reconsidering renewed construction on the line, its usefulness had been eclipsed by other railroads and its day had passed.

The unfinished portion of the BRR begins in Walhalla, South Carolina. In the little community of West Union (a

suburb of Walhalla), an old siding for the BRR leads, as of this writing (2023), to the former site of a sawmill. This short stretch of rails had been the starting point for the aforementioned unfinished portion of the Blue Ridge line planned across northwestern South Carolina, northeast Georgia, western North Carolina, and on up to Knoxville.

At the time of its last inspection, this section of siding did not appear to have been used in quite a long while, as the rails were heavily coated with rust and debris, and the sawmill was closed. However, the rails in the first part of the siding were fairly heavy and there was evidence that this was originally one leg of a "wye" (a triangular arrangement of rails which once allowed the heavy steam locomotives to reverse direction in earlier days).

The first 300 feet of the siding at

The west portal for "Middle Tunnel" of the Blue Ridge has been almost hidden by soil which has collapsed over the tunnel entrance, but spelunkers and other "cave" explorers have retained an opening to the tunnel. The massive obstruction of Stumphouse Mountain and the unfinished tunnel through it, coupled with the onset of the U.S. Civil War, were the death-knell for the Blue Ridge Railroad. (Photo by Ruddy Ellis)

this site appear to have been laid on the original main line grade towards the mountains. There is evidence still of this grade across the road from the sawmill and on through a residential area. The former grade of the old BRR beyond this point has largely been erased by new construction.

Yet another section of the old grade which once existed down from the mountains and around a horseshoe curve is still partially visible. A substantially-long driveway leading to a home at this site exists almost exactly upon the original route of the old grade today.

If one searches a little further, he or she will also find a "cut" (a portion of the line where the original railroad bed required

Explorers of the old BRR often wish to visit the site of Stumphouse Mountain Tunnel.

excavation through high ground) to the north of this aforementioned home, as well as a "fill" (a portion of the railroad bed where low ground or a ford across a ditch or chasm must be "filled in") leading to a culvert site to the south.

When one returns to the paved road in this vicinity, he or she will discover a deep, apparently unfinished cut which stops at the driveway of the aforementioned home just before the paved road. Next to this cut are little signs marking the grade as an official Boy Scout hiking trail. It follows the old line all the way down from what today is known as Stumphouse Tunnel Park. Little evidence of the line south of that point exists today due to modern development in the area.

Stumphouse Mountain

Explorers of the old BRR often wish to visit the site of Stumphouse Mountain Tunnel. At the time of its attempted construction (in the 1850s) – if it had been completed – it would have been (at 5,863 feet) the longest railroad tunnel in the world (over one mile in length).

There are two shorter tunnels through smaller mountains leading up to Stumphouse Tunnel: "Saddle Tunnel," which is 616 feet long, and "Middle Tunnel," which is 385 feet long. The approaches to these tunnels have collapsed into the mouths of the tunnels, rendering them almost unrecognizable today.

Visitors to Stumphouse – who enter at their own risk – should wear rain gear and water-tight boots, and should also

Located on Warwoman Creek near Houck Road, the old mill pictured here was built by Samuel Beck, a captain in the Confederate Army during the U.S. Civil War. It is located in the general vicinity of the east bridge abutment of the Blue Ridge Railroad in Rabun. (Photo by Ruddy Ellis)

obviously carry flashlights. (The Walhalla Light and Electric Company has for some reason not gotten around to stringing exterior illumination into this tunnel.)

The completed portion of Stumphouse Mountain Tunnel measures some 1,600 feet. The interior dimensions of the tunnel are 16 feet wide and approximately 20 feet high.

Another characteristic of Stumphouse Mountain Tunnel (and the reason for the rain gear) is the continuous misting rainfall within its confines, which is a phenomenon in itself. Heavy moist air sinking down vertical airshafts bored from the top of the mountain, cools below the dew-point as it sinks, creating a steady rain inside the tunnel.

Even more interesting, the original tunnel drilling crews dug a total of four of these vertical air shafts from the top

of the mountain down to the interior of the tunnel. The shafts ranged from 161 to 228 feet deep, and enabled the work crews to dramatically increase their work pace. The shafts also provided vents for the wood-burning locomotives' smoke to be vented.

These "exhaust and breathing holes" were not completed without a heavy price. Several workers, according to reports, were killed in accidents. Some either fell into the shafts, plummeting the several hundred feet where they were dashed into the tunnel floor, or else died after being struck by objects falling through the shafts. One individual was scalded by steam from one of the engines used to hoist the buckets of "spoil" from the tunnel which was lifted through the exhaust holes to be discarded outside.

Visitors to this tunnel may also be interested in hiking the short distance

Pictured here is one of the many massive granite stream culverts built by the engineers of the Blue Ridge Railroad. This one was constructed to provide flow-thru for a stream alongside Sandy Ford Road just east of the second ford across Dick's Creek. The roadbed of the BRR passed over the top of this still-excellent culvert constructed over 150 years ago (as of 2023). (Photo by Ruddy Ellis)

over to beautiful Isaqueena Falls, where the ruins of the old Walhalla Water Works dam may be seen.

Middle Tunnel

Energetic hikers can next advance down the Blue Ridge grade to what was known as "Middle Tunnel," a shorter tunnel southeast of Stumphouse Mountain. Middle Tunnel is included in the aforementioned Boy Scout Trail which passes through breath-taking cuts and fills of the old line.

If one visits in spring, wildflowers are in abundance along the trail, including many beautiful "Jack-In-The-Pulpit" flowers. There, however, is also a lot of poison ivy in this vicinity, so hikers beware!

Additional exploration opportunities in this vicinity require a drive

around to a spot near the northwest end of Stumphouse Mountain Tunnel and its long approach cut. This site today is flooded by Crystal Lake. The portal of the tunnel is completely full of water, mud and debris, so that only the rock face above the portal is visible.

If one walks southeast from this portal along a dirt road which appears to run almost exactly above the tunnel, he or she will encounter a crater in the ground which is probably the remains of shaft #4. Approximately 1,200 feet from the portal the hiker will encounter several small piles of rock here and there in the woods, but no real evidence that a lot of digging once took place at this site.

Blue Ridge RR In Rabun

At Stekoa Creek north of Clayton, Georgia, both the plan for the Blue

The massive east abutment of the bridge which was to be completed over Warwoman Creek for the BRR is visible here through the undergrowth. This abutment was completed circa 1859, just prior to the U.S. Civil War which halted construction. (Photo by Ruddy Ellis)

Ridge Railroad and, ultimately, the actual route of the historic Tallulah Falls Railroad (TF) passed over this stream. One can only consider it ironic today that the TF – completed in 1907 from Cornelia, Georgia, to Franklin, North Carolina – succeeded in reaching Rabun County and the Blue Ridge Railroad did not.

The irony of the situation stems from the fact that the 58 miles of the TF included some 42 "wooden" trestles – all of which constantly required maintenance and repair, and constantly engendered danger for the trains and occupants. The trestles were a tremendously expensive proposition which ultimately aided in the demise of the little mountain short-line.

The Blue Ridge Railroad by comparison, whose failure was caused by the advent of the U.S. Civil War, was being built with solid stone culverts and earthen fills across chasms and streams, and was designed to have no wooden trestles whatsoever. Had it been completed, it might very easily still be operational today.

In crossing Stekoa Creek in the 1890s, the TF built a trestle some 30 feet high. A good 50 years earlier, the Blue Ridge had built stone walls on both sides of the creek about 100 feet long. The Blue Ridge Railroad only planned to build bridges over the largest of the creeks such as Stekoa – a circumstance which therefore required the stone walls on either side of the creek.

For any smaller streams, the BRR planned to construct stone culverts covered by massive earthen fills. Amazingly, all of the stone culverts had to be built by hand using only animal-drawn carts! A number of these completed culverts

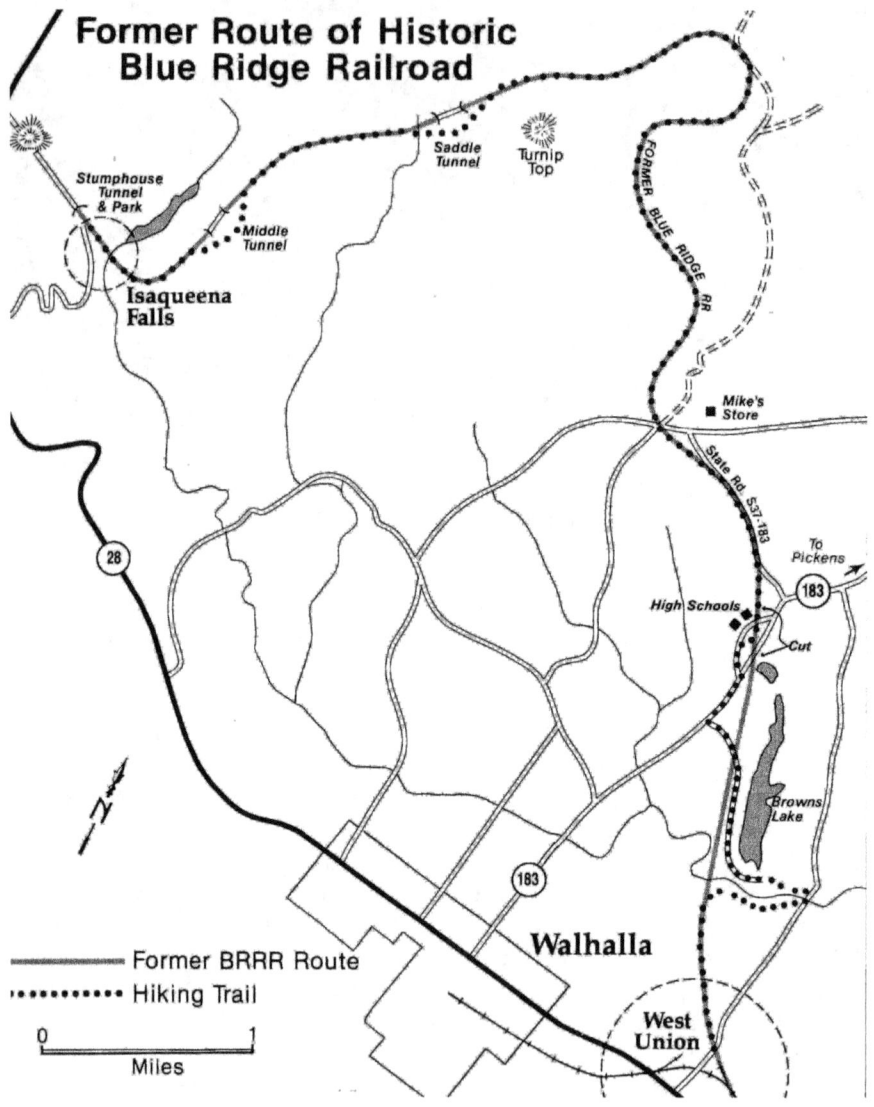

**Former Route of Historic
Blue Ridge Railroad**

Stumphouse
Tunnel
& Park

Saddle
Tunnel

Turnip
Top

Middle
Tunnel

Isaqueena
Falls

FORMER BLUE RIDGE RR

Mike's
Store

State Rd. 537-183

28

To
Pickens

183

High Schools

Cut

Browns
Lake

183

Walhalla

━━━━━━ Former BRRR Route
•••••••••• Hiking Trail

0   1
Miles

West
Union

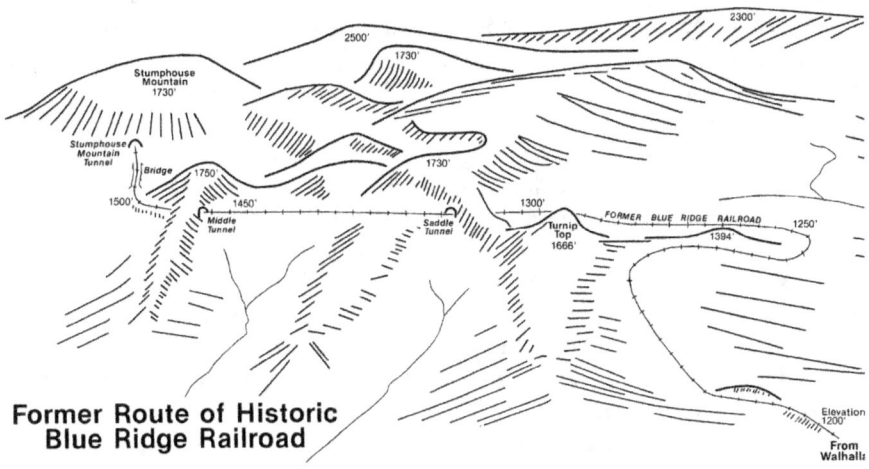

**Former Route of Historic
Blue Ridge Railroad**

may still be seen today, all built of large rectangular stone blocks set without any mortar. This type of fine craftsmanship was standard procedure in the first-class engineering involved in the construction of the Blue Ridge line – sadly, all wasted.

Up at Warwoman Road at Saddle Gap, rail enthusiasts may look down upon the eastern approach cut to Warwoman Tunnel on the BRR. Grades and culverts constructed for the line extend almost as far as the Chattooga River.

A long-standing legend in this vicinity maintains that in the late 1850s, some 41 immigrant Italian laborers were buried in a cave-in inside Warwoman Tunnel. According to the legend, the bodies were left there since work on the project had ceased at about that same time.

More BRR In Rabun

If one drives down Sandy Ford Road (off Warwoman Road), the massive 94-foot-long stone culvert of the Blue Ridge represents the last known remnant of the line in Rabun County.

If one is searching for the spot where the Blue Ridge Railroad had been designed to span the very substantial Chattooga River gorge, he or she must drive to and park at the spot where Bartram Nature Trail intersects with the road. From that point, one needs to hike down to Dick's Creek, then follow the stream to where it flows down Dick's Creek falls into the Chattooga. It was at this spot that a BRR bridge would have crossed the wild and scenic Chattooga.

Construction of the BRR route never reached this point, but a bridge across the Chattooga at this juncture would have been a massive undertaking, particularly for 1850s contractors. Just judging from the topographic maps of this site, the landscape would require a bridge in the neighborhood of 450 feet in length built 100 feet above the river!

Judging from the remoteness this site must have enjoyed in the 1850s, particularly since there were few if any roads – or even pig-trails – in Rabun at this time, the BRR builders quite likely became bogged down in the tunnel at Stumphouse Mountain, and, as such, could not get heavy equipment or building materials around to the Chattooga River gorge, and therefore, no remnants of the line exist at that site today. The most likely bridge site exists between present-day Earl's Ford and Sandy Ford, but there is no indication that any construction whatsoever was attempted in this vicinity.

It seems almost unbelievable today to understand that the charter for the Georgia portion of the Blue Ridge Railroad was granted in 1838, the same year the Cherokee Indians were herded out of Georgia on the shameful "Trail of Tears."

It also seems almost tragic that the Blue Ridge line was never completed, particularly since virtually all of the culverts – constructed of huge indestructible granite stone blocks – are virtually all still serviceable today, an engineering marvel.

Directions:

To reach Stumphouse Tunnel Park, take Interstate 85 north into South Carolina. Take SC 11 to Walhalla, then SC 28 to the park. The entrance to the park will be on the right prior to reaching the Stumphouse Ranger Station.

To reach the Blue Ridge Railroad remnants in Rabun County, take U.S. 23/441 to Clayton. Turn east onto Rickman Road, which joins Warwoman Road. Just beyond the Stockton House Restaurant (a good spot for lunch, incidentally) a side road runs north along Norton Creek. There are stone culvert walls (from the railroad) in the creek and the end of a high fill on the other side of the road.

Continue eastward on Warwoman Road, turning right into the park and drive to the end of the park. Walk up the steps to the railroad grade and read the information signage there. A nature trail leads to the rock face which would have been the east portal of the 1,700-foot-long Warwoman (Stekoa) Tunnel.

Continue eastward on Warwoman Road (about six miles from Clayton) and turn right onto Sandy Ford Road. At the point where Sandy Ford Road take a hard left across Warwoman Creek, continue straight on John Houk Road until you reach the old mill. You will be able to see the old railroad bridge abutment there.

Double back to Sandy Ford Road and continue east. A few miles further, you will be driving upon the old railroad grade. Shortly after that, the grade swings off to the north and to the uncompleted 2,300-foot Wall Mountain (Dick's Creek) Tunnel.

A bit further on, the grade crosses the road and the adjacent creek over another stone culvert.

After fording two creeks, you will see the last stonework at about 9.8 miles from Clayton. Beyond this point is Dick's Creek Falls into the Chattooga River. Good luck!

(Grateful appreciation is expressed herewith to Rutherford L. "Ruddy" Ellis, Jr., a former electrical engineer who was active in the Atlanta Chapter of the National Railway Historical Society for many years. Ruddy learned to love and treasure the north Georgia mountains as a child while visiting his grandmother's cottage on Lake Rabun and attending what once was known as "Camp Dixie" at Wiley. His great-grandmother, Mary Ann Lipscomb, owned a summer home in Tallulah Falls and was a founder of Tallulah Falls School. Ruddy provided most of the information used in this article.)

A Doc Holliday Time-Line In Georgia and the West (1851-1887)

1851: John Henry Holliday was born on August 21, in Griffin, Georgia to Henry Burroughs Holliday and Alice Jane McKey Holliday.

1864: Major Henry B. Holliday sells all his property and moves his family from Griffin to Valdosta, Georgia to escape the Union Army troops advancing on Atlanta.

1866: Alice Jane McKey Holliday, Doc's mother, dies in September. His father re-marries a scant three months later.

1870: Doc enrolls in the Pennsylvania School of Dental Surgery at Philadelphia.

1872: Doc graduates from dental college.

1873: Doc learns he has tuberculosis. Decides to move to the West, and travels to Dallas, Texas.

1874: Doc arrested in Dallas for gambling. Moves to Denison, Texas.

1875: In a New Year's Day shooting, Doc is arrested and charged with *"Assault"* and *"Intent to Murder"* Charles Austin in Dallas. He was tried and acquitted. Following his acquittal, he left Dallas, traveled to Fort Griffin, Texas, where he was indicted yet again for gambling.

1876: Travels to Denver, Colorado, under the identity of "Tom McKey." He is involved in an altercation and knifes gambler Budd Ryan. Returns to Texas.

1877: Doc is arrested three more times in Dallas for gambling. He later meets Wyatt Earp for the first time at Shaughnessey's Saloon in Fort Griffin. Reportedly kills Ed Bailey in Fort Griffin, but no charges were ever brought, so one has to question the validity of the presumed crime.

1878: Doc moves to Dodge City with "Big Nose" Kate Elder (a.k.a. Mary Katherine Harony), where he eventually saves Wyatt Earp's life during an altercation. He travels to Trinidad, Colorado and Las Vegas, New Mexico.

1879: Doc participates in what came to be known as the "Royal Gorge War." He opens a saloon in Las Vegas. May or may not have been involved in the shooting of Mike Gordon. He is indicted once again for running a gambling operation and carrying a deadly weapon. He decides to leave Las Vegas for Prescott, Arizona with the Earps.

1880: Returns to Las Vegas where he shoots Charlie White; the wound, however, is only superficial. No charges were ever brought to bear. He is again arrested for carrying a deadly weapon. Returns to Prescott where he rooms with acting Governor John J. Gosper. He later moves to Tombstone where he is involved in an altercation with Johnny Tyler and a gunfight and brutal fistfight with Milt Joyce where he is beaten senseless. He, nevertheless manages to shoot Joyce in both the hand and the foot. A charge of *"Assault With A Deadly Weapon With Intent To Kill"* was ultimately dismissed.

1881: Doc provides much-needed assistance to his friend Wyatt as the two defend the arrested Johnny-Behind-The-Deuce from a lynchmob. Doc is accused and arrested for robbery and murder involving a stage coach robbery in Benson, but the outlandish charges are dismissed upon examination of the circumstances. Doc is involved in what came to be known as the "Gunfight at the O.K. Corral" which ultimately brought both him and the Earps extreme fame. He was arrested for this shooting and acquitted in the Judge Spicer Hearing and Inquest.

1882: Doc joins Wyatt and Warren Earp, Turkey Creek Jack Johnson, Texas Jack Vermillion, Sherman McMasters and others in what came to be known as the "Vendetta Ride" in Arizona. He was present at the killings of Frank Stillwell, Florentino Cruz, and Curly Bill Brocius, but his actual participation in any of these shootings is unknown. Following these actions, he fled Arizona for New Mexico with the Earp Faction. In Albuquerque, New Mexico, he quarreled with Wyatt Earp during a heated discussion of Earp's latest conquest, Josephine Sarah Marcus. Doc separates from the Earp Faction and travels to Trinidad, New Mexico with Dan Tipton. He eventually leaves there and travels back up to Denver, Colorado, were he is arrested for extradition back to Arizona. Before the extradition can take place, Doc is rescued by Bat Masterson. He leaves Denver to travel to Gunnison, Salida, Pueblo, and Leadville, Colorado, then back to Denver.

1883-1886: Doc lives much of these three years in Leadville where he is involved in his last gunfight as he shoots Billy Allen in Hyman's Saloon. His arrest for the Billy Allen shooting ultimately goes to trial where he is once again acquitted. Doc travels back and forth to Denver several more times. During his final visit to the Colorado capital, he sees Wyatt Earp for the last time. By this point he is reaching destitution, and he is arrested for vagrancy. Chastened, he returns to Leadville.

1887: Doc had seen enough of Leadville, and decides to move to Glenwood Springs where he finally dies of consumption (galloping tuberculosis) on November 8, at the age of 36. He is buried "someplace near Linwood Cemetery" in Glenwood Springs. The exact site of his final remains is a total mystery today.

The Mystery
of Doc Holliday's
Griffin, Georgia Home

*Recent investigations and research on John
Henry Holliday have revealed some captivating
details, particularly as concerns his former
home in Griffin, Georgia.*

Bill Dunn was a man on a mission. A distant cousin to Griffin native John Henry "Doc" Holliday, Dunn made it his goal in life to publicize the truth about his famous forebear – the Southern gentleman as opposed to a reckless outlaw – for posterity's-sake.

As simple as that might seem, it, in fact, is considerably difficult to achieve, especially when dealing with a Western legend whose fascinating life has inspired innumerable interpretations, movies, books and other media, as well as exaggerations and defamation in these media.

Dunn, however, must have luck on his side. Since he began researching Holliday in the 1980s, he managed to uncover quite a bit of previously unknown information pertaining to the dentist-gambler and his Griffin roots.

For instance, Dunn discovered evidence that Holliday actually practiced dentistry in Griffin – a detail heretofore unsubstantiated. He also has researched two "Holliday graves" in the local cemetery believed to be those of Doc's father's slaves, and two other graves in the same cemetery which he maintains are "more than likely" those of Doc and his equally-elusive father.

During their research, Dunn and his fellow Doc "enthusiasts" also discovered the actual site upon which the dentist/gunman's plantation home in Griffin once stood. "This find," said Dunn, "is the most satisfying of all. While the other discoveries happened along the way, this is the one I've been pursuing for decades."

Hitting The Jackpot

John Henry was born August 14, 1851, in Griffin, a west-central Georgia town with a population of 22,000 at the dawning of the 21st century. He was the only living child of Henry Burroughs and Alice Jane McKey Holliday. Prior to

John Henry Holliday was photographed here shortly after his graduation from the Pennsylvania College of Dental Surgery. Had he known what his short life held for him, he no doubt would have been shocked. He lived a scant 15 years after this photo was taken, the last few months of which were spent in Leadville and Glenwood Springs, Colorado. (Photo by O.B. DeMorat)

his birth, a sister, Martha Eleanora, had died at the age of six months.

John Henry was born in a house which once stood at the corner of what today is Tinsley and North 9th Streets, according to Dunn. A modest brick residence now occupies this corner lot. The current residents of this home quite possibly have no clue today that they live on ground once occupied by a Western legend.

John Henry's father had served in both the Indian and Mexican wars by the time his only son was born. Ten years later, the elder Holliday joined the Confederate Army and fought in his third war.

During the decade in-between these two wars, Henry Burroughs had worked as a druggist in Griffin and served as the first elected clerk of court there. His family – though not wealthy – was stable and socially prominent. They attended Griffin's First Presbyterian Church where records today indicate the infant John Henry Holliday was baptized at the age of seven months in 1852.

When John Henry was two years old, the family moved to a 148-acre plantation in rural Griffin. It is the location of this homestead that had eluded historians in the 20th century, and that Dunn had long hoped to find.

"I'd been looking for twenty years," he said. "I'd get close but just couldn't pinpoint the location." Destiny, however, literally walked through his door one day, and Dunn said he still gets goose bumps talking about it.

An employee of Spring Industries – which owns the former Holliday plantation property – had been researching water locations at the site when he reportedly came across a copy of a 140-year-old map. "Bill, I think you'll be interested in this," the worker said as he conversed with him that day.

To his amazement, Dunn discovered the map described in detail the lay of the land of "Camp Stephens," a Griffin-based Confederate Army camp which existed in 1862. Major Henry Burroughs Holliday had sold 137 of his original 148 acres to the Confederate Army for construction of the camp, leaving 11 acres for his family's residence. There, on the map, was clearly listed *"H.B. Holliday's second home."* Confederate Private Asbury H. Jackson had given the original map to Doc's mother in March of 1862.

"You search for something for years, then somebody just walks in and hands it to you," Dunn smiled, still incredulous. To top things off, the fellow who presented him the prized map was a man who had somewhat irritated him the year before at "Doc Holliday Days," an annual event in Griffin.

"This newspaperman asked me about Doc and I pointed him to several experts who were attending the event," Dunn explained. "Instead of interviewing them, he goes up to this fellow (the eventual map-bearer) who had a tattoo of Doc above his ankle. He asked the guy, 'How do you feel about having someone who drank too much, gambled and killed people depicted on your body?'

"Instead of defending Doc, this fellow responded, 'It don't bother me. I do a little of that myself, except for the killing.' Needless to say, I was a little perturbed with him," Dunn confided.

Keeping his frustration to himself, though, Dunn said his resolve paid dividends in the end when the tattooed fellow presented him with the map in the summer of 2002.

Walking Hallowed Ground

The map had barely exchanged hands when Dunn solicited help from two friends – fellow members of the Doc Holliday Society (of which he serves as president) – who were in town that August weekend for Holliday's annual birthday bash.

With Gene Carlisle, a Holliday researcher who has penned a manuscript on the Western legend, Dunn set out hiking. Using the map as their guide, the men followed the old Macon and Western Railroad line toward the house site, battling tree branches, vines and undergrowth as they searched for the site of the old home-place.

Veering off the historic railroad tracks, the men cut their way through one particularly dense area of undergrowth for a short distance before stumbling upon a scattered pile of ancient fieldstones which the men now believe were used in the foundation of the Holliday house.

"Gene," Dunn uttered, barely able to breathe. "I think we've found it."

The next day, Keith Reed – Holliday Society member and the third explorer – entered the wooded area himself at a different angle, hoping to prove Dunn's assumption correct.

"He said he was practically eaten alive by redbugs," Dunn smiled, "but he stepped off the map's directives and landed on the exact same spot, confirming it as the former Holliday home-place."

The site is about two miles from Griffin's town square. Interestingly, Dunn says some earthworks from Camp Stephens – just as they appeared during

Photographed during what appears to have been a public event of some type, this rare historic print shows a portion of the troops at Confederate Fort Stephens near Griffin, Georgia in the 1860s. This camp was located one-half mile east of the railroad and two miles north of Griffin. It was the presence of this camp adjacent to his plantation which motivated Major Henry Burroughs Holliday to move his family, including young John Henry Holliday, southward to a safer locale in Valdosta, Georgia. (Photo courtesy of Confederate Stamps, Old Letters, and History)

the Civil War – remain in the vicinity adjacent to the home-site.

As the war worsened for the South in 1864 – and with the Confederate camp barely a hop, skip and jump from the Holliday home – it does not take a rocket scientist to understand why Major Holliday moved his family to Bemiss (a south Georgia town near Valdosta) that same year, almost simultaneously as William T. Sherman's Army was marching toward middle Georgia.

"Surely," said Dunn, "the major (medically discharged in 1862 due to 'watery dysentery') reckoned Sherman would march right by his home with destruction in mind. Seeking safety, he undoubtedly moved his family farther southward, eventually settling in Valdosta where he acquired more than 2,000 acres and ultimately served four terms as the city's mayor."

John Henry's Georgia

Back in Griffin, Georgia, tangible reminders of Doc's days in this town are abundant even today if one knows where to look. Bill Dunn happily points these out to curious visitors to his town today.

There is John Henry's birthplace on Tinsley Street and the Holliday plantation. There's the former site of First Presbyterian Church where he was baptized. (The Griffin Fire Station stands on this site today.) There's the old Iron Front Building which he once owned and in which he is believed to have practiced dentistry. There also is the old courthouse in Griffin where Major Holliday served as clerk of court. And at Oak Hill Cemetery, there's the final resting place of Doc's sister – and possibly other graves of even more importance.

A bit beyond John Henry's sister's

Henry Burroughs Holliday, John Henry's father, was photographed circa 1852. Despite service in three wars and two stints as mayor of Valdosta, the site of his grave – just as that of his son – is a mystery to historians today.

grave are the graves of Mariah and Harry Holliday, a black couple who, according to Dunn, probably were slaves on the Holliday plantation.

"By all indications," said Dunn, "the Hollidays were good and decent people who cared for their workers." Despite a common tendency to believe that hatred and violence sparked all relationships between Whites and Blacks of the pre-Civil War era, Dunn – just as other Southern historians – asserts that nothing could be further from the truth. He said this was particularly true in regard to the Holliday family.

"Doc, in fact, probably even picked up his card-playing skills from a slave girl – Sophie Walton," Dunn continued, "with whom he often played as a child. She resided at his Uncle John Holliday's farm. According to family tradition, it was Sophie who taught a young John Henry the skills he later used to support himself as a gambler after tuberculosis robbed him of the ability to practice dentistry. She reportedly taught him a number of the tricks of the trade, such as 'skinning' cards and 'the put-and-take' technique of dealing cards."

Doc, the Dentist

One of the most intriguing "Doc sites" in Griffin is the building where he may have practiced dentistry after leaving the practice at which he was working in Atlanta. In a 1940 *Griffin Daily News* article, Judge L.P. Goodrich noted that his father had known the Hollidays. The article goes on to state, "Doc Holliday returned to Griffin after the war and practiced dentistry here in an office in the old Merritt building."

It is a matter of public record that John Henry, in fact, once was part owner of the Merritt building, known in the 1870s as the "Iron Front building." He had inherited half of the property from his mother's estate, and her family – the McKeys – had claimed the other half.

"They actually drew a line down the middle of the building, separating the two halves," Dunn added. "Doc later sold his half for $1,800.00, which was a good price for that property back then." (Equivalent to approximately $43,000.00 in 2023 dollars.)

Dunn said he feels certain Doc practiced dentistry in an upstairs office at the Iron Front. After graduating from Valdosta Institute in 1870, Doc had entered the Pennsylvania College of Dental Surgery from which he was graduated in 1872.

He subsequently returned south and worked for Dr. Arthur C. Ford in his dental practice in Atlanta on Alabama Street, while living with his Uncle John Stiles Holliday a short distance away. *(Interestingly, a portion of this office building still existed for many years on the old portion of Alabama Street preserved in the former "Underground Atlanta" attraction.)*

While Ford attended the Southern Dental Association Conference in Richmond, Virginia in the summer of 1872, Dr. John Henry Holliday was left in charge of Ford's practice. When the elder dentist returned, Holliday was left with time on his hands – time to commute to Griffin to operate his own dental practice, said Dunn.

"If he practiced here, this is where he did it," Dunn said, pointing to four holes in the original wooden floor situated in strategic spots to accommodate a dental chair of that time period. Equally interesting is a tin cylinder discovered under a loose floor plank in this same upstairs room at *Holliday's Portions & Elixirs*, a restaurant that once occupied the old Iron Front building.

"He probably used this for dental supplies or possibly even a hideaway for money," said Dunn who researched the cylinder, stamped *"Great Northern Manufacturing Company, Chicago,"* and found it to be of Civil War-era vintage. Great Northern carried dental supplies among many other items.

"It sure does lend credence to the possibility that Doc practiced dentistry here for two or three months before heading out West," Dunn concluded.

Resting In Peace, But Where?

While history claims that Doc Holliday is buried in Glenwood Springs, Colorado, persistent rumors through the years have suggested that Major Henry B. Holliday in fact brought his son's body back to Georgia for burial. It's

This tombstone which falsely identified (since no one knows for certain where Holliday is actually buried) the grave of John Henry Holliday in Linwood Cemetery outside Glenwood Springs, Colorado, for over half a century, ironically was also engraved with numerous errors of fact about the Georgian, including his birth site, birthday, and the medical school he attended. It, thankfully, was recently replaced with another stone which at least corrected the errors, though it continues to occupy a spot which has not been confirmed as the actual site of Holliday's mortal remains.

one rumor in which Dunn places some credence.

"Yes, I sincerely believe that," he stated emphatically. "Knowing Southern history as I do – and knowing the major had the motive, the money, the mode of transportation, and nothing to stop him – I believe he brought Doc back and buried him under this oak tree," Dunn said, pointing to a stately oak in Griffin's Oak Hill Cemetery. "Until someone proves otherwise to me, I'll believe Doc's buried right here beside the major."

The unmarked twin graves at Oak Hill are compelling. Set off to themselves, they are covered by unassuming concrete slabs with no engravings. Dunn theorizes that Major Holliday either went to Colorado himself or sent a relative to retrieve his son's remains, then buried his boy under the now-massive oak.

Interestingly, a heavy-duty ancient nail is driven, rock-solid, into a sprawling root of the oak, centered above what Dunn believes to be Doc's grave. Dunn conjectures the major quite possibly could have hammered in the nail and used it to work a pulley to lower his son's casket into its final resting place.

"The nail-pulley mechanism would have enabled him to accomplish the two-man job on his own," said Dunn. It's a plausible theory if you believe the major wanted his boy's gravesite to be kept a secret.

Supporting his belief that father and son are buried in Griffin are these notes of interest: 1) While Doc is said to be buried at Glenwood Springs, Colorado, the marker in the cemetery there reads, *This memorial dedicated to Doc Holliday who is buried "someplace" in this cemetery.* It is a fact that no one today knows the actual gravesite – if it exists at all – in Glenwood Springs containing Holliday's last remains. 2) While some Valdostans believe Major Henry Burroughs Holliday is buried in that Georgia town, no one knows the exact location of his gravesite either. Dunn finds it difficult to believe that the grave of a man of his prominence (veteran of three wars and a four-term mayor) would be unknown and unmarked today if indeed it did exist in Valdosta. 3) The twin graves in Griffin are in the Thomas family plot. Dunn said the Thomas and Holliday families were socially connected and the Thomases may very well have acceded to Major Holliday's request and agreed to the anonymous burial of Doc Holliday in their plot.

"Why can't the folks in Glenwood Springs point to Doc's grave?" questioned Dunn. "It's because it's not there. Major Holliday had the motive and the means to bring his boy back to Griffin. A man of Southern heritage would want his son buried near him, and removing him to an anonymous location would prevent the vandalism that surely would have followed had Doc's gravesite been revealed."

> *A man of Southern heritage would want his son buried near him, and removing him to an anonymous location would prevent vandalism.*

Gentleman From Georgia

They say you can take the boy out of Georgia but can't take Georgia out of the boy. John Henry Holliday left the South and lived out West as "Doc" Holliday the final 15 years of his life, but did he long for home?

An 1882 *Atlanta Constitution* interview with Holliday family friend Lee Smith indicates he did. When asked if Doc ever spoke of returning to Georgia, Smith responded, "He would be back here today but for fear of being handed over to the Arizona authorities."

By the 1880s, however, the West had claimed Doc Holliday as its own. He ultimately died in a Colorado hotel on Nov. 8, 1887, tuberculosis finally defeating him.

It's a matter of public record that John Henry died out West, but, if Bill Dunn's theory about the two graves at Oak Hill Cemetery in Griffin, Georgia is correct, the noted gunman did, indeed, come home to Georgia a final time.

Bill Dunn said he likes Tombstone (Arizona) Historian Ben Traywick's description of Doc Holliday best: "He was an orchid in a cactus patch."

Dunn said he once received a call from Traywick when the Tombstone historian was working on his book, *John Henry: The Doc Holliday Story*.

"He asked me to help and I asked him how he intended to portray Doc,"

Dunn recalled. Traywick replied, "As the true Southern educated gentleman that he was."

"What can I do to help?" Dunn said he responded. Published in 1996, the book, to Dunn's delight, "does nothing to discredit Doc."

Known best for teaming with the Earp brothers to defeat the Clantons and McLaurys in the 1881 gunfight behind the O.K. Corral, Doc Holliday became a larger-than-life legend. Over the next century, stories of him would range from fact to fabrication with his reputation as a ruthless gunman dominating. Numerous publications and Hollywood movies would paint the picture of a merciless killer with murder in his heart.

The facts, said Dunn, dictate a different personality – that of an educated gentleman who never abandoned his Southern roots. Either way, the intrigue of Doc Holliday continues, even as it did a century ago.

"This guy from Buckhead called to get information for a report his 11-year-old daughter was doing on Doc," said Dunn. "He said she was infatuated with him and that after seeing the movie **Tombstone**, she could recite all of actor Val Kilmer's dialogue in the movie."

While some insist on portraying John Henry as a killer without a conscience, Dunn vows the dentist from Griffin fired a weapon only when he had to, and he never became comfortable

> *Dunn vows the dentist from Griffin fired a weapon only when he had to, and he never became comfortable with killing.*

with killing. The handsome ash-blond, blue-eyed Georgian who departed his home for the drier climate out West to slow the stranglehold of tuberculosis was most likely "a very typical young guy, mischievous with an out-going personality," says Dunn.

The Stuff Of Legends

Dunn appreciates the comparisons which sometimes are drawn between himself and his famous relative, but he's also serious about the preservation of John Henry Holliday's legitimate legacy.

"Being a relative has little to do with it," Dunn added. "I've got this thing about Hollywood and history. History is more exciting than Hollywood could ever make it. Why they have to exaggerate and fabricate things just doesn't make sense to me."

While his findings do shed light on the history of Doc Holliday, the mystery which pervades his persona is certain to dog this Western legend as long as Hollywood's cameras roll. Whether he's viewed as a Southern gentleman, a Western gunman, a man with a death wish, or a man who dared death to do him in, Doc Holliday remains the stuff of legends. Regardless of later depictions and Hollywood tripe, he began his life as an educated and cultured son of the South from Griffin, Georgia, who lived an honorable and captivating life and died an honorable death.

John Henry Holliday's Final Georgia Possession

It has stood in this middle Georgia town since the days of the Wild West. Indeed, it once was co-owned by one of the most famed old West icons of all time.

allas, Deadwood, Dodge City, Tombstone . . . . The names evoke images of the wild, wild West and the now legendary world of John Henry Holliday. "Doc," however, had another world as well – a Southern world in Georgia where he once lived and worked, and of which remnants still exist today.

These sites include landmarks like the home of his uncle, Dr. John Stiles Holliday, in Fayetteville, Georgia, where the future gunman often visited with his cousin, Mattie; the former Holliday home in Griffin, Georgia, where he was born and lived the early portion of his life; the former Holliday home in Valdosta, Georgia, to which his family moved in the 1860s, fleeing the on-coming juggernaut of Gen. William T. Sherman; and the Griffin, Georgia office building – known as "the Iron Front Building" – where a young Dr. John H. Holliday reportedly once practiced dentistry a short time.

The Iron Front building on Griffin's historic Solomon Street was a portion of John Henry's inheritance from his mother, Alice Jane McKey Holliday. When Alice Jane died in 1867, the building was passed to thirteen-year-old John, with his father, Henry Burroughs Holliday, acting as his guardian over the property until he became "of age."

A Family Rift

A short three months later, Henry Burroughs shocked the Holliday family by quickly remarrying. The unusually-quick remarriage understandably caused a rift within the family, which, in turn, also surprisingly caused John Henry's relatives on his mother's side – the McKeys – to file suit against the Hollidays in an attempt to reclaim what they felt was "McKey property."

The suit was brought by John Henry's (Doc's) uncle, Tom McKey, and was tried in the Lowndes County courthouse in Valdosta. Ironically, this is the same uncle who Doc so admired, and whose name he later used as an alias to disguise his own identity while in Colorado. Even more surprising is the fact that the case, *McKey vs Holliday*, ultimately

This commercial structure was known in John Henry Holliday's day as the "Iron Front Building." He inherited this building from his mother's estate upon her death, and had set up a dental practice here in the summer of 1872. It was at this same time that he learned he had contracted tuberculosis. (Photo by Jackie Kennedy)

proved to be at least a partially-successful suit, causing Alice Jane's estate to be divided equally between the McKey and Holliday families.

This unique settlement included the Iron Front Building in Griffin, of which ownership was likewise divided equally between the McKeys and John Henry. The legal solution had been to literally create a partition down through the middle of the building from room to basement, with the eastern half being returned to McKey ownership, and the western half remaining as John Henry's legal inheritance. Though this suit and subsequent settlement obviously denied John Henry a substantial portion of his "legal" inheritance, history does not record his reaction to the decision or to his McKey relatives who prevailed in the case.

It is likewise unknown today just how

John Henry's mother, Alice Jane, came to own a substantial downtown Griffin property such as the Iron Front Building. It presumably had been in the family for a number of years, with Alice Jane inheriting it following the death of another member of her family who had owned it.

Impressive Asset

The Iron Front was certainly a property worth fighting for. It was an impressive structure, two stories high with an iron infrastructure beneath its fancy red brick façade. Both floors of the building had long multi-paned windows facing the street in Doc's day. They allowed the morning sunlight to stream into the rooms with their hardwood floors and pressed-tin trimmed ceilings.

At the rear of the main floor, a huge mechanical lift carried merchandise from

An infant John Henry Holliday - his painful future worlds away - was photographed with his mother, Alice Jane McKey Holliday circa 1852. In her *Last Will and Testament*, she left the Iron Front Building to John Henry. (Photo courtesy of Craig Fouts Photo Collection)

the loading dock to the second floor sales offices. In Doc's day, the Iron Front was leased out as shop space to various businesses, and brought in good income in rents.

Henry Burroughs Holliday continued his guardianship of the property until his son reached the age of 21 in the summer of 1872, allowing him to legally take possession of his inheritance. At that time, John Henry had just graduated from dental school in Philadelphia, and was working in the Atlanta dental office of Dr. Arthur C. Ford on Alabama Street in the vicinity of what once was the popular entertainment complex of the 1970s thru the 1990s known as "Underground Atlanta."

With his own office building, John Henry enjoyed the unique distinction of being able to immediately open his own dental practice in his hometown, Griffin. It is believed today that he in fact did return to Griffin and open a small practice there for a brief time.

John Henry registered his ownership of the Iron Front Building, in the Spalding County Deed Book in November of 1872. According to old-time Griffin residents, he also did a modest amount of remodeling to the building, adding an exterior iron staircase which rose from the alley beside the building up to the little second floor office where he set up his practice.

Sudden Departure

Dr. John Henry Holliday's shingle, however, didn't hang in Griffin very long. Just a few months later in January of 1873, he suddenly sold his half of the Iron Front Building, and by October of that year, records indicate he was practicing dentistry in faraway Dallas, Texas – the first stop "Doc" made in his countless western wanderings.

What was the motivation for John Henry to suddenly sell his hard-won inheritance and leave Georgia only a few months after opening his dental practice Griffin? Some sources have argued it was the tuberculosis with which he had been diagnosed by his uncle, Dr. John Stiles Holliday, earlier that year. Others claim it was a star-crossed romance with his cousin, Mattie Holliday (daughter of Dr. John Stiles) from which Doc was running.

Whatever the circumstances, vestiges and memories of Doc Holliday remain strong in his Georgia homeland. And visitors to the little second-floor office in Griffin's Iron Front Building constantly imagine what it was like in the days of yesteryear, when a fearless Old West gunfighter was a simple dentist in a sleepy Southern town.

Doc Holliday Leaves the "Old South" for the "Old West"

Though he was a native son of the old South,
John Henry Holliday earned lasting fame in
the old West in the 1880s.

He was born and grew up in Georgia's Spalding County in the small town of Griffin. Later, with the advancing threat of Gen. William Sherman's forces moving through Georgia during the U.S. Civil War in 1864, John Henry's father refugeed the family southward to the town of Valdosta where the youngster spent his formative years, attending the Valdosta Institute and ultimately leaving to attend the Pennsylvania College of Dental Surgery in Philadelphia. Following graduation and a return to Georgia for a short stint to practice dentistry in Atlanta, "Doc" began a vagabond journey to the West, never to return to Georgia.

The wandering Georgian traveled to and took up temporary residence in many towns of the old West. Places such as Dallas, Fort Griffin and Jacksboro, Texas; Pueblo, Leadville, Glenwood Springs and Denver, Colorado; Cheyenne, Wyoming; Deadwood, South Dakota (He reportedly was there when his friend, James Butler Hickok,

was murdered); Dodge City, Kansas; Las Vegas, New Mexico; Prescott, and Tucson, Arizona, and numerous others all witnessed the comings and goings of Doc. No town held him or his interest very long.

Despite all these travels, it was the town of Tombstone, Arizona Territory that truly defined him. The years he spent in this fast-growing gold mining town – while he was still reasonably healthy – gave him the bulk of his lasting fame. And it was for these years that he is best remembered.

By the early 1990s - with the Hollywood release of movies such as ***Tombstone*** (1993) starring Val Kilmer, Kurt Russell, and Sam Elliott – the name "Doc" Holliday had reached almost mythic proportions in the folklore of America, but it was not always so. After the initial newspaper coverage of the actual shoot-out behind the O.K. Corral in Tombstone in October of 1881, much of the fame of Wyatt Earp; his brothers Virgil, Morgan and Warren; and Doc Holliday, died out over

Originally built in 1879 as the Golden Eagle Brewery, this saloon was burned in the devastating 1882 Tombstone fire, but was soon rebuilt in the same spot and renamed the Crystal Palace Saloon. This was one of John Henry Holliday's favorite haunts, and still stands today in the town. (Photo by Olin Jackson)

the ensuing years. After the huge water pump at the Tombstone silver mines failed and the price of silver plummeted in the late 1880s, the town had withered and died, and the exploits of the Earps and Doc Holliday were almost forgotten completely.

With his opportunities in Tombstone "played out," did John Henry Holliday ever once consider returning to his Georgia homeland? The evidence suggests not. When he exited the once-vibrant silver-mining town in 1882, he traveled for a time with Wyatt and Warren Earp before striking out on his own. The Earps – at least Wyatt – didn't mind camping out and sleeping upon the cold hard ground in the mountains of Colorado, but John Henry Holliday was accustomed to a bit more refinery, and

he exchanged this "uncivil" life for the bright lights and gambling mecca of Denver.

Old Tombstone Today

Meanwhile, back in Tombstone, by the 1890s, most of the miners had departed Cochise County (which included Tombstone). Since Tombstone was located in the middle of the desert, most people just boarded up their homes or stores and left town on horseback or in buggies and covered wagons. Most of them also simply abandoned in Tombstone whatever possessions they had been unable to transport to whatever destination they had selected for a new home. A covered wagon pulled by oxen or mules can only haul a limited amount of items, particularly across the arid and dangerous desert.

As a result, the town – despite two major fires – remained for many years much as Holliday and the Earps had left it. There really wasn't any way to steal or even freely take large amounts of the relics left in Tombstone. Who would chance it across the desert? The now-quiet, dusty, and virtual ghost-town existed in this manner for well over half a century – until the 1950s when American servicemen at nearby Fort Huachuca began taking weekend excursions to the historic site. It was also about this same time that several writers – following the success of a nationally-broadcast Western television series based upon Earp – realized the value in publishing the biographies of the old West icons from this town.

Luckily, the handful of local townspeople who remained in Tombstone – which had quite literally become a ghost-town by the 1950s – apparently realized they had a money-maker on their hands. They banded together and created a historic district out of the town, preserving it for future generations – and for the income it could generate.

A number of the very structures which the Earps, Doc Holliday, "Buckskin" Frank Leslie, William Barclay "Bat" Masterson, Ike Clanton, Johnny Ringo, "Texas" John Slaughter, the McLaury brothers, "Turkey Creek" Jack Johnson, "Texas" Jack Vermilion and many other famous and notorious figures of the old West had frequented, amazingly still stand today in Tombstone.

Though it burned in one of the town's two major fires, portions of the original O.K. Corral site still exist, as do the Wells-Fargo building; the billiard parlor (though re-built) in which Morgan Earp was murdered; the original Birdcage Theatre and the original Crystal Palace Saloon in which Holliday, the Earps and all the rest spent years gambling and carousing. Even the home once owned and inhabited by Virgil Earp on First Street still stands (as of this writing in 2023), as do the bank, and other structures.

The Birdcage Theatre is one of the more prominent relics from that day. Built in December of 1881, it was a popular place to enjoy bawdy women, gambling, theatrical productions, and other forms of adult entertainment in old Tombstone. It has been preserved almost exactly as it existed in the 1880s – a museum to the town's famed former inhabitants.

A Life In The West

Holliday was 21 in 1872, when he departed Georgia to begin his travels. Interestingly, though his doctors had told him he had less than one year left to live due to the tuberculosis in his lungs, he, in fact, lived for 15 more years, and in the interim, he traveled throughout the last frontier in the United States, earning a well-deserved reputation as one of the deadliest gunmen to grace the dusty streets of the old West.

Doc was also accused in print and folklore of being testy and irritable, but these were traits he had picked up in his growing impatience with anyone unlucky enough to be perceived as wasting the Georgian's rapidly-diminishing time on this earth. In retrospect, who wouldn't have been short-tempered under his circumstances?

He was also known to be very gracious to those who were courteous to him, and his honor was the most valuable possession he owned. When bullied or persecuted as a result of his frail condition, John Henry Holliday invariably proved to be a game challenger – even if he didn't always win.

Though he often used what was known as a "pocket holster" (actually a reinforced pocket in his coat for carrying a weapon), he was one of the first gunmen to use the new-fangled "shoulder holster," and it has been documented in testimony from both Wyatt Earp and Bat Masterson that he was one of the deadliest gunmen they both had ever known.

Equally amazing, is the fact that Doc Holliday – despite the numerous gunfights in which he was involved – was not killed as a result of his many conflicts. He was seriously wounded at least twice, and at the O.K. Corral gunfight, a round from one of the McLaurys's guns grazed the pocket holster (in his coat) on his hip, giving him a bad bruise and a limp for several days, but he ultimately recovered in each instance. Few other prominent gunmen of the old West – Earp and Masterson interestingly being two of the few exceptions – endured this life without being killed.

The Hotel Glenwood at the corner of 8th and Grand streets was photographed circa 1887, the year of Holliday's death in a single room on the fifth floor of this structure. Holliday was removed from this room the day of his death and taken to a burial site outside town, the specific location of which has been lost over time. (Photo courtesy of Frontier Historical Society)

Wyatt Earp, amazingly, was never even wounded.

All four of Wyatt's brothers were seriously wounded at some point in their lives, and two of them were killed in gunfire. His brother Morgan was assassinated in Tombstone in 1882, and Warren was murdered in a bar-fight in Wilcox, Arizona, just a few miles away several years later. (Even though no one was arrested or charged in the incident, nor any inquest ever held, one can safely claim Warren was "murdered," since he was unarmed at the time, and the .45 round fired at him was intentional.)

James Butler "Wild Bill" Hickok was killed in Deadwood, South Dakota. Johnny Ringo and most of the Clantons and McLaurys were killed in and around Tombstone in the 1880s. William "Billy the Kid" Bonney was killed in New Mexico in 1881. Jesse James, Pat Garrett, Butch Cassidy and the Sundance Kid, Billy Claiborne and many others all also met with bloody deaths at about this same time. Doc and Wyatt, however, seemed almost invulnerable to bullets, despite their lifestyles.

A Friendship With Earp

Doc and Wyatt had become fast friends in Dodge City, Kansas, while Wyatt was a deputy city marshal there. Holliday reportedly came to Wyatt's rescue (possibly saving his life) on two separate occasions – once in Dodge, and once again later in Tombstone – and Wyatt never forgot it. Though they quarreled in 1882 and went their separate ways, the two men remained close friends nevertheless to the end.

Wyatt was quoted as saying he enjoyed Doc's company because the clever dentist made him laugh. Doc was indeed known to have quite a sense of humor, as well as a love of practical jokes. According to one documented account, on one occasion when a stranger rode into Tombstone wearing a fancy suit and derby hat, Doc reportedly followed him throughout the town, gleefully tinkling a miniature sterling silver hand-held dinner bell everywhere the man went – much to the well-dressed gentleman's uncomfortable chagrin.

There is so much history in the little town of Tombstone, that one would be well-advised to spend at least a weekend in explorations there if ever a visit is made to this historic site. Above and beyond the commercial buildings and homes in the town associated with Holliday and the Earps, many other sites in that vicinity were often frequented by other individuals who later gained fame on the frontier.

Ultimately, in their last days in the Tombstone area in 1882, Doc, Wyatt Earp, Warren Earp, Texas Jack Vermillion, Turkey Creek Jack Johnson, Dan Tipton, and a handful of other close friends began what was known as *"the Vendetta Ride."* They in essence hunted down the outlaws who had assassinated one Earp (Morgan) and maimed another (Virgil) for life, and who had been protected for years by a corrupt judicial system in Cochise County. Months later, when much of the outlaw element had been "eliminated" (by what some described as vigilante justice), Doc, Wyatt and Warren left forever, wandering anew in the West, searching for further adventure and income opportunities.

For the rest of their days, both Doc and Wyatt did little more than travel and enjoy life. Neither of them ever owned a home after leaving Tombstone (Doc never owned a home at all, preferring to live in hotels and rooming houses his entire adult life), and they both literally went wherever the wind blew them.

After the Vendetta Ride, Doc, Wyatt, Warren, Texas Jack Vermillion, Tur-

key Creek Jack Johnson and Dan Tipton drifted east to New Mexico Territory. Eventually, Doc, Wyatt, Warren and Tipton drifted northward up to Colorado, to the gold and silver mining towns which offered a refuge from the Cochise County, Arizona authorities, and an opportunity for gambling which the men needed to generate income. The Earps and Tipton spent the summer of 1882 in Gunnison, with Doc traveling down from Denver to visit them there for a brief time.

Final Days

After that time, John Henry Holliday traveled pretty much alone. He had abandoned his female consort – "Big Nose" Katherine Haroney, and spent most of his later years continuing to travel and gamble. He moved through Leadville and other locales before venturing back to Denver.

In 1886 – just a short time before he died – Doc met Wyatt one last time. It was in Denver, Colorado. Doc was extremely ill by that point, and they both knew he couldn't last much longer. According to the memoirs of Josephine Sara Marcus (Wyatt's common-law wife), Wyatt told Doc, *"Isn't it strange that if not for you I wouldn't be alive today, yet, you must go first."*

Josephine said that as Wyatt and Doc parted that day, Doc threw his arm over Wyatt's shoulder saying *"Good-bye old friend. It'll be a long time before we meet again."* Josephine said that at those words, the great Wyatt Earp wept as he watched his old friend walk quickly away in an unstable gait.

Shortly thereafter, in 1887, John Henry "Doc" Holliday passed away in his room at the Hotel Glenwood in Glenwood Springs, Colorado. He was 36 years of age.

The Actual Old West Gunfights of John Henry "Doc" Holliday

The Georgia native was involved in numerous affrays in the Old West over the years, and didn't hesitate to defend himself – usually to great advantage. Nevertheless, many shootings attributed to Doc either never happened at all, or were simply done by other individuals.

John Henry Holliday was born and raised in the Georgia towns of Griffin and Valdosta. His early life was characterized mainly with the modest, refined and educated life of a Southern gentleman. During these formative years, young John Henry – aside from boyhood pranks – was involved in few if any altercations, and was never involved in any incidents involving gunfights.

Following his diagnosis of tuberculosis and his subsequent relocation to states/territories in the American West, however, the circumstances changed. In stature and muscular development, John Henry at best was a slight and somewhat weak-appearing individual, and his tuberculosis made him even more vulnerable. The Old West was populated by and large with rawhide tough, desperate, and dangerous men, many of whom were constantly seeking an opportunity to establish a reputation, particularly if they could bully an individual.

The weak-appearing John Henry Holliday just naturally became a target of these bullies. It also didn't help matters that the Georgian developed a proclivity for alcohol, gambling, and the saloons in which these vices could be obtained, often becoming inebriated and quarrelsome. It was these circumstances which led to many of his conflicts, since, despite his small stature, John Henry was always "game" for a fight if someone wished to press the issue.

In the instances in which John Henry was challenged, he was anything but defenseless. He carried with him almost constantly several deadly weapons, and didn't hesitate to use them – usually to great success. He was a "dead-shot" with a handgun, having honed the skill during his youth and into his young adulthood. He also learned to hide and quickly retrieve for use a small knife which he

412

carried with him at all times. Anyone who chose to attempt to assault or bully John Henry Holliday – particularly in his early years out West – had made a serious mistake.

Over the years, as legends grew throughout the Old West, the reputations of many noted gunmen invariably exceeded the actual circumstances of their experiences quite significantly. John Henry Holliday was no exception, being credited with many more shootings and deaths than the ones with which he was actually involved. . . but that did not in any way diminish the fact that he had successfully defended himself on numerous occasions.

According to Karen Holliday Tanner (*Doc Holliday: A Family Portrait*, University of Oklahoma Press, 1998) who has extensively researched the experiences of her famous forebear, Doc can be documented as having been involved only in the following incidents:

He was a participant in gunfights between himself and Charles Austin in Dallas, Texas; with Henry Kahn in Breckenridge, Colorado; with Milt Joyce in Tombstone, Arizona; and with Billy Allen in Leadville, Colorado. None of these particular shootings involved fatalities, but all resulted in wounded participants.

Doc was indicted in the Austin case and found *"Not Guilty."* In the shooting incident with Milt Joyce a charge of *"Assault with a Deadly Weapon with Intent to Kill"* was dismissed. For the misdemeanor charge of *"Assault and Battery"* Doc paid a $20 fine. He was also fined in the Kahn shooting and acquitted in the Billy Allen shooting.

Regarding the killing of Ed Bailey at Fort Griffin, Texas, and the shooting of Charlie White in Las Vegas,

New Mexico, no charges were ever brought against Doc for those incidents, so they quite possibly were simply considered obvious cases of self-defense.

As a result of her research, Ms. Tanner admits that it quite likely was Doc who ended the days of Old Man Clanton – the leader of the outlaw Clantons in Tombstone, Arizona Territory in the 1880s, but the details are sketchy.

It is a documented fact that Doc definitely fired the shot that killed Tom McLaury, and he delivered at least one of the three fatal shots which ended the life of Frank McLaury in the October 26, 1881 shooting near the O.K. Corral in Tombstone, AZ.

And finally, Doc may or may not have been involved in other killings during what later came to be known as "the Vendetta Ride," when Wyatt and Warren Earp, Doc, Texas Jack Vermillion, Turkey Creek Jack Johnson, Dan Tipton and others sought out the assassins of Morgan Earp and the assassins who attempted to kill Virgil Earp. These vigilante – but necessary – actions ended forever the days of the organized gang of outlaws which had frequented the Tombstone area in the 1870s and 1880s.

So, if one adds up the obvious cases of record, John Henry Holliday can be credited with ending the lives of at least four men – and quite possibly more, since he was involved in the Vendetta Ride which definitely resulted in other deaths of unspecified numbers.

Holliday can also be credited with wounding at least five other individuals. Collectively, in the known gunfights in which he was involved, approximately 10 individuals were either killed or wounded.

The Last Days of Doc Holliday

Though the actual circumstances of John Henry Holliday's last days on this earth have been debated for years, a credible recently-discovered newspaper article possibly describes the actual events, and debunks some previously-held notions.

Some writers and researchers have maintained that John Henry "Doc" Holliday spent his last days alone in the Hotel Glenwood, slowly wasting away until death finally took him. Other researchers, supported by at least one recently-discovered document, however, maintain an entirely different set of circumstances existed. Until recent times, no detailed first-hand account of Doc's last days was known to exist, but a recently-discovered newspaper article may prove otherwise.

According to Karen Holliday Tanner, Doc sent for his long-time consort – Katherine "Big Nose Kate" Harony – when he realized his last days were upon him, and she subsequently joined him and cared for him until he died. However, very little if any corroborating evidence of this or many of the other details of Holliday's last hours were known to exist, that is until discovery of the newspaper article published in the February 14, 1899 issue of the *Sulphur Headlight* of Sulphur, Oklahoma.

The information was detailed by an individual named Origen C. "Harelip Charlie" Smith, who, fittingly, was an ally of the Earps and Holliday during the volatile days in Tombstone, Arizona Territory, in 1880-1882. Smith was a business associate of Bob Winders in Tombstone, and soon had allied himself with the Earps in support of law and order in the frontier town. His days in that town were well-documented, and are a matter of public record today. He was respected as knowledgeable and trustworthy by associates in Tombstone, so there is little reason to doubt his claims.

By coincidence, Smith found himself traveling in the same stagecoach as Holliday to Glenwood Springs, Colorado, in 1887, and even living in the same hotel there as Doc. According to the *Headlight* article, Smith was present during Holliday's dying days and was intimately familiar with the individuals present and the events surrounding this now-famous event.

Later, after moving back to Tombstone, Arizona, Smith, realizing the importance of the knowledge he carried with him, began writing down his memoirs for posterity. He reportedly sought out another old friend – Lundsford Bryant Shockley – to collaborate with him on the memoirs. Though there is no specific reason to doubt his memory or accuracy in describing the final moments, this, perhaps, is nevertheless, an opportunity for imprecise elaboration to have crept into Smith's description of the circumstances as they actually existed during Holliday's last hours.

In 1899, Shockley reportedly shared the portion of Smith's memoirs involving Glenwood Springs with the publisher of the **Sulphur** (Oklahoma) **Headlight**. Why he chose to share Smith's work with this particular newspaper at this particular time is unknown today. Whatever the circumstances, on February 14 of that year, the **Headlight** published the very interesting details of Doc's last days as supposedly drawn from Smith's memoirs.

The article from the **Headlight** is re-published here in its entirety, exactly as written by Smith, with the exception of quotation marks and paragraph delineations for ease of reading. The article is very detailed, and includes considerable information which would have been exceedingly difficult to fabricate, indicating the writer almost certainly was actually present as a witness at Holliday's death. The initial portion of the article was written from the editor's perspective, with the remainder from Smith's perspective. It reads as follows:

"*The story comes to the* **Headlight** *from colleague Lundsford Shockley, resident of the Chickasaw Nations, Ardmore, Indian Territory. It is known that Mr. Shockley came to town by wagon early in the evening and boarded at the Hotel Sulphur Springs in preparation to meet the* **Headlight** *staff.*

"*It is apparent that connections to Mr. [Origen Charles] Smith came from Shockley's days with John Roberts of the [John] Slaughter crew, driving those vast Texas herds up to the San Pedro Valley. Shockley comments: 'We were encamped up in the Sierra Vistas in '81. On the first time out, many of the boys wanted to go to Tombstone and experience the town's pleasures. Tombstone was a mining camp built from the dust much like the old pueblo, Tucson, which offered a cowboy anything imaginable.'*

"*According to Charlie Smith, it was also a community built on politics; 'a common cause of much of the troubles there.'*

"*When upon reading the Harelip Smith papers, I might comment that the significance surrounds the death of John H. Holliday, known as Doc, on November 8, 1887, where Smith occupied a room across the hallway from him in the Hotel Glenwood, some twelve years ago. It is important to note that Origen Smith's recollections serve as a standard account of the dentist's last days in Glenwood Springs who wrote on his Sol Israel stationary on October 8, 1887, that Holliday was confined to his bed by the local physician who had told his mistress: 'I have done all that can be done. It is in John's hands now. And God's.'*

"*Origen Smith gives an account of Doc Holliday's arrival to the mountain resort on May 24, 1887 [as follows]:*

"'*The Concorde coach had slammed into the rocks along the narrow gauge of mountain road near Carbondale, which damaged the wheel at the rear of the coach which suddenly ended their journey until a mechanic could be brought in from several miles distant. The narrow gauge out of Leadville was hard on Holliday and its three passengers but it was the best means of travel for the day.*

"'*The three passengers on the stage*

knew who Doc Holliday was, but I doubt they had heard of Origen Smith when I arrived on the Leadville laundry train with a group of miners who flooded Leadville when Hoarse Tabot [Horace "Haw" Tabor] *discovered the "Matchbox"* [Matchless] *mine. We were packed in that coach like a can of sardines, fighting to get out.*

"'I had boarded the coach heeled but concealed it inside my coat just as Doc had done that day when all hell broke loose down at Montgomery's [the O.K. Corral]. *In Tombstone, I had served as vigilance messenger for Colonel Wm. Herring, a prominent Tombstone attorney who's* (sic) *office located at 534 Freemont, served as a meeting place for many of Wyatt Earp's backers. In 1882, I had been a messenger for Wyatt Earp, joining his federal posse after the death of his brother by cowards.*

"'Experience had taught me for a man like Holliday – who told me once that I should join the game – that he did not fear death. It was the living that he feared most. The fear of not going out game. Many times I had seen Doc cry tears from the agony the dreadful disease scourged him when the whiskey failed to do its work.*

"'The trip from Leadville was hard on Doc. The jolting from the narrow gauge would cause him to cough up pieces of lung and blood. It was about two o'clock when the stage reached the Hotel Glenwood. Kate said it was May 24*th.

> *"'Experience had taught me for a man like Holliday – who told me once that I should join the game – that he did not fear death."*

"'Doc was coughing from almost each breath and upon arrival, had to use his cane to support his weight. He was very frail in body when I saw him, and his hair was a silver gray. His face showed the lines of age and he looked sick in the eyes. His appearance resembled that of an older man, since pulling out of Hooker's Ranch [where the Vendetta riders were temporarily protected in 1882].

"'One might argue that Doc was content in his actions and that his daily consumption of whiskey came to be his only escape from his suffering. I was rightly taken with the general surroundings of Glenwood Springs upon reaching Eighth Avenue, holding my duffle and looking for the hotel.

"'Kate had told me Doc was boarding. All I wanted was to register and find a bathhouse. I had run into Kate in the lobby who had sent this young bellhop, whom Doc had nicknamed Kenny [Art Kendrick], on an errand.

"'The welcome feeling I experienced far exceeded that of Tombstone I soon discovered. The district was full of excitement when the train pulled into the station house. I recall most of all how many people were about on the streets.

"'There was a definite resemblance to Denver; the big blue sky and the "Rockies," that seem to surround the town, which I would soon see was a perfect view from Doc's hotel window.

"'The Denver and Rio Grande was due to arrive the following day [October

5], and the town was full of anticipation of the arrival of the new iron horse. Banners swung across streets, and merchant signs from store front windows. Great expectations filled the streets.

"'I refrained from the moment and walked in the lobby of the Hotel Glenwood. The lobby was furnished with fine "Victorian" trimmings and elaborate knotted-Persian carpets, reminded me of the Cosmopolitan and Grand hotels in Tombstone, and the White Club House Room in Denver.

"'There was this need to put down words on paper since leaving Hooker's Ranch in '82, but it was Kate's enduring patience and devotion to Doc that gave me my inspiration to tell the story.

"'There was a sense of fatalism in Kate's voice, yet talk of the springs which had brought Doc to Glenwood was the last hope the West had to offer a lunger like Doc. I suppose if there was a chance for Doc's health to improve, he would take up its resources in Glenwood Springs.

"'Writing this down is not to judge him for past actions, but to understand him. Doc's memory seemed to be unaffected at times, although he lost much of his lungs over the years out West since leaving his beloved Georgia. I know the whiskey came to be his only escape from the pain that came with the consumption, and his desperate longing for home.

"'There is no doubt that the short time Doc lived inside the Hotel Glenwood, [it] became his sanctuary. What transpired within the walls will leave a lasting impression. One that is etched in my memory.

"'Coming to Glenwood Springs with the miners in October, I found Doc delirious and dying. He had fallen to a pneumonia the local doctor said, and had not spoken a word in weeks. Kate was already there taken (sic) care of him when I arrived. She said Doc had sent word to her in Globe from Leadville and told her he was leaving after a bit of excitement with Will Allen, and was taking a stage to Glenwood Springs, in Garfield County to see if the sulfur springs would ease his consumption.

"'Kate's devotion to Doc was not surprising, for she remained by his side till the end. Doc had tolerated my presence in Tombstone, though suggested I join the game after Morg's death, since Morg and I had a fondness to billiards at Robert Hatch's. Doc was still a young man though he began to deteriorate in Denver and became more advanced as his struggle for pain was no longer at his control. Doc was at the point of never leaving his bed again.

"'I imagine Kate felt helpless not being able to ease his pain. Shortly after Doc arrived, he tryed (sic) dealing faro but no longer could keep up the long hours he was used to in Tombstone, for he tired easily. Walking from gambling house to gambling house became an exhausting event, and the treatments at the springs [never] seemed to have any effect.

> *"But it was Kate's enduring patience and devotion to Doc that gave me my inspiration to tell the story."*

"'Kate was their means for support, for Doc could not work. I would help to bring in money by doing odd jobs around town, and doing mechanic work for a blacksmith shop.

"'Since October, Doc hardly spoke and hardly sat up twice. Kate never wanted to be far from Doc. I consoled her and saw to it no harm came to Doc from the traffic coming and going inside the hotel. Doc had made many enemies in his life and perhaps [because of] the troubles Doc faced in Arizona and Colorado, she still sensed danger to him.

"'A light snow had fallen early in the morning and Kate had to shut the window in Doc's room. His breathing had become shallow overnight and the color in his face had turned pale. It is important to know the last day as I was in the hotel room with Doc and Kate as he clinged (sic) to life.

"'An era was ending Kate thought. I don't write about an era changing, but a man's life who was shaped around it. For Kate the day began to fall apart when I was told that Kate sent for the doctor and that I should return to Doc's room. It seemed strange for anyone beside Doc or Kate to summon me at once. I went, expecting the end had come.

"'In the lobby I had a strange feeling. Instead of the heavy traffic, there was this stillness in the hotel lobby as I hurried up to Doc's room. Then the bellhop told me that Doc was sitting up. I felt relief for Kate. For a moment I thought Doc had cheated death one last time.

"'Doc had been found that morning sitting up by the maid who had awoke (sic) Kate who had slept in Doc's chair that he liked sitting by the window in. The doctor was there when I got there. He was saying something to Kate, but his words didn't make her feel better.

"'For the first time in weeks, the details and the sound of Dr. B.'s [possibly Dr. Baldwin] voice was [sic] clear. She knew the end was upon him. Knowing Doc, I figured he might pull out another winning hand. It was not meant to be. This would be his last game.

"'I did not know the complete story from the doctor who had been making house calls to Doc's room the past few weeks. Though I never doubted his opinion. In the final hour I knew one thing. Doc was about to cash in his chips.

"'There were several Glenwood residents in the room, Sarah Copper [Sarah Field Cooper] and Walter Devereaux, whom (sic) shared a seat with Doc on the Concorde stage.

"'The doctor who had been sent for by Kenny stood over Doc pouring him a tumbler of whiskey, jotting down medical quotes in his notebook. During the final moments, when the end was approaching, Doc turned his head toward Kate and smiled. He turned up the tumbler with great fashion as he always had done in the past.

"'As the light began to fade from his eyes, he took his last breath, and heard him say, "This is funny." Then his eyes stood still, and his body relaxed. Doc was lying on his bed, dead. I remember Kate saying in a distraught voice, "The end of Holliday." The room seemed as lifeless as he was.

"'He had opened his eyes once or twice that morning, but his gaze was clouded. When I saw him open his eyes at Kate, she leaned over him straining to hear something or read something from his eyes. Kate was trying to tell him something, though I doubt he heard her. The Colt, which he employed laid idle in the bureau, retired for all times. "Doc is at peace, Charlie. The worms won't get Doc today."

"'It is unthinkable, but during his time of dying, I realized the loss that Kate

was feeling. In the be-
ginning when I first
met him in Tombstone,
he had been a sporting
man, usually staying
among Wyatt's crowd,
yet everyone who knew
him was certain of his
loyalty to friends.

"Doc didn't have
many friends, and he
showed honor to the
ones he did have. Those
in the room were show-
ing their respect for Doc.
During the moment
when he at last found
peace, and the pain had
left him, I knew he had
found what he longed
for. Doc had died a
slow, lingering death.

"It would sur-
prise him to have es-
caped death so many times, to have died in
a room in Glenwood Springs. At the end
when Doc was gone, the doctor noted the
time of death. "Nine fifty-five, November
8, 1887."

"Preparations were made for a quick
funeral, which would take place in a place
called Linwood, a short distance by hack
at two o'clock the same day. It would be
a quiet procession, with the Reverend Ru-
dolph officiating. His coffin would be elaborate with silver trimmings, donated by
Glenwood's social class and friends he had
made.

"By 11 o'clock, the undertakers came
to remove Doc's body from the hotel. It
was the first time I had seen the physical scars the consumption had left on his
body. The body was taken away. A black
hearse rolled to a stop near the front entrance, and everybody came outside. Those
who were standing on the boardwalk and

> *Doc did indeed
> utter the words
> "This is funny"
> just prior to
> his death,
> acknowledging
> the humor in the
> fact that he
> was dying with
> his boots off.*

those in the street tipped
their hats to Kate as the
hearse drove away.

"Kate left Glen-
wood Springs after Doc's
possessions were in order
to be sent back to rela-
tives in Georgia. It was
a sad parting. I left No-
vember 10th, the day af-
ter Kate. Will stop by
Leadville to see Bob I
think.'"

It is interesting to
note from the above ar-
ticle that several items
which have been ques-
tioned over the years
as to their authenticity
can now quite possibly
be certified as being ac-
curate as a result of this
article.

First of all, this ar-
ticle confirms that Kate Harony did in
fact come to Doc's aid during his last
days, staying with him and caring for
him until the end. The article also gives a
specific date (May 24, 1887) for Doc's arrival in Glenwood Springs. Prior to this
article, it was known only that he had arrived in the spring of 1887.

Also confirmed by the article is the
fact that Art Kendrick (Kenny) – who
long claimed he was the bellhop in the
Hotel Glenwood during Doc's last days
and ran many errands for him – was also
actually telling the truth about those experiences.

Finally, one of the most enduring
legends of the Old West is also put to
bed with this article which confirms that
Doc did indeed utter the words "This is
funny" just prior to his death, acknowl-
edging the humor in the fact that he was
dying with his boots off.

Where Lie The Bones Of John Henry Holliday?

He is one of the most celebrated figures of the old West, but today, "Doc" Holliday's final resting place is completely unknown. . . . or is it?

Many of the locations of the last remains of popular figures from the old West are known quite well today. Interestingly, however, the specific location of the last remains of one of the most famous old West gunmen of all time is a mystery today.

But strangely, that actually isn't that unusual for old West gunmen. They often were buried where they fell – and fairly quickly before putrefaction could set in. Their graves also invariably were very poorly marked for posterity – more often than not without permanent stone markers.

For instance, no one today knows the "exact" gravesite of Billy the Kid – though his is at least known generally. Not so, however for Butch Cassidy, nor the Sundance Kid, nor "Curly Bill" Brocius, nor "Buckskin" Frank Leslie, nor "Turkey Creek" Jack Johnson, nor Warren Earp, and on and on, all of whose graves are a total mystery today. Strange? You be the judge.

Most of these men were intentionally mysterious in life, identifying themselves by aliases, and secretively withholding almost all actual details about themselves for their entire lives. So what's so unusual about that circumstance carrying over into death? John Henry Holliday himself occasionally used an alias when he was "on the run." He also played the facts of his life "very close to the vest" while he was alive, though the mystery about his actual gravesite is just a bit different.

John Henry Holliday's parents – Henry Burroughs Holliday and Alice Jane McKey – were from South Carolina. They provided a good education for their son, but his primary interest was the great outdoors. Nothing interested young John Henry more than hunting, fishing and horseback riding. In time, this came to include the use of firearms.

In 1861, Henry Burroughs Holliday accepted a presidential appointment from Jefferson Davis to serve as quartermaster in the 27th Georgia Infantry, Confederate States of America. After the Battle of Manassas, Henry Burroughs was promoted to the rank of major and fought in the Peninsula

Campaign as well as in the deadly Battle of Malvern Hill.

In 1862, a short time after fighting at Malvern Hill, Major Holliday was forced by ill health – watery dysentery – to leave the army and return to his family in Griffin. He, no doubt, thought death for him was eminent at that time, though he managed to survive. Approximately 26 years later, he would suffer through the mortality of his famous son, John Henry.

Creation Of A Myth

During his lifetime, John Henry was credited with the shooting of a number of men who were actually shot by other individuals.[1] The newspapers of that day, however – in the absence of factual information – invariably chose to fabricate many – if not most – of the details of Holliday's life out West. It just made for better reading, and, subsequently, better sales of their publications.

With its usual artistic license, Hollywood also created a false image and persona for John Henry Holliday. In most instances, it portrayed him as a bloodthirsty and cold-blooded killer.

In reality, of the handful of actual shootings in which Holliday was involved, they occurred because much larger and stronger men – who, due to John Henry's much weaker and therefore vulnerable physical condition – tried to increase their own stature at his expense by attempting to either severely injure him, or kill him outright. These attackers, however, had almost always misjudged their opponent.

Rather than resulting in Holliday's submission or serious injury or death, these attacks invariably ended in either a gun or a knife fight with Holliday virtually always gaining the upper hand. John Henry was weak and small in stature

John Henry Holliday as he appeared in the later years of his life. Even though he was only in his thirties at the time this photo was taken, the vitality of youth apparent only a few years earlier had been drained away by the onslaught of tuberculosis within his body. (Photo courtesy of the Colorado Historical Society)

physically. There was no doubt about that. He, however, had been blessed with strong arms and hands, lightning-quick reflexes, and deadly accuracy with firearms, and he utilized these physical traits and skills time after time when attacked.

Doc Holliday's life contradicts the myth of the man. He was not a ruthless individual, nor was he "blood-thirsty" in nature, nor necessarily evil. "When any of you fellows have been hunted from one end of the country to the other, as I have been, you'll understand what a bad man's reputation is built on," John Henry is reported to have once quipped.

Holliday pursued life under the only circumstances available to him. He sought to remain alive as long as his body would allow him, and along the way, unfortunately, his reputation from incidents in which he was forced to defend himself became twisted and tainted, and

Grand Avenue in Glenwood Springs was photographed on June 18, 1898, a little over 10 years after Holliday's death. The gambler from Georgia strode down this street more than a few times. Visible approximately halfway down on the right side of the street in the distance is the Hotel Glenwood
in which he died.

caused violence to follow him just as do
fleas a dog. This myth of his preponder-
ance or desire for violence is just one of
many which followed him into the grave.

Lost Burial Site

Inaccurate information seemed to
plague Doc in death just as it had in real
life. His obituary was printed in a variety of newspapers, but very few if any of
them printed factual information about
him or his death.

The local newspaper in Glenwood
Springs, Colorado (where he died), stated that Doc was buried "in Linwood
Cemetery," Glenwood Springs, Colorado, at 4:00 p.m., November 8, 1887.
However, the steep trail that led to the
cemetery (which exists on a hilltop
mesa) reportedly was impassable due to
snow and ice on the day Holliday's mortal remains were to be buried.

According to records, Doc was
therefore actually buried in a temporary

grave someplace near the foot of the hill.
When spring and warmer weather returned, even if a burial detail had been
organized to dig up his body (which it
wasn't), no one by that point knew exactly where he was buried – just as they don't
today – though the signage in Linwood
and the media reports of his death have
consistently maintained that he nevertheless is buried "in Linwood Cemetery."

The same Glenwood Springs news-
paper which mis-stated the site of his burial also stated that many friends attended
Holliday's funeral, but since he reportedly
was buried the same day he died, this too
is doubtful.[2] Also, adding insult to injury,
both a monument and Holliday's headstone in Linwood Cemetery contained
numerous mistakes for many years. It was
almost as if his detractors were attempting
to harass him even in death.

Tombstone, Arizona historian Ben
Traywick seemed to state it best: "It is
difficult to see how so many mistakes

The bar inside the Hotel Glenwood in Glenwood Springs was photographed circa 1890s. It, in all likelihood, was visited by Holliday prior to the time he became bedridden in his last days. The rough-looking crew in this photo says it all. (Courtesy of Frontier Historical Society)

could be made on a headstone without trying," he wrote.[3]

Despite the fact that a monument in Linwood Cemetery continues to proclaim that Holliday is buried "somewhere in this cemetery," some historians are convinced he was not.

One account maintains that following the spring thaw in 1888, a relative of Holliday's traveled to Glenwood Springs, retrieved the gunfighter's body, and returned with it to Georgia where it was re-interred in Oak Hill Cemetery in Griffin, his boyhood home.

Bill Dunn, a distant relative of Holliday's who headed up the Doc Holliday Society in Griffin, extensively researched the Holliday family for a number of years.

"There is no doubt in my mind why the people in Glenwood Springs don't know exactly where Doc is buried," Dunn said in an interview in 1999. *"[It's because] he isn't there. Doc is buried right here in his hometown of Griffin. He was originally buried near Linwood Cemetery, but he is not there now. You just don't*

lose the grave of a man who held his celebrity status."

Buried In Georgia?

Some researchers believe that Doc's father, Major Henry B. Holliday (or his emissary) traveled to Glenwood Springs and claimed his son's remains. In retrospect, this is a definite possibility, since transportation of the coffin and remains could easily have been accomplished via the Denver & Rio Grande Western (D&RGW) Railroad which had been completed to Glenwood Springs in 1887 – the year Holliday died and prior to his death. And back in Griffin, Georgia, the train depot was within a mile of Oak Hill Cemetery.

Dunn says he believes that if it was not Major Holliday who retrieved his son's remains, he quite possibly sent his nephew, Robert Alexander Holliday, to perform the task. Doc's consort out West – Mary Katherine Harony – recalled in a later interview that one of Doc's cousins visited him in Tombstone after the shootout at the O.K. Corral.

Dunn says he believes this man was Robert.

Strangely coincidental – or maybe not – is the fact that the final resting place of Major Holliday himself is also unknown today. Considering the fact that Henry Burroughs Holliday was a wealthy landowner, a decorated veteran of three wars, and a four-time mayor of Valdosta, Georgia, it is highly unlikely that his final resting place would not have been clearly marked and definitely known today – unless he intentionally made arrangements to be buried in a secret location for a particular reason.

Major Holliday out-lived his son by several years. He died on February 22, 1893 in Valdosta. Despite many years of searches, the location of his grave has eluded researchers just as has that of his famous son.

Bill Dunn maintains that he has located a marked grave for every Holliday family member in Valdosta and Griffin – except for Major Holliday and his son, Doc. Dunn says he now believes without a doubt he has found the unmarked graves of both in Griffin's Oak Hill Cemetery.

The Plot Thickens

The two graves which Dunn says belong to Henry Burroughs and John Henry Holliday are located in the Thomas family plot at Oak Hill. The families enjoyed a very close relationship, and Dunn says he believes the Thomas family may have agreed to an anonymous burial of Doc in their family plot to avoid vandalism of his grave.

"I believe they buried Doc in Oak Hill when he was brought back from Glenwood Springs, and Major Holliday was buried there when he died," Dunn remarks. "Why would a plot containing expensive marble markers of the Thomas family contain two concrete slab graves

with no marking or identification whatsoever? Could it be that they wanted them to remain anonymous and their last remains protected from vandalism?"

Osgood Miller, an employee of Clark Monument Company for forty-six years, added credence to Dunn's claim. He said he remembered the late Charlie McElroy – who was cemetery superintendent during the 1930s – telling him that Doc Holliday was buried in Oak Hill. Osgood said Charlie even pointed in the direction of the Thomas plot when he made the statement. Several years later, the late Griffin historian Laura Clark pointed out the same area as Doc's final resting place.

Wyatt Earp, who was probably the closest friend John Henry Holliday ever had, died in 1929. Ironically, after all the gunfights in which he was involved, Earp was never once wounded. He died in bed from what undoubtedly was prostate cancer (listed as "prostatitis" on his death certificate).

While he and Doc were both still alive, Earp was quoted as saying "Doc Holliday is the nerviest, fastest, deadliest man with a six-gun I ever saw." And in Denver, Colorado, when last the two met and he realized that his old friend was near death, Earp, with tears in his eyes, also told Holliday that "You saved my life on two separate occasions. Isn't it strange that you must go first."

One can only marvel today that the final resting place of such a celebrated figure of the old West is, for all intents and purposes, completely unknown, as is that of his father, Henry Burroughs Holliday.

Endnotes

1/ John Henry by Ben T. Traywick

2/ Ibid

3/ Ibid

Engineer David J. Fant and the "Valley of Death"

Famed railroad man David J. Fant was known as "the evangelist of the rails" during his lifetime, because he was a Baptist minister in addition to his railroading duties. On a cool spring morning in 1910, his faith undoubtedly earned him deliverance from disaster.

David J. Fant – "the evangelist of the rails" – knew he had a serious problem when old No. 37 began to shake and vibrate terrifically as the huge train he was controlling approached Toccoa Falls in northeast Georgia. The car immediately behind the great engine and tender bobbled and bounced as it left the tracks and began dragging the train down a steep embankment.

Fant had been on the rails long enough to have witnessed his share of the end results of disasters such as this. He had only a moment to utter a quick prayer before yelling for his fireman to jump. Time was obviously of the essence, as they say, and it was quickly expiring for these two men.

Fant was well aware that the huge steam locomotive was about to roll over. It was simply the nature of the beast. When these mechanical giants leave the rails, they rarely remain upright, and when they roll over and hit the ground, the boiling water tanks filled with super-heated steam are always ruptured, and anyone within 50 to 100 feet invariably is delivered to the hereafter, the skin from their bodies instantly boiled and flaying off.

In his desperation in the moment, Fant cried out to the Lord, threw on the emergency brake then closed his eyes and awaited the inevitable. . . .

Dangerous Rails

Seven years earlier in 1903 and almost at this same spot near Toccoa, Georgia, Fant had watched in helpless horror as his dear friend and fellow engineer Ed Miller had died tragically in a similar derailment. Then, only one year later in 1904 – again near this exact same spot – Fant himself miraculously had escaped injury in a similar derailment. Did fate hold a winning hand against him now in 1910?

Fant's exciting adventures upon the endless ribbons of rail and his compassion for his fellow man ultimately earned him a spot in the annals of railroading folklore for all time. And today, as his immense engine leaned to the right side, he was about to add to that legend. . .

There was a pall hanging over the scenic Blue Ridge Mountains as the railroad rose up from the lowlands and forested terrain along the North Broad River south of Toccoa. It was almost like a funeral dirge marching the railroaders to a final destiny.

In today's modern world, rail accidents, comparatively-speaking, are rare. For that reason, when an accident does occur, it's usually a big one, becoming statewide, if not national, news.

Back in Fant's day in the early 1900s – prior to the age of the automobile and practical air travel – the railroads were the only means of quick long-distance transportation. And since the technology of safe rail travel had not yet been perfected, railroad mishaps were much more common – yet they were still big news when they occurred, since they were just as devastating as modern accidents.

From the 1840s to the early 1900s, passenger rail cars were all constructed of wood, not metal. Consequently, when a rail disaster occurred and the momentum of the train was suddenly halted, these wooden cars filled with flesh and bone human passengers would "telescope" or collapse into each other as they collided, crushing each car in succession and mangling the unfortunate passengers inside.

As if that was not bad enough, a wrecked steam locomotive meant a horrible death for many a brave engineer, his fireman, and anyone else within 50 to 100 feet of the steam escaping from the locomotive's ruptured water tanks. If they weren't crushed and killed immediately, the steam would horribly scald them to death. It was a death, the thought of which, caused even tough and hardened trainmen to shudder in fear.

Atlanta-Charlotte Route

The real culprit in these disasters in the early 1900s was the routes traveled by the trains and often the speed at which the trains were required to travel. The railroad construction contractors invariably were forced to wind the route of their rail lines around mountains and across deep chasms, often using construction technology and materials which were destined for eventual certain failure and catastrophic accidents.

In 1856, a company was formed to build a railroad through the Toccoa (Stephens County) area to connect Atlanta and Charlotte, North Carolina with steam locomotive rail transportation. However, according to historian Kathryn Curtis Trogden, a national depression and the Civil War held up this project until sometime around 1873-74.

This Atlanta to Charlotte route was and still is a heavily traveled line even today (2023), since it is the shortest route by rail from the Deep South to the North. It became so popular in the late 19th century that the iron rails were replaced with steel from 1878 to 1887, and the line was double-tracked in 1917.

The "Air-Line," as this railroad was known, skirted the edge of the mountains, a dangerous route in the days prior to the safety measures taken by today's rail transportation companies. In the Toccoa area, the railroad had sharp curves, high wooden trestles, steep banks and other characteristics which made it a perilous trip, especially during heavy rains which caused landslides and destabilized trestles.

Famous Fant

David Jones Fant, an engineer from Atlanta, had earned a place in the folklore of railroading because, aside from his employment as an engineer, he was also a Baptist minister, preaching wherever his time and schedule would allow him. While many of the railroad employees in the early 1900s were a rough, tough, profane lot, with a "live for today" attitude, Fant was a family man, close to both his family and his ministry.

Fant had even met his future wife on the railroad while on a short run on the Atlanta to Toccoa route. He also often ministered to the students at Toccoa Falls Bible College, and would blow his engine's whistle each time he passed by the school, as a call to prayer for his friends there.

As a result of his many and varied railroading experiences, Fant – as much as anyone – was well aware of the dangers of steaming up the Toccoa run. His knowledge of the danger this route represented constantly plagued him, and he also knew that he could be the inadvertent cause of the deaths or injuries to others because of this peril.

In addition to the normal dangers of this route, Fant also had to be on the lookout for other steam locomotives on the tracks, as well as the people and livestock which often strayed accidentally onto the rails. Livestock were big enough to actually derail a train themselves, although it was considered good luck (and good eating) for the engineer to catch poultry in the grill of his engine.

Fant had witnessed the devastating derailment involving engineer Ed Miller, a friend of his, who – only one day previous (through Fant's persuasion) – had attended railroad church for the first – and, as it turned out, the last – time. Fant was running a fast freight and had side-tracked at Toccoa to allow the north-bound No.36 passenger train under Miller to pass.

His fellow engineer, however, never arrived. At Ayersville, six miles up the mountainside from Toccoa, a landslide had caught and derailed the locomotive of the No. 36 at Currahee Crossing.

Wreck of No. 36

Upon learning of Miller's fate, Fant waited only long enough to take on local doctors and nurses, before going to his friend's rescue. As suspected, the wreck was a terrible one.

The huge locomotive with its white-hot steam-filled tanks had been turned over by the force of the landslide, trapping Miller and his fireman beneath it. Unfortunately for them, they were not killed by the impact, but were slowly dying from a complete scalding they had received from the ruptured tanks of boiling water in their engine. The skin, reportedly, was sliding off their bodies, and the colors of their eyes had faded by the time Fant reached them.

The dying Miller, in horrible agony, feverishly beseeched Fant to pray for him. The evangelist engineer pulled out his worn, grease-stained Bible which he always carried with him, and began to read:

"Yea though I walk through the valley of the shadow of death, I will fear no evil, for thou art with me..." Fant read steadily, as Miller's life slowly ebbed away.

On April 28, 1910, near the anniversary of Miller's death at the site, Fant passed through that same "valley of death" once again on a run to Atlanta. He was at the controls of No. 37, heading for Atlanta with his friend and black fireman - Rufus Johnson.

Deliverance

After passing through Toccoa, Fant pushed the old engine up to its cruising speed of 50 miles an hour, in order to accelerate for the climb through the edge of the mountains. Toccoa Falls Bible College rushed by, and it was shortly thereafter, that Fant's world turned topsy-turvy.

Since he was going south on a banked curve at such a high rate of speed, the engine of No. 37 *should* have turned over on the outside of the curve, derailing and trapping Fant beneath his engine. Miraculously, however, the engine fell instead over in the opposite direction, and when it finally came to rest seventy feet below, the evangelist of the rails amazingly emerged from the tangled wreck above the wheels uninjured. Was it a miracle? You be the judge.

Fant immediately began a feverish search for his devoted fireman, Rufus Johnson. He finally found him a short distance away. He, just as amazingly, was also unharmed, but in a state of shock.

The conductor and flagman arrived soon afterwards, and not finding Fant and Johnson, assumed they had met their fate trapped beneath the huge engine. Somehow, this false assumption was reported down the line. The wreck drew headlines in the *Atlanta Journal* where Fant's assumed death was unfortunately reported therein, a mistake which was not corrected before Fant's young son had read it in the newspaper.

Fant's wife, however, had been spared much of the shock. She and their three-year-old daughter, Mary, were on a passenger train that ironically was following Fant's No. 37. Not only did they get to see that he was alright, but were given a tour of the wrecked engine and cars.

The derailment had been a terrible wreck, but, amazingly, no one was killed. Little Mary wasn't even shocked or impressed, remarking simply: "Daddy turned his engine over."

Arriving safely in Atlanta with his family, Fant stopped at the terminus long enough to send a telegram to his friend Rev. R.V. Miller in Hendersonville, North Carolina. It read *"Saved from a serious wreck. Psalms 91:9-12. Continue to pray."*

Miller's reply was: *"Have just learned of your deliverance. Psalms 91:9-12. God answers prayer."*

The passage cited by both these God-fearing men reads as follows:

"Because thou hast made the Lord which is my refuge, even the most High thy habitation; there shall be no evil befall thee, neither shall any plague come nigh thy dwelling. For he shall give his angels charge over thee, to keep thee in all thy ways. And they shall bear thee up in their hands, lest thou dash thy foot against a stone."

A Legend Retires

The late Atlanta historian Franklin Garrett once wrote that the stretch of Southern Railway between Charlotte and Atlanta has never been quite the same since David J. Fant made his last run on September 22, 1939, retiring at the age of 71, after 47 years of service. His narrow escape from the wreck of the Southern Crescent in 1910 made him a legend, familiar to evangelists and trainmen alike throughout the United States.

Interestingly, news media coverage of Fant's miraculous survival of that train wreck was dwarfed the following year by the media circus surrounding the fabled engineer as he had the dubious honor of watching his train being robbed at gun-point near Gainesville, Georgia, by one of the last remaining notorious bandits from the old West – Bill Miner. The *"Gentleman Bandit,"* as Miner was dubbed in newspaper coverage, had migrated to the eastern United States after numerous robberies and murder in the western United States Canada had made him a *"Wanted"* man in those areas.

David J. Fant died in 1965 at the ripe old age of 97. The rails through Toccoa today are not the same in many ways as they were in Fant's day. Modern safety measures and advanced engineering of the routes have virtually eliminated most of the danger, but old-timers still close their eyes when they hear a train approaching, imagining that it is a steam locomotive about to pass through the "Valley of Death." They silently pray that the next sound they hear is not a crash....

Former Stagecoach Route Through the Mountains

It began as a pathway in pre-history, traversed
periodically and seasonally by migrating wildlife.
In pioneer days, early travelers and, later, stagecoaches,
often converted these routes to their use.

It takes a keen eye today, and a reasonably good knowledge of the pioneer history of our state, to find traces of the early toll-roads, but if one knows where to look, they can still be seen in the backwoods. The Logan Turnpike (known originally as "Union Turnpike") was once a well-traveled wagon road over Tesnatee Gap, providing a lifeline for commerce and transportation between Blairsville (in Union County) and Gainesville (in Hall County).

To pay for its construction and maintenance, the Logan had both a toll-gate and a gate-keeper who collected a fee from everyone who used the road. Modern highways built across the north Georgia mountains in the 1930s ultimately eliminated the need for most of the old toll-roads, and it wasn't long before routes like Logan fell into disuse and

abandonment, but they once were vital travel venues.

Today, very few north Georgians are even aware the old toll-roads ever existed at all, and fewer still can claim to have traveled over one of these old routes prior to the time that our modern highways usurped the usefulness of these early thoroughfares. One individual who could however, was Charles Roscoe Collins of Choestoe.

Known to family and friends as "Ros," Mr. Collins was appointed official historian of Union County by Georgia Governor Zell Miller during his term in office. Interviewed for this article prior to his death, Ros's memories provided a colorful roadmap for a time in our state's history which has long departed.

"I went over the Union Turnpike many times with my father, James J. Collins, in our two-horse wagon," recalled

Though remnants of the old pioneer-era Logan Turnpike are still visible in the mountains of Union County, much of the route has been obscured over the passage of time by logging roads and access trails. One distinct characteristic of the turnpike, however, is the many boulders lining the route which were removed to the sides of the road annually as they were revealed by cattle, horse, and wagon traffic.

Collins. "My job was to 'brake' the wagon. I'd cut some blocks of wood to use in scotching the wheels down the steep grades. In the wintertime, I had to go ahead and break up the ice on streams so the horses could get across. These were hard jobs for a slip of a boy."

Once, before the turnpike closed (circa 1925 when U.S. Highway 129 was opened across Neel Gap in north Georgia), Ros Collins made a wagon trip on the old trail by himself. He was about seventeen years of age at the time.

"The experience was a sign of 'having arrived,' of being grown up and responsible enough to manage the team and wagon alone, sell the farm produce at the market in Gainesville, and purchase 'store-bought' supplies at wholesale houses for re-sale in father's country

store at Choestoe," he smiled in remembrance. "The round trip took five days."

Origin of the Routes

The Union Turnpike over Tesnatee Gap is one of the earliest official travel routes ever cleared in the state. In the *Digest of Laws of the State of Georgia for 1821*, the following notation may be found: *"John Lyon, Joel Dickerson and Company shall hereafter be a body corporate by the name and style of the Union Turnpike Company, for the purpose of constructing a turnpike road from Loudsville in Habersham County, through the Tesnatee Gap in the Blue Ridge Mountains, by way of Blairsville to some eligible point on the northern boundary of this state in a direction toward the Tellico Plains in the state of Tennessee."*

Specifications for the turnpike were for a width of twenty feet with twelve feet of causeway. The owners/contractors of the route forbade any canal, railroad or other road being constructed within ten miles laterally of the turnpike for a period of fifteen years. This no doubt was done to discourage competition against this toll-road, at least until its owners could make back their investment in this public conveyance.

Construction of Union Turnpike apparently began immediately. Indians were still in the mountain areas in 1821, and, as was customary in road-building projects, the course of the Union Turnpike followed an Indian trail.

The early footpaths of the Native Americans had often been adopted from trails through the mountain passes which had been originally trampled down by animals – usually buffalo, elk, or some other hooved animal – in their seasonal migrations. These animals instinctively knew the easiest and safest routes across the mountains, and their trails subsequently were naturally adopted by the Native Americans for their trading and warring purposes.

The Union Turnpike was completed the same year it was chartered. Despite its early construction, it was paralleled across another ridge by an even older road, chartered in 1813, known as the *"Unicoi Turnpike."* The course of this early mountain road extended from North Carolina down across Unicoi Gap, through Nacoochee Valley (in present-day White County, GA) and on into present-day Clarkesville in Habersham County.

Remnants of this trail may still be viewed today in the Sautee-Nacoochee Valley. A short portion is clearly visible in the lower front yard of the popular Sautee Inn. Though chartered in 1813,

Photographed here circa 1920, are Homer Nix and a "Miss Satterfield." They stand in front of the old Logan home near the toll-gate of the Logan Turnpike. Travelers - both coming and going - were required to pause at this spot to pay fees. The ten-room log lodge at this site known appropriately as "Logan's Lodge" reportedly was a favorite of South Carolina Senator and former U.S. Vice-President John C. Calhoun who often traveled the turnpike to check on his gold mine in Dahlonega.

the route was actually cleared in 1812 by a group of coastal merchants seeking an inland trade route into the area.

The early mountain turnpikes usually acquired their names from a prominent mountain gap through which they passed, from a nearby landmark – or from a prominent landowner.

Logan Turnpike

Frances Logan was born July 18, 1802. He was the son of James and Nancy Edgerton Logan. He had migrated from Rutherford County, North Carolina, leaving March 1, 1822, and

A circa-1920s view of the Gainesville, Georgia town square at which much of the products produced in Tennessee and extreme north Georgia were sold in pioneer days. Gainesville was the southern terminus of the Logan/Union Turnpike.

arriving on March 10 at Nacoochee Valley in north Georgia's present-day White County.

Logan had made the trip to Georgia via the Unicoi Turnpike, and was one of a number of pioneer settlers who had chosen to leave North Carolina for the valleys along the Chattahoochee River in Habersham County (in a section later renamed White County).

Frances Logan's land was physically located north of Cleveland in the Loudsville community. According to records, he married Hulda Powell on August 12, 1825.

Three years later in 1828, an event on the Logan farm set off a chain reaction which was unprecedented in the area. One of Frances Logan's slaves discovered a gold nugget in nearby Duke's Creek. The precious lump weighed some three ounces, and ignited a gold rush of

amazing proportions at the same time as a similar strike and rush were occurring just a bit southward in what came to be known as Dahlonega, Georgia.

Other discoveries were soon made along the Chattahoochee River, Bean Creek, Black Branch, Hamby's Ford, Town Creek and adjacent locations in White. Within a short period of time, the "North Georgia Gold Rush" was in full swing, and thousands of gold-hungry prospectors and businessmen were setting up operations from all directions to seek a share of the riches.

Gold played an important role in the development of both the Union and Unicoi Turnpikes. Gold ore obtained in the early days of mining in the area was hauled over both routes to Bechtler's Mint in Rutherford County, North Carolina, where it was processed. The valuable cargo was guarded with great caution along the trip. This arduous trek later became unnecessary with the construction of the U.S. Branch Mint in nearby Dahlonega, Georgia.

When Major Willis Logan, a son of Frances Logan, purchased extensive lands on the south slope of the Blue Ridge Mountains in western White County, the name of the Union Turnpike over Tesnatee Gap was changed to "Logan Turnpike." Records show that Major Logan paid $3,000 for the rights to the road. He then owned a charter to its operation for some thirty years. Members of his family continued to operate it right up to the days when U.S. Highway 129 was opened across Neel Gap in 1925.

After Major Logan's ownership was established, the route of "Logan" Turnpike extended from Loudsville in White County northward over Tesnatee Gap, by Ponder Post Office, on into Choestoe, where it connected with the old Union Turnpike – a length of seven and one-half miles.

A stagecoach line made regular trips from Augusta, Georgia, to Athens, Tennessee, on this turnpike. Major Logan had a stagecoach stop or "stand" (as it was called in pioneer days) on the route, and frequently accommodated overnight boarders.

Tolls for the road were collected at Major Logan's stop. The charges varied according to the type vehicle, the purpose of the travel, and the number of livestock used to pull the vehicle:

*Wagons with four wheels and drawn by four or more horses or oxen were charged two cents per mile.

*Four-wheel carriages termed "pleasure vehicles" paid three cents per mile.

*Jensey wagons (those drawn by only two horses or mules) and pleasure carriages with only two wheels (buggies) were clocked for one and one-half cents per mile.

*Ox-drawn carts were one-half cent per mile.

*Cattle driven over the turnpike had additional special rates.

Jack Shuler and his family lived at the foot of Tesnatee Gap on the Logan Turnpike. They operated the Ponder Post Office and a store, and farmed the nearby bottomlands.

Shuler was employed by Willis Logan to maintain the Turnpike. He worked for seventy-five cents per day. When his sons worked, they received ten cents per day for their labor, even when they were grown to manhood and could pile rocks and move brush with the best of workers.

Edward Shuler, a son of Jack, remembered working on the Turnpike. "While our bottomlands were drying out before another plowing, we boys put in time with Father, working on the Logan Turnpike from its foot to its top at Tesnatee Gap.

"We took up large rocks from the road which had sharp points poking out of the ground and piled them or threw them over the banks down the mountainside. We opened ditches that had become clogged with rocks and sticks and leaves. We filled up low places that had been washed out by rains or hollowed out by wagon wheels, and smoothed them out."

Legends on the Turnpike

A favorite story of both Ros Collins and Edward Shuler about Logan Turnpike happened at the point called Big or Spiva Bend. A man named Newt Spiva was a deserter during the U.S. Civil War. He had been hiding out in the mountains. The "Home Guard," (a group of men loosely organized on the pretense of protection for the homes and property of those who had volunteered for service in the Confederate forces), surprised Spiva as he sat on a big rock outcropping. They ordered him to raise his hands and surrender, but he refused to be taken captive, preferring instead to die at that spot, and they accommodated him.

Spiva Bend on Logan Turnpike had the most hazardous curve to negotiate – particularly if one was transporting a large load. Ros Collins tells of a huge steam boiler constructed at the gold mines in Coosa District of Union County west of Blairsville. Tom Collins (Ros' older brother) and two others, Perry Hood and Tom Calloway, had been hired by a Mr. Jarrard to transport the bulky contraption across Tesnatee Gap to his place on Town Creek near Collins Mountain in White County.

A special wheeled vehicle had been made to bear the boiler. Three yokes of oxen (large steers) pulled the unwieldy rig onto which the boiler was strapped.

When the men arrived at Spiva Bend, it appeared that they would have to dismantle the boiler to get it around the gigantic rock alongside the narrow road. With true mountain ingenuity however, the men used a series of winches in strategic locations to move the boiler past Spiva Bend. The effort required so much time and energy that the men camped at the Bend that night, and proceeded on across Logan Turnpike to the Jarrard place in White County the next day. The precious cargo arrived safely and in one piece.

Tesnatee Gap rises 3,138 feet, the highest point on the toll-road. The famed Appalachian Trail now crosses near this spot. Ros Collins identified another milepost near here.

"The Runyon boys were hanged from a chestnut tree here," he explained, matter-of-factly. According to folklore, the Runyons were also hiding out in the mountains for a transgression, and apparently were also captured by the Home Guard. They were hanged as an example from the branches of the giant chestnut.

"As a lad, every time Dad and I came along this place, I had a horror of seeing the Runyon boys' ghosts seeking revenge," he said.

(Editor's Note: It seems proper to point out here that in many instances, the "Home Guards" of Civil War days were often little more than a self-appointed group of opportunists supposedly serving duty by defending the home front. In reality, they quite often represented little more than an assemblage of vigilantes and outlaws, taking the law into their own hands and taking advantage of unprotected property, guarded in most instances by little more than women and children.)

As might be expected, the few old-timers who still remember Logan Turnpike have colorful stories to tell of the early days along the historic route. Characteristically, a number of the common stereotypes of wagon-train travel also hold true for the trail.

Life on the Turnpikes

Travel along the turnpike usually followed a pattern. Wagons banded together and journeyed as a group from Choestoe to Gainesville, according to Mr. Collins. The largest group usually consisted of approximately thirty wagons (which would have been quite a procession).

The first day's travel took the wagon train to Mile Branch north of Cleveland, where the group camped for the night. The next day got them to Gainesville where they stayed overnight at either Bell's or Simon's Wagon Yards. There, they sold chestnuts, animal skins, farm produce, and sorghum syrup. They traded as much as possible for merchandise to stock the country stores.

The return trip also took two days. The entire episode was usually planned to extend from Tuesday through Saturday. Mondays were used to load the wagons for the out-going trip, because the mountaineers were strongly opposed to working on Sunday, considering it the Lord's day, Collins noted.

Jud Duckworth once made his living as a wagon driver on the Turnpike. Employed by merchant Virge Waldroup, Duckworth made weekly trips across Tesnatee to Gainesville. His large covered wagon, drawn by four iron-gray mules, regularly transported heavy loads.

On the way south, Jud said he carried live chickens, eggs, and various

The ever-adventurous Roxane E. Durfee amazingly drove her *Overland Roadster* - an early version of the off-road vehicle - over Tesnatee Gap on the Logan Turnpike in 1917. It was the first time an automobile had navigated that rough route. After successfully completing her trek, she parked the vehicle (pictured) on the town square of Blairsville, Georgia.

produce from mountain farms received "in trade" at Waldroup's General Merchandise. On the return trip, the wagon was loaded with hardware, dry goods, and staples such as coffee, sugar, and rice. The driver also became the source of news from "down south," so he had to have a good memory.

Ros Collins and others in Blairsville today remember the first automobile driven over Logan Turnpike. The year was 1917, and the car was an Overland Country Club Roadster owned by Mrs. Roxane Durfee of Atlanta.

When Mrs. Durfee – an obvious adventuress – came to the toll gate at Loudsville, the gatekeeper reportedly was perplexed, because no fee had ever been established for motorized vehicles. After much argument, an agreement was struck for a fee of fifty cents – a cost which remained in use for the remainder of the life of the old turnpike.

Following a great deal of trouble with over-heated brakes, dangerous pot-holes, hazardous curves and frequent stops, Mrs. Durfee finally appeared at the Christopher Hotel in Blairsville – nerves somewhat frayed and frazzled. Her snappy gray roadster, however, with its red wire wheels and white convertible top, seemed none the worse for wear. Mrs. Durfee probably didn't know it at the time, but her trip undoubtedly signaled the beginning of the end for the turnpike, since the age of motorized transportation inevitably required a more accessible route.

To reach the site where the old Logan Turnpike Toll Gate and the stagecoach stop once stood, travel northwest from Cleveland, Georgia, on U.S. Highway 129 for approximately eight miles. Turn right onto Kellum Valley Road and proceed northeastward for approximately two miles. On the right, a sign with the words "Toll Gate" marks the historic spot.

The two-story Logan home-place which served as a hotel, stagecoach stop and toll-gate, is long gone today. On its former site, a newer home erected at a much later date and the adjoining toll-gate site were purchased in 1947 by Mary Mathis of Americus, Georgia, and Washington, D.C., as a future retirement residence. Four Mathis sisters – Mary, Rebecca Kimmel, Sarah Ethier, and Lynn McKay – spent May through October there annually until all of the sisters had passed away with the exception of Sarah. Sarah continued to live – well into her 90s – at the old Toll-Gate site in a modernized home with her daughter, Marion Crawford.

The Logan Turnpike was officially closed on Independence Day, 1925, but until the U.S. Forest Service barricaded the road in 1981, four-wheel-drive vehicles still traveled the 7.5 miles of the route regularly.

Today, a hike up the old road is still a challenge, but well-worth the trip, offering numerous scenic vistas of small waterfalls and the flora and fauna of the Blue Ridge Mountains along Town Creek. All along the old turnpike, piles of rocks and boulders serve as silent reminders of the days long ago when Jack Shuler and his predecessors kept the old Logan Turnpike passable by piling the obstructing stones to the sides of the road. Today, the old route has receded into the mists of time.

The Murder Of Union County Sheriff Charles L. Hill

The law enforcement domain of a rural mountain sheriff is, more often than not, a reasonably peaceful pursuit. The years immediately following the U.S. Civil War, however, were anything but peaceful. In fact, they were an exceedingly dangerous and deadly time for the entire Southeast. Union County Sheriff Charles L. Hill, had hardly been on the job six months before his life was quickly ended.

The old U.S. Civil War-era William Campbell property is quiet today. The Campbell cabin still existed until the 1980s, when it finally collapsed from neglect and rot. The property is located in a small valley, coursed by Crane Creek in the western portion of Towns County, just a few miles east of the Union County line "as the crow flies." No sign whatsoever hints that in 1867, this was a killing ground, when Campbell, a settler in the area, shot down 27-year-old Union County Sheriff Charles Hill in the prime of his life.

Charles Leonidas Hill had moved with his parents to a farm on what today is known as Mauney Road in the northern end of Union County. His father, Felix Walker Hill, and mother, Elizabeth, had migrated from Snow Hill, North Carolina, to north Georgia, perhaps seeking a new start in what they assumed would be a peaceful locale during the traumatic years immediately following the Civil War. If this was the case,

then the lawless north Georgia environs was an exceedingly poor choice for resettlement.

Hill's two brothers, Adam C. and Napoleon B. also came to Union County to live. It is not known today exactly when they moved to the area, but the family had become known well enough for Charles to be elected county sheriff of Union in 1866. Perhaps no one else wanted the job in the outlaw-infested area.

Charles's law enforcement career in north Georgia, like his life, would be short-lived – barely six months in length. His responsibilities on May 14, 1867, required him to apprehend and arrest William Campbell from his cabin on his Towns County farm. Normally, an apprehension of this nature would not involve the use of "deadly force," but these were anything but "normal times."

No one seems to recall the crime that Campbell had committed. Perhaps someplace deep in the Union County Sheriff's homicide records there is an accounting of this incident.

The only explanation that might be offered for the unusual circumstances in which a Union County sheriff might venture to make an arrest on Towns County soil, is that Campbell must have committed some offense in Union County. Nevertheless, under those circumstances, this arrest should have been the task of the Town's County Sheriff's Office.

In those highly lawless days in north Georgia, jurisdictional lines may not have been as strictly observed nor procedure as cautious as is the case today. In 1867, Towns County was but eleven years old, having been created from portions of Rabun and Union counties in 1856. Perhaps under the circumstances, the boundaries were blurred.

Prior to the formation of Towns County, Campbell's cabin would, in fact, have been on Union County soil. Perhaps Sheriff Hill was not even aware his quarry was located in a different county. Perhaps he didn't even care. In those days, outlaws were everywhere, and law enforcement in the Deep South was a tough, hard business.

Whatever his reasons for his method of apprehension of Campbell, Charles Leonidas Hill must have been a dedicated sheriff to pursue his man across the county line, particularly if he was aware that he was making an arrest beyond his legal jurisdiction. No one

Perhaps Sheriff Hill was not even aware his quarry was located in a different county. Perhaps he didn't even care.

will ever know what was on Hill's mind on this early summer day in 1867, when he left Union County with his deputies to arrest Campbell. He possibly was merely determined to allow nothing to stop him in the successful completion of his responsibilities.

Campbell's cabin was a two-story log structure that had been built at the base of a mountain a few yards from Crane Creek. If a settler had no fresh mountain spring or deep-water well from which to draw his drinking water in those days, a fresh mountain stream was a worthy substitute.

According to Howard Nichols – who had inherited the farm from his father Adam Nichols – the Campbell cabin had a porch across the back which faced the mountain trail down which Sheriff Hill descended that fateful morning. The structure's two rooms were divided, with a shared chimney between them. Each room could be entered only by outside doors as was customary in many cabins at that time.

Nichols, who learned the story of the murder from his father, says Sheriff Hill had apparently sent word to Campbell that he would be coming that day to make the arrest. Hill reportedly bravely instructed his deputies to wait for him at the ridgetop while he proceeded alone down the mountain path to arrest Campbell.

Perhaps Hill felt that Campbell

could be taken without resistance if he (Hill) went alone to persuade Campbell to give himself up. Campbell, however, apparently had a different agenda. He must have observed Hill's approach with extreme trepidation, apparently very determined to put up a vigorous resistance.

One has to remember these were the days immediately following the terrible U.S. Civil War times when bloody deaths were an everyday common occurrence. Most men were accustomed to an immediate defense of themselves – with deadly weapons – if an attempt was being made upon their lives or their freedoms.

According to details of the incident as described by Mr. Nichols, Campbell reportedly grabbed up his pistol, opened the door to the cabin slightly, and warned Sheriff Hill not to proceed any closer. Campbell shouted that if Hill would only leave him alone, he would depart the area in the morning, and never again return to the north Georgia mountains. Otherwise, Campbell warned, he would shoot Hill if he had to, although it was not his wish to do so.

In retrospect, depending of course upon the crime which Campbell had committed, Sheriff Hill might have been wise to allow him the requested latitude. If he did so, however, the good sheriff would have had some explaining to do to his deputies – possibly to the detriment of his law enforcement career.

After considering these circumstances, Sheriff Hill apparently misjudged his quarry, and kept walking. It is not known whether or not Hill had carried his weapon down to the cabin with him, but he evidently did not think Campbell would shoot him.

As with most unusual incidents of this nature in which the details were not carefully recorded at the time, several different versions of the story have been handed down through time and folklore. Another version of this incident at this juncture, as told by Roy Mauney of Blairsville, great-nephew of Charles Hill, maintains that Campbell refused to come out of the cabin, forcing Sheriff Hill to take an axe from a nearby wood-pile to break down the door. At this point, Campbell reportedly fired his pistol through a hole in the door, striking Hill at point-blank range.

Whatever the circumstances, Campbell reportedly did fire his pistol into Hill's abdomen, mortally wounding him. Campbell then made his escape from the area. In retrospect, Hill had simply used poor judgement and paid a very stiff price for it.

Sheriff Hill also, unfortunately, did not die immediately. He was carried, probably by his deputies, in a wagon to his father's home in Union County. This trip which Hill was forced to undergo that morning, undoubtedly was made either in agony, or in a state of unconsciousness, travel being what it was in those days on the crude very bumpy mountain roads.

According to the Towns County indictment handed down against Campbell for Hill's murder in the May term of court that year, Campbell had *"feloniously, willfully, and with malice aforethought"* taken *"a certain pistol of the value of $10.00"* and shot a *"leaden ball"* into the belly of Charles L. Hill, near the navel, giving Hill *"one mortal wound of the breadth of one inch and of the depth of ten inches, from which Hill languished and lingering did afterwards die."*

It is not known whether Hill's death finally came from blood loss, infection, or other complications, and it is not known whether any attempts were made by a surgeon or surgeons to remove the lead ball. In the 1860s, with a wound of that nature, an extremely painful lingering death was almost an inevitability. Hill, if he was conscious, must have known he was going to die.

It is interesting to note that the indictment of Campbell contains an obvious error, since it states that Hill was shot by Campbell on the 19th of May, and died after a period of lingering on May 17th. The inscription on Hill's tombstone indicates he died on May 17th, so the date of the shooting as stated in the indictment quite likely is an error. Hill most probably was shot on the 14th, since local folklore maintains that he clung to life for three days after being wounded.

Campbell, meanwhile, made good his escape, abandoning his wife, children, and all he owned forever. His ultimate destination and any other circumstances surrounding the remainder of his life from that day forward remain a mystery today. Though Towns County indictments charged him with murder, robbery, assault and battery, Campbell was never found, and therefore never stood trial on the charges.

According to Mr. Nichols, sometime in the 1980s, a woman who claimed to be a descendant of William Campbell, stopped by his farm wishing to see the place where Campbell had lived. The woman explained to Mr. Nichols that the only information the Campbell family had ever received of William Campbell was that he had gone West.

Information in a Towns County deed indicates that in the October term of court in the county in 1882, William L. Sutton was appointed administrator of the estate of William Campbell,

whom the deed lists as "deceased," empowering Sutton to sell the property. Since Campbell's family never learned of his whereabouts, he apparently was declared legally dead in order to allow the family to liquidate his assets.

Whether Campbell never returned because of his demise, or because he did not intend to stand trial for the murder of Sheriff Hill will never be known. In any case, Campbell either willingly or unwillingly made good on the promise he made to Hill before he shot him.

No doubt the Hill family suffered along with Charles as they nursed him in his last three days. Felix, his father, was 53, and Elizabeth, his mother, was 48, when they laid their young son to rest in Antioch Cemetery, five miles north of Blairsville, Georgia, near the Hill family's farm.

This was the second tragedy the Hill family had experienced in less than a decade. A daughter, Ursula Elizabeth, born in 1842, had died on October 27, 1859, at the age of 17 years, one month and 21 days, according to her marker - less than eight years before Charles himself would join her in the cemetery. The cause of her demise is unknown.

It may be that the loss of his sister at an age so near his own gave the 20-year-old Charles a sense of his own mortality. One, however, can only speculate.

The gravestones of Charles, his mother, father and sister, all bear inscriptions of short verse and the amount of time, counted to days, that each lived, indicating perhaps, that they valued and took note of each day the deceased had spent among loved ones.

Though the verses upon their parents' headstones are now unreadable, one can still, with great difficulty, make out the inscriptions upon Charles's and

Ursula Elizabeth's markers - inscriptions which would seem to indicate the family's feeling of ultimate triumph over death.

Charles's marker reads: *"God, my Redeemer, live (sic) and ever from the skies, look (sic) down and watches my dust till He shall bid it rise."*

Ursula Elizabeth's reads: *"Companion, earth and worms shall but refine this flesh till my triumphant spirit comes to put it on afresh."*

The stones of Charles's parents - Felix and Elizabeth - (though not identical) match each other's, but differ from the two matching stones of their children. Likely, by that time, readily available marker designs had changed, or perhaps they were selected to be different from the children's.

It is interesting to note that the mother's stone should break style from the others in bearing the notation at the top: *"Sacred to the Memory of Elizabeth, wife of Felix Walker Hill."*

Since Felix died August 24, 1883, at the age of 77 years and 17 days, Elizabeth, who died November 15, 1896, at the age of 85 years and 82 days, would have outlived Felix and therefore would be most likely to have chosen the headstones for them both. From the inscription on Elizabeth's marker, however, it would seem that perhaps some other family member chose the headstones, unless Felix and Elizabeth chose their own stones in advance of Felix's death.

If Charles or young Ursula Elizabeth were ever married or had children, there is no record of either circumstance. The name Hill still survives in that section of Union County, however, and the cemetery markers attest to the fact that there have been several Charles Hills, most likely named after the young sheriff who had no children of his own.

Besides the stories handed down from generation to generation, and the lonely gravestones in Antioch Cemetery, the only other lasting reminders of the fateful event are the doors of the old Campbell cabin and the old fireplace hearthstones which were preserved on the Nichols farm. The doors still serve their function on the Nichols barn and storage shed. It is impossible to know which of the four is the door behind which Campbell stood as he fired the round into Hill's midsection. The surface of their rough boards has been worn and weathered smooth in the past 150+ years.

The old hearthstones, have, for years now, served as the entrance steps to the old home of Mr. Nichols's father. It is interesting to imagine that once an ordinary man named William Campbell and his family warmed themselves and cooked their supper upon a fire made on these stones.

It is equally interesting to note that once, behind one of the now innocent-looking old doors, a desperate Campbell clutched a $10.00 pistol which he fired to fell an unsuspecting Sheriff Charles Hill.

It seems doubly tragic to think that on a summer day more than 150 years ago, when all life was budding anew against the back-drop of the beautiful Blue Ridge Mountains, a young sheriff made a terrible mistake in judgment which ended his life.

When William Campbell pulled the trigger on that fateful day in May of 1867, he not only took the sheriff's life, but sealed his own fate as well. So far as is known, he never again saw his family, friends, or his snug little cabin in the beautiful north Georgia mountain valley.

The Tragically Short Life of Byron Herbert Reece

*Tormented by an illness from which he could achieve no relief,
and a desperation to record for posterity the constant lyrical music
within his soul, Byron Herbert Reece created a remarkable legacy
of poetic compositions before ending his life.*

He is not well-known today in literary circles. Though his remarkable poetry lives on, he personally is almost forgotten except by the few remaining Georgians who knew him. In his day, however, the late Byron Herbert Reece was a rising star in the literary world – among the best in the business at lyrical poetry. Today, his ballads and sonnets still irrepressibly haunt the thoughts and touch the souls of those who read them.

During his short life, Byron Reece listened to the melody of Wolf Creek almost every day as it sang against the rocks in the bed of the stream on the Reece farm in a community known as "Choestoe" in north Georgia's Union County. He was a keen observer of nature, and a person of deep introspection, and his poetic works reflect these characteristics. Words obsessed him, and he expressed them to an incredible degree during his short lifetime.

Despite his innate talent, Reece was nonetheless an extremely-poor farmer tilling the soil on his small family farm for many years before the voices in his lyrical works found the public's ear. He followed the plow by day, and at night in his attic room beneath a tin roof, he worked at a fever pitch – sometimes into the wee hours of morning – penning the lines which gave meaning to his otherwise dreary life.

The lyrics of hundreds of poems eventually were wrested from his soul. The mode best-suited to his nature was lyrical poetry, ballads and sonnets. The themes which hammered at his thoughts were "death," "the changing seasons," "wind," "the passage of time," and "the brevity of things held dear": life, love, beauty, and innocence. Many of these thoughts tortured Reece in life, and continue to haunt today's readers years after the talented poet's tragic demise.

After nights short of rest, and long in writing, Reece characteristically arose to a new day of turning the rich creekside alluvial soils, running a harrow to smooth it, seeding it in the springtime, cultivating it in the summer, and harvesting the crops it produced in summertime and autumn.

Other farm tasks demanded his time and attention too. He cut wood to fuel the hearth against the cold and wet autumn, winter, and spring weather. Another size of wood was needed for the cook stove.

Reece also attended each day to the farm animals with which he felt a special rapport. The tasks vying for his energies seemed endless, a condition reflected in his poetry:

"With fence to mend and cows to tend,

And care of wheat and corn."

*["The Stay-At-Home" in **The Season of Flesh** (1955)]*

Reece was born September 14, 1917, to Emma Lance and Juan Reece in a log cabin, long since vanished, which once stood on land now covered by Lake Trahlyta at Vogel State Park near Blairsville. He had one brother, T.J., and three sisters, Eva Mae, Jean and Kate. Another sister died in infancy.

Emma Reece recognized the precociousness of her son early-on, and encouraged his curiosity. She read to him from the King James version of the **Bible** and other meager sources such as John Bunyan's **Pilgrim's Progress**.

Before "Hub" entered the Primer Class at Choestoe Grammar School, he could read the **Bible** and had read **Pilgrim's Progress**. The sonnets of Shakespeare and lyrical ballads were also a part of his repertoire. And all the while, the rhythms and cadences were building and growing in his mind.

Choestoe, the place of Reece's birth, is a Cherokee Indian word which, roughly translated, means *"The Place Where Rabbits Dance."* In his poem by the same name, he writes:

"It's not that rabbits ever really danced here,

Though sometimes, in the dusk, when nothing happens,

We could believe they danced and wish them dancing;

They came to sport forever in the name our country bears,

One that the Indians gave it."

*["Choestoe (The Dance of the Rabbits)" **The Prairie Schooner** (1944)]*

Reece was strongly attached to his Choestoe home, his parents and the farm. Slender and frail by nature, he nonetheless learned to shoulder his weight of the farm tasks while pursuing his education.

Dr. J.M. Nicholson, who was both principal and teacher at Union County High School, took an avid interest in young Hub Reece when he entered the school. Nicholson provided books for Reece to read and encouraged his literary talents. While other young males of his day demonstrated interest in little more than mischief, Hub was concerned almost solely with his studies.

During his teen years, especially after crops were laid by, Reece sometimes spent stretches of sixteen hours reading by kerosene lamp after the sunlight had faded. He avidly read the works of English and American poets.

Mrs. Dora Allison Spiva, Reece's high school mathematics teacher, recalls that his proficiency lay in literature and humanities, not in mathematics. "He seemed to understand the basic principles of mathematics," she explained, "but apparently saw no need for learning algebra. However, in the final analysis, he was a good, well-rounded student, because he came out second, the salutatorian, in a graduating class of nineteen."

Mrs. Spiva also remembers Reece in another light. Having been a neighbor to the Reece family in Choestoe, she recalled his serving as a lay minister at the Salem Methodist Church. "When the regular pastor was not present, Hub preached," she added. "His sermons were filled with appropriate illustrations, and were at the same time both simple and truly profound."

Louise Dyer, a schoolmate of Hub Reece's at Union County High School, remembered that he was not a mixer and did not initiate conversations with other students, yet he would talk when questioned. "We used to sing on the school bus returning to Choestoe in the afternoons," she said. "Hub would ask us to be quiet. I could never figure whether it was because he didn't like the song we favored – a gospel song, 'O Why Not Tonight?' – or whether our poor singing and noise disturbed his efforts to read as we bumped along the rutted roads.

"In high school, we were awed by his ability at poetry," she continued. "His first poem was published in the *North Georgia News* in 1934, and was entitled 'Return To Remembrance.' I remember wondering then how he could write such a beautiful poem."

Leon Colwell, another schoolmate at Blairsville, recalls Reece's interest in memorizing poetry, and encouraging others to do the same. "I can still quote Shakespeare's *Sonnet 116*, and others, which I memorized at Hub's insistence. He showed me that loving poetry was not 'sissy,'" Colwell smiled. "I attribute my life-long love of poetry more to the peer encouragement of Reece than to any one particular teacher."

"I recall that we spent the school years of 1930 through 1935 together at Blairsville (Union County) High School," said Dale Elliott, another former classmate of Reece's. "When we were in the seventh grade, Hub was real interested

in aviation and was a great fan of Charles Lindbergh. He talked about and even sketched some rough plans for a glider.

"Many have said that Hub was withdrawn and always, even in a crowd, seemed to be in his own world, not too much disturbed by what was going on around him," Elliott added. "That's true. He was a thinker and a philosopher who continually pondered the tragedy, beauty and mystery of life, and to really know him, you have to read his poetry."

Byron Herbert Reece entered Young Harris College in the fall of 1935, and attended there intermittently for about four years, working on the college farm to earn his tuition and board. When his family suffered illness, however, he withdrew from college to return to the family farm to help out there.

Reece himself suffered from poor health, and it was not unusual for him to experience periods of depression, as well as doubts about his abilities as a writer. In one fit of despondency in 1937, he tragically burned all the poems he had written prior to 1935.

The Quill Club at Young Harris College was a source of inspiration for Reece. After an absence of almost three years, he returned to study at the college in 1938. He worked for a dollar a day on the college farm and also received a scholarship.

Philip Greear, a college mate of Reece's, and a long-time friend who also worked with him on the college farm, wrote the following account in *"A Poet Among Us"* in **Enotah Echoes**, the Young Harris College newspaper, dated October 4, 1938:

"Fourteen years later (after his birth), with an urge bred by surroundings of irresistible mountain beauty, Byron began writing, writing poetry; and it was good poetry. So good, that three years' development produced publishable verses. In the

short time since 1934, when the first piece was accepted, he has had thirty-one pieces published... Byron Reece is an oddish sort of boy, who is little seen on campus because of his timidity and his yearn for study."

Jack Biles of the Quill Club recalls that most of the poetry written by members of the club was "God awful," but Hub's offerings showed "talent or genius or whatever you want to call it. Hub was writing a high caliber of poetry and we were writing rather absurd verses."

The late Ralph McGill, former editor of the *Atlanta Constitution*, wrote of meeting Reece the first time. McGill had gone to Young Harris College to speak.

He reportedly inquired of Professor W.L. Dance whether he knew a young poet named Reece from Blairsville who had a poem published in *Mercury* magazine. Dance told McGill that Reece was one of their students, and took him to the dormitory room to meet Reece. Following introductions, McGill inquired if Hub would read one of his poems, but, noticing the poet's hesitancy in front of his two roommates, the editor respected the young poet's mountain reticence and deferred the reading until later.

Ralph McGill proved to be one of Reece's staunchest supporters. The friendship helped eventually to catapult Reece into the limelight of literary fame when his first book, *Ballad of the Bones and Other Poems* was published by E.P. Dutton and Company, New York, 1945. By January, 1946, the book had entered its third printing. The poet dedicated it *"To Juan and Emma."*

Ethelene Dyer Jones lived on a farm adjacent to the Reece farm in Choestoe. Her father, J. Marion Dyer, also a dirt farmer, read the *Atlanta Journal* daily, and especially the Sunday edition, to follow the latest literary criticism of his neighbor's work.

Mrs. Grapelle Mock, a teacher at Union County High School, took young Ethelene to interview the "poet among us" for the school column in the local newspaper. Seeking some word of advice from Reece for struggling English students in high school and would-be writers, they received his sage response: "Read the great literary masters. It is from them you learn technique, style, truth. And if any among you would write, then write, write, write. Don't hide your light under a bushel, but bring it out for all to see. Don't be afraid of criticism – whether constructive or destructive – but profit from it."

Reece had been discovered by famed Kentucky poet, Jesse Stuart, who had read the Georgian's lyrical ballad *"Lest the Lonesome Bird"* in *The Prairie Schooner* in 1944. He wrote to Reece asking for samples of his poems.

In a crowded country store/post office in Riverton, Kentucky, Stuart read the sheaf of ballads and lyrical poems sent to him. Greatly impressed, he wrote, *"The poems held me while the customers pushed around me, stepping on my toes, trying to get waited on while I sat there obstructing their passageway. Here, I thought, is a poet."*

Stuart sent Reece's poems to his own editor at Dutton. The contact proved valuable for Reece. Dutton subsequently published six of his books: *Ballad of the Bones and Other Poems*, (1945); *Bow Down in Jericho*, (1950); *Better a Dinner of Herbs*, (1950) (a novel); *A Song of Joy and Other Poems*, (1952); *The Season of Flesh*, (1955); and another novel *The Hawk and the Sun*, (1955).

At the outbreak of World War II, Byron Herbert Reece volunteered for service. He was rejected, however, because of *"a nervous tic"* in his face. It was a great disappointment to the young man to be ineligible to serve his country. Did he still harbor dreams of becoming a pilot? We'll never know.

Reece returned to Choestoe. His parents, who by this time both suffered from tuberculosis, were in great need of his help. He farmed the land and continued to write his poems and novels by night.

By this time, his sister, Eva Mae, had become a teacher. Hub also had tried teaching for a time in the rural school in the northwestern end of Union County at Zion School. He, however, wrote to his friend, Philip Greear, reporting: *"I am still unhappy at school teaching, as I would be at anything more than likely. I hate to stay in a schoolroom all day, hate it to such an extent that I get nervous and snappy like a big dog confined to a narrow cage."*

It was the Reece home that was Hub's ultimate refuge. Loretta Odum Loudermilk of Epworth, a relative of Reece, remembers stopping there frequently as a child to visit "Aunt Emma and Uncle Juan." "Daddy, Uncle Juan and Hub went out to look over the crops or down to the barn to see the cattle. Maybe they stood down by Wolf Creek and talked," she stated.

"My fondest memory is of Aunt Emma taking me, a little child, down the steps from the 'front room' to the kitchen," Loudermilk added. "The kitchen had a dirt floor, but it was hard-packed and always immaculately clean. There, Aunt Emma always had something enticing to eat in the 'warming closet' of the wood stove. It might be a stacked June apple cake, or some 'sweet bread' sweetened with sorghum syrup. She would go to the spring house and get me a glass of cold milk to drink with the sweet treat."

Mrs. Loudermilk remembers the house as being very modest, heated by a single fireplace in the front (living) room, and the wood stove in the kitchen. Over the dug-out kitchen room was a bedroom, and off the living room was the larger bedroom, with entry to the attic.

It was the attic in which Hub found true refuge from some of his depression. From there, a small window at either end looked out on Blood and Slaughter Mountains towering above, and on Wolf Creek cascading northward on a downgrade from its spring somewhere beneath Lake Trahlyta.

On the east side of the house, close by it, ran the paved road – Highway 129 – that led across Neel's Gap. After the road was built, the name of the gap was changed from its Indian designation – "Walasi-yi" or "Frogtown Gap" – to the current name of "Neel's Gap," to honor the engineer who had laid out the road. It was a pet peeve of Reece's that an authentically-original place name which had been handed down through a century or more of tradition would be changed to honor a 'mere person.'

With the advent of ***Ballad of the Bones***, life became more complicated for the farmer-poet. His farm-work still came first, since book royalties and other income from his writing still were not sufficient to fully support him, but he was gaining more and more attention in the publishing world.

Reece eventually was much in demand at book dinners and autographings. His natural shyness made these appearances occasions of dread, and his gradually-declining health made them even less appealing.

Because of his growing illness – by this point he also had contracted tuberculosis for which there still was little treatment – and general temperament, Reece constantly lived with the spectre of death, and much of his writing reflects this theme. One or both of his parents had passed the tuberculosis on to him and he suffered from it increasingly.

He was admitted to Battey State Hospital in Rome, Georgia, on February 8, 1954, for treatment, but could bear the lonely confines only so long. Only four poems emerged during this period of enforced rest. One of these works - *"Underground,"* reveals the pathos and dispirited condition of Reece as he is compelled to be absent from the mountains he loved so dearly:

> *"In that subterranean city*
> *To which I came at last*
> *A ghost walked, and was pity,*
> *And the ghost walked past and past.*
> *At the middle bells, at midnight,*
> *Help! cried a bundle of bones."*

One morning, early in May, before nurses made their morning rounds, Reece dressed in his worn and weathered mountain clothing and walked out of Battey Hospital, continuing across the mountains northeastward back home. With continued medication at home, he improved somewhat, but his weight remained at a gaunt 125 pounds, and the disease still pervaded his lungs. His constant state of depression worsened even more with his mother's death from the disease on August 20, 1954.

Hub gave little notice to the accolades which followed his being presented the *Michael Strange Memorial Award* for his poem, *"The Betrothed from the Grave,"* published in **Poetry Digest**, nor to the rave notices by his editors at Dutton upon receiving the manuscript for **The Season of Flesh**. By this time his royalties had increased considerably, and he had used a portion of the funds to pay for the construction of a warm snug house for Juan and Emma. Now that his beloved mother had passed on, the house was strangely quiet. Even the central heat could not replace the warmth that had permeated the little house by the road with its attic where he had been so inspired in years past to write the faultless lyrics of his ballads and sonnets.

Reece now had contracts for books of poems and novels, but his productivity was hampered by his own emaciation, stark loneliness and grief. Accustomed to being a loner, he could not talk of the dark thoughts that stalked his mind "like a baying hound" as his disease continued to plague him.

In the years that allowed him, he shared his expertise on creative writing by serving as poet-in-residence at various colleges. Emory University, the University of Georgia, and Young Harris College each included him among their faculties at one point or another. He also traveled to the University of California at Los Angeles in 1950 to lecture.

Reece was twice the recipient of the prestigious *Guggenheim Award*, and was nominated for the equally-prestigious *Pulitzer Prize in Poetry*. The second *Guggenheim Award* was a grant for $3,000.00 in anticipation of a projected novel, **The Ax and the Sword**. Hub traveled to the writers' and artists' colony at Pacific Palisades, California, hoping to work on the novel there. He returned to Georgia, however, when the fall leaves were at their most flamboyant in Choestoe Valley. He took many photographs, explaining, "I want to preserve intact what I have seen to pass it on to others."

He again took a teaching job at Young Harris College. As a teacher, he brought out the best in his students, urging them on to greater creativity and study. Sherry Welch, though not having him as an instructor, remembers seeing him around campus. "He was a chain-smoker," she says. "Outside the classroom, as he walked between buildings, he always had a lighted cigarette. He often had bouts of coughing, and his respiratory ailment worsened with the onslaught of winter.

He was so thin it seemed a strong breeze on campus would have swept him away."

Reece attended the graduation exercises at North Georgia College in Dahlonega where his sister, Eva Mae, was graduated *Cum Laude* on June 1, 1958. He then returned to Young Harris where he finished grading his students' final examinations to prepare their grades for the records.

Terry Reece, nephew of Byron Herbert Reece and son of T.J. Reece, wrote his recollections of the last time he saw his Uncle Hub:

"I am now of the same age as Uncle Hub when he died. Like the polite neighbors, I say 'died,' because killing one's self is still not acceptable behavior; I suppose it never shall be.

"The Sunday before he ended his life was a gloriously beautiful day. When you're a ten-year-old boy, most of them are, aren't they? I was playing with my cousins along the banks of Wolf Creek which rushed by just a few feet from Hub's door. We would throw a tin can in the water and attempt to sink it with stones before it disappeared under the thick mountain laurel with its cargo of 'enemy troops.' No electronic toy of today could even remotely compete with the imagination of a child of the '50s.

"Uncle Hub came up beside me and hugged me. He is often written of as being lean and frail, and he was, but in the eyes of a ten-year-old boy, he was strong and powerful and comforting. He gave me a shiny half-dollar to ride J.O. Fowler's horses at Vogel State Park. He then proceeded to do the same thing with the other nieces and nephews.

"If God could have given the wisdom of a forty-year-old man to a ten-year-old boy, I would have known this wonderful man was telling me goodbye. I would have seen the pain and loneliness in the dark eyes. It is obvious even in the photographs of that period. But God, in his infinite wisdom, never intended for a ten-year-old boy to carry such

a burden. I went to Vogel and rode a horse, and I never saw Uncle Hub alive again."

In the same room where his mentor, Professor W.L. Dance, had ended his life twelve years earlier, Reece committed suicide on June 3, 1958. He left no death note. Dr. Robert Andress, dean of students, and Professor Fred Edmiston, found Reece's body full-length on the apartment floor, with a bullet wound through his left lung. Dr. Andress noted, *"Reece's face bore a serenity and composure which had not been evident in a long time."*

Ralph McGill wrote, *"All of us have within us (the capacity for) an inexplicable loneliness. Byron had the mountain silence... What fires of resentment at his fate burned in his brain none of us ever knew. But that he was a Prometheus bound to the harsh rock of tuberculosis, the vultures of a cruel fate pecking at his liver, was undoubtedly true.*

"He had a growing fear of the future. He was afraid of becoming a burden - of being unable to care for himself. Fires other than tuberculosis were burning within him and consuming him.... He was weighted with a great sense of insecurity.... What happened was that the frail mechanism swiftly was running down.... Loneliness came about him like a fog. Life is a candle in the wind, another poet has said. For him, the cold winds had begun to blow across that River Jordan, about which he had written so often in his poems. He snuffed it out himself, without that last, helpless waiting." (**Georgia Review**, WTR, 1958)

No greater, more appropriate epitaph could one man create, than the epigraph written by Reece himself in **Bow Down In Jericho**:

"From chips and shards, in idle times, I made these stories, shaped these rhymes;

May they engage some friendly tongue When I am past the reach of song."

Civil War Abode from Yesteryear:

The Gordon-Lee Mansion

An antebellum home and gristmill in northwest Georgia around which a portion of the U.S. Civil War raged in September of 1863, are the only structures to survive the bloody Battle of Chickamauga.

This magnificent home in northwest Georgia is silent more often than not these days, used mainly as a property rented for weddings and receptions. Though now peaceful and serene, it was once the scene of some of the most grisly activities imaginable of mankind, when the Battle of Chickamauga in the U.S. Civil War raged within its midst in 1863.

Nestled deep within the beauty of the fiefdom of Chickamauga – a tiny northwest Georgia town separated from Chattanooga, Tennessee, by the well-known Chickamauga-Chattanooga National Military Park – this antebellum mansion is the only structure that survived the now-historic battle.

In its worst hours, it was used as an emergency surgery ward for the removal of ruined legs and arms of soldiers wounded in the desperate battle between the Blue and the Grey. According to descriptions passed down through the years, there were so many amputations that a horse-drawn wagon would pull up to the French doors of the library, be filled to the brim with arms and legs, and then pull away just moments before another cart would take its place.

Originally, the land rising above the lush banks of Crawfish Springs was home to the Cherokee Indians, and a Cherokee log courthouse from the tribe's last years of civilized effort in Georgia in the later 1830s, once existed at the site. When Andrew Jackson drove the Indians from their homes during the now infamous "Trail of Tears," ownership of the property was assumed by White settlers.

In 1840, James Gordon, a Scotsman who had earlier migrated from Virginia to Gwinnett County, Georgia, with his brothers Charles and Clark, bought 2,500 acres-worth of lottery tracts near the lush springs with funds he had acquired through his newly-thriving business – nearby Gordon Mill. By 1847, James, most likely a millionaire at that point by today's standards, built the imposing brick house – known locally as "The Mansion" – as a plantation home. It was the envy of much of north Georgia.

Unfortunately, the Walker County courthouse in Lafayette which housed the area's documents was destroyed by fire in 1883, so little is known today of the births, marriages and deeds of the well-known Gordon family. We do know however, that James and his wife Sarah had six children: Thomas, William, Mary, Elizabeth, James, and Sarah.

When James died in 1863, just months before the Battle of Chickamauga, his daughter Elizabeth and her husband James Morgan Lee (who was already a partner in the thriving nearby Lee and Gordon Mill) took over the house, and the Lees expanded the property realm to 5,000 acres. The mansion, to which area residents by then often referred simply as "the Widow Gordon House" or "Crawfish Springs," became home to the Lees and their six children – Gordon, Tom, Clarkie, Sarah, Molly and Pearl. At one time, the property also was home to 45 to 50 slaves.

The mansion's most famous owner – Gordon Lee – would soon be elected to the U.S. Congress, serving Georgia's 7th District, but that was still a bit in the future. Gordon was just four years old at the time of the bloody Battle of Chickamauga in September of 1963.

"I was in but one battle, but that was the great battle of Chickamauga," a whimsical Lee later wrote. "I was in the Union lines at the beginning and in the Confederate lines at the end. I did not desert; but I was one of the few who stayed where they were when the Confederates advanced. For several years after this military service, I was spanked at home and flogged at school, just as if I had not been a veteran."

By 1863, most of the homes in Chattanooga and the surrounding towns had been confiscated by men in blue uniforms. Before everything was "said and done," some 37,000 men had died during a 40-hour engagement over the days of September 19-20 in the terrible Chickamauga battle.

After taking over the property, Union soldiers evicted the Lees to initially convert the home into a command headquarters for General William Rosecrans, leader of the Union Army of the Cumberland. Chief of Staff James Garfield, who would later go on to become the nation's 20th president, also moved into the home. The Gordon-Lee mansion was chosen for service in this regard because of its ideal location near "good water," and was soon transformed into the Union's primary hospital, with six tents pitched on the grounds and the slave cabins emptied to make room for the wounded.

"As the battle progressed, the situation at the hospital became even more desperate," writes Dr. Frank Green, who purchased the mansion in 1974, long after the Lees had departed. "Longstreet had arrived with fresh troops that were thrust into the center of the Union lines. The pace of activity at Crawfish Springs was heightened, if that could be imagined.

"The library of the mansion was an unbelievable sight as an operating theater," Green continues. "The surgeons, without anesthesia, were amputating destroyed limbs in attempts to save lives. (One can only imagine) the cries of anguish and the frustration of those

The Gordon-Lee mansion was chosen for service in this regard because of its ideal location near "good water"

When James Gordon died in 1863, just months before the Battle of Chickamauga, his daughter Elizabeth and her husband James Morgan Lee (who was already a partner in the thriving nearby Lee and Gordon Mills) took over the house as the war eventually raged around them. The Lees later expanded the property realm to over 5,000 acres. The mill is photographed here circa 1860s.

caring for the wounded and dying; the floors slippery with blood."

During the battle, Lee's daughters, who, along with the rest of the family, were allowed to stay in one of the slave cabins, copied down messages scribbled upon the walls of the house by dying men in a last desperate attempt to reach out to their families as they succumbed to their injuries. The mansion was eventually captured by General Braxton Bragg's Southern troops.

Years later, a woman from the Midwest arrived on the steps of the Gordon-Lee mansion, looking for evidence of her missing son. James Lee, who reportedly was sitting on the front porch at the time, graciously invited the visitor to search the house and grounds. Soon, a scream pierced the still Georgia air, and Lee rushed to one of the out-buildings.

He found the woman kneeling before one of the inside walls of the building on which someone – undoubtedly her son – had written his name, address, and military company - in blood.

James Lee died in 1889 of, as the ***Daily Times Chattanooga*** reported, *"typhy-pneumonia, leading to a malignant form of lung affliction which resulted in consumption."* His wife, Elizabeth, died 14 years later, in 1903, and their son – Gordon – became a U.S. Representative the next year.

The congressman, who married Olivia Berry of Newnan, Georgia – reportedly the wealthiest woman in Georgia at the turn of the century – enjoyed close personal friendships with four U.S. presidents – Theodore Roosevelt, William H. Taft, Calvin Coolidge and Woodrow Wilson.

When son, Gordon Lee, died in 1927, his spinster nieces – Sarah and Pauline Gaskill – assumed possession and came to live in the house. At the turn of the century, bathrooms with claw foot tubs, wooden toilets and pedestal sinks had been added, and the old double-front porches had been torn away.

In 1974, after the death of the last family member (the Lees had been childless), Dr. Frank Green, a Chattanooga dentist, purchased the famed structure and restored it to museum quality with pieces more reflective of the Civil War era. Green unveiled the Gordon-Lee Mansion during the nation's bicentennial in 1976.

"I had been interested in history and particularly the Civil War, and I enjoy antiques," Green stated at the time, "so it fit right in with my interests. And in a moment of madness," Green added with a grin, "I bought it."

For 13 years, the Gordon-Lee Mansion served as a gathering place for craft fairs, guided tours and archaeological digs, but up-keep on the home was expensive, and in 1989, Green realized that the 5,000-square-foot structure would need to generate additional income to help support itself. He said he mused at the time, "Why not a bed and breakfast inn?"

Green explained that though he was extremely proud of the furnishings in the house, many of which were museum-quality, he had hesitated about making it a bed and breakfast for that reason. Nevertheless, sound business acumen required the home be a money-maker, so it served ably as a popular bed and breakfast for a number of years, attracting guests from all walks of life.

During those years, the facility was patronized by the likes of Maureen Reagan, daughter of U.S. President Ronald Reagan, and Jack Carter, son of U.S. President Jimmy Carter. Many others gratefully paid for the opportunity to overnight in this magnificent dwelling from yesteryear where mint juleps were once enjoyed on the veranda.

"We felt like guests in a private home," wrote one visitor. Another penned, "Thank you for allowing me to step back into, in my opinion, the most romantic period of our nation's history."

All good things, however must come to an end, and so also did the "Gordon-Lee Mansion Bed and Breakfast." It soon, however, found new life as a wedding venue.

No matter what time of year, the upstairs museum always stirs memories of the site's historic past. Guests of the mansion – whether they like it or not – take a step back in time in a room filled with such Civil War artifacts as the breastplate of a Union soldier with the bullet still lodged in the emblem; a tree limb hammered with bullets and missiles from all directions; and an artificial arm, all of which serve as striking reminders of one of the bloodiest chapters in our nation's history.

Guests of the mansion – whether they like it or not – take a step back in time in a room filled with Civil War artifacts.

Historic Helen and the Gainesville-Northwestern Railroad

*Built in the early 1900s, this mountain short-line
railroad was a mainstay for mountain communities
between Gainesville and Robertstown for some 37 years.
In the early 1930s, with its lifeblood gone and
suffering from the effects of the Great Depression,
the line went out of business and slipped into history.*

Byrd-Matthews Lumber Co., one of the largest lumber mills east of the Mississippi in its day, opened in Helen, Georgia, White County, in 1912. It was the same year the hydro-electric dams were built on the Tallulah River to silence the great falls there. These were very "industrial days" in the once-quiet and sleepy confines of northeast Georgia. Along with the harvesting of the huge stands of virgin timber in White County, came a "first" for the county – the railroad.

In order to get the huge trees harvested by lumbermen down to the mill, and then to get the lumber products to market after they had been milled, Byrd-Matthews Lumber had to have a reliable method of transporting the lumber. A new railroad – the Gainesville-Northwestern–fulfilled this need.

The advent of this railroad was a momentous occasion, because it brought with it not only a method of transportation for the lumber, but also for passenger train service as well. Suddenly, area residents all up and down the line could obtain products which had previously been completely unavailable to

Engine #203 of the Gainesville-Northwestern Railroad pulls into Nacoochee Station in the early 1900s. The depot pictured here still stands as of this writing.

453

Byrd-Matthews Lumber Company was photographed circa early 1900s. A side-track of the Gainesville-Northwestern Railroad used to transport lumber to market via the main line is visible foreground.

them, and they also were able to send their own products to new markets back down the line.

After reaching Gainesville, Georgia, the thousands of board feet of lumber from Byrd-Matthews was then transferred to other railroads for distribution throughout the United States as well as to foreign markets. Lumber production was big business in north Georgia when virgin timber was still abundant in the early 1900s.

The "passenger" aspect of the Gainesville-Northwestern Railroad (called G&NW) provided "an excursion service" to and from Gainesville for residents along the line. It also made the shipping of freight and the availability of postal services extremely convenient for the first time. The run began at the old Gainesville Depot (which

still stands as of this writing in 2023) and made stops at Bradford Street Station (removed long ago), New Holland (also gone), Clark (gone), Autry (gone), Dewberry (gone), Brookton (remnants still survived until just recently), Clermont (long gone), County Line (gone), Mossy Creek Campground (long gone), Meldean (gone), Cleveland (long gone), Asbestos (gone), Mt. Yonah (gone), Nacoochee (still exists as of this writing in 2021), Helen (gone), and Robertstown (also gone). Gainesville, Brookton, Clermont, Meldean, Cleveland, Nacoochee, Helen, and Robertstown were agency stations, and the train made regular stops at them. The others were known as "flag stops," (where stops, amazingly enough, were made if the train was "flagged").

"Back in the day," Mr. T.B. Henderson owned a general merchandise

The dilapidated remains of the Gainesville-Northwestern Railroad depot at Brookton, Georgia, were photographed on the "wagon side" in 1972. This station, one of the last standing, sadly has since succumbed to the ravages of time and nature. Out of a total of 17 stations which once dotted the countryside on the Gainesville-Northwestern line, Brookton was one of eight "Agency Stations" which received a higher priority. The remaining nine stations were known as "flag stops," and were of lesser importance. (Photo by Grant Keene, Cleveland, GA)

store next to the Nacoochee Station. This building still stands today (as of this writing). It is the old brick building near the intersection of Highways 75 and 17, near the Nacoochee Indian mound. Mr. Henderson's daughter (a Mrs. Davidson) provided the following information:

"The Nacoochee Post Office was located in the general store and my father (Mr. Henderson) was postmaster there. He also served as rail agent at the Nacoochee Station. His duties included the issuance of tickets and the posting of freight bills. Most of the merchandise in my father's store came in by rail from Athens or Gainesville.

"Father was one of the few persons in the area who owned an automobile.

Sometimes passengers coming in on the train would need transportation to one of the 'resorts' in the area or to a friend or relative's house. After arriving at Nacoochee Station (which also still stands across Hwy 75 from the old general merchandise store), my brother – Bon – would drive the travelers to their destination."

Mrs. Davidson explained how she helped her father in the store, post office and at the little railroad station. She remembers that in the store, they sold groceries, hardware, men's, women's and children's clothing, seeds and fertilizer, all mostly delivered by rail. She said that Mr. L.G. Hardman (whose beautiful historic home – once known as "West End" – also still stands near the intersection

Byrd-Matthews Lumber Mill produced 125,000 board feet of lumber per day when operating at maximum capacity. Pictured here is an aged photo of the immense storage yard of this lumber at what today is Helen, Georgia. The Gainesville-Northwestern Railroad was a vital cog in the movement of this immense stockyard of product to market.

of Hwy. 75 and 17) shipped butter and milk from his dairy by rail to Gainesville, and Mr. "Simp" Logan shipped asbestos from his asbestos mine by railroad. This, of course, was long before science had revealed the destructive aspect of asbestos to human lungs.

Mr. Henry Davidson, who became the husband of Miss Mary Lula Henderson, was one of the many who helped to build the railroad from Gainesville to Robertstown. His brother, Mr. George Davidson, was engineer on the train and Mr. Paul Westmoreland was the fireman.

The railroad brought many visitors to the White County area. Major resorts included the Alley House (present-day Old Sautee Inn); Nacoochee; the Henderson Hotel in Cleveland; and the Mitchell Mountain Ranch in Helen. Most of these historic structures – save the Old Sautee Inn, the historic Hardman House and its out-buildings, the old depot building, and a few others – are now sadly long gone.

The Gainesville-Northwestern Railroad continued its 37-mile run from Gainesville to Robertstown until 1930. Shortly thereafter, when the seeming inexhaustible supply of virgin timber had in fact been depleted almost entirely, the railroad, with its life-blood gone, was discontinued. The tracks were taken up; the railroad rights-of-way reverted back to private ownership, and the Gainesville-Northwestern Railroad disappeared from White County and receded into history.

Tales of Historic Logan/Adair Mill

*Most of the old gristmills in Georgia are gone today -
victims of abandonment, "freshets," weathering, and "progress."
Prior to 1945 however, they were a staple in food production,
particularly in the South. And just as do most of these ancient
edifices, Logan/Adair Mill has quite an interesting history.*

Gristmills once proliferated at almost any spot where water power was available and grain crops were grown in abundance. For those who owned them, they were a permanent income-stream and automatic source of food where grain crops were grown in abundance. Logan/Adair Mill in what today is Georgia's White County was a prime example.

Corn was *the* primary staple crop of the South in the last century and was on the table in some form or fashion at almost every meal. Fresh roasting ears ("roastineers" to Southerners) were an eagerly anticipated summer treat – except by snaggle-toothed youngsters missing their front teeth who thus could not manage biting into a golden ear of corn-on-the-cob dripping with home-churned butter. What a treat!

Perhaps the most versatile of all grains, corn was eaten as cornbread, spoonbread, "johnnie cakes," hominy grits, fritters, mush, muffins, hush puppies, and was also made into batter for delicious fried items such as fish. Before the corn could be used for these treats, however, it had to be ground into meal, and every settlement needed a gristmill and miller for this service.

As of this writing in 2023, Logan/Adair Mill – one of the few remaining examples of this slice of history in Georgia – has not been used in almost 75 years, but still stands today on Town Creek. It is a picturesque landmark – one of the few in Georgia that has managed to survive the years.

According to the late Dr. George Adair, a former veterinarian in White County for whom Logan/Adair Mill was last named, the first mill on that site was built in the 1850s and was known simply as Logan Mill. Adair described how many years ago, he was told by a Mr. Ridley from Lumpkin County that his (Ridley's) grandfather had erected the

Logan Mill was the nucleus of a busy trading center known as Kimsey, Georgia, in pioneer days of what today is White County. It was vital to early rural farming families such as the one pictured here. Mount Yonah, a prominent landmark in White County is visible in the background.

mill for Major Will Logan who immigrated to this area from England.

Edd Ridley of Dahlonega confirmed that his great-grandfather, Alex Ridley, did indeed build the mill prior to the U.S. Civil War, securing the rafters with hickory pegs. Large hand-hewn beams still visible beneath the mill were probably part of the original structure, which was enlarged in later years to accommodate a flour mill.

The original dam at the site was 50 to 60 feet upstream from the present-day dam, and was built of poles and known as a "pole dam," a commonly-used alternative to the expensive stone dams. It had penstocks (gates used to control the flow of water) on either side connected by a gang-plank which enabled one man to operate both sluices. One penstock provided water to turn the millwheel, while the other allowed water to run through another millrace to the water-house, a rectangular tank about 8 feet wide and 10 feet deep used to operate a sawmill on the opposite side of the creek.

The drowning scene from the major motion picture *"I'd Climb The Highest Mountain,"* starring Susan Hayward, William Lundigan, Gene Lockhart and Rory Calhoun, (Readers please see *"When Hollywood Came to Film 'I'd Climb the Highest Mountain'"* in the White County section of *Mystery & History in Georgia, Volume I*), filmed in 1950 at Nora Mill in White County (which also still stands near Helen, Georgia) quite likely originated in author Corra Harris's best-selling book *A Circuit Rider's Wife* (on which the movie was based) from a tragic incident she and her Methodist

Abandoned at the time this recent photo was taken, historic Logan-Adair Mill on Town Creek in White County is a picture-perfect landmark. It is believed that a tragic drowning which actually occurred here in 1885 and was witnessed by author Corra Harris, became the basis for a drowning scene in her best-selling book, *"A Circuit Rider's Wife,"* and, subsequently, the major motion picture *"I'd Climb The Highest Mountain,"* which was based upon her book and filmed in White County in 1950.

minister north Georgia circuit-riding husband may have witnessed which actually occurred at Logan Mill in June of 1885.

At that time, Will Logan's young son, Charley, was a frequent visitor to the mill and enjoyed watching all the activity. One day, during one of Charley's visits, the miller missed the boy and began searching for him. To his indescribable horror, he reportedly discovered Charley's hat floating in the sawmill water-house – an ominous sign of possible trouble.

Charley's lifeless body was ultimately recovered from the millpond. He was buried at Mt. Pleasant Methodist Cemetery beside other Logan relatives. He was just under 7 years of age when he drowned.

A kneeling lamb adorns his headstone at Mt. Pleasant on which is inscribed the following heart-breaking epitaph:

"Sleep on in thy beauty
Thou sweet angel child.
By sorrow un-blighted
By sin undefiled."

Will Logan is believed to have been the son of Francis Logan who came with a large party of settlers to the Nacoochee Valley from Rutherford County, North Carolina, in 1822. He eventually settled near Loudsville and operated the tollgate for the Logan Turnpike.

According to interviews with the

Will Logan's son, Charley, who was tragically drowned in the millpond at Logan/Adair Mill in 1885, was buried at Mt. Pleasant Methodist Church Cemetery in White County.

late John Helton and Gordon Winkler, Will Logan wound up with the ownership of the tollgate after his father's death. (Readers please see *"Retracing the Logan Turnpike"* in the Union County section of *Mystery & History in Georgia, Volume II*).

In its heydays, Logan Mill was the nucleus of a busy trading center which had its own post office known as Kimsey, Georgia. According to local tradition, more trading supposedly occurred at the mill than at the county seat of Cleveland, since the gristmill was nearer the Logan Turnpike, causing it therefore to enjoy a steady stream of wagons bringing produce from Union County who bartered at the mill.

In addition to the mill, the community included a blacksmith shop, as well as Will Logan's three-story mercantile building. A wooden trough supplied the Logan's house with running water year-round from a spring high up on the side of the mountain, and in the wintertime, that water reportedly was so cold, it would curl your toes.

The first miller at the site is believed to have been Ben Campbell, who operated the little enterprise prior to the Civil War. Just as did many men in his day, though he owned no slaves and didn't believe in the institution of slavery, Ben nevertheless risked losing his livelihood, his defenseless family, and his very life by leaving to fight in the war. The majority of Southern combatants in that war did so for reasons other than the issue of slavery, contrary to popular opinion. Fortunately, Ben later returned safely after the war to resume milling operations.

According to Dr. Adair, the top portion of the Dutch door to the mill was covered with names, most of which were scratched in the wood by "loafers" waiting to have their corn ground. Written in bold letters as wide as a finger on one spot were the words "Ben Camel," possibly a reference to the miller's speed (or lack thereof) in his milling.

Other early millers were Marion Crumley, Jim Nix, and John Allen (known as "Buggar John") who operated the mill for sixteen years.

Following Will Logan's death, the property was purchased first by J.W. Henderson and known as "Henderson Mill," and then later by Lee Kytle and known obviously as "Kytle Mill." The mill was also once known as "Robinson Mill" during the thirty-five years that John Robinson was at the helm of the business, even though it was still owned by Lee Kytle.

Robinson was assisted by his grandson, Milt Robinson, who lived with him most of his life. The younger Robinson continued to operate the mill after his grandfather's death at the age of 93 in the early 1930s. Milt, however, must have found that the milling occupation did not agree with him, because he moved away from the area in 1937.

John Robinson was the miller when George Adair first visited the mill in 1921. "It took me three hours to get there from Cleveland in my Overland automobile," Adair recalled wryly, "because I had to ford three streams and kept getting stuck in the low ground!

"Will Logan's house and store had both burned a few years earlier, so I stayed with Miller Robinson in his house on a bluff across the creek. I remember the house really well because the ceiling of the large original one-room portion was made of hand-dressed boards that must have been a foot-and-a-half wide.

"Water for the house was brought across the creek in a wooden v-shaped trough," Adair continued. "The only way across the creek was a foot-log, which John Robinson had secured with a chain on one end to keep it from washing away during floods."

George says he came to know about the mill when his uncle, Dr. E.F. Adair, and his partner, Frank Edwards from Athens, purchased the property circa 1910 as a portion of 1,600 acres on which they planned to establish a trade school for boys where they could work to pay for their education.

The late George Adair, photographed in 1995, lived to be 100 years of age, passing away in 2002 at his White County, Georgia residence. He was the last miller at Logan/Adair Mill, operating the business until 1943, at which time he elected to pursue his original profession - that of a veterinarian.

"As it turned out, Kellum (*) and his wife bought land up the creek and got a school going first, so Uncle Gene and Edwards dissolved their partnership and divided up the property," George explained. "Uncle Gene got the mill property, and I eventually acquired it from him.

"I had the present rock and concrete dam built in 1930 after a big freshet washed out the old dam and millrace," George added. "I also replaced the old hand-made wooden mill-wheel with an undershot turbine wheel and took out the flour mill, since farmers had pretty much quit growing wheat in these parts.

"My wife, Sewell, and I moved permanently from Elberton to the mill in 1937, and I operated a gristmill, sawmill, and even a planing mill for a few years. A feed mill I added in a shed on the side of the mill-house also washed out in another big freshet, and I never put it back. I saw the water rise knee-deep in the millhouse even though it stands high off the ground on rock pillars. That was a scary lot of water!

"Miller John Robinson's bell had long since disappeared, so I started looking for a replacement for people to ring when they brought corn to be ground," Adair smiled. "Once when I had gone back to Elbert County to doctor a man's cow, I noticed an old bell lying on the ground. It was made of solid brass and had 'Troy, New York, 1856' embossed on the side. It had been used on the ferry that crossed the Broad River in years past.

"Times were hard in those days, and the man was glad to give that old bell to me in exchange for treating his cow," Adair laughed. "Unfortunately, the bell was stolen from the top of the mill one day while I was away.

"We lived in the mill house for a few years until we built another house close by. I used some Elberton granite to give additional support to some of the native rock pillars. A man from Blue Ridge bought the wheel after I quit milling and set it up on a creek in that area. I later heard that his mill burned, and I've often wondered what became of that old millwheel.

"I operated the mill until 1943. By that time, corn mills had gone out of style because folks were buying loaf bread at the store instead of baking corn bread. I was much more in demand in my profession as a veterinarian than as a miller... but that's another story."

(Author's Note #1: Logan/Adair Mill and its scenic waterfall can still be seen as of this writing (2023) on Mill Lane off Adair Mill Road which runs between U.S. Highway 129 and Town Creek Road in White County. Some of the surrounding property has now been sold to developers and divided into lots in a new subdivision appropriately-named "Adair Mill Community.")

(Author's Note #2: (*) The "Kellums" to whom Dr. Adair referred were Med R. and Elizabeth L. Kellum (the niece of Andrew Carnegie). Following the purchase of 1,000 acres of land 10 miles north of Cleveland, the Kellums became aware that existing educational facilities were inadequate for the mountain children of the area. They founded a school built on top of Pinnacle Mountain and hired teachers to staff it. Pupils included underprivileged children from Atlanta, as well as local youngsters. In 1924, the Kellums set out on a trip around the world in a private yacht and, strangely, never returned to White County. The school burned to the ground in 1928.)

Last Days of the Confederacy
And Vanished Treasury Gold

*During the dark closing days of the U.S. Civil War, casks
of gold and silver coins comprising the Confederate Treasury and
the assets of several Virginia banks – a glittering hoard worth
untold millions of dollars today – were spirited across the Carolinas
and northeast Georgia in a last-ditch effort to avoid their confiscation
by Federal authorities. Portions of these funds ultimately simply
disappeared into thin air in the confusion of a mass exodus.*

On April 2, 1865, in the closing days of the U.S. Civil War,
Confederate President Jefferson Davis and his Cabinet were finally
forced to admit the obvious. Little hope
remained for the Confederacy, and with
Union troops kicking down the doors
of Richmond, Virginia, Davis, accompanied by his Cabinet and most-trusted
assistants, fled – via the nearby Danville
railroad depot – the soon-to-be-burning
city around 8:00 p.m. At approximately
midnight of that same evening, the Confederate Treasury, as well as almost half
a million dollars in gold and silver specie (coins) composing the assets of several of the banks of Virginia, were also being transported as quickly as possible on
the same rail line.

By this point, the Southern populace and its starving, diseased, and ravaged armies had become the hallmark
of a dying nation, and lawlessness erupt-
ed freely throughout the southland.

Fleeing southward into Georgia, Davis
hoped to avoid being arrested by Federal
authorities and somehow make it to Texas where he planned to reestablish the
Confederacy.

Davis's remaining Cabinet was
composed of Secretary of War John C.
Breckinridge, Secretary of State Judah
P. Benjamin, Secretary of the Navy Ste-
phen R. Mallory, and Acting Secretary
of the Treasury John H. Reagan. Other
cabinet members resigned and fled as the
group later crossed into South Carolina.

Preserving the Treasury

The Confederate Treasury alone
was comprised of a fabulous cache of
silver and gold coins; silver and gold
bullion; $600 to $700 million dol-
lars-worth of Confederate treasury notes
(dropping in value like cow flop by the
hour); 16,000 to 18,000 pounds sterling in Liverpool, England, acceptances; a chest of silver jewelry donated by

An engraved portrait of Lieutenant Commander William Harwar Parker (CSN). It was the intrepid Parker who, with 50 midshipmen guards, was charged with actually transporting the Confederate Treasury from Richmond, Virginia, to a safe site for temporary storage and who ultimately refused to abandon it until it could be returned to the protection of Confederate Cabinet officers. (Photo courtesy of Mark Waters)

Confederate devotees; and more. The value of the gold and silver items (coinage, bullion and jewelry) being spirited southward was estimated at that time (1865) to be in the realm of $500,000.00 to $527,000.00, a treasure which would be worth well over $9,000,000.00 in 2023 dollars. Interestingly, those virtually worthless Confederate paper funds would also be quite valuable in today's collectors' market.

This assessment of the Confederate Treasury does not begin to consider the total actual worth of this breath-taking treasure trove, since the $500,000.00 (equivalent to $9,000,000.00 in 2023) provided almost unlimited purchasing power in 1865. If discovered today with

provenance to this incident, the collectors' value of these extremely rare and historic coins would be astronomical.

Captain Micajah Clark, Confederate Acting Treasurer, maintained meticulous records (outlined below) of the entire dispersal of the Confederate Treasury, so in actuality, there is no mystery as to what ultimately became of these funds. Nevertheless, some portions of his accounting – just by virtue of the *size* of some of the individual dispersals, as well as the final disposition of those dispersals – have in fact caused those portions of the funds to fall into the realm of "mystery" today.

The monumental task of protection and transport of this immense treasure had fallen to Captain William Harwar Parker (CSN) and his 50 midshipmen guards. Though almost all of the men were less than 18 years of age (and some reportedly no more than 14 years old), those who had chosen this group for this task seemingly could not have made a better choice, particularly in view of all of the intelligence and non-stop vigilance necessary to avoid the thousands of Federal troops, bounty hunters, and general bushwhackers eager to gain control of this valuable cargo. Though largely forgotten today, the logistical criteria and expertise necessary to accomplish this feat of avoidance can only be acknowledged as one of the truly amazing achievements of either side during the entire war.

Prior to its ultimate dispersal to loyal supporters and staff, this gold and silver comprising the Treasury would undergo an amazing 33-day odyssey across South Carolina and Georgia zig-zagging back and forth across the Carolinas and northeast Georgia countryside in avoidance strategies. Due to the expert technique and unwavering dedication exercised by the Confederate Navy midshipmen, the Confederate Treasury was never close to being intercepted by Federal troops, despite their heavy presence in the vicinity.

According to historian and researcher Marshall P. Waters III, PhD, of Washington, Georgia, the train containing the Treasury (as well as the assets of the banks of Richmond, Virginia) was moved onto a railroad siding in Danville, Virginia, where it sat from April 3-6. During this pause in travel, treasury clerks wisely exchanged – with all comers – paper Confederate dollars for silver coins, offering the swiftly-depreciating Confederate paper at the rate of $70 to $1. The Confederate clerks and bankers were well aware that the value of the Confederate paper currency was dropping steadily by the moment, and they hurried to convert the funds as quickly as possible.

"Near 6:00 p.m. on April 6, Captain Parker was ordered to move the Treasury (and banks of Virginia assets) by rail to Charlotte, North Carolina," Waters wrote, *"and to store these funds within the safe confines of the Mint there. Prior to departing the rail siding, the Confederate Treasury was counted for the first time by Senior Teller Walter Philbrook. It reportedly contained a total of $327,022.90."*[1]

From Danville, the treasure train continued to Greensboro, North Carolina. It was there that, according to records, approximately **$39,000.00 of the Treasury was paid out to Major General Joseph E. Johnston's (CSA) troops** at the rate of $1.15 per soldier. This payment rate is obviously a very paltry sum in modern times, but in 1865, one dollar was the equivalent of approximately eighteen dollars in 2023. That amount also had much greater purchasing power in 1865 than in 2023, particularly for the

Major Gen. John C. Breckinridge was forced to pay out a significant portion of the Confederate Treasury funds to a mutinous cavalry unit traveling with, and supposedly protecting Confederate President Jefferson Davis and the Treasury. (Photo courtesy of Mark Waters)

ragged, penniless, and desperate troops comprising the Confederate forces at that time.

When Jefferson Davis and his entourage reached Sandersville, Georgia, on May 6, 1865, it apparently had become obvious that there would be no easy route to Texas. At that point, **$35,000.00 was removed from the Treasury** *"for later use by President Davis and his Cabinet"* **and sent to a destination in Florida "for future needs."**

The ultimate disposition of this $35,000.00 (equivalent to $619,500.00 in 2023 dollars) is unknown today. At no time did Davis ever have any of the Confederate Treasury in his personal possession, nor were any funds discovered with him or his entourage when he was later captured in Irwinville, Georgia

Photographed circa 1900, some thirty-five years after the close of the U.S. Civil War, the depot at Washington, Georgia, was still standing and active. It was into and out of this depot that millions of dollars in gold and silver coinage were shipped in a desperate bid to prevent the Confederate Treasury and funds from six Richmond, Virginia banks from falling into the hands of bounty hunters and pursuing Federal officials. (Photo courtesy of Mark Waters)

on May 10, 1865. These funds therefore were either hidden in some secret spot and forgotten, or were taken and spent illicitly by "trusted officials."

Meanwhile, from Greensboro, the treasure train had proceeded to Charlotte, North Carolina, and from there to Chester, South Carolina, where any/all serviceable rail lines ended. At that point, the Treasury was *off-loaded* onto horse-drawn wagons which then proceeded toward Newberry, South Carolina upon exceedingly rough pioneer trails. Today, one cannot conceive of the virtual impossibility of securing healthy horses and the necessary wagons at this late stage in the war, when virtually all equine-related stock had either been killed in battle or butchered for the starving Confederacy. This feat, accomplished over and over again by Parker and the Navy midshipmen, must truly be acknowledged as a small miracle.

Destination Quandary

At Newberry, the treasure was *again loaded* back into a railroad boxcar and transported to Abbeville, South Carolina, where it was then *off-loaded once again* onto horse-drawn wagons, with the parties then proceeding overland to Washington, Georgia. The wagon train crossed a pontoon bridge near the tiny burg of Vienna, South Carolina

(Author's Note: This site is today beneath the waters of Clark Hill Reservoir on the Savannah River), arriving at Washington on the afternoon of April 17.

According to Capt. Parker's personal memoirs of this event, the Confederate Treasury and assets of the banks of Virginia were at this point *unloaded yet again* from the wagons and transferred to *"a local house,"* described in more recent years as *"the Heard House"* on the public square in Washington. In point of fact, *"the Heard House"* is the descriptive name which was assigned "post-war" by writers and researchers to describe the home owned by Dr. J.J. Robertson, the lower floor of which served, strange as it may sound today, as the Bank of Georgia Branch in Washington.

When Parker learned here that troops commanded by Major General James H. Wilson (US) were approaching Macon, Georgia (to which Parker had originally planned to travel to deposit the Confederate Treasury), he altered his plans to travel instead to the Confederate Depository in Augusta, Georgia. This was just one of countless logistical nightmares he and his young charges encountered and somehow successfully navigated. Federal forces and other pursuing authorities had become so numerous across the South by this point that it shocked those fleeing their pursuit.

From Washington, the Treasury's circuitous route found it being *loaded yet again* into railroad boxcars for transport to Augusta where it arrived on April 18. Several days later, when Augusta itself was threatened by Federals troops, Parker, amazingly, decided he had no alternative but to *again load* the Treasury back onto still more railroad boxcars and convoy back to Davis and his Cabinet, since he (Parker) was out of options. Worse yet, at this point, the leader of the

midshipmen had no firm idea of Davis's actual location.

Parker, nevertheless correctly guessed that Davis was moving south toward Abbeville to join his wife. In his pursuit of Davis, the intrepid Naval captain amazingly returned *yet again* to Washington by rail on April 23rd where he *re-loaded yet again* the Treasury back onto horse-drawn wagons, and set out *yet again* for Abbeville, South Carolina, on April 28. Upon his arrival at that destination on the afternoon of April 29, and being unable to locate President Davis or any members of his Cabinet, a no-doubt totally-frustrated Parker, uncertain of a further course of action at that point, apparently simply wisely decided to remain where he was until he might gather further intelligence on Davis's location. He ordered his men to *unload yet again* the Treasury from the wagons and store the immensely-valuable hoard of gold and silver coins in a warehouse on the town square.

Meanwhile, at 10:00 AM on May 2, Davis's entourage finally reached Abbeville. Confederate Navy Secretary Mallory accompanying Davis ordered Parker to transfer the Treasury to Acting Secretary of the Treasury, John H. Reagan – an order to which Parker no doubt happily and wearily – yet quickly - complied.

By Mallory's order, the corps of Navy midshipmen were also disbanded and instructed to proceed to their respective homes – their service done. These 50+ young men, most of whom were threadbare and shoeless by this point yet continuously loyal, devoted and dedicated to their mission, had walked from Chester to Newberry, South Carolina, then from Abbeville, South Carolina to Washington, Georgia, and back yet again from April 12 to April 29, none ever once shirking their duty of protection of the Confederate

Treasury nor voicing any known complaints despite their constantly-miserable circumstances.

The harrowing nature of the mission of Captain Parker and the Confederate Navy midshipmen cannot be over-emphasized. Aside from their responsibilities in guarding the golden treasure, they were also totally responsible for the logistical requirements involving the safe transport of the gold, a task at which they proved to be astoundingly adept. "It should be noted that the weight of $250,000.00 in silver dollars is approximately 9,555 pounds (4.78 tons)," historian Waters adds.

At 11:00 PM on May 2, President Davis and a small party set out from Abbeville toward Washington. Separately, Confederate Secretary of War Major General John C. Breckinridge also soon departed after having ordered that the Confederate Treasury be *loaded once again* onto horse-drawn wagons and accompanied by a contingent of Confederate cavalry troops.

On the evening of May 3-4, 1865, after having crossed the Savannah River, the cavalry troops who had been accompanying Davis and the Treasury cross-country finally began having reservations about their dedication to the task at hand. They knew this immensely-valuable horde of gold they were guarding could be intercepted and taken from them at any time by a significantly-larger army of Federal troops of which the numbers were growing daily. They also were hungry, sick, extremely poorly supplied, dressed in rags, penniless, and finally of the decision that they should be granted their "share" of the Confederate Treasury before they were overtaken by Federal troops. They, therefore, confronted Major Gen. Breckinridge (CSA) in whose charge the Treasury was traveling.

Treasury Dispersal

At this point, the Treasury had been reduced to approximately **$253,000.00** (as valued in 1865). Try as he might, Gen. Breckinridge ultimately was unable to stave-off the demands of the cavalry troopers and was forced to pay out approximately $26.00 to each man in the 4,000-man unit (some accounts maintain approximately $50.00 each to a 2,000-trooper unit), which came to a total of approximately $108,322.90.[2] After being reduced by this amount, the Confederate Treasury now held approximately **$144,700.00** in Confederate gold and silver – the equivalent of approximately $2.56 million in 2023 dollars.

The payout of these funds to the Confederate cavalry troops reportedly was made from the parlor window of the Mrs. David M. (Susan) Moss house in Lincoln County, Georgia (approximately 3 miles from the Savannah River). Amazingly, it would later be learned that the troops in this payout included some twenty First Ohio Cavalry under the command of Lieutenant Joseph A.O. Yeoman (USA) who were actually Union Army spies disguised as Confederate cavalry who had been secretly moving with President Davis and his escort party. *(Yeoman and his men later applied for and received a portion of the reward money for the capture of President Davis. However, the fact that Davis and his entourage were able to flee almost to the Florida state line prior to their capture speaks volumes as to the poor espionage talents of Yeoman's unit.)*

That night, Gen. Breckinridge wrote to Davis: *"Nothing can be done with the bulk of this command. It has been with difficulty that anything has been kept in shape. I am having the silver*

The three separate trips in which the Confederate Treasury was desperately transported back and forth to Washington, Georgia are depicted on this map. (Map courtesy of Mark Waters)

paid to the troops and will, in any event, save the gold and have it brought forward in the morning, when I hope Judge (Treasury Secretary John) *Reagan will take it. Many of the men have thrown away their arms. Most of them have resolved to... make terms. A few hundred men will move on and may be depended upon for the object we spoke of yesterday (i.e., escaping to Mexico)."*

Jefferson Davis, meanwhile, traveling separately from the Confederate Treasury and its escort, arrived in Washington, Georgia, in the late morning of May 3. While there, he conducted his final Cabinet meeting and issued his final orders of the Confederate government in the Dr. J.J. Robertson home (a.k.a. the Heard house), which also housed the aforementioned Bank of Georgia branch building on the Washington, Georgia, town square. Among other directives,

Davis instructed Major Raphael Moses (CSA) to carry $40,000.00 to Augusta for distribution to returning Confederate soldiers.

According to researcher Waters, "Not long after Davis and his small group departed Washington, Georgia, the wagon train transporting the Confederate Treasury arrived at Brigadier General Basil Duke's camp about a mile NNE from the Washington Public Square. Here, beneath the shade of an elm tree, Captain Micajah Clark (CSA), now the Acting Treasurer, dispensed what remained in the Treasury to various Cabinet members, officers, soldiers, naval personnel and others in the service of the Confederate government."

Those paid included:

$150.00 ($50.00 each to S. Brittain, Jas. Miller, and J.B. Macmurdo of the First Auditor's Office;

$300.00 to Captain Given Campbell (CSA) for payment to Presidential Scouts at Abbeville;

$300.00 to Lieutenant Bradford (CSA) for payment to the marines at Abbeville;

$520.00 to Captain Joseph M. Brown (CSA), acting quartermaster, for services of the Quartermaster's Department;

$806.00 to Quartermaster General Alexander Robert Lawton (CSA) for payment of five commissioned officers and 26 men under Brigadier General L. York's Louisiana Brigade;

$1,000.00 to Major General John Breckinridge for transport to the trans-Mississippi Department;

$1,500.00 to John F. Wheliss (Captain Parker's paymaster) for payment of the midshipmen and other Naval scouts

The 1817 Wilkes County Courthouse on the Washington, Georgia town square was photographed here circa 1880. This structure was demolished in 1904. In 1865, in one of his last official acts as president, Jefferson Davis instructed that Confederate bonds, paper funds, and other documents be burned in front of this courthouse on the town square by Major Raphael Moses (CSA). These acts were witnessed by the Secretary of War John C. Breckinridge and the Postmaster General John H. Reagan. (Photo courtesy of Mark Waters)

at Abbeville (about twenty days' pay each);

$2,000.00 to General Braxton Bragg for transport to the trans-Mississippi Department;

$3,500.00 to Acting Secretary of the Treasury John H. Reagan (taken by Federals at Irwinville);

$6,040.00 ($1,510.00 each to Colonels William Preston Johnston, Francis Richard Lubbock, Charles E. Thorburn, and John Taylor Wood;

$40,000.00 (transported to Augusta, Georgia) to Major and Chief of Commissary Raphael Moses (CSA) to help paroled soldiers and stragglers who were passing through that town. (Davis's last order.);

$86,000.00 in gold and bullion was made to Lieutenant Commander James A. Semple (CSN). This last dispersal – the final payment made by Acting Treasurer Clark – has been associated with deceit since the day it was made. Semple, who apparently was a highly-trusted officer, had been directed to transport these funds to Charleston or Savannah to be shipped to Bermuda, Nassau or Liverpool, where they were to be deposited into an account in the name of the Confederate government.

Semple, however, apparently chose to disobey that order, and instead gave **$27,000.00** to Edward M. Tidball and **$25,000.00** to William F. Howell (Varina Davis's brother). Both were naval purchasing agents under Semple. The logic for their entitlement to these funds is unknown today. The remaining **$34,000.00** apparently was simply kept by Semple for his own personal use;

And finally, there was **$2,584.00** for which there was no accounting whatsoever, but which may simply have been consumed by miscellaneous expenses encountered enroute to Washington. In that day and time, however, even excessive travel expenses would have been impossibly-pressed to consume $2,584.00 for travel from Richmond, Virginia, to Washington, Georgia.

As is obvious from the detailed accounting above, virtually none of the funds from the Confederate Treasury actually "disappeared." Nevertheless, there were some dispersals – for instance the $86,000.00 assigned to Lieutenant Commander James A. Semple and the $35,000.00 supposedly sent ahead to a destination in Florida for President Jefferson Davis – which remain a mystery today. In all likelihood, those funds were simply taken contrary to directive and intended purposes and personally utilized by the individuals to whom they were entrusted during the turmoil and confusion of the last days of the Confederacy.

Davis's Final Acts

Many Confederate government documents and items of former value were ordered by Davis and his Cabinet to be destroyed prior to their departure from Washington. Confederate bonds, paper funds, and other documents were burned in front of the courthouse on the town square by Major Raphael Moses (CSA). These acts were witnessed by the Secretary of War John C. Breckinridge and the Postmaster General John H. Reagan.

Though, as explained above, Davis's original destination had been Texas, the growing cordon of Union troops and Federal authorities had forced the Confederate president to alter his route and flee instead toward Florida. Even as he had departed Richmond, Davis knew Georgia – with its heavy infusion of and occupation by Union Army troops – would be difficult, if not impossible, to cross without being captured.

Davis's last official act as President of the Confederacy had been to appoint Capt. M.H. Clark (CSA) as Acting Treasurer of the Confederacy. After he had realized how undependable the cavalry unit "protecting" him actually had become (and indeed, after they had essentially mutinied), Davis had ordered that the troopers be released to proceed as they saw fit. It was either that, or jeopardize the safety of the funds remaining in the Confederate Treasury at that time. *(Author's Note: It quite likely was due to this peril for the Treasury demonstrated by the cavalry troops that Davis and his Cabinet ultimately decided to disperse the funds completely.)*

History has demonstrated that in times of war and national disaster, the trustworthiness of formerly loyal assistants often "falls by the wayside," as demonstrated by the Treasury funds with which several trusted aides obviously absconded in those dark days of 1865. Once those funds were divided among Davis's Cabinet officers and trusted assistants such as James Allen Semple, no further record or mention of them has ever been discovered.

Composed of gold and silver coins, the $86,000.00 taken by Semple would, as described above, have been exceedingly heavy, requiring at minimum some type of horse or mule-drawn wagon(s) for transport. In other words, it would not have been a simple matter to secretly spirit these funds away, yet that is exactly what seems to have occurred – unless these funds were somehow hidden and later secretly retrieved (or not) by the absconders.

Interestingly, even though the previously-described $2,584.00 – for which there is no accounting in the final reckoning of the Confederate Treasury – would be mere "pocket-change" to many individuals today, the coins themselves – if discovered today – would, again, be an almost priceless treasure for the afore-mentioned reasons.

The ultimate destination of the $27,000.00 and $25,000.00 and $34,000.00 (totaling $86,000.00 entrusted to Semple) which had been ear-marked for the "new" Confederacy remain – as stated – a mystery today. Perhaps Semple remained honorable in his actions and the funds remain in a hidden cache even today.

There also was no final accounting for the ultimate disposition of the 16,000 to 18,000 pounds Sterling in Liverpool, England acceptances. Just as with the many other mysteries surrounding the old Confederacy during the closing days of the U.S. Civil War, the truth regarding these outstanding funds may never be known.

Davis directed Breckinridge to take command of the five cavalry brigades which had been riding with the party. He (Davis) went off separately with an escort of about 350 horsemen. Of these 350, Davis quickly discharged all but about ten devoted volunteers. Breckinridge continued southward, amazingly evading Federal patrols, and managing to escape to Florida, Cuba, Great Britain and ultimately Canada.

Meanwhile, Jefferson Davis was not as successful in his evasive efforts. His wagon-train composed of the ten Confederate cavalrymen remaining as his protective escort, three of his military aides, and various servants, teamsters, and secretaries continued southward out of Washington on May 5. For security purposes, Davis traveled separately a short distance away from the group accompanying him.

The deposed Confederate President crossed the Oconee River below the Dublin Ferry, then proceeded to the southeastern edge of the town of Dublin. He never entered the community, but remained at a site in the area now bounded on the north by Madison Street, east by Decatur Street, south by the railroad, and west by South Franklin Street.

The wagon train accompanying Davis pulled into Dublin late Sunday morning. In those days, Dublin was a bare village which had practically become a ghost-town during the war. The group continued on, ultimately making it as far as Irwinville in south Georgia before being intercepted and captured.

Virginia Banks' Gold

The hoard of Confederate Treasury gold is often confused with the assets of six state banks in Richmond, Virginia – the Bank of Virginia, the Bank of Richmond, the Bank of the Commonwealth, the Exchange Bank, the Farmer's Bank, and the Trader's Bank – which traveled in the same general vicinity of the Confederate Treasury. U.S. Court of Claims documents indicate the assets from these banks were valued at that time at $450,000.00 in gold specie which had been quietly transported out of Richmond and on to Washington (Georgia) simultaneously with the Confederate Treasury funds in the closing days of the war and deposited into the vault of Washington's Bank of Georgia Branch.

When Jefferson Davis departed Washington, Georgia, on May 5, officials with the banks of Virginia – apparently concerned with the security of the banks' funds – surprisingly attempted to ship those assets *back to what then was the totally-insecure and Federally-occupied Richmond.* Under any other circumstances, such an action would

The "Heard House" is the reference identity assigned "post-war" by writers and researchers to describe the home owned by Dr. J.J. Robertson, the lower floor of which served, strange as it may sound today, as the Bank of Georgia branch in Washington. It was into this branch bank that Judge William W. Crump deposited nearly half a million dollars in gold coin (as valued in 1865) comprising the funds of six banks of Virginia. This building was also the site of the final Cabinet meeting of Jefferson Davis and what remained of the Confederate government in 1865. The "new" Wilkes County Courthouse was constructed upon this site following the Robertson House's/Heard Building's demolition in 1904. (Photo courtesy of Mary Willis Library, Washington, GA)

have been sheer financial suicide for the banks' funds, but at the helm of this wheeling and dealing was an individual by the name of Judge William W. Crump, president of the Bank of Virginia and Assistant Treasurer of the Confederacy.

Since he had realized he would be unable to "hide the Virginia banks' funds" from Federal authorities, Crump had hit upon a new strategy, that being to return to Virginia where he intended to "come clean" with Federal Provost authorities and plead his case as an innocent "civilian." In so-doing, the ingenious banker hoped to officially sever any association of the $450,000.00 with

the Confederacy, and have it certified for what it actually was – private property. Had his idea worked out as planned, it would indeed have been a crackerjack scheme. There is, however, an old saying: *"Man makes plans. God laughs."*

Much of what actually transpired in this incident has been obscured down through the years in folktales, rumor and half-truths. At least two separate and distinct explanations for the actual location of the ultimate initial theft of the gold from the banks of Virginia have persevered for well over 158 years now (as of 2023).

One account maintains the treasure was transported successfully to the vicinity of the old Chennault plantation once owned by John Chennault approximately 17 miles northeast of Washington, Georgia, where it was plundered and partially stolen by thieves. The two-story Georgian mansion (circa 1853) at this plantation – which is still in existence (as of this writing in 2023) and privately-owned today – was constructed atop a prominence overlooking the crossroads of what today are State Highways 44 and 79.

Another more logical and well-documented account (herewith) maintains that the group transporting the

Confederate President Jefferson Davis conducted the last meeting of the Confederate government in Washington, Georgia. The Confederate Treasury had followed close behind him to Washington. These funds ultimately were taken to an isolated location outside Washington and divided among Davis's Cabinet members, Army assistants, and other trusted advisors and staff. The group then disbanded and departed Washington, seeking to escape pursuing Union troops and bounty hunters. (Illustration courtesy of GA Dept. of Archives & History, Atlanta)

Richmond banks' gold made it as far as the home of Mrs. David M. (Susan) Moss, three miles from the Savannah River and approximately one mile beyond the Chennault plantation. Both accounts maintain the wagons with their golden treasure circled up in a horse lot for the night.

No matter which account one chooses to believe, the treasure definitely traveled toward this destination on May 24, 1865. Present-day GA Highway 44 which winds by the plantation mansion was the main thoroughfare – albeit little more than a dusty trail – between Washington, Georgia, and what remained of the once-thriving river-port town of Petersburg during Civil War days. It carried a steady stream of paroled Confederates heading for Washington and its rail spur which would carry them home to all parts of Georgia and Alabama. To a man, these troops were ragged, starving, destitute, war-weary, and absolutely desperate.

Accompanying this treasure (which, as described above, was being shipped back to Virginia) was a group of smartly-dressed bankers selected by the aforementioned Judge William Crump. These wealthy businessmen from Richmond knew their credibility was at stake should they fail to return the gold specie to the banks from whom it had originated. The treasure convoy was escorted by a squad of Federal cavalrymen acquired by the resourceful Crump, all of whom were headed to a military pontoon bridge across the Savannah River to the Abbeville, South Carolina, rail-head.

The assets which these men escorted – hundreds of thousands of dollars in gold coins – were packaged in wooden casks and heavy crates loaded into wagons, and were, understandably, a substantial burden for the draft animals pulling the wagons. The Abbeville, South Carolina-bound group hoped to soon be leaving that town by rail to return to the former Confederate capitol of Richmond and the banks whose funds they were guarding and transporting.

A general sense of unease pervasive among these riders stemmed from their realization of what they suspected was a growing threat on the horizon which they had noticed. A party of Confederate renegades who obviously had been tipped off to the treasure were shadowing the slow-plodding wagons which had departed Washington that morning. The entourage had hoped to make it to the relative safety of the military pontoon bridge across the Savannah by nightfall, but their unusually-slow rate of travel had delayed them, and they ultimately were forced to stop short of their destination to camp for the evening.

According to long-time Washington, Georgia resident and historian Waters, instead of overnighting at the Chennault plantation as has been reported in some quarters, the group almost certainly stopped instead at what was known as the Moss house. "Bank officials present at the time of the robbery remembered the site being the yard of 'William Moss,'"[3] said Waters. "This was most likely the home of Mrs. David M. (Susan) Moss, approximately one mile down the road beyond the Chennault home toward the Savannah River. It, coincidentally, was the same site where Confederate Secretary of War John C. Breckinridge had earlier paid out $108,322.90 (in silver specie) of the Confederate Treasury from the parlor window to mutinying Confederate cavalry troops on the evening of May 2nd-3rd.

"It is hard to believe that even after sundown," Waters continued, "(intelligent) bank officials could confuse the

Chennault house – which is columned and two-storied – with the Susan Moss house (no longer in existence) which was a simple (one-story) farmhouse with a porch."

The question of whether the gold convoy overnighted at the Chennault plantation or at the Moss home has been a matter of conjecture for many years. Whatever the circumstances, owner John Chennault was known to be an amiable and welcoming host during these terrible times who did not deny hospitality to the poor and desperate travelers and war-weary troops streaming daily down the dusty road beside his home.[4] His kindnesses, coupled with his residence quite near to the robbery site, would later unfortunately earn him several days of torture and imprisonment at the hands of a mad-man.

The 11-man squad of Federal cavalrymen escorting the wagons containing the gold undoubtedly knew their journey was a perilous one. History does not record the name of the sergeant commanding these troops, but he no doubt had been watching the cloud of dust from the renegades following the wagons, and ruing the day he had been near enough to be assigned as an escort to the bankers.

When the men had departed Washington earlier that day, the town had been filled – just as it had been for weeks – with ex-Confederate soldiers, most of them Kentucky and Tennessee cavalrymen – all battle-toughened men who had suffered long and hard, and who knew how to fight viciously. Judging from the appearance of the bankers and the military escort accompanying the obviously heavily-laden wagons, it would have been a simple matter for lawless renegades to deduce that the cargo was a valuable commodity had they not already been tipped off to that fact back in Washington. They had not wasted any time in planning their assault of the gold treasure train.

Theft of the VA Gold

The sergeant in charge of these men no doubt knew they would be "easy pickings" if they were attacked by a substantial number of determined outlaws. He, however, apparently was just as determined not to be caught flat-footed. Near sundown, he ordered the teamsters to drive the wagons into a fenced horse-lot and to draw them into a circle.

As explained above, whether this horse-lot was located at the Chennault plantation or the Moss farmhouse remains a matter of conjecture today. These two sites, nevertheless, were within approximately one mile of each other, and research has indicated the robbery site almost certainly was the Moss farm.

The cavalrymen, teamsters and the junior tellers bivouacked with the wagons in a defensive posture. The Federal pickets guarding the gold wagons no doubt nervously watched the flickering fires of the renegades in the distance through the trees as the moon rose that night.

Evening ultimately passed into early-morning. Whether the pickets were careless in their vigil, or merely fell asleep on their watch is unknown today. Whatever the circumstances, in the early morning hours, the troopers and bank tellers were suddenly and shockingly awakened by a tremendous tumult of countless hoof-beats, insanely-sounding screams and shouts of men, all punctuated by gunshots. The Federal troopers – completely overwhelmed in an instant according to reports – were horrified, and simply broke and ran.

The mounted attackers – spectral images and shadowy figures in the pale moonlight – steadily assaulted the wagons, jumping upon them and tearing into the casks of gold and silver coins and scooping them out by the double-handfuls into haversacks and saddlebags. Images on foot teemed around the wagons like wolves upon a feast – hacking and slashing at the casks and crates of treasure they had discovered to their great delight – all done with no opposition whatsoever.

Cursing and shouting, the men reportedly fought amongst themselves for the booty. They stripped the coins from the heavy containments, and loaded them as quickly as possible into whatever they could be conveyed by mounted horses, cackling and screaming insanely in their obvious amazement at the riches. In the process, hundreds of the gold coins reportedly were scattered haphazardly across the ground in the darkness.

According to later testimony, *"they waded ankle-deep in gold and silver, filling their haversacks and pockets as they went. They tied bags of gold and silver to their saddles."*[5] And then, just as quickly as they had appeared, the hoard of thieves were gone – hooting, laughing, and screaming maniacally as they dashed into the concealment of the thick forest, undergrowth and darkness.

Totally aghast, the remaining junior tellers and bankers could only watch as the renegades departed into the nearby timber. The riders spurred and whipped their mounts up the roads and across the fields toward the river and the creek fords. Their lathered horses galloped to the jingle of silver and gold coins, many of which continued to be sprinkled across the countryside as they were jostled and tossed from the loose containers.

Despite the diabolical nature of

Photographed circa 1913, Warthen Store may or may not have been in existence when Confederate President Jefferson Davis paused May 5, 1865, to purchase supplies in Warthen as he fled Federal forces who were in hot pursuit. (Photo courtesy of GA Dept of Archives & History, Atlanta, GA)

this incident, not a single drop of blood was spilled. The Iowan troopers and the teamsters who had been assigned to transport and protect the gold were nowhere to be found. They reportedly did not put up any resistance whatsoever, and basically fled in terror in the face of the sheer overwhelming number of maniacal raiders. Where and when they (the Iowans) stopped running history does not record.[6]

With the first rays of early dawn, the Virginia bankers took stock of their losses. The horse-lot and the surrounding yard literally glittered in the morning sunlight with stray silver dollars and five- and twenty-dollar gold pieces, as did the road and fields into the distance.[7]

According to records, the bankers amazingly managed to collect more than $40,000.00 (in face value) in odd coins lying scattered about on the ground.

Ex-Confederate Brig. Gen. Porter Alexander would later recover approximately $70,000.00 from a portion of the thieves who resided in the nearby Danburg community, bringing the total initial recovery to $110,000.00.

A later accounting would also determine that, in their rush to plunder, the thieves had left behind an additional amount of the treasure untouched in the cases and casks in the wagons, and these funds would ultimately make it back to the banks in Richmond. This amount, however, was still far short of the original $450,000.00 treasure originally spirited out of Richmond in the evacuation.

Origin of the VA Gold

So. . . How did the $450,000.00 in gold and silver coins from the Virginia banks come to be crated up in wagons

This artist's depiction of a Southern plantation mansion of the 1860s is quite similar to the mansion at Chenault Plantation outside Washington, Georgia, near where the robbery of the gold specie from the banks of Virginia occurred in 1865. (Engraving courtesy of GA Dept. of Archives & History, Atlanta, GA)

which ultimately were robbed and pillaged at a quiet Georgia backwater near Petersburg on the Savannah River? Why was it there? Who stole it?

The answers are rooted in the twilight days of the Confederate government. Strapped for cash and desperate for funds to revitalize a dying war effort, the Confederacy had turned to the private sector. On March 14, 1865, the Virginia State Legislature had authorized a loan of $300,000.00 in hard money to the Confederate leadership if it could somehow be properly collateralized – bankers as they are, being somewhat sticky about such matters. In order to accomplish this, the state of Virginia borrowed the funds in a loan which was to be secured by two million pounds of cotton held in various local warehouses.

With the collateral and loan ap-

proved, the banks which handled the state of Virginia's finances began scrambling to scrape up the necessary hard money (read: gold and silver specie) from smaller banks and private holdings. At the helm of this wheeling and dealing was the aforementioned Judge William W. Crump. Shrewd and competent, Crump made easy work of a hard job, but the ever-shifting winds of war soon made him regret his assumption of this task.[8]

By this point in the war, Richmond, Virginia, was under siege by the Union Army. *"It is just a matter of time,"* wrote Gen. Robert E. Lee (CSA) depressingly to Jefferson Davis.[9] Despite still-high hopes in some quarters as March waned, a gloomy reality soon began settling over the Confederate capital. With the city's fall imminent, the Confederate

Congress had adjourned and fled – without finally authorizing surety (the two million pounds of cotton) for Virginia's loan.

As a result of all of the above, the deal for the collateral and hard cash for the Confederacy suddenly collapsed, leaving the Virginia bankers totally flustered – but flush with an amazing amount of hard currency they had collected from the state's banks. What were they to do? They were now suddenly in possession of hundreds of thousands of dollars in gold and silver, with their enemy – the Union Army – poised to sweep into their city at any moment, at which point the funds would be confiscated.

Crump knew the Confederate Treasury Department had plans to remove the *government's* specie and bullion reserves southward, so he made similar arrangements to spirit the Virginia banks' funds out via the same pack-train. It was either that, or sit idly by as Federal officials rode in and took the gold and silver as spoils of war, and he wasn't about to allow that to happen.

As Richmond was gradually being burned and looted, Crump and his hand-picked cadre of bankers gathered their new-found wealth – a sum amounting to approximately $450,000.00 – and smuggled it through the bedlam, loading it into the same railroad boxcar into which the Confederate Treasury funds had been loaded. How ironic that the very funds the Rebel government had so desperately needed a few months earlier were now traveling in concert on the same train with that government's Treasury, yet the gold was now essentially useless as the Confederacy collapsed around them.

Near midnight, the treasure train filled with the Confederate Treasury's and Virginia banks' funds creaked out of the dying city. Dawn would find a Union flag flying over the former capitol as the remnants of the Rebel government sought an escape southward through Georgia.

The Midshipmen

As previously explained, this train moving across southern Virginia with all this Confederate Treasury gold traveled under the authority and protection of the officers and midshipmen of the Confederate Naval Academy. Lieutenant Commander William H. Parker, superintendent of the Confederate Naval Academy, ten officers of his faculty, and fifty of his midshipmen – cadets ranging in age from seventeen down to fourteen – had been assigned the task of arranging the logistics and protection for the funds.

These young guards probably never inspired Judge Crump with much confidence, but Parker's fledglings proved to be more than up to the task, providing the most reliable protection the banks' funds would ever have. They never wavered in their commitment or reliability.

Parker pushed his command steadily southward, staying well ahead of the Federal cavalry sweeps out to net the fleeing Jefferson Davis who was moving his refugee government along the same route. When the rail lines ran out in Chester, South Carolina, Parker and his staff switched the treasure to horse-drawn wagons and continued southward, utilizing whatever backroads were available for concealment. Davis and his advisors had also earlier transferred to horses but had taken a separate alternate route.

The lieutenant quickened his pace as rumors of what – and how much – he was carrying became more widely known. In order to make escape as difficult as possible for Davis and his Cabinet, U.S. President Andrew Johnson and federal authorities had been widely circulating information which announced the huge value of the Confederate Treasury accompanying Davis, and the fact that any captors of the Rebel president would be rewarded with a share of the gold.

"One hundred thousand dollars Reward in Gold will be paid to any person or persons who will apprehend and deliver JEFFERSON DAVIS to any of the military authorities of the United States," Johnson announced. *"Several millions of specie reported to be with him will become the property of the captors..."*

The farther south Davis and the Confederate Treasury traveled, the taller grew the tales in the telling of the golden hoard. This made Parker and his staff's task of successful transport of the Treasury doubly difficult, because he gradually had to fear not only the pursuing Federal troops, but the growing number of desperate renegades as well. He nevertheless remained confident – as he later noted in his memoirs – that if attacked by anyone, that *"we could give a good accounting of ourselves."*

Davis and his entourage, meanwhile, had traveled across South Carolina toward Georgia. He initially was destined for Texas. The Treasury was destined for the protection of a secure lock-up in Macon, Georgia, but Parker altered this route after learning that Federal troops were headed toward that objective. As an alternate destination, he chose the Confederate Depository in Augusta, Georgia, to secure the Treasury. Due to the ever-changing nature of the Federal drag-net in pursuit of Davis, however, the plans changed almost daily.

Crump, his bankers and the bank funds, accompanied by Parker and his Confederate Naval Academy midshipmen, reached Augusta on April 18. Upon arrival, Parker received instructions to disband his command, but realizing the desperate nature of the circumstances (since Augusta was also under imminent threat by that point from Union troops), he made the decision to disobey orders for the first time in his life, refusing to abandon his duty to guard the Treasury. This was just too much gold to leave unguarded.

Why the Confederate government cabinet officials believed they could simply dump the Confederate Treasury in Augusta and then somehow later retrieve it unopposed from Texas is unknown today. Suffice it to say that confusion reigned supreme in those dark days. Whatever the circumstances, Parker wasn't having any of the disbandment orders.

In the final analysis, after foregoing both Macon and Augusta (since both were about to be occupied by Union troops) as safe harbor for the Treasury, Parker, as detailed above, decided he had no choice but to retrace his route back northward in the hope of tracking down Davis and turning the Treasury over to his staff. As for Crump and the Virginia banks' treasure, he decided to remain – at least for the immediate future – in Augusta. This, however, would soon change as well.

Hiding the Gold

It wasn't long before Crump also reconsidered the plan of remaining in Augusta. He had discovered that officers of no less than twelve Tennessee banks were already hiding over $500,000.00 in specie in Augusta, and that they feared Federal officials already had them targeted. Crump immediately decided that Augusta therefore was far too dangerous for temporary concealment of the Virginia banks' $450,000.00 in gold. With his options becoming more limited by the hour, Crump found himself retracing his route with the funds back to Washington.

Avoiding the railroads this time, Crump and the bankers moved their trove once again through the back country, arriving in Washington on May 3. The small, remote town of 2,200 residents was the political and commercial center of a fairly wealthy farming district – but, unknown at the time to Crump, it also was a Union Army target.

The community itself had been little touched by the war. General William T. Sherman or the bummers who followed in his wake hadn't quite reached out that far.

The converging roads and the Georgia Railroad spur line made Washington a natural way-station for anyone bound for someplace else in an attempt to escape the war. In the full flower of spring and absent the destruction of the war, the hamlet offered memories of happier times to many of the war-weary Confederates passing through it.

Given his desperate situation, Crump can almost be excused for misjudging Washington's presumed virtues. Almost. If, however, he had carefully and systematically weighed the little town's assets and liabilities with his usual shrewd banker's eye, he almost certainly would not have found it to be so comforting a haven.

To begin with, Robert Toombs, the former Confederate Secretary of State, Brigadier General and all-around secessionist firebrand had been nursing his bruised ego in Washington – his hometown – for over two years. And Confederate Vice-President Alexander H. Stephens – though not fleeing arrest – was also ensconced in his home only nineteen miles away in Crawfordville. Both were top Federal targets of arrest.

Had he adequately sized-up the situation, Judge Crump would have figured both men as the liabilities for safety they represented. What's more, he ought easily to have reckoned that Washington's transportation hub circumstances would likely draw President Jefferson Davis through that vicinity as well, and virtually anyone should have deduced that Davis would have Federal hounds hot upon his trail.

As it happened, only a few hours after Crump and his party had stored their banks' gold in the Washington branch of the Bank of Georgia, Davis and what remained of his government rolled into town. Judge Crump requested a meeting with Davis to discuss his dilemma, but the president of the dying Confederacy had enough problems as it was. He had no interest whatsoever in taking on new ones from Crump, and therefore declined to meet with the banker.

Since the assassination of Lincoln, the Federal dragnet for Davis had been steadily tightening, and he knew he would have to lighten his load if he were to have any hope at all of escaping his pursuers. He had thus ordered what remained of the Confederate Treasury – which had caught up with him in Washington – to be divided among his Cabinet officers, trusted assistants and military attaches who then all rode off in different directions, planning to regroup in Texas.[10]

Federal Protection

Crump and his associate bankers now knew that Washington would shortly be overrun with Federals searching for Davis. And even before Davis had departed, Crump had learned still more disturbing news. Some of Davis's escort had mutinied and demanded part of the Treasury in payment of back wages. Now the whole countryside in Wilkes County and beyond was aware of the treasure-trove in town.[11] It was quickly becoming obvious to Crump that his problems were about to become too great to overcome.

On May 6, 1865, Federal cavalry entered Washington, Georgia, and seized any property with even a whiff of the Confederate government about it. The $450,000.00 in gold sitting in the Washington branch of the Bank of Georgia smelled fairly to high Heaven of the Confederacy.

On the advice of his host, Judge Garnett Andrews, Crump had decided to try his new strategy – that being to return to Virginia and plead his case that the banks' funds were "private" funds, unassociated with the Confederacy. As explained above, had this idea borne fruit, it would have been ingenious, but instead, it resulted in disaster – at least on a partial scale.

On May 18, two more bank officers fresh from Virginia and the meeting with the Federal provost authorities reached Washington. They carried instructions from Judge Crump and official Federal *"Letters of Transit"* signed by Major General Marsena R. Patrick, the Federal Army's Provost Marshal General.

Against the longest of odds, Crump had actually seemingly accomplished his objective. The bankers would not only be allowed to transfer the specie back to Richmond to its rightful owners, they would be given a Federal military escort to guarantee safe delivery! What could have been better? Crump no doubt was feeling much more confident

at this point, but, unknown to him, dark clouds were continuing to gather upon the horizon.

Happy to have their money back nevertheless, and eager to set off for Virginia, the bankers in Washington set out almost immediately. Though the mode of transport is uncertain, they quite likely had obtained mule or horse-drawn wagons – since all that weight could not be simply transported upon the backs of their horses – and at mid-morning on May 24, they embarked for the railhead at Abbeville, South Carolina, their problems seemingly diminishing by the hour.[12]

However, if the bankers had hoped to steal away unnoticed, their hopes had been in vain. Gold has a way of diminishing any possibility of secrecy almost from the get-go. It is extremely difficult to hide its existence, particularly if more than one person is involved with it. And that brings us full-circle, back to the Confederate renegades' attack and theft of the gold near Petersburg at a tiny burg known ironically as "Graball," Georgia.

Years after the gold had been looted that night by the former Confederate soldiers, Lewis Shepard, a Tennessean from Vaughn's brigade, recalled (without owning up to any involvement in the incident himself) what happened after word of the gold had spread:

". . . Some of the officers and men of Vaughan's brigade became appraised that a train of specie was being carried North under Federal guard, and they jumped to the conclusion that it was the property of the Confederate government which the Federals had captured. They concluded that their . . . . hard service for the Confederacy entitled them to a share of this gold and silver provided they could . . . (succeed) in securing it from the Federal guard. . . They

organized an expedition with the view of capturing this money and followed the (wagon)-train until a favorable opportunity of attack presented itself. . . ."[13]

Partial Gold Recovery

In the early afternoon of May 25, following the theft of the Virginia banks' gold, Brigadier General Edward Porter Alexander and a band of paroled Confederates cantered toward the site of the gold theft which, as explained above, was almost certainly the Moss home. Just as all the returning Confederate veterans, these men also were ragged, starving and destitute. Nevertheless, they, just as Gen. Alexander, were – for the most part – also very good and honorable men.

Following the trauma of the assault and robbery of the gold, Alexander – due no doubt to his uncompromising honor – had either been recruited by the bankers, or had volunteered outright to help recover the stolen gold and silver. The brilliant 30-year-old engineer who had risen through the ranks to Confederate general, had returned to Washington barely three weeks earlier from the very painful surrender at Appomattox Courthouse in Virginia.

Alexander's remarkable knowledge and astute management of the artillery for Longstreet's Corps had made him one of the Confederacy's most respected soldiers, and a near-legend around his hometown. More importantly, his reputation for integrity and bravery was beyond reproach. If there was one man in the community who might carry weight with any raiders remaining in the area, it was Alexander.

The young general had gathered six members of his former Irwin Artillery company and had pushed on immediately for the site of the robbery, adding eight

more recruits to his band as they passed through the Danburg community. Also along was Judge William M. Reese, a local magistrate, to provide any necessary warrants and official sanction if Alexander was required to make arrests and take back the loot by force. Reese, as a Confederate magistrate appointee, ironically had no legal authority any longer

Brigadier General Edward A. Wild was a rabid abolitionist from Massachusetts who held a deep, burning hatred for all White Southerners, slave-holders or not. He had lost an arm at Gettysburg, and the wound fostered an addiction to laudanum (opium) that exacerbated his already deeply-disturbed mentality into an obsession with the infliction of pain upon others. He caused untold misery and despair in using extreme torture in an attempt to extract information about the stolen assets of the banks of Virginia from residents in the vicinity of the Moss home and Chenault plantation. (Photo courtesy of Mark Waters)

to issue any warrants or to be involved in any other legalities since the Confederate surrender, but he accompanied the group nonetheless.

"We came upon a party of guerrillas who had about $80,000.00 of the money in charge," Alexander recalled in an 1881 interview. *"They said they did not know it was private property; believing it to belong to the Confederacy, they thought they were as much entitled to it as anyone else. . . but being convinced that it was private property, they were willing to surrender it."*[14]

The fact that these desperate renegades were eventually willing to part company with $70,000.00 of their ill-gotten gains is amazing in itself, and a testament not only to the respect Alexander engendered among his neighbors, but also to the honor of the men who returned the gold. Men had regularly killed and been killed for far less money during good times prior to the 1860s, and this theft recovery was being attempted during some of the darkest most desperate days to date in the United States.

The initial confrontation between Alexander's men and the renegades took place with guns drawn, but luckily, no shooting occurred. Alexander could see other raiders gathering and watching from the shadows, and he shortly became certain there were too many others he could not see. He wanted the money, but not at the risk of serious injury or death of a number of his men. He was ready for an end to the conflict pervading the South.

Since he was badly out-numbered, Alexander soon came to the conclusion that any of the stolen gold which was not voluntarily surrendered would not be pursued. He simply had not anticipated the sheer number of outlaws with which he now was confronted. For the

same reason, he knew it would be imprudent – if not downright foolhardy – to attempt to make any arrests for the theft. Besides, money or no money, Alexander had little taste for arresting Confederates – even guerrillas – who would ultimately face Federal martial law.

When he had collected all of the gold and silver that the men were willing to surrender, Alexander returned to Washington to report to Crump. After turning over the recovered gold, ex-Confederate Brigadier General Edward Porter Alexander returned to his ancestral home in Washington which still stands as of this writing (2023) on what today is Alexander Drive.

All told, the bankers had now – according to U.S. Court of Claims official records – recovered approximately $110,000.00 of the stolen funds. They also retained possession to a substantial amount of the funds in the casks and cases in the wagons which the thieves had never touched. Though this was far short of the original $450,000.00, Crump undoubtedly didn't feel quite as bad. Had he been able to see a bit into the future, however, he, no doubt, would have been crestfallen.

A Damned Yankee

Brigadier General Edward A. Wild was that sort of "damned Yankee" whose very name Southerners for three generations after the war couldn't hear uttered without feeling compelled to spit. A rabid abolitionist from Massachusetts, Wild held a deep, burning hatred for all White Southerners, slave-holders or not.

He had lost an arm at the battle of South Mountain in Maryland, and the wound had fostered an addiction to laudanum (opium) that twisted Wild's already demented mind and constantly stoked the fires of his hatred to a white-hot heat. Wherever he served, Wild cut a swath of wanton destruction and cruelty against prisoners and civilians alike.

In Virginia in 1864, several random hangings of Confederate prisoners, with Wild personally acting as hangman, prompted his then-commanding officer, Major General Benjamin F. Butler to write Secretary of War Stanton: *"I wish Wild were elsewhere. He has no common sense."*[15] The mild, almost passing nature of this criticism can only be interpreted as a ridiculously weak effort at a rebuke of an individual on the edge of madness who should, at the very least, have been relieved of his command (which eventually did occur).

Wild had come to Washington, Georgia, to investigate several lynchings, but when he learned of the looted treasure train, the lynchings suddenly were forgotten. He became fixated upon the massive gold cache and the capture of the raiders involved in its theft. The local population quickly began to experience Wild's cruel hand.

The twisted brigadier general began by arresting the Virginia bankers and confiscating their recently-recovered $110,000.00 in gold and silver, despite their legitimate and official *"Letters of Transit"* which had earlier been issued by Union Provost Marshal General Marsena R. Patrick. In his uncontrolled lust for violence, Wild filled the county jail and several temporary jails with suspects.[16]

It was out of these circumstances that one of the numerous mysteries involving the Richmond banks' gold originated. It is unknown today why the portion of the gold and silver coins left behind untouched in the wagons by the thieves (approximately $159,929.90 according to records) was returned to the possession of the Richmond banks, and yet the $40,000.00 recovered from the thieves' droppings on the ground and the $70,000.00 recovered by Brig. Gen. Alexander were confiscated by Federal officials, but that apparently is what occurred. History does not record the exact circumstances of these two separate caches of funds, or the specific logistics involved in their apparent separate journeys.

For several weeks, the insane Gen. Wild and his men ravaged the countryside in Wilkes County in an effort to root out any of the stolen funds remaining in the hands of any renegades or guerrillas. When his efforts bore no fruit, he was emboldened to more brutal actions and cruelty.[17]

In mid-July, a former slave once owned by John Chennault made her way to Wild's headquarters, possibly seeking some type of vengeance against her former owner. She accused Chennault not only of taking part in the raid conducted by the thieves, but also of hiding a great deal of the loot himself. With the woman, Angelina, in tow as a guide, Wild led a detail to the Chennault plantation where he intended to initiate a painful interrogation.

Brutal Torture

When they arrived at the plantation, Wild's men opened accounts by killing the Chennault children's dog, shooting and stabbing the animal to death in front of the children. The men, laughing and jeering, ignored the desperate pleas from the weeping and distraught children as the poor animal was cruelly tortured and dispatched.

For his part, Wild arrested John Chennault and his brother, Dionysius, as well as John's 16-year-old son, Frank, and set about meticulously torturing the

Brig. Gen. Edward Porter Alexander, a native of Wilkes County and noted artillerist with Confederate Gen. James Longstreet's army, was instrumental in the recovery of a portion of the tens of thousands of dollars in gold coins from the banks of Richmond which had been stolen by thieves. (Photo courtesy of Mark Waters)

three in order to extract confessions and/or any information concerning the location of any hidden loot. The "prisoners" were taken to a nearby wood-lot, where the first punishments were meted out.

"They tied their hands behind them and then hung them up by their thumbs with their feet off the ground," explained Mary Ann Chennault Shumate in a later interview who was seventeen at the time of Wild's tortures. *"My brother and father said the pain was so great that after the first time they begged the Yankees to shoot them dead rather than suffer so a second time. . . . Their hands were so black and swollen that it was a long time before they could use them again."*[18]

According to later reports, the torture being administered by Wild and his men continued throughout the day and into the night. When torturing the Chennault family proved futile (since they were innocent and knew absolutely nothing about the stolen gold), Wild

turned to torturing John Chennault's body servant, Tom, who ironically was Angelina's son (causing her, no doubt, to greatly regret her earlier false accusations).

Meanwhile, back inside the plantation house, more of Wild's men and Angelina heaped abuse upon the other Chennaults. *"Some of the soldiers came into the house cursing and abusing Ma and the children,"* Mary Ann Chennault Shumate continued. *"They took Ma and me and Aunt Deasy* [Ardesia (Mrs. Dionysius Chennault)] *and shut us up in a room and forced us to strip off our clothes while Angelina came in and searched us."*[19]

A number of the former Chennault slaves managed to spirit the younger children away to the neighbors or to their own cabins. In the end, all that Wild could seize were the Chennault women's few pieces of jewelry and $150.00 in coin the Chennault brothers had accumulated.

All six Chennaults – John, Dionysius, their wives, Mary Ann and Frank – ultimately were hauled to Washington and illegally imprisoned for no reason whatsoever. Amazingly, as cruel as were Wild's torturous tactics, they were nowhere near as criminal as the abuses in other quarters where rape, assault, theft, arson, and beatings were standard fare across north Georgia and Alabama in particular where lawlessness reigned.

The Chennaults remained in prison for several days while Judge Garnett Andrews of Washington traveled to Augusta to plead their case before Wild's superior, Major General John B. Steedman. Andrews, much respected in Washington though he had remained a staunch Unionist, was perhaps the only person in a position to offer the Chennaults any hope. He returned to Washington with Col. E.I. Drayton of Steedman's staff.

"Colonel Drayton behaved very

gentlemanly and sent us back home, just as soon as he could finish investigating the case," Mary Shumate added. Drayton also returned the Chennaults' money and jewelry as well and freed the rest of Wild's prisoners, including the Virginia bankers, but unfortunately for Crump and the bankers, their gold apparently was too much of a temptation and Drayton refused to return it.[20]

Interestingly, though Wild was not present to witness it, his torture of the Chennaults ironically may actually have yielded the results he sought. *"A good many others* (who did have portions of the stolen gold and silver coins) *when they saw how things were going, they got uneasy and gave up their shares,"* Shumate said, *"and so the Yankees got a good deal of it back."*[21]

Thankfully, those remaining in Wilkes County were spared any further cruelties by the obviously unbalanced Brigadier General Wild. After learning of the extent of the attrocities meted by the mad general and his troops to innocent civilians, Major Gen. Steedman instructed that Wild be arrested at Augusta on July 31. He was sent to Washington, D.C. for formal inquiry shortly thereafter, subsequently removed from command by General Ulysses S. Grant, and mustered out of service on January 15, 1866.[22]

"Federal" Theft of Gold

Under orders from President Andrew Johnson, Maj. General Steedman transferred to Augusta, Georgia, the earlier-recovered $110,000.00 gold and silver funds from the banks of Richmond. It shortly thereafter was transferred from Augusta to United States Treasury officials in Washington, D.C. As a result of Judge Crump's agreement with Provost Marshal General Patrick (USA), the Virginia banks petitioned President

Johnson and the Secretary of the Treasury to have these funds returned. Following a full investigation, Johnson, the Secretary of the Treasury, and the U.S. Attorney General all collectively held forth in March of 1867 that the specie was indeed private property and that the banks were entitled to have it returned.[23]

Secretary of War Stanton, however – as many powerful Federal officials continue practicing to this very day – had his own agenda, and simply refused to obey official law. He called upon his "Radical Republican" allies in Congress to alter the mandate handed down by Johnson, the Treasury and the attorney general, and on March 22, 1867, the U.S. House passed a resolution claiming the Virginia bankers' funds for the U.S. Treasury.

The U.S. Senate proved equally co-operative with Stanton, passing an identical resolution the following day. In both instances, the margin of votes clearly indicated to President Johnson that he would lose a fight to sustain a veto if he pressed the issue, so he signed the bill into law.[24]

The seizure of the Virginia bankers' specie fit a pattern Stanton had vigorously mandated in the war's waning days. On May 14, 1865, he had cabled Major General James H. Wilson (US) at Macon, Georgia, instructing him to move at once against Augusta and confiscate the assets of the various Tennessee banks known to be on deposit in that town.

After that, any funds to which a Unionist Tennessean could establish claim were returned to that individual, but those funds of any other Southern residents or commercial businesses were simply deposited into the U.S. Treasury. This pattern was played out all over the old Confederacy. It was inarguably outright theft, and served to emphasize the hypocrisy of politics, but the funds were considered "spoils of war," and there simply was no way to fight it.[25]

It was for this and many other reasons that the deep wounds of the U.S. Civil War were so painfully slow in healing, causing unimaginably cruel suffering felt in many quarters until the 1890s. Outrageous taxation on Southern properties and the denial of legally-elected representatives in the U.S. Congress, caused untold numbers of families to lose all they owned, creating beggars by the thousands.

The legal fight over the funds from the Virginia banks didn't end with the acts of Congress. Lawsuits ground on for twenty-six years as first the banks, and then their receivers, brought claim after claim for the return of the funds. Finally, on June 22, 1893 – almost 30 years after their theft by the Federal government – the suits were settled when the U.S. Court of Claims ruled that the receivers of the Bank of Virginia were entitled to recover a grand total of $16,987.88.[26]

In the end, though a large portion of the Virginia banks' gold assets were permanently confiscated by the U.S. Federal government as "spoils of war," and another large portion was stolen by thieves, some of the gold – as described above – nevertheless did make it back to Richmond intact. These funds, as explained below, amounted to "approximately" $159,929.90. So how much of this tremendous treasure is still actually a mystery today?

A Legend for the Ages

Almost from the moment the din of the shouting raiders and their pounding horses' hooves died away, the tales of "lost treasure" began growing thick as the cotton which once graced the fields and vales of the Wilkes County countryside. So, . . . How much of the gold and silver specie from the banks of Virginia funds – which originally totaled approximately $450,000.00 – was actually lost to and never recovered from the thieves who attacked the wagon-train that fateful night? That information is sketchy at best today, but an approximation, according to researcher/historian Marshall Waters is as follows:

"IF $450,000.00 was the total original amount being transported by the bankers when they fled Richmond – and this figure might not be totally accurate," says Waters – "the Wilkes County thieves who attacked the treasure train that night definitely did NOT leave with the entire $450,000.00 (or whatever the exact sum may have been).

"According to the Virginia bankers' records of the incident (as explained above)," Waters continues, "approximately $40,000.00-worth of the coins were left scattered upon the ground at the robbery site. Records at the U.S. Court of Claims also indicate that $159,929.90 was later taken to the railhead at Abbeville then on to Richmond, so one must assume that those were the funds which were never even removed from the wagons that night by the bandits.

"Then there was Brig. Gen. Porter Alexander and his men who recovered approximately $70,000 from the thieves from the Danburg area who had participated in the robbery then returned their stolen funds. This $70,000.00, coupled with the approximately $40,000.00 picked up on the ground, totaled a little over $110,000.00 which was returned to the Bank of Georgia Branch in Washington (and later confiscated by the U.S. government).

"If one assumes the $159,929.90 supposedly taken to Abbeville, plus the approximately $110,000.00 supposedly returned to the Bank of Georgia Branch in Washington (and later confiscated by Federal officials) are true and reasonably accurate figures, then this sum total is approximately $269,929.90," Waters

This pontoon ferry on the Oconee River was photographed circa 1914. It was via a ferry just such as this forty-nine years earlier on May 6, 1865, at Ball's Ferry a short distance away, that Confederate President Jefferson Davis and several men in his escort crossed the Oconee, then proceeded to the southeastern edge of the town of Dublin, Georgia. (Photo courtesy of GA Dept. of Archives & History, Atlanta)

adds. "And if $450,000.00 was the accurate amount originally in transit with the Virginia bankers, it then follows that there was approximately $180,000.00 taken by the thieves in Wilkes County that night for which there has never been any accounting whatsoever."

It, interestingly, is this $180,000.00 portion which left the most enduring legacy in the folklore of the Washington, Georgia, area with its now-renowned legend of the "lost gold of the Confederacy." Years later, right up to the present-day, local folklore continues to attribute the wealth of a local landowner or businessman in Washington or the near vicinity to *"that gold stolen back during the war."*[27]

Modern discoveries have added to the folklore. Young boys seining a creek for fish in recent years discovered several

gold "Double-Eagles" in the creek waters – much to their delight. Were these lost by one of the wagons crossing the creek on that fateful evening, or were they among the hundreds of coins which tinkled from the filled saddlebags and haversacks upon the galloping horses as they fled the robbery that night?

Today, the now-historic (and legendary) Chennault mansion can still be seen by driving northeast out of Washington on GA 44, or by turning south onto GA 79 off GA 72 twelve miles east of Elberton. The mansion was recently restored and is privately owned as of this writing (2023). It is important to emphasize herewith that although some of the incident – particularly some of the tortures administered by Brigadier Gen. Wild (US) and his men – occurred at this plantation, research has indicated the actual theft of the banks of Richmond gold quite probably took place approximately one mile away at the Moss farmhouse.

Are there still coins sprinkled in the fields, or in the streams and upon the hillsides from that night so long ago – or perhaps even hidden away in a cave somewhere in the Wilkes County vicinity? Only one way to find out, but you better ask permission before you go traipsing illegally across private property in that area. The insane ghost of old Brig. Gen. Eddie Wild just might still be in the area!

(Grateful appreciation is expressed herewith to writers/researchers Marshall P. Waters III, Ray Chandler and Robert S. Davis, Jr., who researched and provided details regarding various segments of the mystery of the Confederate Treasury gold and the theft of the banks of Virginia gold near Chennault Plantation in Georgia's Wilkes County.)

Footnotes:

1/ Clark, Captain Micajah H. (CSA), *"The Last Days of the Confederate Treasury and What Became of the Specie,"* Southern Historical Society Papers (1881), Vol. 9, No. 1, Page 545, reprinted, Broadfoot Publishing Company, Morningside Bookshop, Dayton, OH (1990)

2/ Parker, William Harwar, *Recollections of a Naval Officer, 1841-1865, p 379,* Charles Scribners' Sons, New York (1883)

3/ Davis, Robert Scott, *"The Georgia Odyssey of the Confederate Gold,"* Georgia Historical Quarterly, Vol. LXXXVI, p 575, No. 4, Winter, (2002)

4/ Ashmore, Otis, *"The Story of the Virginia Bank Funds,"* Georgia Historical Quarterly, p 179, (December, 1918), Ashmore cites letter from Mary Ann Chennault Shumate.

5/ Davis, Burke, *The Long Surrender,* p 185, Vintage Books, New York (1985)

6/ The Iowans presumably made their way back

to the 22nd Iowa Infantry Regiment, which was enroute to Augusta at the time. However, a search of the official records turns up no report filed by Captain Abraham referring to the incident or the fate of the detail.

7/ Ibid, Davis, Burke, p 185

8/ Ibid, Ashmore, Otis, p 190

9/ Ibid, Davis, Burke, p 17

10/Hanna, A.J., *Flight into Oblivion,* pp 88-93, Indiana University Press (1959), and Ibid, Davis, Burke, *The Long Surrender,* pp 123, 129-130.

11/Ibid, Davis, Burke, pp 114-115.

12/ Ibid, p 184

13/ Willingham, Jr., Robert M., *No Jubilee: The Story of Confederate Wilkes County,* p 197, Wilkes Publishing Co., Washington, GA (1976)

14/ Ibid, Ashmore, Otis, pp 174-175

15/ Nolan, Dick, *The Damndest Yankee: Benjamin Franklin Butler,* pp 242-243, Presidio Press (1991)

16/ Andrews, Eliza Francis, *The War-time Journal of a Georgia Girl, 1864-1865,* Ardivan Press, Macon, Georgia, (1908); reprinted (1960)

17/Ibid, Davis, Burke, pp 186-187

18/ Ibid, Ashmore, Otis, pp 180-181and Andrews, Eliza Francis, *The War-Time Journal of a Georgia Girl, 1864-1865,* Ardivan Press, Macon, Georgia (1908); reprinted (1960)

19/ Ibid, Ashmore, Otis, p 181

20/ Ibid, Ashmore, Otis, p 182

21/ Ibid, p 183

22/ Casstevens, Frances H., *Edward A. Wild and the African Brigade in the Civil War,* p 231, McFarland & Company, Inc., Jefferson, NC, (2003)

23/ Ibid, Ashmore, Otis, pp 186-188

24/ Ibid, pp 190-197

25/ *Official Records of the War of Rebellion, Series I, Volume 49, Part II* (Correspondence), p 799. General Wilson acknowledges cable from Stanton and discusses its contents.

26/ Ashmore, pp 196-197

27/ Ashmore, p 172

About The Author

R. Olin Jackson founded *Legacy Communications, Inc.*, in 1985, where he became the award-winning executive editor and publisher of his flagship creations – *North Georgia Journal* and *Georgia Backroads* magazines. During his tenure at *Legacy*, Olin was the recipient of a number of awards from the *Magazine Association of Georgia (MAG)* for excellence in publishing.

Olin parlayed his magazine publishing business into a long and fruitful career before selling it in 2005. *Georgia Backroads* is now under new ownership and enjoying its 37th year (as of 2023) of publication. It is one of the longest-running magazines in the state.

Olin also wrote/co-wrote a selection of books, including *Moonshine, Murder and Mayhem in Georgia* (2003); *Tales of the Rails in Georgia* (2004); *Georgia Backroads Traveler* (2005); and *Georgia's Doc Holliday* (2006) among others.

In 2021, Olin founded *Whippoorwill Publications, LLC*. His current projects within that realm include: *Mystery & History in Georgia, Volume I* (2022) which was honored with a *Five-Star Award* by *Readers' Favorite* book awards (available at *Amazon.com* and *Barnes&Noble.com*); and *Some Genealogy Keys to Some Georgia Family Trees: Histories and Genealogies of Assorted Jackson, Fricks, Neel, Anderson, Jordan, Gravatt, Hudgins, Tanner, Pettyjohn and Rogers Family Lines* (2023) (also available at *Amazon.com* and *Barnes&Noble.com.*).

Other works scheduled for release in 2023 include *Memories of Army Life and MPs of the 529th: The Story of the Top MP Company in the U.S. Army*; and a selection of original poetry entitled *After All That We've Been Through*.

Olin is married to the former Judy Grizzle of Dahlonega, Georgia. The couple make their home in Roswell and Rockmart, Georgia. Olin also has a son – Burke – by a former marriage.

Supplemental
Bibliographical References

1/ Amerson, Anne Dismukes, *Dahlonega, Georgia: Site of America's First Major Gold Rush* (2013), Chestatee Publications

2/ Bartow County Genealogical Society, *Bartow County Heritage Book* (1995)

3/ Cain, Andrew, *History of Lumpkin County, 1832-1932* (1979), The Reprint Company Publishers

4/ Coulter, E. Merton, *Auraria: The Story of a Georgia Gold Mining Town* (1956), UGA Press

5/ Dabney, Joseph E., *Mountain Spirits* (1974), Bright Mountain Books

6/ Davis, Donald E., *The Land of Ridge and Valley, A Photographic History of the Northwest Georgia Mountains*, (2000), Arcadia Publishing

7/ Dickens, Jr., Roy, *Cherokee Pre-History* (1976), University of Tennessee Press

8/ Dillman, Caroline M., *Days Gone By: Alpharetta and Georgia* (1992), Chattahoochee Press

9/ Ehle, John, *The Trail of Tears* (1988), Anchor Books

10/ Foster, Jr., W.A., *Paulding County: Its People and Places* (1983), W.H. Wolfe Associates

11/ Furnas, J.C., *The Americans: A Social History of the United States, 1587-1914* (1969), G.P. Putnam's Sons, New York

12/ Garrett, Franklin and Rice, Bradley, Atlanta Historic Society, *Atlanta History, A Journal of the South* (1980)

13/ Glover, V., James Bolan; McIntyre, Joe; and Rebecca Nash Paden, *Marietta 1833-2000*, (1999), Arcadia Publishing

14/ Harris, Corra, *A Circuit Rider's Wife* (1998), University of Georgia Press

15/ Head, Sylvia Gailey, *The Neighborhood Mint* (1986), Gold Rush Gallery

16/ Hicks, John D., *The Federal Union (Second Edition), A History of the United States to 1865* (1952), Houghton Mifflin Company / The Riverside Press Cambridge

17/ Jackson, III, Ralph Olin, *A North Georgia Journal of History, Vol. 1* (1989), Legacy Communications, Inc.

18/ Jackson, III, Ralph Olin, *A North Georgia Journal of History, Vol. 2* (1991), Legacy Communications, Inc.

19/ Jackson, III, Ralph Olin, *A North Georgia Journal of History, Vol. 3* (1995), Legacy Communications, Inc.

20/ Jackson, III, Ralph Olin, *A North Georgia Journal of History, Vol. 4* (1999), Legacy Communications, Inc.

21/ Jackson, III, Ralph Olin, *Moonshine, Murder & Mayhem in Georgia* (2003), Legacy Communications, Inc.

22/ Jackson, III, Ralph Olin, *Tales of the Rails In Georgia* (2004), Legacy Communications, Inc.

23/ Kloeppel, James E., *Georgia Snapshots* (1994), Adele Enterprises

24/ Kollock, John, *These Gentle Hills* (1976), Copple House Books

25/ Lyle, Katie Lecher, *Scalded to Death by the Steam* (1988), Algonquin Books

26/ McRay, Sybil, *A Pictorial History of Hall County* (1985), Taylor Publishing

27/ McRay, Sybil and James Dorsey, *Windows of Memory, The Hall County That Was* (1989) Chestatee Regional Library

28/ Mooney, James, *Myths of the Cherokees and Sacred Formulas of the Cherokees* (1982), Charles & Randy Elder Booksellers

29/ Ritchie, Andrew Jackson, *Sketches of Rabun County History*, 1819-1948, Copple House Books

30/ Roswell Historic Society, *Roswell: A Pictorial History* (1985)

31/ Sargent, Gordon, Polk County Heritage Committee, 2000, *The Heritage of Polk County, 1851-2000*

32/ Sawyer, Gordon, *Northeast Georgia: A History*, (2001), Arcadia Publishing

33/ Shadburn, Don L., *Cherokee Planters in Georgia, 1832-1838*, (1989), W. H. Wolfe Associates

34/ Shadburn, Don L., *Pioneer History of Forsyth County, Forsyth County Heritage Series, Vol. 1* (1981), W.H. Wolfe Associates, Roswell, GA

35/ Sherman, Gen. William T., *The Capture of Atlanta and the March to the Sea* (2007), Dover Publications, Inc., Mineola, New York

36/ Tate, Luke, *History of Pickens County* (1987), The Reprint Company Publishers

37/ Walker County Historic Society, *Walker County, Georgia Heritage, 1833-1983* (1984), Taylor Publishing Company

38/ Webb, J.A., *History of New Holland, GA* (1985)

39/ Wells II, Ridley, *Old Enough To Die* (1996), Hillsboro Press, Franklin, Tennessee

40/ Whitfield-Murray County Historical Society, *Murray County's Indian Heritage* (1987), W.H. Wolfe Associates

41/ Williams, David, *Georgia Gold Rush* (1993), University of South Carolina Press

42/ Williams, Harry T.; Current, Richard N.; and Freidel, Frank; *A History of the United States to 1876* (1959), Alfred A. Knopf, New York

Full Name Index

Subject Index